I'll

Build a

Stairway

to

Paradise

I'll
Build a
Stairway
 ### to
Paradise

A Life of
Bunny Mellon

MAC GRISWOLD

Farrar, Straus and Giroux
New York

Farrar, Straus and Giroux
120 Broadway, New York 10271

Illustration credits can be found on pages 537–539.

Library of Congress Cataloging-in-Publication Data
Names: Griswold, Mac K., author.
Title: I'll build a stairway to paradise : a life of Bunny Mellon / Mac Griswold.
Description: First edition. | New York : Farrar, Straus and Giroux, 2022. |
    Includes bibliographical references and index.
Identifiers: LCCN 2022023649 | ISBN 9780374279882 (hardcover)
Subjects: LCSH: Mellon, Paul, Mrs. | Upper class women—United States—
    Biography. | Gardeners—United States—Biography. | Women gardeners—
    United States—Biography. | Philanthropists—United States—Biography. |
    Women philanthropists—United States—Biography.
Classification: LCC CT275.M469122 G75 2022 | DDC 361.74092 [B]—
    dc23/eng/20220706
LC record available at https://lccn.loc.gov/2022023649

Our books may be purchased in bulk for promotional, educational, or business
use. Please contact your local bookseller or the Macmillan Corporate and
Premium Sales Department at 1-800-221-7945, extension 5442, or by email at
MacmillanSpecialMarkets@macmillan.com.

www.fsgbooks.com
www.twitter.com/fsgbooks • www.facebook.com/fsgbooks

1 3 5 7 9 10 8 6 4 2

For Bunny Mellon

He had what is always very attractive in anyone,
which is self-indulgence carried to extremes.
—LUCIEN FREUD ON OSCAR WILDE

CONTENTS

ACKNOWLEDGMENTS

As fact, fiction, and legend boiled over after Rachel Lambert Mellon's death in 2014, I began to explore her 103 years, helped by scores of people who had known her. Bunny herself provided two years of informal meetings in the nineties in her houses and gardens in Virginia, Antigua, and Cape Cod. Those conversations (and long phone calls), along with her extensive private journals, garden records, and letters from more than two hundred correspondents, form the spine of this book. Her daughter, my friend Eliza Lloyd Moore, opened up her memories of her mother; my own memories of Bunny's husband Paul Mellon also warmed this account. Pieces of the puzzle came in from Eliza's brother Stacy "Tuffy" B. Lloyd, III, her half brothers Tim Mellon and Robin Lloyd, Bunny's niece Lily Lambert Norton, her nephew Gerard "Barnes" Lambert III, and her grandson Thomas Lloyd. Georgiana McCabe, a goddaughter of Paul's, and Eliza's husband, Derry Moore, offered observations both cogent and funny. Ann Hudner related her own perceptive story of Eliza.

I owe a great debt to those who worked with Bunny over the decades: her legal counselors Alexander Forger and Jane MacLennan, Paul Mellon's great friend and coauthor John Baskett, and Bunny's longtime library staff, especially Tony Willis and Nancy Collins, without whom this book wouldn't have been possible, as well as Kimberley Fisher and Ricky Willis. Interviews with Dita Amory, Willis van Devanter, and John Saumarez Smith, who worked with Bunny in the early library days, were enlightening, as were conversations with

Lucia Tongiorgi Tomasi, who wrote two of the four Oak Spring garden catalogues. Sir Peter Crane and his wife, Elinor Crane, also offered assistance of every kind, including wide-ranging access to the library holdings, and Peter kindly read several chapters. Max Smith allowed me to use his measured drawing of the walled garden at Oak Spring. Caroline Kennedy graciously gave permission to quote from her mother's letters.

I interviewed many who worked with Bunny closely at Oak Spring—her touchstone and experiment station. The cast, indoors and out, include Ronnie Caison, Nelly Jo Thomas, Skip Glascock, Ron Evans, Bill Keyser, J. D. Tutwiller, Boyd Pauley, Randy Embrey, Jay Keys, and Shirley Glascock. Ernie and Carol Bugg identified photographs of Paul's racehorses.

Daniel Sutherland recorded and explained Bunny's creation of South Pasture on Nantucket. Artists and craftspeople such as the framer Bill Waller and the weaver Sam Kasten, and Barrie McIntyre and Imogen Taylor of Colefax & Fowler, offered insights on Bunny's working methods and taste. Akko van Acker led me through Bunny's Paris apartments. Erroll Manners and James Godfrey placed Bunny as a porcelain collector in historical context. Tiffany's Allen Nissim opened the Schlumberger record books and workrooms. Above all, Bruce Budd's help in describing his thirteen years as Bunny's decorator and friend was paramount in understanding the evolution of Bunny's eye and her complex character.

Bunny made a striking impression on those she met. Anecdotes and stories, long and short, and surprising nuggets of information came from Paris Fields, Cristina de Heeren, Lucie Kinsolving, Liz Garvin, Bunny Williams, Diane Brown, Kerri Gonzalez, Martin Filler, Babs Simpson, Ann Jackson, John von Stade, Arthur Reade, Bee Dabney Adams, Barbara Burn, John Barnes, Cabell Williams, Elizabeth Locke, Mitchell Owens, James Taffin de Givenchy, Jean Vanderbilt, Dr. Bruce Horten, Cathy Graham, Anne Bass, Camilla Chandon de Brialles, Kathe Scott, Alix Diana, Felicia Warburg Rogan, Paul Richard, Charlotte Moss, Guy Trebay, Linda Hackett, and Bonnie Burnham.

At the National Gallery of Art, I reached out to Anne Halpern on the Mellons' acquisitions; Mary Morton sketched Ailsa Mellon Bruce as a counterpart art collector, and Kelly Burton made photo research effortless; Joseph Krakora and Ginevra Higginson described their encounters with Bunny. At the Virginia Museum of Fine Arts, Mitchell Merling, Kristie Couser, Jennie Runnels, and Colleen Yarger dug into their archives, while Pamela Reynolds boosted my interest in Bunny's style. Igor Uria Zubizarreta at the Cristobal Balenciaga Museum and Foundation answered questions. I am extremely grateful to William Seale, Lydia Tederick, Marcia Anderson, and Elyse Werling at the White House Historical Association. At the Center for Advanced Study in the Visual Arts, my friend Therese O'Malley was helpful in placing Bunny as a book collector. At the New York Botanical Garden, Gregory Long and Susan M. Fraser showcased Bunny's botanical art and her great discernment. Darcy Reid Trick burrowed into the Perry Wheeler papers at the Library of Congress. Sotheby's Elaine Whitmire, Frank Everett, and Darrell Rocha helped with details of the November 2014 auction of Bunny's effects. Arlyn Levee, Judith Tankard, and Patricia Jonas located landscape design records; Maral Kalbian produced architectural materials.

Editor Ileene Smith at Farrar, Straus and Giroux knew I should write this book before I did, and has guided me gently all the way. Assistant editor Ian Van Wye has provided support speedily and tactfully. Leslie Kazanjian judiciously copyedited the text, Rima Weinberg and Judy Kiviat proofread, Maxine Bartow straightened out the notes, Bri Panzica oversaw the production editorial workflow, and Songhee Kim created the handsome design. For technical assistance I've relied on Charles Grubb, Mike Avery, and Sheryl Heller. Literary agent Jeff Posternak has patiently followed this long road with good humor and advice.

In a flash of inspiration, Frederick Seidel provided the title—and encouragement, as ever and always. The gallant John Wood Sweet has read every word—even written a few of them—and supplied the basis of the jacket design. Jon Galassi read the entire manuscript. Wendy Gimbel, Rose Emery, Anne Isaak, Maggie Lidz, Holly Wright, Cathy Cochran and Liz Addison (who were my Virginia refuge), Sara Lee Barnes, Margaret Keith, Marella Caracciolo Chia, Leslie Close,

Deborah Nevins, Susan Weitz, and Barbara Dixon and Christopher Dixon all read chapters. Eleanor Reade was a useful skeptic; Steven Kossak and Tim Lovejoy were saturnine observers of art and society.

Early excitement and encouragement came from Henry Wiençek and Donna Lucey, Liz and Lawrence Banks, Colin Bailey, Elizabeth Neff, Andrew Wylie, and my old friends David Norman and Selina and Gordon Rainey. DeCourcy McIntosh opened the Knoedler Gallery doorway that led to Bunny's active art collecting. Janet Bruce was the book's design godmother and delineated Evangeline Bruce's importance. A support team of other friends included Linda Donn, Greg Fitch, Bean and Charlie Carroll, Anka Begley, Carol Williams, Grace Tankersley and Nicholas Quennell, Holly Wright, Cordelia and James Gelly, and Susana Leval. If I've omitted anyone who helped me in these eight years, this seventy-nine-year-old's memory most deeply apologizes for the lapse!

My daughters, Belinda and Anna Brown, bemused by my choice of subject, have remained loyal and loving. Finally, during the last four years I've depended on the invaluable counsel, stable environment, and deep affection provided by my friend and partner, Stockton Illoway, to get this book into print.

I'll

Build a

Stairway

to

Paradise

Bunny Mellon, icon and woman, looks down over the walled garden
at Oak Spring from her dressing room window in 1961.

Introduction

My first encounter with Bunny Mellon was in the 1950s; she was the mother of a school friend. At the time Mrs. Mellon was not yet famous, as she would later become, for her art and book collections, for her gardens and homes, for her uncanny ability to stage a social or political extravaganza yet remain out of the spotlight. Even so, she did make an impression. After all, how many other mothers invited their daughter's classmates to line their driveway and wave when the queen of England rolled in for tea? Over the years I remained friends with her daughter, Eliza. Then, in the 1990s, Bunny asked me to help her write her memoirs—she knew her life was the stuff of legend, but she also knew she needed assistance—and in the process I began to learn about her in a new way. Our project was interrupted in 1999 when Eliza suffered a terrible accident. She was hit by a truck while crossing a street in Manhattan and suffered a severe brain injury. Left quadriplegic and unable to speak, my school friend would spend her final years sequestered under her mother's anxious, hopeful watch. During that time, although I was unsuccessful in prompting Bunny to complete her memoirs herself, she and I became close.

As a friend, Bunny was not a legend but a person. Still, as an icon of style, Bunny was one of the last examples of something that doesn't really exist anymore. She falls into a category, deserved or not, of rich and outrageous American women of the twentieth century, one that included the renowned—such as the tobacco scion Doris Duke and the Baroness Pauline de Rothschild (née Potter)—and the less so, such as "Gertie" Legendre, the big-game hunter and adventurer. Bunny was contained, careful, polite, and grand, but not heedlessly so. Her vast wealth meant that she could afford the great gesture, psychologically as well as monetarily.

However, any comprehensive examination of Bunny Mellon's life and sorrows—including this book—must also take into account a certain zaniness. I fell on this example in Sag Harbor, New York, far from Bunny's usual haunts and more than half a century after we first met. To this day there are hundreds of similar tales rolling around like loose pearls on the streets of commerce and high society. This single anecdote mirrors dozens of others in which she, like a Charles Perrault character, transforms herself into a fairy godmother.

One wet and windy winter day in 1995, Bunny, then in her eighties, headed to the shop of the antiques dealer J. Garvin Mecking on East Eleventh Street. There she was waited on by the antiquarian Paris Fields, who was minding the store.

"It was raining and snowing," Fields told me. "A woman came into the shop, soaked, running with water. She said she was waiting to meet a friend. I helped her take off her coat and shoes. I thought she was a homeless person until I saw that her raincoat was lined with sable. My mother once said, 'No one must know that your coat is lined with mink.'

"I said to my visitor, 'I see your coat is lined with sable!' and I asked her name.

"'Call me Bunny,' she said.

"'I can't call you Bunny,' I protested to the elderly woman.

"'Why not? Everybody else does.'

"She picked out a few things to buy, and then announced, 'I have no money.'

"And so I gave her a cup.

"She asked, 'What is the cup for?'

"I jokingly replied that she should go out in the street and find some change.

"She replied, 'Whenever someone gives you something, you must always give something back.'

"She took two bracelets out of her pocketbook and handed them to me. 'Try them on,' she urged. So I put on the red one. Then she insisted that I put on the green one, too.

"'It's Christmas,' I said.

"'That's better,' she said.

"I went into the back of the shop to make some coffee for us. My partner took a look at the bracelets and hissed, 'Those are *real*; you can't keep them.'

"I hadn't realized they were authentic Schlumberger pieces.

"When I returned with our coffee, Bunny said, 'He's having a show in Paris, you know; I'll fly you over.'

"This 'show' was a retrospective of the famous jewelry designer Jean Schlumberger's work at the Musée des Arts Décoratifs. I said, 'You'll fly me over?'

"'Yes,' she answered. 'I have a plane; we could fly over and you could see the show; I can have you back here in a day or two.'

"I marveled, 'You have a *plane*?'"

"At that moment a gorgeous but very upset blond guy came into the shop," said Fields, who recognized him as Akko van Acker, a fellow antiques dealer working in Paris.

"I couldn't find a place to park," grumbled van Acker, clearly unhappy that Bunny and Fields were apparently becoming fast friends.

Fields replied, "I don't know who she is! She has no money and only says her name is Bunny."

"You can't call her that!" van Acker snapped. "She is Madame Mellon."

Oh!

"Of course, I gave her back the bracelets," Fields said, "but a few days later a drawing arrived . . . seventeenth century, of a garden, in a Lowy frame."

It was the start of a long epistolary friendship accompanied by a sporadic stream of gifts.

Paris Fields's story concentrates much of the Bunny I knew as a friend and came to know even better as my subject. The spontaneous kindness, the faith in what she had been taught as a child—you must always give something back—resulting in a gift no one else could give. The naked speed of entry into intimacy, friendship. But also the woman still uncertain of herself, even at eighty-five, who needed to impress. Imperiousness. Excess. Loneliness. A need for solitude that she both rejected and embraced—why was she flying to Paris alone? A display flashed only occasionally, like the sable lining. A breeziness that comes from an utter confidence in what wealth can—and should—provide. The sound of her voice. Robert Isabell, the florist and event planner who was her last great passion, said in astonishment, "You talk like Noël Coward." The playwright's brittle, funny chat, the epitome of performance, often came naturally to Bunny; Coward, like Adele and Fred Astaire, was her old friend.

What Fields's story doesn't convey is Bunny's belief in beauty as a practical, working construct, a vehicle to another world, whether it was into a magical private event such as her daughter's 1961 debut or at JFK's grave site in Arlington National Cemetery, where, at his widow's request, she transformed a handsome public tribute into an inward, thoughtful reflection of the man himself, conjured up by an assemblage of worn-looking Cape Cod granite set in a nest of flowering trees.

Rachel Lambert (Lloyd) Mellon is now chiefly famed for her style, for making a religion of domestic understatement, a rigorous simplicity of a very expensive and beautiful kind. Over more than half a century she created a hushed and extremely private domestic universe at eight different houses staffed by as many as 350 employees. Within those creations she wanted to alter mundane reality not just for herself but for those who would share it. Perhaps without ever understanding how or why, her circle of family and intimates felt sheltered within a witty, elegant, and yet seemingly casual world that hadn't changed much since the eighteenth century.

Bunny Mellon elevated "the decoration of houses"—the phrase Edith Wharton and Ogden Codman, Jr., used—to the level of a Zen koan. Was she a person who, in another era, could have run a nation instead of making a fetish of home decor and the history and practice of gardening? How much of her restraint was constraint—and was she herself aware of it? This book explores both her achievements and her limits.

For her time Bunny Mellon did breathtakingly well by all her advantages—intelligence, talent, energy, health, and great wealth—almost always, and intentionally so, without public fanfare. Her husband Paul Mellon's millions (and her own very substantial inheritance) gave her considerable freedom to do what she wanted. She chose to remain an amateur, but she performed at a professional level in whatever she undertook, and she was honored on two continents for her work. The world-famous architect I. M. Pei once told the award-winning fashion designer Bill Blass that, in his opinion, "she's the greatest landscape gardener and architect in this country. She knows flowers, gardens, buildings, decoration, and pictures. It [her knowledge] is absolutely complete."

Best known are her accomplishments as a gardener and the designer of the White House Rose Garden for the Kennedys in 1961; less known are her abilities as the designer of a score of private gardens that remain to be documented. The relationship between Bunny's design abilities and her book collecting culminated in a celebrated garden library in Virginia, an assemblage that currently holds more than nineteen thousand objects: artworks as well as rare books and incunabula. Because she celebrated intellectual and artistic connections that few others observed at the time that she began collecting, in the late fifties, and because she was able to follow her own omnivorous habit, her holdings extend to botany, natural history, travel, architecture, the decorative arts, and the classics, as well as garden and landscape.

She also had an enormous effect on her second husband's deservedly famous art collection. She first gravitated to the French Impressionists in the 1950s, finding that the clarity and complications of their take on the natural world mirrored her own. Among the thousand-plus paintings and sculptures the two of them gave to the National Gallery of Art in Washington, D.C., are hundreds of Impressionist works, great and small. Bunny also kicked off the Gallery's acquisition of modern paintings with a private opening dinner in 1973 at the Gallery, where she hung two of her own Rothkos as if to say, "See, these belong here too." Her second trove of art is a collection of jewels that she donated to the Virginia Museum of Fine Arts. These impossibly refined works by Jean Schlumberger portray infinitely small and precious aspects of the natural world.

But this biography is meant to be less a catalogue of Bunny Mellon's collections of treasure (or her wardrobe, sometimes admirable, sometimes perilously close to dowdy) and more of an inquiry into how and why she became the woman she was. Of course I follow the signposts of her parentage and her childhood, her education, marriages, children, scandals (there were two), and the friendships made and frequently lost. Being dropped by Bunny Mellon was like being felled by a velvet-covered brick.

Along with the details of her correspondence with hundreds of people, letters now also housed in the Oak Spring Garden Library in Upperville, Virginia, the best insights into Bunny's life and emotions are, perhaps, her own, found in her private journals, complete with cross-outs, misspellings, hesitations, and revisions.

Like many celebrities, Bunny was acquainted with or known to countless people who considered her to be a friend or whom she merely met, or who saw her at public events, or who were sparingly granted interviews. The curtain wall fronting the Mellons' home on East Seventieth Street in Manhattan can stand as a metaphor for their insistence on personal privacy. Paul Mellon, philanthropist and co-heir to one of America's greatest business fortunes, set down their feelings on the matter when he wrote, "Privacy is the most valuable asset that money can buy."

Bunny dedicated the second of her four descriptive library catalogues to her husband of fifty-one years. The first honored her grandfather, Arthur Houghton Lowe; the third, her "dear and loyal friend" Jacqueline Bouvier Kennedy Onassis; and the last, her daughter, Eliza Winn Lloyd Moore. Each name represents a chapter or chapters in Bunny Mellon's life.

She pushed far past her high school education, armed with a keen and judicious eye, an intense curiosity, and a practicality that had begun with her growing plants from seed when she was eight. Decades later, she would closet herself for hours with John Fowler, the principal decorator of the famous interior design firm Colefax & Fowler, in order to learn exactly how to make a silk-and-satin curtain tassel. It may sound absurd to hear that a woman whose properties were cared for by hundreds of skilled employees could and did do any gardening on her own, but to watch Bunny Mellon shaping a boxwood with her garden shears (or with nail scissors, as I saw her do) was to glimpse her firsthand expertise. Her many bold architectural sketches, dashed off in a letter or on the back of an envelope, light up how design seldom left her mind.

The kind of freehanded spending that would allow Bunny Mellon to give away two Schlumberger bracelets on the spur of the moment was balanced by an intense, almost puritanical desire to engage her own creativity directly, even in the smallest details. It is as if she valued her ability *to do things herself* as a counterweight to her status as an heiress. In contrast, Bunny once dismissed the discerning eye of the New York philanthropist and eminent collector of French decorative arts Jayne Wrightsman by saying, "Everything she does she's read how to do it, or had someone tell her how it should be done."

Bunny Mellon's long life stretches back to what we call the Gilded Age of America's youth before World War I or the enactment of a federal income tax law, an era of excess in almost every arena. Yet Bunny would prize simplicity in all fields of design, in the garden and out.

In 1932, when Bunny was a young woman on the brink of her first marriage, Edith Wharton wrote about how Henry James had conjured up the past, summoning his vanished New Yorkers in all their "old follies, old failures," as well as their "old lovelinesses . . . a long train of ghosts flung with his enchanter's wand across the wide stage of the summer night . . . wavering and indistinct at first . . . and then, suddenly, by some miracle of shifted lights and accumulated strokes, there they stood before us as they lived, drawn with a million filament-like lines . . ." that manage to be both sharp and dense. Bunny Mellon deserves such a portrait.

On the eve of her marriage to Paul Mellon in 1948, she saved and marked with the date a poem by Gloria Kommi, "Time Shall Be Ended," and she kept it all her life. The last lines are:

> Did you expect too little or too much?
> Now you are wise with flight: all this you know.

PART I

Childhood
and
Family

1

Becoming Bunny

"I was born 92 years ago in N.Y.C. at the corner of 66th St. & Madison Ave.," wrote Bunny Mellon about August 9, 1910, her birthday, not forgetting to mention that the address, 777 Madison Avenue, was, even then, "considered an important architectural achievement." The ten-story red-and-white French Gothic building remains one of the most eye-catching and sought-after residences in the city today, where the antique-jewelry dealer Fred Leighton's vintage pieces glitter in the curved ground-floor windows. When Bunny began to write about her life, she started with this building where she was born.

"My mother, caught by surprise on her way to East Hampton, went through the unexpected ordeal—at 2 A.M." It was no doubt seen as a great inconvenience for her mother, having to stop for the birth when she was on her way to the Hamptons. Later, Bunny said she was told that she was born on the kitchen table and that she was nicknamed "Bunny" by her nurse, who said she looked like one. Her birth certificate doesn't give her weight but does offer the occupation of her father (the business mogul and Renaissance man Gerard B. Lambert) as "architect." Bunny would follow in those footsteps: her second husband, Paul Mellon, in one of his bursts of light verse, would call her "Building Bunny," and she herself saw architecture and garden design as her best means of personal expression. (She also apparently inherited her father's extravagance, along with his inventive practicality.) While she would determinedly remain an "amateur," her skills and drive would lead her to design not only her own gardens and properties, but also the White House's Rose and East Gardens and dozens of lovingly detailed private gardens for friends.

Bunny adored handsome, dashing men, starting with her father and ending with Robert Isabell, king of New York's event planners. The exceptions were her "Grandpa" Lowe and her husband of fifty-one years, Paul Mellon—both good-looking, powerful men, yes, but both less showy than many of her other male friends or companions. Both men also had a keen eye for the absurd and a sense of whimsy, qualities she prized in anyone, friend or lover, male or female.

Gerard Barnes Lambert, born in 1886, never had to worry about money. In his memoir, *All Out of Step*, published when he was seventy, he describes how he and his five siblings, all born in St. Louis, thought of "the mysterious institution known to us children as 'the Lambert Estate.' This, like a horn of plenty, spewed forth the money for every need. I recall no discussions at any time of economies."

Gerard B. married the nineteen-year-old redhead Rachel Parkhill Lowe, from Fitchburg, Massachusetts, in 1908, the year he graduated from Princeton University. The couple took an extended European honeymoon, and on their return to the United States, he headed to the Graduate School of Architecture at Columbia University for a brief two years. He then fled architecture's heavy math and engineering requirements and went to New York Law School, another short-lived venture. He enlisted in the military in 1917 (when Bunny was seven), eager to go overseas again, leaving behind both a huge unfinished house in New Jersey and an undercapitalized foray into timber and cotton in Arkansas. As he himself admitted, "Up to this time I had, of course, no business experience whatsoever, nor did I know anything about lumbering or cotton."

After the war, however, Gerard B. turned out to be very good at making money—once he found someone else to run the Arkansas project. To trim expenses, he moved his wife and children (now including a brother and a sister as well as Bunny) from Princeton, New Jersey, back to his hometown of St. Louis for a year in 1922, where he took the family business, Lambert Pharmacal Company, in hand. He discovered he was an advertising genius, transforming Listerine, a surgical antiseptic—the Lamberts' solid but lackluster pharmaceutical performer—into a bestselling mouthwash. (Sir Joseph Lister, the British pioneer of antiseptic surgery, had developed an effective but corrosive carbolic; Bunny's grandfather Jordan Wheat Lambert had earlier bought the use of Lister's name to use it for his own, milder, disinfectant compound.) In 1921, Gerard B., a *Mad Men* prototype, created a striking campaign to popularize the then-arcane term "halitosis." Through his in-house advertising agency of Lambert & Feasley, he pitched his mouthwash sales to single women (and a few wretched men) who were frantic to get married and unable to find a mate, presumably because of bad breath. It was Lambert who coined the phrase "Often a bridesmaid, never a bride." In just seven years annual profits rose from $115,000 to more than $8 million. Bunny was often called "the Listerine heiress" in print but sailed on past that without much comment; her sister, Lily, on the other hand, was dubbed the "halitosis heiress" by none other than the gossip columnist "Cholly Knickerbocker," and it rankled.

Although he left Listerine behind in 1928, selling his shares of Lambert Pharmacal, Gerard B.'s luck, judgment, and intuition continued to hold: he sold out of the stock market in early 1929 and suffered no losses. By 1931 he was president of the Gillette Safety Razor Company, and had turned the troubled firm around with the famous "Blue Blade," a razor blade coated in an instantly recognizable blue lacquer.

Following the birth of Bunny's brother, the Lamberts' mademuch-of Gerard Barnes "Sonny" Lambert, Jr., in 1912, had come sister Lily, born at the Plaza Hotel in 1914. (Until the Lamberts took up residence in Princeton at the house they were slowly building, they had lived in multiple rental houses on Long Island and rented apartments in New York City.) Lily "was a very beautiful baby, and the doctor remarked to me, at two in the morning, that we would have to build a Chinese wall around her someday," wrote Gerard B.

Bunny, age four when Lily was born, quickly learned that now she was neither the most beautiful of the Lambert children, nor the cherished male heir. How to distinguish herself? She developed a determination to do things her own way, to think things out for herself and

Bunny shows how to size someone up when you are under ten years old.

yet keenly observe and learn from others. She was quiet in public, as a female of her day, age, and class was trained to be. She smiled and kept her own counsel. Her voice was almost as soft as that of Jacqueline Kennedy, who became her best friend and soulmate, but behind it—just as Jackie did—Bunny developed drive and ambition, backbone, grit—whatever you care to call it—and the organizational abilities to successfully deploy those qualities.

When Bunny was forty-six and had been married to Paul Mellon, her second husband, for eight years, her father wrote, "She was a fat, chubby little girl, but she soon lost that and became the slim, tall, and dignified person that she is today. She has the most original mind of any one I know and has exquisite taste." She was sent, by her own choice, to a finishing school, Foxcroft, as a sophomore. A clue to her later interests and aptitudes is found in her resounding score of 92 on a history-of-art final in her senior year. Bunny's grade in business arithmetic, which required administrative skills as well, was also excellent. She would certainly know how to hire, train, and organize a superb staff—at least half of running a business—although the ledger side was something she would prefer to ignore. By 1929, the year Bunny left school, the mold was set.

Eleanor MacKubin, a housemother and riding teacher (then as now, riding and having your own horse at the school were distinguishing features of the Foxcroft curriculum), wrote frequently to Bunny during vacations and for a few years after she graduated. MacKubin, a recent Foxcroft graduate herself, loved Bunny and had high hopes for her—mostly to do with finding a suitable husband—and their friendship and closeness in age meant she felt free to counsel her young friend on personal matters. She asked Bunny why she some-times picked a fight with a friend without any apparent reason, adding that, given Bunny's "forceful disposition," she herself couldn't imagine "fighting with you over anything." Prophetically, she added, "It would be sad indeed if you lost a friend you love just through your love for fight—or your desire to be right" over "whatever it is that makes you fuss over nothing."

"Whatever it is" was hardly nothing. At home, Bunny had received little counseling about relationships. About her father she wrote, "We never really talked . . . never discussed life or anything to do with it. He was preoccupied with his interests—but his interests included a way of life—of living—and I lived within this orbit. I was surrounded by beautiful things, an excitement of people, my cousins—all boys who played the piano, drums and loved music—and aeroplanes."

Bunny said that her mother, Rachel Lowe Lambert, known as "Ray," "was passionate about two things only: dress and religion." She was nervous, said Bunny, and sometimes "hysterically threatened sui-cide." Bunny told me that once, out of patience, she had cruelly said to Ray, "Go ahead, do it." Her relationship with her mother would always be cool, and, for better or worse, it taught Bunny how to ef-ficiently edit out of her life those she didn't need or like as well as those she sensed didn't like her. In later years, though, she did visit Cape Cod, where Ray, divorced from Gerard B. in 1933 and married to the widower Dr. Malvern Clopton (who had first married Gerard B.'s sister, Lily, since deceased), had a summer house.

Gerard B. had employed the country house architect Harrie T. Lindeberg to build the family's giant (192 feet long) pillared home on a 400-acre holding in what were then the outskirts of Princeton, New Jersey. Named Albemarle after the Virginia county where Lam-bert had spent his childhood summers, the place was barely finished in 1917, just as the United States entered World War I. During the four years of construction, Gerard B. and Lindeberg had played with proportion and scale—the front columns were built and rebuilt four times—a habit of persistence in "getting it right" that Bunny was to copy in her own architectural career.

"Being a child not much noticed by my family in this house, I

Billowing boxwoods like those at Albemarle became
Bunny's lifelong go-tos for a garden.

was freer than either Lily or Gerard to live in it," Bunny recorded
in a reminiscence about her father. For company, Bunny turned to
the objects around her, which she observed intently. And like many
children of her class and period, she remembered sadly the day her
nanny left. Bunny waited at the stairs leading down from the third
floor. "We had the top floor of a house in Princeton . . . I was waiting
for the governess. First came a big black trunk. [Then] Flora Adam
[descended]. I named one of my cows after her. She won a great prize
in Maryland."

Loneliness, nannies, governesses, the nursery floor at the top of the
house, one's own herd of prize cows: Downton-Abbey-in-America.
Even though Bunny Mellon was not the reclusive person she was
often reputed to be in the press and, indeed, led a lively, international,
modern life, she never entirely left the insulated world in which she
was born: orderly, Edwardian, and, most important, unburdened by
concerns about money or class.

In the early decades of the twentieth century, the flat green fields
that ran west from Princeton to the Delaware River made perfect

airstrips for fiercely enthusiastic aviators such as the Lamberts. Bunny's uncle Albert was the first to fund Charles Lindbergh's transatlantic flight, as well as the first pilot, writes Gerard B., to loop the loop, turning his plane upside down, pasted into his open cockpit by the thrust of zero gravity. St. Louis's airport—originally known as Lambert Field—still commemorates Albert; it is named St. Louis Lambert International Airport.

Bunny's "cousins who loved aeroplanes" considered it great sport to take a biplane up. A woman who later developed a fear of flying and needed constant hand-holding to do so was fearless as a girl. George Lea Lambert, Albert's son and her favorite cousin, once asked her, "Hey, kid, want to fly to Lawrenceville?" (Lawrenceville, home to the eponymous boys' prep school, is a small hop from Princeton.) When she instantly agreed, George Lea tied her into the passenger cockpit with her sweater, and off they flew. Crashes were common, however, and deaths not unexpected. Bunny was nineteen in 1929 when, as Gerard B. wrote, George Lea was coaching a young flier from the back of their two-seater, and his student froze at the controls. The plane dived to the ground, killing both men.

Four months after George Lea's death, Bunny sent her bouquet (orchids and pink roses) from her Virginia coming-out party to be placed on George's grave in the Bellefontaine Cemetery outside St. Louis. George Lea's few surviving postcards to Bunny give no sense that he was more than cousinly in his affections, but the numerous black-edged cards and notes sent to her after his death tell us that others knew that Bunny's affection for him ran deeper. He was the first man to feature in a series of either imaginary romances or deeply romantic friendships she would have in her life. She loved being in love—when she was in love, everything was easier, she said.

Her Grandpa Lowe, her maternal grandfather, is the only person who ever seemed to love her unconditionally and pay her close attention. He urged her to stand up straight and to improve her handwriting—"ask Mother to give you a little sharper pointed pen." Once she sent him a report card from her grade school, Miss Fine's, in Princeton; he wrote it was "splendid" when he returned it to her. One wonders if anyone else even acknowledged her report cards.

Gerard B. actually wrote that his coddled front lawn of creeping bent grass at Albemarle "received more loving thought and attention than the inhabitants of the house." Though meant as a joke, the remark also carried some truth.

When Bunny was eleven, Grandpa Lowe finished his account of a wildlife death struggle on the farm by saying, "Bunnies are always in danger of being caught and eaten . . . Foxes and Eagles have different names, like Selfishness and Thoughtlessness. Don't let either kind get you." But soon after her fourteenth birthday, he gave this child—so grim-looking in her early photographs—license to' enjoy herself. "Don't be [completely] unselfish," he instructed her. "Sometimes people think themselves above the simple lovely sweet things in life as they pass out of childhood into girlhood and on into Ladyship." Bunny followed that instruction faithfully. Throughout her life she was not so "unselfish" as to deny herself the plain, ordinary pleasures of life, whether sunshine or fresh air or glorious green trees (all of which were probably in Grandpa's mind as he wrote); one of her most refreshing qualities was her visible enjoyment of these "simple things." She also appreciated the less simple pleasures that came to her later, such as two houses by the sea, an apartment in Paris, a great painting, or the very expensive fabrics used to make her clothing—no matter how much she had to pay to ensure that they were perfectly "simple and lovely."

It's not hard to see why Bunny wrote often of her childhood summers spent with Grandpa Lowe in Fitchburg and in West Rindge, New Hampshire. However, except for a few reminiscences of time spent in France or on Cape Cod much later in her life, she never got any farther in her autobiography, as if her later experiences, her often warring emotions and complex existence, couldn't measure up to the simplicity and directness of her relationship with her maternal grandfather.

A stapled booklet she made, titled "A Visit to the Land of Totem Poles," records Bunny's six-week summer trip in 1923 with Grandpa Lowe and her family to Banff and Yellowstone National Parks. The colored pictures of totem poles she drew are charming, but it's the last page that catches a reader: "and as all stories end we lived happily ever after. The End."

Her earliest dated letter to Grandpa Lowe, written when she was eight, after she'd spent the summer of 1918 with him, is playful and radiant with affection, as was his reply. "Dear Bunny, Your grand-pa is lonesome for his playmate." He describes how he misses her when he reads his morning papers or feels the morning sunshine. There is no "little girl for him to dream about when he takes his nap" or to greet him with a kiss. It's clear they enjoyed a very close, affectionate relationship unlike her contact with either of her parents. Bunny missed him too: "I saw my grandfather's smiling kind eyes beneath his heavy white eyebrows," she wrote. "He would often say nothing, but put his arms around me, nodding his head in strong affirmation—and send me on my way."

In another letter, Grandpa values what she valued in herself throughout her life—her imagination—which would lead her to create a refuge in a vast collection of fairy tales and a world-class botanical library. "My dear Bun, I loved your fairy story . . . I am glad you have imagination." He adds that her "little story about being taken up into the clouds and . . . spending the night in cloud beds in the care of angels is really beautiful," then tosses in one of his mild jokes: "I can't go because I snore too loud." Grandpa's quips must have delighted Bunny in a family that didn't do much joking. Although Gerard B. in his memoir is a self-described "charming scamp," his tricks were not intended to amuse his children.

Bunny prized her grandfather for sharing with her the rural outdoors he loved. Writing later from her splendid house on East Seventieth Street in Manhattan, she begins, "Every summer Grandpa would say on some morning at breakfast, 'Bun, it's time to climb the old mountain.' Grandpa was born in a farmhouse in a field below Mount Monadnock in New Hampshire—The mountain was part of his life & strength." The two of them stayed in a cabin high up in the pastures. An early riser, Bunny would dress quickly and go outdoors even before her grandfather was up.

"The day for the climb came in mid-August." They drove north across the state border, then up toward the farm, where they left their touring car—driven by Sterling, the chauffeur. Then Grandpa "would tie a ribbon around my waist with a tin cup, give me a few graham crackers, put a small pack on his back, take his sturdy stick & up we would go. The trail was clear, but often we were distracted by a tree different from the rest, [or by] wild flowers or large rocks—and wandered off.

"This was the best part of the climb—*discovery*. My Grandfather's enthusiasm like the sunlight coming through the trees has never left me. Once coming to a corner where the ferns and trees were greener and fresher, we discovered a clear small spring trickling down through the leaves—the water was like crystal—I loved it so much. 'Now, Bun,' Grandpa said with a smile, 'you can use your tin cup.'" On the terrace of the Virginia library Bunny built to house her botanical collection stands a stone water trough fed by an ordinary metal pipe; from the pipe handle hangs a plain tin cup for the thirsty wayfarer.

It was then that Bunny "fell in love with the joy of space—with shadows and special trees—with the sound of clear water in the small brook—one could drink it lying flat in the cup of one's hands," she wrote. "But it was the sky, that great space—ice blue, lazy blue, dark blue, full of stars—angry or hidden by fog—what a little world we are, looking at that sky. Space, and how to use it, for me, is the beginning of every garden . . ."

On the high, clear-cut tract that her grandfather had bought expressly to reforest, a farmer had dug the holes for thousands of bare-root seedling pine trees. In those summers between the ages of eight and thirteen Bunny began to notice patterns of plant growth. She also loved to design fantasy gardens in a twelve-inch by twelve-inch sandbox—a gift from Grandpa Lowe. She found she enjoyed designing and making things with her own hands: in the Fitchburg garage workshop she fell upon "hammer, saws, nails, and also bits of wood" to make "small boxy wooden things (representing houses)." By her early teens she would stand over workmen in Princeton, directing them how to build her playhouse with its thatched roof and fenced garden.

At Albemarle, where the landscape architecture Olmsted firm created the gardens between 1913 and 1930, young Bunny closely observed someone she called "the Dutchman"—Jacob Sloet, from the Netherlands—as he planted the elaborate flower and shrub borders. Later, when Bunny was designing and planting the White House

Rose Garden, she said Sloet had been the first person to teach her in depth about plants and gardens.

Throughout her life Bunny was drawn to figures (almost all men) in various fields of design. She felt comfortable with them, respected them, admired them—even loved some of them deliriously and possessively—for their excellent taste and ingenious skills. It almost goes without saying that by the time she was "Mrs. Paul Mellon," she commanded the attention of designers of all kinds who had reached the pinnacle of success. Her checks to them were large, whether to John Fowler of Colefax & Fowler, king of London decorators, or Jean Schlumberger, the French jewelry designer of Tiffany & Co. fame, or the much-lauded couturier Hubert de Givenchy.

Her beloved grandfather Arthur Houghton Lowe (1853–1932), the son of a Scot, moved to Fitchburg, Massachusetts, as a small child from a farm in West Rindge, New Hampshire. He worked in his father's meat and produce business until he became the agent and manager of the Parkhill Manufacturing Company and married the boss's daughter, Annie Parkhill, Bunny's "Grandma." Lowe merged two Fitchburg milling companies to concentrate on the production of fine ginghams and went on to buy another mill in the South, as well as a wide swath of prime Arkansas cotton land to supply his mills. In Fitchburg alone, the company employed more than a thousand workers at its peak.

When Grandpa Lowe and Bunny took their 6:00 a.m. summer constitutionals together to the old family store in Fitchburg, Bunny wrote that he always introduced her with a "sort of royal gesture" to those they met on the walk.

Lowe's sweetness notwithstanding, he was still a classic late-nineteenth-century American industrialist and businessman who kept his hands on the levers of power whenever possible. He served in executive offices in local banks and power companies, became alderman and then mayor of Fitchburg, and played a major role in every national organization that dealt in cotton or its interests.

As chairman of the nation's cotton tariff committee, in 1921 Lowe argued cannily and guardedly before the House Ways and Means Committee for protectionist policies for the fine fabrics he and his cohort produced—and he defended a wage reduction of twenty-two percent in New England cotton mills such as his own. At the same time he was philanthropic, privately and locally, presenting Fitchburg with the Lowe Playground and Parkhill Park, serving in local welfare projects, and helping construct a new building for the high school from which he graduated in 1871.

Both of the men who most shaped the young Bunny Lambert's views—her maternal grandfather and her father—were political creatures. In different ways each subscribed to advice Grandpa Lowe gave Bunny as a child, which stayed with her all her life: "What you can do for your country, do it."

Lowe and Lambert were both confident in their power to influence political events and organizations. President Teddy Roosevelt made a brief train stop in Fitchburg in 1902, and some twenty thousand citizens turned out to greet him with flags and a pageant. Nevertheless, the president found time to sit in a rocker on Arthur Lowe's front porch for a private chat. And among Bunny's anecdotes, she recalled how "Grandpa took me to Calvin Coolidge's office" (when he was governor of Massachusetts), then went on to describe how Coolidge gave her crayons for her to use for drawing on the floor. Later she told Caroline Kennedy that she had sat on Coolidge's lap.

As for Lambert—appropriately enough for a man who couldn't stop building his own palatial residences—his first foray into politics was a public housing scheme in Princeton. In 1938 he came on board the Federal Housing Administration as an informal advisor, convinced that private investment could produce good-quality low-cost housing as economically as could government funding (which he frowned upon). His "Lambert Plan" was designed to shelter investors with tax-free bonds and produce good investments for them while keeping rents stabilized. In the case of the single such project Gerard B. created, the handsome ten-unit Franklin Terrace, he was both investor and landlord. Although Lambert hoped his development plans would be well received by the Roosevelt administration, he later wrote that the First Lady thought his scheme was "just a plan to provide some tax exemptions for [his] own investments," which—considered narrowly—it was.

Bunny's father then turned back to something he was far more familiar with—polling—following on his widely tested and effective advertising campaigns for Listerine and Gillette. For the 1940 presidential campaign he compiled data and ran public-opinion surveys for Thomas Dewey, who ran as a Progressive Republican. After Dewey lost the nomination, probably because of his noninterventionist stance as Hitler advanced across Europe, Lambert was kept on as a pollster by Wendell Willkie, who became the Republican nominee. Willkie trod the line between progressive and conservative Republican, picking and choosing his issues and declaring the nation should do all it could to help the Allies "short of war." He lost to FDR, the incumbent running for a third term.

As a woman of thirty-one, married and living in rural Virginia, Bunny would describe herself in a Foxcroft newsletter as "very active in the Willkie campaign." So did two of her former Foxcroft School classmates, who were also close friends: Eleanor Schley (Todd) and Kitty Wickes (Poole). The three of them were the only respondents to the 1941 alumnae bulletin to link themselves with political activities.

How Lambert ran his polling is also of interest regarding Bunny Mellon's much later, off-the-record contributions to the former North Carolina senator John Edwards when he ran for the Democratic presidential nomination in 2008. (She gave $3.5 million openly to his campaign and another $725,000 in private personal support.) Lambert ran his political affairs in secrecy. He asked Robert W. Goelet— yachtsman, financier, a leading light of New York society, and one of the largest owners of real estate in New York City—for help. Goelet offered the Dewey campaign staffers use of the mezzanine floor of Carlton House on East Sixty-First Street, next door to the Ritz Tower on Madison Avenue, where Lambert kept an apartment. A passageway ran from the Ritz to the Carlton, and "waiters in livery came through . . . to our quarters and served us dinner" in "the resplendent living room" of the Carlton suite. Lambert proudly contends that "during the whole time [of the campaign operation], I don't think even a reporter knew of our hide-out."

His polling data was often correct—and often depressingly so, as both of the presidential candidates he worked for lost, and Lambert's last polls had predicted they would. As for whom he employed, Lambert was no piker there either: two of his best hires had been trained by George Gallup, founder of the American Institute of Public Opinion, to take surveys on a national basis.

Bunny Lambert Lloyd Mellon enjoyed her proximity to power; she was fascinated by power, wanted to see how it worked, wanted it for herself. Of course, as a woman of her time, she expected to stay in the background, not assume public office or be in the news, but she was well aware that money, large amounts of money, could at least put her on the path to power.

"Dear Old Bun . . . one of the most beautiful winter days God ever made . . . Lincoln's birthday . . . He was one of the greatest men of our country," Grandpa Lowe wrote to his granddaughter, advising that she "read about him." She did. She also kept a clipping of something Abraham Lincoln had said. "I do the very best I know how—the very best I can; and I mean to keep doing so until the end. If the end brings me out all right, what's said against me won't amount to anything." Lincoln apparently said this during the fraught war months of 1864, when he was being painted by the portraitist Francis Carpenter. "If the end brings me out wrong," the president concluded, "ten angels swearing I was right would make no difference."

Throughout her life, Bunny was no stranger to criticism—which had started early. Many who met her—and many who had once been her friends but were "dropped" without explanation—saw her as cold, cutting, and selfish. However, those few to whom she was loyal for life viewed things differently. That circle was small but featured notable— and often witty—figures in the arts and design worlds, and they stayed mum about Bunny to protect her privacy. She held on to the Lincoln quote perhaps due to a feeling that he had given her a route to follow, wherever it led. But that is not to say that she admired herself. She needed Grandpa Lowe's stability and praise, and she needed the domestic perfection she created around her to find happiness.

After her noteworthy childhood, after Foxcroft, after her debut and a couple of trips abroad, one with classmate Kitty Wickes, during which Bunny found that France was going to matter to her as much as Virginia; after she had learned to be an adequate rider and had her jodhpur boots made by the prestigious bespoke London bootmaker Peal & Co and had the shape of her narrow feet recorded in one of Peal's "Feet Books"; after she had tasted the pleasure of her decorative arts "eye" and skill in redesigning parts of her childhood home, Carter Hall, for her father; Bunny would be ready for the world. She would be ready for the world she created for herself, one where "we lived happily ever after. The End." That "End" would be only the beginning.

Bespoke jodhpur boots from Peal & Co in London
are still preserved at Oak Spring.

2

Crafting Happiness

The young Mrs. Stacy Lloyd, at left, endures the formality of a family photo shoot at a Christmas ball.

An unfortunate photograph of Bunny at a ball at Carter Hall in Virginia on December 30, 1933, shows her arm-in-arm with her brother, Sonny (Gerard Barnes Lambert, Jr.), and her sister, Lily. The dance had been planned for the previous year to celebrate her wedding but was hastily called off after her grandfather's death, when festivities were curtailed for mourning. This photograph speaks of a woman being launched into a destiny for which she's not, perhaps, ideally suited or prepared, where she wonders if she will be able to distinguish herself. Bunny is tall, thin, distant, hollow-eyed, and unsmiling—with schoolgirl hair. Good-looking Sonny holds the stilted pose stylishly, his hands crossed over his white-tie waistcoat. Lily, perfectly composed, looks down through her enviably thick, dark lashes, smiling confidently, perhaps at the pleasure of being photographed and the dancing to come. Their father reproduced this photo in his memoir and rather apologetically noted, "Flashlight photos are cruel."

Bunny would later stage-manage her infrequent press appearances. She hired the best photographers, such as Horst P. Horst, Henri Cartier-Bresson, Louise Dahl-Wolfe, and Toni Frissell. For a 1968 story in *The New York Times*, she made certain that the best at taking "candids," Fred Conrad, was assigned. Rare was the real "candid" that found its way into print. Bunny preferred to be the producer, not the play. In the White House restoration, in her friendship with Jacqueline Kennedy, at the Potager du Roi at Versailles, even in her own library, where for portrait photographs she would often shelter herself behind a beautiful volume, she ensured her invisibility as much as possible.

Carter Hall's nine thousand square feet were not ideally suited for big dancing parties—the late-eighteenth-century rooms were too small. In Southampton or Tuxedo Park at the time, if your grand country place happened not to have a ballroom, the wealthy would erect a temporary one outdoors, complete with tent, hardwood dance floor, chandelier, hot-water radiators to ward off the cold (powered by a separate oil furnace nearby in a garden), garlands of smilax, family portraits temporarily hung on the canvas walls, a silk-covered sofa for tired dancers or their chaperones—all neatly whisked

Carter Hall's two-story colonnade shines in the midday sun.

away after the party. But even in rural Virginia in the foothills of the Blue Ridge Mountains, Bunny noted how to do things right and replicated them for spectacular parties of her own.

Bunny's father had bought Carter Hall, the resplendent late-eighteenth-century house built by one of his remote ancestors, Colonel Nathaniel Burwell, in Millwood, Clarke County, in 1929. Gerard B. enthusiastically harked back to those Virginian connections through his mother, Eliza Winn of Richmond, and said he'd bought the place "to keep it in the family." Through his purchase of Carter Hall, Bunny began shaping her lifelong identity as that of a Virginian instead of thinking of herself as a displaced New Yorker living in a big house in New Jersey.

Her great-great-grandfather was the American painter John Wesley Jarvis. One of his sons, Charles, also an artist, painted a small but gripping portrait of the fiery Kentucky statesman Henry Clay, which now hangs in the Oak Spring Garden Library. Gerard B., ever thorough in his desire to display his prestigious roots, hung at Carter Hall six other portraits by one Jarvis or the other, some inherited from his mother and the rest purchased. Besides those of family or connections, the collection included one of Andrew Jackson and another of Daniel Webster. Young Bunny had a chance to recognize these movers and shakers of her nation as her intimates in her own house.

Understanding how to move among the famous, the accomplished, and the titled had inevitably begun for Bunny after her graduation from Foxcroft in 1929. She had been schooled for it on the debutante circuit, meeting eligible young men and taking in, as only she could, the theatrical effects that transformed ordinary rooms into starry fairylands. What she remembered most, however, were the difficulties of being too tall (five feet, nine inches), her fear of rejection, and the pathetic advice to make oneself popular: "'If you dance longer than five minutes with the same man, apologize & say you must make a telephone call & go to the ladies' dressing room a while—come back smiling & you will be a success.' I took this seriously and took hidden in my evening coat pocket some knitting."

On the debutante circuit she met people who would play important roles in her life, among them the syndicated columnist Joseph Alsop, whose Georgetown garden she would design, and the classical architect H. Page Cross, who would ultimately work with Bunny on three of her residences. Her official debut, attended by a platoon of Princeton boys, took place at Albemarle on October 26, two days before the stock market crash of 1929. Though her own kin did not suffer, many of her close friends' families lost all their money. The relatives of Henry Parish, Jr., who was soon to become the husband of the influential interior designer Dorothy "Sister" Kinnicutt, Bunny's Foxcroft schoolmate, were among them. Sister Parish got her start on her new married life by running a tiny decorating shop in Far Hills, New Jersey, found she loved being in business, and never looked back. Her firm, Parish-Hadley, redefined old-time patrician coziness as "American Country" for several generations.

Yacht racing was popular among the rich and famous, and Bunny's father went all out, in his usual way, to make himself known in such circles and to enjoy himself at the same time. In 1927 he bought from Cornelius Vanderbilt, commodore of the New York Yacht Club, what was, according to Gerard B., the most famous racing yacht in the world, the schooner *Atlantic*. Racing thereafter became Gerard B.'s principal passion, along with building big houses. *Atlantic* was but the first of a series of storied craft he bought and raced. Bunny would be drawn to the sea and boats all her life.

Bunny's father coaches his elder daughter
in the fine points of sailing a yacht.

During the summer of 1928, which the family largely spent following Gerard B.'s yacht races around Europe, the Lamberts passed several days in Santander, the Spanish summer royal capital, as guests of King Alfonso XIII, waiting for the fabled *Atlantic* to arrive from America as the expected winner of an ocean-crossing race. Although *Atlantic* didn't win, the king gave Gerard B., the dashing skipper he admired and whose great yacht he might have admired even more, a silver trophy anyway. And why not? He was the king. Bunny called the gigantic trophy the "umbrella stand."

Nobody would ever accuse Bunny Mellon of being a wit, but her casual, offhand delivery, her ability to cut life down to size, to at least *appear* to take herself lightly, became a habit. In February 1930, Bunny and her Foxcroft friend Kitty Wickes took a trip to Spain, Turkey, and North Africa. (Kitty and Bunny remained close all their lives.) This was not your usual European grand tour, however, since both girls had already spent considerable time abroad. On school vacations Bunny had stayed with Kitty's family in their house in Paris and their château in the country. Such visits stoked her enduring love for France and French culture: Bunny's heartfelt paragraphs about Chartres Cathedral had already been published in the 1929 Foxcroft yearbook.

Bunny's somewhat more scattershot record of her 1930 trip with Kitty hits some of the high points. She said they were chaperoned by "a World War I nurse—Miss Strang spoke French and was very reliable. She was also a hot shot trained nurse." The trip was "laid out for us I don't know how. February to spring, we went up the Bosporus. We went on big boats, got off big boats, went up the Nile on a *dahabiyeh*. We went along with the shepherd and met people." The American debutante would revisit the region decades later with Hubert de Givenchy.

During the next two years, between other debutante parties, Bunny spent a great deal of time at Carter Hall. She observed—and assisted—as her father and Harrie T. Lindeberg thoroughly renovated—some say defaced—the great Virginia house, removing the original exterior stucco of the stone structure to make it look more ruggedly "period." Indoors, only the paneled dining room remained untouched. The renovations included everything needed to upgrade to early-twentieth-century great-estate standards a house whose conveniences dated from the late 1800s. They added not only a heating plant but also a wet bar, a wine cellar, and plenty of bathrooms, some with heated towel racks. They converted the east outbuilding into a guesthouse with two bedrooms and baths above a cozy living room with an existing ten-foot-wide fireplace. The stables were outfitted for Bunny's hunter, and the great barn was renovated to become staff quarters. The threesome "restored" the smokehouse and retained the barred-windowed estate's jail, perhaps for a frisson of danger. They replaced the main building's stairs with a "flying" staircase like the grand one at Shirley, one of Virginia's great tidewater plantations.

Meanwhile, Bunny continued to educate herself about gardens and plants. At Carter Hall, she worked on both the home's grounds and the wider landscape that sloped toward the Shenandoah River. Sometime in the 1830s a Mr. Spence, a Scottish gardener, had graded the land into three shallow terraces, commonly called "falls," which were often built below grand houses of the period, especially in the South. The top level nearest the house was reserved for a flower garden and the lowest for vegetables. (Bunny, however, would always grow flowers and vegetables together.) In 1908 a previous Carter Hall owner had hired the eminent landscape architect Warren Manning (who had originally trained with the Olmsted firm in Brookline, Massachusetts) to make a garden plan, which apparently was never executed. Then in 1932 Gerard B. called in the Olmsted firm itself to make a master plan and execute it, just as he had done in Princeton at Albemarle. Olmsted sent one of their top men, Percival Gallagher. However, when Gerard B. received the estimate, he, a man who never seemed to stint on expense, was shocked at the price. Even the intervention of Bunny's beloved Jacob Sloet, who explained that Gallagher had selected "specimen stock," didn't help. Relations with the firm were permanently severed.

During their renovation process, Bunny, her father, and Lindeberg did reconfigure the garden, however, replacing its pond (alive with two-foot-long carp) with a swimming pool, and planting many boxwoods, which became talismanic evergreen shrubs for Bunny. All her life, any garden she designed had to have roses, apple trees, and box, like those of her childhood home in Princeton. When in 1934 she and her first husband, Stacy Lloyd, came to live at Carter Hall, she was already an ambitious enough gardener to feel that a greenhouse was also a necessity. She designed and built a small stone potting shed and greenhouse next to the garden. Later, at Oak Spring, Bunny would replicate features of its design and scale, such as the potting bench with fold-out bins for compost and soil.

The years between Foxcroft and her marriage in 1932 were busy ones for Bunny. In addition to the upheaval of the Virginia renovation, Bunny saw the dissolution of her parents' marriage (not that she was heartbroken about it, given her cool feelings about her mother). Rachel sued for desertion—apparently the quickest way to get a divorce at the time—and Gerard B. left for the required two years and lived at the Ritz-Carlton Hotel in Boston.

David Banks, longtime family butler and young Bunny's trusted counselor

Bunny became the de facto mistress of Carter Hall, since her mother lived mostly in Princeton. In Virginia, Bunny turned to another father figure, someone who would be part of her life for forty years until his death in 1969. David Banks, born and raised in Millwood, Virginia, became the butler first at Carter Hall, then at Oak Spring, and in the summers at the Mellons' house on Cape Cod—foremost among the many servants who would work for Bunny Mellon. But Banks was more than merely staff. Though he was only six months older than Bunny and in her employ, he cast a stern eye on her young male visitors at Carter Hall, and if one didn't meet his standards, he'd comment, "T'aint quality, miss." And she listened.

Like most upper-class American

children of her period, Bunny was brought up almost entirely by servants, including a Scottish nurse named Randy and the governess, Flora Adams. The skilled stable hands at Foxcroft, in her day and in mine as well, were almost all Black. For many of us girls from the Northeast, those grooms, who kept the private horses some brought to the school each year, might have been the first African Americans with whom we had ever spoken, or whom we respected absolutely.

Bunny loved and trusted those who looked after her, made the rules, and enforced them, but she was not equipped either by upbringing or education to formulate progressive ideas about race and social justice. Whatever thoughts she did have had little bearing on her personal relations. Bunny was no mean-spirited racist. However, the numbingly large fact that she had more clout, fame, or social standing than any Black person she encountered—until she flew down in the Mellon plane with Jackie Kennedy to attend Martin Luther King, Jr.'s, funeral in 1968—ensured she didn't *have* to consider the national framework of racial prejudice.

As a child she'd been shocked by the black-and-white photographs her father kept of events at Lambrook, his cotton plantation in Elaine, Arkansas, when a 1919 union face-off between Black workers and white management culminated in the death of five white men and perhaps hundreds of Black Arkansans. Gerard B., who had created the miserable working conditions that led to the outbreak, was never charged. Nonetheless, whatever his blinkered outlook on race, he was apparently aware enough to film not only the devastation of the white supremacist riots but also the ramshackle hovels themselves. Bunny later wrote how those haunting pictures remained in her memory.

Far from such considerations of race, a decade later Bunny rode lightheartedly to hounds, complaining in a 1931 letter to Stacy Lloyd (by that time the two were informally a couple) only that some red-faced Jorrocks straight out of the pages of Surtees had cracked his whip at her—perhaps even touching her surprised horse with the tip of his lash—and snarled "Get out the way!" Apparently hounds had roared off on a hot scent and she hadn't made room fast enough to suit the eager Mr. White behind her.

Stacy, a consummate horseman, a seasoned foxhunter, and a man in love sympathetically wrote back: "I do hope you told Mr. White just where to get off for using his lash a bit too freely. It was a mistake of course, but all the same I would like to go at him with a whip for being so damn careless with his. After all a lady can choose her own place in the field, and she does not have to be in the first flight [at the front of the pack, with the most experienced hunters] all the time." Then, in the same sentence, he turned gracefully to his beloved's character:

> Though I suspect you, my darling, this time of deliberately not getting up [into the first flight] because you were being told in probably no uncertain language to do that very thing. My darling, bad girl, how I do love you for just those qualities of yours. If you did not have them and were not so stubborn and willful, I don't think I would love you half so much. But with them I respect you and most of the time do what you make me which is excellent. All my love, precious, Stacy.

Bunny rides sidesaddle across the Virginia hills in 1935.

3

"The Most Beautiful Playboy"

"He was the most beautiful play-boy in Philadelphia" is how Bunny described her first husband to me in her old age. In his courtship letters—we don't have hers—he continually recognized her strength of character, boldness, and willfulness. Then, dutifully, charmingly, conventionally, he pursued her. Bunny later admitted to loving Stacy better than she did her second husband, Paul Mellon.

A native of Philadelphia, Stacy Barcroft Lloyd, Jr., was born in 1908 to parents whose forebears were founders of the Quaker city. His father was a banker and president of the Philadelphia Savings Fund Society and a direct descendant of Thomas Lloyd, deputy governor under William Penn. One

Life is sweet: Stacy Lloyd in white flannels aboard Gerard B. Lambert's fabled yacht *Atlantic*

of his mother's ancestors, Anthony Morris, was Philadelphia's second mayor; Stacy's great-great-grandfather was Captain Samuel Morris, commander under General George Washington of the First Troop

Philadelphia City Cavalry in 1774. His mother, Eleanor Burroughs Morris, born in 1881, was the seventh generation of her family to be raised in the 1786 Reynolds-Morris House, one of Philadelphia's most imposing Federal residences, a monument to the family's mercantile wealth and power. It added to Eleanor's lustrous pedigree that Dr. Samuel Fuller, aboard the *Mayflower* as the only physician, was also one of her antecedents.

Young Stacy went to grammar school in Philadelphia and in 1922 went north to St. Paul's, the prestigious boys' boarding school in New Hampshire. Apparently he played almost every sport and excelled at them all. He crewed competitively for the school and played hockey and football on the top teams; his less athletic endeavors included being a field marshal and serving as an acolyte in the school's High Episcopal services. He was active in both library and literary societies. Though not "a facile scholar," as St. Paul's headmaster wrote in his recommendation letter, Stacy would "do credit to Princeton," where he applied and was accepted at once. No doubt because of his irreproachable background, patrician looks, leadership ability, and winning personality, Stacy sailed through the secret "bicker" process to become the president of Ivy, the oldest undergraduate "eating club," Princeton's equivalent of Greek-letter clubs and secret societies and the place where a young man made his lifelong friends. (Ivy membership was apparently the ultimate stamp of approval for Gerard B. Lambert's new son-in-law, as evidenced in Gerard B.'s memoir.) F. Scott Fitzgerald's 1920 characterization of Princeton in *This Side of Paradise* as "the pleasantest country club in America" is likely an apt description of Stacy's Princeton as well. (As the then-president of the university, John Grier Hibben, remarked, "I cannot bear to think that our young men are merely living four years in a country club.") Stacy would go on to a graduate law course at the University of Pennsylvania, while simultaneously rowing his heart out on the Schuylkill River to prepare for the 1932 Olympics single scull.

It is impossible to find anyone on the record—or even off it—who ever said a bad word about Stacy Lloyd, Jr. "Grace is the greatest artistic effect of the Old Money class," wrote Nelson Aldrich in *Old Money: The Mythology of America's Upper Class*. When Bunny married

Stacy, she had discerningly married the genuine graceful article. All the more interesting to explore why she later divorced him.

It would have been easy for Bunny and Stacy to meet once he entered Princeton. In fact, the two may well have been pushed together, both being eligible and of the right age, either during his college years or when she came out in Virginia. Stacy was surely wanted in every debutante's stag line. A debutante attended not only the private parties of her friends in her coming-out year but also the whirl of annual cotillions sponsored by elites in every major city, such as the "St. Cecilia Ball" in Charleston, South Carolina, the "Bachelors' Cotillion" in Baltimore, Boston's "Debutante Cotillion," and New York's "Junior Assembly" and "Infirmary Ball." Hoariest and most impenetrable for outsiders were the "Philadelphia Assemblies," first conducted in 1748. Admission to these affairs followed strict rules, but if your name appeared in the *Social Register* or the *Blue Book*, you were an easy in, and certainly Bunny was an easy in.

Two years after her debut, on October 8, 1931, the date of the first of his letters that Bunny kept, Stacy found himself startlingly ill, sitting in a wheelchair on the boardwalk in Atlantic City. He was recovering from a bout of sickness that had been diagnosed as a heart attack but was probably peritonitis. (Rapid heartbeat, shortness of breath, and exhaustion can be equally symptomatic of heart failure and appendix troubles; Stacy's appendix was removed five months later.) His hopes for the 1932 rowing Olympics faded, as did his efforts to take a law degree.

Ever inclined to see the bright side, however, Stacy told Bunny that he was "lucky to be laid up . . . I feel sure that my heart attacks and sickness have been the luckiest things that have happened to me in more ways than just being lucky to have survived them." He told her that finding the "enjoyment . . . of hours alone with a good book or a quiet place and after thoughts . . . cannot be equaled by the thrill of a horse leaping over a fence and following hounds." She had apparently written to him about more adventures in the hunting field. "But now my darling I have rambled on about myself," he concluded, "and have not written a word about the only interesting and very wonderful fact of my life which is you . . . do please be careful of yourself my precious angel and save up your rash actions until later when we can do them together."

Through the following months, they corresponded, talked on the phone, visited each other in Princeton and in Ardmore, Pennsylvania, on the Main Line, where his family lived, and at Carter Hall, where they spent the Christmas of 1931 with her mother. When Bunny entertained a weekend crowd of "beaux" at Carter Hall, Stacy was, or pretended to be, jealous. One rainy day in early December when he was still studying for his degree, he wrote,

> And so the day is just pleasantly drifting by as the fine clean rain that we need so badly comes washing down. I have on some comfortable old clothes and I only wish that I could put on my old boots and go flashing across the grey wet hills with the rain beating down on my face the way we did one Friday a long time ago. And you were such a good sport about getting your clothes wet although they were the only ones you had. Yet you did not care at all and were perfectly bully. Oh my darling girl I do love you for the good sport that you are. Some day we will go out and walk the hills again together.

He worried about his uncertain health and even his future, writing in a slightly later letter, "I would love to go to a party with you and have a whale of a time. But you know as well as I do that I am not nearly well enough to do that and will not be for another year." He wasn't well enough, he said, and would have his hands full studying. He was even doubtful whether he would "ever be strong enough to do that properly let alone anything else." At that point, in early January 1932, Bunny had decided to travel abroad. "So my darling go and have a grand time for I will be waiting for you with all my love, Stacy."

Once he had recovered, he wrote about what he wanted from life, saying,

> You are perfectly right about people having to learn how to live. They do, you know and most Americans don't know how. There is an art of living . . . just as there is an art of loving by

considering the other person first and trying to understand them first before yourself . . . Must stop, will be waiting for you on the fifth [of March] please don't change plans. all my love angel, I adore you, Stacy.

Giant hothouse plants, orchids, and torrents of
white satin freeze the young couple in place.

Nine months later they were married on November 26, 1932, at Trinity Episcopal Church in Princeton. The headmaster of St. Paul's School performed the service jointly with Trinity's rector. Lily was maid of honor, and Morris, Stacy's brother, the best man. The bride wore a long-sleeved, high-necked heavy cream satin gown with a train and carried lilies of the valley, flowers she'd always loved, and orchids, which she later said "made her nervous," as they were too fancy.

Gerard B., continuing his enforced absence from New Jersey, made a swift appearance at the church to give his elder daughter away. He wrote, "I crossed the state line feeling as if I should be under heavy guard, changed into my striped trousers down at the Princeton Inn, gave my daughters away [he performed the same act for Lily a year later] . . . and departed immediately after the ceremonies." The imposing lineup of groomsmen, including Nelson A. Rockefeller, found no bridesmaids to accompany Bunny up the aisle, however.

On October 30, a month before the wedding, *The Philadelphia Inquirer* had announced what was to be a very large affair, with ten bridesmaids, including many of Bunny's Foxcroft classmates. But just two days before that announcement Arthur Houghton Lowe, Bunny's beloved grandpa, had died in Fitchburg. The day after his death flags flew at half-mast, and the crowd at his funeral overflowed the city's Congregational Church. Bunny's brother, Sonny, was one of the pallbearers. (Out of respect for Arthur Lowe, the bridesmaids didn't march up the wedding aisle on November 26, but Bunny's mother-in-law-to-be helped out by giving the would-be bridesmaids a pre-wedding luncheon.) Among the banks of cut flowers stood a grove of "graceful young pine trees raised by Mr. Lowe from seedlings and transported from New Hampshire to lend their forest beauty to the formal rites."

The meaning of that small forest grove ran deep for Bunny. Recalling a childhood memory about her New Hampshire trips with her grandpa, Bunny wrote,

> When a match company had laid waste to the adjoining forest [near his cabin in New Hampshire] he bought this unwanted land and replanted it. The farmer dug the holes—I, aged ten— followed with a bundle of seedling pines, dropping one in each hole. Then Grandfather secured the earth around them—we planted thousands of trees. At the end of each summer he had engraved on a boulder how many were planted, and the year.

"For my grandchildren and great-grandchildren," he smiled.
The boulders are still there.

She quoted him saying, "This is a great country we must take care of it."

Stacy's mother, Eleanor Burroughs Morris Lloyd, born in 1881, would prove to be a formidable mother-in-law. She spent her life in the club and charity circuit limelight of her native city, doing good works and bolstering historic preservation. Like her son, she was a hardworking, top-ranked member of many social, philanthropic, and cultural organizations—always the most exclusive ones—in whose causes she believed. Her gardening credentials were impeccable. She chaired the New York Botanical Garden's women's advisory council, was a charter member (1913) of the Garden Club of America, and held various posts in the Horticultural Club of Philadelphia. No doubt she was a very good hands-on gardener. But perhaps Eleanor was on Bunny's mind when she wrote how amazed Leon Zach, president and fellow of the American Society of Landscape Architects, was a year or so after the White House Rose Garden was finished when he interviewed Bunny, only to find that she was no "pompous blue-haired garden club woman." Hidden "producer" that she preferred to be, the new Mrs. Lloyd would not follow the public path of her mother-in-law.

After the young couple returned from a honeymoon that finished in Honolulu, Stacy's parents surprised them with the gift of a fully furnished house in Ardmore, Pennsylvania, uncomfortably close to the senior Lloyds. "Even the lilies of the valley looked starved in this place," said Bunny, who was determined to find a way out. "Secretly, we looked for another house," she added, and they quickly found one in Paoli, Pennsylvania, near Radnor, "on a piece of land that had been bought just to save the hunting country—we were given it for free & I set about redoing it."

Innately attuned to interior design and style, Bunny had also picked up on the latest trends. During the European yacht-racing summer of 1928, Bunny, age eighteen, had traveled in England with her family. They visited Cliveden, home of Viscountess Astor, Gerard B.'s old Virginian friend Nancy Langhorne. "Nannie's boy," as Gerard B. called the young Hon. William Astor, asked Bunny to cut his twenty-first-birthday cake. Nancy was the arbiter of opulent country-house chic, but it was Syrie Maugham, mother of one of Bunny's best friends, Liza Maugham, who introduced to the fashionable world the hot new style of "distressed furniture"—part of today's "shabby chic"—pieces that had been stripped and pickled into instant old age. Maugham's brilliantly lit drawing room in London, decorated in all white with mirrors, had been an instant sensation in 1927.

"I bought a bed for 11.00 and set it out in the sun to bleach," Bunny told me. This was probably her first stab at furnishing a house with pieces meant to look as if they had aged comfortably through the decades. She added, "I made the hangings and curtains myself." One day, when everything was ready, Bunny recalled, "I sent Stacy with the key to give back to his mother, to tell her, 'We have found a place in Radnor.'"

By then Bunny had completely charmed her mother-in-law's jolly father, Effingham Buckley Morris, a beloved Philadelphia figure and apparently a man not averse to making waves when he felt like it. "Mr. Morris always gave a big Christmas lunch," Bunny recounted. "But that year he decided not to: 'I would like to have lunch with Bunny and Stacy,' he said. Walking behind him on Christmas Day came the caped footman bearing the goose on a platter. 'I have come to have Christmas lunch with you,' announced Mr. Morris who proceeded to cut up the goose."

Bunny had made her position clear, and Effingham Buckley Morris was happy to play along. As she saw it, Stacy was to be hers exclusively, and Mrs. Lloyd's efforts to keep her son close were interference—like that of other women, wives and girlfriends especially, that Bunny would see as "interfering" in her relationships with men. Had Eleanor Lloyd taken Bunny's measure regarding her abilities and interest in design when she provided her darling son and his mate with that fully furnished house as a wedding gift? In hindsight such a gift to a woman destined to be one of the greatest style icons of the twentieth century looks like a disaster. Even seen through 1932 eyes, it's hard to conceive of a young woman who wouldn't at least have raised an eyebrow at this apron-strings attempt.

By 1934 the pair were living at rural Carter Hall, far from the social center of Philadelphia's Main Line. Stacy bought the old local paper, *The Clarke Courier*, and Bunny contributed four articles about gardening, including one called "Chewing and Sucking Bugs."

Over the course of the first years of his ownership, Stacy wrote columns on local, national, and even international politics, as well as the Great Depression, its labor issues, and finance. Bunny volunteered her design eye for the local Middleburg school grounds. The couple attended the Roosevelts' 1939 New Year's Eve dinner at the White House, but in general these Virginia days were troubled by little outside their own lives until the first year of World War II. Foxhunting remained an obsession for the pair, a three-times-a-week ritual in fall, winter, and spring, as two local packs met on alternate days in the beautiful countryside to find their quarry. (To those who find the sport cruel, American sportsmen like to say that their hounds rarely catch their prey, as every fox knows a handy groundhog hole.)

The Virginia Piedmont was by the 1930s decidedly "horse country." A post–Civil War population of cattle and subsistence farmers and formerly enslaved people by then included racehorse owners, breeders, trainers, and foxhunters. Many of them, horsey or not, like Gerard B. Lambert, had come from the North to enjoy the mystique of the South and to become "Virginians," their expensive pastimes fueled by industrial fortunes, many of them rooted in the nineteenth century. Paul Mellon, already a horseman, and his wife, Mary Conover Brown, who learned to ride despite the dangers that horses posed to her asthma, were among them. The two couples became friends.

The Mellons' American saga began in 1818 when Andrew and Rebecca Mellon, along with young Thomas (1813–1908), emigrated from Ireland and settled in a log cabin in western Pennsylvania, farming 160 acres. As a young man Thomas left the farm, went to university and law school, opened his own firm in 1870, and founded the T. Mellon & Sons' Bank in Pittsburgh in 1870. Over the next decades the great money-making machine that became Pittsburgh saw the Mellon family—including Thomas's son Andrew W. Mellon, Paul Mellon's father—investing shrewdly in coal, in what became Alcoa; in steel (U.S. Steel); and in oil, with the Rockefellers (Standard Oil).

As U.S. Secretary of the Treasury (1921–1932), Andrew W. Mellon served under three presidents, and in 1937 he founded the National Gallery of Art (NGA). In 2014 the Mellon family held a $12 billion fortune, the nineteenth-largest family net worth in America, one greater than that of the Rockefellers and Kennedys combined, according to *Forbes* magazine.

In 1931, Andrew Mellon had bought the nucleus of what would become his son's prized 4,500-acre swath of central Virginia: 400-acre Rokeby Farm in the broad valley between the Blue Ridge and the Catoctin Ridge of the Bull Run Mountains, just southeast of Upperville. The purchase was initially spurred by the proximity of Ailsa Mellon, Andrew's only daughter, and her husband, David Bruce, who lived in Washington, D.C., only fifty miles away.

Bruce, born in Baltimore, had dropped out of Princeton to serve in World War I and then headed for the bar, practicing in Maryland and Virginia. After his marriage to Ailsa, he had the funds to buy back Staunton Hill, a splendid neo-Gothic pile built by his grandfather some two hundred miles south of Washington, D.C. Now a Virginian, he won a seat in the state legislature. In D.C., he played a major role in the National Gallery of Art, Andrew Mellon's dream for the nation. David Bruce and Paul Mellon became lifelong friends; Bruce's divorce from Paul's sister in 1945 never ruffled their long relationship or their joint dedication to the NGA.

Nora McMullen, Andrew's divorced wife, who hadn't ridden a horse since she was a girl, found she loved foxhunting and kept a stable of hunters at Rokeby Farm. Paul Mellon came to join his mother for weekends from the job he so disliked at the Mellon Bank in Pittsburgh, and thus his close association began with the area and with the sense of freedom and joy horses would bring him all his life. Andrew Mellon died in August 1937, and the following year Paul and Mary Conover Brown, whom he had married only two years earlier, left Pittsburgh forever and moved to Rokeby Farm, while his mother moved to Connecticut.

Shortly before his father's death, Paul, with Mary's help, had at last cut through the memories of his dark and lonely childhood as the only son of Andrew Mellon and his scalding memories of his parents' public and angry divorce in the course of which his mother attacked his father publicly in the press, a rare event in that period. The press had a field day. By 1934 both Paul and Mary had read Carl Jung's *Modern Man in Search of a Soul* and subsequently underwent psychoanalysis with him. In order to talk with his father, Paul set down a long memo to himself that clearly relies on what he had absorbed from Jung. "The years of habit have encased me in a lump of ice, like the people in my dreams," he wrote, "and when I get into any personal conversation with Father I become congealed and afraid to speak . . . it will be frightfully hard to thaw myself out and actually be able to feel my real emotions and actually say them to him." In his memoir, *Reflections in a Silver Spoon*, he limned his childhood house in Pittsburgh as a place that had given off "a feeling of silence and gloominess." In one of his kinder descriptions of his father, Paul described him as "a thin-voiced, thin-bodied, shy, and uncommunicative man," who, "were his early life better understood . . . might provide clues to help explain his withdrawn character, but, as things stand his personality remains an enigma."

In the memo, written when he was twenty-nine years old, Paul explains how strenuously he wants "the mass of accumulations, the complications of our holdings" to "be taken care of by trusts or competent persons . . . I do not want to be harassed . . . by the great problems of taxes or by the very dangers and hazards of business competition and natural changes." He found the self-confidence to write, "Perhaps I am not meant to do anything very important or startling in this world but I do know that I will have very engrossing interests if I am only able to grow into them myself. Perhaps I will only be a gentleman farmer or a sportsman." Not only would he find those "competent persons" to take care of his family fortune by his forties, but he also would find those "engrossing interests" and become one of the greatest philanthropists of the twentieth century. Not least, he would also become "a gentleman farmer" and "a sportsman" on the grandest scale.

Mary Conover Brown was not a country girl, nor was she familiar with inherited wealth. The daughter of a Kansas doctor, she had found her way out of the Midwest, graduating from Vassar, where she

Paul and Mary Mellon at his childhood home on Woodland Road
in Pittsburgh before they moved to Virginia in 1938

had majored in French and loved piano and singing. Classmates recalled that "she led the singing [of the college glee club] like someone possessed—vibrant, tense, gesturing in a staccato way," all part of
her "joyous spirit," as someone who "jumped into all gaiety and gave
enormously to it, with an instant laugh and quick remark. Everyone
loved her." Then off she went to the Sorbonne, and in 1929, back in
the United States, following a year of graduate work at Columbia,
Mary married Karl Brown, an advertising man. They were divorced in
1933. She went to work at a small avant-garde New York gallery that
attracted artists such as Isamu Noguchi, Fernand Léger, and Walker
Evans. Another who wandered in was John D. Barrett, Jr., future
president of the Bollingen Foundation, which Paul Mellon funded to
sponsor projects in the arts and humanities. In that same year, 1933,

Paul and Mary were introduced over drinks in New York City by Lucius Beebe, Paul's roistering, openly gay Yale classmate; the three headed through Central Park to the Casino nightclub, where they were greeted with a bottle of champagne, the traditional gift to those who arrived first in a sleigh in the first snowstorm of the year. The couple married in 1935 and honeymooned aboard a houseboat on the Nile.

A dramatic 1937 portrait by the English society painter Gerald Brockhurst shows Mary in a dark green cloak against a pale gray sky. Mary said to a friend, "I hope one day I grow up to that portrait." She wears her shiny brown hair in a curly bob; her brooding eyebrows curve over dark, intense eyes. Her wide-boned face is handsome, vivid. Hanging from her wrist is a charm bracelet, probably a gift from Paul that Mary mentioned as a talisman in a letter to Jung. Her looks couldn't have been more different from Bunny's.

Mary, unlike Bunny, had a less than consuming interest in houses, which she saw as places to live rather than as symbols of self or a way of life. Soon after their move to Virginia, they had hired one of the best-known architects in the nation, William Adams Delano, of Delano & Aldrich, who designed perfect country estates from soup to nuts—gardens, doorknobs, and all. (Delano also renovated neo-Gothic Staunton Hill for the Bruces.)

Paul's was the guiding hand in the creation of the Brick House in Upperville. The Georgian-style mansion that Delano designed was closely modeled after Hammond-Harwood House in Annapolis, recognized as one of the most beautiful eighteenth-century residences in America. Paul had seen it during his brief stint in the classical graduate program at St. John's College in 1940, from which he regularly returned home for weekends to Mary—and foxhunting—until he departed for military training. Paul had already purchased the farm called Oak Spring, adjacent to what would become the Brick House estate. But the country life Paul and Mary planned, like the young Lloyds' life, was in jeopardy, as all four were aware. War was on the way.

4

The Mythology of Contentment

Bunny's first independent landscape, Apple Hill, cascades down toward the bottomland (seen here with a dog for scale).

Half an hour away across the Shenandoah River, in Millwood, David Greville (1934–1996), Lord Brooke, later the 8th Earl of Warwick, arrived in 1942 as a young war refugee sent away from German bombing to stay with the Lloyd family as Stacy went overseas to join the war effort. David was the first of the boys Bunny "adopted" as her own and cared for, perhaps more assiduously than she cared for her own son, Stacy Lloyd III, born in 1937 and known as "Tuffy." (The actor Frank Langella, an acquaintance of her daughter, Eliza, would be her last such "adoption" of a young man.) Lady Charlotte

Fraser, David Greville's daughter, wrote to Bunny after her father's death in 1996, "All the fond memories that are reserved for a parent Daddy held for you." She continued, "I adored Rosie [David Greville's mother]. She was naughty and witty and so beautiful but she was not a good mother. She terrorized my poor papa to her dying day."

Seven-year-old "Brookie" was part of the general evacuation of English children during and following the London Blitz in 1941. Ever mindful of his birth, as an adult he prefaced his sharp-eyed memoir with a seventeen-page genealogy that traces his paternal descent to Charles II in five different ways—through the king's various mistresses. His mother's family, he was careful to point out, was "far below the other side of the family in rank."

For much of his four childhood years in America, David stayed with Bunny in Virginia. His memories of that time stand out. "I always like to say that until 1944 or 1945 the Old South had not really changed since the days of Reconstruction," he wrote. "Carter Hall was an old southern estate standing well on a hill in beautiful parkland near the Shenandoah River . . . The village was Millwood a sort of Tobacco Row at a junction of the road going west to Ohio through the mountains and another going north into West Virginia."

He remembered going over the first line of the Blue Ridge Mountains to visit the next village, White Post, where

> you had the feeling that nothing had changed; there were dirt roads, with old trucks and cars, certainly, but also quite a lot of horse carts and buggies. People still wore very formal old clothes. Old people sat on porches with rocking chairs and plants and spat into cuspidors. The old relationship between white and black people had not really changed. At a farm party children still played the games they had always played: the young black men chased greased hogs and climbed greased poles for silver dollars; and the black people sang the traditional songs to banjos.

Bunny Lloyd was part of this nineteenth-century, Reconstruction-era rural Virginia. It would be a mistake to think that she ever lost sight of it, even as its outward signs were passing away and as she traveled into the galactic worlds of international fashion, art, and style.

Bunny told me about Tuffy's birth at Carter Hall on September 23, 1936, clearly an old-Virginia event. A big mint julep party was taking place downstairs in the grand front hall where a band played while she was in labor in a room at the top of the sweeping staircase. The attending obstetrician was enjoying the juleps and the music. Neighbor and close friend Liz Whitney, married to the millionaire sportsman "Jock" Whitney and soon to be Tuffy's godmother, was upstairs with Bunny and the nurse. Finally, Liz stuck her head over the balcony rail and yelled, "Hey, doc, you better come up, the head's out"—a grittier tale about the real Mrs. Stacy Barcroft Lloyd, Jr., and Mrs. John Hay Whitney than the lofty refinement of those distinguished names might usually acknowledge.

Bunny was serenely aware of class structure and quite comfortable with her place in it—at the top. Thus, without any embarrassment she could tell such an anecdote and then artlessly remark on the butler David Banks's place at the birth in language that is jarring in its assumptions today.

"When my son, Stacy, was born," wrote Bunny, "he sat outside my bedroom until the nurse brought the baby out. Then he reached out his arms and said 'Can I take the young gentleman to his room?' Needless to say, they were like brothers—Stacy nicknamed him 'Buddsie' for 'My Buddy.'" In Bunny's mind the then-twenty-six-year-old Banks, a generation older than Tuffy, had three personas: he was trusted almost as a father figure by Bunny, a beloved playmate for her son, and nonetheless always and unmistakably a servant.

Indeed, even when Bunny Mellon managed 350 employees at "the farm" or any of her five other residences, she treated all those who worked for her with courtesy, respect, and affection—unless or until they took a false step. Those who didn't execute their jobs perfectly—beyond perfectly—or got too familiar or told stories to outsiders or the press were quickly but quietly sacked. She loved Brookie for understanding such exigencies of class—and for being a Warwick as well as for being himself. Her world, and his, was one where quite as a matter of course your "war refugee" was a titled little boy instead of a Cockney kid from East London. Bunny once airily summarized David Greville's family by telling me that "Shakespeare said they were the kingmakers. Much more elegant than the royal family." (The latter referred to the Windsors, with their unfashionable and suspiciously German Saxe-Coburg background.)

Left to right: Possibly the widowed grandmother Mrs. Arthur Lowe; Stacy; Bunny; the baby's nurse; godmother Liz Whitney with Tuffy in her arms; Stacy's mother, Mrs. Lloyd; Bunny's father, Gerard B.; and his second wife, Gracie Mull Lambert, gather at Tuffy's christening.

In the spring of 1937, little Tuffy's christening party was held at Carter Hall. A commemorative scrapbook shows it was cold enough for everyone to wear coats; the trees had not yet leafed out. The party stands on the front steps of the house anyway, enjoying champagne in the thin sunshine. Bunny grins shyly, looking very pleased. For some of the pictures she took off her hairy tweed balmacaan, showing off a girly, short-sleeved, busy flower-printed dress with a ruffled bosom and pleated skirt. Liz Whitney, the godmother, holds Tuffy; Mrs. Lloyd wears a smart dark hat tilted to one side. Stacy looks thrilled and a bit dazed in some of the pictures; in another, he smiles at his father-in-law holding the baby. Gerard B. is proud. A *boy*.

Left to right: Grace Mull Lambert, Bunny, and her husband, Stacy, survey
Bunny's new kingdom from the ridge above the site of Apple Hill.

Sometime that afternoon, Stacy and Bunny, accompanied by Gracie Lambert, Gerard B.'s second wife, took a walk to survey their new house site. In February, they had bought a ten-acre sliver of land. The new place, which they would call Apple Hill, was adjacent to Carter Hall (but was not a gift from Gerard B.). The tract was carved out of the adjoining estate, Mt. Airy, and the Lloyds had paid for it themselves. Following the line of a tumbledown stone wall, a grassy track led down to Apple Hill from Carter Hall. The high point of their new property, a rocky ridge to the north, overlooked a wide meadow edged by woodland. To this day, Apple Hill is stamped with all the trademarks of Bunny's later ventures: a perfect site; a spring and pond; gardens; a greenhouse; and a stable and stable yard. It was her first attempt to create a complete "life" and to begin to establish a mythology of contentment.

The Lloyds chose Charles N. Read from Rhode Island as their architect, rather than Lindeberg, who perhaps was too busy—or too expensive. Or too grand? Charles Read, like Gerard B., his fellow

Princetonian and contemporary, had followed up his education with classes at the École des Beaux-Arts in Paris. Like Gerard B., he took an interest in archaeology and all things classical. He had also worked under Lindeberg at Albemarle. Previously, Read had been employed by Guy Lowell, the Boston turn-of-the-century architect who brought the Beaux Arts into the American garden, with pillars, balustrades, terraces, and plenty of marble. But not a trace of the Beaux Arts style appears at Apple Hill in house or garden.

Ellen Biddle Shipman, the prolific American landscape architect famed for opulent flower bed plantings and harmonious estate garden plans, was briefly hired. Shipman created several gardens and farm estates nearby from start to finish, but at Apple Hill she designed only a garden fence and a decorative gate. Bunny read Shipman's writings and left notes in the Oak Spring library about how to make such Shipmanesque features as grass steps. The concept of surrounding a house with a series of "garden rooms" was already generally in play, but Apple Hill's herb garden, off the living room terrace, with its Colonial Revival design and plantings, surely owes its inspiration directly to Shipman.

A woman who commanded the language of architecture and space, Bunny answered the grandeur of Carter Hall with a firm no when she created Apple Hill. Its comfortable Pennsylvania farmhouse style clearly prefigures Oak Spring, her first landscape essay as Mrs. Paul Mellon. Handsome, beautifully scaled, and well-lit downstairs rooms included a tiny kitchen no bigger than a closet, the prototype for what Bunny called a "cook out," where she could make a cup of tea in solitude. Upstairs, a rabbit warren of small connecting bedrooms far out of parental earshot was no doubt perfect in the Lloyds' eyes for children and servants.

Brookie remembered Apple Hill as very beautiful. Bunny "had used a great deal of local stone and had whitewashed it, mixing local clay in with the whitewash to give everything a battered old look, and she was a very keen gardener. At the bottom of Carter Hall there was a huge spring which had been dammed up, the sides built up with the loose stone walls of the area to form a pond. It had huge trees hanging over it and was incredibly cold and clear. When we were stiflingly hot in mid-summer we used to swim there, or in the local stream which ran through the farmland . . . I do remember the feeling of organization, of happy busyness," he continued. "Stacy had a horse-drawn sledge, and [in winter] cars went slowly with their chains on . . . And we snowballed and built ice-houses."

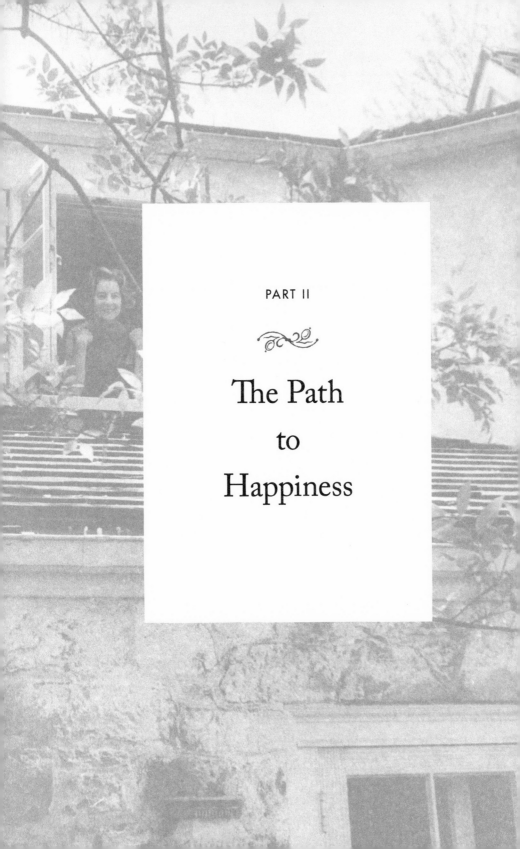

PART II

The Path
to
Happiness

London, War—and Women

By early 1941 the timeless Virginian world Brookie described had begun to break apart under the pressure of the mounting European conflict. The life of his mother, Rosie, in those years encapsulates the hectic flavor of the Lloyds' circle as it whirlpooled into wartime haste, bravery, derring-do, hilarity—and tragedy. Rosie had married the dashing 7th Earl of Warwick in 1933. After producing the all-important heir (little Lord Brooke) and divorcing the earl in 1938, Rosie married the far more dashing combat pilot Captain Billy Fiske later that same year. Son of a well-to-do New England banker, Fiske, a brilliant Olympic athlete and aviator, was one of the first Americans to enlist in the British Royal Air Force (RAF). America was still stridently isolationist, so Fiske pretended to be Canadian. In July 1940 he jubilantly joined the "Millionaires' Squadron," so called as many were well-heeled, high-living young men who quickly gained a reputation as daring fighters. On August 16, Fiske's squadron destroyed eight German aircraft but his fuel tank caught a bullet. Instead of bailing, he nursed his flaming plane over some hedgerows and back to base, hoping to save his aircraft. He died of his wounds two days later.

Rosie arrived in Virginia less than a year after her husband's death. Her American friends rallied around. Liz Whitney, Tuffy's godmother, gave Rosie an old farmhouse, Peach House, on the Whitneys' huge horse farm, Llangollen, not far from Apple Hill. Bunny, already known as a gardener, offered her old friend Rosie both advice and some of her own roses and perennials. But Brookie writes that

Whitney, a noted horsewoman, often visited on her hunter, "which would clump around the garden, probably doing a fair amount of damage . . . Their friendship cooled . . . Liz Whitney was not happy at the success of the mother, a beautiful young widow in Virginia with young me . . . She was evicted by the sheriff & our possessions were sold on the lawn . . . Later they made up." It is typical of Bunny's mischievous sense of humor that she kept the July 1941 eviction notice, along with an eight-page inventory of the contents of Peach House. Rosie had gleefully crossed out the feather duster and thirty-six bottles of delicious Charmes-Chambertin, noting that they "Didn't go!" Rosie's Virginian idyll had ended, and off she went, back to England.

Army instructor Paul Mellon is ready to teach horsemanship at Fort Riley, Kansas, in 1942.

Paul Mellon had enlisted in the army a month earlier and was given a cavalry assignment after reaching out to Major General George S. Patton, nephew of a foxhunting neighbor, for help to get what he wanted. Paul was sent to Fort Riley, Kansas, and emerged in March 1943 as an officer, a second lieutenant teaching the military seat and elementary jumping to raw recruits unfamiliar with horses. A couple of steeplechase friends found their way into one of his platoons. Superb and confident horsemen, they found the "military seat," with its buttocks-up posture, absurd, and Mellon found himself—probably rightly—hesitant to correct them. In his memoir, Paul tells with characteristic modesty and understatement the story of his military service mostly as a series of pratfalls, which is one way to handle the enormity of war.

The real death and destruction of the coming combat had been on Paul's mind even before he enlisted, however. Only days before the London Blitz began in September 1940, while the city was bracing itself for Luftwaffe attacks and possible German invasion, Paul had written to the lord mayor. He offered to buy an ambulance for the Red Cross Fund in memory of Andrew Mellon, "to express what would have been my father's deep sympathy for the English cause" and his own. The lord mayor wrote back to ask if Paul's letter could be published; the assent was accompanied by a check for $22,000, enough to buy ten ambulances. Six months after Paul enlisted, the war came to the United States after the Japanese attack on Pearl Harbor on December 7, 1941.

In the fall of 1942, on September 18, Stacy Lloyd, Jr., left Apple Hill, his beloved horses, his newspaper, *The Clarke Courier*, his fledgling magazine, *The Chronicle of the Horse* (which survives today)—and a wife who was eight months pregnant. Bunny left the farm soon after that to stay at her father and stepmother's house on Kalorama Circle in Washington, D.C., to await her second baby. The much-cherished Eliza was born on October 27 in the city's dilapidated Garfield Memorial Hospital, where for lack of space she was stashed in a room along with the floral arrangements destined to be delivered to patients.

By June 1942, President Roosevelt had already created—not without difficulty, given a noninterventionist Congress—the Office of Strategic Services (OSS) under the leadership of Col. William "Wild Bill" Donovan. The forerunner of today's CIA, the OSS was originally set up to collect and analyze strategic information required by the Joint Chiefs of Staff and to carry out special operations not already assigned to other agencies, such as the FBI. The OSS was soon empowered to carry out every kind of secret activity—espionage, counterintelligence, propaganda, and covert action.

Paul Mellon's brother-in-law, Col. David Bruce, was engaged in covert activities even before Pearl Harbor, making himself familiar with the various British spy agencies (none of which was particularly welcoming to American intelligence efforts). Acting as an American Red Cross war-relief observer in England, he was photographed among a group of journalists watching RAF and Luftwaffe planes duel above the White Cliffs of Dover in August 1940. Among the combat-helmeted group, Bruce stands out in his bowler and chalk-striped English suit.

Quick-witted, charming, ambitious, yet understated, Bruce had served in the army courier service during the Paris Peace Conference at Versailles in 1919 and briefly in the American consular service in the 1920s. He knew the diplomatic players and the ropes. He was equally at home in European and American high society. Donovan would soon make him head of OSS secret operations in Europe. He would become perhaps the most able and certainly the best-connected of all the American spy organizers who navigated the narrow, contentious channels of American and British intelligence abroad.

Donovan and Bruce recruited to the infant OSS many of those whom the journalist and satirist Malcolm Muggeridge called the "*jeunes filles en fleur* straight from a finishing school, all fresh and innocent." Bruce's biographer retailed them as "a glittering pool of talent—academics, entrepreneurs, Ivy League Republican bankers, left-wing labor attorneys, anyone with a particular skill to contribute"—as well as sportsmen (aka gentlemen of leisure), scientists, frequenters of nightclubs, and journalists and writers of every kind. The index of David Bruce's memoir reads like a compilation of America's *Social Register*, *Debrett's Peerage*, the *Almanach de Gotha*, and the *New York Post*'s Page Six. These freshmen, plus a very few women, included Stacy Lloyd and Paul Mellon.

By mid-October 1942, Stacy was working in London for the OSS. Rosie Fiske, who had been back in England since October 1941 after Liz Whitney kicked her out, wrote reassuringly to the very pregnant Bunny: "I promise I'll look after him for you. I think he likes his job and is quite happy . . . Bless you and don't worry he is OK we both love you." Rosie offered Stacy her own flat, because she had moved to the country accompanied by her personal maid, Green, renting a house that came equipped with a cook, a parlor maid, and a gardener.

Instead, Stacy first lived in the house of another upper-crust American horseman, the half-English Raymond Guest, second cousin to Winston Churchill, polo player, horse breeder, and bon vivant. Bruce, not given to exaggeration, described Guest as bringing to any situation "his usual ebullient self, as if he contained enough vitamins to supply a nation of people with vitality." (Guest, an officer in the U.S. Navy, soon became the OSS naval chief in Europe.) Stacy was finding himself in a familiar world but one now lit with the glamour of secrecy, danger, and the knowledge that he was on an important mission.

Back at Apple Hill in Virginia as winter came on, Bunny's life felt very different. She had her hands full with a newborn, Eliza, her five-year-old son, and little Brookie. Not that she had no help: in addition to David Banks, whom Brookie also recognized as "the mainstay of the house," there was a staff of five: Bunny's maid, Evelyn; a cook and her nephew who helped out in the garden; and, wrote Brookie, "a disagreeable Swiss governess full of Republican spirit who lectured me about the King at breakfast before Bunny came down." Eliza also had a nanny. But the old life that circled around Stacy was gone; only the constant stream of letters between husband and wife remained.

Rosie and Bunny's correspondence also went back and forth between England and Virginia. "Stacy is fine and under my maternal wing," wrote Rosie ten days after Eliza's birth. "We think and talk of you to the distraction of everybody else but we know best all blessings love." The cable, sent to Bunny at her father's house in D.C., where she was recuperating from childbirth, was signed by both Rosie and Stacy. In the same cable, Rosie said she was happy to be Eliza's godmother and that she and Stacy were dining together that night. They would also spend Stacy's first birthday and first Christmas abroad together. Even as Stacy was sending Bunny a constant cascade of information and affection, so was Rosie. "Stacy is away on a course . . . Don't worry it's only a lecture course!" she wrote on January 8, 1943.

Rosie may have intended only to reassure and support her friend Bunny, but her messages also indicated how very close she and Stacy had become during his year in London training to be a secret agent. On March 4, Rosie wrote, "I promise Stacy is fine & well . . . I see him usually every day so do know what I am talking about."

Care packages, often waylaid by wartime customs, also made their way across the ocean. Clothes rationing had been in force in England since June 1941. In that same March 4 letter, Rosie asked Bunny to send her some of the impossible-to-find necessities for which all

Englishwomen were begging, such as stockings. Rosie wanted silk ones, "6 or 7 pairs." She also asked Bunny for "six yards of pink satin or crepe de chine, peachy pink or white for petticoats . . . 2 boxes of black Rimmel's [mascara]" and "ready-made white silk long-sleeved tailor-made shirts with plain collar to wear with a tie. Bust 36," she specified. The gorgeous Rosie was about to do American Red Cross canteen work in London—a sought-after, high-visibility wartime job for a fashionably patriotic woman—and one requirement was looking good.

Stacy let Bunny know that "the silk stockings were the most immense success, she was chortling over them and the eye black. As to the pants you sent her," however, "I . . . doubt very much if she wears them. I believe Rosie is probably the Minute Man type or the Boy Scout who must always Be Prepared."

By August 1943, Rosie was able to give Bunny the news that Stacy had "been away on a three weeks' course as I cabled you and has since returned, very well, and full of the life he led at the barracks." In her cable, sent on August 30—with belated birthday greetings to Bunny (who took her August 9 birthday very seriously all her life)—Rosie noted that Stacy had returned from the course as a "perfect physical specimen." She signed off with "devoted love always."

In the meantime, Paul Mellon had sailed from Boston on May 1, 1943, as a security officer on a freighter, part of a huge 150-vessel convoy. Paul briefly taught calisthenics to the navy gun crew aboard and eventually landed in Cardiff. He was first assigned to tend victory gardens in American army camps, then rerouted to London to an office job that he felt wasn't what he wanted to be doing for the war any more than the gardening or the calisthenics. So he contacted his brother-in-law, David Bruce, for help—and Stacy Lloyd, Jr., then working in Special Intelligence (SI). After Paul went on various interviews, it appeared that his French wasn't good enough to qualify him for SI; by late July he found himself in the OSS in yet another desk job. He and Stacy had moved in together, first to a flat, then to a house they shared.

"He and Paul have moved into their new home," Rosie informed Bunny in a long typed letter, "which is . . . so much nicer than

Raymond [Guest]'s house." She told how the two men had warmed up what they thought was a saucepan of stew left for them by their housekeeper but that turned out to be what she'd left for the cat. Stacy also related the story to Bunny, and Paul Mellon repeated it in *Reflections*. Clearly it *was* worth a big laugh all around at a time when English food had reached new lows, thanks to rationing.

Hilarity and a British stiff upper lip were both much needed. Although the German raids had lessened for a while by August 1943 and British spirits were still high, much of London had been badly damaged. Nearly thirty thousand Londoners had been killed and fifty thousand severely wounded in the 1940–41 blitz. A million and a half people were left homeless. Nine miles of London's East End, the docklands so vital to Britain's survival, had been set ablaze. Deep bomb shelters had not been completed, and the biggest tube stations, including Sloane and Trafalgar Squares, where Londoners spent many a night waiting for the all clear, had been struck. Other London landmarks that had been severely damaged included Buckingham Palace, Parliament, Whitehall, the National Gallery, the BBC in Portland Place—and Savile Row, where, as a matter of course, Americans such as Stacy Lloyd, Jr., Paul Mellon, and David Bruce, like their British counterparts, attended their tailors' shops to be fitted for their chalk-striped suits, riding clothes, and morning coats.

David Bruce's first goals as head of the OSS's European operations were to meld cantankerous British and American intelligence groups, share intelligence, and raise the OSS's profile as a legitimate information-gathering agency. He also began a round of meetings to plan for the Allied attack that would begin a year later on June 6, 1944, D-Day. The OSS's new venture, the Morale Operations (MO) Branch, founded a month after Bruce's arrival in England in February 1943, would produce and disseminate undercover propaganda to use against the Axis powers. Stacy, now assigned to MO, took part in the planning. If not at OSS headquarters, meetings invariably took place in the upper-class watering holes of London, such as traditional men's clubs, Claridge's, and the Ritz. "It seemed very natural to be back at the Ritz, with its usual hall porters, indestructible old servants, and moths flying out of every stuffed chair," recalled Bruce.

A favored spot for David Bruce and Stacy Lloyd to meet was Buck's, lively and informal, the "youngest" of the men's clubs, where at the "American bar" (bars being a fairly new thing) the "Buck's Fizz"—half champagne, half orange juice—was first concocted. P. G. Wodehouse modeled his fictional Drones Club on Buck's.

To Bunny, Rosie described the hectic London parties she and Stacy attended together in the summer of 1943. At one party she confessed she "looked pretty slick" in a red chiffon dress worn with a glowing tan—"I've burned the whole bee you tiful body a glorious golden brown"—achieved by sunbathing naked on the roof of a British officers' mess in Devonshire. Rosie's own riotous gatherings must have sounded impossibly glamorous to Bunny, stuck in far-off rural Virginia: at one, besides the ever-present Stacy, the guests included stars such as the comedian Bob Hope and the screen idol Clark Gable. Rosie herself left around two in the morning, but later gathered that the party swirled on until 7 a.m.—"a success, I feel."

Even while reassuring his wife, Bunny, at home in Virginia about her friend Rosie Fiske's loyalty, Stacy, in London in 1943, did have to admit that Rosie's past reputation had been "a very very gay one and it is going to be very hard for her to live down, if she ever does."

"The war was an irresistible catalyst. It overwhelmed everything, forced relationships like a hothouse, so that in a matter of days one would achieve a closeness with someone that would have taken months to develop in peacetime," remembered Kay Summersby Morgan in a memoir of her wartime affair with Dwight D. Eisenhower. Or, as the American journalist Harrison Salisbury put it: "Sex hung in the air like a fog."

Bunny did have her suspicions about the relationship between her husband and her close friend—anyone would have on reading letters like Rosie's—and English gossip columns whispered about a liaison.

Stacy hastened to calm his wife down, writing, "Now Muff don't have a fit over Rose. She is absolutely loyal to you to the last dot." He hustled to mention other less high-flying, more respectable friends, "who are not at all the utter spoiled socially minded ones but very nice and sensible. Lady Patricia Ward who works on Lord Beaverbrook's paper . . . the Countess of Munster who is a big tall ungainly girl who runs a farm with her husband in the country . . ." But then Stacy notes, "Rose gives little dinner parties almost constantly," something that could hardly have reassured his wife. He added that Rosie frequented "very nice places" and that Churchill's close friend "Lord Beaverbrook and any number of other high government people like her a lot and have her to dinner. She is behaving very well," he went on, claiming that despite her wild reputation, she "seems to be living a very sensible life."

Stacy had rumors of dalliances buzzing around him, but Paul Mellon went farther. "Uncle Paul [Mellon] had an English girl: Valerie Churchill-Longman," recalled Paul's goddaughter, Georgiana Drake Hubbard McCabe. "Valerie came over to the USA at the end of the war, and Chauncey [Chauncey K. Hubbard, Georgiana's father] and a bunch of their friends went to the dock when the ship came in and persuaded her to go home."

From January 1943 and on through the summer, Stacy took top-secret training courses in espionage. Although Bunny was kept vaguely aware of her husband's activities through his letters, she was getting restive. From Rosie's letters, as well as Stacy's, wartime London looked like an exciting place. Why not leave the children at home and join her husband? Work in the American Red Cross like Rosie and other friends? Stacy nixed the suggestion, which was entirely reasonable. When Bunny insisted that he then take a leave and come home, he told her that he couldn't, and, what was more, he couldn't tell her why. Nothing could have enraged her more.

Instead, in the summer of 1943, a group of three women and six

Bunny with her children and friends in the summer of 1943
in Watch Hill, Rhode Island

small children rented one of the worn, slightly uncomfortable shingled "summer cottages" so typical of WASP-y seaside resorts in New England. In a group picture taken on the front steps, Bunny Lloyd was doing what many an upper-class American woman has done since the nineteenth century: spending the summer alone with her children while her husband was elsewhere, at work or at play. The two other women, both close English friends of Bunny's, were spending the war in safety in the United States with their children. Brookie, who was often kept busy pushing one of the little girls in her pram during what he described as a long summer, is absent from the scene.

Bunny later recollected that for the three mothers their Watch Hill, Rhode Island, escapade was like camping—"we slept three women to a bed," like a pajama party. In the photo, Liza Maugham Paravicini, the daughter of W. Somerset Maugham, cocks her head smilingly at the photographer. (Liza had not yet left her first marriage to become Baroness Glendevon). Bunny, who admired Liza prodigiously until their friendship mysteriously vaporized in the 1990s, told me, "She writes better than her father!"

Liza's letters in the Oak Spring Garden Library, while they don't bear out that outrageous claim, make very good reading. They are those of someone who at thirteen had already been described by the British fashion photographer Cecil Beaton as "unique, wise, sophisticated, yet very childish." In the photograph, Liza, always a great dresser, is wearing a marvelous plaid pinafore that shows off her very small waist.

Rosie Clyde, who "played the piano like George Shearing and was much in demand for weekend parties," according to Liza's daughter, Camilla, wears one of the blousy gabardines so popular in the 1940s and sports a pair of low-heeled spectator pumps, brown and white and very chic.

Bunny, totally absorbed in the barefoot, smiling, eighteen-month-old Eliza on her lap, looks comfortable in a full dark skirt and a striped shirt with a Peter Pan collar. She has rolled up her sleeves and is wearing a pair of shapeless white espadrilles—she had not yet become a style icon.

On August 14, 1943, Rosie Fiske wrote, "I have not had a letter from you for damn nearly two months, please Bunny. I rather suspect that you are having a wonderful time at your summer residence and cannot find the time to write. My very best love to you and the other girls. I long for a letter so sit down now." Even as Rosie wrote lighthearted letters to her best friend about London life, one wonders if she might have been sleeping with Bunny's husband. Stacy's reassurances to Bunny that nothing had gone on or was going on with Rosie fell flat. He continued to tell his "dearest Hun Bun" that Rosie "is one of the very best and most devoted friends you will ever have." Bunny told me she never entirely believed him but would not say more.

6

The Field of War

Stacy Lloyd, Jr., Paul Mellon, and David Bruce had all been schooled for war according to the same rules of life, but among them Stacy had exceptional "street smarts." Unlike Paul Mellon, he was also an all-round athlete who had loved sports and excelled at them in school and college. Elite prep schools such as St. Paul's and Choate (Paul Mellon's beloved school) and Ivy League universities (Princeton for Stacy, Yale for Paul) took it as a given that they were to produce leaders and confident judges of men. They were meant to rapidly take charge of any situation no matter how unlikely, frightened, or inept their teammates might be. Stacy was also a quick study in what Paul Mellon described as "cloak-and-dagger activities."

In his flight suit, Stacy Lloyd, Jr., center, prepares for action with the OSS.

As for Paul, it is hard to tell what his undercover abilities were from his memoir, where he often modestly presents himself as a bemused participant. When in September

1943 he at last got away from sorting papers and pay scales, he was sent to a field training course in Hampshire where OSS recruits had to learn such skills as killing silently, breaking and entering houses by night, using explosives, and "crossing streams by cable hand over hand with a Sten gun hanging below one."

Meanwhile, Stacy—with a full year of similar OSS training under his belt—was dispatched to Algiers as a member of the staff of "Wild Bill" Donovan, now a general. North Africa was the OSS's first engagement as an arm of the military at war. To the surprise of the competitive British intelligence services, the OSS had proved useful. After Mussolini fell from power in late July 1943, Eisenhower, in command of Allied forces in the Mediterranean, was ordered to proceed at once to recapture Italy. Salerno, the first place the opposing forces met on European soil, was a disorganized disaster for the Allies, but in the mayhem Stacy capably reorganized an oddball crew of resistance fighters, writing to Bunny that he'd received a battlefield promotion to lieutenant colonel. In Naples, his next stop, even though Southern Italy was in Allied hands by early October, Stacy was begging for supplies, including jeeps, maps, and even shoes for his threadbare agents. By November he was back in England.

There he secretly trained OSS agents to infiltrate the French battleground. As the date for the invasion neared, the OSS broadened preparations, offering a "progressive and complete training in various English grand castles and castellated manor houses for agents recruited in Algeria." In March 1944, from his secret training place in the shires, Stacy had written, "Dearest Hun Bun I have not been able to write you for six days which is a tremendous lapse of time . . . I have been living in a tent outside of a colossal house somewhere in England," a house big enough to require "a good half hour to walk through all of the rooms."

In late March, Stacy was given a two-week leave. On his return to the United States, he briefed the Washington higher-ups, then headed for Bunny and Apple Hill. Virginia's spring was in full flower. Tuffy, a somber little boy, was seven years old; his sister, Eliza, was now a dark-haired, ravishingly chubby toddler. The ever-sanguine Brookie was nine. Bunny was thin and anxious. Everyone was waiting, sensing that the big assault on Europe would happen soon, but when? Lieutenant Colonel Lloyd had already served for eighteen months overseas. He again kissed his wife goodbye. On April 8 he headed back to England for final preparations. Eight weeks later came D-Day, the Allied invasion of Normandy on June 6, 1944.

David Bruce was a superb storyteller. In his wartime diaries, published as *OSS Against the Reich*, he regaled his readers with a minute-by-minute account of the summer days in London after D-Day and on OSS movements through the fall as they followed the Allied troops and the retreating Germans. Paris was Bruce's holy grail, where he and Ernest Hemingway, acting as a war correspondent, would "liberate" the Ritz Hotel on August 25, ordering up fifty martinis from the imperturbable Claude Auzello, manager of the hotel since the 1920s. (Bruce also visited the perfume house of Guerlain, where M. Guerlain presented him with a bottle of Shalimar, the house's flagship scent, perhaps [or perhaps not] for Evangeline Bell—who had been recruited by the OSS to create convincing aliases for agents parachuting into France. She and Bruce would marry when the war ended.)

En route to Paris, David Bruce, at left, then the commanding OSS officer in the field in France, stops with Ernest Hemingway, at right, for a drink.

Bruce's reports from the field—rapid, wry, colorful, detailed, and sometimes hilarious—were eagerly anticipated and read in the Home Office. But his terse, elegant reporting offers little room for sadness or horror, only for facts and observations. When on June 13 the first "doodlebugs," the initial phase of German pilotless missiles, fell on London, killing one hundred people and seriously wounding five hundred, Bruce wrote only that "after today it is likely that AA [anti-aircraft] fire will no longer be directed against these pilotless planes . . . because AA [are] rarely able to hit them, and unless they were exploded in the air, it did no good to bring them down as they naturally explode upon impact." London lay defenseless against the buzz bombs screaming in.

Stacy huddled with Bruce about creating propaganda intended to look as if it was written by their opponents—so-called black propaganda—to be distributed as leaflets behind the German lines. He got firsthand advice from Count Paul Münster, a German aristocrat and a friend of the Duke of Windsor, who had served four years as an officer in the German army during World War I and was apparently well aware of how best to induce Nazi soldiers to revolt or surrender.

In early July, Bruce got the okay to begin the French mission, so Stacy and a French liaison officer headed across the Channel immediately to set up their MO team. Within a month the OSS was ensconced in five comfortable "villas" they had commandeered as their continental base in Saint-Pair-sur-Mer, a picturesque resort in Normandy. In nearby Saint-Malo, however, "the shelling and bombing is heavy," noted Bruce calmly, adding nonetheless, "Nothing could testify more strongly to our overwhelming mastery of the skies than the freedom and insouciance with which our armadas of trucks, bulldozers, and other automotive equipment of every kind roll in their thousands along the roads."

Stacy shines as an almost miraculous forager in Bruce's account. The countryside was thick with mines and with the enemy, who were torturing and killing as they retreated, but Stacy never failed to find a secure place to house and feed his weary group of spies. No one knew better than Stacy the old Napoleonic saw that an army travels on its stomach. His team pushed on during the late summer and fall of 1944, making it eventually through the forests of the Ardennes to Luxembourg and Belgium. Bunny had no idea what his classified work was. Top secret.

By August 15, Stacy had seized a large, comfortable house in the countryside near Angers, which, Bruce wrote,

> is part of the so-called "Garden of France" . . . Great expanses of wheat fields, orchards, pastures and forests stretch on either side of us . . . The apples are just beginning to acquire a pinkish tinge, and the wheat stubble and sheaves are a mellow gold. Many peasant families keep Belgian hares in little cages where they fatten for the table . . . vines grow . . . in rows within well-tended vegetable patches. Under the sun it is a smiling countryside . . . Here and there along the road is a destroyed house or hamlet, or a burnt-out truck or tank.

Stacy operated independently, keeping in touch by radio. Often Bruce couldn't find him—sometimes "the bird had flown" from his safe house. From a café terrace in Le Mans, only 132 miles west of Paris, as he waited to meet Stacy, Bruce admired the pretty young Frenchwomen who managed to remain stylish in wartime. At midnight, Bruce's elusive quarry suddenly turned up, and together Stacy and he concocted leaflets, "one of them purportedly signed by General Rommel, saying the German cause is hopeless and advising surrender."

On August 18, Bruce moved MO operations north to Chartres, taking all the equipment to churn out his leaflets. At one point on the way to a nearby command post, the group saw "a dozen dead German soldiers and three or four Americans. [B]loated, stiffened, and their skins black." In Chartres itself, French Resistance fighters fired on what they believed were German snipers in the spires of the cathedral, Bunny's lodestar of beauty and civilization, but did little damage. In the town of Rambouillet, Stacy and Bruce visited the French wounded lying in their hospital beds. To their horror they discovered that most of the injuries had been caused by American bombs or by American planes strafing German equipment on the roads. One young woman who was caught in an American plane's machine-gun fire had had to have her feet amputated. "C'est la guerre," she told her visitors.

At last on August 25, General Charles de Gaulle marched into Notre-Dame Cathedral for a Te Deum mass to celebrate the liberation of Paris. The war was not over for Stacy, however. At the end of September, as the Allies slowly beat their way toward the German border across the Low Countries, the days grew short, and heavy autumn rains began, flooding the countryside. The golden weather and the ebullient sense of a harvest earned when they landed in Saint-Pair-sur-Mer in July had disappeared. Stacy and his team were in Luxembourg City, where OSS colonel K. D. Mann had enjoyed one of Stacy's "living off the country banquets." Mann, who, like Stacy, had served in Algiers, noticed a change in Stacy. He was thin and both physically and mentally worn, Mann said. In October, Mann wrote to Bruce that Stacy needed to be relieved. In a later letter Mann revealed to Bruce what he hadn't previously disclosed about Stacy: Mann had been in Washington, D.C., that October and dined with Bunny, who told him she was about to have a hysterectomy. In his letter to Bruce, Mann also said that she was anemic and in an unsettled mental state. Bunny said she wanted to keep her condition and the operation a secret.

The news nonetheless reached Stacy. The operation was a success, and Bunny rested up at her father's house on Kalorama Circle before going back to Apple Hill and the children. Stacy telegrammed Bunny on December 6, saying he would come home if she needed him. Ten days later, during the nightmarish fighting in Belgium, Stacy wrote to tell her how much their reunion would mean to him. Virginia and Bunny must have looked like heaven. It took six weeks from that last letter for Stacy to reach the United States.

Paul Mellon's summer and fall of 1944 had been very different from Stacy's. A week after D-Day he found himself in the English Midlands in a clandestine training house, waiting to head overseas. For foreign agents like the Algerians whom Stacy had decanted into Liverpool, this had been strange territory. For Paul, it was practically home ground. Around him, as they traveled toward Southampton, lay countryside he had ridden over in pursuit of the fox, crashing through hedges and galloping across grassy fields, and the stables where his steeplechasers had trained.

Paul's first foray in France resulted in a near-lethal case of pneumonia. He was remanded to England to recover and eventually sent on a stretcher train to a hospital in far-off Shropshire. Valerie Churchill-Longman (who, like Rosie Fiske, also worked for the classy American Red Cross operation in London) raced to him there. By October 1944, Paul was ready to return to action, although, as he wrote, he "had missed the big push across France." Some of his OSS colleagues had been decorated, including Stacy, whose MO unit Paul finally joined just before the Battle of the Bulge in December. The Germans had waited until bad weather gave them an advantage. Dense fog prevented any use of superior Allied air defense. "Weather was a weapon the German army used with success," Field Marshal Gerd von Rundstedt later said. In the near-Arctic conditions some American tanks froze to the ground and had to be chiseled free. The Allies, including behind-the-lines MO units, were forced to fall back. Stacy and Paul ended up some thirty miles behind Stacy's previously hard-won outpost.

As he admits in his memoir, Paul didn't think much of MO in general and even less of its disinformation leaflets. However, when Stacy flew back to Virginia in late January and Paul was made commanding officer of the unit, he wondered if in fact there weren't ways to use black propaganda after all. But during the final mopping-up operations against German forces in France, in a Bordeaux vineyard, a French soldier following Paul's MO team was blown up by a booby trap. Paul wrote later that for himself at least, at that moment his "playing at war, playing at propaganda artists, was thoughtless and foolish." He and his team returned to Paris.

On May 8, 1945, V-E (Victory in Europe) Day, the Germans surrendered. By now, Paul had been promoted to major. For his service he received two Bronze Stars and the silver parachutist's badge he had coveted, and he was commended as an "excellent, all-round field officer" in his discharge papers. He sailed on May 22 aboard the SS *Île de France*, arriving at his house on East Seventieth Street in Manhattan "a very different man from the raw recruit who had left for Fort Riley four years earlier."

Stacy had returned to the sleepy Shenandoah Valley, to Bunny and their children and to his old life. Uneasily he wondered if, after all he'd seen and done, running two local newspapers would be enough to occupy him. Certainly he felt financially strapped: he had already borrowed $30,000 to pay for expensive changes to the garden and house and was startled by Bunny proposing a new roof for a house less than ten years old.

But there in Millwood, on November 2, 1945, nine months after his return, Lieutenant Colonel Stacy Lloyd, Jr., was pinned with the glittering red, white, and blue star of the American Legion of Merit, awarded for "exceptionally meritorious conduct in the performance of outstanding services to the United States." He would also receive France's Croix de Guerre, the bronze Maltese cross awarded for bravery and gallantry.

David Bruce—and to a lesser degree, Stacy Lloyd and Paul Mellon—even at war, knew precisely what they ate, what they drank (often right down to the vintage year), and what they saw, including the breeds of cattle and the flowers in the fields and gardens they motored by in France. They had all been well schooled not to consider such things as "niceties," but rather as the very stuff of life. Knowing how to live extremely well was part of who they were. The women they married had been schooled in the same way, though their formal education had in most cases been sheared off at the age of eighteen or nineteen. These men had now seen firsthand that the "stuff of life" could also include death on the battlefield and the sure knowledge that they might be the next casualty. Thus, the scope of their lives had widened. But the war had also rocked women. Women like Bunny had found the solitary space and time to consider their lives, what they had been and done so far, and what they could be and do.

7

The Chase and the Wedding

"They kept her body sitting up in bed for days. Mr. couldn't get over it. They had dinner parties downstairs" is how Nelly Jo Thomas, who was born next door to Oak Spring in Upperville, Virginia, recalled Mary Mellon's death in 1946 and the events that followed it like one long, continuous wake. "That coffin went to the old graveyard on the place in a wagon drawn by horses." Today Nelly Jo seems an Appalachian portrait from a distant past: long, pale gray face, knob of gray hair, wearing a plain gingham wash dress and an old cardigan as she sits commandingly at her kitchen table, where we talked. At the age of fifteen she was already working for the Mellons when Mary died.

On October 6 the huntsman had called it a day, gathering his hounds together to head back to kennels. Mary started homeward, joined by Paul, who had enjoyed the sport from close behind the field master. Mary usually "hilltopped," staying behind the thick of the hunt on a quiet horse. She had been told she should avoid horses altogether because her asthma was exacerbated by horse dander, but the life she had married into was intertwined with riding both in Paul's Virginia and in the English countryside. Paul and Mary were trying to resume the life they'd had before the war.

But in the grip of a sudden asthma attack, Mary lost her breath and slipped off her saddle. She gasped for a car to take her home. Paul galloped ahead to get one. Forrest Dishman, the head groom who had accompanied her hunting, held the horses while they waited, according to Nelly Jo. "We took her upstairs," she went on, "and I brought up a supper tray." Paul eventually went downstairs to let Mary rest. But he hurried back up to her bedside after the children's nurse rushed in to tell him that things were worse. Mary, only forty-two, turned to Paul and breathed her last words to him: "And I had so much to do."

Even for the very rich, like Paul and Mary Mellon, a gulf had opened between men who had seen indescribable horror and suffering in the war and women who, notwithstanding a large household staff (however decimated by wartime call-ups), had found independence in a life that had previously circled around the needs of a husband. Paul was mustered out in August 1945, and by early winter the couple found themselves bored and restive in the house they had bought in Hobe Sound, Florida.

Paul was "restless and irritated by the life there," as he writes in *Reflections in a Silver Spoon*. Indeed, he covers his relationship with Mary, her death, and his subsequent remarriage in seven pages, as contrasted to the twenty-two he devotes to his war service in the same chapter. Still, those few pages are among the most clear-sighted in his memoir. This intensely private man draws his first wife as if from a distance with even strokes of love, dislike, and discomfort. (Speaking literally, it *was* a great distance: *Reflections* was published in 1992, when he was eighty-five years old and Mary had been dead for almost half a century.) Paul describes her as a forceful personality but one with a sense of humor. Although sometimes bossy, he says, she was also compassionate, intelligent, and a feminist. She was proud of her time at Vassar. Her French was vivid if ungrammatical. She was occasionally impulsive—Paul tells how she sometimes woke up their daughter, Catherine, to take her on midnight pony cart rides in the moonlight. He also writes that, for Mary, "the present was never as real to her as the future, and it was as though she always felt the present was holding her back."

With Paul at war, the future had actually become the present for Mary, especially with her deep involvement in the Bollingen Foundation's publishing program, the Bollingen Series, funded by Paul and named after the Swiss village where Jung lived and where both Mellons had spent time in psychotherapy. Ongoing projects Mary oversaw included translations of the collected works of Carl Jung and *The*

I Ching, books such as Joseph Campbell's *The Hero with a Thousand Faces,* and no-strings-attached fellowships for promising young authors such as Malcolm Cowley and Denis de Rougemont, the Swiss cultural theorist and writer. De Rougemont wrote that the "cultural provinces of the vast kingdom that Mary administers alone while her husband is at war" also included responsibilities at the National Gallery of Art, two universities, and the Red Cross.

Mary thrived in the heady Bollingen atmosphere. The series would later go on to publish hundreds of works across a broad spectrum of the arts, social sciences, and psychology. During the war, however, one of Jung's close associates was investigated by the FBI, and the entire project was briefly curtailed. Jung's extensive correspondence with Mary cooled. It's no wonder that by 1946, as Paul writes, Mary felt "an overwhelming sense that her intellectual interests and publishing projects with the Bollingen Foundation were withering on the vine," which served "to force her into a state of unrest and depression." He finishes his description, a loving warts-and-all eulogy, by writing, "I have a very strong feeling that eventually we would have stuck it out."

Paul and Bunny had known one another socially from at least 1938, when the young Mellons moved permanently to Virginia. Their links were foxhunting and other horsey events, dinner parties in each other's houses, and then the local war efforts. They might already have met even earlier, on Paul's weekend visits to his mother at Rokeby Farm beginning in 1931, the year before Bunny married Stacy. Their children were close in age. Bunny was sufficiently intimate with Mary to have designed a garden for her at the Brick House, but its whereabouts are unknown, unless a sunken metal drain and a curving, lumpy ridge in the lawn just outside Delano's brick-walled enclosure are clues to a vanished circular garden. Whatever the nature of Paul and Bunny's friendship had been, now the distraught Paul found Bunny "very kind and understanding" over his distress after Mary's death. That is all he wished to say about their courtship; the actuality was very different.

I asked Nelly Jo after Bunny's death how Paul and Bunny became close. She did not answer directly. Instead, she said that "when Mr. and Mrs. were courting," Bunny would come over from Apple Hill and "put Eliza into Mr. Mellon's bed for her nap." *Not a hot love affair* is how I read Nelly Jo's cautious comment, but a respectable family in the making.

Bunny herself held to her own vague description, variously couched to different friends over many years, that her first marriage had fallen apart because of the war. She told me she found some wartime love letters to Stacy; she never said from whom. Nancy Collins, her nurse and close confidante, confirmed the same thing: yes, there had been letters, Bunny told her too, and no, not a one was ever found. Looking back at the tumultuous year and a half between Mary's death and her own divorce and remarriage, Bunny may have searched for a respectable reason for leaving her husband that would satisfy both her sense of self and some sort of general propriety.

Standard gossip has held that Bunny seduced Paul, an unconfirmed story retailed by Martin Filler, the art critic who was a friend of Paul's. "When Bunny asked for a divorce," recalled Filler, "Stacy, startled, evidently said, 'But, Bunny, don't you love me?' Bunny answered, 'I do love you, Stacy, but I want to be Mrs. Paul Mellon.'"

Marriage was a business for women like Bunny, and often the only business for which they were adequately prepared. Bunny was groomed for a "good marriage." Prestige and education—the latter a word that encompassed far more than her few years of accredited schooling—entitled Bunny to power, although only of a certain limited kind. Beauty, which Bunny did not have, and even wit, in measured quantities, were important also, but money was key. More money meant more power, and Paul had entrée to a life that made rural Virginia look very limited.

While Paul introduced Mary—and would then introduce Bunny—to vast opportunities through his unimaginable wealth, each woman in turn led him to other worlds. Mary guided him into intellectual and psychological explorations with Carl Jung that ultimately made Paul uncomfortable, as he recalled in *Reflections*. But in creating and supporting the Bollingen Foundation, he got his first taste of the kind of scholarly endeavor that eventually and most productively led to the founding of his Yale Center for British Art, and CASVA, the Center for Advanced Studies in the Visual Arts at the National Gallery of Art.

Bunny's greatest gift to Paul would be opening his eyes to the pleasures of collecting the works of art to which she was instinctively drawn—the Impressionists and Postimpressionists. It is difficult to assess her precise influence, but it is safe to say that the aggregate collection the two eventually gave to the National Gallery would have been much poorer without her passion.

In Henry James's *The Portrait of a Lady*, Isabel Archer is given a fortune, and the world watches to see what she will do with it and with the supposed independence it offers her. Bunny Lambert Lloyd used Paul Mellon's fortune to create a private universe, one that she would control. "I know what I want to get done," she said to me in 1995, some fifty-odd years after her marriage to Paul. Her Janus eyes looked backward at what she had done and forward to the decades she would still have to exercise her powers.

I asked the British photographer Derry Moore, now the 12th Earl of Drogheda and Bunny's former son-in-law, if he knew why the Lloyds divorced. Derry, astonished, said, "Why, because of Paul!" Derry then related a telling anecdote. "Eddy Warburg once told me that he dropped in on Bunny, who was a friend, and found her in tears. [Edward M. M. Warburg of the eponymous banking clan and a major arts patron and philanthropist was probably visiting his brother, Frederick M. Warburg, who kept a hunting box in Middleburg.]

"'What's the matter, Bunny?' Eddy Warburg asked. She told him that a small parcel arrived every day containing another jewel from Paul. Looking up at Warburg, she added, 'He's drowning me in diamonds.'" Derry paused, then added, "She couldn't resist."

Paul would indeed pursue Bunny. In early spring 1947 the pair met secretly in New York City at the Ritz, walking out in the mornings to find the world transformed by their love. In Virginia the pair spent fierce nights of lovemaking in the old Fletcher log cabin at Oak Spring, where the bright flames flickered on the ceiling.

Only a few months later, in the fall of 1947, Bunny separated from Stacy. She had made a difficult decision but it seems she was not entirely sure of herself, nor of the future she had chosen. She left Virginia to await her divorce decree in Florida. Her official residence was her family's house in Palm Beach, but she also spent time in Princeton, staying with her mother. Paul had kept the house in Hobe Sound, forty-five minutes away from Palm Beach, and they used it as a hideout. Paul was rightly terrified of the press baying at his heels, as they had done since his birth. Already by October the secret was out: gossip columns reported friends prophesying, "The late Andrew Mellon's son Paul will remarry. The bride will be Rachel Lambert Lloyd of the antiseptic tribe."

A week after her divorce decree was announced in Palm Beach on March 9, 1948, and after she and Paul had happily planned a quiet trip abroad together, Bunny must have had second thoughts. She suggested that they travel separately. She would not be alone, however. Conveniently, her Foxcroft classmate "Sister" Kinnicutt, now Mrs. Henry Parish II, was upping her decorating game. Starting in 1933, Sister Parish had been doing up the houses of friends in Far Hills, New Jersey, her home territory. And what had begun as a way to make pin money and amuse herself soon became a profitable business. She and her husband, a stockbroker who had lost considerable wealth in the Wall Street Crash of 1929, now needed the income she might provide. So she was eager to head to England with Bunny to meet the leading lights of the interior decorating world.

Sister particularly wanted to meet John Fowler, who had joined Lady Sibyl Colefax, whom Bunny knew well, to form the fabled firm of Sibyl Colefax & John Fowler, *the* English tastemakers of the postwar twentieth century. Then, because of Sister, Bunny also met John Fowler, who became her first bona fide decorating mentor, and from then on she understood that domestic decoration—interior design—was, like garden design, a legitimate art form with meaning and integrity. And if she married Paul Mellon, she would have the wherewithal to do whatever she dreamed of.

Paul agreed to her terms, hoping that time and distance would resolve Bunny's doubts. His own traveling companion was his daughter, Cathy, twelve years old. Aboard the RMS *Queen Elizabeth*, father and daughter enjoyed the two luxurious staterooms he had booked for himself and Bunny. He wrote to her that the seaborne cabins would have been perfect for a pair of lovers. He also reflected on his hopes not just for tenderness and intimacy but for calm after the fireworks and shock of their new passion for each other. Sleepless nighttime hours aboard ship gave him plenty of opportunity to reflect on himself, on her, and on their volatile new relationship.

The comic aspect of their situation seems inescapable, as two luxury ocean liners steamed briskly across the Atlantic, carrying letters *poste restante* between the lovers. (Once in London, Bunny stayed at Claridge's, while lovelorn Paul sought companionship to occupy his days, dining and lunching with Bunny's close friends Liza Maugham and Rosie Fiske, or making himself more comfortable with a few of his own old buddies from the war and the sporting world. One of these was a Virginian friend of his sister, Ailsa, Nancy Yuille, who had married "Dicky" Adare, later the 6th Earl of Dunraven; Paul and Mary had visited them in Ireland on a hunting expedition in 1936. Paul and Cathy attended the Grand National, that fearsome and storied four-mile steeplechase in Liverpool, and spent Easter weekend at a friend's Scottish castle. Then father and daughter were homeward bound on the RMS *Queen Mary*.

Did Bunny find their monthlong separation as anxiety-producing as Paul? His idea of English pleasures was very different from hers, which involved spending time in the international café society to which her father had introduced her. Paul felt that the rush and chatter of that fast, aristocratic company caused Bunny to float away in one of her "magic balloons." As a man quite accustomed by the time he was forty to getting his own way, Paul now, even in Bunny's absence, had the opportunity to better comprehend the strong, gifted, and stubborn woman he had fallen for so quickly. Jungian analysis had made him value self-exploration, and he hoped it would help him resolve any difficulties that might arise in this new life he longed for.

Bunny seemed to suffer no such inclination to closely examine her feelings about her divorce from Stacy or her affair with Paul.

Paul made it home to the Brick House, which was crowded with weekend guests for the Piedmont Point-to-Point meet. He then rushed up to Bunny when her ship docked in New York and then hustled back down to Virginia. Although by this time both realized that the news of their relationship was widespread, like many celebrities they wanted to keep their movements quiet. Paul cautioned her to use a fictitious name if she sent him cable messages, as he had to pick them up at a local store.

On May 1, 1948, Paul and Bunny walked through the columned

and crested doorway of 24 East Eighty-Second Street, one of the former bijou private houses of the Upper East Side, around the corner from the Metropolitan Museum of Art, and up they went to the apartment of Mr. and Mrs. Henry Parish. That afternoon they were married under the benevolent eye of Sister Parish, who was a witness. Bunny was thirty-eight, Paul forty-one. Years later, even though Sister and Bunny were no longer in close touch, Sister sent Bunny her copy of the stock printed booklet containing the Reformed Church in America standard service they had used, and the church certificate of marriage—a far cry from the elaborate Episcopalian ritual of Bunny's wedding to Stacy Lloyd in 1932. Bunny's mother was a witness, too: she supported her daughter in her search for a new life. Gerard B., Bunny's much-revered father, who had himself been divorced, nonetheless saw fit to disapprove of his daughter's divorce. He refused to attend the ceremony.

Mr. and Mrs. Paul Mellon soon left for Virginia to disentangle themselves from their separate former lives. The newlyweds, especially Paul, hoped for blissful solitude together, at least for a while. In a shipboard letter written on his return trip, Paul had painted what he hoped to find with Bunny: a life without compromises where the touchiness, the self-pride, the memories of past experiences they had already faced would melt away in loving one another.

The happy couple in 1959, with Bunny in Balenciaga

The Marriage and the Troubles

"When I came over the mountains in 1949 from Millwood . . ." is how, some fifty-five years later, Bunny began one of the many unfinished stories of her life. The ten miles along Route 50 to Upperville had been a dividing line between past and present. As Bunny made this momentous trip, she was happy and finally sure of herself. She was traveling on the wings of high hopes for herself and her new husband. She had tested herself—and Paul—by saying that she needed more time to think. The time she had spent steaming back and forth across the Atlantic with Sister Parish had reinforced the decision she had made to leave Stacy and Apple Hill behind and embark on a new life with this man who was so clearly enthralled with her and would give her his undivided love.

Previously, Bunny's Virginia geography had been confined by the shorter trajectory from Millwood to Middleburg, where Charlotte Haxall Noland continued to reign over the Foxcroft School she had founded in 1914. "Miss Charlotte," as she was always known by her students and alumnae, was happy to see Bunny successful in a new, larger, and more influential sphere. Ever true to her maxim of "Be loyal to the royal in yourself," the redoubtable headmistresss had no quarrel with marrying well. Many others also saw the new marriage as a good move.

On their honeymoon, partly spent in Scotland, Paul and Bunny visited her childhood nurse, Randy. Bunny told me that Randy whisked her off to the kitchen "to help make the tea" but that Randy was more interested in the immense size of Paul's fortune than in whether the new couple was really in love. Randy wanted to make sure that, this time around, her Bunny had the best.

Bunny and her children moved from cozy Apple Hill, set in its valley sheltered by woods, to big, echoing Brick House above the immense green spread of Rokeby Farm's four hundred acres. Already Rokeby was swelling into a kingdom that employed hundreds of artisans, farmers, gardeners, housepainters, carpenters, masons, grooms, and horsemen, as well as household staff. (Paul would buy up farm after neighboring farm, eventually consolidating more than 4,500 acres, all under conservation easement.)

Built as an exact copy of Annapolis's stately Hammond-Harwood House (1774), Paul and Mary Mellon's Brick House was never a comfortable fit for Bunny, and she was determined that this, her third monumental home, would be her last.

Without much success, Bunny and Paul tried to unite their two families. Bucolic photographs of their four children—his son, Tim, and daughter, Cathy, and Bunny's Tuffy and Eliza—show them posed seated against a Rokeby haystack (piled up expressly for the photo shoot). Their faces seem both bewildered and blank. Bunny much later told me, "I can take care of a plant better than I can a dog or a child." She had few illusions about herself in this regard.

Bunny and her children—Tuffy, second from left, and Eliza, far right—and her new Mellon stepchildren—Tim, far left, and Cathy, second from right—against a haystack at Rokeby Farm

Lambert family events also remapped Bunny's world. Her stepfather, Dr. Malvern Clopton, had died in April 1947, when Paul and Bunny were in the midst of their love affair. Bunny had never been especially close to Clopton, but he had been a familiar figure in her life since childhood. More affecting was the death of her brother, Sonny, who had perished in a plane crash in October that same year, just as Bunny was starting her divorce proceedings in Florida. Two months later, Gerard B. and his second wife, Grace Mull, sold Carter Hall, perhaps as Gerard's expression of grief that his only son would never inherit the house he had fantasized as his family's ancestral Virginia homestead. Or perhaps, as the incessant builder he was, he just wanted a new endeavor, which he found in his eccentric new house in Palm Beach, which faced freshwater Lake Worth on one side and the Atlantic Ocean on the other.

In early 1949, Stacy Lloyd, Jr., married twenty-year-old Alice Babcock from Long Island, who was described as attractive and a superb horsewoman. Stacy brought her to Apple Hill and its little square garden set with heart-shaped beds Bunny had lovingly created.

Newly married to Paul Mellon, Bunny found her compass widen well beyond Virginia and New Jersey. At first they lived in New York City—in Paul and Mary's old house on East Seventieth Street—and Paris, where she and Paul took a penthouse apartment in the Crillon. Paris was still recovering from the war, and the Place de la Concorde was somberly blackened with soot; André Malraux's program to return the noble stone facades to their original creamy color would only begin in 1962. But the city's fountains glittered, and its lights gleamed against the darkness. Paris was giddy with relief and pleasure, and so were Bunny and Paul.

The pair frequented art galleries in both Paris and New York, sounding out with each other what they liked best. It became clear that Bunny had a very discerning eye. Whereas she and Stacy had collected horse and hunting prints on a minor scale, now she and Paul, with his unlimited funds, began to collect far more broadly, more opulently. Bunny turned Paul's eyes for the first time to pleasures outside the peaceful English landscapes that had meant so much to him since his childhood years spent in England and toward the freshness of the French Impressionists and Postimpressionists. They were new to her as well, but she caught on fast.

In the fifties, Paul and Bunny sketched out their characters and roles within the marriage. In 1951, Bunny embarked on her first ambitious building program: a new Episcopalian church in the village of Upperville. The original plan had been to get rid of the termites and shore up the old church, but Bunny had an entirely different idea: to build an exquisite but simple French country church, "a haven for rest and peace," where, as she wrote, "the meanest peasant and the highest aristocrat are one." Although dedicated to Mary Mellon, Trinity Episcopal Church would be Bunny's testament to her love for France. It would be designed by the architect H. Page Cross in close collaboration with Bunny, whom he had known as a friend since her debutante days in Southampton. It was to be Cross's first endeavor for the

Mellons, but he soon effectively became their go-to architect for all major domestic projects.

Trinity itself would take nine years to complete, and, when finished, the edifice would turn out to be grander than most provincial French churches. One startled visitor drove along Route 50 into what was then the slightly shabby post–Civil War, post–Great Depression village to find "an abbey close" consisting of "a[n] enclosed sandstone complex of two buildings as well as a church and connecting cloister." He experienced the time warp most first-time visitors feel at the site. Travelers, he wrote, "may wonder whether they have passed through some odd dimension," ending up in a version of medieval France. He called the church "a marvelous hodge-podge of first-rate American and European carpentry, stonework, ironwork, carvings, and furnishings . . . its builders were the skilled residents of the area . . . the windows were made in Amsterdam; the tower bells cast in England; the wrought-iron 'Peace Angels' a gift from a thirteenth-century church near Dresden; the brass and iron furnishings importations from eighteenth-century England, France," and other European countries.

By the third year of their marriage, Paul had come to better understand his powerfully effective new wife's character and drive. He underscored a last line in a note he wrote to her to accompany the gift of a fantastic jewel: "You came in like a lion, so you may come out like a lamb." With regard to building an entirely new church, he had told her he would fund it but that he had too many of his own projects to take it on with her. Then, as a man already used to wielding power and money, he diplomatically cautioned her to tread softly, because she "would experience, most of all, the mixed thoughts and emotions of members of the Parish where you have just become a new member."

It was a busy first five years of marriage. Paul began to give his money away in earnest. His initial large-scale foray into environmental conservation was saving fragile Cape Hatteras, the first national seashore, funded in 1952 by two Mellon foundations (his sister, Ailsa's, Avalon and his own, Old Dominion) jointly with the state of North Carolina. Paul also took on the joint mastership of the Piedmont Hunt in 1954. Bunny, who had given up horses herself after the birth of Eliza, dutifully followed the hunt in her car. Paul rode his chasers in local amateur races; his breeding and training stables expanded. For her part, Bunny began to collect books with a bigger budget than she'd ever enjoyed: mostly on horticulture, botany, gardening, and design. She would broaden her acquisitions to include travel accounts and the illustrated fairy tales that had always meant so much to her.

In 1957, Bunny went to Paris on her first couture trip, meeting both the Spanish fashion designer Cristóbal Balenciaga and the young French one Hubert de Givenchy through her ripening relationship with jewelry designer Jean Schlumberger. She began to "dress for the world," as her librarian, Tony Willis, would so aptly put it. Brooches were in fashion: Paul commissioned a tiny espaliered apple tree pin with ruby fruit and diamond leaves from Fulco di Verdura, a jeweler he would always patronize. A chastely beautiful Schlumberger piece in diamonds and platinum, with the looseness and irregularity of a living blossom, was shaped like the wildflower Queen Anne's lace and was the first piece of the hundreds of examples of his work that Bunny would own. She carefully tagged it "first gift from Paul."

The Brick House was the setting for a huge gathering of horse folk following the last point-to-point steeplechase to be held at the original Rokeby Stables site across the road from Oak Spring. In 1955, Bunny planned and orchestrated her first big social event: the coming-out party for her stepdaughter, Cathy Mellon, held in the Broodmare Barn at Oak Spring with a tented dance floor laid over the yard's central lawn and hot-walking ring. Paul's growing worth and weight as a Washington, D.C., public figure and a lifelong Republican can be measured by the massive turnout of Eisenhower's first-term cabinet members at the dance. That same summer Brookie turned twenty-one, and Bunny flew to England to be there for the occasion. Brookie asked Bunny—not his mother, Rosie—to coach him on the speech he would deliver that evening at Warwick Castle to the assembled townspeople and his tenants.

But despite all this activity, it was a very unhappy time for Bunny, as I was to find out, first when I tried to help Bunny with her auto-biography in the 1990s and then more fully when I began the research for this book. Already, Paul and Bunny's marriage was strained to the breaking point. In the 1990s I had begun to wonder if there was an important story about their courtship and marriage that was different from the brief account Paul offers in his 1992 memoir: "Having known each other so well for so long, we decided to marry . . . she has pro-vided my life with a stability and security it had not known before, and she and I had been careful to allow each other to develop our own interests." I wondered at the stiffness of that passage but recognized that Paul, whom I admired, was a private man telling his own story.

As I interviewed Bunny about her many men friends—the closest of soulmates and colleagues, the romantic fantasies, the lovers—she also told me that she and Paul eventually had come to lead quite sep-arate lives. They had had terrible troubles, but they had worked them out, she said. (Along with everyone else, I had read the 1969 article by Sarah Booth Conroy in *The New York Times* about the unshakable sta-bility of the Mellon marriage and the peace and beauty of Oak Spring and its gardens and landscape.) That article had the same deliberate air as a rare statement from Buckingham Palace on the royal marriage in 1957, when rumors were rife about the Duke of Edinburgh's wild behavior: "It is quite untrue that there is any rift between the Queen and the Duke."

But then, over a long evening Bunny and I spent together in An-tigua in 1996, when everyone else had gone to bed, Bunny began to elaborate on what had happened. "Our marriage wasn't happy after five years," she began. First came the warring schools of psychother-apy. "Paul broke with Jung after Mary's death from asthma and went to a Freudian therapist in Washington, Dr. Jenny Waelder-Hall, with whom he was in analysis for twenty-one years," she said. (Paul, in his memoir, recalled the number as eight years but noted that the ses-sions were spread out irregularly over a long period.) At the same time Bunny also went into Freudian therapy briefly, with another practi-tioner, but, according to Paul, it was too impersonal a treatment for her to endure for long.

The fifties was still a world where expensive wives, however diplomatically and insincerely, almost always deferred to their well-heeled husbands. As for therapy, the general run of marriage counseling in the fifties basically involved telling the wife it was all her fault and treating her depression, anxiety, and "frigidity" with one of the psychopharmaceuticals new to the market—Miltown and other "mother's little helpers."

Bunny said nothing on that Antigua evening she spent with me about Paul's unsuccessful attempt to convince her of the efficacy of Freudian analysis. Instead, she continued calmly, "Almost at once Hall told Paul to stop having sexual relations with me." I didn't question Bunny's statement—after all, the arrogance of mid-twentieth-century psychiatry was breathtaking. I also wondered if this was just a convenient way to describe an emotional distance that Paul, and perhaps Bunny also, had wanted.

The reasons he gave, Bunny told me in a disconnected bunch of phrases that seemed impatient and dismissive, were a "mishmash about his early childhood, a governess, neglect, and an unloving mother." Paul's memories of his parents' very public divorce and custody battle, and the looming presence of Nora Mellon's scoundrel lover, the English Alfred Curphey, had played a huge role in shaping his miserable childhood. Paul's relationship with his implacably stony and deliberately unemotional father, even after his treatment with Jung, had left him with little ability to figure himself out until he started his psychoanalysis in Washington.

Bunny's childhood had not been altogether easy either, although she was not one to dwell on it. She was the least loved of the three children, she said. Bunny had turned a lack of affection into a sort of freedom.

That evening in Antigua, Bunny continued to tell me her story. "Then I asked Paul, 'Do you want a divorce?' He said, 'No, you take care of the children, and you'll have all the money you want. You will be Mrs. Paul Mellon.'"

Bunny had calculated her risks. She had married a man with a pathological dislike of publicity—not surprising, given his parents' very public divorce. But if Paul divorced her, Bunny could become a laughingstock, a woman who had divorced a perfectly nice husband and then been divorced by one of the richest men in the world. And although she was an heiress in her own right, Bunny's funds were nothing compared to Paul's. According to the first Fortune 500 listing, Paul was the fifth-richest person in the world in 1957. So Bunny did "take care of the children," in her own fashion, and certainly she would have all the money she wanted. She agreed to Paul's bargain. She did not want to relinquish the chance to remain Mrs. Paul Mellon with all that the position offered.

Not long after she and Paul had navigated their way to this truce, Bunny wrote in her journal about her feelings on receiving the queen of England at Oak Spring. On the day of the royal visit she had been very nervous and tried to steady herself.

"Standing alone in the hall, how my heart pounded . . . I wanted the queen to play her role and I mine, calmly. I believed in her. She was disciplined . . . She had courage. She would never stoop. And she was sad," Bunny wrote. What a commentary. She wanted to go forward in her life with steadiness, discipline, and courage just as the queen had done after reports of her husband's alleged high jinks aboard the royal yacht *Britannia* in 1956.

In short order a lot of real estate changed hands, perhaps as much in the service of increasing their separateness as in their desire to create summer and winter escapes, a common pastime for the rich. By the midfifties Bunny had created the house at Oak Spring, and the family had left the Brick House behind. Paul had bought the oceanfront acres at Oyster Harbors, in Osterville on Cape Cod. H. Page Cross—with Bunny—built their summer retreat there, finishing in 1955. Bunny had made a start on their Antigua winter hideout, again with Cross. In New York, Paul bought the adjacent house on East Seventieth Street. For two years, while renovations were ongoing, the couple spent their time in Manhattan in two apartments in the nearby Carlyle Hotel—but not before Bunny had carried out some architectural changes and had both apartments repainted.

Whatever else went on between the couple, Paul appeared to be tickled and amazed by what Bunny accomplished. She consulted him on every construction move—often to a contractor's frustration with the glacial pace—and both took pleasure in the process.

BUNNY SAVED SEVERAL of Paul's long, anguished letters from those difficult times in which he laid out details of their deteriorating marriage and what he felt was her determination to wreck it. He acknowledged his moodiness, his quick temper, his sense that she brushed away his feelings and derided his convictions, and above all he admitted to his jealousy of her continued deep affection for Stacy Lloyd. On the other hand, he didn't overlook Bunny's touchiness and what he saw as her inability to comprehend anyone who was significantly different from her—meaning himself. In their first years of marriage he had reveled in her intense sexuality, but now he found himself frozen and impotent. He continued to be drawn to her native sense of beauty and to what he, a rather emotionally defended man, saw as her grace and ease with other people. He was envious of her unveiled kindness and ready sympathy for others. Why not for him, was his bewildered cry. Most of all he found himself desperately enraged that he couldn't seem to be the person she wanted him to be, someone charming, intelligent, lighthearted, and hardworking, someone he knew within himself he could be.

What Bunny wanted more than anything else was for Paul to quit his analysis in D.C. with Dr. Waelder-Hall, a prominent child psychologist trained by Freud himself. (Bunny and Paul dubbed her "Mother Goose.") Bunny strenuously believed that Hall's real purpose was to alienate husband from wife. (This, of course, came from the Bunny who saw all other women as rivals.) Paul sensibly defended his treatment, writing that it was much more about him than about them. He asked that they talk about it seriously once more, saying that if she really wanted him to give it up, he would do so, without ever mentioning it again. Whether they had that conversation or not, Paul stuck with his analysis.

He made at least one more unguarded plea to enlist Bunny as his partner rather than as his chilly adversary. He wanted her to believe that he was trying to be a good man, he wrote. As it was, he felt like a pariah and saw that they were becoming more and more estranged, without any way to regain their old ways of loving each other. In one letter to his "darling Bun," Paul had fully acknowledged an insecurity he called both deeply ingrained and unpardonable, but at the same time he put the burden of their failure almost entirely on Bunny. He didn't mention his ongoing treatment but did ask repeatedly for her patience. What he wanted was to be reassured that she really loved him; if she did, he was certain he could become the man she thought she had married. He would thaw not only sexually but in every other way. It seems, however, that this did not happen.

Was her refusal to comprehend his need for psychological treatment what made him draw back, or was the context much larger? Was Bunny in fact incapable of giving him the kind of love he wanted, the love he'd described in his courtship? Before things soured, Paul Mellon thought he had truly found security and happiness at last.

Bunny had come into the marriage as the person she would be all her life: someone who was far more interested in moving forward than in analyzing what lay behind her. In a very real sense, she and Paul were at cross purposes. In addition to being courageous, Bunny was stubborn; Eleanor MacKubin, her teacher at Foxcroft, had gotten it right: "It would be sad indeed if you lost a friend you love just through your love for fight—or your desire to be right . . ."

Neither Paul nor Bunny wanted to call it quits, even though the basis of their relationship had completely altered. In *Reflections*, published in 1992, Paul described their long marriage as a partnership. For him, for her—for them—this would be an acceptable structure, an old-fashioned marriage based on common interests, using strategies to which they had grown accustomed: Bunny knew how to coax and threaten; Paul knew how to rage (in private) or be silent and moody.

Bunny told me that after the rift with Paul, she "found a girl for him," meaning Dorcas Hardin, who would become Paul's lifelong mistress. If Bunny's memory can be believed, she didn't have to look very far. Dorcas's brother-in-law, Taylor Scott Hardin, the twin of her D.C. physician husband Dr. B. Lauriston Hardin, was a member of Virginia's horsey set. Diana, Dorcas's daughter, also went to Foxcroft, graduating a year ahead of Eliza and me in 1959. Dorcas Hardin owned a fashionable clothing boutique in Georgetown.

"Dorcas was fabulous-looking, tall, not thin but not fat either—well rounded, I guess you'd call her," said one of my Foxcroft classmates whose family was friendly with the Hardins. "She had auburn hair in a pageboy, was pretty but not movie star pretty, and was always stunningly dressed and incredibly chic. She gave great dinner parties." Despite her profound deafness (Dorcas learned to lip-read to compensate), "she wanted to be with people all the time." She was a beloved D.C. society figure. "She was naughty and fun—always laughing. I mean, she was somebody's mother, but she was still a kick . . . There was an amazingly good energy around her all the time. And she noticed how you felt; she would say, 'What's the matter with you?' then pat your cheek."

Dorcas Hardin in the place to be in Washington, D.C., in the 1960s—her Georgetown shop

Dorcas was also alert to small things, to fashion statements perhaps not yet considered appropriate but that were fun and edgy. "When my younger sister wanted to get her ears pierced," said a diplomat's daughter who worked in Dorcas's boutique in the summer of 1972, "and our mother said no, Dorcas said, 'Of course she should get her ears pierced.'" Others remember Dorcas's great eye and her ability to be plainspoken without causing offense: "If you picked out clothes that didn't suit you, Dorcas would say, 'No, that doesn't look right.'"

When Paul was eighty-four, the art critic John Russell wrote, "Unlike many people who have always been able to do more or less what they liked, Paul Mellon gives the impression that he enormously enjoys his life, is content with the way in which he has conducted it and is never bedeviled by regrets." In fact, Paul had worked carefully to achieve what he wanted after a childhood and life as a young man in which he had had to contend strenuously with his frigid and almighty father. And Paul knew what he wanted. His early letters to Bunny express how well he understood himself as a man who wanted very badly to be intimately connected with someone, to find the exhilaration and rush of happiness he had found with Bunny in 1948 and for the first few years of their marriage. In Dorcas Hardin he rediscovered that laughter, sex, coziness, and empathy. Dorcas seems to have released in Paul the certain knowledge of who he wanted to be, the man he felt he truly was.

None of this could have been easy for Bunny, neither the problem nor her claim of a practical solution—finding a mistress for her husband. She kept Paul's later letters as well as his early ones. Whether she reread them or not, I don't know, but if she did, when she read one he had written in the middle of their troubles, in which he asked her to believe that he loved her deeply and would always be good to her and always faithful, I can hear her indrawn breath. Their relationship by 1961 was solidifying into a workable mechanism with many compromises on each side. It seems almost inconceivable that two such passionate people could settle for this. And yet the opportunities for other kinds of freedom, and for other relationships while they yet remained in the marriage, were partly what made it work.

So every year, Paul went to England for racing and hunting in their allotted seasons, Bunny to Paris for the spring and fall couture showings. Paul spent more time in D.C., she in Paris. She bought her first Paris apartment (over Paul's objections) on Avenue Foch. Together and separately, they dived deep into the international art market. They spent time together in Antigua in late winter and on Cape Cod in July and August. Christmas was always at Oak Spring, the heart of it all. Like state figures, they displayed themselves together at signal events, such as art openings where their collections were on view, and the biggest races where Paul's horses were running. And like all state figures, they had separate bedrooms—as did many upper-class Americans, copying European tradition. They did all these things with the self-discipline, assurance, and stubbornness that characterized each of them.

For fifty-one years they would pay attention to one another with a constant stream of letters, notes, and gifts, especially from him to her. They would make much of holidays and birthdays. Paul Mellon's light verse made him the Ogden Nash of millionaires. The beautiful surroundings Bunny created made their life appear seamless from decade to decade. Their struggle to stay together would be remarkable, touching. They had grasped that living apart would keep them together.

FOR PAUL, BEING "careful to allow each other to develop our own interests" meant Dorcas. For Bunny, it meant a long cavalcade of interesting and talented men—almost all gay, except, perhaps, for Jean Schlumberger, the jewelry designer who, by all reports, occasionally slept with women but who, like most of the others, had a male life partner, Luc Bouchage.

What all these consummately creative types felt for Bunny was affection and admiration amounting to awe for what she was so easily able to provide for them—not just luxuries like a ride in the Mellon plane or a vacation at the Mellons' sublime getaway on Antigua but a wide scope of opportunities in which they, as top practitioners in their own fields (jewelry design, landscape architecture, couture), could achieve magnificent results that also interested her.

To judge from Bunny's affair with Schlumberger and her sexually fueled but unrequited infatuation with Hubert de Givenchy in the seventies, it's clear she was open to men other than Paul Mellon. In 1970, as she was about to fly off to Tunisia with Givenchy and his partner, the designer Philippe Venet, she made some notes in one of her many journals. One sentence drew an implicit comparison between Paul and Bunny's new love, Hubert. About Hubert she wrote, "He has not a trace of those qualities that one must ignore because of their roughness or because their sound or way of moving causes pain."

Bunny flew off to Tunisia in a transport of happiness about Hubert, a man whose "thoughts and way of doing things literally make me helpless and weak with joy—I am drowned suddenly with all the expressions and thoughts of another human being that I feel myself & try to do for others I love."

Givenchy and "the French family" he and Bunny would create cruised the eastern Mediterranean in 1971; his sketch captures the lightness of his friendship with Bunny.

PART III

Bunny's
New Path

❧ 9 ❧

Finding the Way

As part of her new partnership with Paul, Bunny moved her daily life to a realm that no one else could match in scale, expense, taste, or imagination. Beyond the sphere of perfectly executed and unique buildings, interiors, gardens, and landscapes, she was finding a farther reach of occasions and events, both public and private. Paul gave her free rein, marveled at what she did, often helped her, and sometimes made light of her escapades.

Bunny gave a coming-out party, a ball, for her daughter, Eliza, in 1961 that was really a coming-out party for herself as a maker of magic. No one who was there on that June night ever forgot it. Cathy Mellon's debutante party in 1955 had been beautiful and extravagant, but it had not been like this. Over a hundred workmen and scenic painters toiled for more than a month to create this one-night stand. She was at last building her "stairway to Paradise," to quote the Gershwin song.

Efforts were made to keep the event private, but the press got in anyhow. The intrepid Dorothy McCardle, *The Washington Post*'s society reporter, was spied crawling behind farm hedges and through the *Rosa multiflora* thorns to get a glimpse of the "village"—fifty multicolored canvas pavilions straight out of the Field of the Cloth of Gold— that was erected in a pasture for all the young men. Shower and toilet facilities were housed in still other tents, along with valet services to press dinner jackets and shine evening pumps. Oak Spring's internal roads were asphalted for the evening and then quickly returned to their country gravel surfaces once the party was over. A plane that buzzed the circle of tents managed to snatch a blurry aerial shot that was published in McCardle's syndicated column. McCardle, like a retriever with a bird in its jaws, trotted forth to tell the world in print that Eliza's debut was a first in every way—principally that it was the first to cost a million dollars—and that Anne Ford's debut, held a week later, was a piker's performance at a mere $280,000.

Billy Baldwin, the dean of twentieth-century decorators, said that by the year of Eliza's party, Bunny's taste had already become legendary (especially in regard to her whispered-about gardens that only a few had seen). "Everybody always spoke of Bunny Mellon with a slightly hushed breath; not fear, really," Baldwin wrote in his autobiography, "but almost reverence. Certainly her word would always be the final one."

Who was Bunny's intended audience for this party? The politicos, financial heavyweights, local gentry, international horsemen, and the upper crust of London and New York who had attended Cathy Mellon's party would not necessarily have seen or cared what Bunny was up to, except to say that Eliza's ball was magnificent and must have cost a million bucks—something they could easily have learned from the papers. But in claiming her public role as one of society's arbiters, Bunny was also setting a hurdle of taste and expense that Dorcas Hardin would not be able to cross.

Bunny's new target was the world of fashion and style. Among others at Eliza's ball was the Franco-Russian baron Nicolas "Niki" de Gunzburg, one of the twentieth century's most important style arbiters. The baron had spent the last of his considerable inheritance in Europe on a summer costume party in 1934 set on an island in the Bois de Boulogne that he wrapped—in a pre-Christo flash of inspiration—in white velvet, shore to shore, surely just the right snowy setting for guests tricked out as members of the Habsburg imperial court. Nobody ever forgot that party either. By 1961 the baron had gone to work in America, taking his perch as fashion editor at *Vogue*, where he reigned for a quarter century.

With Eliza's party, Bunny was joining the ranks of impresarios like de Gunzburg who would stop at nothing to achieve an effect, creating a performance that lives forever as history and is transmuted into a symbol of a certain time. (The Black and White Ball thrown by Truman Capote in 1966 for Katharine Graham was another such performance.)

ELIZA WINN LLOYD, age nineteen, had spent the year following her graduation from Foxcroft in France, where efforts were being made to mold her into a lady. Cheering letters from various itinerant teachers went regularly to Bunny, one saying how happy Eliza was that her mother was coming to Paris to visit (rooms were reserved for Bunny and her maid at the Crillon), another that Eliza had been to the theater with "Johnny" Schlumberger, Bunny's new friend as of 1954. Eliza learned to speak French fluently although never entirely correctly. "Son accent est incontestablement meilleur," said Madame Bourdet-Pléville, with whom Eliza boarded. She took in the sights of Paris and enjoyed the cooking of Mme Bourdet-Pleville's "domestique, Alice." A French friend of Hubert de Givenchy's, Marie-Hélène Bouilloux-Lafont, carried her off for a haircut "so her hair doesn't fall in her face." (Eliza spent a lifetime tossing back that dark hair—her characteristic gesture.)

In Paris, her mother's friends discovered that Eliza was original, spontaneous, enthusiastic; "elle est très attachante," one said, something all found true about Eliza. Just as she was at school, she was guileless and good-natured. Once in a while she seemed shy and temporarily wordless—then she would burst out with a droll, seemingly unconnected remark that somehow *did* fit the moment better than anything anyone else had said. In May 1961, just before Eliza returned home to Virginia, Mme Bourdet-Pléville wrote to Bunny thanking her for the invitation to Eliza's coming-out party but sending regrets that she was too far away to attend. Then she took her pupil for a tour of "les plus beaux châteaux de la Loire" and sent her off.

When Eliza got home, she was aghast at the scale of "her" party. She had known her mother was busy with the arrangements, but she had no idea *how* busy. It was usual for a debutante at her own party not to know many of the guests, since she was being introduced to "society," but seven hundred people?

My twenty-nine Foxcroft classmates and I had arrived at the school in the fall of 1956 at thirteen or fourteen or even fifteen, ranging in maturity from mere children to knowing young adults. Our characters changed almost from day to day. But a particularly varied and indistinct Eliza emerges from my own and my classmates' memories of her, as if she was hard to grasp or as if she was a shadow—until she danced or acted onstage, and then, much later, when she defined herself as an artist.

Before her coming-out party on June 16, 1961, at Oak Spring, Eliza practices the Charleston in her bedroom with the ultimate high kicker and an old friend of Bunny's, Adele Astaire.

The Eliza I remember at school screened herself behind a booming laugh and a way of seeming constantly surprised by life. Alix Clark, a classmate, said that Eliza "didn't make a lasting impression. She was reticent, reserved, withdrawn, reluctant to expose who she was in a way that we didn't understand. Tall, physically solid, not willowy, not beautiful, with that goofy haircut, she was a dear, dear person, a country girl, someone we loved and had fun with."

She had "big dark beautiful cow eyes," remembered another classmate, Kathe Gates. "The whites were very white, and with that straight black hair she was striking." After supper at Foxcroft and before study hour, "Eliza and I practiced theatrical stuff on the school auditorium stage," said Gates. "We turned on the Victrola and danced around the room—she was a good dancer without having a dancer's figure."

Eliza and I had first become friends because we were so often "grounded" together—confined to school grounds on weekends when other girls got to go away or even just to Middleburg for lunch. Eliza was grounded for bad grades, I for general insubordination and untidiness (such as underpants and bras not folded correctly in their drawer for daily inspection).

Eliza and I were aware, without ever saying so to one another, that she was a perpetual outsider, walled off from our peers by the greater wealth and prominence she did not want to acknowledge. She made up for it by acting out. She was intentionally comical in a pratfall kind of way that shielded her from serious contemplation.

We had, of course, discovered something of who Eliza was in our sophomore year when Queen Elizabeth and Prince Philip visited the Mellons, because the event took place more or less before our very eyes: from the pasture fences that lined Oak Spring's driveway we had watched the queen's Rolls cabriolet make its way to the house. Impressed by this regal vision, we were then herded back to school. Eliza was allowed to remain for the family tea party that followed the queen's visit to Paul's stables.

A month or so before the queen came to tea, Bunny had written, "My daughter never ceases to give me joy . . . She has her own ideas, her own code, and her own high sense of values. As someone once said to me, she is an ancient child." The two of them were sitting in the Oak Spring kitchen that day, wrote Bunny, "making damson jelly and relaxing in the joy of a peaceful country existence." Then she said to her daughter "that it was too lovely to be believed," just the two of them, alone together with nobody else around. "Yes," said Eliza soberly, "and the queen for tea too."

That remark captures another aspect of the Eliza I knew, the struggle of the "ancient child" to deal with the uncomfortable double quality of the gauzy life her mother insisted on creating—both art-fully simple and grand. Eliza mostly said nothing about it but made intermittent efforts all her life to free herself of her mother's direct influence—a difficult quest due to the scale of her mother's life and her powerful grasp of details.

In her own way, though, Eliza sometimes stood her ground. Bunny had coached her fifteen-year-old daughter on how to behave at the royal tea party, and Eliza was taught the ritual of pouring tea for guests. But Eliza caught the Duke of Edinburgh by surprise after he dropped a lump of sugar into his tea, and she noted sharply, "I'm supposed to do that." He loved it! No wonder he was ready with the right reply at the end of the afternoon when she said, "See you later, alligator."

Eliza was essentially indifferent to and numbed by her coming-out party. She later told her husband, Derry Moore, that when someone she didn't know had approached her to ask who the celebration was for, she'd pointed at a pretty girl nearby and said, "It's for her," and walked away. (Eliza and Derry would marry in 1968 and divorce in 1972.)

The mysterious château, lost in time and the forest

Then there was the decor. Her mother had forcibly dragged the Brick House—and the fields and pastures of Oak Spring—into a France that had never existed: the land of Alain-Fournier's cult novel *Le Grand Meaulnes* (*The Wanderer*). First published in 1913, for the past century the book has been synonymous for many readers with lost love, lost innocence, nostalgia, and the mysteries that lie between childhood and maturity. A boy at the edge of manhood stumbles through a forest one night, loses his way, and finds a crumbling, magical château in the woods, a party, and love.

The day after Eliza's party, Evangeline Bruce, the wife of David Bruce, wrote,

> Darling Bunny—I only today remembered that the Meaulnes was the inspiration for the party—just as I was trying to describe it to Marietta [Tree] . . . you made it just that, the furthest-from-reality evening there ever was. The beautiful groves and mysterious buildings did filter through to one's consciousness, but nothing was insistent—surely the most successful kind of planning and bearing your stamp.

(Already by 1961, Bunny's style had evolved to what she would later famously describe as "Nothing should be noticed.")

Bunny and Evangeline, known to her friends as "Vangie," had been friends since Bunny's days as Mrs. Stacy Lloyd. Stacy Lloyd and Bunny Mellon were godparents to the Bruces' son David S. Bruce, who was born in February 1948, the same month that Bunny and Stacy's divorce was finalized. The tall, beautiful Vangie (vividly languid in photographs, with amused, alert eyes) was "Madame Ambassadress" to perfection and a skilled diplomat herself: intelligent, multilingual, empathetic. When she attended Eliza's party, her husband had just taken up his London ambassadorship, a preface to his serving in the same position in France and West Germany. Because Vangie understood to her core what had happened to Bunny's marriage, she knew how lonely Bunny was. Bunny was grateful: throughout her letters (naturally many fewer in Bunny's papers than Vangie's

hundreds) run her thanks for Vangie's presence here, there, and everywhere when Paul was "away again," as Bunny wrote to her.

I am not sure that any of Eliza's Foxcroft classmates, including me,
got it about *Le Grand Meaulnes* as the theme of her debutante ball or
whether that mattered at all. The famous interior decorator Billy Baldwin, who wrote that he had been invited as "the same old thing, the
extra man and the dancing man," and who only met Bunny for the first
time at the ball, did not mention the book, but he certainly got Bunny's
drift. He noticed that the "garden side of the house had been entirely masked by a giant slipcover upon which was the drawing of a French châ-
teau" and that it seemed "that everything had been there for
a long time, and you found yourself walking around in
the marvelous atmosphere of the eighteenth century, but
transformed into a wild lively result."

In the receiving line at the Brick House, with squeals
and shouts of pretended surprise, we Foxcroft girls
greeted Eliza, who had left the dinner party we had all
attended at Oak Spring only minutes before. Now she and
her mother stood inside the cavernous front hall, which

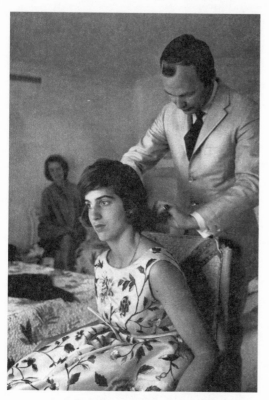

Kenneth, society's hairdresser, styles a
doubtful Eliza's hair. Bunny watches.

was grandly empty except for a jungle painting by Henri Rousseau.
Eliza wore the long white satin dress sprigged with red and green that
another classmate, Dixie Burden, and I had cooed over in her bedroom
when she put it on. Her mother wore a shadowy orchid chiffon—not

that Dixie and I noted this detail; we simply read about it later in the papers like everyone else.

From there we stepped outside into the tent and the party. Alix Clark, who was short and voluptuous, said she felt she had looked like an upside-down tulip in her knee-length bouffant dress. We all wore beehives, the standard hairdo for girls with long hair. I ate nothing, thanks to the extremely tight merry widow I was wearing under my dress, even though the steaming omelets prepared by the "omelet king," Rudolph Stanish, which were served before daylight arrived, smelled so good.

We strolled through what seemed to be a French village—a reminder of the one young Augustin Meaulnes had left for the bewildering forest, which here was skillfully represented by real tree trunks topped with wire cages filled with, and made invisible by, bunches of glossy lemon leaves. We walked along sidewalks lined with stage sets of very French shops, consulted an astrologer in a booth, listened to a honky-tonk piano in a bar, sat down for a minute in a replica Petit Trianon, and danced with an army of boys, many of whom we didn't know, to big bands that never stopped playing all night. Was it Emil Coleman? Or Count Basie? Peter Duchin, son of the society bandleader Eddy Duchin and then a very young man, played the piano in yet another alcove.

Bunny had invited Evangeline to change in her own room at Oak Spring (Bunny's maid, Dudley, had helped her dress); she was seated next to Paul at dinner. When she drove off to Washington at three in the morning, she later wrote to Bunny, she'd had another ghostly view of the boys' tent city, "pennants bravely streaming in no wind," a perfect *Grand Meaulnes* touch. Evangeline also wrote that the party's "cosy atmosphere" owed much to the presence of Bunny's "older friends from all over."

However, Eliza's classmates, me included, didn't find the party "cosy" and didn't take in much about the decor except that it was beautiful and not like any other deb party we'd ever been to. Although few of us were acutely aware of the larger universe of politics and business most of our parents inhabited, one was quite at home with "older friends," especially in the D.C. world of politics. Her father had served in the navy during World War II, then under President Eisenhower as secretary of the navy and subsequently as secretary of defense until John F. Kennedy won the 1960 election; he and his wife necessarily lived in D.C.

When the high-flying Kennedy years began, the couple, like other professional Washingtonians, quickly absorbed the need to mix politics and high style as society eased itself away from the dowdy Eisenhower years. The wives went to Dorcas Hardin's eponymous Georgetown boutique, which she first operated out of her own home and then from a separate house on Wisconsin Avenue, to find the latest American couture, which arrived weekly from New York: Mollie Parnis, Norman Norell, Halston—a roll call of American fashion in the fifties and sixties. Bunny might have worn some of their clothes if she weren't already dressing in French haute couture. She did not need to patronize Dorcas Hardin's shop.

"D.C. was power," said the daughter of the secretary, who was also one of the daughters of Dorcas Hardin's friends working at her shop during summer vacations. "All the fancy people came in, and Dorcas was one of them. In the fifties she dressed them for all the charity balls, the embassy affairs in the beautiful French and British embassies, and for the art openings. So there she was at the start of the party that was the sixties." Describing what it was like to work for Dorcas, she sounded as thrilled as she had been then, saying, "Once I was in the shop alone, and the White House called! It was the First Lady! She wanted a Mainbocher coat! So when Dorcas came in, I was able to say casually, 'Oh, by the way, Jackie called . . .'"

By the time that nineteen-year-old was dancing at Eliza's debutante ball, she knew that Paul Mellon and Dorcas Hardin were having an affair, because, as she said gravely to me some sixty years later, "My parents said I was old enough to know such things."

That night, when Bunny and Eliza stood together to receive their guests, Paul went off through the crowds to greet them and to admire and smile at what his wife had created. Bunny and Paul, these two immensely gifted and stubborn people, faced the voids and inadequacies of their marriage, but they had found a way out of their dilemma, and a very conventional way it was: a mistress for Paul.

Bunny found different ways to compensate, among them exercising her remarkable ability to retreat into fantasy and creative play, spending whatever it took—since she had it to spend—to perfect what she wanted, such as this *Midsummer Night's Dream* confection of a coming-out party. She was also finding ways to build an interior life apart with secret meanings: at the heart of the story of *Le Grand Meaulnes* is the bitterness of a love lost and never found again.

That night at Eliza's party, all the Hardins were invited, and Dorcas was there, according to the society columns, although her name isn't checked off the main gate guest list. Society's delighted whispers about the affair and the reports of occasional sightings of the lovers together in public were Bunny's to deal with for more than thirty years.

A sense of society's complicity comes with just one story: At the shop, Dorcas had a desk in an alcove off the main salesroom in the front. Behind were dressing rooms, storage, and lingerie. The back wall of the lingerie area was sheathed in mirrors; one concealed a nearly invisible door into a closet that held only a phone. Usually it was closed. "One day, when too many mammoth clothes boxes had arrived from New York, we needed the space, so the door was open," one young summer employee remembers, "and all of a sudden, the closet phone rang. I went in to answer it, just as someone else pulled me away and called out urgently, 'The phone is ringing—the phone is ringing!' Dorcas sprinted into the back closet, closed the door, and did not emerge for some time. No one said a word about it, and we continued chatting and unpacking as though nothing at all had happened. I was totally mystified. Some days later a fellow employee told me that phone was the one on which Paul Mellon called her. No one was to discuss it or the affair."

But this affair was a very public one. Paul and Dorcas were seen together in D.C. and New York hotels. He also had family dinners that included her; he introduced her to his bosom friend the English art historian John Baskett, who liked Dorcas very much. Bunny told me that "even though everyone in Washington at the big dinners and receptions that I arranged said, 'Oh you'll win,' I felt very alone." Imagine how humiliating it must have been for Bunny to have the state of her marriage and her husband's affair (with a woman generally acknowledged to be more popular than she was) bandied about by "everyone in Washington." No wonder that Bunny, always a reserved person except with a few close friends, kept her guard up, often appearing expressionless and forbidding. "The only person who was wonderful, truly human, understanding, and sorrowing was Evangeline Bruce," Bunny told me.

At her daughter's ball, however, Bunny was on a sure footing, and everything went off like a dream. About an hour after dawn, to tell us the end of the party was near, fireworks exploded against a nursery-pink-and-blue sky over the pastures stretching south of the Brick House.

Bunny, the great impresario, had found her power: she had blown us along on the wind of her imaginings, had taken us to a faraway place, and had even carried the unwilling Eliza along with her on a cloud of make-believe.

10

Life in Pictures: Degas—and Rothko and Braque

A gift of Edgar Degas's black-chalk drawing
started a great collecting collaboration.

Another part of Bunny and Paul's new bargain was "looking at pictures," as Paul called their pastime, pursuing the art they wanted and buying it. The pattern had started before their marriage. A Degas drawing of a jockey for $575? That was what a "Mrs. Stacey Floyd" had paid in July 1948 in West Palm Beach. The sale was handled by Knoedler's, a New York art dealer well known since the mid-nineteenth century for selling old masters to American millionaires. According to the account book in which the sale was recorded, the name was sometime later corrected to "Stacy Lloyd." The description "now Mrs. Paul Mellon" was inserted on January 31 the following year.

By July 1948, Bunny and Paul had been married for some two months. Perhaps "Mrs. Floyd" had bought the drawing earlier in 1948, before her divorce from Stacy was finalized in March. My own belief is that Bunny bought the Degas as a present for Paul when the divorce papers had not yet come through and the two were in Florida together, secretly, waiting to marry, and had strolled into a gallery to which Knoedler supplied art.

The drawing is described as nine-and-a-half by twelve inches, according to the sales listing, and is titled simply *Jockey* as per Knoedler's sales book. A search through the immense number of Mr. and Mrs. Paul Mellon's gifts to the National Gallery of Art doesn't reveal a Degas drawing of that size or by that name. However, the Mellon collections at the Virginia Museum of Fine Arts (VMFA) in Richmond do reveal a drawing titled *Seated Jockey* of almost the right dimensions. The inscription on the packaging in which it arrived from Paul's collections in the Brick House reads "From Mrs. Mellon to Mr. Mellon."

Still, it's not possible to absolutely confirm that this is what Bunny gave Paul, as the size is off by three-eighths of an inch. What is not mysterious about the purchase is the name change in the account book itself. I see Bunny's transformation into Mrs. Paul Mellon on this page as an announcement of a new life together. Her eye, her ambition, along with Paul's fortune and his quick comprehension of how his wife saw art and how he could too, would take them into new arenas of collecting. Of all the French artists whose works and subjects she might have chosen in 1948 to interest Paul Mellon, a Degas *Jockey* would have been a safe bet. A dedicated horseman and breeder, he had begun to collect English sporting art in the 1930s.

Degas would weave a continuous thread in their lives. Paul once said his favorite painting at the National Gallery was Degas's *The Dance Lesson*. Another, *The Riders*, was part of a large 1999 bequest made following his death. Seven horses move across a racecourse toward the start—one is rearing slightly; another hangs back from the crowd.

This is a country race meeting—in the background is a thin line of spectators, no viewing stand. And beyond? Only a valley, a stretch of low hillside, and trees. It is France, of course, but for the newly-weds this work could have called up memories of early spring point-to-points in Virginia in the first days of their marriage, when Bunny attended the local races in a bulky double-breasted tweed coat with a Peter Pan collar to watch Paul racing and smile admiringly at him as he accepted the silver plate.

Bunny was left a life interest in *The Riders*, so it went to the National Gallery only in 2014. It remained over the Oak Spring dining room fireplace until the house contents were sold after her death.

Degas's works—finding them, authenticating them, buying them, displaying them, donating them in groups and singly—would be one of the many Impressionist threads the Mellons pursued together. In 1955—"just for something to do," as Paul writes in *Reflections*—he and Bunny strolled into the Knoedler gallery on East Fifty-Seventh Street in Manhattan. About seventy small wax models of dancers and horses in various attitudes (and states of deterioration) stood on a table. Most were less than thirty inches tall, with a few taller ones, the tallest being the *Little Dancer Aged Fourteen* at thirty-nine-plus inches. Today, she is one of the most famous and best-loved sculptures in the National Gallery's collections.

These blobs of pigmented beeswax, air-dried clay, plasteline (a nonhardening clay), animal fat, rope, and wire had been shaped into almost-living forms by Degas's aging hands. He had left the odd fin-gerprint as he worked. In these curiously constructed creatures, wrote Paul, "one could feel the grace, the tension and the movement of the dancers and the horses."

Paul and Bunny were hooked. The great Mellon/National Gallery of Art authentication machine swung into action. By December 19, with a preliminary report in hand, experts looked into the mod-els' history and questionable durability. On February 3, 1956, John Walker, then senior curator at the National Gallery, was able to write, "Mr. Mellon . . . authorized me to make an offer through Mr. Coe Kerr of Knoedler & Company for these waxes." The price was $400,000. As they began to seek export permission from France, the Louvre asked for two figures as a gift. Paul gave them four, following the example he'd set when asked for an ambulance for Londoners in the Blitz: he had given enough money to buy ten.

After the sculptures' inaugural display at the Virginia Museum of Fine Arts in 1956, the Mellons wanted to live with them in Virginia before they went to the National Gallery of Art. The Brick House was transformed into a state-of-the-art, climate-controlled art gallery. John Baskett, the English art historian who became Paul's curator and eventually the co-author of his memoirs, unpacked them.

In 1964, Bunny lined an upstairs room with silk velvet of wisteria-pod green. The roll of the fabric as it flowed down the walls had a silvery hue like that on the back of a leaf. Against one side of the room she arranged the horses; against the other sides, the dancers. Each figure stood on a nearly invisible shelf projecting from the wall.

Straight ahead as you entered the room hung the grimly truthful oil painting *Scene from the Steeplechase: The Fallen Jockey*, which depicts an Armageddon of galloping horses jostling for position. One rider, the brightest spot on the canvas in his soft pink racing silks, lies on the ground, unconscious if not dead. Both Paul and Bunny could have witnessed a similar instant in real time at any race meeting.

In the middle of the room stood the *Little Dancer Aged Fourteen*. The space was small, or it seemed so, because of the explosive beauty of what it held. It was quiet in there; you could watch the figures prance, gallop, dance, and stretch their limbs. This treatment was akin to a museum installation. Rarely, if ever, did Bunny and Paul display any of their other precious collections this way. Every visitor to Oak Spring relished the sight of one small Impressionist work or another parked somewhere in the living room. Most took note that van Gogh's *Green Wheat Fields, Auvers* hung over the living room mantel unframed, showing the rough edges of the canvas where it had been tacked to the stretcher.

Bill Waller, a Virginian picture framer who did a lot of work for the Mellons, recalls that Monet's *Still Life with Bottle, Carafe, Bread, and Wine* hung on the back wall of the Oak Spring Garden Library's kitchen in Bunny's day, mirroring the scene it enlivened. "At waist height, unframed," Waller said, "anybody could have knocked against it in that busy kitchen." Apparently, nobody ever did, not even during the hours when the staff all pitched in—and still do—to make lunch for themselves and for any visitors studying in the library.

Paul and Bunny knew they were stewards, custodians, of the fine art they collected. Bunny's take on a garden, published in *Vogue* in 1965, holds true in a larger sense for her life and how she saw it: "Its greatest reality is not a reality, for a garden, hovering always in a state of becoming, sums up its own past and its future."

HOW DID BUNNY turn Paul Mellon, who previously had had eyes almost entirely for British painters such as Stubbs and Constable, into a collector of French Impressionists? They didn't write letters to each other explaining how and why, but Paul later credited Bunny with "90 percent" of his interest in French art.

Paul told the Mellon family biographer Burton Hersh that in the 1950s Bunny "drew my interest toward a . . . vision and technique that was like a new wind blowing through musty galleries . . . The artist applied his pigment in fragmented dabs so that the eye of the beholder mixed the colors." That's a very good description of what Paul Cézanne's justly prized *Boy in a Red Waistcoat* must have looked like to Paul Mellon. The art critic Meyer Schapiro wrote that Cézanne's art "lies between the old kind of picture, faithful to a striking or beautiful object, and the modern 'abstract' kind of painting, a moving harmony of color touches representing nothing." Understanding a "moving harmony of color touches" had bridged Paul's old and new ways of seeing art.

Paul's agent at the Sotheby's auction in London in 1958 exceeded Paul's instructions for his maximum bid for *Boy in a Red Waistcoat* by "quite a large amount," as Paul wrote. Still, Paul said he had no reason to regret the huge outlay—at $616,000, then the record for a single painting. One of his favorites, it hung in the house on Whitehaven Street in Washington, D.C., until it went to the National Gallery in 1995. The graceful and diffident young man in the Cézanne painting was apparently a talisman for Paul, perhaps a mirror of his own understanding of who he was and what he was coming to know about art. *Boy in a Red Waistcoat* eventually served as the frontispiece of Paul's funeral service program. When a memorial event was held in the NGA's East Wing after Paul's death, the *Boy* appeared on the cover of the program.

Bunny's turn to the Impressionists followed her governing subject: the garden, its history and plants, its tools and implements, the intimate landscape of a fallow field or a farm lane that often included farmers, scenes so often chosen by Impressionist plein air artists. She had an excellent eye, perhaps a gift from her childhood solitude, when observation was everything. She wasn't a scholar, as she herself often admitted; instead, she was a visual learner, which would serve her well as a collector. The directness of some of her choices seems to express in an unspoken language what she knew about herself and her life.

The collector and curator of the National Gallery of Art John Walker, writing about the Mellons, asked, "What causes their instinctive selection of one painting rather than another? . . . I think it is often, as with myself, empathy, an imaginative identification with the subject represented . . . art as the embodiment of memory, not the remembrance of actuality . . . this I think is at the base of their aesthetic response."

Images of a caged bird, or of an empty cage, held special meaning for Bunny. In thinking about her life and her marriage, Bunny even called herself—rather improbably, it may seem to many less privileged than she—a bird in a cage, but a cage with an open door. She could always fly out, she told Bruce Budd, her interior decorator during the long stretch of her life after Paul's death. But, she added, she could—and would—always return. As a talisman for herself, Bunny hung a birdcage close to one of the wooden panels in the Oak Spring greenhouse vestibule that were painted by Fernand Renard, a French trompe l'oeil specialist, who incorporated the objects that meant the most to her, composing a "visual biography" of her life.

What else did Bunny see in the art she bought? Was it the arc of aesthetic perfection she followed throughout her life? In the many portraits of solitary women and domestic interiors that she bought or Paul gave her, did she see a shadow figure—herself—between the painted image and her perception of it?

The dilemma that Bunny lived out is perfectly encoded in the art critic and writer John Berger's immortal paragraph about women in *Ways of Seeing*:

> A woman must continually watch herself . . . And so she comes to consider the surveyor and the surveyed within her as the two constituent yet always distinct elements of her identity as a woman . . . She has to survey everything she is and everything she does because how she appears to men, is of crucial importance for what is normally thought of as the success of her life.

A draw for both Bunny and Paul was the beach, limitless, liminal, recalling childhood, that early stage of life when everything can seem possible, boundless. "The Mellons . . . have the largest collection of beach scenes by Boudin I have seen anywhere," wrote John Walker. "Sand, sea, sky, as he painted them, aren't these the elements of their childhood experiences, reminders of the happiness of their youth?" In the New York house the dark, twisting staircase was brightened with a festive toile de Jouy wallpaper and hung with about a dozen Eugène Boudin beach scenes that only a few people would ever see.

The Mellons had begun collecting art in the fifties, when psychotherapy, in thrall to Freud, began with an exhaustive examination of the patient's childhood. For Paul, that world opened up through psychoanalysis. As we have seen, Bunny disdained the formal distance of Freudian analysis. She turned instead to astrologers, horoscopes, *The Witches' Almanac*, or Beverley Newton, the Virginia psychic she once called her own "witch on retainer." From the 1980s on, the two spoke nearly every day until Bunny's death.

Which is not to say that Bunny didn't make efforts to understand herself better. In the early 1970s, Bunny had consulted a Dr. Carl Lambert (no relation), an English psychiatrist. Dr. Lambert was enlisted to work with Eliza as well as with her mother. Lambert was invited to accompany his mother-and-daughter patients to the South of France with Eliza's husband, Derry Moore. Over lunch, Lambert once privately told Derry, "It's a court and the discipline is ruthless," so it's not clear how well treatment succeeded for either patient.

By 1966 the several hundred nineteenth- and early-twentieth-century French works owned by Mr. and Mrs. Paul Mellon represented one of the most important private collections of Impressionists and Postimpressionists in the nation. That year, Paul and Bunny joined his sister, Ailsa Mellon Bruce, to mount an exhibition to celebrate the twenty-fifth anniversary of the National Gallery of Art. Of the 246 works on display, 184 belonged to Bunny and Paul. The paintings, oil sketches, watercolors, gouaches, and drawings included Degas's *The Fallen Jockey*. John Walker thanked the three donors for the pleasure they were generously giving the public, noting also that for them it meant living with bare walls and lonely rooms. One such room was the little green gallery of waxes at the Brick House.

One might think that, by the mid-1960s, Bunny had satisfied her need for as thorough an art education as any amateur of her stripe—a woman with a high school education, a sheltered upbringing, and some Grand Tour–style travel abroad—might hope for. But she had studied great works carefully with Paul and on her own; discussed them with others; coveted, chased, and bought them; hung them as she and Paul liked. And she appears to have—always—paid close attention to what was being said about them.

In 1969 she attended a lunch to celebrate an opening at the National Gallery, smartly understated in a black suit and hat that set off her dazzling twenty-millimeter pearls. (That's close to an inch across, each.) She sat next to Lord Kenneth Clark, by then well known for his television series *Civilisation*. As one reporter wrote, "Mrs. Mellon voiced the unspoken thoughts of most of us on the recording of events that have led Western civilization from the collapse of Rome to the present: "We get a chance to learn so much without having to admit what we don't know." Bunny was often playing catch-up with her limited education, and she played it very well.

"CHAQUE COLLECTION DOIT avoir son oeuvre maitrêsse," wrote Hubert de Givenchy to Bunny Mellon in June 1971. That every collection must have its crowning work was Hubert's lesson for his new friend. For Bunny, Givenchy was her next move in developing her eye for art.

They had first met briefly in 1954 in Paris though Schlumberger; now, after Cristobal Balenciaga's retirement in 1968, she would become Hubert's client and friend. She swiftly gained a new ally and companion as well as an entirely new look to her wardrobe. In his first letter to her after their meeting, Givenchy wrote, "Several times you said with so much affection, you got a new friend in me, I am sure you understood that I had the same feelings for you."

Six-foot-six, broad-shouldered with narrow hips and burning blue eyes, Hubert de Givenchy, who lived to be ninety-one, was also lucky enough to have a magnificent French nose—rather the same beak as seen in portraits of François Premier—which he wielded very nonchalantly. Bunny and Hubert would develop a relationship that she viewed as a unique love affair, and he, a gay man, as the warmest

Hubert de Givenchy knew the art world, as well as all the international gossip, intimately.

and closest of friendships—except for his devotion to Audrey Hepburn, his muse, whose "little black dress" in the opening scene of *Breakfast at Tiffany's* in 1961 had won him worldwide fame.

Hubert was born into the *gratin*, the French upper crust, as the second son of Lucien Taffin de Givenchy, into a family neither rich nor grand despite their name. He also grew up learning that on his maternal side he was the youngest offshoot of not one but two important families in the fluidly connected, centuries-old worlds of the decorative and fine arts in France, the Diéterles and the Badins.

Both of Hubert's polymath great-grandfathers, skilled artists in many fields, served as administrators of the Gobelins and Beauvais tapestry works. Hubert's grandfather Jules Badin (d. 1940) followed family tradition at Beauvais and married Marguerite "Béatrice" Diéterle. Their daughter, Béatrice Badin, married Lucien Taffin de Givenchy, and after Lucien's death from influenza in 1930, the widowed mother and grandmother raised Hubert and his older brother, Jean-Claude, in the family house in Beauvais.

In the lofty, closed world of the decorative arts, these people understood the value of making beautiful things. They were masters and cognoscenti of design and materials, and Hubert was proud to learn the skills of pencil and shears. He would develop an extraordinary eye for sumptuous textiles as well as a cut-to-the-chase clarity in design.

In 1970, Bunny was looking beyond Impressionism. Paul admired only a few modern artists: the sculptor Barbara Hepworth, the painter Ben Nicholson, and the sculptor John Skeaping, all British. Bunny went for Abstract Expressionists, color-field painting, the New York School, and other modern masters, French as well as American. Hubert was delighted.

The story was that Givenchy took Bunny to Mark Rothko's studio after the artist's death and that the visit was her first encounter with Rothko's work. However, Bunny was quite capable of seeing new things herself. Mark Rothko had died by suicide in February 1970. By April 20 of that year, a memorial exhibition of ten Rothkos was briefly installed on the third floor of the Museum of Modern Art.

Rothko was already regarded as one of the greatest artists of his generation; he had been given his first MoMA show (fifty-four works) in 1961. Bunny—and certainly Paul—would not have had much interest then. But Bunny, in telling me how she bought her paintings, said she'd seen that 1970 memorial show. Hubert recalled that Bunny had sent him a postcard of a Rothko that belonged to the architect Philip Johnson, suggesting that the two of them visit Rothko's studio. (The two Rothkos that Johnson eventually gave to MoMA were both in the 1970 show.)

In early fall, the two friends walked around the corner from her house on Seventieth Street to Rothko's studio on Sixty-Ninth Street between Lexington and Third Avenues. As Bunny described the studio interior to me, she made it sound like a big mess. "Canvases were in a pile on the floor, un-stretched. First I bought one for $150,000 then twelve others between twenty and thirty thousand." (Givenchy, with a much smaller budget, also reserved one—later saying that "at that time Rothko was not so expensive"—a work he later gave to the Fondation Beyeler in Switzerland.)

The power of being able to make such an enormous purchase was exhilarating. The memory stuck with Bunny for life. In her various renderings of the story—over the years she repeated it several times to me—she was so excited that she exaggerated the number of paintings, changed the dates of her various acquisitions, and salted her versions of the story with a variety of prices.

It was her habit, Bunny said, to call "the bank or Paul's office" to run her large purchases by them, whether for books or paintings. "I kept calling [to give them the numbers], and Paul finally called me himself and said, 'What's going on, Bunny? That's an awful lot of money.' I explained who Rothko was and that the prices seemed low. 'They sound like a good buy,' he finally said." Paul Mellon didn't dicker about prices when he was buying art. However, he generally took the time to look at the market and was well advised—and, as he wrote in his memoir, he usually conferred, catalogue in hand, with Bunny. In this case he seems to have trusted his wife on the basis of her phone calls and just said yes. (Paul may have known about Rothko, however vaguely, from the notable art collector and critic Duncan Phillips, who had created a special Rothko Room at the Phillips Collection in 1961.) Or perhaps Paul's fraught bargain with Bunny—"You'll have all the money you want"—was the reason for his ready acquiescence.

The first three of the nine Rothkos Bunny eventually bought included the 1955 *Yellow, Orange, Yellow, Light Orange*, estimated in the 2014 Sotheby's sale of her effects at $20,000 to $30,000. It went for $36,565,000. Even discounting the rise in the art market by 2014, it had certainly been "a good buy."

Another letter from Hubert written very soon after their visit congratulated her on her purchases: "How much I liked going to see all those paintings with you! I am so happy that you have chosen several for your collection, as you have done so well. I love how you choose with precision and at the same time with certainty."

In the spring of 1971, Bunny bought four more Rothkos at low prices from the Marlborough gallery, including *White and Greens in Blue* and the monumental ten-by-fifteen-foot *No. 20*, better known as *Yellow Expanse*. These two paintings would eventually be sold privately shortly before her death for a reported $300 million. David Anfam, the authority on modern American art who wrote the Rothko catalogue raisonné, said that *Yellow Expanse* was "the jewel in the crown" of Rothko's oeuvre. It was certainly the jewel of Bunny's Oak Spring Garden Library, where it lit up the space like dawn breaking.

"The lawyers came after me [from the Rothko estate]," Bunny continued, "but I hadn't done anything wrong." She hadn't—she had simply bought the works on the terms offered by Mark Rothko's executors. The Marlborough gallery had bought one hundred Rothkos—reportedly some for as low as $18,000—from the estate. They also took a commission of fifty percent on almost seven hundred more.

Bunny's purchases stood out as prime examples in the suit the Rothko children brought against their father's executors, claiming that they had "wasted" the estate to enrich themselves. Kate and Christopher Rothko won, but Bunny didn't have to return her paintings. For the first time she had engaged the brilliant Alexander Forger of Millbank, Tweed, who defended her successfully and never left her side as her lawyer throughout the rest of her life.

Hubert de Givenchy knew all the art dealers in France as well as many in the United States, whom he frequented when he came to visit his clients. (He had many American clients besides Bunny.) He went to all the exhibitions, visited all the galleries and antiques shops, and remarked on what he thought Bunny might like, including upholstery fabrics, furniture, or blue-sprigged eighteenth-century Chantilly dinnerware.

After yet another visit to Marlborough with Hubert, which included a look at some Abstract Expressionist paintings by Franz Kline (she bought two), Bunny wrote, "Hubert comments [on their] strength—delicacy—quality in everything—understanding of color—shapes—it is all these things in life that I want to talk to him about." With Hubert, Bunny knew the thrill of being in the presence of someone who could unhesitatingly identify much of what he saw and explain why he loved it. Bunny was apprenticing, learning visually and first-hand from those who knew more than she. She never talked about what she learned. She simply demonstrated that knowledge with her choices. (She seldom discussed what she spent, either, except in the most general terms, and it appears that very often she didn't pay attention to cost at all.)

Bunny wanted more from Hubert than he could, or would, give, however. She continued in the same journal entry about Hubert and that 1970 visit to the Marlborough gallery, writing that "he is never alone and one is pulled back from deep thoughts to say something polite to the third person—the thread is lost and a half finished thought is left to be dissolved in tears later when the soul can hold no more."

Bunny fell hard for her men—at least those she was attracted to after her marriage with Paul went cold—in a primitive (maybe "undivided" is a better word for it) and possessive way. Each of Bunny's many romantic friendships moved purposefully forward thanks to a liberal application of her funding and the electric jolt of her joyful, collaborative spirit. These connections were also often patron/client relationships. But you could also call them violent crushes. Bunny wanted each "romance" to go further, be deeper. She wanted a flirtation, a frisson of sensuality, often heightened with the muskier tones of sexual flirtation. She was aware of the dangers of her desire, though, writing in 1969, as soon as Hubert de Givenchy had begun to work on her wardrobe, about her new bond with him, "I hope my enthusiasm will not damage this new and heavenly relationship."

Within Bunny's family circle not everyone was completely enthusiastic about the handsome, courtly Frenchman. Eliza told me she and Paul called Hubert the big poodle and dubbed Akko van Acker (the Dutch antiques dealer in Paris who became Bunny's obsession in the 1990s) the little poodle behind their backs. That said, Hubert became Bunny's most cherished companion for many years.

Bunny loved to track down treasures—especially if it involved a trip somewhere with Hubert. In early 1971 she mentioned that she'd be interested in buying some of Georges Braque's work. At once Hubert organized a trip to Provence, to Fondation Maeght, whose founders, the dealers Marguerite and Aimé Maeght, were his close friends. Accompanying the two collectors, as he often did, was Philippe Venet, also a couturier and Hubert's lifetime companion, who was often a thorn in Bunny's side just because he was present, interfering with her communion with Hubert.

After visiting Beauvais, Hubert's birthplace, they flew off for the South of France—"all excited as we flew to [the] Coast," as Bunny wrote in her journal. They had rented a villa where everyone in the party stayed, including the Mellon pilots, Walter Helmer and Art Ray, "who were rather stunned" by the grandeur of their housing. (This was the Mellon plane's first transatlantic trip.) But, Bunny wrote, "Walt falls into the joy of it." She had already done so herself, writing, "[Hubert's] joy of sharing joy becomes part of me. And one sees and feels nothing but the weightlessness of complete happiness." After lunch at Roderick "Rory" Cameron's famous Villa La Fiorentina in Saint-Jean-Cap-Ferrat, one of the great expatriate gardens of the French Riviera, they headed for Saint-Paul-de-Vence, up in the hills.

They stopped in at the rosy little auberge La Colombe d'Or, famed as the retreat of the entire French art contingent during World War II and ever after. Miró, Picasso, Braque, Léger, and Giacometti—all were friends or at least acquaintances of Hubert's from whom he bought paintings and sculpture. "Everyone knows and loves Hubert," Bunny wrote. This Provençal excursion was a huge pleasure for a woman who spent so much time creating events, planning and anguishing over every detail of how a life should be lived.

Then it was time to visit the Maeghts—and the Braques. "We go to the Foundation for lunch" is all she wrote. But in 2012, Hubert told the columnist and art critic Susan Moore that "Bunny bought four or five Braques that afternoon. That was what my life was like: I would visit a client for a fitting and we would end up doing something completely different. Life is marvelous!"

Georges Braque's *Les Deux Oiseaux* sold in Sotheby's 2014 *Masterworks* auction of Bunny's property for $1,325,000, more than double the top estimate. Of the Braque paintings that Bunny bought, it was the most striking. To see those two massive black birds flying together into a thick, stormy sky is to see creatures flying free. No cages. She hung the painting in the guest cottage at the Cape Cod house, which often became a refuge for her friend Jackie Kennedy after her husband's assassination. At Oak Spring Farm, another Braque bird, *Nocturne*, flew across the tall white end wall inside the "Basket House," the roof of which is shaped like an overturned basket. Inside, the high vaulted ceiling was hung with straw baskets— and a few birdcages.

Braque had refused to assign any symbolic meaning to his series of bird images. But for Bunny, equipped with her own private "bird in a cage" symbolism, they might have been reminders of the marvelous trip to Provence, where she briefly found what she always craved—the "weightlessness of complete happiness."

11

Bunny and the Modern Museum

Rothkos, Braques, and Klines: buying multiple works by an artist became Bunny's pattern. Among other modern masters she collected were Nicolas de Staël and Richard Diebenkorn. She purchased many of de Staël's abstract landscapes and beach scenes in different mediums. Most wonderful is a still life, *Le Saladier*, which depicts a single glass bowl frosted with cold and filled with lettuce so crisp it seems phosphorescent. It originally enlivened the dining room of Bunny's cool blue dining room on Avenue Foch.

She bought eight Diebenkorns between 1974 and 1984, finishing with a blowout sweep of three works in May 1984. It's easy to see what drew Bunny to Diebenkorn. The artist's horizon lines, his awareness of light, his lucid structural framing, and his worked surfaces incorporating layers of paint and other materials, as well as collage, twin remarkably with Bunny's way of seeing and creating gardens and landscapes accretively. No wonder she wanted to collect his works, although where to hang them was a different matter.

Tony Willis, head librarian at the Oak Spring Garden Foundation, who has a near-photographic memory of where paintings were hung in all the various buildings at the farm, recalls seeing only one Diebenkorn on a wall, however. He said that "Mrs. M. hung it in Eliza's quarters at Spring Hill," the house on the property that Bunny fixed up as a private nursing center for her badly injured daughter after her accident. According to Willis, the other Diebenkorns were stored in a barn.

Joseph J. Krakora, longtime National Gallery of Art executive, recalls that "one of her great Diebenkorns hung front and center, directly behind the director's desk," both in J. Carter Brown's day and Earl A. Powell III's. So why did she sell it instead of leaving it to the NGA? Krakora and I agree she wanted to fund her Oak Spring Garden Library. "I'm not surprised she stuck to her guns," he said, because it was clear that, "in making decisions, she took no back seat."

The de Staëls and the Diebenkorns were all auctioned at Sotheby's in 2014, adding considerably to the millions ($218 million in total) destined to endow the Oak Spring Garden Library and Bunny's family foundation. The sale of five de Staëls and eight Diebenkorn oils and gouaches realized somewhat over $36 million. The two Rothkos she gave to the National Gallery were foundational to that institution's first foray into collecting modern art. The rest were sold privately or at auction. The writer Meryl Gordon, in her book about Bunny Mellon, notes that the three Rothkos that were sold privately before the Sotheby's auction neatly erased a $250 million bank loan Bunny had taken out very late in life *and* left enough funding to ensure that her bequests were paid.

It's no surprise that the first comprehensive show of American abstract art had already taken place at the Museum of Modern Art in 1951—modern art being its mandate, after all—nor that 1961 was the year for Rothko's turn for a solo show there. At the Metropolitan Museum in 1969, Director Thomas Hoving gave Henry Geldzahler, then the curator for twentieth-century art, the chance to bring the Met up to speed with *New York Painting and Sculpture: 1940–1970.*

The National Gallery also came late to America's modern art party. "No living artists" had been the rule until Chester Dale, a trustee and later president of the NGA, bequeathed his world-class collection, including Braques and Picassos, in 1962 at his death. The rule was hastily amended. And in October 1973, Bunny played a role in bringing the institution up to speed. She installed two of her new knockout Rothkos in the gallery's entrance hall to the preview dinner for seventy the evening before the exhibition opened. Six more glowed on the dining room walls, so all collectors, all cognoscenti, all possible donors, all important museum people could see them. All the works were on loan for the night.

On the tables were small wooden sculptures by Betty Parsons, the New York gallerist and artist who had first nurtured Rothko and many other Abstract Expressionists. Another of Parsons's contributions to the education of Bunny Mellon was a list she sent to Bunny—at Bunny's request—of important living artists, from Robert Rauschenberg to Louise Nevelson, Helen Frankenthaler, Willem de Kooning, and Andy Warhol. Bunny made sure they were all sent invitations. Many attended that evening, along with such D.C. worthies as Chief Justice Warren Burger, who was also chairman of the National Gallery board—and Robert and Ethel Scull, early New York collectors who had fallen upon the Abstract Expressionists before they were famous and had then raced on to scoop up the best of Pop Art. The Sculls were fresh from the successful sale of fifty of their finest works at Sotheby's only a week before the National Gallery opening.

That October evening, Ethel Scull wore a black jersey T-shirt, a Halston, that was screened on the bosom with the medallion of her husband's Checker Cab company, "Scull's Angels," the profits of which had helped the couple become the notable collectors they were. Bunny felt secure in her Paris couture but surely took notice. Paul Mellon, president of the gallery from 1963 to 1979, graciously recognized the late inclusion of modern works in the nation's art museum by saying in his introductory remarks that before the show went up, contemporary artists "probably would not have wanted to be shown dead at the National Gallery."

The twenty-six works in the show, with the exception of Jackson Pollock's *Blue Poles*, belonged to private collectors. Paul Richard, the art critic for *The Washington Post* between 1967 and 2009, pointed out that the National Gallery did not own any Abstract Expressionist works, had not bid on any of the best works at the Scull auction, and did not as yet have a curator of twentieth-century art. The exhibition, which Richard saw as uneven, was an announcement of intention, not realization.

While the Sculls transformed the art market, the director J. Carter Brown brought the concept of the blockbuster show to the National Gallery of Art and, with it, the idea of a museum as a social space. At the beginning of Brown's tenure as director in 1969 the NGA was all columns, marble, and chaste gray walls, promoting a somber experience more like a visit to the bank or a dutiful stop along the standard "Trip to the Nation's Capital" pilgrimage than a joyful immersion in art. It was J. Carter Brown's job—and policy—to heat things up. He turned to Bunny Mellon, among others, for help.

Paul Richard was not an admirer of Bunny Mellon, finding her cold and always discovering a way, in my phone interview with him, to return to Paul Mellon and his warmth, his modesty, his humor, his humanity, his generosity. When I asked Richard if Bunny Mellon was a generous person, he didn't answer me. I accepted his silence: her generosity was private, singular, exclusive, and until quite late in her life she had to ask Paul for every cent she spent for charity—if she didn't want to spend her own money, that is.

Richard did, however, agree enthusiastically that both Bunny and J. Carter Brown loved "events." Creating an arena for such events and the exhibitions they supported was partly why there was a push to erect the gallery's new East Building, the construction of which began in 1971.

The National Gallery was also being forced to recognize a more diverse audience. While pointing out that "the Gallery needed space for traveling shows," Richard notes that the NGA was a "classical art institution—therefore, white—in a city with an eighty percent Black population." After Martin Luther King, Jr., was assassinated on April 4, 1968, the riots in Washington, D.C., were among the largest and longest in the nation. In 1970, the minute after he had become director in 1969, J. Carter Brown installed a huge exhibition of African sculpture in the West Building. "The NGA was saying, 'We may not collect this stuff, but we value it,'" said Richard.

What Bunny knew about race in America came from her personal connection with her Black employees, but she also witnessed the rage and grief in Atlanta at first hand. She had flown Jackie Kennedy in the Mellon plane to Dr. King's funeral. Making their way through the crowds from the Kings' home, where the two women had stopped to pay respects to Coretta Scott King—author, activist, and wife of Dr. King—to the church was slow and frightening. The driver impatiently honked his horn until Jackie "jumped forward . . . tapping him on the shoulder, [and] said, 'Stop blowing that horn! This is their town.'" In the huge bowl of Ebenezer Baptist Church, Bunny sat next to Bobby Kennedy, who identified the public figures "settling around us (like flocks of migrating birds)." What Bunny remembered most was the music: "Few instruments, just voices numbering a hundred or more. The voices sounded to come from distant lands, from seas, deserts, plains, lakes, and mountains." Back in the plane, they "settled down to silence and calm. Bobby Kennedy had left us to walk in the famous march behind the mule team to the cemetery."

The private preview dinner for the African sculpture show was another first for the National Gallery. "No food allowed in the exhibition rooms" was the stern lede in *The New York Times* on January 26, 1970, a piece about the preview party to be held in rooms holding the Widener Collection in the West Building. But that evening the massive Renaissance table, china, and tapestries Joseph Widener had collected had been whisked away from the caterers' candlelit tables, food, and drink.

The evening proceeded, but not without a hitch—Bunny's absence. Paul told the guests that she had broken her ankle a month earlier in Antigua, working in the garden, watering flowers in the dark. Bunny always walked fast and often didn't seem to care what might be in the way. Although she was a festive person who loved giving pleasure and creating pleasant surprises, Bunny didn't particularly enjoy being onstage herself. In this case, breaking her ankle—however painful— left her safely out of the picture, something she privately might have preferred.

The challenge in helping J. Carter Brown at the National Gallery was how to transport Bunny's private sense of theater to such events at a modern museum. She often attacked problems of scale with massive stands of greenery and informal arrangements of flowers that brought the eye down to the dinner table. When Russia sent priceless Impressionists and Postimpressionists to the United States, for the preview dinner in April 1973 Bunny used brilliant red tablecloths centered with rustic straw baskets filled with flowers that she said would "make it look like springtime in Moscow."

Bunny's preview dinners and luncheons at the National Gallery, particularly in the 1970s, advertised exhibition themes to very important donors, visiting diplomats, and weighty politicians in an attractive yet subliminal way. The entertainment mimicked that of being a guest in a rich person's home: calligraphed invitations, name cards on the tables, careful seating arrangements, and perfect timing of all service, so that no one could complain that the ice was not cold enough. At the other end of the art spectrum, the 1965 creation of the National Endowment for the Arts began to influence public engagement with museums and their funding. Museum boards expanded beyond families of their donors to corporate elites, who realized they could monetize visitors' experience with cafeterias, restaurants, and shops. Museums soon offered massive merchandising campaigns and branding opportunities.

Genevra Higginson, chief of protocol and director of special events at the NGA in the 1980s, told me that Bunny put extra time and effort into the 1985 exhibition *Treasure Houses of Britain*, a loan show built around English country house architecture and culture over five centuries. Joseph Krakora thought *Treasure Houses* had particular appeal for Bunny because it exemplified her own ideal mix of humble objects and grand ones, returning her to a world she had known with her British girlfriends, a place and an upper crust she was utterly familiar with. And she wanted to demonstrate that Americans could carry off this scene too.

"The Gallery had invited all lenders to the exhibition and had expected some twenty or so to come," said Higginson. Instead, 150 arrived—dukes, earls, counts, marquesses, marchionesses, as well as some plain old squires, knights, and their ladies—the lot expecting to be wined, dined, and fêted during their stay in town.

D.C. sprang into action. One Friday night, according to the *Los Angeles Times*, they "spread out to 42 different dinner parties in private homes, given by the likes of Sen. Jay Rockefeller (D-W. Va.), *The Washington Post* Chairman of the Board Katharine Graham, Maurice Tobin (former chairman of the National Theater), and socialite Oatsie Charles." Bunny gave a dinner at the house on Whitehaven Street. Both there and at the National Gallery, where august guests sat shoulder to shoulder at dinners in the West and East Buildings, the place settings, conversation, and tiaras sparkled.

Not everything went flawlessly. Krakora recalled that the gallery had asked the palace staff about receiving lines for Charles and Diana, the prince and princess of Wales, and was frostily told, "We don't do receiving lines; we do crescents" (where guests form curving lines on each side of a room, and royalty moves along them, murmuring to each person). Krakora said to himself, "This is America; we don't do crescents." He was right. When the prince and princess of Wales emerged into the atrium space of the East Building, the crowd behaved like "locusts coming out of the woods—people climbing on planters, craning their necks."

The follow-up to the opening came on Sunday, when the young royals visited Oak Spring for lunch, the only such private event of their four-day stay in D.C. It was a very different occasion from the teatime visit of twenty-eight years earlier, when the queen and the duke of Edinburgh had toured the farm and Foxcroft girls had lined the drive.

By 1985, Bunny's concept of what was appropriate for a royal event had expanded. A Kublai Khan pleasure dome—a latticed pavilion, not a tent—bloomed on the terrace overlooking the spring that gave Oak Spring Farm its name. Bunny didn't hesitate to break through a sturdy stone wall of her house to unite the partygoers within and on the terrace.

Bunny's walled garden that November day in 1985 provided a fall tapestry. Clouds of blue—Michaelmas daisies, the plucky late-autumn asters that are an English favorite—accompanied annuals and other perennials grown in pots and set into the bare spots, just as Ellen Shipman's writings had taught Bunny to do long ago at Apple Hill. A carefully pruned specimen of one of Bunny's favored tree species at Oak Spring, the fearsomely thorny trifoliate orange, stood (and still stands) on the terrace like a tamed unicorn in a medieval tapestry.

Paul Leonard, the good-looking decorative painter and interior designer who'd gotten his start painting sets for the film, opera, and TV director Franco Zeffirelli, was on hand. Leonard and his business partner, William Strom, had been on Bunny's payroll for fifteen years beginning in 1961 and were given an apartment in one of the Mellon buildings on Manhattan's Upper East Side. Leonard had long been far more than an employee or one of Bunny's walkers—a role he sometimes took on. He was a fun-loving playmate, a confidant, a "finder" and art advisor, and a real support in troubled times—a close friend, in other words. But Bunny had emotional boundaries, and if a friend crossed those invisible lines, even unthinkingly, he or she was coldly dismissed—as was Leonard when he married the British graphic designer Valerie Pedlar in the mid-1970s. Bunny's men were hers. They were not to be shared with anyone—especially not with other women.

But that fall in 1985, Leonard was nonetheless suddenly reinstated as if they had never parted to help Bunny create the mise-en-scène for British royalty. Like others she cut off, Leonard returned to the fold with apparent joy when Bunny relented, discovering she needed him. Now, all that remains to anchor the memory of that day at Oak Spring are four heavy yet graceful metal dining chairs that Leonard painted in rich browns, greens, and blues. The library staff uses them for lunch at the simple oak table framed from trees cut on the farm.

Leonard had also played a role in Bunny's own "curatorial staff" for National Gallery events. Another mainstay for these affairs was Perry Wheeler, the soft-spoken D.C. landscape architect who helped her with the White House Rose Garden and many private landscapes and gardens. Of one National Gallery lunch in 1972, *The Washington Evening Star* wrote, "Mrs. Mellon, who usually arranges every detail and every flower for her parties, refused to take credit for the blossom-filled baskets on the tables. 'Perry Wheeler, who is a great landscape artist, did them,' she said, adding, 'He helps me very often; I don't have to explain a thing. He always knows just what I want.'"

In terms of imagination and inventiveness and extra hands, what Leonard and Wheeler did for her National Gallery preview events, the gallery's design team of Gaillard Ravenel and Mark Leithauser did for the exhibitions themselves, starting in 1970. In 2011, Leithauser said, "I think what you want to do as an exhibit designer is to make the work feel at home." He added, "Let the painting do the work, and let the colors of the wall fall off." Which is exactly what

Bunny and Paul Mellon did in their houses with Cézannes and van Goghs and Manets: let the paintings do the work.

We can follow Bunny's career as a collector through the art that she and Paul ultimately gave to the National Gallery of Art, through what she sold at auction in 2014 as her property, and through what the NGA lists in her name alone. In 1983, after the discovery of Paul's prostate cancer, the Mellons gave ninety-three additional works to the National Gallery, including six Monets and two Gauguins.

Paul's reckoning of how much Bunny contributed to the collection varied from time to time, but in a 1983 interview with art critic Paul Richard, he said that she "has had an enormous impact on the collection." He estimated that she had chosen twenty percent of the art, he himself another twenty percent, and that "picking the other sixty percent was really a joint endeavor."

Despite Paul's description of which of them was responsible for what, however, Bunny remains shadowy as a collector. The eighteen gifts whose credit line reads "Collection of Mrs. Paul Mellon"—five Netherlandish still lifes, ten Calder sheet metal cutouts, and two large

At Paul's retirement as chairman of the National Gallery of Art on May 3, 1985, he and Bunny toast each other. She holds a folder about the event under her arm; he wears the blue cross of an Honorary Knight Commander of the British Empire.

Rothkos, part of her 1970/71 expedition—give a clue to the throughline of her taste over the years but not to her powerful agency in buying hundreds of Impressionist and Postimpressionist works with her husband.

Bunny, both as a donor and as a patron, was unlike her sister-in-law, Ailsa Mellon Bruce. The National Gallery's current curator of French art and the head of the department, Mary Morton, described Bruce's attitude as a case of "aggressive resistance to recognition of spectacular acts of generosity" in a talk and a biographical essay accompanying a 2014 exhibition of the gallery's small Impressionist pictures.

Ailsa Mellon Bruce was born in 1901, Bunny in 1910. Both were the eldest children of powerful, wealthy men. Morton charts Bruce's collecting life primarily through the male figures who most supported her: her brother, Paul; her husband, David Bruce; Lauder Greenway, her companion of many years after her divorce from David Bruce; and John Walker, the director of the National Gallery throughout her collecting life.

Most twentieth-century women of their class and wealth acted through men. Even after Bunny struck out on her own to collect works that Paul didn't like, Paul paid for them. She agreed with Ailsa that her role was a supporting one, not separate from her husband's. In museum credit lines, Bunny usually becomes "& Mrs. Paul Mellon." About Ailsa Bruce, Morton quotes a reporter for the *Washington Star* who, after Bruce's death in 1969, wrote, "She was that most valuable of donors, the one concerned with the emerging of the museum's total collection rather than with her own identity within that emergence."

Comparisons with three other noted women collectors are telling. Isabella Stewart Gardner, Louisine Havemeyer, and Jane Meyerhoff couldn't have been more different from Bunny in their collecting, museum gifts, and presentation of self.

Gardner's Boston museum, in architectural style and content, sharply and intentionally reflects an ornate and eccentric personage who was following her tutor, the American art historian Bernard Berenson, and her own eclectic interests in Italian art. (Initially, it was funded with a $2 million bequest from her father.) "Mrs. Jack [Gardner]" reveled in publicity.

The suffragist Louisine Havemeyer and her husband, the industrialist and sugar magnate H. O. Havemeyer, collected art together for forty years. Louisine's collecting had begun in the 1870s in Paris with her friendship with Mary Cassatt, who introduced her to French art, and Louisine took the lead in the couple's acquisitions. In 1929 her children donated some two thousand works on canvas and paper, sculpture, and decorative art to the Metropolitan Museum of Art.

Close to a century later, in 1958, Jane Meyerhoff of Phoenix, Maryland, north of Baltimore, bought a black-and-olive Rothko for $3,000 in New York. Jane later recalled, "When I got it home and showed it to Bob [a successful real estate developer in the post–World War II years], he said, 'I can't believe you spent $3,000 on something that looks like this.'" Like Louisine Havemeyer, Jane Meyerhoff took the lead in the couple's acquisitions.

All three women shaped their collections in ways Bunny did not, but their husbands lacked the close identification with and family ties to an institution that Paul Mellon had with the National Gallery of Art. John Gardner, H. O. Havemeyer, and Robert Meyerhoff were generally content to step back from the limelight and keep a low profile. No way would Paul Mellon have wanted to step back from his involvement with the National Gallery.

Paul's goddaughter Georgiana McCabe met I. M. Pei, the architect of the National Gallery's East Building, at the reception following Paul's interment in the private Mellon plot at Trinity Episcopal Church in Upperville, Virginia, in 1999. (I remember that Paul's casket was draped with a magnificent pall—a horse blanket in Rokeby's dark gray and yellow racing colors—part of the endless procession of meaningful details so characteristic of Bunny's work. Over a glass of Nicolas Feuillatte champagne, Bunny's preferred marque, everyone there was able to rejoice in every single thing they knew and loved about Paul Mellon.)

In talking about the NGA's East Building, Pei began by telling McCabe, "Every great building has a great patron." Then he went on about the construction process. "My people went and researched the Tennessee quarry from where the pink marble came for the West

Building. The quarry had closed." Pei and his team then had to make a decision to go for a different color, as they couldn't find a match. "I told Paul the quarry had gone out of business. He said, 'I guess we'd better buy it.' He was willing to go for the two-year delay this entailed as 'it was the right thing to do.'"

"The right thing" would also mean choosing the right plantings for the building. Dan Kiley, famous for his French-inflected modernist work at American institutions, was the landscape architect for the new building, but "Bunny was very involved in the East Wing building process," said Genevra Higginson. She pointed out, as just one of many details, that "Bunny chose the highly fragrant tea crab apple, *Malus hupehensis*, for the terrace outside Paul Mellon's office." *M. hupehensis* was another favorite Bunny used on many of her jobs, including at Oak Spring.

Bunny's designs for the gala opening dinner were precisely tuned to Pei's odd-angled building and its airy lines. No ordinary circular or rectangular dining tables would suit the irregular space, Bunny decided. Instead, the two hundred guests sat at specially constructed triangles, trapezoids, and parallelograms. The white tablecloths specially woven by Bunny's protégés Nantucket Looms were crisscrossed with narrow bands of her favorite blue. The large windowpane check brought a breath of spontaneity, a picnic air, to the evening.

Evangeline Bruce reported that the French arbiter of taste "Bobby" de Margerie, later ambassador to the United States, said, "I think the evening at the Gallery was perfect, and the most perfect thing there was Mrs. Mellon."

The silky, ankle-length dress with short sleeves that Hubert de Givenchy made for Bunny for the gala black-tie opening of the East Building in 1978 is loose, almost formless, and gathered at the waist not with darts but with a ribbon. It seems to move, even in still photographs. Against a white background, its uneven red and blue stripes look like brushstrokes on the flowing fabric. Perhaps not many of the partygoers took in that dress as the tribute it was to what the evening celebrated—I. M. Pei's innovative new building and the twentieth-century art it contained. It was also as red, white, and blue as the

Paul, standing next to Eileen Pei, cracks a half grin at the photographer, Diana Walker, daughter of his mistress, Dorcas Hardin, while Bunny talks composedly with her friend I. M. Pei, the architect of the East Building of the National Gallery, at its opening on June 1, 1978.

American flag and as American as the music the guests enjoyed: that of the American jazz clarinetist and bandleader Benny Goodman.

Given Bunny's pleasure in planning surprises, was it at all remarkable, really, that she had secretly collared Paul's favorite musician to surprise him with his favorite jazz? The crowd danced until two in the morning. Andrea and Lavinia Currier, Ailsa's granddaughters, were there. Jackie Kennedy was there, and so was "the cream of the art world, a mixture of artists, collectors and patrons of the arts, with nary a political figure in sight," noted Barbara Gamarekian, an arts and society reporter for *The New York Times*.

Despite all the action on the dance floor, the brilliant company, the banks of lush greenery, the hurricane lamps glowing, all eyes had to have been drawn to Robert Motherwell's magnificent *Reconciliation Elegy*. Specially commissioned for the East Building's opening, it commanded the west wall of the lower atrium level. Big black shapes almost touch, then don't, against a white background tenderly hued with clouds of almost pink and blue.

Motherwell wanted the painting to read as "open and freely made, like an enormous sketch." A similarly large commission on which he had worked spontaneously, without extensive preparation, had proved a clumsy failure. For *Reconciliation Elegy* the artist had decided, he reported, to "proceed otherwise . . . to use every technical resource at my command to give spontaneity, that is, the illusion that the work was both conceived (which it was) and executed (which it nearly was) with total immediacy in one energetic day." In fact, it had required three years to conceive the original sketch and then nine months from that sketch through all the various stages of painting to carry the work to completion. Such apparently "flawless performances of effortlessness" were what Bunny also strove for, as if all of life, the private and the public, could be—had to be—conveyed in a single compressed if ephemeral gesture.

Motherwell also explained that the problem he faced in *Reconciliation Elegy* was "in the midst of architectural grandeur to strike a personal note, the note of the human presence . . . of a twentieth-century solitary individual, that terrible burden . . . and somehow make it public, too." One could argue that Bunny Mellon also often faced her own interior tension between the solitary burden and the public image.

I. M. Pei understood what Bunny strove for. In January 1979, after all the East Building hoopla, he wrote a note of thanks to her for a gift—what it was isn't clear—saying, "Who else but you could have thought of so appropriate a memento! It sums up without words so poignantly the hectic but joyful months of working together to bring our long journey to such a happy ending. With much affection . . . yours . . ."

Pei and Bunny became real friends. They had known one another at least since 1968, when Pei laid out the first conceptual designs for the East Building while simultaneously working on the Paul Mellon Arts Center at Paul's alma mater, the Choate School in Wallingford, Connecticut. But still earlier, in 1964, Pei had been selected as the architect for the John F. Kennedy Presidential Library and Museum in Boston. Jacqueline Kennedy had made the ultimate choice of the as-yet-comparatively-unknown Pei, saying, "I decided it would be fun to take a great leap with him." Inevitably, as Jackie's closest friend, confidante, and advisor on all architectural and landscape projects, Bunny must have been in on the discussion.

Pei watched Bunny in action on the difficult JFK library site on Boston's windblown Columbia Point, overlooking Dorchester Bay and the Atlantic. Fifteen feet of earth and topsoil covered the former landfill. Dan Kiley was chosen as landscape architect; Bunny, working with Kiley, was instrumental in the plantings, which included dune grasses both to hold the soil in the constant winds and to evoke the Cape Cod that she knew Kennedy had loved. At the library's opening ceremony, Bunny, her face glowing with delight, sat between Pei and his wife, Eileen.

Bunny and Pei corresponded sporadically over thirty years, writing short communiques to each other about such topics as wind power on Antigua, the stone facings on the weirs of rivers in New England, and his firm's other projects, such as three buildings at the Christian Science Center in Boston. He expressed hope that she would approve of the Belgian landscape designer Jacques Wirtz's Carrousel Garden connecting the Louvre Museum, and Pei's glass pyramid, with the Tuileries.

She had indeed noticed "the planting of the Carrousel gardens radiating out from your 'Grand Louvre' now full of space and light. It seems like the sun is shining there at last after 200 years." In the same letter she says, "Dear I.M., I become a vulgar American in Paris when I boast that you are my friend." They treasured their friendship, their shared understanding of materials and construction, and their respect for one another.

Artists, architects, artisans, craftsmen—I. M. Pei; Edward Larrabee Barnes, the American architect who designed Bunny's Oak Spring Garden Library; and Paul Leonard—as well as the gifted masons, painters, woodcarvers, and metalworkers at the farm—are only a few with whom she shared that respect for materials, construction, and ability. It is not far-fetched to say that Bunny Mellon proudly felt that she, as a landscape gardener and a bona fide "dirt gardener," was their colleague as much as she was an arts and fashion patron, a society figure, and for fifty-one years the wife of Paul Mellon.

Sometime in the 1970s, when both the NGA's East Building and the JFK Presidential Library were in the works, I. M. Pei told Billy Baldwin, who had also worked with Bunny, that she was "the greatest landscape gardener and architect in this country. She knows flowers, gardens, buildings, decoration and pictures. It is absolutely complete."

∽ 12 ∾

Johnny and the Jewels

Bunny's introduction to the meaning and value of perfection—and the pleasures found along the way—had begun with the French jewelry designer Jean Schlumberger in 1954. "Johnny" was born in the same year as Paul Mellon, 1907, into a well-to-do textile family in Mulhouse, a grimy industrial city in the Alsace plain in northern France. He escaped to Paris to join the rarefied creative bubble of the couturiere Coco Chanel, the writer and critic Jean Cocteau, and the artist Christian Bérard—and the circle of eccentric and fashionable aristocrats, such as Vicomtesse Marie-Laure de Noailles, who were friends and patrons of Surrealists such as Salvador Dalí and Man Ray. In the frenetic, prewar 1930s, Schlumberger created his first designs—elaborate costume jewelry crafted from flea-market finds for the Italian fashion designer Elsa Schiaparelli.

Sexy and feline—Bunny later described him to me as a black cat—Schlumberger was apparently fought over by men and women alike. He first moved to the United States in 1940 and briefly opened a boutique on Fifth Avenue. When the war came, he returned to France to join the fight, survived Dunkirk, and served with the Free French in England under Charles de Gaulle.

When the war was over, Schlumberger again emigrated to the United States and set up a jewelry workshop on East Sixty-Third Street in 1947 with a nephew of the French couturier Paul Poiret, Nicolas Bongard, who became Schlumberger's longtime business partner. In 1956, Schlumberger was hired by Tiffany & Co., which gave him access to the firm's storehouse of fantastic gemstones and offered him a real footing as an artist. Later he and Lucien "Luc" Bouchage, an artist and a photographer, became life partners.

According to Bunny, the shop on Sixty-Third Street is where she met Johnny. Once, she told me in what she called her "go do something nice for yourself story," just when things were beginning to go badly with Paul, she "pulled herself together," took the children to the doctor in New York, and allowed to him how she herself was feeling low. The pediatrician, probably no stranger to the spending habits of rich young mothers, then facetiously asked, "Do[n't] you have any money?"

Bunny went home, she told me, "and I put on a Schiaparelli suit and a red velvet beret and went to Schlumberger's on Sixty-Third Street. I ordered a necklace from a nice tall man. Soon afterwards," she continued, "I went a second time—this time I was helped by not-as-good-looking a guy, so I asked him, 'Could I please speak to Mr. Schlumberger?' He replied, 'I am Mr. Schlumberger.' Oh."

Bunny ran into Schlumberger again in New York in 1955 at the bedside of the dying Syrie Maugham. After the visit she and Schlumberger went out to lunch. Bunny now found the man so attractive, she asked Rosie Fiske, still in the 1950s a close friend, whether she should go further. "Darling," said Rosie, "I went to Schlumberger, and all I can say is, bash on!" (Meaning, in British slang, "Go for it, baby." Maybe Rosie and other women *did* have flings with Schlumberger; at any rate, Rosie, true to form, named her storied house in the South of France "Domaine de Bashon.")

So next Bunny went to the theater as a foursome with Johnny, her great friend Liza Maugham (later Paravicini, later Hope), and Mainbocher, the couturier. "Finally," said Bunny, "he had tea with me by himself. Liza was upstairs, making sure I went through with it." Whether the tea party did the trick or not, it seems pretty clear that the pair became lovers.

Between April and early May 1956, Bunny went on a spending spree, with Paul's willing financial assistance and encouragement and Schlumberger's collaboration. The Tiffany order book for those weeks records that "Mrs. Mellon came in to discuss with Schlumberger" a pair of bracelets of multicolored stones with butterfly motifs (they tremble over flowers). She placed a firm order a week later.

During the same meeting, she was shown the design for a woven-gold cigarette case with cabochon sapphires and said she would "take it as soon [as it] will be completed." She also commissioned a magnificent turquoise and diamond necklace named "Leaves" for delivery in November.

She ordered a cocktail ring with an "Abeilles Impériales" design, featuring gold and diamond bees clustered around a canary diamond that she already owned. She and Paul came in together to look at a ninety-four-karat Kashmir sapphire known as "The Dancing Girl of India." Schlumberger would put the stone to good use for her. "Both liked it very much," the order book notes, adding, "we ask 275,000.00 . . . Mr. M. will give us a reply shortly if he'll take it or not" ($275,000 is the equivalent of $2.5 million in 2018). At one point, according to the order book, they took the stone home with them.

Black-clad Johnny stands on the back steps of his Manhattan house.

Exotic, exciting, unpredictable, and imperious, Schlumberger was a new experience for Bunny Mellon. He surely was the first man to whom she was attracted who was not like the tweedy gentlemen of her world. "He always wore black," she said, "and sometimes when the phone would ring, and there was nobody there, I knew it was Johnny."

Sometime soon after they met, Schlumberger began Bunny's transformation into a woman of fashion—clothes to measure up to his jewels. "Oh, look at that weed crawling up your dress—you can't wear these clothes," he once said to her, she told me. She never mentioned what she was wearing to bring on that outburst, but I'd have to imagine it was a busy but otherwise unremarkable flowered cotton print like the one she wore for Tuffy's christening in 1937.

The obvious step was to get her to Cristóbal Balenciaga, the Basque fisherman's son who had become the king of Paris couture, opening his own salon in 1937. The famous French fashion designer Christian Dior would describe him as "the master of us all." In the 1950s and '60s, Balenciaga (b. 1895), Schlumberger (b. 1907), and Givenchy (b. 1927) reigned as the three musketeers of high style. When Bunny was on a trip to England in 1954, Schlumberger had Balenciaga send his head fitter to London, who measured her for a maquette (a couturier's fitting mannequin for an important private client).

Bunny was tall and slim with long hands, narrow size 7.5 feet, a slender neck, small wrists, and good posture. During her twelve years with Balenciaga, she remained quite thin. Never a clotheshorse, she was a practical dresser who liked outfits of great beauty and originality constructed for ease of movement—that is, designed by a master and crafted by top seamstresses in unusual fabrics ranging from specially woven linen and cotton to embroidered brocades.

Later that year two dresses and a three-quarter-length coat for autumn arrived in what Bunny remembered as "a fascinating black fabric. I have to admit I loved it." In 1956, Schlumberger took her to view Balenciaga's fall collection, where she fell for the muted colors and arrestingly severe but flattering designs. She ordered an evening dress, a country suit, and another coat, all of which Schlumberger had sent to her from his friend Cristóbal's atelier.

And then, a year or so after she had become a regular client, "Cristóbal came to a fitting. The seamstress fussed over the details of my dress before he arrived," wrote Bunny later, recalling that the two conversed in their own versions of rather halting French. "That evening Johnny called to say Cristóbal had asked if we could come for the weekend." (With his partner Ramon Esparza, Balenciaga had a weekend retreat near Orléans in the farmlands of the Loire Valley.)

"Balenciaga met me at the door of his house," she continued.

"He had an amused smile on his face when he greeted me, saying in French, 'You are very well-dressed, Madame.'" I have to bet she was wearing Balenciaga.

She admired her guest room details of "heavy linen sheets, beautiful big towels, Balenciaga soaps, and bath scent"—a version of her own refinement. The American men Bunny knew, generally speaking, were used to having women attend to such details. Men were expected to admire decor or take it for granted, but they understood it wasn't theirs to arrange. (Her father was an exception.)

This atmosphere—an unabashedly although nominally closeted gay society created by powerful, gifted, and successful men with perfect taste—was very different from what Bunny was accustomed to, but she readily grasped the pleasures it had to offer. She may also have understood that for such men pleasure of all kinds was often to be taken for granted wherever you found it. "Johnny had the room next to me," she added. After she dressed herself in a casual evening gown, a yellow and ochre Balenciaga dishabille, she descended to the living room to find the three men waiting for her and for their host's special martinis.

She left the retreat with seeds of the first white wild *fraises des bois* she'd ever seen and propagated them at Oak Spring, where they produced the fragrant little strawberries for many years. Balenciaga often invited her back for weekends, and she also visited him at his seaside house in Getaria, his Basque birthplace.

Bunny quickly became the first private client in line at Balenciaga, visiting the collections as soon as they had been shown to commercial buyers. Making her clothes was a cottage industry: she had a separate workroom and a dedicated team of seamstresses. The costs were enormous and included American Airlines fees. Conservatively estimated, Bunny's wardrobe ran to about $150,000 a year, or close to $3 million in 2022.

Schlumberger was a constant presence during her years as Balenciaga's client: if she couldn't make it to a collection herself, he would work with the director of the salon, Renée Tamisier, to choose what he thought would suit her. Great attention was paid to the arrangement of jewels—Schlumberger's jewels. Instructions could be included: the note for one blue strapless evening gown advised that it be worn with a necklace. Both the necklace—and the neckline—were to be held in place by a concealed strap. Another time, Mlle Tamisier sent a letter to Bunny accompanying some sketches of her orders, writing, "On [the sketches of] various dresses, you will find a little swatch of fabric, indicating which coat you should wear with them," as if Bunny were a magnificent life-size doll.

Looking back at her last season of being dressed by Balenciaga, Bunny recalled her farewell visit to his salon, which was closing. "On a summer afternoon his Paris studio was silent and empty," she wrote, "no more design boards, each covered with fabric swatches, buttons, feathers and ribbons. A solitary rack held the American Airlines uniforms he had just finished."

Balenciaga made her take off what she was wearing and put on a model's smock because, he said, "th[at] dress is too large on the shoulders, Bunny." He ripped open the seams himself to repair the garment and sent her home in a denim skirt of hers that had been sent back to the atelier to copy and one of the stewardesses' blouses.

Then he took her by those shoulders, thimble still on his finger, and said, "Now you leave exactly as you arrived . . . nothing here has changed your character." For Balenciaga, what you wore could never change the inner human truth. The next morning that farewell gift— her dress, remade by the master himself—arrived at her door before ten o'clock.

Bunny felt the same reverence for Schlumberger and his artistry. In her little cubby of an office upstairs in the library at Oak Spring, Bunny hung two small black-and-white photographs of Johnny. In one he stands somewhere in Bali in 1954—he was always traveling to exotic places for inspiration—Bali, Cambodia, Nepal, Kashmir. He wears wrinkled khakis, a black T-shirt, a half smile, and is smoking as usual. He is totally absorbed by a band of small monkeys climbing all over him. The other is a closeup of his hands working on a drawing.

For Bunny, the image would have been a talisman, a sign of the importance that knowing how to work with your hands—as he did on the page, as she did in the garden—held for her. Schlumberger was not a jeweler but a jewelry *designer*. The very best fabricators and

The art and artistry of Jean Schlumberger began with a pencil.

goldsmiths and artisans were hired from all over the world to work for him in Paris or in New York in the Tiffany workshop. Nicolas Bongard, trained as a jeweler, guided the transmutation into precious metals and stones of what poured out of Schlumberger's fantastic imagination onto sheets of paper. The transaction was organic and involved the client as well as the artist and the artisans who all contributed to the alchemy.

Bunny's collection of Schlumberger was the largest in the world—all of it purchased for her by Paul. Paul was happy to visit Schlumberger's quiet little boutique at Tiffany's to vet the important pieces, sometimes with Bunny but also without her. On occasion Bunny mentioned she'd like him to see what she wanted; at other times someone at Tiffany's would let him know. On a lesser scale, the same game was played with Dorcas Hardin.

This roundabout delivery is startling—an old pattern dating to the time when women lost control of their money through marriage. Bunny had her own considerable fortune—but apparently it wasn't part of the bargain she and Paul had struck. Ultimately, Paul had control.

A representative selection—140 pieces—went to the Virginia Museum of Fine Arts in Richmond and in 2017 was displayed in a full-scale show at the museum. By making the gift, Bunny wanted to underline her belief that Schlumberger was no mere jewelry designer, he was an artist. He fashioned many simple enamel-and-gold clip earrings for her—Bunny never had her ears pierced; like many American women of her class and generation, she thought it tacky. The collection also includes an ornate, Byzantine-looking pectoral cross fit for a Russian Orthodox bishop. Athough she had built her country church in Upperville to the glory of God, she was a fervent High Church believer in the beauty of religious ritual and symbol.

She always had a cross hanging above her bed, and this confection was the one that hung in Virginia and then was popped into a sleek gray metal jewel box and locked up by her lady's maid, Nelly Jo Thomas, whenever Bunny left Oak Spring. Five-and-a-half inches long, it was designed in 1960. Heavy sapphire and aquamarine wings like those of an archangel or a bird of prey sprout from the cross's arms, even though it looks far too heavy to fly—the shaft is made of countless closely set emeralds. Diamonds blink here and there. Catherine the Great and her magnificent, commanding collection of jewels come to mind.

The day after Bunny's death in Virginia, Bunny's nurse, Nancy Collins, and Tony Willis, her librarian, hurried from the library to the house, where others of Bunny's staff were already throwing things out, much to their distress. They collected all the locked jewel boxes (crafted in the metal shop on the property) from under her bed and in the closets to take them to the secure vaults in the library. Then they opened the lids of the built-in chests set beneath the window seats, just to be thorough.

All the windows in all of Bunny's houses were recessed to hold pairs of specially made folding wooden shutters, louvered or paneled, that controlled light to just the right degree. A window seat was built into each recess. Sometimes these built-in storage chests contained books or papers or caches of rare fabrics—pieces of old chintz faded to just the right shade of pale, bolts of early-nineteenth-century toile de Jouy printed with fairy-tale fêtes galantes, and ancient, jewel-toned paisley shawls. Bunny used them to upholster pillows and small pieces of furniture (a rage that had started with Syrie Maugham and Nancy Lancaster).

In Bunny's bedroom Nancy Collins noticed a little wooden knob inset flat into the setback on one side of a window, below the level of the closed chest lid. She pulled it, releasing the hinged cover of a shallow hidden compartment. Presumably, the only people who knew about it were the carpenter and Bunny, like a Pharaoh and his mason, who constructed a secret tunnel leading down to the crypt—but without the same ending for the carpenter as the Egyptian mason, who was buried with his lord. Inside was a thin locked jewel box containing Jean Schlumberger's great necklace of 128 sapphires of various colors wreathed in fine diamond branches, the tendrils of the sapphire flowers. Bunny called it "Breath of Spring." Nancy thought it would be too prickly for comfort.

In the pitiful, ever-hopeful codicils of Bunny's will that follow the downhill track of daughter Eliza's life as she lay, largely unresponsive, for eight years, one reads that this great necklace was destined to go to Eliza at Bunny's death. No one who knew Eliza could imagine her ever wearing such a thing or even having an occasion to wear it. Bunny herself saved Schlumberger's bravura pieces only for great occasions; she was photographed wearing "Breath of Spring" on Paul's retirement as president of the National Gallery in 1985.

Still more astounding is Schlumberger's golden sunflower, crafted in eighteen-, twenty-, and twenty-two-karat gold. In Bunny's walled garden at Oak Spring, a blaze of different kinds of sunflowers, ranging from three feet tall to over six feet, grows against a whitewashed wall. Schlumberger's sunflower is only a little over seven inches. Where a living sunflower has a heart of black or red seeds, this one is centered with a huge jewel—today an amethyst but originally the sapphire known as "The Dancing Girl of India" that Paul and Bunny had taken back to the New York house to consider. The soil in the pot it sprouts from is composed of black garnet ore, but the pot itself, caged in gold straps, is a plain old clay pot from Bunny's garden.

I can imagine how Bunny and Schlumberger took pleasure in this creation, and in the drawing that started the process of making a *gage d'amour* for a woman who loved gardens, including fantasy ones like those in Marianne Moore's poem, "with real toads in them." So it was not just the opulence, the extravagance, the unbridled Madame de Pompadour quality of Bunny's spending—such as the the numerous Schlumberger lapis-and-gold cigarette boxes for the Mellon plane—that was shocking; it was also the use of Black human figures as decorative objects. Eighteenth-century-style ornaments were crafted as miniature blackamoors in turbans and jewels, evocations of the exotic African servants ubiquitous at European courts. (Schlumberger's figures who carry gold baskets on their heads evoke not only those enslaved people but also the Antiguan women who were Bunny's well-trained servants—in uniforms designed by Givenchy.) In the pleasures of inspiration, of creation, and of being outrageous, anything could be grist for the mill.

Some half a century later, the retired Mellon chief pilot of many years, Walter Helmer, called on Mrs. Mellon at Oak Spring. Afterward she wrote to him:

> Seeing you was like going back to days of great happiness. Flying to Guadeloupe to go grocery shopping . . . Today is different. I wonder if we went back to Guadeloupe and I went to the [Île des] Saints on a sailboat with Johnny, if it would be the same. [She was 100 years old when she wrote this!] Johnny was adventuresome. We would go to a house in the mountains there for a day or two surrounded by iguanas and a shower that was a bucket of water that you overturned with a rope.

"The Saints," a scattering of volcanic, almost uninhabited islands in the Lesser Antilles, lie just south of Guadeloupe, where Schlumberger and Bongard had a house. An expedition to the Saints was a respite from a respite, a rural place to get still closer to nature. But fresh water was scarce—hence the "bucket of water," which was probably rainwater collected in tropical storms—and Bunny's iguanas were a rare species not found elsewhere in the Caribbean—still rarer when

Bunny and Johnny on a plane
with a trove of orchids

seen in miniature on a Schlumberger brooch. Delicate orchids, also rare, sparkled and twined like jewels in the trees: the fringed white, the daddy-long-legs, and the yellow dancing lady. Johnny was as absorbed in what he observed outdoors as Bunny was. Schlumberger's friend Diana Vreeland, the noted fashion journalist, once said of him, "He so well understands the fantastic beauty of the world that he is not a fantasist. The world is a fantasy; Johnny is a realist."

Just that kind of grounding reality is found in a brief thank-you note he wrote to Bunny. After a visit to Bunny's gardens at the Mellons' winter vacation house in Antigua in 1974 he wrote, "My darling . . . I found fascinating your tropical gardening, in white and green—it is a real challenge in a nature in which plants have a tendency to bloom red if they can—in order to attract more easily the attention of the humming birds . . . So much love darling, Johnny."

"Johnny and I learned [about nature] without being taught," Bunny once said to me.

Certainly their friendship had its longueurs—years when they didn't correspond or see one another much. It could be revived, however, by another commission, by something to look forward to. Then Johnny had a stroke in 1974, and although he recovered somewhat, he was left unable to draw. His career was over.

He moved to Paris, leaving in his nineteenth-century clapboard house at 160 East Ninety-Second Street what he now knew he could no longer use: a collection of rare books about birds, insects, flowers, fish, and sea animals he had relied on as inspiration for his designs. Without the fever of commissions or a visit to the Caribbean, Bunny and Schlumberger saw one another less. And Bunny herself was knocked down by a serious illness (probably cancer, but nobody's talking) in 1978.

By 1979 they were back in touch, and they resumed their friendship but never with the same heat. Bunny's journals are instead filled with outpourings of love and complaints about Hubert de Givenchy and contain little about Schlumberger. I think the essence of their relationship was concentrated in the work, and in the charged times they spent together.

Two months before his death on August 29, 1987, Bunny visited Johnny in the hospital in Paris. Janette Mahler, Givenchy's secretary, who kept in touch with Bunny on details large and small, wrote, "I know how much pain your visit to Mr. Schlumberger must have caused you . . . but know that you must have given him such pleasure in coming to see him."

Janette was deeply fond of Bunny, but as a longtime fashion professional fiercely loyal to the House of Givenchy, she truly believed that a fine appearance—in a Givenchy creation, *bien sûr*—was crucial. She wanted her clients to look good, to look their *best*. Janette hated to think of Bunny so deeply upset and sorrowful after the hospital visit partly because, she also wrote, "you are so beautiful when you are happy, and when you laugh." While not conventionally beautiful, Bunny could appear so when animated, decisive, sparked by something or someone. She must have looked lifeless, drained, gray, and lonely after her final visit to someone she'd loved (and been loved by, in his own fashion) for more than thirty years.

Ten days after Schlumberger's death, Luc Bouchage was cleaning out Johnny's cupboards and closets in the Paris apartment, and he wrote to Bunny, "Everywhere, I keep finding letters from you—recent and past . . . a few photographs as well. But you know, the one he always had of you, in his passport case, whenever he traveled, I put with him—so that is gone."

By early 1989, Bouchage was in New York, cataloguing Schlumberger's drawings at Tiffany's. He also gave Bunny the first news of the show in Paris, *Un Diamant dans la Ville*, which would open in 1995 at the Musée des Arts Décoratifs, the repository of Schlumberger's three thousand drawings. "Jewels have such a precarious life," he wrote. "Either they get lost, stolen, or broken up because someone thinks they are old fashioned—so that the drawings are Johnny's opus." Certain she would lend her own pieces and perhaps hoping she would contribute funding, he added, "I am sure you can help this show so much when it finally gets on the way by your wonderful eye and knowledge of how it should all be done and presented." The Virginia Museum of Fine Arts lent the cream of her collection to the Paris exhibition and others, keeping alive the memory of the man's genius.

This wasn't the first time Bunny and Bouchage had worked together on a project for Johnny. She had offered advice and workmen to remodel the kitchen and create a studio addition to the East Ninety-Second Street house that Schlumberger had bought not far from Spanish Harlem in 1956. In the 1970s, Schlumberger spent a great deal of time working there.

As usual Bunny had imagined the project fully. Also as usual, she was a perfectionist, and cost—not entirely her cost, it appears in this case—was no object. But Bouchage politely wondered if sending her own carpenter to plane the floors was entirely necessary, as Schlumberger would surely use carpet throughout.

Bunny envisioned the studio as "a gay, informal little room to play with," but her plans for kitchen counters and windows were practical. He should have one counter where he could arrange flowers, she wrote, and enough windows to make it well lit but with one "perfectly good solid wall on which to display his plates or anything he chooses."

She sketched a back stoop curving down from the house, making a bottom turn into a garden. She suggested a little greenhouse next to it, against a wall of the house, writing that that would mitigate the looming height of the addition. The greenhouse was never built, but the steps and the "Dutch" door, one of her telltale architectural signatures, remain today. Bunny's projects for her friends were her way of expressing not only her love and involvement but also her skills, something she considered integral to her authentic self.

Schlumberger was buried on the cemetery island of San Michele in the Venetian lagoon, along with other great twentieth-century figures in the arts, such as Igor Stravinsky, Sergei Diaghilev, and Ezra Pound. For Bunny—friend, patron, and lover—Schlumberger had transformed nature into the golden creatures of Yeats's hymn to Byzantium "to set upon a golden bough to sing . . . Of what is past, and passing, and to come."

13

Clothes and the Man

Jean Schlumberger had taken Bunny to meet his friend Cristóbal Balenciaga in 1956; in 1968, on Balenciaga's retirement, the fashion designer
had walked her across the street to Hubert de Givenchy's atelier. At each
house, Bunny ordered twelve to thirty-five designs every season, some
of which were reproduced in different colors and fabrics. She bought
four versions of the same Balenciaga coat in December 1957, for example. Once Bunny found a becoming style—a skirt with a waistband,
a tailored top, a coat to match a dress, many separates—something
Givenchy introduced in his first collection in 1952—she stuck with it.
A redingote, a fitted dress or coat, would be made in hundreds of variations over the years.

The clothes the two couturiers crafted for Bunny were elegant but
easy, occasionally even fanciful. Although she made several appearances on the Best-Dressed lists she was never "fashionable," just very
well dressed. The occasional dash of The Gap or Orvis or Land's End
kept this grand wardrobe grounded even as Bunny moved on from
New York's Hattie Carnegie, the first designer she'd patronized as
Mrs. Lloyd.

Bunny's relationships with the Three Musketeers of Style stretched
far beyond buying and wearing their beautiful creations. In 1991,
Bunny wrote in her journal that what had fascinated her most were
not the beautiful clothes Balenciaga and then Givenchy made for her,
but sharing "our lives & imaginations." She added, "Minds that create
often salute each other with an exciting & simpathic [*sic*] curiosity."

Bill Waller, the Virginia picture framer, was speaking as Bunny's equal when he said, "Some clients—not many, but some—work *with* the artist or craftsman. Sometimes they need to be talked out of their ideas. Sometimes their ideas work."

By the time Bunny Mellon and Hubert de Givenchy met, Bunny, who was already recognized for the White House Rose Garden, had created a masterpiece—Oak Spring Farm in Upperville, Virginia— and was refining her style into modernism on Nantucket. Bunny understood that Hubert, with his remarkable taste and eye, would recognize and appreciate the details that she had silently fashioned in landscapes and gardens.

A dashing young Givenchy cuts a swath to the top
of the couturier hierarchy.

Hubert de Givenchy at twenty-five was that rarity, a couturier who owned his own firm. From the start he had a financial backer, someone who believed in his talents, in Hélène Bouilloux-Lafont. After Bunny became Givenchy's client, she and Bouilloux-Lafont became friends. The two women, Hubert, Philippe Venet, and a few others reveled in calling themselves "the French family" as they traveled together on vacation jaunts, hiring a very grand private yacht to sail along the Turkish coast, or visiting Tunisia, or staying at the Mellons' Antigua hideaway.

Lighthearted Bouilloux-Lafont added an irreverent note to "the French family." Once, when she knew Bunny was coming, she and Hubert posed enjoying a cup of tea as the display in the window of the chic little shop she ran for a while.

Bouilloux-Lafont was also perfectly capable of sending Bunny a postcard of a School of Fontainebleau portrait: a stark-naked young woman with a knowing eye wearing a lot of jewelry, whom she naughtily labeled "Bunny." When Bunny made her twice-yearly visits, Bouilloux-Lafont often ran errands for her; Bunny responded with thoughtful presents from the gobsmacking to the practical: a gold Schlumberger box or a two-volume French/English dictionary, the latter especially useful, since Bouilloux-Lafont's English was apparently sketchier than Bunny's French. "The French family" depended chiefly on Franglais.

As her new French life developed, some of Bunny's old friendships dimmed or disappeared, a pattern that continued for the rest of her life. Similar transitions happen in many lives, although rarely in such numbers. In Bunny's case there was seldom an obvious rupture, just a remarkable and complete absence; discarded friends often had no clue why they had fallen out of favor. And if she did explain, it wasn't necessarily the whole truth.

Most startling to me was the case of her steadfast friend Liza Maugham, Baroness Glendevon, whose daughter Camilla Chandon de Briailles (wife of the Moët et Chandon heir) was one of Bunny's goddaughters. (While Paul and Bunny were courting, Liza had been one of two friends of Bunny's, the other being Sister Parish, whom Paul really trusted and liked.) When I asked Bunny about the rupture, she scornfully crossed Liza off the list with a single remark: "Spoilt pretty lady."

Camilla said that since her childhood Bunny had truly been her "fairy godmother." She and her sister Caroline went to Eliza's *Grand Meaulnes* coming-out party in 1961 and were then flown to New York (with Adele Astaire also aboard the plane), where the girls were booked (at the Mellons' expense) at the Drake Hotel. "There were two little purses on the dressing table with five hundred dollars each for us to spend," recalled Camilla, adding, "Amazing to think of all that in the middle of arranging the fabulous party, typical of Bunny's thoughtfulness . . . Caroline had never been to America before, and she wanted us to have a good time." How, indeed, did Bunny think of this stuff? But in the 1990s, Bunny's friendship with Camilla's mother vanished. Even when Liza died in 1999, Bunny never got in touch with the family. Likely a part of what made her disappearance so painful for anyone she dropped was the crushing *absence* of that kind of fairy-tale magic Bunny often supplied.

Paris and "the French family" provided a trouble-free respite from Bunny's own family circle, where relationships had often been fraught. Bunny had never been close to her mother or to her sister, Lily. Her relationship with her stepson, Timothy Mellon, had been troubled almost from the start, according to early letters from Paul. Eliza and Derry Moore divorced in 1972, and at some point thereafter Eliza stopped speaking to her mother; the breach lasted for many years while Bunny, inconsolable, continued to reach out to her daughter. Eliza seldom responded; she was trying to create a separate life for herself.

In my few conversations with Tuffy, he made it clear that Eliza was the favored child. In 1973, Bunny, who had sent stepdaughter Cathy Mellon off with Senator John Warner in a charming Cape Cod wedding sixteen years earlier, saw Cathy and Warner divorcing while at the same time Tuffy was marrying Anne Emmet Pepper, a member of the old D.C. Eustis family, whose best-known member was William Corcoran, founder of the Corcoran Gallery of Art in 1869.

Anne was a Foxcroft schoolmate of Eliza's; Anne's uncle was David E. Finley, Jr., the first director of the NGA and a close friend of Paul's; Oatlands (built in 1798, an exact contemporary of Carter Hall), the Eustis family's plantation, was only twenty miles away from Oak Spring in Upperville; Anne's father, Grenville Emmet, Jr., had gone to school with Stacy Lloyd. Thus the regal family circle was very, very small, and none of the players shared Bunny's acute interests in gardening or collecting (books, furniture, porcelain, art, or design of all kinds, from architecture to couture).

For Bunny, the form of carefully curated events such as family weddings and funerals may have had additional meaning beyond the emotions that propelled them. She expertly took charge of and managed such events, including the funeral of her own mother, Rachel Lowe Clopton, in 1978. She had also supported Paul in mourning his mother, Nora, who had died in 1973 in Roosevelt Hospital in New York City. Bunny, remembering Nora Mellon's lonely demise, would later write in her journal that Paul should not die as Nora had. Bunny was determined that he would die at home.

EVEN THOUGH PAUL was against her buying an apartment in Paris, Bunny was clearly already thinking about it in October 1970, when Hubert sent her a hand-sewn linen booklet, one of several such booklets he sent to the Crillon, where she had stayed (always with her personal maid) ever since her honeymoon trip with Paul. The pages were blank, Hubert wrote, so she could sketch "plans for your new house . . . with much affection, Hubert." By 1971, Bunny had bought her apartment at 84, avenue Foch and would spend many enjoyable years perfecting the renovations. Couture had opened the door to an absorbing new life that was at the same time a continuation of two old passions: la belle France and the building and decoration of houses.

By 1974, Hubert was very successful, and had found the perfect "maison de campagne." He fell for the Manoir du Jonchet, two hours south of Paris, a magical Renaissance château encircled by forest and gardens. Over the following years he and Venet did a top-to-bottom restoration, from the roof and six-foot-tall fireplaces to the floors, where he took up the wall-to-wall carpet and laid massive worn stone pavers that were polished every week. He repaired the walls of the moat and folded some later additions seamlessly into the ancient fabric of the place, as careful about those details as he was about every design detail for his couture collections. He reinstated the ancient *potager* garden and renewed the chapel.

Bunny was, of course, happy to help. (She had already advised him on his first, more modest country house in Jouy-en-Josas, in the southwestern suburbs of Paris.) At Le Jonchet, Hubert laid out a special bedroom for her in which every possible upholstered surface, not to mention the curtains, was covered with a blue and white print of not-quite-recognizable flowers with a faintly medieval air. Bunny reciprocated with "the poppy room" for Hubert in the guesthouse at Oak Spring, as well as a bedroom in New York. Few other guests—only the favored or distinguished—ever slept in either of these special chambers.

Hubert at ease in the bedroom at the Manoir du Jonchet that
he and Bunny decorated using a single fabric

How did Bunny define the look she wanted? What should the image of the wife of one of the richest men in the world be? Not horsey, although all her life she kept her canvas Foxcroft riding raincoat; it was handsome, heavy, blocky, with interior straps for the rider's legs and a waist-high split up the back with a flange to keep the rider dry. Not flowery—Bunny's look under Givenchy's tutelage became very un–Laura Ashley—unless the flowers were abstracted, formalized. She almost never wore pants, at least not in public. She was smart enough to know they didn't suit her as her hips and thighs broadened over the years.

Her clothes, like those of all rich women in service to a husband and society, were a uniform of a sort. And she had to be well prepared for all occasions. But why did she order forty-eight pairs of navy blue silk panties from the best Paris lingerie shop? In case they wore out? To have about a dozen for each of her houses? Probably, just as she ordered the same dress in different colors and fabrics for her various homes. It's as if her clothes were saying, "I have better things to do than to be outrageously fashionable or to follow trends."

Her style evolved with the shift from Balenciaga to Givenchy. She had worn Balenciaga's splendiferous printed silk velvet evening gown cut with a small train to a National Gallery of Art opening in 1966, two years before the designer's retirement. The fabric is outrageous— blue and green fantasy leaves and branches, small orange berries, glints of gold thread on the beige background. In one photograph of the event, where Bunny and Paul

Lady Bird Johnson greets Paul and Bunny Mellon, with her gaze on Bunny's splendid gown.

are walking over to greet Lady Bird Johnson, the First Lady's eyes are entirely on the dress rather than on the illustrious donors to the exhibition.

Hubert's clothes for Bunny were more lighthearted than Balenciaga's. The extent and detail of the kingdom of fabrics entranced both Hubert and Bunny, and they played in it like children with very expensive tastes. In 1970, the year Hubert sent Bunny the little linen notebook, Janette Mahler, his secretary, in an urgent letter, asked her if she wanted sixty-one yards of cotton sprigged with delicate branches in black and blue—for curtains, she writes, or any other decorating effect. If so, M. de Givenchy was prepared to offer it to her at a "very advantageous price."

Not long after their Rothko foray in New York, Hubert made her not one but two "robe soir Rothko," one in crepe printed in a "Rothko orange," chestnut, and black, the other in organza with a matching cape in prune, greenish black, a dense, subdued blue, and, once again, "Rothko orange."

Her shoes were made by René Mancini, the Italian shoe designer in Paris favored by many couturiers. Janette Mahler, who was in charge of pulling together "touts les accessoires boutique: sacs, ceintures, bijoux, etc." for each of Bunny's outfits, sent her three pages of Mancini designs in a range of silk and velvet, goat, and black crocodile. Once a package of the bespoke footwear went missing, and panic ensued, with plans for replacements already in the works just as the parcel was found. In October 1977, Bunny ordered twenty-two items through Janette.

Once an order was shipped to Virginia—customs for clothes and accessories were punctiliously paid, even though the items would travel on the Mellon plane—care for all the clothes fell to her lady's maid, Nelly Jo Thomas.

In her job interview with Bunny, Nelly Jo quoted her boss as saying, more or less, "I want that little schoolgirl because she don't know nothing and I can teach her my way." Bunny was a hands-on teacher: "I did flowers," continued Nelly Jo, "and she taught me the right way to do laundry; how to make a bed right; how to cut roses." Nelly Jo learned everything from how many sorrel leaves from the Oak Spring garden were needed to make a pot of soup to "how to curtsy to the Queen of England."

Fiercely proud of her job, Nelly Jo did not leave her position until 1983, after thirty-five years "in service." Ladies' maids were expected both to divine their employers' wishes and to keep their secrets. Their world was thus enmeshed with that of their employers'.

A lady's maid like Nelly Jo had to be up to dealing with any emergency. On one occasion Paul and Bunny had a fierce marital disagreement when they were having dinner upstairs alone together, on trays. "He grabbed the front of Mrs.'s dress and tore it all the way down . . . he was pretty rough," remembered Nelly Jo. "Mrs. said to me, 'I think you better get rid of this.'" Naturally, Nelly Jo burned it. She knew Bunny's heartaches and recalled her saying sadly but defiantly that Paul "goes his way; I go my way."

Although Bunny might say wise things in her nineties to a lovelorn friend, like "Don't make a man your only focus," she often asked her nurse and confidante Nancy Collins to recite the litany of her great loves, always saying, "Don't forget Paul." So which man did Bunny love best? Stacy? Paul? Johnny? Hubert? Bunny loved the lift of being in love with a man, and at one point she confided to her journal that she wanted to talk to a therapist about the difficulties of loving "two at once."

Hubert de Givenchy became the mainstay of her life for decades, but she remained married to Paul. Once, arriving in Paris, Bunny found her Avenue Foch residence flooded with flowers from Hubert. "Je suis si heureuse!" she wrote in a journal entry in the mid-1970s. She added that when he called that afternoon, it was like "a clear bell ringing with joy." They went out to dinner that evening to a favorite restaurant—"our table saved in the corner." Over dinner, they talked about his house, Le Jonchet, and how to decorate it—"how we would do the Grand Salon." But most of all, that evening was precious because of "his desire to talk—thoughts coming from deep within."

They were linked by more than her incredible yearly couture outlay or the use of the Mellon plane or his visits to her extraordinary houses and gardens, which he prized, or even the junkets and camaraderie of "the French family." Bunny was proud to put her skill at landscaping to work for Hubert. In a four-page letter written in 1973, Hubert lays out how Bunny was helping him knit the château together with its surroundings. He hurries outside every weekend to see what has happened, he writes, and loves the new proportions of a wall and the protection it gives to him so close to the house. Then he says, "Thanks for all of that because without you I would never have found a solution . . . There is a whole harmony I never had the luck to discover before I knew you."

But they also depended on one another during the crises of their lives in ways that had little to do with clothes or garden design. Bunny was much more volatile emotionally than Hubert, who, in his correspondence, appears to have been solid and optimistic. If she drove him crazy sometimes and demanded more of his time than he could spare, he was too much of a gentleman to let it show. In September 1986, Bunny was upset about something—major or minor, it's not clear what—and Hubert fired off a telegram that read: CHERE BUNNY, NE SOYEZ PAS TRISTE, DANS LA VIE TOUTES LES CHOSES S'ARRANGENT. [*DON'T BE SAD, IN LIFE EVERYTHING WILL WORK OUT.*]

But even this sanguine, practical, and hardworking man sometimes needed comforting himself. After his mother's death in 1976, Hubert wrote to Bunny, "I take you in my arms . . . you have been near me . . . I couldn't speak. Yesterday I began to speak," adding that he'd communed with his mother's spirit and that it felt like a prayer. He concluded, "Now I am sane. I am not happy but I can work."

Givenchy by that time was universally recognized as a brilliant businessman as well as a fashion star. "I am not happy but I can work"—work was his salvation, and his work patterns were inviolate. The fashion writer Carol Mongo recalls, "While preparing his twice-yearly couture collections, Givenchy is incommunicado, completely losing himself in work. For hours on end, his models walk, stand and sit while he discusses patterns and sends the muslin prototypes back to the workroom for alterations before the ideas cool."

Bunny knew she wasn't his only important client. Besides Audrey Hepburn, who was his muse and friend, his clientele included Lauren Bacall, Ingrid Bergman, Leslie Caron, Maria Callas, the Duchesse de Cadaval, the Baroness Liliane de Rothschild, Gloria Guinness, Babe Paley, Daisy Fellowes, Mona von Bismarck, Princess Grace of

Monaco, and Jackie Kennedy, both as First Lady (the president worried about the costs of her couture getting out to the public) and as Jacqueline Kennedy Onassis.

The very possessive Bunny might want to stamp Hubert somehow as hers alone, but that would never be possible. Her first requirement, never mind how romantic and fanciful, was for constancy, for a constant lover, for a *chevalier sans peur et sans reproche*, someone who would completely carry out her concept of noblesse oblige.

A photograph of her at a benefit fashion show in Washington, D.C., on a sweltering September day in 1970 (two years after they met), has Bunny in a dark blue long-sleeved top, navy-and-white plaid skirt, a dark blue hat, and a knifelike profile. Givenchy sports a double-breasted tan suit. Bunny made a point of telling a columnist that they were flying off to Cape Cod after lunch, adding, "It's too hot to stay in Washington . . . I wouldn't have come out in the heat today for anyone but him. He's my good friend."

Sometimes the *chevalier* illusion grew thin, and when it did, Bunny skewered Hubert and what she saw as his insincerity in her private journal. Her account of a fitting appointment that wasn't exclusively hers runs like this: "'Je vous aime tellement tellement.' [That "I love you so much" was Hubert, before he walked her into a fitters' room.] I sat down on a small gold chair in a particularly dark, small cabine [dressing room]—was handed a large book on art—and told he would return. He forgot to turn on the light . . . My only sentence . . . was 'You must be kidding,' an American phrase of astonishment I might never have imagined [me saying] before, I guess. Slowly I listened to the sounds of women in the two adjoining cabines . . . I knew it wasn't an imaginary experience. And that a shock had taken me through a new door." That shock and recognition was that she wasn't the only one and that she wouldn't unfailingly receive special treatment.

Bunny always relented, however. In April 1976, for Givenchy's spring collection show, the Waldorf Astoria ballroom was filled to capacity with seven hundred fashion lovers. (The first "Actual Black Male Supermodel" twirled Givenchy's chiffon-clad mannequins.) The tall, delicate table arrangements were designed by Bunny with Robert Perkins, her favorite New York floral designer. All the dogwood, lilacs, and calla lilies were brought in from her farm. Planning was key: one of the very large glass greenhouses on the Rokeby side of the property must have been set aside well in advance to raise enough white callas for this event.

That night, Givenchy headed off to Infinity, New York's ragingly fashionable nightclub, which had opened only six months earlier in a former envelope factory on lower Broadway. "In this club you would see gays, straights, transvestites, bisexuals, movie stars, paupers, everything . . ." remembered the owner, Maurice Brahms, adding, "Givenchy used to bring in Bunny Mellon . . . She'd come in for fifteen minutes just to make him happy."

Several weeks after they flew off together to Cape Cod to beat the D.C. heat in 1970, Bunny confided to her journal: "Hubert is my strength—of imagination . . . His sensitivity and gentleness are like arrows fine sharp and painful reaching inside me like a god seducing a mortal."

An undated postcard demonstrates how able he was to tamp down her extreme neediness, to keep their relationship on an even and deeply loving keel—as a friend, but not as more than that: "Dear Bunny, thank you for your truthful and touching letter. I am not frightened by your affection, quite the contrary, I am proud and happy . . . What a fine day we all had together. See you this evening . . . —Hubert."

About Bunny and her preference for gay men, Bunny's son-in-law, Derry Moore, said a telling thing. "Barbara Hutton, a great friend of my mother's, was the same. Also a very rich woman. Gay men can never possess them—and they can never be betrayed by them. *And as gay men they can never truly be possessed, which is also part of the charm for the very spoilt.*"

Hubert was able to overlook the neediness, the bad temper, and the selfishness he must have seen in his friend from time to time. Besides love and care over many years, the two (mostly Bunny) sent one another apple tarts, an iris transported across a fair expanse of two continents and an ocean to find a home in Virginia, bunches of bluets, a Virginia ham, a pair of prie-dieu kneelers for the chapel at Le Jonchet, scarves by the textile designer Sophie Grandval, and a great *citronnier* (lemon tree) for the big hall at Le Jonchet. Presents flowed back and forth across the ocean or door to door in France: a little portable greenhouse, verbena, flowers, flowers, flowers. Apples from her orchard (to Paris, really?), a "petit poisson," and carpets for the car . . . and that's only a partial list.

In 2010, Bunny reached her century mark. She was losing her eyesight to macular degeneration and had someone on her staff (probably her librarian, Tony Willis) type a letter on Oak Spring Garden Library letterhead. She could still see enough to write the salutation and the closing herself.

> Dear Hubert, Our conversation this morning took me back to the many years we have had together—whether you're helping me with the hem on my dress or we're sailing along the coast of Turkey. It also reminded me of the night you came to pick me up at dinner around 11:00 p.m. in Paris and we went dancing. You are a marvelous friend and we will always be together. All my love xx & a kiss, Bunny.

PART IV

Oak Spring
Farm
in Virginia

14

An American Pastoral

For the fifty-one years of their marriage, whatever their other romantic entanglements, their rifts, and their quarrels, Paul and Bunny continued to work together closely in Virginia. In their different ways—she with design, he with horses—they were creating the ultimate private American pastoral.

A three-quarter-size replica of John Skeaping's statue of champion Mill Reef dominates the hot-walking ring at Oak Spring's Broodmare Barn.

Bunny had already tested her strengths at siting and scale at Apple Hill. She had a taste for abstraction and simplification, and she also trusted her ability to create structure using the horizon and the existing landforms. She had certain rules that had worked for her in the past: every great landscape architect knows her own strategies—and knows also how to guard herself from being too formulaic. She was unafraid of making mistakes and bold in correcting them to create an innate sense of harmony.

By the time Bunny was 101 years old, she had given up gardening herself and was being driven around the place by Nancy Collins. A holly that had grown too large stood crammed up against one of the house gables. "Cut that down," Bunny said. Nancy was aghast at the instant decision to take down a tree that had been there, as far as she knew, since the 1950s. Bunny did not explain the accuracy of her judicious eye, but she knew it was right and simply said, "If I don't do it, who will?"

Of course, she also had enough money to do anything. Billy Baldwin, the New York decorator, wrote that Bunny said to him more than once, "Oh, come on, Billy. Let's take a chance. You aren't sure, and neither am I." Then, if she wasn't entirely pleased with their efforts, she declared, "It didn't work," and they'd start over.

Bunny's Upperville, Virginia, canvas was divided into two parts: Oak Spring Farm is located east of Rokeby Road, while Paul's Rokeby Stables lay to the west. Rokeby was Paul's—with certain exceptions, principally the big greenhouses. Oak Spring was Bunny's—except for the Brick House, which she had so happily left for the renovated and enlarged Fletcher log cabin, later known as Little Oak Spring, in 1955. Every acre was safely in conservation easement.

While Paul's activities mainly took place at Rokeby, he wrote that "the paddocks and fields near the house are reserved for horses in order that we may have the pleasure of seeing them from the house or when we go for a walk." Oak Spring and Rokeby were yoked under the supervision of Ron Evans, who oversaw carpenters, electricians, fence builders, mechanics, and painters—everyone except the gardeners, who worked directly for Bunny.

The first glimpse of this very carefully wrought American landscape comes on the drive along Rokeby Road, which treats you to a bucolic stretch of fields, woods, and ponds. Immediately inside the main entrance to Oak Spring Farm—just a break in the fieldstone wall—stands a small white pavilion. A severe speed bump more or less forces you to stop. An affable, ruddy-cheeked older man wearing a blazer, tie, and gray slacks steps out to ask your business with a very Virginian accent.

Neither Bunny nor Paul wanted the feeling of being in a "gated community." Instead, at every one of the many Oak Spring entrances, rather than anything as offensive as a gate stands one of these well-proportioned little white buildings equipped with an intercom to the house and a security center. Many of the men whose services, including overnight patrols, were paid for with Mellon money were former CIA hands. All were armed, trusted, and well rewarded.

In the 2014 Sotheby's auction of Bunny's art, household effects, and jewels, the presence of seven sturdy Rolex Oyster Perpetual Explorers might have seemed simply an example of insatiable accumulation, but, in fact, the Mellons often gave Rolexes to trusted employees. These timepieces may have been kept on hand just in case they needed more.

In one of her garden notebooks Bunny had jotted, "Enclosures guard against many things." The Bunny I knew was indeed given to frights about security and safety, albeit with, perhaps, a somewhat primitive sense of what that "security" might mean: she kept her Schlumberger collection under her bed in locked boxes made by the farm's metalworkers and carpenters.

Once you have passed scrutiny at the entrance, imagine you are visiting the Mellons at Oak Spring anytime between 1955 and 2016, when the properties were put up for sale after Bunny's death. The drive rises gently, skirting a tall grove of oaks on the right and running close to a pasture on the left. A priceless Thoroughbred mare or yearling is grazing. Each shade tree in the pasture, just as in English parks, is protected by its own little fence, which keeps livestock from rubbing against the bark. Here on the drive there is no glimpse of a main building: the Brick House, with its imposing, brick-walled formal garden and a clock tower, lies invisibly off to the right behind the oaks.

The graceful, farm-based landscape that today appears unchanging sometimes seems too uninflected to bear the immense load of memories it carries. At the top of a hill, one way takes you to the livestock barns and past the old walled farm cemetery where Robert Isabell, society's foremost florist and event planner in the 1980s and the greatest of Bunny's latter-day romantic passions, is interred. Beyond is a small farmhouse that became Tuffy Lloyd's house in his final years. Another route takes you down a steep hillside and across a Goose Creek floodplain to Spring Hill, where Eliza would live out her days as an unspeaking quadriplegic.

SOMETIME IN THE 1990s the Mellons' Gulfstream jet brought Eliza and me from New York, touching down on the long turf landing strip. The plane's cabin was hung with small, airy works by Pablo Picasso, Paul Klee, and Ben Nicholson. Bunny, in a warm and serviceable brown jacket, stood by her aged green Volvo wagon, waiting with a smile on her face as Eliza and I crossed the grass. Tendrils of hair escaped from under her beret into the December breeze. She looked very old but very lively.

Something else came into focus for me: I saw, as if for the first time, that the trees lining the airstrip, the drives, and the pasture fences all looked like the very best editions of themselves—the perfect lindens, oaks, maples, and hickories. The architect John Barnes, whose father, Edward Larrabee Barnes, designed the main Oak Spring Garden Library in 1980, remembered one visit. Over lunch with Mrs. Mellon, he discovered that she "had spent most of the morning on a walkie-talkie with an arborist sitting in a tree a mile and a half away. He was shaping it to create her perfect viewshed." He added that for Bunny Mellon, "whatever was in sight was part of the garden."

Bunny was convinced she could divine the innate character of each species of tree and reveal it in the specimens shaped by her private arborist, Everett Hicks, and his assistants. However, repeated and extreme pruning over time runs the risk of shortening the life of a tree. A lighter hand can sometimes at least slow this outcome.

Bunny's extreme need to prune and shape, combined with her ability to satisfy her own dreams, extended to her ideas for her children.

Over the old chestnut rails past the two trees and on to the Blue Ridge

I think both Tuffy and Eliza suffered for it, however gentle her hand. She expected them to absorb all the minutiae that interested her. Tuffy told me that when he was ten or eleven, his mother asked him to come with her to supervise a load of coal pouring endlessly into the Apple Hill cellar. Her answer as to why they had to do that was to make sure the lumps of coal were the right size. "If they are too small," she told her bored little boy, "they won't give out enough heat," adding, "I'm learning too, Tuffy." Of course, the children were also the beneficiaries of what extraordinary family clout could provide. While it seems almost a normal thing for Stacy Lloyd to use his connections to help his son get a State Department job, it's quite another to build a well-equipped home stage inside a barn on the Mellon farm, where a teenage Eliza, in a brief fantasy of a career onstage, played Sammy Davis, Jr., in her own top hat and bespoke tails.

Returning to the top of the steep hill overlooking Goose Creek, one can choose between the way to the Brick House and a grand

and formal way of life or to Oak Spring, simpler and cozier, which Bunny and Paul enjoyed. Oak Spring is only one of the seven residences Bunny designed over her lifetime. Along with the New York house on East Seventieth Street, it is also the only one that reveals Paul's specific tastes and interests.

The turn for Oak Spring is marked by a life-size bronze horse, *Sea Hero*, by the British sculptor Tessa Pullen, and a sweeping view in every direction. Paul, a brilliant equine matchmaker, had bred Sea Hero, but neither he at age eighty-six, nor Sea Hero's trainer, Mackenzie "Mack" Miller, at seventy-two, had been particularly sanguine about the horse's chance of winning the Kentucky Derby, which neither man had ever won.

Still, the two old horsemen headed off to Kentucky on May 1, 1993, harboring secret hopes. Bunny, who was no longer paying much attention to racing, decided to go at the last minute. She grabbed her hat and hopped aboard the Mellon plane. After the joyful upset victory (Sea Hero had gone off at 13 to 1), the party flew back to the farm, Bunny holding fast to a flower from the traditional garland of red roses that blankets a Kentucky Derby winner. Paul had exuberantly pulled it out and handed it to his wife. It was, after all, their forty-fifth wedding anniversary.

HEADING DOWN THE drive to Oak Spring for the first time, you might almost wonder where the house is. The hodgepodge assemblage of low white buildings is half-hidden in the fold of a hill and blurred by a small orchard. A tall oak Bunny planted near the spring gave the place its name.

When I had stood on the post-and-rail pasture fence along that drive with my Foxcroft schoolmates in 1957, I certainly hadn't had eyes for anything except the queen's Rolls-Royce slowly traversing the gravel. The queen, a horsewoman since childhood and a fancier of fine horseflesh, was curious to see Paul's stables and breeding establishment, but what she saw must have surprised her in its modesty.

Bunny's close friend Liza Maugham, by then Lady Glendevon, moved in court circles in London. She wrote to Bunny after the royal visit that "my mother-in-law . . . sat next to Prince Philip at dinner, and he talked about their trip to Virginia in the most glowing terms . . . After dinner my mother-in-law had a chat with the queen, and she was even more enthusiastic . . . she said that it was such a relief to meet an American millionaire who was not 'purse proud'—her expression . . . She . . . 'loved the prettiness and simplicity of the house.'" (Had Bunny's whitewash trick fooled her?)

Simplicity derived from open space designed to lead to stillness and tranquility is key to Oak Spring's extended pastoral of fields, woods, and farm buildings. The same simplicity governs a sketch of

Bunny sets forth, loppers in hand, to do the hard work of heavy pruning.

the racecourse at Newmarket Heath by the eighteenth-century British artist George Stubbs, whose works Paul collected. That exquisite little image, *Newmarket Heath, with a Rubbing-Down House,* now at the Yale Center for British Art, has been rightly described as being about "nothing."

Stubbs's "nothing"—a wide expanse of horizon, sky, and distance viewed over rough grass—extends across half the painting. The other half is anchored by a solid little brick house where grooms washed off horses after a race. For the English art historian Martin Myrone, the work displays "the power of art to project an image of order." For Bunny, order in the physical world was also achieved chiefly with air, light, and space.

In designing a garden, as she wrote in one of her books, Bunny began with the same elements that Stubbs used in his sketch: "When I see any landscaped area for the first time, I automatically look for . . . how much sky, how much air. Then the shape. Is it cut up into bits without any thought of Line or patterns."

In the 1980s, when Bunny thought most intently about writing a gardening book, she looked back at how she had taught herself landscape design, writing, "I hesitated to use the word 'landscape' until a friend explained the origin of the word to me. Since then it seems a little better—but is it a picture or a live landscape? It should evoke a sense of pleasure calm & wellbeing. This changes with each individual and that is why this is a book of collected suggestions not rules."

Paul, writing a decade later, looked back at his childhood memories of England before World War I, before his parents divorced: "Somehow at this great distance it all melts into a sunny and imperturbable English summer landscape. There seemed to be a tranquility in those days that has never again been found and a quietness as detached from life as the memory itself."

The power of art to project an image of order. Bunny sought her perfect order in coherent landscape form. Paul looked back to what had been the only happy days of his childhood. Something else that powered the couple's creation of "the farm" was a desire for the wholesomeness of the seasonal round as it figures in country pursuits, as well as the contentment that a grand self-sufficiency can provide. Hence their storage spaces, such as the honey house, smokehouse, apple house, and so forth—even though they only spent a certain number of months a year at Oak Spring.

Over time, every square foot of their vast landscape was created or worked over as part of a project, a jigsaw puzzle of the very best pieces that would fall harmoniously into place as a whole. What was "the best" was always the question.

Without doubt it was hallmarked by a quiet exclusivity. For instance, the American artisanal cheese movement, the long-ago beginning of today's locavore passion, started in the 1970s in Vermont and California, and Bunny jumped aboard. Her Oak Spring Dairy delivered milk to a few locals in old-fashioned glass bottles, as well as farmstead cheeses. In the center of the circular green label Bunny designed for her wares was a husky oak tree. (The same iconic oak was embroidered on her table linens and stamped in a faint lavender lusterware hue on the tiny coffee mugs Bunny had made for the Garden Library.) The cheese maker Allen Bassler made more than a dozen varieties, of which the plain yellow cheddar, aged for a year in a small garage that had been transformed into a cheese "cave," was the best. I don't think Bunny's cheeses matched the explosion in American excellence that has followed, but they were admirable—and they were *hers*.

The dairy is hidden behind another log cabin at Oak Spring—not the one that became the Mellons' residence, but one where Nelly Jo's grandmother lived, across Goose Creek. Bunny, who loved playing her own version of dollhouse with the outbuildings, as if imaginary families lived in them, eventually restored and reimagined this particular cabin down to the last teaspoon. In this case, however, the inhabitant she envisioned had not been imaginary; she had lovingly planned it for long visits by Jackie Kennedy, her best friend.

"I always hoped Jackie would stay here," said Bunny as we traversed spaces where the standard openings for trays were cushioned with felt in the exact same cobalt as the blue-and-white squares on the floor painted by Paul Leonard. Jackie, who had died of non-Hodgkin's lymphoma only two years before Bunny showed me the cottage, did make occasional visits to the farm to join local foxhunts and to spend time with her friend. After Jackie's death, the cabin sat vacant. Bunny sometimes offered it to others for long stays—including me—saying, "It has plenty of room for your girls." The place still felt as if it were waiting for someone to live there, or, as Eliza uneasily once said, "Where's the whoever to fill it?"

The cabin crouches on a hillock over a steep drop to the farm road. The front porch hung out uneasily until Bunny put in a landing and steps and stabilized the miniature landscape with a big pillow of her all-time favorite shrub, boxwood. She also planted a cascade of shocking pink Nerines that tumbles down to the road in August.

In the Mellons' self-sufficient universe, acquiring the best became expected, ingrained, something to be done without remarking on the effort or the money it required. Skip Glascock, who started working for the Mellons in 1976 and is now the head electrician for the Oak Spring Garden Foundation (OSGF), set up a database in 1997 to record electrical data for the property, including the Rokeby greenhouses and every tenant house. "It included a record of all materials and parts—*but it did not have a column for price*," Skip remarked.

Glascock remembered the trial run of Bunny's newfangled apple-washer-cum-dryer. It was taking quite a while, he said, to produce the final result: shiny apples bobbing along a small conveyor belt and down into their winter storage in the Apple House. The noise was incredible, but Bunny was mesmerized. Paul, on his way to the nearby Broodmare Barn, heard her call, "Paul, Paul, come over here! You must see this!" So Paul diligently came over to observe. A rapt Bunny wouldn't let him leave. Finally someone else walked past, said Skip, and Paul waved frantically for relief.

For Paul, the real sign of an orderly landscape was an immaculate stable and barns. The brass always had to be shined, the fences freshly painted. "He was as particular and had as sharp an eye as she," said Bill Keyser, the farm's head painter for thirty years, recounting the springtime public stable visits that benefited Bunny's Trinity Episcopal Church in Upperville. "From March to Memorial Day they primped every detail. He would come down to see what they'd done the day before the opening, would walk through, say, 'It looks fabulous!' and walk out."

Keyser also described what else made the place look good: "We had fourteen painters for the one hundred and twenty-five buildings on the place. There were fifteen miles of fence to paint—and Mr. Mellon did not want creosote. Tractor trailer–loads of paint came in yearly, and we spent about a hundred and seventy-five thousand per annum on paint."

In Meryl Gordon's biography, Bunny suddenly orders a hill to be moved "to achieve the best visual effect." But Bunny's intentions for her landscapes were deeply considered. I was there the day she directed David "Sammy" Copenhaver, known as "Sam the grader," as he followed her hand signals and the occasional word to remap the slope and outline of that hill. This was no mere rich woman's whim. Naturally, part of the exercise was to improve the visual effect, but Bunny and Sam's underlying purpose on the slope southwest of the library was more practical: to increase the flow of a hidden spring, carrying it down to an outlet and a stone channel that runs parallel to the library entrance. The hillside is filled with pipes.

After you've settled your things into the guesthouse, you can once again follow the drive out to the nearby hill where the library stands. Walking up the carefully preserved old-time cart track with its two graveled ruts for the wheels and a crown of turf (which keeps the roadbed from eroding), you pause to admire the building.

But only when you are walking back down the hill do you perceive at a glance what is surely the best view of Oak Spring, now the headquarters of the Gerard B. Lambert Foundation. It is revealing that the most eloquent vista Bunny Mellon ever sculpted is not from the house where she lived for fifty-nine years but the fluid panorama she saw walking home from her private library.

The whitewashed assortment of buildings cozied down between a pasture and a wood is so startlingly beautiful, it stops you in your tracks. That view of an Oak Spring "village" was featured as a spread in the Sotheby's 2014 sale catalogue. A journalist friend who worked

Oak Spring "village" seen from the Garden Library

for *The Washington Post* visited for the first time recently and then rhetorically asked me, "But who lived in this village?" While Bunny's vision of her village was one that served a community, an organism serving many purposes and people, Bunny's perfect rendering of a village in fact primarily served the goals of only two people. It was feudal.

15

Say It with Flowers: The Walled Garden

The walled garden at Oak Spring provided Bunny with an intimate canvas. For her opening stroke she created the perfect forecourt, a space meant for the practicalities of arrivals and departures: hello and welcome, and thank you for coming.

The design follows a Renaissance formula: it is wide and long enough to tip the elevation of the house onto it, creating a sense of stability. The space is sheltered from the north wind by the shoulder of the hill in which the house is set and by the bulk of the building

Oak Spring's welcoming front courtyard

itself. In summer, long, cool tree shadows cross it from the west. Low boxwoods soften the edges of the big pavers, creating a subtle sense of ease and plenty. The front door is very wide.

Over the finely painted Regency bench where you throw your coat when you enter hangs—what? A Cézanne? The van Gogh that you might expect in the home of the most powerful husband-and-wife art-collecting team of their day? No, such important works hang almost unobtrusively elsewhere. Here is a pleasant painting by a comparatively unknown French Cubist, Roger de La Fresnaye. If you stare at it long enough, what first emerges is a depiction of a watering can.

Turn away from the La Fresnaye in this pale, open space, and you face the door to the garden. Dead ahead through the workmanlike wooden garden gates—open by day and closed by night against deer, rabbits, and groundhogs—is a glimpse of a prized allée of 'Mary Potter' crab apples that leads to the greenhouse. Each gatepost is topped with a statue—not a cute garden sprite or a rare eighteenth-century Flora or Pomona but a groundhog and a rabbit, the work of the twentieth-century American sculptor Jane Canfield. Over the garden wall is a glimpse of a very American red silo and the peak of an old cow barn. Bunny's earliest sketches of her proposed garden include both silo and barn—a deliberate reminder that you are at Oak Spring *Farm*. Two terraces ease you down the hill; as you descend, the farm view disappears.

The first terrace is embraced by the wings of the house—to the west is Paul's office complex, while to the east is the service wing. A couple of steps down take you to a wider second terrace that establishes the garden's traffic patterns. Some of the terrace pavers of a local material, greenstone, are very heavy rectangular slabs four feet long.

When the terrace had just been laid, the story goes, the stones were arranged with their longer sides running north/south, from the house to the garden below. Bunny took one look and had the biggest pavers lifted and relaid so their longer sides would run east/west, parallel to the length of the house. How easy it would be to say, "What an extravagant gesture, just for the look of the thing, and who would even notice?" But the wide horizontals unobtrusively keep the eye steady, keep the terrace calm and stable.

Head down the terrace steps, and now you are in the garden itself, safely enclosed by high stone walls and six small buildings with varied rooflines that point this way and that. One is a storehouse holding a cache of honey produced on-site; from its gable a clock chimes all twenty-four hours, like a French village church bell that regulates the entire day by the ecclesiastical hours. At night you either swear when it keeps you awake in the guesthouse, or you turn over, wrapped comfortably in the sound.

The narrow guesthouse front door facing the honey house is dwarfed by a fat five-foot-tall boxwood with tiny leaves, a plant sport (a genetic mutation) named 'Tide Hill' grown by Bunny's favored nurseryman, Henry Hohman, on Maryland's Eastern Shore. Once you know that 'Tide Hill' grows less than half an inch a year—and even if you don't know what size it was when planted—this creature tells you about the passage of time. Bunny used it in every one of her gardens, buying it in quantity, just as she did every plant she favored.

Given her wealth and the fame of her horticultural prowess, visiting gardeners can be surprised to find no expansive spread of flamboyant deep borders à la Christopher Lloyd. Instead, narrow, very flowery edgings are contained by expertly pruned low cordons of apple trees, an homage to Jean-Baptiste de La Quintinie, Bunny's seventeenth-century French god of the espalier technique.

In February 2018 a crew of gardeners from Le Potager du Roi at Versailles (which the Mellons helped restore in the nineties) arrived to do a little corrective pruning. They reduced the height of the cordons, which had grown to over two feet, to the original seventeen inches, resetting the scale and tone for the entire enclosure back to Bunny's original. "A garden, hovering always in a state of becoming, sums up its own past and its future," she wrote in the pages of *Vogue* in 1965.

What is most unusual about this garden is the conversation it carries on with Bunny's library, not only with La Quintinie's publications but also with many other rare books, especially the French ones that Bunny collected. If you spend a few hours looking at such works, or at the hundreds of eighteenth- and early-nineteenth-century prints and watercolors in the Oak Spring Garden Library, you will feel you have "entered the picture" when you walk back into the garden.

Water is strategically used in four locations. A little canal—a runnel—divides the big lawn from what used to be "the boys' house," envisioned as a sort of modern-day *garçonnière*, or bachelor quarters for young men—guests or family—at a château.

With evident relief, both parents had felt that the time-honored English upper-class system of sending boys as young as eight away to school would solve a big problem. Paul agreed with Bunny that Tim was a very difficult child. So in 1953, ten-year-old Tim had been sent to Fenn, a boys' boarding school for the elementary grades near Boston. By 1955, the year the Mellons moved permanently from the Brick House, Tuffy, at nineteen, was finishing his boarding school experience at Middlesex, and "the boys' house" was a roost for his vacations. By the 1980s the place had completely outlived its original purpose and served as an auxiliary guesthouse.

The second glint of water is a shallow dipping pool under a shady tree. The adjoining little garden is a talisman reminder of Apple Hill. There Bunny had small brick-edged, heart-shaped flower beds; here, the shapes are butterflies. The third water feature is a reflecting pool in front of the Basket House that is crossed by a narrow stone causeway—the only overtly dramatic effect in this garden. The fourth water feature is a central stone well in the middle of the vegetable beds. By the time Bunny laid out these beds, the ornamental farm, or *ferme ornée*, that included a vegetable garden as part of the design, was long established at great estates in Europe, Britain, and the United States.

Oak Spring's vegetable beds are both for show—they are seen on any walk through the garden—*and* for the kitchen, unlike the beds of European gardens, such as that at the Château de Villandry, where no one dares pick a single leaf. Preserving the pattern while simultaneously eating the cabbages or broccoli is no mean trick. But because Oak Spring had large, well-staffed production greenhouses across Rokeby Road, it was possible to pop a new specimen into the garden when cabbage or broccoli was on the menu. Pattern always won out, and the waste could be incredible.

Once, I was startled to find an entire row of cabbages grown slightly too large for the design piled up behind the garden in a wheelbarrow. The good news was, they were destined for compost. But still. The rows of lettuces or carrots are easier to deal with: plant thick and thin continually. One wall bed was once entirely devoted to sorrel, grown from special French seeds with extra zing. Nelly Jo said, "Mrs. would say, 'Go get me so and so many leaves of sorrel to make a soup,' and I would go out and pick 'em."

Bunny was clearly a knowledgeable gardener by the time she asked Nelly Jo Thomas to pick sorrel. As Bunny Lloyd she had gardened at Carter Hall, the site of her first greenhouse, but then at Apple Hill, her second garden was a big jump up. The siting of the house and the landscape design, which exist to this day, are brilliant; the plantings are renewed from Bunny's long seed lists.

Bunny had loved Apple Hill and had hated to leave it. No matter what the circumstances are, anyone who makes a garden with blood, sweat, money, and, above all, time always feels regret at abandoning it. Bunny's ten garden books are like a diary or scrapbook (some remain to be cataloged). From a newspaper she clipped "Time Shall Be Ended," a poem by a Gloria Kommi, and at some point marked it "1948," the year that she married Paul Mellon and "went over the mountains" to her new life.

Paul had pushed her urgently to marry him, but it's clear Bunny had had her doubts. Kommi's poem begins, "Leaving the lovely house with leaf-green tiles, windows above washed apple blossoms . . . how the hills will hurt your throat . . ." Apple Hill, nestled in the Blue Ridge Mountains, is a lovely house indeed, and branches of apple blossoms do still hang under its windows.

I asked Bunny once what it was like to become Mrs. Paul Mellon, remembering that at their breaking point in the 1950s she had said she was ready to leave him if he wished, and he had said no, he wanted her to stay. As usual, she answered me with an anecdote, and as usual, the anecdote had an edge. "Yes, I have made choices," she answered, a choice that defined herself and her terms. "When I was just married to Paul, I thought about all the social people in New York—and said to myself, 'Oh, I can't be bothered with Babe Paley.'" (Barbara "Babe"

Cushing Paley, like Bunny, had just married her second and much richer husband, William S. Paley, already president of CBS.)

"Then Babe called me one day," Bunny continued, "and said, 'I'd like to have you help me make a garden like the beautiful gardens you've done.'" (Paley had attended Eliza's coming-out party at Oak Spring, and Bunny's work at the White House for the Kennedys had been well publicized.) Surely a perfectly kindly way to reach out to Bunny, Paley must have thought. But Bunny's answer to a woman who was loved by everyone who met her couldn't have been more dismissive: "All right, Babe, I'd love to help you—first, go somewhere on the place, only 15 x 15 feet. Work with something simple and do it all by yourself."

I think that was Bunny's way of saying that she didn't have time for people she privately judged as being unable to do anything for themselves, above all in the garden. Even Babe Paley should do it the hard way and alone, according to Bunny. But I conjecture that more lay behind her cold response in this case. While Bunny attended Capote's famous Black and White Ball in honor of the *Washington Post* publisher Katharine Graham at the Plaza Hotel in New York in 1966, Paul did not. At that time, whispers were circulating in society about Paul's well-established affair with Dorcas Hardin, while Paley's life with husband Bill was beset by his affairs with other women. Surely aware of their similar marital woes, Bunny was perhaps distinguishing herself from Paley by throwing down the gauntlet in the garden arena, where she knew she had already won.

Babe Paley would go on to hire the legendary British landscape designer Russell Page to create Kiluna, on Long Island, one of the most poetic gardens in America, a magical woodland sloping down to a still pool. And she herself did learn to garden, though it seems unlikely she did so because she was sparked by Bunny's note.

"Never stop learning" was one of the rules Bunny herself set down for the gardening book she never published. (By 1948, when she and Stacy divided the Apple Hill library, she already owned ninety-one gardening books.) When, on a visit to England long after she became Mrs. Mellon, she trailed her great friend Evangeline Bruce around Nancy Lancaster's romantic Haseley Court gardens, where deep borders overflowed the beds, spilling onto the path in the English manner, Bruce and Lancaster threw botanical names at each other. Bunny, who was unfamiliar with many of the plants, took notes, doggedly spelling everything as she heard it. On seeing Lancaster's clary sage, *Salvia sclarea* var. *turkestanica*, Bunny wrote down "turkey stantica," looked it up later, and planted it often at Oak Spring. Still later, in the summer of 1963, Vangie would take Bunny to Vita Sackville-West's famed gardens at Sissinghurst Castle, another important step in Bunny's garden education.

Phlox was a flower Bunny knew well. It was actually the first one she remembered; a stand of white phlox on Long Island in the thousand-acre compound of her godmother Madeline Dixon in North Haven, across the bridge from Sag Harbor. The perfume of garden phlox is heady and intoxicating; it stops you in your tracks. Three-year-old Bunny had stood mesmerized beneath that tall "forest of phlox," which she "loved more than anything." Bunny remembered her nurse telling her not to touch but touching anyway. She also remembered putting the phlox she picked into the dog's water bowl to keep it alive.

She had observed nature's processes since she was eight years old, walking her grandfather's pastures on Mount Monadnock in New Hampshire. "It was during these hours alone that I began to notice how things grew," she wrote, "some near to a wall for protection, others in the open field. Stronger where the cows had been—spindly and fragile otherwise." She had noted how animal droppings released fertilizers that left rings of bright green grass.

Natural process was what she drew on first in design. Much later, with landscape architect Perry Wheeler's help, Bunny made a garden for her friend Kenneth Battelle (society's hairstylist) on Fire Island. At his waterfront property she wanted to preserve the feeling of wildness behind the house: the sparse, sandy landscape with its low, twisting shadblow trees—what she called its "shad forest"—and "the process of nature" that had created the space. On Nantucket, at her own beachfront property, she was equally careful to preserve the native plants and salty atmosphere.

She also prized pattern. While the limewashed stone wall at the

far end of the Virginia garden featured large groups of lilies and sunflowers in every shade from white to a brownish-black blaze against
the equally white blaze of the wall in summer, in winter the pattern
of fruit trees espaliered against the wall became crucial to the garden.

Peak seasons in this garden were spring and early summer, after
Bunny and Paul returned from Antigua, and fall, after a Cape Cod
summer. Christmas was always celebrated at Oak Spring. In winter, the
structures and boundaries of the garden are defined by walks, steps, and
the bare forms of incessantly pruned branches. Boxwoods, hollies, and
other broadleaf evergreens come into focus. By December the flower
garden mostly moved indoors: exotic plants all grown in the Rokeby
greenhouses warmed the house with masses of color and hints of
exotic perfume.

In another set of notes for her proposed gardening book Bunny
wrote that boundaries, whether walls or hedges, should be "high
enough [for the viewer] to see only sky," which is the case in this garden once you step down from the second terrace. You don't see how

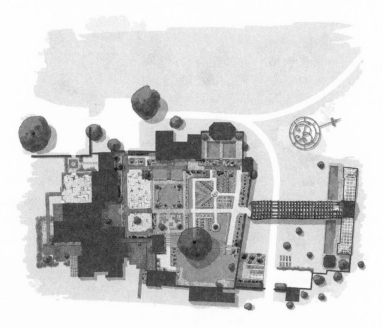

A measured, hand-drawn plan highlights the intricacies of Oak Spring's enclosed
garden, which isn't as symmetrical as it appears on the ground.

the wall slants off to the northwest, making the garden's geometry vaguely trapezoidal.

Why would anyone, especially Bunny Mellon, do this? It was no whim. After what had been called the "Fletcher cabin" was rebuilt as "Little Oak Spring," its garden retained exactly the same shape as the present one extending from the cabin's back door. The heart of today's Oak Spring stands on the footprint of the old log house, which was moved on rollers across the road to the Rokeby side of the property.

The log cabin, even with some additions, had proved too small for the family of six (two adult Mellons and four children, plus a nurse) who had moved into it from the Brick House early in the 1950s, so architect H. Page Cross was hired to enlarge the old cabin still further to fit Bunny's specifications. The family, which hopscotched back into the Brick House while construction took place, finally returned permanently to what would henceforth be called Oak Spring in 1955. But Bunny, who apparently had had enough architectural symmetry at the Brick House and Carter Hall to last her lifetime, stuck with the old garden's dimensions and askew plan, thus guarding her memories of happiness there with Paul before their marriage. The outlines of cabin, garden, and the main path can clearly be seen in a 1937 aerial view.

Paul and Bunny's private life is also encoded in other ways at Oak Spring. By 1951, she had been champing at the bit to start the renovations that would transform it into the house it is today. Unable to start on those major architectural renovations she longed for, because Paul had told her in no uncertain terms that they would have to wait, she began in the garden, planting masses of roses—climbers, shrubs, rugosas. The quantities tell you something about her pent-up desire and the scope of her plans. Before the taste for "old garden roses" with their heady fragrance and hundreds of petals was revived, Bunny was planting varieties such as the carmine moss rose 'Souvenir de Pierre Vibert,' hybridized in 1867.

She also included more modern red roses, such as 'Blaze' and 'Chevy Chase,' vigorous, long-blooming crimson ramblers that are less susceptible to disease but, unlike the old roses, have almost no fragrance. In 1951, she planted those red roses for Paul, who loved the color. When 'Blaze' bloomed over the years, Paul often commented on "his" rose, outside a dining room window.

Forty years later, on Paul's eighty-fourth birthday, one of his presents was a replacement red climber, which was duly labeled "Paul's Rose Tree" and planted in the same spot against the smokehouse wall. He also always had red carnations in his bedroom; even after his death Bunny made sure fresh ones were kept in place. (The conversation between husband and wife apparently never ended.)

As the 1950s advanced, however, Bunny kept pushing to expand the house. The only way to know how the battle of wills was resolved is to look at the eventual outcome: the removal of the family from the Brick House back to the completed house in 1955.

By 1961, Paul's relationship with Dorcas Hardin was in full swing. Bunny would provide the most perfect comforts of home for Paul, but she also turned to creating a new "family" of friends and to searching for her perfect cavalier lover.

SOMETIME IN THE winter of 1966, Bunny penned a long letter to Perry Wheeler, her friend and garden-making partner, about the heavy undertow of her life. On the lone surviving page of that letter, she wrote, "Old DorcASS [spelling and capitals are hers] is still plugging and it is such a Bore. What she is really doing that I resent is making Paul a fool, and taking from him all feelings of appreciation for the true, real, and simple happiness of life."

In 1969, Bunny did an unprecedented thing. She gave the journalist Sarah Booth Conroy an interview for *The New York Times* that stands as the most complete statement she ever made about the "true, real, and simple happiness of life" at Oak Spring, what it meant to her, and her relationship with her husband, which—in public, at least—both parties had determined would endure.

"I've never given an interview before . . . But my husband and I talked it over the other day, and we said we were tired of reading in the press all sorts of wrong things about the way we live. A woman reporter calls my husband periodically to ask when we are getting divorced. My husband said, 'Perhaps it's because they really haven't seen the way we live.'"

Included in the day-long interview—which included a lunch at Oak Spring that was a surprise to Conroy—was the story of Bunny's friendship with Jackie Kennedy, told in the pages of a scrapbook that Jackie had made for Bunny, filled with photographs as well as sketches of the Rose Garden.

About the scrapbook and the struggle the bereaved Jackie had with William Manchester over the publication of his book *The Death of a President*, the only thing Bunny said to Conroy was, "When all that William Manchester business was happening, Jacqueline Kennedy was serenely pasting these pictures of Jack Kennedy in the book for me."

During the year leading up to Manchester's publication in April 1967, Jackie and the author, whom she and the president's brother Robert had commissioned to write the official account of the assassination, had a battle that erupted in banner headlines. She had poured out her most searing and intimate memories, somehow expecting the book to appear as a sober record that would lie quietly in the JFK Library. When she learned that *Look* magazine would serialize Manchester's work, she was horrified at the anticipated popular publicity and outraged by the largest fee ever paid for a serialization, $665,000—which would go not to the JFK Library but to Manchester himself. (Manchester had received a reasonable advance that looked modest by comparison.) She offered him a million-dollar kill fee for the serial. He refused. She sued to stop the book's publication in December 1966 but settled hours before the trial was to begin in January, after she returned from a holiday with the Mellons in Antigua, where she had given Bunny the scrapbook as a Christmas present. Changes to Manchester's manuscript submitted by Jackie and the other Kennedys were made, seven disputed pages were cut from more than six hundred, and both book publication and serialization went forward. By summer, more than a million copies had been sold.

Gardens could sustain the soul, was Bunny's message to Conroy, as could Oak Spring's mown pastures, its tiny homegrown asparagus at lunch, and—for the Mellons—the greater comforts that money and discernment could buy: rare books, fine horses, Givenchy garden hats, and the ability to buy a Mondrian in Paris and bring it home on their own plane.

Bunny's picture of a well-planned life included the couple's four children, all grown and seemingly settled in 1969, as well as her astounding certitude, as she and Conroy returned to the house after a post-lunch stroll through the garden, that she "almost could do this work alone if we lost our money tomorrow."

Her bravura performance for Conroy is punctuated by other occasional misstatements, as when she claimed that she and Paul had built the Brick House together "some twenty-one years ago," when, in fact, she was referring to her move, in 1948, into the house built for Mary, Paul's first wife. Bunny also claimed that she had "grown up at Carter Hall," when, in actuality, her father had bought the place when Bunny was nineteen. Bunny finished her interview by telling Conroy, "This is the way I really like to live. With this peace."

Erasure, selection—these, as well as truth and desire, determine how anyone's memories arise, but Bunny's memories also involved construction; for example, how she bridged her sorrows to present her life—even, at times, to herself—as a fairy tale of happiness, contentment, and stability.

Bunny felt protected from troubles—and perhaps even from the knowledge of her own exaggerations—in her gardens, where she could exercise her own proven skills and control the space around her. There, she could have what she wanted, and no one could say no.

Because Bunny became renowned for every kind of expenditure and yet insisted on her privacy, the gossip columnists, frustrated by the lack of information, habitually took an envious stance. Bunny once told her librarian, Tony Willis, who became a close friend, that "jealousy wears many hats."

Yet despite her lavish living, Bunny was also practical—in a certain highfalutin way. In Bunny's list of gardening rules, she conceptualizes in a practical manner: she wants to teach new gardeners how to "think three feet," meaning how to measure by eye in the first stages of planning. Always aware of the psychological impact of a garden, she also wants her imagined readers to know that every detail—light and reflected light, the airiness or bulk of particular trees and plants, even a broken branch—might arouse sadness or happiness. And after all those considerations, one shouldn't forget to buy pencils and a ruler.

Borders as narrow as those in the Oak Spring walled garden—often only about twenty-eight inches deep and meant to be viewed from both sides—are a challenge to create: plant choices must fit a certain range of scale in height, breadth, and foliage. There is no room for drifts or masses here. Bunny often mentions how important it is to vary leaf sizes, or, as she puts it, to "slip in some large leaves." Plantings have to be seen from many angles. She adds, "Allow plants to roam a bit—flax daisies columbine *Phlox divaricata*—like clouds to float over an organized design—lasting 3 weeks or so," and then advises herself, "Cut back—watch where they seed for another year."

Gardeners at least since the legendary Gertrude Jekyll and William Robinson have been allowing self-sowing plants to grow freely in gardens; this is nothing new. But as your gaze travels across Bunny's walled garden, you may have a vaguely hallucinatory experience, as if a cloud in shades of silver, gray, white, pink, and blue were floating around you about two feet above the actual garden. Substantial groups of taller plants, such as her childhood white phlox, hold their own against newcomers such as the gray-and-white-striped thistle *Eryngium bourgatii* "Graham Stuart Thomas's Selected Form," named after the great twentieth-century English plantsman.

Self-sown everywhere also is a small, luscious apricot poppy, a gift from the French art expert Gérald Van der Kemp, who not only masterminded the restoration of the interiors of Versailles and saved the *Mona Lisa* from destruction by the Nazis but also restored Monet's gardens at Giverny. He thanked Bunny for her financial help by sending her some of the painter's poppy seeds.

The number of plants Bunny tried out is staggeringly ambitious: someone on the garden staff alphabetized and typed *fourteen* pages of all the *blue* flowers grown at Oak Spring in 1970, from in-ground perennials to bulbs both tender and hardy to greenhouse plants. Seed sources and bloom times are also listed. My best guess is that this was a comprehensive overview of what was tried, what succeeded, and what may have failed over time, not what was blooming in that year alone. Along with seeking out the best plants or the best seeds, Bunny also found the best people to work for her. I remember thinking that the gardeners at Oak Spring were handsome farm boys straight out of Virgil's "Georgics"—then discovering that more than one of them had a degree in horticulture. (Bunny often paid for schooling for those who worked for her.)

And then there was Everett Hicks. In her list of gardening rules, where Bunny writes "Never end learning," what follows is "Love to prune," followed simply by "Mr. Hicks." At Oak Spring, Hicks's testament to that exhortation is the monumental crab apple arbor; it took him many years to patiently train the stiff tree branches to follow, inch by inch, the curve of the twelve-foot-tall steel frame he built. The first volume of the four Oak Spring Garden Library catalogues is *An Oak Spring Sylva*, on the highlights of Bunny's collection of books about trees and arboriculture, which is dedicated to her grandfather Lowe, the first person in her life who loved trees with a passion as great as hers. Hicks was the second.

Hicks's arbor also enfolds memories from a wartime letter from Stacy about a "terraced garden with two rows of apple trees done in an arbor" with "box on the inside of the tunnel," something that Bunny never created at Apple Hill but reimagined at Oak Spring. He also described other apple trees first trained on wires that had grown to be freestanding, so they resembled "very knarled [*sic*] old men with their hands above their heads." In other words, they formed what is called a "Belgian fence." Bunny's apple cordons at Oak Spring around the beds of the enclosure are miniature versions that use the same training technique. Like any efficient hunter-gatherer, she used everything that appealed to her in her garden.

Beyond novel ideas and fond memories, essential for Bunny's kind of gardening were the four industrial-strength greenhouses at Rokeby Farm, originally built for Paul and Mary Mellon in 1940. (Today, the average residential greenhouse runs five hundred to one thousand square feet; the square footage of Rokeby's is slightly over nine thousand.)

A more ornamental but still practical greenhouse stands outside Oak Spring's garden walls at the far end of Everett Hicks's crab apple arbor, where two small glass wings flank a central conservatory pavilion. The interior paneling was painted by the French decorative artist Fernand Renard with elements large and small that document Bunny's life—her wedding and engagement rings slung on a piece of string so she could garden without getting them dirty, for example; a bunch of feathers; a pair of secateurs (pruning shears); a basket of apples; a worn blue trowel; a little basket fish trap from Jackie Kennedy with Jackie's note attached.

The glazed wings were used for display and as resting places for some of the topiary herb trees after a stint in the house or library. The greenhouse's finial/weather vane is a lead vase of flowers designed by Johnny Schlumberger, who carefully included one lead flower lying on the roof as if it had fallen out or was yet to be added. "I prefer imperfect perfection," as Bunny said.

Bunny's two-page list for June 1977 of "plants to propagate" includes white strawberries—maybe the descendants of those she gathered at Balenciaga's country retreat in the fifties—and *fraises des bois*, "the red ones," she adds.

In the late seventies and early eighties, Bunny sometimes ordered plants by the dozens from catalogues, particularly those of Wayside Gardens and White Flower Farm, but most of what went into the ground at Oak Spring was raised in Virginia.

Bunny was once again following in the footsteps of Ellen Biddle Shipman, the landscape architect who had designed a gate and fence at Apple Hill. In the early twentieth century Shipman was one of the first professional women to train as a landscape architect at Radcliffe, which was then called the Harvard Annex. Shipman's initial jobs had been for friends in the summer colony of Cornish, New Hampshire, where she and the architect Charles Platt met. By the time of her divorce from Louis Shipman in 1910, she already had a significant reputation as a garden designer. Platt provided the architecture and important client contacts; she provided deep horticultural knowledge and formidable garden-design abilities. Shipman soon branched out on her own, however, and by her death in 1950 she and her all-women firm had designed more than 650 residential gardens across the nation. It's possible to imagine how—before her marriage to Paul—Bunny Mellon might have partnered with an architect as a professional garden designer.

By the early 1980s, Bunny's skills and self-confidence had matured, as revealed in her architectural sketches and planting schemes. To judge from her astute comments—additions, deletions, questions— penned on a French nursery's two-page list in 1981 for Givenchy's Le Jonchet, she really knew her plants and how to place them where they would thrive.

Over the course of thirty years, Bunny was awarded many honors that testified to her skills. The list is long for someone who generally preferred to stay out of the limelight. Among the most prestigious are La Croix d'Officier de l'Ordre des Arts et des Lettres in 1995 for her work and financial help at Le Potager du Roi at Versailles, and the Royal Horticultural Society's Veitch Memorial Medal, given annually to "persons of any nationality who have made an outstanding contribution to the advancement and improvement of the science and practice of horticulture."

In the United States, the Missouri Botanical Garden granted Bunny its Henry Shaw Medal, which singles out those who have made "a significant contribution to environmental objectives" as well as to horticulture and education. In 1965 the Massachusetts Horticultural Society, the oldest in the nation, gave her its Gold Medal, bestowed on the "man or woman, commercial firm or institution in the United States that has done the most during the year to advance the interest in horticulture in its broadest sense." She received it for her "original design and planting of native plant material" at "the seashore estate of Mr. and Mrs. Paul Mellon."

When the American Horticultural Society selected Bunny for its Landscape Design Award in 1987, she joined a list of professionals to receive it, including the landscape architects Thomas Church and her friend Dan Kiley, as well as a few other notable amateur gardeners.

She won for her topiary trees and her cyclamen when her gardeners took collections of her greenhouse plants to the big flower shows in New York and Chicago. The Virginia Museum of Fine Arts conferred its Webster S. Rhoads Medal on Bunny for her patronage, which began with her joint gift with Paul of Impressionist and Postimpressionist works in 1985, went on to her promised gift of her Schlumberger jewels, and concluded with artworks from her estate in 2014. Not surprisingly, many are landscapes or floral still lifes, including a tiny painting by van Gogh of disheveled daisies tumbling over the edge of a commonplace clay pot—it hung in Bunny's bathroom at Oak Spring until her death.

Educational institutions honored Bunny too. In 1987, Bunny's alma mater, Foxcroft, recognized her for the beautiful courtyard design that fronts the library she and Paul gave in memory of Paul's great-niece, Audrey Bruce Currier, who, with her husband, Stephen Currier, was lost when their private plane vanished in the Bermuda Triangle in 1967. At the edge of the low-walled enclosure, Bunny's classmate and greatest friend at school, Kitty Wickes (Poole), is remembered with a lead sculpture of an open book lying on a wooden bench under an apple tree, Bunny's all-time favorite for comfort and solace. Many of the shrubs were chosen for their fragrance: the sun beating on the courtyard pavers draws out their powerful scent; the surrounding walls form a bowl that retains the mingled perfumes. In her address to the school about the garden, Bunny was characteristically modest: she mentioned that she had darned Kitty's socks while Kitty helped her with her schoolwork.

She received an honorary Doctorate of Sciences in 1973 from Sewanee: The University of the South, and an honorary Doctor of Humanities in 1983 from Randolph-Macon College, from which her grandfather Jordan Wheat Lambert had been graduated and where he had first exhibited the flair for chemistry and business that made the Lambert family's initial fortune with Listerine. In a photograph, "Dr. Bunny," whose father had felt that girls didn't need to go to college, wore the traditional black robe and a big smile under her official mortarboard as she accepted the honor.

In 1990 the American Academy in Rome saluted her for, among other things, her "leadership in the patronage of scholarship and the pursuit of the fine arts in their many manifestations," leadership still bearing fruit in Oak Spring Garden Foundation (OSGF) projects and at the Gerard B. Lambert Foundation.

A snapshot shows how Bunny beamed with pride in 1999 when the Rhode Island School of Design (RISD) made her an honorary Doctor of Fine Arts for her work in landscape design. Roger Mandle, the former head of the institution, was surprised to find her both graceful and humble about her accomplishments, adding that he didn't experience her as intimidating—except by example.

Her first symbol of national recognition, and perhaps the one she cared about most, had come in 1966, when the U.S. Interior Secretary Stewart L. Udall gave her the Conservation Service Award. In his speech, Udall said, "The nation will be ever indebted to you for your gift of talent to the design and development of the Rose Garden and the Jacqueline Kennedy Garden at the White House." More personal is a framed photograph of Udall with Bunny (who wore short white gloves, a sleeveless dark top, and a knee-length tweedy Balenciaga skirt), in which she is flanked by the White House staff and many of those who worked on the gardens. Udall scribbled a more heartfelt message on the photo: *For Bunny—my kind of conservationist!*

A beaming, white-gloved Bunny receives a Conservation Service Award with four others on March 15, 1966, for her White House gardens.

Had Bunny ever *wanted* to hang out her shingle, or was it more her style, given how she lived her life, to work for friends when and if she pleased? The gardens and landscapes of her own houses are as professional as those of any licensed practitioner, as were her White House projects. (For much of her work Bunny relied on Harvard-trained Perry Wheeler for professional advice and scaled plans.) Early women garden designers such as Beatrix Farrand and Ellen Shipman did their work first for family members and neighbors and through their social contacts. Bunny's niece, Lily Norton, suggested that if Bunny and Stacy had remained married, she might have been more inclined to accept paid commissions.

A garden for Hattie Carnegie in Middletown, New Jersey, at her house—Four Winds, named after a perfume she created—has vanished. Bunny, who bought clothes from the New York designer up through her marriage with Stacy, remembered the year when she advised Hattie Carnegie on a garden as 1933. However, Carnegie and her husband didn't buy the property on Walter Field Road until 1936, and their house—the second on the site, as the first had burned— wasn't completed until 1938. Bunny remembered also that she told the couturiere she had to make a choice between buying a horse or new clothes. If the more likely date was 1938, perhaps refreshing her wardrobe after the recent birth of her son seems a possibility. Whatever the date, and whether Bunny did more than advise Carnegie to plant roses and a double row of apple trees—both stalwart features of most of her designs—it seems clear that Bunny felt that her funds were limited. She chose a matching Hattie Carnegie dress and jacket. "We agreed it was a success on both sides," Bunny told Paula Dietz of *The New York Times* in 1982.

In the late thirties or early forties, Bunny Lloyd designed a garden, so far not formally recognized as her work—what she called "her first paying job"—for her aunt Emily Milliken Lambert, wife of Gerard B. Lambert's youngest brother, Wooster. The Edgehill garden's many sections envelop a small stone farmstead in Paris, ten miles east of Millwood. How the gardens link the house to its stone outbuildings is entirely reminiscent of Oak Spring, and the subtle curves of the grading are recognizably Bunny's. She included the apple orchard that still stands in front of the house in her late-life private summary of her five most significant works. She wrote that every garden, public or private, should produce "a feeling people can take home—can copy—or remember later with a positive and thoughtful recall . . . an atmosphere that inspires and one can relate to."

On an evening in Virginia long after Bunny had been publicly recognized by I. M. Pei as "the greatest landscape gardener and architect in this country," mostly for her work on Kennedy projects, Paul Mellon mentioned to me how lucky Bunny was always to have known what she wanted to do, as if he perceived how different his early life had been from hers. Over a lifetime of celebratory poems he rejoiced in her talents, although always in the context of their private houses and gardens. In his memoir, where he describes how they collected art together, he touches on "how much her imagination and visual acuity have influenced me," adding, "It is not widely known enough that she is an amateur landscapist and gardener (although of professional capability)." He finishes the passage by saying, "To see at first hand any of her personally designed and self-worked-in gardens is in itself an immersion in what art can mean."

Dr. Bruce Horten, who became one of Bunny's serial confidants beginning in 1985, when they met, told Meryl Gordon that he remembered Paul's attitude toward his wife's work differently, saying, "He'd ignore her or laugh at her interests . . . but he had that very patrician way of being amused, a beatific smile. He was very, very polite."

John Baskett, who with Paul wrote *Reflections in a Silver Spoon* and who knew Bunny well, told me he is convinced that Bunny was just as content as Paul to remain an amateur. It is true that this suited Bunny in the sense that she could do what she wanted without the constraints a professional practice would entail, but I believe she also wanted her public landscape achievements, such as those at the White House, to be recognized as what they were: as good as the work of any professional.

Bunny's personal sphere was almost entirely domestic: it included the staff and gardeners at all the Mellon domiciles as well as the Oak

Spring Garden Library. Those with whom Bunny worked to create those domains, such as architects, contractors, and every sort of artisan—after consultation with Paul, and with him paying all the bills—were also hers to command. But her artistic sphere also encompassed recommendations, designs, and planting of other properties besides the White House gardens and her own, although research remains to be done to identify some of those projects.

Two typed pages of brief biographical notes are the closest approximation to a professional résumé that Bunny left in her papers. Undated but clearly dictated in her last years, they state the following: "Rachel Lambert Mellon grew up in Princeton & Millwood. The gardens and libraries of her father's houses were inspiration for interest in horticulture and landscape design." The sketch continues to her formal education: Miss Fine's school in Princeton, followed by Foxcroft. It includes a mention of gardens designed "first for family and friends" but without mentioning any names. Following a request of President Kennedy to design the Rose Garden, she designed the Jacqueline Kennedy Garden at the White House and then, later, JFK's grave in Arlington. At the John F. Kennedy Presidential Library she planted "dune grass facing Boston Harbor for sea and wind." She "helped restore gardens at Carter Hall" and "in France Hubert de Givenchy's Le Jonchet near Romilly-sur-Aigre. Presently preservation of rural landscape in Virginia and Nantucket moors and wild flowers. Antigua: subtropical garden. Now listed as living on the farm at Oak Spring."

The self that Bunny presents in her gardening notebooks is livelier than the Madame Tussaud–like figure often presented of an imperious grande dame famous for her spending. In her notebooks, an empathetic Bunny takes on the role of gardener-cum-psychologist. "I will write down thoughts and ideas to awaken or bring back long-forgotten dreams," she writes. "Very often people will say, 'That's it,' and take off from there on their own."

Like any good designer, she wants to know who her clients are: "apart from the many differences of location soil climate etc., many differences come from the personification of those involved, how they see it, their needs & way of life." She looks for her clients' favorite

In 1964, the French portraitist Mati Klarwein, who also painted Jackie Kennedy,
included a slice of the Mellons' Antigua view, upper left, and Oak Spring's
young crab apple arbor, upper right.

plants: the American prairie black-eyed Susan, *Rudbeckia hirta*, for
wildflower enthusiast Lady Bird Johnson in the East Garden of the
White House, or herbs for Jackie Kennedy Onassis on Martha's Vineyard, or a "shad forest" for Kenneth Battelle. "Finally," she wrote, a
garden design must reflect "the honest belief and vision of one person."

16

Walking Through the House

Seclusion and repose were easily found at Oak Spring. "I walked into the Oak Spring guesthouse—it was a transformative experience," remembered Paul's goddaughter, Georgiana McCabe, looking back at the winter of 1963. "Imagine a filthy, icy, wet February day . . . stepping into that guest cottage meant I entered a space of effortless beauty and tranquility. The entrance hall was tiny. A huge Chinese bowl filled with dozens of flowering paper-white narcissus, green moss tucked around them, sat on a plant stand, filling the space with a promise of spring and the fragrance of both the earth and the flowers. Upstairs, every inch of the walls, including the fronts of built-in drawers, was covered with a blue-and-white toile de Jouy. That blue filled the room—the bedspread, the chair upholstery, the table covering on the round table by the window—even in the bathroom the blue toile continued.

"On another visit, at dinner, I asked Bunny about that blue, said it was so beautiful. She warmed up slightly—she was always so cold with me—and said, 'Billy Baldwin did that.'" Bunny was not going to be on her best behavior with the nineteen-year-old daughter of one of Paul's closest college friends, men who often said how much they had loved Mary, men like Chauncey K. Hubbard, Georgiana's father, who, on his visits to the farm, would take Paul off to the Red Fox Inn in Middleburg, where they would drink and reminisce about the old days in the war and the old, old days at Yale. Bunny *was* willing, however, always to give credit to Billy Baldwin or any of the other distinguished and talented decorators, fabric designers, furniture makers, plantsmen, floral designers, and artisans with whom she worked—the people to whom she was closest.

Georgiana had never forgotten the experience of opening that guesthouse door. Outdoors lay "brown fields, fallow earth, bare trees," but inside those walls she found "the vibrancy of the unexpected bulbs, their abundance . . . a guest was surrounded by the power of a world of visual beauty, of comfort, not so different from the effect of the garden without, had it been a different season . . . Bunny had set an unforgettable tableau."

The guesthouse had five bedrooms, with a different color scheme for each, a wallpapered and carpeted bathroom en suite, all but one with a tub, and a slipper chair next to the tub. (Men, as well as women anxious to preserve their hairdos—Kenneth Battelle was often flown down from New York—took baths in those days.) Art, some of which was worth millions, hung on the walls; the charmingly worn American hooked rugs on the floors were worth a ransom. A service kitchen with plenty of light stood (and still stands) behind the staircase. In the Mellons' day it was equipped with enough flowered china that all guests could have breakfast in their rooms simultaneously. (Lunch was the first public meal of the day, at which Bunny would appear.) Another ground-floor bedroom and bath—then used for staff—were attached to the kitchen. As in England's grand houses—just as at Downton Abbey—your bag was unpacked by that staff, and if what you'd brought with you had a spot or a tear or needed pressing, it was silently whisked away and returned before it was needed.

The handsome, upright, blue-eyed Shirley Glascock ruled the guesthouse. She is one of three generations of Glascocks who worked for the Mellons and continue to work for the foundation today. Nineteenth-century deeds for Oak Spring are signed by Glascocks. "Mrs. hired families," said Nancy Collins—families both white and Black. Skip Glascock, the head electrician, added that a prime reason for hiring family members was to avoid having to place public advertisements in the papers, part of the Mellons' encompassing privacy blackout.)

Guests didn't have to watch Shirley Glascock's lightning-swift wardrobe appraisal, because when they arrived at Oak Spring, they entered through the wide front door of the main house, while their bags, as at some boutique hotel, were removed to the guesthouse. When they did retire to the guesthouse, they walked through an opening in a low wall separating the forecourt from the stone courtyard, where herbs and well-behaved wildflowers were encouraged to grow in the cracks between the pavers.

By now, imagine that you have driven in through the pastures to the quiet safety of the house folded between its hills. You have taken your first walk through the walled garden, and both experiences have sensitized you to what you now see. You recognize Bunny's greatest design strength indoors and out: her ability to position anything—structures, hills, roads, posts, trees, and garden walls or chairs, sofas, Cézannes, and china bowls—so as to seem inevitable. Everyone who entered her precincts, whether or not they completely took in what she had done, felt a sense of warmth and comfort. Sam Kasten, an internationally known weaver and designer who got his start with Nantucket Looms and who visited all of Bunny's homes except her Paris apartment, recalled, "There wasn't a chair anywhere that you couldn't sit in all day and read a book."

Sun floods the Oak Spring front hall.

The front hall, which holds Bunny's basket of garden tools, also displays the outdoor paraphernalia of both people who lived there. Paul's worn velvet hunt cap has a downturned ribbon at the back to signal its owner is a master of foxhounds, as do his perfectly treed boots. On the floor is a basket for whichever in the long succession of small dogs is in residence. Arcane bits of sporting equipment hang from pegs: a wicker creel for a fish from the stream, a leather sandwich case to hang from your saddle while you are out hunting. Paul and Bunny knew and loved the language and equipment of English and American upper-class country life.

An umbrella stand displays an assortment of taller garden tools, umbrellas, and a shooting stick. (One of two such assortments would be estimated at $400 to $600 and would sell for $8,125 at auction in 2014.) Under a mirror on a sideboard sits an overflowing basket arrangement of garden flowers, along with Bunny's wide-brimmed straw hat or, in winter, a prize greenhouse specimen. A single high-backed armchair is upholstered in a riotously rosy floral chintz.

What transports this assemblage out of the ordinary? First, consider the intention and the quality of each thing, no matter how subtle. That armchair is a soigné Louis XV bergère in walnut that was sometimes draped with yards of untailored fabric as if to say, *This is about to be slip-covered—this is ongoing—I am not finished here.* The garden has come indoors too: specimens of lusty herbs with aromatic foliage nice to touch and inhale are poised strategically about in stone or ceramic cachepots. One of the expertly barbered plants is a small "herb tree," as Bunny called her two-foot-tall round topiaries, each of which required several years of painstaking clipping to shape. They became her talismans and are now a commonplace of floral and interior design.

Then consider the overall effect. The world-renowned decorator Bunny Williams, often called the standard-bearer of cozy upper-class interior design and comfort after fifty years in the trade, summarized Bunny Mellon's interiors by saying she created "an American version of English country house style. She was an editor; nothing was placed by chance. Her taste was clean, almost Scandinavian, pared down, and modest—cottons and baskets, not ormolu, brocade, and gilt. No William Kent chairs. Most wealthy Americans of her day (beginning in the sixties) were likely to say, 'What's *that* all about?' Her houses were for *her*. She was no Brooke Astor, entertaining twenty-four for dinner three nights a week." Williams ended her assessment with, "Bunny was a sculptor, sculpting space."

But then, it goes almost without saying, there was the art. Where Nancy Lancaster, owner of the English decorating firm Colefax & Fowler, would have hung a splendid eighteenth-century gilded mirror, Bunny and Paul (who marched around the house with his own hammer and nails) hung one of the aforementioned masterpieces.

From the hall, a left turn will take you to Paul's study, meant for reading and writing, thought and withdrawal. The frames of bookcases, windows, and even radiator housings are finished with tiny Gothic arches worthy of the cloisters of Yale University or Clare College, Cambridge. At Yale, in 1929, Paul won the first McLaughlin Memorial Prize in English. He then attended Cambridge, where he mostly enjoyed himself with crew and foxhunting. At both institutions he had written a fair amount of light verse and pondered a lot about what to do with the rest of his life. He became an eminently civilized, capable man with a highly developed sense of humor whose memoir made light of his whopping charitable contributions to the arts, education, sciences, and conservation and preservation. The walls are painted a cheerful chartreuse as if to demonstrate that Paul didn't take himself too seriously.

Some of the study's ornamental woodwork was carved by one of the permanent staff of farm carpenters. Bill Keyser, the Oak Spring head painter, said that the carver, "Junior" Hanback, was "the son of Charley Hanback," the contractor for Trinity Church and JFK's grave. Keyser is careful to note that "Junior" was the master craftsman who also "carved the wheat sheaves at the farm 'in his spare time.'" The ornamental wheat sheaf reliefs, Virgilian symbols of plenty and peace, are seen here and there on overdoors and mantels. Keyser adds dryly that Hanback "was not a fast mover," meaning that the Mellons gave him the time he needed and respected his talent as a craftsman and an artist.

Off the main hallway lies the "Sunday kitchen," where, after most weekend guests had left, Bunny tied on her apron and did a little light cooking, Marie Antoinette style (much of the prep was done beforehand), although she was in fact a good enough cook to start from scratch if she wanted to. Paul did the washing-up, I am told. Blue-and-white tiles clothe the stove's exhaust fan hood and the walls; the farm-made wooden table seats six in a pinch; a small blue-and-white porcelain stove stands to one side.

Bunny was fascinated by the miniature, including dollhouses. She wrote, "They are not only play for young children but are very important as a way of opening up a child's imagination that continues forever and ever. It is living with your ideas but all in miniature . . . How you would like it—it is all possible." This can be read in two ways: either the dollhouse might teach you that everything in life can be manipulated or allow for the kind of imagination that Bunny developed in a lonely childhood, being encouraged to build play gardens both in Princeton and in Fitchburg, and fostered by her love for Arthur Rackham's phantasmagoric illustrations. Up the hill, in the garden library, what looks like a vertical file opens up into a surprise (no small part of the pleasure): the tiny rooms of a beautifully furnished dollhouse, a fantasy life hidden in a cool, well-organized ground-floor office.

"Design is about discipline and reality, not about fantasy beyond reality," said Sister Parish's coolly modernist partner, Albert Hadley. "Glamor is part of it," he cautioned, "but glamor is not the essence." Bunny admired Hadley and absorbed some of his astringent style.

Now, at drinks time, you pass a small staircase as you head for the living room. Light falls into the stairwell from a window halfway up. Bunny, like Thomas Jefferson, appeared to think that sweeping staircases were a waste of space, an unnecessary display. In the stairwell on a table stands a hybrid creature under two feet tall carved in dark wood, a monkey footman wearing a frock coat. His mouth is half-agape in what passes for a smile to show his white teeth as he bows slightly, ceremoniously presenting you with a platter, a large mother-of-pearl shell. His shapely legs terminate in all-too-human feet—and shackles.

The monkey footman is what in eighteenth-century France was called a "singerie," a "monkey trick," as seen at the château of Chantilly in lighthearted murals of monkeys in human dress. But this small being is no mere ornament: he is an offhand but devastating commentary on service and servility and servitude. His pearl shell was meant to receive calling cards from visitors; today from some he gets a chuckle and from others an unnerved glance.

Continuing down the hall you pass a changing parade of small treasures: an old master drawing or two, the Welsh artist Gwen John's *Leaves in a White Jug* (Paul's anniversary gift to Bunny in 1968), perhaps two tiny gouaches of fluffy Portuguese water dogs, a Balthus sketch of a girl, a Boudin seaside. Stepping down into the living room, you must move around a large blue-gray French escritoire that sticks out into the main area. Bunny has placed the desk perpendicular to the wall, gently sculpting the space, guiding you to face the fireplace.

The van Gogh is hung unframed, a frequent habit with the Mellons.

This is a moment of recognition. Over the mantel hangs van Gogh's *Green Wheat Fields, Auvers*, a magnificent turbulence of brushstrokes now hanging in the National Gallery of Art. Candy Camp, a Foxcroft classmate of Eliza's and mine, came for lunch one Sunday with a few others of us. Realizing there were an awful lot of pictures on the walls, Candy politely asked Eliza, "Who paints?" "Nobody here," said Eliza, "Da buys them at the store." "Da," as Eliza called her stepfather, repeated the anecdote quite often. Once, when he and I were looking at the van Gogh, he said, "For me the story is a gentle put-down for those of us who worship art too much."

To the right of the fireplace behind the sofa where Bunny usually sat is a concealed door that reveals a small bar. Paul's specially mixed martinis and Bunny's champagne are at the ready. (Daiquiris were another of her go-tos.) Because Ronnie Caison, the butler, brings you your glass of champagne on a small silver tray with a napkin, you might have missed the label on the bottle: *Brut Champagne Nicolas Feuillatte Réserve Particulière: Sélectionné par Paul Mellon esq.*

Nicolas Feuillatte was friends with Jackie Kennedy, played golf with Aristotle Onassis, and was patronized by Princess Diana, who served his rosé at receptions. None of them had asked Feuillatte to privately label twelve hundred half bottles to keep in reserve in France. "You have only to telephone my office," Feuillatte wrote, "to have them sent to you by the case."

Feuillatte's champagne is now the most popular in France, but it wasn't in 1977, the year Bunny placed her order. Feuillatte then had a single vineyard and was bottling only for the cognoscenti. Bunny, ever specific about details, asked if the bottles could be splits. No, said

The private label for Bunny's Nicolas Feuillatte champagne

Feuillatte, champagne made in such small bottles cannot really be "du bon champagne." And certainly, he added, "It would not be suitable for the labels to say that this inferior champagne had been "selected by Paul Mellon esq." Certainly not. So Bunny went for half bottles, the larger size ensuring adequate fermentation.

In his first letter to Bunny, Feuillatte had the temerity to tell her he would write to her in French, because, he said, "I think this would be a good thing for you, as there is nothing better than practice." Feuillatte became Bunny's friend, and she visited him in Tunisia. She liked men who knew the best, made the best, and were firm in their executive convictions.

Bunny was something of an executive herself, running an operation with many independent contractors working on different projects in different states or countries simultaneously to carry out her vision. It seems no exaggeration to say that if Bunny had been born half a century later, she might have escaped being merely a rich man's lonely, isolated, and ambitious elder daughter, simply excellent marriage fodder for a wealthy male of her own class.

Babs de Menocal Simpson, the great twentieth-century editor and arbiter of style, was Bunny's friend for decades—until, like many others, she wasn't. But Babs—she was always Babs, even more often than Bunny was Bunny—bore no grudge against her former friend. Babs told me in a rather formal way that she had "great fondness and respect and [had] a great friendship." When I spoke with her soon after Bunny's death in 2014, she mentioned that Bunny had indeed designed a garden for her in Amagansett, in the Hamptons, but she wondered why every obituary she had read had focused so exclusively on Bunny's gardening prowess. "Bunny was so much more than that," she said.

Ronnie Caison, the distinguished butler and major domo who still works for the OSGF today, announces dinner. As you continue through the house, the hall widens before the dining room to accommodate a George III display case. One of the wonderfully frivolous objects in the house, it has an illustrious pedigree. Sibyl Colefax, the original owner of Colefax & Fowler, had it in her stock of furniture when Nancy Lancaster, Paul and Bunny's old Virginia friend, joined the firm as partner in 1944. Bunny bought it after her marriage to Paul—and promptly lopped off the Chippendale-style crests. Tiny Gothic frills trim the cream-painted shelves; the sides are latticed. Every shelf holds replicas of vegetables and fruits—soft-paste porcelain sculptures from every noted eighteenth-century English and European factory. A small melon-shaped tureen has a perky puce snail for a knop. Naturalistically modeled cauliflowers, cabbages, and lettuces all open up to become tureens. Twelve pairs of asparagus tureens tell you you have entered the realm of an omnivorous collector.

"They are some of the finest wares made by the most important of English porcelain factories," says Errol Manners, a porcelain specialist in London, who points out that they are "some of the first porcelains to depict botanically correct specimens mostly taken from drawings by [the German] botanist G. D. Ehret and published by Philip Miller of the Chelsea Physic Garden." As such, he adds, "they are true documents of the eighteenth-century Enlightenment." (Georg Dionysus Ehret is considered one of the greatest botanical artists of all time.)

Manners continues, "The taste for Chelsea porcelain was widespread among wealthy East Coast collectors and mirrored a similar taste in England (the Queen Mother favored the Chelsea botanical wares painted with accurately depicted specimen plants)." When her daughter the queen came to tea at Oak Spring, Bunny was careful to show her the cabinet and its precious contents.

After dinner walk a few steps up the hill to the Oak Spring Garden Library to follow the trail to the full-blown Enlightenment, featuring many Ehrets and several rare copies of Philip Miller's *The Gardeners Dictionary*, first published in 1768, which offers "the Best and Newest Methods of Cultivating and Improving the Kitchen, Fruit, Flower Garden, and Nursery . . ."

In the dining room, a long serving sideboard made from oaks felled in the Oak Spring woods runs along one wall. What is served could be what the British call "nursery food"—simple, sustaining fare—although you may eat it off plates painted in 1800 that are centered with a coat of arms depicting a tiny green topiary tree just like the liv-

Pierre Bonnard's *Still Life with Dog*, flanked by four of Georges Seurat's tiny but significant oil studies, hangs above a red-and-yellow japanned Regency faux-bamboo bookcase acquired through Syrie Maugham. The arrangement of objects on the marble top is balanced but not symmetrical.

ing specimens dotted throughout the house. If it is beef stew, the recipe harks back to pre–Julia Child's day: "Marinate the cubed beef in A.1. sauce and Worcestershire" is how it begins. Eventually the usual vegetables, plus a bay leaf, beef stock, and Clamato are added. Broccoli from the garden piped with mashed potatoes is served with vinaigrette or hollandaise—Eliza once helped herself to both. The wine might be a Mouton Rothschild. If there are baked apples and rice pudding for dessert, they are made by Ronnie Caison's grandmother.

Those baked apples will be followed by a demitasse, then a stroll across the garden to sleep in luxurious D. Porthault sheets that have been turned down by Shirley Glascock or one of her helpers. It is hard to remember that this same lifestyle—with variations of climate, scale, and locale—is available, with staff always ready to go, at Bunny's other residences across two continents: on Cape Cod at Oyster Harbors; at King's Leap on Antigua; in Manhattan at 125 East Seventieth Street;

in Washington, D.C., at 3055 Whitehaven Street; in Paris on Avenue Foch or later the rue de l'Université; and on Nantucket at South Pasture.

In 1957, someone with a gimlet eye of her own—Jackie Kennedy—spotted many of Bunny's special touches at Oak Spring and recognized that they were in service to a larger ideal.

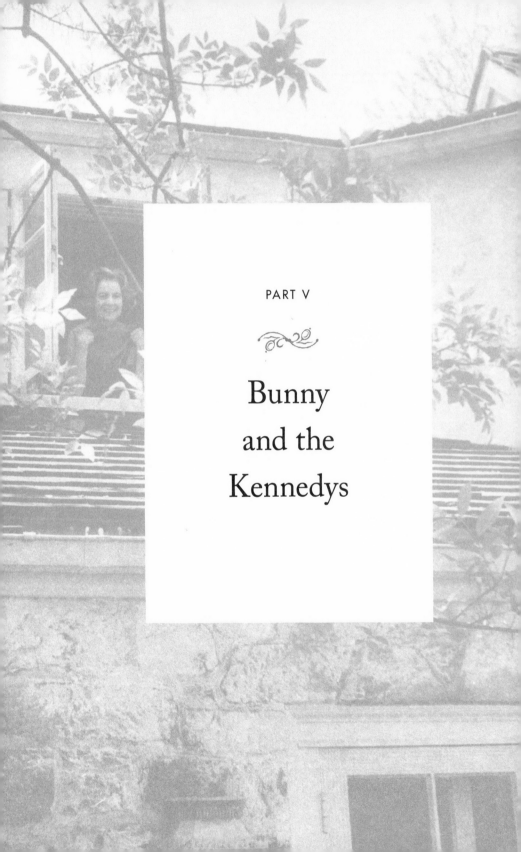

PART V

Bunny
and the
Kennedys

17

Bunny and Jackie: A Friendship

While Bunny was coming to grips with the changes in her marriage, she met the woman who would become her best friend, Jackie Kennedy, wife of the dashing junior senator from Massachusetts. JFK had just published *Profiles in Courage*, a volume of studies of senatorial political bravery that had won the 1957 Pulitzer Prize and would help him in his run for the presidency.

They met in 1958 when Adele Astaire Douglass, an old friend of Bunny and Paul's and then a Virginia neighbor, brought her guest

Garden flowers loosely arranged in a grand agate-surfaced footbath,
piles of books in no particular order, Bunny's hat, and a basket
of her gardening tools greet visitors in the front hall.

Jackie to Oak Spring for tea not long after the birth of her daughter, Caroline. Jackie took it all in—the relaxed style, the magnificent art, *and* the stale candies in the antique jars—as she told Bunny in a phone call the next day. That funny, sharp-eyed—and bold—observation was what won over the wary Bunny, and before long she agreed to help Jackie with her Georgetown house, with the White House Rose Garden, and with the restoration of the presidential mansion itself.

The two women took to one another at once. Jackie found a parent who suited her better than her own mother, the socialite Janet Lee Bouvier Auchincloss, while Bunny gained a daughter very different from Eliza. When in 1968 Eliza married Viscount Henry Dermot Ponsonby Moore, better known as the photographer Derry Moore, Bunny would draft Jackie's children, Caroline and John, then eleven and eight, as flower girl and page boy (in knee breeches, British court style for little boys). Each also found in the other a sister more compatible, loyal, and loving than her own.

Bunny had the Pittsburgh Mellons to deal with; Jackie had the football-playing Kennedys and their constant togetherness in Hyannis Port, which she often found trying. The two women managed to make light of the issues in their own difficult marriages: Paul's relationship with Dorcas Hardin, and JFK's omnivorous promiscuity. (the Kennedy biographer Sally Bedell Smith quotes Jackie as saying to Ted Kennedy's wife, Joan, "All Kennedy men are like that . . . You can't let it get to you, because you shouldn't take it personally.")

Bunny, nineteen years older than Jackie, could take on the role of teacher and exemplar at one moment and then shift to become the cozy, sympathetic friend to whom Jackie poured out her heart. Sometimes Jackie became Bunny's advisor. Bunny said that Jackie "was always telling me what to do—like a nanny—& I didn't always listen—She would say—'all your ducks are swans'—you should not believe some people!"

In 1995, George Trescher, New York's top event planner, sent a note to Bunny along with a clipping from his interview with *W* magazine. Trescher—with Bunny in her special role as collaborator/director—had orchestrated Caroline Kennedy's wedding in 1985. Trescher mentioned how surprised he'd been at first to find that "Mrs. Mellon," a woman whose acquaintances and the press had led him to believe was distant and cold, was in fact "warm & funny" once he got to know her. Bunny answered him, writing "so was she [Jackie]—we saw life like that," going on to add that no matter how self-importantly people took themselves or their doing, "we could see the simpler side, and wondered why the fuss?"

Bunny contrived not to understand why it was difficult for "serious people" to grasp what the "simpler side" was for her and her friend—two women who, by birth, wealth, and their grasp of power, were essentially living on another planet. Bunny went on to sketch her friend as one who "had a mischievous side—& twinkle in her eye . . . She minded her own life and she felt deeply . . . We talked for hours—on nothing and never gossipped [sic]. She was loyal beyond anything—and we gave each other space. That was the best part. that & her sense of humor."

The two shared a childlike imagination and enthusiasm that, as Jackie herself said, "seems to flicker out in so many adults." J. B. West, chief usher at the White House during the Kennedy administration, watched Jackie at play with her children on the South Lawn and observed that she was "so happy, so abandoned, so like a little girl who had never grown up." Billy Baldwin, albeit a shameless gusher about clients he loved, accurately described the same quality in Bunny when he wrote that "one of the incredibly rare qualities of this incredibly rare woman is her ability to empathize with another's enthusiasms"—at least with enthusiasms like his own.

More prosaically, Jackie and Bunny's shared foundation of WASP taste and attitudes included a dedication (an idealized post–World War I preoccupation) to husband and home, an attitude that reached its apogee in America in the 1950s. Bunny poured her nesting urge into the creation of many perfect houses for Paul and the children. However, her best and dearest "families" were made up of friends who shared her passions and tastes. Her rarefied style sometimes reached a point where the real people in her life, such as her children, seemed to become doll-like figures for her to mold and shape.

In Jackie's case, it was her main article of faith that a woman's job was to raise the children, and if she made a mess of it, the rest of what she did amounted to nothing. Sally Bedell Smith quotes Jackie as telling a journalist right after the election that she "'would describe Jack as rather like me in that his life is an iceberg. The public life is above water—& the private life—is submerged—I flatter myself that I have made his private life something he can love & find peace in—comfortable smoothly run houses—with all the things he loves in them—pictures, books, good food, friends—& his daughter & wife geared to adapt to his hours when he comes home.'" Bunny gave Jackie confidence in her chosen role, helped her enhance the president's home even more, and provided her a friendship like no other.

Beneath their perfect society manners and oddly similar whispering voices ran an electric current of power. They could move, manipulate, and cut—with finality. Billy Baldwin, who saw Bunny at work at Oak Spring, wrote about her affectionately but clearly: "You *know* that she loves every chair, you *know* that she feels tenderly about every single blossom, and you *know* that she rips out anything that she doesn't like, not with violence or cruelty but with the simple determination to eliminate it. Hers is a regime of no tolerance for the mediocre." She had little patience for those she considered superficial or boring and chose her friends carefully. Both she and Jackie were crowded by more people than they had time for.

Bunny's eye for space and proportion and what could be made of them was matched by Jackie's discernment about people and events and how best to employ and "frame" them. In 2004 in the opening essay for the Metropolitan Museum's exhibition *Jacqueline Kennedy: The White House Years*, Arthur Schlesinger, Jr., who was Jackie's friend and ally, wrote that "underneath a veil of lovely inconsequence she developed a cool assessment of people and an ironical slant on life. One soon realized that her social graces masked tremendous awareness, an all-seeing eye, ruthless judgment, and a steely purpose."

The two women enjoyed dismissing people who thought they had the right to intrude on their friendship and privacy. One small but bracing example that Bunny related to me was about the renowned poet Robert Lowell, who ran into the two women one afternoon—Bunny didn't say where—and asked, "Could I have dinner with you girls?" clearly imagining that of course they would want to do so, as almost anyone else might have. According to Bunny, Jackie said coolly, "'Absolutely not.' Lowell then said, 'Well, what *are* you going to do?' Jackie answered him by saying, 'Well, we've got it all planned,' and that was that."

Their particular combination of money (Bunny's) and fame (Jackie's) made them formidable. The historian William Seale, a longtime observer of Executive Mansion occupants in his post at the White House Historical Association, remarked, "Jackie didn't have money. She was a poor Bouvier, by the standards of the society in which she moved. She had political and social power but not financial power." Although Jackie's friendship with Bunny ran deeper than access to Mellon money, once Jackie was no longer in the White House, she became aware of the ease that assets like Bunny's offered—such as the peace and privacy of the Mellons' house on Antigua, where they retreated in the first traumatic days of January 1964.

Eliza, Bunny, and Jackie sit at breakfast at King's Leap, Antigua.

After JFK's death and the subsequent assassination of Robert Kennedy, Jackie needed protection beyond what the Secret Service could provide for her and her young children, and she also needed a well-financed husband to support her in style. She found both in Aristotle Onassis. After his death in 1975, it was probably no accident that Jackie turned to Bunny's lawyer, Alexander Forger, to secure $200 million, far more than Onassis had decided to settle on his wife.

Only two years before Jackie won her settlement, Paul Mellon, for the first time and thanks to Forger, had settled an annual $500,000 on Bunny, allegedly "for charity," meaning that she no longer had to ask her husband for every cent she spent. Forger, then at the white-shoe law firm of Milbank, Tweed, eventually worked exclusively for Bunny, who set up an elegant office for him and his staff on West Fifty-Seventh Street in New York City.

Given Paul and Bunny's emerging stature in philanthropy and the arts, and Jackie's celebrity, when Bunny and Jackie joined forces for a cause, they invariably succeeded. On Halloween in 1961 the Wildenstein & Co. Manhattan gallery opened a charity exhibition of Schlumberger's jewels, which included some of Bunny's pieces. This was the first time that Bunny clearly laid out her conviction that Schlumberger should be treated as an artist, not just a fashionable jewelry designer. Bunny and Jackie dined at Johnny's small clapboard house on East Ninety-Second Street before heading to the gala, the proceeds of which would support the preservation of Newport, Rhode Island's, trove of eighteenth- and nineteenth-century architecture.

With Jackie in the White House, Bunny was again happily en-gaged with the glamour of politics, something she'd once enjoyed while sitting on Calvin Coolidge's lap as a child. Later that same first year of the Kennedy administration she sat at the president's table at a state dinner for Puerto Rico's governor, and when the cellist Pablo Casals played after dinner, she knew she was witnessing a powerful blend of political power and high culture. This exposure whetted her appetite for political influence, an appetite she would eventually seek to satisfy in her relationship with Senator John Edwards.

Bunny's actual reimmersion in politics had come in November 1960 in the presidential election, when she voted as a Virginian for Kennedy, although she apparently didn't change her party affiliation and become a Democrat until she met Richard Nixon in 1972. Stepping up to the polls with Paul, Bunny said, she found she didn't have anything to write with. She turned to her husband, a lifelong Republican, who said he certainly wasn't going to lend her *his* pen! Bunny told me that a Black voter just leaving the polls handed her his pen and said with a wink, "Here, missus, use this." This was Bunny's adult baptism into the importance of her vote.

Bunny was a society figure with an almost pathological dislike for publicity, a trait she shared with her husband. Repeatedly in her letters over the years, Jackie apologized for the attention that being her friend brought Bunny. "I know you'll hate . . . the fact that you are splashed in the *Daily News*," she wrote to accompany a piece about RFK's funeral that she mailed to Bunny. At the age of ninety-five, however, Bunny's secret support for John Edwards's mistress and child would bring her a certain notoriety—and a visit from the FBI—that she would quite enjoy. She classed her deception as fun, and with a "Why not?" air she dismissed Edwards's infidelity to a dying wife as the sort of thing one might expect from an attractive man like him.

Jackie, on the other hand, was an outright celebrity, and she quickly gained a new kind of celebrity—or notoriety—when she married Aristotle Onassis. Joseph Campbell, the twentieth-century writer on myth best known for *The Hero with a Thousand Faces*, saw what he thought might be the dangers of Jackie's life after JFK's assassination. He warned her that she should shun celebrity and stick to becoming a myth. Jackie did neither. The Kennedys were aghast at her unwillingness to cultivate her myth as JFK's widow and even more upset that she would marry a Greek shipping magnate, Bunny told me. She also said that she ran interference with the Kennedys regarding Onassis before Jackie's 1968 marriage to him.

The two women often celebrated their summer birthdays together. For Bunny's sixty-ninth, Jackie gave her an illustrated edition of Emily Dickinson's poems. In it she wrote:

> Bunny—on your birthday. You are a poet like Emily Dickinson in your gardens, in your houses, in the way you see nature and all of life. She kept her gift private from the world and so

have you. But so great a talent could not remain forever hidden and neither will yours. With love and inexpressible gratitude for all the joy and help you have always given me. Jackie August 9, 1979.

Jackie honored her friend's creative achievements—something that Bunny welcomed. She had been raised in a family that believed a woman should not advertise herself, and yet it's clear that she wanted some sort of recognition for the importance of her work, especially for the Rose Garden. Ironically, Bunny's own interiors and her landscapes, public as well as private, were purposefully designed not to draw attention to themselves. Instead, they were subtly made to complete a special sense of place. Sometimes Bunny felt very alone in her effort to maintain this balance. Yet when Sam Kasten of Nantucket Looms, a company that wove custom fabrics for her, wrote her that his visit to the Garden Library at Oak Spring was a life-changing event, she called him in tears. "Nobody really notices what I do," she said.

Jackie excitedly attends the Princeton Library's 1989 opening of *An Oak Spring Garland*, the first public exhibition of works from Bunny's growing collection.

Bunny and Jackie often turned to each other when they were depressed: Jackie wrote to Bunny in 1976 that she wanted to have a little boat and learn how to sail so she could anchor off Oyster Harbors. "I want to come back to see you, and be near you again. You don't even have to talk. I'm not sad—not really . . . I want to live again. I want to come back." Another note from Jackie that Bunny inserted into one of her little blue daily datebooks went the other way, with Jackie comforting her friend about some problem and telling her, "Don't worry, we will just beat the world back again."

When in 1989 Jackie looked back at their years as friends, she wrote, "Ever since I've known you (33 years ago this spring) you have meant as much to me as any person in my life." Thanking Bunny for her love and care, her wise and strong support, and for all she had meant to the Kennedy children, Jackie closed with, "I want you to be as happy as you make me."

Jackie and Bunny sometimes looked for happiness together on real estate adventures, finding the escape they dreamed of. After Gerard B.'s death in 1967, they prospected on Nantucket, where Bunny bought two hundred acres of coastal heathland and old pasture with the money her father had left her.

In turn, after 1979, when Jackie bought Red Gate Farm on over three hundred acres on Martha's Vineyard, Bunny cleaned up and edited the straggling old farm-scape without overmanaging it and guided Jackie to the well-known architect Hugh Newell Jacobsen, who designed a plain, cedar-shingled Cape Cod house. As it was being built, the two women considered its furnishings. Bunny opined that one's bed was important, because "it held so many thoughts." Jackie agreed, saying, "It is a celebration, a bed," and then Bunny decided they should design one for her.

Bunny's presents were more extravagant than Jackie's and often featured a surprise. The Mellons gave Jackie a birthday party in 1966, three years after the assassination, at their home in Oyster Harbors. The guest list entailed flying in many of the D.C. and New York regulars who had danced at Eliza's coming-out party; the band played foxtrots from the Great American Songbook before moving on to rock and roll; and the food was delicious—striped bass, lamb, string beans, salad, peaches. Only Bunny could have thought of the perfect finale: as dinner finished, Jackie's beloved White House chef, René Verdon, who had been secretly flown up to cook the birthday feast, appeared like a rabbit pulled out of a hat.

Tales straight out of *A Thousand and One Nights*, some true, some apocryphal, gathered around the pair and their friendship. When Jackie left her straw hat on Nantucket after one of their lunches, Bunny sent the plane straight back from Cape Cod to fetch it. "What extravagance," breathed Jackie, or so the story goes. If true, it's also possible to look at it as just one more example of both Bunny's fierce determination to finish a thing, to make it perfect, and her determination to go the distance for her friend.

Tiffany & Co.'s Pierce McGuire recalled that Mrs. Mellon described how she and Schlumberger had collaborated on the design for his famous *paillonné* enamel bangle and that she had given Jackie the first one. Jackie wore hers so often that the press dubbed them "Jackie bracelets." But was a paint box filled with rubies, sapphires, and emeralds instead of pigments another Bunny gift? That's the story. One day these gems may turn up, but my take is that the fantastical yet practical Bunny might just as likely have given Jackie a solid gold Schlumberger box of *real* paints.

The scale of Bunny's wealth meant she could indulge herself in over-the-top moments, as when she treated a magnificent Milton Avery painting that hung in her house on Nantucket as merely a snapshot of herself and her friend Jackie. Two women sitting close together overlooking Gloucester Harbor while one sketches and the other looks on admiringly became "Jackie and I on the Dock." Or, to say it more simply, Bunny enjoyed the thought of their friendship when she looked at the painting. She didn't think it trivialized Avery—and if it did, that didn't matter, as it was hers.

The two women took art lessons from Oliver Smith, the scenic designer for American Ballet Theatre who was most famous for his magical Broadway productions: *West Side Story*, *Brigadoon*, and in 1960, *Camelot*, the basis of Jackie's enduring reimagining of her husband's brief presidency. They often painted together on Cape Cod: in the Garden Library at the bottom of stairs to Bunny's study hangs a summery watercolor of a pale blue hydrangea in a pot. Although charming, it's hardly a match for the other treasures on those walls, but it was painted by Jackie and was therefore another precious reminder of their times together.

Even as a child, Bunny had depicted her surroundings in sketches and paintings. As an adult, her fluency with pencil and ink led her to illustrate her letters, underlining the emotions they expressed. She often developed her garden designs on paper, with particular attention to scale.

Both women shared a profound belief in the absolute ability of style to carry real meaning. "Style" included a great deal more than the cut of clothing or a period of interior decoration. Every choice of a color was eloquent. Bunny considered white to be the most significant color. In going through her papers in the months after her death, I found that she had wrapped many important keepsakes, such as gifts from her Grandpa Lowe, in white paper and tied them up with a blue ribbon, using the two colors as signals to show how precious the things were to her. For Jackie, too, "white was the most ceremonial color"; her strapless inaugural ball gown was white, with a small white ribbon cockade at the waist—homage to the France she loved.

Wendy Gimbel, a biographer, critic, and redoubtable interpreter of the meaning of fashion, remarked that the clothes in the 2002 Metropolitan Museum's Costume Institute show, *Jacqueline Kennedy: The White House Years*, were dowdy. I agreed but said, "But she had to dress for Peoria." Wendy, who knew Jackie well, shot back, "She didn't know there was a Peoria."

Jackie had, in fact, quickly come to understand that she had become "a piece of public property" and that there was a pressing need to have what she wore in the White House years be a uniform. Jackie's wardrobe of "state clothing," as she called it, was like that of Queen Elizabeth II in its clear, solid colors and off-the-face hats but modernized with cleaner lines and greater ease of movement. At the time, what kept most of us from seeing the dowdiness was the luster of

No better armor than a watchful friend: Bunny quietly walks with Jackie from the funeral of Martin Luther King, Jr., at Ebenezer Baptist Church in Atlanta.

glamour conveyed by Jackie's trim, big-shouldered, athletic figure—and then, in rapid hindsight, the burnished armor of tragedy. Her close friendship with Bunny would give her the privacy, affection, and depth of understanding to help bear the weight of that armor.

18

A Garden for the President

"The President was precise," Bunny wrote later in one of her many gardening journals. His was a tall order. This president wanted function and beauty and historical meaning, a lawn big enough to hold a thousand people, a new set of steps to the Oval Office, a continuous display of floral color, and a garden reminiscent of colonial American gardens that would evoke lofty memories of Washington and Jefferson's dreams for their new nation. The very regular features of Bunny's design define the dignified "palace garden" that JFK told her he wanted after he'd seen similar examples in Europe.

John F. Kennedy understood how Europeans deployed their magnificent outdoor spaces to display ageless beauty and sophistication, as Charles de Gaulle did at Versailles in May 1961. In Vienna the following month the gardens of Schönbrunn Palace offered the new American president a reassuring sense of civilization, as well as room to breathe and walk after his punishing session with Nikita Khrushchev. Columnist Joseph Alsop, the first to interview JFK following that encounter, later recalled, "After that . . . he really began to be president in the full sense of the word."

As the first politician to recognize the advantages of television, JFK also saw within the tattered remains of the first Mrs. Wilson's 1927 West Garden the possibilities for a stage from which public events would be broadcast worldwide. In asking Bunny Mellon to create this setting, he had hired the perfect impresario to create the mise-en-scène for a new political discourse.

As gardens go, the Rose Garden is small. The entire enclosure measures 125 by 90 feet and is visually narrowed by 12-foot-wide planting beds on the long sides. It is only half the size of the rectangular and similarly formal enclosed garden of Paris's Palais-Royal, where colonnades tie the surrounding architecture to the garden plantings just as the White House's north colonnade and four deciduous flowering magnolias tie the Rose Garden together. At the east end of the garden and against the backdrop of the White House stands Andrew Jackson's living memorial for his late wife, a Southern magnolia planted in 1829 whose foot-wide, lemon-scented white flowers still stand out against the shining evergreen leaves in midsummer.

From the Teddy Roosevelt administration onward, the Rose Garden has been a real "working garden" in the sense that it must always look splendid and perfectly groomed. In Bunny's design, the crossing patterns of severely clipped boxwoods of various sizes and the straight lines of enclosing low hedges hold the eye even in winter. Under the

In an old overhead photo, the very French gray and silver patterns
of the 1962 Rose Garden design come through clearly.

two lines of crab apple trees that connect the White House residence with the West Wing, the open diamond shapes of Bunny's favorite box, 'Kingsville Dwarf,' and santolina, a bright silver herb, are planted with perennials—tulips and other seasonal bulbs—chrysanthemums, and bedding-out annuals.

But where are the roses? Bunny's detailed planting plans in fact show only fourteen such plants, placed judiciously among twenty-two other species. Ellen Axson Wilson's garden had held rows of bushes and standardized roses, but while many rose cultivars produce flushes of bloom, few provide the continuous floral show needed for a comparatively airless, confined space in D.C.'s humid summers. So Bunny set out her design as her guide Ellen Shipman had taught her, with other plants in high and low clumps of contrasting color and foliage, often using taller roses to highlight pattern. It is an expert's way of making a flower garden and one that requires constant maintenance.

The four deciduous magnolias anchoring the corners of the rectangular space are the only unrestrained, irregular, apparently freely growing plants—a brilliant stroke effected by a woman who knew her trees. Only when you walk slowly along the colonnaded walk or down the steps leading from the president's Oval Office and across the lawn, however, can you understand the brilliance of using those particular magnolias, of placing them as Bunny did. Their height minimizes the elevation of the bulky White House, and their craggy gray tracery softens its wedding-cake whiteness. She herself was well aware of this and was quite insistent that the creamy pink flowers were not really the point, as they either fade in a single hot April week in D.C. or, more often than not, are ruined by frost. She also valued the ever-changing shade patterns and the visual spaces the branches created.

Bunny might have thought back to the August day in 1961 when she and JFK had sat apart from the rest of the picnic guests in what she called a "small, fisherman-[type] house built into a dune on the Seapuit River" at the Mellon retreat on Cape Cod. They had faced each other at a table covered with her signature blue-and-white checked cloth. In an often-reproduced photograph, Bunny, fifty-one years old and elegant in a skirt, T-shirt, and Balenciaga beach hat, leans hard into what she is saying to the president, gesturing fluently with her narrow, muscular, suntanned hands. The young new president, in his dark glasses, is listening as intently as a schoolboy.

An inspired Bunny tells the president about the garden she sees in her mind's eye.

Bunny's day had begun confidently. She had been in her bedroom overlooking Nantucket Sound where she always had breakfast. A picnic on the beach was planned with the Kennedys and the Grahams. Philip Graham was then the publisher of *The Washington Post* and JFK's friend, advisor, and occasional speechwriter, while Katharine Graham, daughter of the owner of the paper, Eugene Meyer, was still a stay-at-home wife. The Grahams had rented a summer place in Cotuit, not far from Hyannis Port.

As was usual every summer, Bunny's household staff, headed by David Banks, Bunny's most trusted domestic lieutenant and mentor since she was a teenager ("He watched over me like a Lion"), had come up from Virginia. David Banks's father, Frank, had worked at Carter Hall as Gerard B. Lambert's shepherd, according to Bunny, while his niece, Gladys, who had been trained as a cook by her mother, Banks's sister, was making corn soup, a favorite of the president, for a lunch that would also include steamed clams and champagne.

Then the phone rang. "It was Jackie," Bunny wrote.

"'Jack's going to ask you to do something for him—promise me you will do it. He wants you to design a garden for him at the White House.'

"'Where?' I asked.

"'Beside his office.'

"She was breathless and in a hurry. Before I could answer, she had hung up."

"How can I cope with a garden of this size?" Bunny wondered to herself as she sat on her bed and looked out at the water. "Technical things like drains, water pipes, etc., must be considered and drawings made—I have never had any formal schooling in landscape design, which would have helped me now."

Bunny pulled herself together, yet again remembering Grandpa Lowe, who had told her, "We are all part of this country, and if we have something . . . to contribute . . . we must." Before long, Bunny found for herself three perfect assistants—aides-de-camp, colleagues, friends.

The first of these was the tall, gentle landscape architect Perry Wheeler, who was born on a farm outside Atlanta and trained at Harvard's Graduate School of Design. Wheeler's assets included Southern manners, notable taste, and a privately scathing sense of humor as well as sophisticated horticultural knowledge. While his portfolio included work at the National Arboretum and Washington's National Cathedral, he is chiefly known for the Rose Garden and for the plantings that he laid out with Bunny at the JFK and Robert Kennedy grave sites in Arlington National Cemetery. Acting as design associate and as a contractor for her, he also contributed to the landscape of the Mellons' Trinity Episcopal Church in Upperville and scoured nurseries for her gardens in Virginia, New York, Antigua, and the Cape. (Additionally, he provided Bunny with the best gossip when he found it, and in her letters she asked if he had heard any lately.) He had signed a contract with the Mellons in 1959 to help Bunny renovate gardens at Paul's two houses on Whitehaven Street in D.C. (one to live in, the other to hold Paul's ever-growing art collection). Wheeler also collaborated with her on a score of gardens for close friends up and down the East Coast. Besides the Martha's Vineyard landscape for Jackie and Evangeline Bruce's Georgetown garden, most notable were projects for Joseph Alsop and for Babs Simpson of *Vogue* and then *House & Garden*.

Stylish as most of Bunny's clients were, they knew little about gardens, so they often felt that what she and Wheeler did could only be the work of magicians. Wheeler's ability to translate Bunny's drawings and what she envisioned into scale renderings was absolutely necessary to her success.

Bunny put Wheeler on an annual retainer to be paid half yearly and eventually gave him and his partner, Dr. James M. Stengle, several acres at Oak Spring to build a house, Spring Hill. However, it seems that Wheeler had his own opinion about being paid for the White House work. In June 1963, when the Rose Garden was entering its first full year, Bunny sent him "a very small compensation for the work, time, inspiration and heart you put into the gardens at the White House" (and asked him not to tell Jackie that she had done so). It's clear he hadn't received payment before that, since Bunny wrote, "you cannot go on helping and living on air." However, at the bottom of a later undated note from Bunny that accompanied a "second little [payment]," he wrote: "returned to Mrs. Mellon," perhaps seeing his work on the Rose Garden as his own gift to the country.

The other two people who were indispensable for carrying out her plan for the Rose Garden—and for what became the Jacqueline Kennedy Garden on the east side of the White House—were both government employees, each an expert in his field and, just as important, masterfully tactful. Both understood the bureaucratic challenges of a job at the White House, where lawns and plantings were ruled with military precision by the National Park Service.

J. B. West, the chief usher who had held the position since 1957, ran the White House and knew what was going on outside as well as indoors. Bunny described him as the one who "knew all the intricacies of staff management, the ways of past families, the protocol, and the tiresome details. His smile and calm never left him; Jacqueline Kennedy and I often wondered what would really shake Mr. West." West actually became easygoing enough with Bunny to tease her; at one point when she had been sick, he sent a note, writing that "it has

been much too long since we have seen you around the mid-town estate" [meaning the White House]. Hurry and get well so we can have
our cocktail party in the garden, or at some other beautiful spot in the
Nation's Capital." While the Rose Garden project was underway, security was tight: the area was sometimes called "Mrs. West's Garden"
or some other nickname meant to flummox the press.

Beneath the West Colonnade, Irvin Williams and
Bunny discuss the next steps.

The other essential person was the West Virginian Irvin Williams,
a gardener whom Bunny found working with aquatic plants in a remote,

government-owned nursery on the Potomac River. She apparently instantly recognized him as just the man for the job·(a job that would last fifty years). In her essay about the Rose Garden and the assassination of President Kennedy for the 2002 Metropolitan Museum catalogue on Jackie Kennedy's White House years, Bunny described Williams as "a devoted and extraordinary man," a friend of hers and of the Kennedys, who always forgave "dogs and ponies for trespassing [on JFK's pride and joy, the Rose Garden lawn] and redoing the damage without a word." (The Kennedys were unique as a First Family in inviting a pony, Caroline's Macaroni, to graze the lawn.)

In his service to the Rose Garden, Williams did a lot of other things "without a word." Bunny was on her annual sojourn in Antigua as the March window to plant the magnolias while they were still dormant dribbled away, day by day, and the National Park Service "boys" responsible for the job insisted that the idea of trees should be abandoned entirely, especially the one in the northeast corner, where, they said, there were too many cables underground to dig safely. In a long letter to Bunny on March 8, Wheeler pointed out that if that were the case, if she threatened "to redesign the entire project," they would back down. They did.

After hearing their continuous objections about the trees, Wheeler wrote, "I will get in touch with Mr. Williams, since he seems to understand this problem and knows more about the effect you want than any of the others do." According to Linda Jane Holden's book on Bunny's gardens, "Mr. Williams conducted a stealth operation. With as little fuss as possible, he had the trees transferred . . . in the dead of night." Photographs of the trees on-site show giant balled-and-burlapped roots eighteen or so feet in diameter and about four feet deep—certainly there wasn't much for the "boys" to do but plant them at that point.

As Bunny well knew from her own gardens, once a design is laid out on the ground, minor adjustments can be crucial. She recalled that as the work began, she and Williams "realized the garden needed to be wider than the plan called for." They asked the job crew "to remove the measuring string on the south boundary over another eighteen inches . . . They said 'No' and went back to work . . . As soon as they left for lunch, Mr. Williams quietly went over, measured the additional eighteen inches, and moved the string!" Nobody noticed when they came back, Bunny continued, "or if they did, they said not a word . . . We got our way," she concluded, "the Irv Williams way."

Williams and Bunny were working off a plan drawn by Wheeler that was based on detailed watercolor sketches she had sent to President Kennedy late in January 1962. Unusually, she had signed her full name, perhaps for her the equivalent of a professional landscape architect's "block," the cartouche stamped on every plan that comes out of an office.

Bunny was awed and thrilled at the honor and responsibility that she had been given in getting a commission for a garden for the president of the United States. However, nothing was going to upset her annual program for spending the first months of the new year on Antigua, recovering from the elaborate Christmas celebrations she always orchestrated at "the farm." But the Rose Garden was much on her mind: while on Antigua she was able to study a preliminary plan of the area that Perry Wheeler had measured in November 1961.

The president gave the okay for the drawings in two days. He requested that Bunny complete the garden in four months and keep costs down by using the National Park Service for labor. Work began on March 19, 1962, once the president had signed off on the modest $23,458 estimate.

Bunny was not used to operating on a budget. It's probable that she contributed more than Wheeler's initial "salary" to the job, just as she often quietly did on projects that Wheeler installed for her friends. In this case, she at least paid lip service to the idea of a budget, noting in a fall planting memo that certain tulip varieties should be planted "if not too costly. If so, perhaps other similar varieties might be substituted."

The planting beds were spaded and fertilized, the irrigation system was installed, and the lawn area was dug to a depth of four feet and the earth replaced with topsoil. It was almost time to begin planting. However, just as the National Park Service "boys" had warned on March 31, an underground cable was cut by a gardener's shovel. And it was not just any cable. The "hotline" to the Strategic Arms Command had been severed, causing a "red button" government tremor at the height of the Cold War. "The scene was suddenly alive with security guards," Bunny wrote. At Andrews Air Force Base, warplanes were hastily recalled from the tarmac. Digging and preparation for the opening of the garden nevertheless continued. For her part, Bunny passed it all off lightly, later laughingly telling an interviewer, "A war was avoided."

Two weeks later, on April 15, came the Bay of Pigs, President Kennedy's botched clandestine invasion of Cuba manned by a brigade of Cuban exiles that collapsed spectacularly after only two days for lack of American air support. But Bunny and Irvin Williams kept on working tranquilly in the garden, moving plants, pruning, and deadheading, to make it perfect for the April 24 unveiling and for the heavy schedule of events the president had already lined up for the rest of the year. He was proud of his garden and wanted to show it off.

Curiously, there was little mention of the garden's opening in the press—*The Washington Post* merely announced two weeks later that the "garden has bloomed back into official business." By early October the garden had been the location for a clutch of prestigious ceremonies, including a twenty-one-gun salute on the White House lawn for Premier Ahmed Ben Bella of Algeria that terrified young John Kennedy, who was watching from his mother's arms inside the hedge of the Rose Garden.

Then, in mid-October, just the time of year when bags of bulbs arrive to plant for spring, came the discovery of Russian missiles in Cuba poised within striking range of the United States. The Strategic Air Command moved to the highest military alert short of all-out war. Over a thousand bombers and almost two hundred intercontinental ballistic missiles were put on alert. More than one hundred thousand combat-ready army infantrymen were deployed to ports along the East Coast. Nuclear submarines were moved into position. The U.S. Navy set up a blockade to stop Russian shipping. Russian warships headed for Cuba. Attorney General Robert Kennedy, almost as deeply involved in the crisis as his brother, held clandestine meetings with Ambassador Anatoly Dobrynin. Russian warships turned back on October 24, but when an American U-2 spy plane was

downed over Cuba, events began to spiral out of control. Secret negotiations designed to save face and to avoid nuclear war hastily took
place, and on October 28, Khrushchev agreed to remove the missiles.
Secretary of State Dean Rusk said, "We're eyeball to eyeball, and I
think the other fellow just blinked." In private, President Kennedy
told his friends, "I cut his balls off." Meanwhile, Bunny and Williams
kept on with their work in the garden.

The next autumn, on September 9, 1963, Bunny sent a memorandum to Williams preparing not only for the late-fall season but also
for the spring to come. It covers sixteen points, beginning with Williams's request for her to send him the key to her seasonal plantings.
She will provide fully grown clumps of white fall anemones from Oak
Spring and from Rokeby; she notes that early lilies are to be followed
by white *nicotiana*, the tobacco plant. And she will see about a bench
to hide a manhole cover . . .

Bunny wonders if it's worth trying martagon lilies again, since
"they were unusually small and did not show up very well." The native
Allegheny martagon (*Lilium superbum*) was a Jefferson favorite. At
the outset of the project Bunny had given a modern copy of Jefferson's
own garden book to the president, who wanted to have flowers that
both Jefferson and Washington had planted. (During the entire Rose
Garden design process, Jackie had repeatedly stepped back: Bunny
was her closest friend, but the garden she was designing was the
president's.)

Bunny's memo names another five lilies to be planted and others
that are simply listed as "green ones" and "some bright orange ones."
Tragically, the president did not live to see any of his lilies flower the
next summer.

On November 22, 1963, President John Fitzgerald Kennedy was
assassinated in Dallas. Jackie and the children were expected to move
out of the White House quickly to make room for the new president,
Lyndon Johnson, and First Lady, Lady Bird. Averell Harriman, then
serving in the administration, moved hastily out of his Georgetown
house so the bereaved Kennedys could move in. Bunny quietly called
on Billy Baldwin for help to make the place feel more like home.
When Jackie bought the house facing the Harrimans' several months

later, Baldwin continued working for her. At Jackie's request, he made the children's rooms replicas of those in the White House and hung gorgeous apricot silk curtains to screen the interiors from the huge crowds that assembled on N Street every day.

AS EARLY AS the spring of 1962, JFK had the thought of creating a more informal garden on the east side of the White House, a place, as Bunny recollected in 1984, that would be an oasis for his family. Bunny and Jackie began planning a few weeks later. Preliminary work had begun by 1963 but was not far advanced. Two weeks after JFK's death, Lady Bird Johnson invited Bunny to meet with her at the White House. "It was a hard decision to return to the White House so soon after Mrs. Kennedy had left," Bunny later wrote, but she agreed to Lady Bird Johnson's request to complete the job.

A spirit of lightness—of make-believe and play—had propelled the plan for this second garden, which Bunny and Jackie had envisioned as a more relaxed, feminine area, with a space big enough for croquet, children's games, a splashing pool, beds of herbs for the White House kitchens, and a latticed pavilion for a First Lady's traditional agenda of lunches and teas. Both women were aware that the glazed colonnade walk from the east public entrance would soon see increased traffic, because Jackie's White House restoration was under way by November 1961. A line of lindens, shaped and pruned to eight feet tall, would provide some visual protection from the new visitor flow and keep the airless passageway somewhat cooler in the summer.

As was so often the case with Bunny's work, the design started with a tree: a tall topiary holly in a Maryland nursery. It had reminded her of the Red Queen's croquet grounds in Disney's *Alice in Wonderland*. (The film, with its catchy satirical ditty, "Painting the Roses Red," had been released in 1951.) As planted, the huge fancifully clipped hollies and lindens were oversize versions of the small standardized herb trees Bunny grew for all her houses and gardens.

Over protests from Jackie, who said that she only wanted her name "scratched on the back of a bench," a silver plaque engraved with a short inscription in Bunny's hand that dedicated the space "to Jacqueline Kennedy, with great affection, from those who worked with her in the White House" was fixed to a column in the garden. The April 1965 opening was quiet; Jackie's mother, Mrs. Auchincloss, stood in for her, and Paul Mellon, Bunny, and Everett Hicks, her arborist, arrived in a trio of Rolls-Royces.

In taking on a public commission that would have been a prize for any garden designer or landscape architect—gardens for the president of the United States, and in particular the very public Rose Garden—Bunny discloses a boldness and a measure of self-confidence she seldom revealed publicly. But is the Rose Garden her best work, her most original work? It is easily matched by the siting and landscapes of Oak Spring and the landscape of the South Pasture park on Nantucket, the sweep of the JFK memorial library entrance, and his Arlington Cemetery grave site. Is it perfect for the site and its purpose? Yes. Above all, Bunny had listened carefully to the president. She had done something she intuitively understood how to do: pay attention as raptly as the president had listened to her at that picnic table on Cape Cod. And then she had acted with what Paul most admired in her: "the directness and sheer ability of someone who gets things done."

By 1966, Bunny Mellon, then fifty-six years old, had finished her White House garden projects. She had also worked with Jacqueline Kennedy on the restoration of the White House and had comforted her through the days after the assassination. But before she received the Department of the Interior's Conservation Service Award that year for both the White House Rose Garden and the Jacqueline Kennedy East Garden, her credentials were scrutinized by the renowned D.C. landscape architect Leon Henry Zach.

As then-president of the American Society of Landscape Architects (ASLA), Zach was asked to interview Bunny, because the ASLA "felt there must have been a ghost designer" for the White House work, as Bunny wrote in a memoir fragment.

His temperament and background made him an interesting choice to interview a woman of great wealth and social standing who, without professional training, had taken on the redesign of one of the most visible areas of the White House grounds—and succeeded brilliantly.

Leon Zach (1895–1966) was what you might call a "company man." After graduating from Harvard and Harvard's Graduate School of Design, he worked for the Olmsted firm and became a partner, leaving Boston in 1938 to work for the War Department in Washington, D.C. He served actively on the historic Dumbarton Oaks estate's museum, garden, and library advisory board; Bunny would later serve on the library committee, the first woman to do so other than founder Mildred Bliss. But while Dumbarton Oaks had represented the apogee of American Country Place culture, the Country Place Era had ended. During the booming post–World War II years, landscape architects mainly found jobs in the public sector and large-scale residential development.

"At first I could not take it seriously," Bunny wrote, but at Perry Wheeler's urging, she agreed to meet Zach in the Rose Garden. Bunny described him as "a nice man," who, she imagined, "had expected sort of a pompous blue-haired garden club woman who did not really plant on hands and knees. We talked, it was very easy, he asked where I studied and I said 'never.' Responding that I had just lived in my father's house [Albemarle in Princeton] and had learned by the things that happened there, I explained that its garden had been designed by Olmsted in Boston and I tagged along to listen to the nice Dutchman in charge."

Zach smiled when she told him her story, and then he said, "I was an apprentice on that job. I learned from the same plans when I was a very young man." Jacob Sloet, Bunny's "Dutchman," had been his teacher too.

Professional validation was one thing; it was another to be recognized in public by her husband for her work. I once asked Bunny what Paul thought of the Rose Garden. She began by talking about the difficulties of balancing the White House installation and Paul's demands on her time. "Paul was very old-fashioned," she said. I asked her what that meant. "Well," she flashed back, "when I was doing the garden at the White House, I'd rush in and he'd say, 'Now sit down, you haven't time to dress. I know where you've been.' I'd think to myself, my goodness, all I've been doing was a garden for the president of the United States and I'm treated as though I'd been smoking behind the barn."

Sometime in February 1963, Paul visited the Rose Garden for the first time. He must have admired what he saw, because in April, at the opening of the exhibition *Painting in England 1700–1850* at the Virginia Museum of Fine Arts, he stood up in front of many landscapes by Turner, Constable, Hogarth, Blake, and other great British artists he had collected to declare Bunny "a brilliant artist in her own right in the fields of gardening and architecture."

THOSE WHO WORKED for the Mellons knew without having to advertise it that they did first-rate work and were valued for it. They formed a skilled *equipe*, or team, that had the confidence of any great sports team that jogs onto the field prepared to win. Bill Keyser, the longtime head painter at Oak Spring, glowed when he admitted to me that artisans from the carpenters' shop and the sheet metal shop had anonymously produced materials for the White House.

However, any Mellon employee—no matter how talented, trusted, and hardworking—who blabbed to the press was fired. Bunny told Joan Holt, one of the Metropolitan Museum of Art editors who worked on the catalogue for the 2002 exhibition *Designing Camelot*, that a certain reference to a longtime farm employee in Bunny's essay must be cut. He "had <u>nothing</u> [underlined three times] to do with the W.H. Gardens except drive me in with my plants to Washington," Bunny wrote. He then "had talked too much" about the role he'd played and was let go.

Bunny was determined to keep the record straight about her most prominent commission. After the employee was dismissed, Bunny went on, he had even written "an article bringing himself into the Rose Garden . . . This is where History gets mixed up so often and goes through years before it is cleaned up. I don't want the Rose Garden mixed up." Bunny almost never explained her actions directly when she fired an employee or dropped a friend. But here, in a professional setting, she must have felt she needed to do so. "Sorry to be so fussy!" she added.

While Bunny was willing to receive public credit for the Rose Garden, the assistance she gave to Jackie on restoring the White House as a showplace and as a residence was mostly behind the scenes. During the two and a half halcyon years of the White House restoration under the Kennedy administration (January 1961–November 1963), Bunny was a member of Jackie's Fine Arts Committee, a society of equals in social standing, wealth, and contacts. Unlike the others, however, Bunny mostly worked with Jackie through letters and phone calls, not through meetings, acting as her informal wish-fulfillment agent while at the same time making the Rose Garden for JFK.

19

"America's Country House"

In August 1960, Bunny returned from one of her couture fittings in Paris to find panicked phone messages from Jackie Kennedy. Apparently, Jackie had at last understood that her husband might well win the presidential election. When Jackie asked her what she could possibly do with "that big house and all those curtains," she was asking the right person.

For Bunny, this was no more complicated a project than the organization of each of her own homes to afford a comfortable, pleasurable life like the British country squires and French aristocrats on their estates in the provinces had created for themselves for hundreds of years. Like those country palaces, the White House has always relied on a large skilled staff. Enslaved Africans were in domestic service from the start and had also been among the laborers who quarried the stone to build the mansion. Even though the White House was, by Inauguration Day 1961, embedded in a city mired in poverty and stark racial divisions, Bunny and Jackie viewed the iconic presidential dwelling as it had been in Washington and Jefferson's day: a grand country house.

In the essay Bunny wrote for the catalogue of the 2002 Metropolitan Museum's Costume Institute show of Jackie's White House wardrobe, she respectfully credited Jackie with the image of the White House as a "large southern mansion." It seems far more likely that Bunny herself, who had lived at eighteenth-century Carter Hall, an archetypal "Southern mansion," as a nineteen-year-old and had learned there how to be the perfect chatelaine, was the one who suggested the idea of what she later called, in talking with me, "America's country house."

Both Bunny and Jackie understood the dual iconographic value of the White House as the home of the current president of the United States and as a symbol of the nation. Jackie's restoration was meant to reveal to all Americans and to visitors and tourists a long and distinguished history made visible in material objects and their surroundings. She needed her friend Bunny to help her.

What the "New Frontier" (JFK's slogan for the challenges facing the country) gang thought of the Eisenhowers' decorating style can be gathered from Katharine Graham's letter to Bunny written soon after the inauguration, an event Bunny had missed because she was recuperating from surgery, perhaps her hysterectomy.

Graham described for Bunny "the first quiet family supper" in the White House two days later. The guest list of six included Joseph Alsop, whose chastely green D.C. garden Bunny had designed. Alsop—a columnist, a friend and booster, and a most accomplished snob—took a peek at the furniture arrangements left by the Eisenhowers. "'Dahling,'" he reported to Graham, "'I wish you could see it upstairs. Just like the royal suite in the Muehlebach Hotel. [Eisenhower came from Kansas, and the Muehlebach was Kansas City's best.] There is a huge dresser against the door in the President's room that closed up the opening to Mamie's.'"

As the restoration began, the "large Southern mansion" that Bunny and Jackie envisioned was enveloped in, as Bunny wrote, "a new atmosphere" that "blew through the White House like wind with a clearing sky . . . Windows were soon opened . . . Fireplaces and chimneys were cleaned so fires could burn in all the rooms as needed . . . Cupboards and warehouses were opened to search for historic treasures." After the State Dining Room was transformed with white and gold, "the existing party chairs were sad, not suitable for the new cheerfulness," Bunny continued, so "traditional chairs used in Paris for such occasions were ordered and made in France."

In July 1961, before those French chairs arrived, came the hasty loan of Bunny's own chairs, 140 or so of them (plus Bunny's yellow tablecloths), which were trucked over to Mount Vernon for a state dinner, the first ever held outside the White House, to honor the president of Pakistan, Mohammed Ayub Khan. (A year earlier, Bunny had purchased and imported 150 handsome iron chairs for $18,000, so she had plenty of seating available to lend her friend.) This was a level of entertaining that Jacqueline Kennedy hadn't faced before on a regular basis. Neither "Black Jack" Bouvier, Jackie's father, nor her mother, Janet Auchincloss, nor even the Kennedy family would have had such a huge set of chairs at the ready.

Bunny's greatest gift to her friend Jackie as First Lady was her ability to warm things up. When the first Christmas rolled around in 1961, Bunny enlisted the scenic design team of Paul Leonard and Bill Strom, who had painted the sets for Eliza's June coming-out fairy-tale extravaganza only months before. They decked out the sweet-scented eighteen-foot-tall balsam in the Blue Room in a new way and without any "vulgar" tinsel or glassy balls or string after string of cold white lights. Such a tree had never been seen before in this official setting.

When *The Washington Post* noted that the decorations were "less colorful and lavish than in previous years," Pamela Turnure, Jackie's press secretary, countered by saying they were "in the manner of an

Caroline Kennedy, an unidentified friend, and Jackie's dog Clipper check out the first Kennedy Christmas tree in the White House in 1961.

American country home." From every twig hung gingerbread cookies, candy canes, furry toy mice, wooden nutcrackers (the theme Jackie chose was Tchaikovsky's ballet *The Nutcracker*) along with tiny straw baskets, birds, angels, and alphabet blocks, most of them made by elderly or disabled American craftspeople. The lights, shaped like small candles, glowed softly, and the simple star atop the tree was made of straw. The tree was an irresistible draw for four-year-old Caroline Kennedy, who "kept inventing little plots of how to take candy & toys off the tree it was forbidden to violate," as her mother wrote to Bunny. To deck other rooms of the mansion, Oak Spring staff hauled in freshly cut Virginia red cedars, holly, and mistletoe from the farm.

By December 1962, in addition to taking on the design and execution of the Rose Garden at the president's request, Bunny had been a member of the White House Fine Arts Committee, which was quickly formed after the inauguration in January 1961. The twelve members, most of them antiques enthusiasts without any special training, were to raise the funds for the acquisition of historic furnishings. Their wealth and connections ensured that the White House restoration effort would not need to go back to Congress for additional money.

Jackie's initial idea had been to restore the mansion to its origins in 1800, when John and Abigail Adams moved into the new house. Henry Francis du Pont (1880–1969), the venerable and august collector of American antiques and Americana who chaired the committee, swiftly saw that part of his job would be to shield Jackie and the restoration from public criticism. Was most White House history going to be obliterated in a frenzy for purity? Two eminent consultants (Lyman Butterfield, editor of the John Adams Papers, and Julian Boyd, editor of the Thomas Jefferson Papers) drafted a treatise on the evolving, living nature of the White House as symbol as well as residence that helped Jackie do a U-turn. Knowing it was imperative to find furnishings from different administrations, she enlisted *Life* magazine as her mouthpiece, saying, "The public should have no fear that we might restore the building to its earliest period . . . or fill it with French furniture." Jackie did in fact include as much French furniture in "the People's House" as was decently possible.

Bunny's activities for various committees were often deliberately veiled. Jackie understood why and wrote to her, "I so often feel badly that in return for all you give you often receive only the things that are most distasteful to you—that terrible spotlight that is the onus of our friendship."

Following the gauzy thread of one very French acquisition leads to Bunny and the splendid fifty-three-piece suite of gilded furniture ordered by President James Monroe in 1817 from the Parisian *ébéniste* (cabinetmaker) Pierre-Antoine Bellangé for what is now known as the Blue Room, Jackie's favorite. After a pier table, apparently the solitary remaining Bellangé piece of the White House suite, was located in off-site storage, restored, and publicized, private donors contributed four of the original chairs. (The Daughters of the American Revolution owned yet another, but even a plea from du Pont to lend it to the White House failed.) Charles Francis Adams IV, a direct descendant of John Adams and a member of the Fine Arts Committee, leapt in to pay for the reproduction of eleven matching chairs.

Charles Francis Adams IV and Bunny had known one another since they were children. His father, Charles Francis Adams III, Secretary of the Navy under President Herbert Hoover and a famed yachtsman who was known as the "Dean of American helmsmen," had coached Gerard B.—and Bunny as a young girl—on the finer points of sailing his three-masted schooner, *Atlantic*. In a 1997 unpublished

Carved and gilded in 1817, parts of the Bellangé suite found a new life in the Kennedy years.

reminiscence, Bunny wrote that Adams had "taught me at an early age how to sail." Aboard *Atlantic*, the great yachtsman had cautioned her, "Never forget that the sea will always have the last word." Then he consoled her, adding, "Sailing a boat has all the elements you need to know about life." Nothing was publicized about this two-generational connection to the Adamses, but the relationship speaks to the hushed stratosphere of American aristocracy.

There is certainly nothing democratic about the Bellangé suite. If anything, those finely carved and joined sticks of beechwood speak less to the concept of "the People's House" and more to the imperial aspirations of a mighty new nation in the making. The surviving arm-chairs and their new companions were reupholstered in 1963 with silk as blue as a Kansas sky, specially woven with a golden eagle on the back and seat. Jackie and Bunny spoke the silent language of things down to the last nuance.

Henry du Pont had enlisted an auxiliary advisory committee (including Butterfield and Boyd) of eighteen scholars and museum directors and curators eminent enough in American history, culture, and the decorative arts to supply academic authority to the restoration and to ensure nationwide representation and to help make the White House "a symbol of cultural as well as political leadership," as du Pont wrote. Although Bunny wasn't officially a member of this committee, nor of yet another group that du Pont formed—the Special Commit-tee for White House Paintings—she contributed to both.

From the first, Jackie wanted Bunny in on all decisions—including her okay on samples chosen by the American Institute of Interior De-signers for the ground-floor library upholstery. "A telephone message from the White House . . . indicates we may show you samples of ma-terials," wrote the interior decorator Jeannette Lenygon to Bunny in early October 1961. Bunny promptly got herself to a midtown Man-hattan antiques shop, approved the samples collected there for her viewing, called Jackie, and then gave Mrs. Lenygon her answer.

As for the contents of the library, James T. Babb, Yale University Librarian, who chaired a small committee for the restoration proj-ect, wrote to Jackie that he had "discussed the matter with Mrs. Paul Mellon, in Upperville, and she urged me to write you about it." Instead of the standard "collection of the great American books in original condition" to be displayed as "an exhibition piece in the White House," the new library should be a useful reference tool for the president, his family, and the official White House staff, wrote Babb. He surely knew that a reference to Mrs. Mellon as Mrs. Kennedy's close friend would help in making such a shift.

The paintings committee also faced plenty of difficulties. At that time the White House art collection consisted mostly of portraits, many of them of previous presidents, often of dubious artistic value. Chaired by James Fosburgh, a painter, an art historian, and a collector, the committee included a number of other serious collectors with deep pockets and phenomenal social pull. Within two years they had amassed more than 150 works, including landscapes and still lifes, for the White House. It's not clear that Bunny was a de facto member of the committee (she doesn't appear in the only photograph of the assembled group), but the Rembrandt Peale portrait of Thomas Jefferson as vice president that she and Paul quietly gave in December 1962 proved to Jackie that "the effort of our painting committee . . . at last . . . has been made worthwhile," as the First Lady wrote to her friend.

Rembrandt Peale, a son of the better-known Charles Willson Peale, had painted it with the fresh vision of youth (he was twenty-two) for the Peales' "Museum and Gallery of the Fine Arts" in Baltimore. The museum closed in 1829; when the surviving works were sold, the portrait was bought by Charles J. M. Eaton of Baltimore in 1856 and was hung in the library of the Peabody Institute that Eaton founded until it was "rediscovered" in 1959 through the research of the editors of the Jefferson Papers at Princeton University. Until 1962 the only life portraits of any of the first six presidents in the White House collections had been those of George Washington. Now Jefferson, whose civilized architectural enhancements to the White House Jackie admired, would have his place too.

The response to national press announcements of the mansion's restoration also produced an astonishing number of antiques and family heirlooms and what could only be called "finds" from within the White House itself. All were gathered for evaluation in the old Map Room, which began to look like the site of a high-class rummage sale.

William Voss Elder III, who became the second White House curator, remembered the process: "You had to make decisions yourself . . . You knew if someone wrote in and offered a plate from the Andrew Jackson administration . . . you just said, 'Fine.'"

First of the three design principals to appear on the White House scene, even before there was a Fine Arts Committee, was Bunny's Foxcroft friend Sister Parish. Although Bunny and Parish were beginning to drift apart as friends, it was Bunny who had introduced her to Jackie when JFK was the junior senator from Massachusetts. Parish, who by 1961 was well established in American society's decor hierarchy, renovated and redecorated the dismal White House family quarters on the second floor in chic but comfy haute-WASP fashion.

Parish blew through the entire $50,000 overall budget intended for the White House in just two weeks. Jackie was undaunted, telling the chief usher J. B. West, "I know we're out of money . . . but never mind . . . we're going to find some way to get real antiques into this house." More funding to carry out the restoration would soon arrive from the well-heeled members of the Fine Arts Committee and their friends.

Henry du Pont took on the role of chairman when he was eighty-one years old. Through his ninety-seven rooms of American furniture at Winterthur (his Delaware estate) and the decorative arts program he established there in 1952, he had extended the concept of historical integrity to include period rooms. He also understood what Jackie Kennedy wanted, who she was, and what he was up against. Jackie came to visit Winterthur on May 8, 1961. John Sweeney, then Winterthur's senior curator and a member of the Fine Arts Committee, recalled du Pont saying before the visit, "I have a feeling that her real interest is in French things; she doesn't believe that you can have a really swell house with American furniture, and I want her to see that you can."

While the White House State Rooms display distinct periods, only the Green Room, a Federal parlor, follows du Pont's desire for an all-American room. Du Pont, who was creating period rooms at Winterthur, believed in historical accuracy. When he said, "If you go into a room and right away see something, then you realize that that [something] shouldn't be in the room." At Winterthur he was seeking to re-create an eighteenth-century life as he carefully researched it from inventories and correspondence, then reassembled it for his own pleasure and the instruction of his visitors. A look at Bunny's own eclectic interiors reveals no "period rooms" in which furnishings and effects are assembled to create a sense of a certain era. However, although her language was different from du Pont's, she meant much the same thing about the importance of decorative unity when she said, "Nothing should be noticed."

The role of the third major figure in the restoration, the internationally known interior designer Stéphane Boudin of Maison Jansen in Paris, was largely kept secret, as it would have been a huge political gaffe to have the public know how deeply a French decorator was involved in redesigning the country's most precious national symbol. As it was, word did get out, but Jackie always maintained that Boudin had created what she called in 1980 "a sense of state, arrival, and grandeur."

The grand oval Blue Room, the principal receiving room on the first, or State, floor, was Boudin's masterpiece. Against the walls of self-striped cream silk stood the Bellangé chairs and, in the center, a round table draped with a skirt. The first skirt—proposed by Sister Parish—was gold silk damask trimmed with tassels in the same color: Boudin described it as a "fat Spanish dancer" and produced a lustrous blue velvet version as a replacement. The Blue Room did not meet with du Pont's complete approval, however. J. B. West remembered that du Pont could be heard muttering his disdain every time he entered the room.

The various contretemps that occurred because of the very different design philosophies of the principals—Parish, Boudin, and du Pont—were masterfully handled by Jackie, Jayne Wrightsman, who had introduced Boudin to the project, and William Elder. Kennedy and Wrightsman wrote soothing letters to Parish when she threatened to quit over Boudin's attempts to "Frenchify" the place. Bunny steered clear of the intrigues.

Keeping Parish on the job was vital, as her roster of wealthy clients—Astors, Loebs, and the like—were needed as contributors. So in addition to the private quarters, she took on and was credited with the decor of the so-called Family Dining Room on the State floor below what essentially became a smaller state dining room once the private quarters were finished. Parish's friend, client, and

Fine Arts Committee member Jane Engelhard and her husband, Charles, underwrote the forthrightly American scheme: warm, bright yellow walls, American Federal furniture, and American art. But Boudin left his fingerprints on every room, including this one, where the cheerful, rose-garlanded, pink-and-gold carpet was designed by Maison Jansen.

In the end, the uneasy threesome was able to move the Kennedy "restoration" forward with great success. Sweeney said du Pont knew that his recommendations as chair were not always followed and that the furniture arrangements he put in place were frequently altered after one of his visits. Boudin supplied a true reflection of Jackie Kennedy's taste and glamour, du Pont's status had given the project the pedigree of historical accuracy, and Sister Parish had supplied American comfort and low-key elegance.

A few days after the Jefferson portrait arrived, Jackie described how Perry Wheeler and Cathy Mellon Warner, Paul's daughter, who was then married to Senator John Warner, had sat at a diplomatic luncheon together "under Jefferson's watchful eye" in the State Dining Room. That day Jackie also saw in use for the first time the vermeil flower "baskets" Bunny had given the White House. "Well, they are absolutely unbelievable, Bunny, and *everyone* noticed them . . . people you couldn't think would notice a piano if they fell over it." Chief Usher West certainly noticed. Jackie wrote to Bunny that Mr. West "came in yesterday and poised on one foot—eyes rolled backwards in his head in ecstasy—hands clasped" and said, "'Has Mrs. Kennedy SEEN Mrs. Mellon's baskets—oh they are SUPERB!'"

Bunny later wrote that the Kennedys' new entertainment style at the White House meant that the mansion was now "full of pleasure and celebrated the importance

A vermeil basket for flowers crafted by Tiffany & Co., New York, 1962, one of twenty-four, the gift of Bunny Mellon to the White House Collection

of [all] the guests." Instead of the enormous military or boardroom U-shape favored by the Eisenhowers and previous presidents that celebrated the importance by rank of those who sat nearest the presidential couple, suddenly there were round tables for ten or twelve. This, of course, meant there was a need for lower, more informal flower containers.

In July 1962, Tiffany & Co. had written to Bunny that their factory had been able "to avoid a very large tooling cost to apply against a relatively small number of articles" that Bunny had requested. A little lower and smaller in diameter than the stock item that Tiffany carried, the new vermeil containers were adapted to their new purpose and made with solid, rather than wicker-like, sides so they would hold water. Presumably because less work was required to make them, and because of their size, the price was, accordingly, $95 cheaper per container than the stock items. Bunny ordered twenty-four, and $8,640 was the total for this Christmas present for Jackie (and the White House). Jackie finished off her ecstatic thank-you letter with, "I just hope someone gives *you* what you want for Christmas."

The vermeil containers are still regularly in use today. On my visit to the White House in May 2019, Lydia S. Tederick, then acting curator, led me to the flower room next to the hidden corridor along which JFK walked daily to the indoor swimming pool in the West Wing to join selected female staffers for invigorating swims in the buff. Ms. Tederick and I did not discuss those visits, but when we got to the flower room, there sat one of Bunny's vermeil baskets on the counter. It was still filled with a loose arrangement of pink tulips, sweet peas, and jasmine from a dinner the night before. One of the in-house florists working there also showed me an empty one and let me pick it up. Made of solid silver and washed on the outside with gold, it weighed more than two pounds.

Jackie, who relished the grandeur of that gold and silver, deeply admired how Bunny provided the things that no one else had thought of or could supply. "Some people give State Rooms," Jackie wrote, "but you make the flower room for Mr. Young—and find him to put in it. Everyone else comes heralded by trumpets through the front door—and there you are in working gloves fixing all the flowers for a state dinner." At that time the ground-floor Flower Room that Bunny installed opened out into the Rose Garden, so a few blooms and leaves could always be picked to loosen up the florist's arrangement. Bunny taught the chief floral designer Elmer M. "Rusty" Young how to create bouquets like her own; he stayed through the Nixon administration.

The most enduring evidence of Bunny's influence on the White House is thus paradoxically also the most ephemeral—those flowers. I think a direct connection can be traced between the opulent informality Bunny introduced to White House floral decoration and a diminutive Ambrosius Bosschaert the Elder still life of variegated tulips that she and Paul bought in 1948, the year they married. This work on copper stands as the supreme exemplar of how Bunny, throughout her life, thought flowers should be arranged: loosely and airily, as if they were still magically growing in a garden together, regardless of their actual bloom times.

By December 6, 1963, when the recently widowed Jackie Kennedy left the White House, the Executive Mansion had achieved legal status as a museum with a curator, a guidebook, and its own nonprofit organization, the White House Historical Association. Jackie had walked the American public through the house on television, proudly showing off the culture and history of the country and the treasures that had been unearthed and acquired. Despite the daily dramas and outsize characters involved, Jackie had succeeded in giving the White House the historic luster it deserved. As she left the mansion, Jackie penned a note to Lady Bird Johnson: "You will be remembered as the one who PRESERVED it. Each room has all the historic pictures and furniture it can hold."

THROUGHOUT THE THREE breathlessly short years of the White House project, Bunny had a particular knack for filling a need just as the need was felt, producing on cue precisely the right artisan, such as her Cape Cod upholsterer, Lawrence J. Arata. In an oral history interview held by the JFK Presidential Museum and Library in Boston, Arata recalled that "when Mrs. Kennedy started the restoration program [in 1961] . . . Mrs. Mellon spoke to Mrs. Kennedy, and that's how I came to the White House . . . I have both of them to thank for the biggest break in my life." On arrival he was quietly installed in the Executive Mansion: "They gave me a beautiful room on the third floor, and I had my meals in the White House also." He stayed for another two years in his upstairs lair, moving out when he married a White House secretary in February 1963 but continuing with White House work until 1977.

Arata's skills were soon needed for more than upholstery in the sad days of late November 1963. Around nine on the evening of November 22, he was asked to return to the White House to drape the windows, mantels, and chandeliers in black, finishing up around 4:30 a.m., "just as Mrs. Kennedy accompanied the body to the White House." What he used was "plain, black cambric," the material, he said, that a professional upholsterer uses to finish off the bottoms of chairs "in the correct, old-fashioned way." He had ordered a hundred yards only a few days before. Most people thought it was silk, he remembered, but "Mrs. Kennedy wanted it very, very humble, the same as Lincoln's funeral."

Bunny's description of the terrible days of President Kennedy's assassination and his burial in Arlington Cemetery in November reveal that she knew her value as a witness and that she was determined to set down her part as she remembered it, clearly and briefly. She was on Antigua when the news came crackling through the radio from Martinique. Her friend Paul Leonard, the decorative artist, had climbed off a ladder, run outside to find Bunny, and brought her in to listen to the news. Leonard remembered that all Bunny could say, repeatedly, was, "I must get home for Jackie." Quickly she telegraphed Perry Wheeler, writing, LEAVING ON FIRST PLANE TODAY GIVE MY LOVE AND THOUGHTS TO ALL WE WORK WITH MUCH LOVE BUNNY.

The weather was bad, so it wasn't until the morning of November 24, two days after the tragedy, that she could get to New York on the earliest flight, which arrived at 11:00 p.m. The Mellon plane was waiting on the tarmac to take her to D.C. through a heavy storm that Bunny said mirrored the "horribleness of the occasion."

"I arrived at the North Portico of the White House at 2:00 a.m. The steps were lined with Marines. They clicked their heels as I passed, going up alone. Mr. West opened the door . . . he had been sitting nearby waiting for my arrival. After embracing me, he said, with tears in his eyes, 'Mrs. Kennedy is asleep now but would like for you to be at the Capitol tomorrow morning at nine to organize the flowers.' I asked him if I could go in and pay my respects to the president." She and West went into the East Room, where "at each corner of the casket stood a motionless guard from each of the four services . . . Holding tight to Mr. West's hand, I said my prayers." That was the last moment of quiet reflection she would have for days.

Over the next painful forty-eight hours Bunny did the two things she knew she could do best to help her friend. Even though she had no expectation of direct contact with the former First Lady, she went ahead and made sure that all would be as she knew Jackie would wish. Bunny kept the arrangements simple at the Capitol, where the body of the president lay in state, and in Saint Matthew's Roman Catholic Cathedral, where the requiem Mass was said. She made sure that the overwhelming tide of floral tributes coming from all over the world was massed on the Arlington hillside like "an enormous blanket," leaving the grave itself as stark as the nation's grief.

On Sunday night Bunny listened to her friend speak of the assassination. Ben Bradlee, JFK's close friend, then a reporter for *Newsweek*, had listened to the same agonizing recital of the story and said that Jackie was "trying to get rid of it by talking of it, by emptying herself."

Jackie then asked Bunny to go to the Rose Garden to pick the last flowers of the year for a small basketful "like the one you sent to the hospital when Patrick died." (The Kennedys' infant son, who survived for only two days, had been born on August 7, 1963, barely four months before his father was assassinated.) Jackie told Bunny that at the bottom of the basket "somewhere scrunched down" she should "put in your own note to Jack. Stick it in with the moss and the wet"—a symbolic burial. Scissors in hand, Bunny went to the garden. "It was almost pitch-dark," she remembered, and very late in the year for much to be flowering, but she found "dozens of white roses in bloom," a few hardy blue salvias, and some chrysanthemums.

She snipped berries from the trees and supplemented what she found in the Rose Garden with flowers that she had sent from her greenhouse in Virginia, adding duplicates of what she had planted for the president.

The next morning, Monday, November 25, the sad little floral tribute Jackie had asked her friend to arrange almost didn't make it to the dead president's grave, because the army detail at Arlington refused to let Bunny approach the site. Then a Secret Service agent recognized Mrs. Mellon and handed her little basket of flowers over to another agent, who carried it directly to the bier. Bunny remembered, "It was there, because Jackie told me she saw it." Bunny could not stay to see the coffin lowered into the grave. Instead, she and Paul had to head to New York to see a friend in the hospital, first lingering near the TV set at the airstrip to watch the ceremony from there.

The story of Bunny and Jackie at the White House is the story of a Bunny Mellon who came into her own both as a friend and as an expert in many fields that all required astounding confidence in her own abilities and huge expenditures when she felt they were needed: the vermeil centerpieces, the Peale Jefferson. Jackie called the Peale portrait *le comble*, the apex of the White House restoration. "Do what you can for your country," said Grandpa Lowe. Even after the state funeral and the burial at Arlington, Bunny was not yet finished with all she could do for her dead president, for her grieving friend Jackie, or for her country.

20

Arlington Cemetery: Portrait of a
Landscape Gardener

Bunny had to prove her abilities and skills as a landscape designer all over again at JFK's grave. The president is honored with an eternal flame on the high, grassy hill below Arlington House in the great war cemetery that overlooks Washington, D.C. His wife and his two infants are now buried with him. At the Oak Spring Garden Library, two copies of the intensively researched seventy-six-page final report for the grave's design sit on a shelf. However, for four years after the acceptance of that document by the U.S. government in November 1964, the site itself continued to see many changes that deeply and subtly affected the structure of the landscaping and the graves, creating the quiet power that so movingly affects visitors. As completed, it stands as Bunny Mellon's great contribution to American public life.

Levels rise gently from one to the next and on up to the graves set on a rectangular terrace beneath Arlington House, once the home of the Confederate general Robert E. Lee. When JFK, a passionate reader of American history who abhorred the general's cause but admired his bravery, visited the house and looked down over the metropolis, he had been struck by the splendor and scope of the view. He felt it told the American story in a series of monuments encompassing the height of the nation's achievements and wide spaces that were a reminder of the democratic breadth of the American citizenry. From that vantage point, one's gaze now travels from JFK's grave over Memorial Bridge (a symbol of reconciliation between North and South) and the Lincoln Memorial, then is caught by the Washington Monument and the green length of the Mall to end at the dome of the Capitol. The vista of the city stretches out for miles around and beyond.

When Secretary of Defense Robert McNamara and Robert Kennedy visited Arlington the day after the assassination, they too were struck by the grandeur of what they saw. The president's brother had persuaded Jackie that instead of Holyhood Cemetery in Massachusetts, where her tiny son Patrick had been buried only fifteen weeks earlier, the nation's hallowed military cemetery was where her husband should lie. Patrick's remains and those of his stillborn sister would be brought to join those of their father.

From the cemetery road, a visitor climbs to a broad grass circle bounded by a granite walkway, entering through an off-center opening that fits the steeply ascending topography. (In 1971 the site was made ADA-compliant at the request of Senator Ted Kennedy.) Until the 220-year-old Arlington Oak was felled by Hurricane Irene in 2011, an imposing American native post oak had dominated the circle, a comforting living presence offering protective shade. A sapling grown from an acorn of that tree has since been planted to replace it.

Where the Kennedys rest at Arlington National Cemetery is peaceful: the picturesque hill and the pink granite paving from West Falmouth, Massachusetts, around the graves owe their soft contours to Bunny Mellon's work on the site.

The next level up, a paved ellipse, is bounded by a low granite wall carved with quotations from President Kennedy's speeches. The play of curves between the wall and the circle below offers a graceful contrast to the miles of gravestones in military rows below. The heart-stopping view downward from the center of the low wall around the circle is on an axis with the long view that cuts through the forests of the cemetery to the Capitol far in the distance. Looking upward, however, the angled view of Arlington House is slightly cut off by a living hump of green lawn.

That calming, oblique view of the hilltop—and the eternal flame—were what gave the grave its special meaning for Jackie and the room for reflection that she needed. Although Bunny first began to work on the burial place in 1964, her work to grade the hill would not be completed for five years. The architect John Carl Warnecke, whose firm was selected to design the site, wrote to Bunny in early March 1964 asking her to review and consult on the design studies, essentially a commissioning letter. Her first active work on the project was confined to the selection of trees and shrubs.

As the nation's grief crested and the sense of loss sank in, the demands to have the memorial reflect both that grief and that loss had also grown. Concepts considered for the grave included a cross, a pavilion, a massive headstone, a sarcophagus, a sunken tomb, a raised tomb, and sculpture. The Mausoleum at Halicarnassus, one of the Seven Wonders of the Ancient World, and President Ulysses S. Grant's domed and columned tomb on New York's Upper West Side were both considered as models but rejected. Scores of other architects, landscape architects, and artists of every kind, including calligraphers, were consulted. Stonemasons weighed in, as did liturgical experts. Isamu Noguchi advised getting rid of the flame, saying it was kitschy, and recommended a sculptural cross.

Winston Churchill's burial in January 1965 beneath a plain slab in a country churchyard put pause to the most elaborate plans. Warnecke and his partner, Michael Painter, the firm's lead landscape architect, were creating a calm, beautiful, modernist setting for a memorial, but by 1966 it became apparent that what it lacked was a sense of Kennedy himself and his link to history. At Jackie's behest, Bunny began to work with the firm and with the Army Corps of Engineers on more than the selection and installation of plant material.

The same scenarios that had unfolded with Bunny's work at the White House now took place at Arlington. When others had proposed bad ideas for the Rose Garden, Bunny—sometimes with Jackie, or Wheeler or Williams—had quietly exerted pressure to find a better solution. When President Kennedy's naval aide had ordered the Rose Garden to be planted entirely with poinsettias for Christmas without consulting anyone, Jackie had written a stiff letter stating that Bunny was the advisor on all planting and that there was "a year-round plan for every blade of grass or flower that shall be planted on these grounds."

When construction of a tall building on Lafayette Square with windows that overlooked the garden had threatened the president's security, planting a "tall heavy tree in the center of the north bed" of the Rose Garden was recommended by others as protection. Bunny and Wheeler simultaneously arrived at the idea of planters on the roof of the colonnade leading to the Oval Office instead. Because of the shortened perspective lines from the building's windows down into the garden, low wooden boxes filled with tall plants were all that was needed to obscure the view, Wheeler wrote, adding that "they can be moved around to give the most effective screening." The perspectival screening trick worked just fine. So that Bunny could have a secret laugh, J. B. West kept the peremptory order to plant the "tall, heavy tree" without delay.

Such experience in dealing with bureaucratic power on the Rose Garden job would help Bunny fulfill this still more important and more public effort, where she worked with Warnecke, JFK's old friend, and with other members of Warnecke's acclaimed firm, as well as with officers of the U.S. Army Corps of Engineers who were in charge of the construction.

The major difference between the Rose Garden and the Kennedy tomb jobs, however, was the amount of construction at Arlington that had already taken place by the time Bunny was called in. Eventually, with great effort and at considerable cost, gleaming white marble gave way to granite from Maine, the tough New England stuff used throughout the nation for war monuments, banks, government buildings, and seawalls.

"Since we are anxious to get the white marble changed or softened down, would you be good enough to have one of the squares on the job done in a 9-point finish?" runs a September 1966 memo from Bunny to Michael Painter. To do the work, Bunny chose a D.C. stone company that had been "so helpful to me in an earlier project," perhaps the Mellons' Trinity Episcopal Church in Upperville.

After a look at an unsuccessful marble sample, Wheeler wrote to Bunny, "It seems that now 'they' are more than willing to cover the white marble with gray granite or any other stone you decide on." It wasn't until five years after the assassination, however, that bulldozers arrived to take away the last of the Vermont marble used for steps and platforms, replacing it with Vinalhaven, Maine, granite at a cost of $77,180, not including "the resodding, replacing of shrubbery, etc., that may be damaged or destroyed while performing the above work."

The plan for the actual grave plot on the rectangular top level was also revised: the first idea had been to plant it with fescue, the grass JFK himself had tried so carefully to protect in the Rose Garden. In the scrapbook documenting the creation of the Rose Garden that Jackie gave Bunny in the spring of 1963, Jackie wrote, "He has had barricades made—and placed at gaps in the hedge, to keep his family, his animals, and the members of his administration from wearing a path in the grass." But it turned out that fescue didn't take heat well, turning spotty and brown.

Luck and Bunny's exacting eye led to a more inspired solution than grass of any kind. In the summer of 1966 on Cape Cod, the place that Kennedy had loved, she spotted an old barn foundation of pinkish-gray granite. As was often the case, Bunny's joy at finding something perfect was infectious: O. D. Garland, the Falmouth, Massachusetts, antiques dealer who shipped the stone, jubilated that a current load he was trucking to Virginia would be "even more beautiful!"

In Upperville, Charles Hanback, the contractor responsible for Trinity Episcopal Church, prepared the stones to fit the pattern Bunny had created for the tomb. A memo from Bunny to Michael Painter directs "Hanback's bill for stonework, etc.," to go to her.

Bunny and Jackie together found the right vessel for the eternal flame: an old millstone of the same rosy Falmouth granite as the pavement. In 1967, John Warnecke congratulated Bunny, writing that he had "lived with the flame as a design element for the better part of three years now" and that the "great, old, round stone in its straightforward simplicity couldn't be more perfect." Bunny wrote back, putting her finger on exactly why the stone had special significance for Kennedy's burial site, "as it comes from Cape Cod and is a symbol of simple men, the sea, and history." (Jackie had called her husband, who had served heroically in the U.S. Navy, a "simple man.") Ever practical, Bunny also wrote, "It may, however, need a lining of some sort of metal to protect it, and I am discussing that with Perry [Wheeler] and Colonel Charles this morning."

How the millstone would fit into the pavement was key. A model, full-size if possible, was part of Bunny's process for any important design element, whether for a kitchen wall for her house on Nantucket that would be mocked up ten times in plywood, or a scale model of a garden pavilion. (Landscape gardener Beatrix Farrand and her client Mildred Bliss had done the same thing for features at the Blisses' Georgetown estate, Dumbarton Oaks.) Bunny wanted to make sure the proportions in "real life" were what she envisioned, and she had the time and money to experiment and revise her design at full size on the ground.

When I saw the photograph of a curious feature half-sunk in the surface of the old family graveyard at Oak Spring in Linda Holden's *The Gardens of Bunny Mellon*, I had to smile. I'd seen it often, walking with Eliza up to the cemetery, a good place to catch a breeze. I had thought it was a cover for some sort of underground cistern but never thought to ask Bunny about it. Suddenly I realized it was Bunny's "mock-up" of the Kennedy grave site! Among the trees and the graves of men and women who had once farmed Oak Spring sat a mossy square of rough-cut granite pavers centered with a worn millstone.

After many trials, in early February 1967, the perfected gas nozzle for the eternal flame was brought to Arlington, where an expert from the Institute of Gas Technology installed it. At last various jerry-built solutions for keeping the eternal flame "eternal" had given way to a permanent one that would withstand the elements—although nothing could prevent chance events like the group of Catholic schoolchildren putting out the flame while trying to bless it with holy water. In the Garden Library are copies of eight letters about the flame, whose height shrank from eight inches to three as the effect was trialed over the following summer. Army Corps of Engineers correspondence seems most concerned that the flame be visible from a maximum distance, which to others on the project didn't seem the main point.

For Jackie, who in 1961 had stood by her husband's side with Charles de Gaulle at the Arc de Triomphe's Tomb of the Unknown Soldier, the Arlington flame stood for the "something living" that she wanted for her husband's memory. With an elegance of style that meant so much to Jackie (and to Bunny), the French had solved the difficulty of "eternity" by having a veteran come every evening to rekindle the flame in a stark but dignified ceremony.

Bunny also wanted to soften the grave's appearance. Granite edges were ground down at her suggestion, while billowing *Osmanthus fragrans*, one of her favorite hedging choices, replaced a wall. A small moat also vanished. She nixed lowering the stone border around the grave platform: "I tried your suggestion of lowering the stone border but . . . it created yet again the hard, sharp line we were trying to avoid," Bunny wrote to Warnecke. In the same letter, she set out what I consider to be her guiding principle for any project: "Landscaping is often not following a set of plans, but rather of creating a feeling. This can only be done by degrees, the finding and planting of key trees, followed with other more available ones."

In designing her own gardens and landscapes or those of her friends, Bunny did not operate at the pace of a professional working on commission. Sometimes she must have driven Warnecke and the rest of the firm crazy. In Perry Wheeler's papers is one very brief, undated note to that effect. Wheeler asked someone—perhaps Warnecke—if he should show some plan or drawing to Mrs. Mellon. Scrawled in large letters in blue marker is the answer: "NO."

Over the course of several years JFK's tomb and the approach to it were nestled among flowering trees. "The men working on this project

The Watering Can, 1913, by Roger de la Fresnaye (1885–1925), 35 × 79 in.
(National Gallery of Art, Collection of Mr. and Mrs. Paul Mellon)

The front hall, Oak Spring, Upperville, Virginia (Michael Dunne Photography)

TOP: A cheerful Cubist work announcing Bunny's passion for the garden dominates the entryway room. BOTTOM: A plain brick floor and a settee ready to receive coats, hats, boots, shooting sticks, and what have you speak to a life of easy country comfort—and style.

The living room, Oak Spring (Michael Dunne Photography)

Green Wheat Fields, Auvers, 1890, by
Vincent van Gogh (1853–1890),
28½ × 36 in. (National Gallery of Art,
Collection of Mr. and Mrs. Paul Mellon)

*Still Life of Oranges and Lemons with
Blue Gloves*, 1889, by Vincent van Gogh
(1853–1890), 18⅞ × 24⁷⁄₁₆ in. (National
Gallery of Art, Collection of
Mr. and Mrs. Paul Mellon)

Sunny slipcovers, no-color walls, regular placement of comfortable furniture—
even the handsome clutter of daily life—all recede in the presence of one of the
most famous and best-loved Impressionist works hanging nonchalantly over
the mantel. Look left for *another* Van Gogh, in which worn blue gardening
gloves bring Bunny Mellon to mind.

Warwick Castle, 1748–1749, by Canaletto (Giovanni Antonio Canal) (1697–1768), 28½ × 47³⁄₁₆ in. (Yale Center for British Art, Paul Mellon Collection)

Paul Mellon's New York City study (Michael Dunne Photography)

Paul Mellon could glance up from his New York City desk to join the strollers, fishermen, and a pensive dog, at right, in the imaginary world he loved best, eighteenth-century rural England.

1969 (winter blue), 1969, by Ben Nicholson (1894–1982), 32⅝ × 33 in.
(Yale Center for British Art, Paul Mellon Collection)

Dune Cottage, Oyster Harbors, Cape Cod (Michael Dunne Photography)

A spare seaside retreat is furnished with New England country furniture and calmed by the soft geometries of Nicholson's blue, brown, and white. Jackie Kennedy Onassis and Bunny spent many hours here together.

Jasmine (Breath of Spring) (necklace); Jean Schlumberger (1907–1987), Tiffany Schlumberger, France; colored sapphires, diamonds, 18 karat gold, and platinum; 1966 (model 1962); 1¾ × 19 in. (Virginia Museum of Fine Arts, Collection of Mrs. Paul Mellon, 2015.77 / Photograph by Travis Fuller)

A necklace fit for a queen: The forthright bling of sapphires contrasts with naturalistic diamond tendrils, buds, and blooms, a design powered by the artist-jeweler's force of imagination.

A Young Daughter of the Picts, ca. 1585, by Jacques Le Moyne de Morgues (ca. 1533–1588), 10¼ × 7⅜ in. (Yale Center for British Art, Paul Mellon Collection)

A force of nature: This rare late-sixteenth-century drawing is no portrait of Bunny—or of any real person—but among the flowers on her "body suit" are Bunny's favorite blue cornflowers at waist and wrist. The artist Le Moyne was attached to a French colonizing expedition in 1564 that visited the Timucua of Florida, whose women tattooed their bodies.

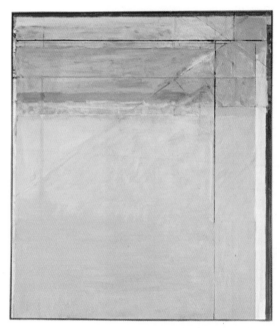

Ocean Park #61, 1973, by Richard Diebenkorn (1922–1993), 93 × 81 in.
(Property from the Collection of Mrs. Paul Mellon, Sotheby's, 2014)

"Shells" (pill box), late twentieth century, Jean Schlumberger (1907–1987), Tiffany &
Company (manufacturer), 18 karat gold and shells, ⅝ × 1⅜ × 1⅜ in. (Virginia Museum of
Fine Arts, Collection of Mrs. Paul Mellon, 2015.152 / Photograph by Travis Fullerton)

Painting and pillbox share startlingly rich worked surfaces and eloquently
rigorous form, pared to ultimate simplicity. Diebenkorn's successive limpid
glazes do not hide what lies beneath; the surface of the box only slowly reveals
the tidal beach. The Diebenkorn is one of eight that Bunny owned; her collection
of Schlumberger extended to close to a thousand pieces.

Untitled, No. 20 (*Yellow Expanse*), 1953, by Mark Rothko, 117 × 175 in.,
shown here in the Garden Library (Photograph by Clive Boursnell)

"Chaque collection doit avoir sa maîtresse," said Givenchy to his new friend Bunny;
this Rothko indeed crowned her collection.

Roses de Nice on a Table, 1882, by Henri Fantin-Latour (1836–1904), 10⅜ × 16½ in.
(National Gallery of Art, Collection of Mr. and Mrs. Paul Mellon)

Embroidered silk evening shoes on a George III Axminster carpet
(Property from the Collection of Mrs. Paul Mellon, Sotheby's, 2014)

A heap of old roses took pride of place on the wall of Bunny's private office at the top of her library tower—and her bold understanding of such suffused color sometimes swept down to the tips of her shoes.

The Basket House at Oak Spring, exterior

The Basket House at Oak Spring, interior

The harmonious exterior offers no clue to the chaos of creation that occasionally overcame the interior. In Georges Braque's powerful painting, one of a series titled *Les oiseaux*, a bird flies on serenely against the moon.

Newmarket Heath, with the King's stables rubbing house at the finish of the Beacon Course, ca. 1765, by George Stubbs (1724–1806), 12 × 16 in. (Yale Center for British Art, Paul Mellon Collection)

The art critic Tom Lubbock, writing for *The Independent*, observed that the empty turf racecourse George Stubbs depicted is "bathed in a soft morning light, like holy ground, like a famous battlefield," then added: "A picture of nothing? Stubbs' painting is one of the greatest compliments ever paid to a place."

Mechanical building at South Pasture, Nantucket, Massachusetts (Photograph by Daniel Sutherland)

Bunny used the elegant hipped roof, a standard stripped-down architectural form, for outbuildings. Space, light, and the horizon line were the starting points for any landscape or garden she designed.

Le saladier, by Nicolas de Staël (1914–1955), 21½ × 25½ in.
(Property from the Collection of Mrs. Paul Mellon, Sotheby's, 2014)

15, rue de l'Université, interior (Oak Spring Garden Foundation, Upperville, Virginia)

The artist's celebration of the simplest of the domestic arts—fresh lettuce in a bowl, waiting to be dressed—followed Bunny from one dining room to another in her Paris apartments, and then to Oak Spring.

Chez la modiste, by Edgar Degas (1834–1917), 24¼ × 29 in. (Virginia Museum of Fine Arts, Collection of Mr. and Mrs. Paul Mellon, 2001.27 / Photograph by Travis Fullerton)

Reflection, self-reflection, a woman absorbed in herself, a painter ultimately absorbed in abstraction—one of Degas's best works was hung in each of Bunny's Paris apartments in turn, but never in any other of her homes.

Marguerites, by Vincent van Gogh (1853–1890), 13 × 16½ in. (Virginia Museum of Fine Arts, Collection of Mr. and Mrs. Paul Mellon, 2014.207 / Photograph by Travis Fullerton)

Bunny so loved Van Gogh's handful of daisies that she hung it in her private Oak Spring bathroom, where it remained above the bathtub, steaming gently for years without any severe damage.

The bar corner, Oak Spring
(Property from the Collection
of Mrs. Paul Mellon, Sotheby's,
2014)

*A Still Life Study of Insects
on a Sprig of Rosemary, with
Butterflies, a Bumble Bee,
Beetles and Other Insects*,
1653, by Jan van Kessel the
Elder (1626–1679),
4½ × 5½ in. (Property from
the Collection of Mrs. Paul
Mellon, Sotheby's, 2014)

In the living room, a tiny nature study such as this hung on the wall next to
Bunny's usual seat by the fire.

George Moore in the Artist's Garden, ca. 1879, by Édouard Manet (1832–1883),
21½ × 17¾ in. (National Gallery of Art, Collection of Mr. and Mrs. Paul Mellon)

One of the great trove of French nineteenth-century paintings collected by
the Mellons, Manet's searching portrait of his friend the Irish writer adds
informality to the severe and magnificent French dining room.

125 East Seventieth Street, a table set for dinner (Michael Dunne Photography)

Bespoke French linens, French wines, and the practical French habit of upholstering dining chairs in leather.

A George III–style cream-painted standing bookcase at Oak Spring
(Property from the Collection of Mrs. Paul Mellon, Sotheby's, 2014)

A George III–style cream-painted standing bookcase at Colefax & Fowler
in London in the 1940s (Photograph courtesy of Barrie McIntyre)

In the late 1940s, one of Bunny's earliest forays at Colefax & Fowler, the British
decorating firm that dominated twentieth-century elite taste, produced a Gothic
china bookcase. Bunny sheared off the crocketed top and loaded the shelves with
a choice selection of her important porcelains.

are highly qualified and understand this form of landscape planting," Bunny assured Warnecke. Irvin Williams found some specimens on Daingerfield Island in the Potomac River, where they had found three of the Rose Garden magnolias; Perry Williams and Everett Hicks selected other trees and shrubs at nurseries Bunny often used. Hicks, an arboriculturist, also wrote to her with a long-term maintenance plan for every plant on the site.

Everett Hicks, recognizable as one of those long, lean arborists who seem to ascend trees as easily as angels ascend clouds, came into Bunny's employ as a seasoned professional from the Davey Tree Expert Company in 1961 and remained until 1989, when he retired. During those twenty-eight years, he worked with Bunny on all of the Mellon properties in the United States and Antigua and absorbed all the flora and climate information needed for each location. Hicks had shaped the magnolias in the Rose Garden before working on the Kennedy grave.

In late November 1966, Bunny extended her reach over the job still further to shaping the topography of the site. She directed the grading of the big grass circle herself, to the embarrassment of the Army Corps of Engineers and Warnecke's firm. The gifted Michael Painter was tasked with writing a handsome "eat crow" letter. "I think the grading of the 'great circle' area at the Kennedy grave worked out beautifully," he wrote. "Your idea of the grading of this space was excellent, and your supervision of the work was very skillful." He went on: "It was not until November 19 that I learned you had directed the work yourself . . . Unfortunately, it was not until October 26 that the Army Corps of Engineers finally accepted the idea that the work be personally directed in the field in lieu of the work being staked out by surveyors working from engineering type drawings."

Painter had already worked with Jackie Kennedy on John Warnecke's successful design of Lafayette Square Park facing the White House, so he knew how to work with bureaucrats such as the Army Corps of Engineers. They had charge of the Arlington site and provided the labor for the installation; nonetheless, his frustration shows through in this letter. Still, there was little room for overt disagreement over such a weighty public project, and the letters between Warnecke and Bunny are professional in tone. (Bunny's are polite but firm as she communicates her ideas.)

Letters continued to go back and forth between Bunny and Warnecke as the day for the project's completion neared. He wrote to Bunny on March 14, 1967, congratulating her on the choice of the millstone and the site plantings that Perry Wheeler and Everett Hicks were continuing to carry out. He suggested a "final review" very soon with all parties involved.

That evening Kennedy's casket and those of his infant children were quietly exhumed from the temporary grave some twenty feet up the steep hill that led to Arlington House, where they had lain for more than four years, and were brought to their permanent resting place. The pink granite pavers shaped to fit Bunny's pattern were carefully fitted over them. The eternal flame flickered from the millstone.

At seven o'clock the next morning Cardinal Richard Cushing of Boston, the Kennedys' old friend who had married Jack Kennedy and Jacqueline Bouvier fifteen years before, blessed the site. A driving spring rain drenched the private gathering attended only by Jackie, members of the Kennedy family, and President Johnson. The entire ceremony took twenty minutes.

Bunny answered Warnecke's letter promptly, the day after the interment. She wrote that it wouldn't be necessary to bring Painter back east from California at this time: "There is very little more we can do until fall, as we are at the end of the planting season." Covering all bases, she noted that everyone was "on schedule with the promised work, and both Secretary McNamara and Jackie seem pleased. Any meeting, therefore, would not be necessary before midsummer. *This will also give me time to grade and work out the hill below the Lee Mansion* [Arlington House], *which is so important to Jackie . . .*" [italics mine]. Some grading of the hill to soften its steepness had been done, but the site still looked precipitous, and the columns of Arlington House rising above it were cut off at the wrong angle. Bunny copied all principals involved—McNamara, Wheeler, Lieutenant Colonel Charles of the Army Corps of Engineers, Everett Hicks, and of course, Jackie.

Jackie wrote to Bunny on March 17, sending her a news photo of the gravestone and the bunches of flowers they had laid on her husband's gravestone, perhaps on the day after the interment. "This is what I wish I could paint for you," she begins. "Your flowers"—which were the blue cornflowers both she and Bunny loved—"are on the left, then McNamara's lily of the valley, then Bobby's carnation [Bobby Kennedy]—and my lily of the valley" and then a "little handful of crumpled moss" from one of Bobby Kennedy's daughters. She finished by saying "I keep thinking of Cardinal Cushing's prayer—'Be at peace, dear Jack, with your tiny infants by your side, until we all meet again—above this hill and beyond the stars.' He said that because of the way you made 'this hill.'"

ROBERT KENNEDY, IN a letter written shortly after his brother's death, had told Bunny that she was "the single most influential individual in President John Kennedy's administration. President Kennedy spent more time worrying about the Rose Garden and how the two of you were going to manage it than he did about the Cuban missile crisis or Berlin and what he and Bob McNamara or Dean Rusk were going to do." (Construction of the Berlin Wall began in August 1961, just as President Kennedy was listening to Bunny at the picnic table.) Robert Kennedy concluded, "In addition—you made everything cheerful and pleasant—for him and everyone—So from all of us, thank you and Love, Bobby."

The playfulness and tenderness of this brief letter are characteristic of the lightness that Bunny—and the Kennedy brothers and Jackie—were somehow able to conjure up even at somber moments. From childhood onward, Bunny had learned how to downsize important events in order to be able to deal with them capably. RFK's tenderness for her was a feeling she returned with a clarity of affection she shared with only a few people in her life.

His death in June 1968, two months after that of Martin Luther King, Jr., brought back to Jackie all the lost hopes they had had for those brief "shining years." In a long letter she wrote to Bunny soon after Robert Kennedy's funeral train had slowly rolled to Washington, the tracks lined with "all the people who had no other friend—who loved Bobby" and with "the poor hopeless ones who had lost Dr. King," the widow turned to her greatest friend and thanked her, not just for the Rose Garden, but for helping her husband, the president, comprehend that a garden is more than flowers—it can stand as a symbol. "You did that for him . . . he wouldn't have known how without you." For Jackie the Rose Garden expressed all that JFK had "hoped our country could be as it had been dreamed at the beginning."

The double tragedy—first Reverend King, then Bobby, Jackie's chief support after her husband's death, the one in whom rested the nation's hope that the dream would go forward—opened Jackie's wounds afresh. That August, on the Cape, two months after she had written her long letter to Bunny, Jackie realized that one last symbolic action remained to make her husband's grave complete. She wrote to Jean Schlumberger, who had been asked to design a grave plaque carved with a wreath of flowers. The project had been set aside, she said, apologizing for the delay—"we were too wounded." She asked that he add a cornflower, the blazingly blue country flower that was one of Bunny's emblems, as a tribute to her loyal friend who had helped her shape and comprehend the hours, days, months, and years of sorrow and loss. In the end, only the drawing remains. The plaque was never made, as if it were too much for the unembellished grave site. As if enough had already been said.

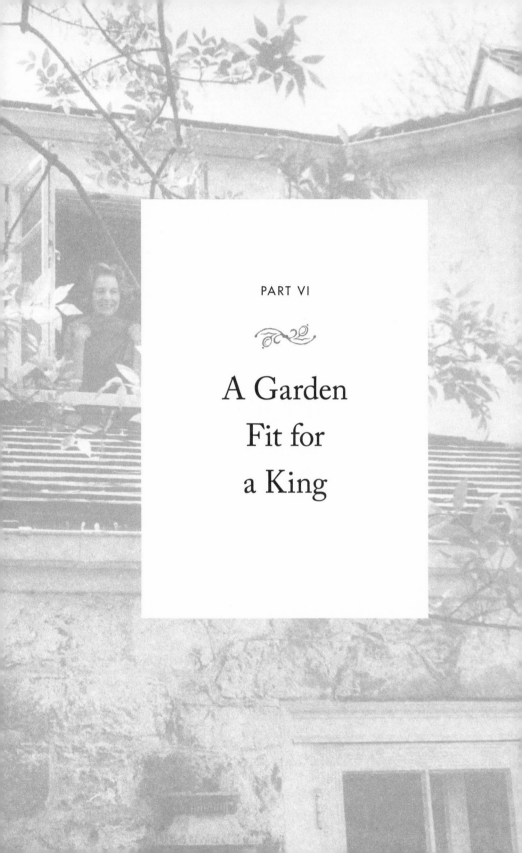

PART VI

A Garden
Fit for
a King

21

Le Potager du Roi

By 1971, Bunny had done it. She had an apartment of her own in Paris. Paul had been against it; Stoddard Stevens, her husband's foremost legal counsel and a fierce guardian of Paul's fortune, had been against it. Her European axis hadn't begun to shift to Paris away from her old friends in England until the 1950s, when she met the first two of her Three Musketeers of Style: Schlumberger and Balenciaga. Until she bought her 84, avenue Foch apartment, she would take rooms at the Crillon for herself and her maid when she came for fittings with Balenciaga and then, after 1968, with the third "Musketeer," Hubert de Givenchy.

Givenchy gave her entrée to a Paris beyond her schoolgirl imaginings. It was he who had helped her find her first Paris apartment and then her second, at 15, rue de l'Université. His secretary, Janette Mahler at the House of Givenchy, often carried out Bunny's personal commissions. Hubert himself introduced her to artists and gallerists and antiques dealers and restaurants and the world of the haut monde who were only too delighted to meet Madame Bunny Mellon.

The world of couture, of course, had already heard whispers about the size of her orders, but in 1971 she was probably best known as the wife of the American millionaire Paul Mellon, whose diminutive bay colt Mill Reef had crossed the English Channel in October to win the world's richest Thoroughbred race, the Arc de Triomphe. Like the English Grand National (which Mill Reef also won in 1971) and the Kentucky Derby, the Arc is a national cultural event, not just a horse race. The stands at Longchamps in the Bois de Boulogne were jammed with what James Brown, writing for *The New York Times*, called "the swells, the greats, and others" who had flown in from all over the sporting world, as well as the president of France, Georges Pompidou, and his wife.

Bunny's husband was also a well-known international public figure in the worlds of art collecting and philanthropy. Although her intimate French circle was small, and she only rarely appeared at grand events, she was acquainted with some of the other celebrated American women who had married European aristocrats and moved there. She already knew Pauline Potter, who had worked as head of the couture division of Hattie Carnegie in the forties, when Bunny had been a customer, and who later became the Baroness de Rothschild. Joan Dillon, granddaughter of Treasury Secretary C. Douglas Dillon, a member of the Kennedys' inner circle in the early sixties, became the Duchess of Mouchy and Poix. Unlike these social icons, Bunny Mellon had been more of a legend than an actual figure in France.

Shortly after she bought her first Paris apartment, Hubert introduced her to what would become her most important French project, the restoration of the Potager du Roi, the vegetable garden of the king of France. As Bunny told *House & Garden* in 1988 in an article called "Mrs. Mellon's Secret Garden," she and Hubert had spent a cold afternoon in Versailles—not at the Sun King's vast, glittering palace but at the farmers' market, shopping for vegetables, cheese, and fruit.

As they were finishing up, Hubert suddenly said, "Come with me." They drove a few blocks and left the car in a dark, narrow street. Without telling her where they were going, he led her into a courtyard enclosed by ancient, white-stuccoed stone houses and up the front steps of one whose front door was unlocked. The house seemed deserted. Without asking any questions about where they were, she followed Hubert inside and down an empty corridor to another door, a glass one. "It was late autumn, a faint mist was beginning to shorten the last light of day," she recalled, and through that mist and raking light she saw "an uninterrupted space so great that a far row of houses beyond a wall was silhouetted by the glow of the departing sun."

Out that door and down "a pebbled ramp covered with moss and dried leaves" they walked, into "a forest of espaliered fruit trees towering high on the surrounding walls . . . where . . . pears hung from the small twigs that climbed the walls or covered the trellises" that outlined beds of winter vegetables.

Hubert was already aware that Bunny, by then famous for her work at the White House, never went into any of her gardens without a pair of secateurs in her pocket and that pruning a fruit tree was her special joy and skill. Hubert must also have known of her love for fairy tales and her fascination with Alain-Fournier's *Le Grand Meaulnes*. He may also have sensed that, to anchor her new life in France, she would need a project. Standing in the centuries-old royal kitchen garden without knowing what it was, Bunny was nonetheless spellbound: "For one who had struggled with this form of horticulture, the garden had the unreality of a dream."

On they walked, through "acres of thoughtfully pruned fruit trees and carefully tended vegetables . . . standard trees of plums, apricots, and apples" that "had been pruned that day, leaving wreaths of small branches on the ground where the mist had formed droplets of water that glistened." The gardening staff, even in the face of the crumbling walls and general desuetude of the vast garden, were plying their skills. Bunny and Hubert traveled on through stone-roofed tunnels "cluttered with wheelbarrows and watering cans" that were connected to yet other gardens, "walled rooms of small grass-filled meadows with now and then low wild white asters." Hubert said nothing. He did not explain the garden or disturb the silence; he "understood the pleasure and the mystery of adventure." At last they circled back to a closed gate that stood "at the end of a wide walk between two high walls covered with ripe pears . . . The gate held the secret to the garden. Woven into its painted blue ironwork held together with rust but still bordered with gold were the initials of Louis XIV."

Here was the misty forest of Charles Perrault's "Sleeping Beauty" come to life. Here were the trees like "gnarled old men with their hands in the air" that her first husband, Stacy Lloyd, had seen at a garden in England, trees like the ones that Bunny was then slowly shaping into an arbor at Oak Spring. And here Bunny had also unmistakably found what she would later describe as "a gardener's conception of *Le Grand*

Meaulnes," her own private vision of a mist-wrapped France that never was.

In the Oak Spring Garden Library is an undated guidebook—a leaflet—"Monsieur de la Quintinye à la Grille du Roy," a guidebook that Bunny inscribed with her name and the date: Paris 1972, which must mark the date of her first visit. It would take a quarter of a century for the two friends to carry out what was to be Bunny's new project.

After that first visit to the Potager du Roi, Bunny started thinking more broadly about kitchen gardens. She began to collect books related to the gardener of the king's *potager*, Jean-Baptiste de La Quintinie. The undeniable decay of the garden as she first saw it with Hubert worked on her active mind. She began to think about taking it on as a project. She researched her 1988 article heavily and wrote a dozen drafts; by 1990 she was developing a plan.

It's such an innocent midcentury American thing to do: fix things that need fixing, just as the Marshall Plan did for Europe after World War II. Still, those in charge at Versailles soon realized that Madame Mellon was *special.* It was as if she were born for this task. A *potager* must be practical and well designed, and it depends on gritty handwork. Bunny also knew how to find the experts and how to woo additional financing. In 1990 the preservation world still believed that having taste and money gave an individual permission to commandeer public spaces. (It would be impossible today, for example, for one person to take over the restoration of Notre-Dame Cathedral.)

With the *potager,* Bunny had also hit on a gardening trend that would bloom in the 1980s. The idea of a plot for growing fruits, vegetables, and herbs as an important part of any upscale country house came about partly because the gardener Rosemary Verey, after the death of her husband in 1984, turned professional and began to design ornamental kitchen plots like her own at Barnsley House in Gloucester, England (inspired by the early-twentieth-century one at the Château de Villandry in France), for American and British clients. The fame of the Potager du Roi would spread the style still further.

Louis XIV's kitchen garden is wedged between the town of Versailles, the south flank of the château, and the "Pièce d'Eau des

Suisses," a forty-acre ornamental pond designed by the landscape architect André Le Nôtre that extends the château's southern vista. The earth from the excavation that was carved out by the King's Swiss Guards from 1679 to 1682 to create the new pond was dumped as fill into the swampy ground that would become the *potager*.

After the king and his entire court moved permanently from Paris to Versailles, the palace population stood constantly at about three thousand. It was the king's duty to feed his court as well as himself. The old produce garden of a mere ten acres at what had been Louis XIII's simple hunting lodge at Versailles was clearly inadequate, so Jean-Baptiste de La Quintinie went to work in 1678 laying out the twenty-three acres of what is the *potager* today, although, even in full production mode with a staff of thirty gardeners, much of the court's food was brought in from outside.

The *potager*, which is as geometric as any other section of the Versailles gardens, is divided into squares—some large, some small— and among these are the walled grassy plots centered with a single fruit tree and starred with the last white asters that Bunny and Hubert walked through. Some of the squares and avenues are set off by Belgian fences: dwarf fruit trees planted at regular intervals and tied onto five-foot-tall *V*-shaped wooden trellises. Eventually the branches grow to cross one another and make a diagonal lattice pattern. Surrounding other beds are low cordons, little trees grown on single main stems about two feet tall that branch out to either side to touch the adjoining cordons. Together these tree-training methods can produce an amazing amount of fruit in a small space. A big shallow pool, a *bassin*, or bowl, lies in the middle of what is called *le grand carré*, the central quadrangle.

As in the other garden features of Versailles, the final touch of enchantment had once been supplied by a fountain: a sparkling *jet d'eau*. By the time of Bunny's visit, it no longer spouted above vegetables and fruits. But still ripening on trees and against walls were many kinds of fruits in season, including the thin-skinned green *bon Chrétien* pears and the misshapen, fragrant yellow Calville *blanc d'hiver* apple, which is sometimes eaten with knife and fork for dessert in France. Today tons of those apples and pears, along with a wide range of vegetables in their season, are sold from the back entrance to the *potager* on rue Hardy while the rest goes to wholesale markets. The entire operation is overseen by the French national schools of horticulture and landscaping.

On the back of the photograph of gardeners gathering apples at the Potager du Roi, Bunny proudly noted, "Gift of the gardeners."

Nicolas Fouquet, the finance minister of France, had dared to build a château, Vaux-le-Vicomte, bigger than anything the twenty-two-year-old King Louis XIV had imagined for himself, with gardens that were just as spectacular. In 1661, Fouquet's great fête, held at Vaux, was the last straw. The minister was removed from his post for embezzlement and was ultimately banished for life. The king carted off his former official's tapestries and statues and even his potted orange trees. He also appropriated the artists who had created Vaux. The architect Louis Le Vau, the garden designer André Le Nôtre, and the painter Charles Le Brun were dispatched to Versailles to make the king an even bigger, better palace. The king also nabbed Fouquet's talented head kitchen gardener.

Before he began work on the *potager* garden at Versailles, Jean-Baptiste de La Quintinie had trained as a lawyer, then worked for an aristocratic family in Paris as a tutor, then had become that family's gardener when he found his true interest: horticulture. After travels in Italy to see the famous gardens there, he visited England to see what his fellow countryman André Mollet, royal gardener to the Stuart kings, was doing. (The English king asked La Quintinie to stay and work for him, but the Frenchman said no.) He had also created *potager* gardens for various dukes and princes—and for the minister of finance, Colbert, who had succeeded Fouquet. His fame as a master gardener grew: Colbert presented La Quintinie to his monarch in 1670 and created a position especially for him: *directeur des jardins fruitiers et potagers de toutes les maisons royales.*

Not for another seven years, however, did work on the new kitchen garden begin in earnest. From then until his death on the job in 1688, La Quintinie worked intensively on growing every kind of produce in and out of season, early and late, using walls to catch the heat of the sun and as windbreaks to protect tender plants.

He was obsessed with discovering new techniques for coaxing plants to produce the most appealing, the most delicious fruits and vegetables—and the most unobtainable. He kept notes on every aspect of gardening: planting and transplanting, amending and preparing the soil, installing drainage systems—a must on the swampy site—and experimenting with new plants as they began to arrive from all over the world. He kept an eye out for what varieties were best, and, above all, he learned about grafting.

Grafting—inserting exactly the right kind of young twig of one tree under the bark of a rootstock of another so the transplant, known as the scion, will grow as if it were on its own roots—was considered the highest of the garden arts. It is not quite as simple as it sounds, and for a culture not so very far away from the Middle Ages, it seemed a bit like magic.

Bunny, a dedicated reader of fairy tales, had grown up beguiled by the sprites, goblins, and monstrous twining trees and roots of the fantastical twentieth-century English illustrator Arthur Rackham. In what seems like an implausible twinning of fairy tale and the story of the Potager du Roi, Paul Mellon had bought the entire contents of Rackham's studio in 1971 as a present for his wife . . . and only a year later Bunny found herself walking through a mysterious glass door into what for her was the reality of that world.

One of La Quintinie's friends was Charles Perrault, who invented a new literary genre, the fairy tale, writing *The Tales of Mother Goose* (which included "Cinderella," "Sleeping Beauty," "Puss in Boots," and others). Perrault had been Colbert's assistant and was La Quintinie's fellow member in the French Academy of Sciences. When La Quintinie's book, *De l'instruction des jardins fruitiers & potagers*, was edited and published by his son Michel two years after his father's death, Charles Perrault wrote a dedicatory poem. In 1984, in the midst of her research on the Potager du Roi, Bunny bought a copy of La Quintinie's book, a first edition stamped with the magnificent royal coat of arms of Louis XIV's brother, Philippe d'Orléans.

Much later, once the project was well underway, Bunny wrote to one of those working with her on the restoration, Bertrand du Vignaud de Villefort, that she had seen the garden "in the spirit of the ancient Fairy Tales . . . It was like a silent treasure for me. Jean de La Quintinie became one of my dear Historical friends along with Robert Louis Stevenson & Thomas Jefferson."

Bunny herself knew all the different ways that people learn to garden: by making play gardens as a solitary child, by observing Jacob Sloet of the Olmsted firm at her father's place in Princeton when she was an equally solitary teenager, by reading all the books she could find on the subject, and from actual practice.

La Quintinie, a fan of classical writers such as Pliny the Elder, had learned about gardens in much the same way. In her *House & Garden* article, Bunny wrote about her idol, La Quintinie, noting that he would "spend his free hours in the study of botanical and agricultural books."

Louis XIV, who loved to stroll around his gardens with his retinue, wrote *La Manière de Montrer les Jardins de Versailles*, his own guide to exactly where to walk and where to pause to see his favorite views. The king loved to survey the checkerboard of his *potager* garden from the broad terrace that the architect who succeeded Le Vau, Jules Hardouin-Mansart, had built on the south side of the château.

Today a statue of La Quintinie surveys the garden from that

high post. In his left hand, against his breast, he holds a skinny little branch—a fruit tree graft ready to insert—and in his right, a grafting knife: he is ready to perform the magical work of transmuting one kind of tree into another.

When the king visited his gardener, he walked through the blue and gold gate twined with his initials that one of the top metalworkers of the day, Alexis Fordrin, had forged for him—the only original iron gate remaining at Versailles. By the time Bunny saw the gate in 1972, it was rusted shut. The *bassin* was crumbling, and the walls carrying their precious hand-wrought tracery of fruit trees were decaying.

Could she wave a magic wand over the place to restore it to its former glory?

She could, but it took a lot of waving. She and Hubert traveled to see other *potager* gardens, including the one at Vaux that La Quintinie had designed for Fouquet before his fall. Ever thorough, Bunny sent a draft of her *House & Garden* article to her friend and enthusiastic admirer Emmanuel "Bobby" de Margerie, who "went over it with me to check out any historical mistakes etc." De Margerie, who had been head of the museums of France since 1975 (and later served as ambassador to the United States), subsequently introduced Bunny to the director of the Versailles museum complex, Jean-Pierre Babelon.

In the summer of 1990, Bunny wrote to Babelon about the Potager du Roi: with her help, she suggested, "the garden might be returned to its original perfection." Babelon was eager for her assistance. He invited her on a tour of the *potager* and also showed her a brilliantly realized model of one of the great fountain showpieces of Versailles's gardens: the Encelade. Babelon might also have wanted to test if she wished to go further in restoring the gardens of Versailles. But Bunny essentially said, "No, I'm interested in the Potager."

Bunny proposed that the first step to raise interest and attract funders for the restoration would be to commission a model of the *potager*, which, she suggested, would be "within her possibilities" to donate. By September of that year she had written to Versailles's chief architect, Pierre-André Lablaude, to commission the maquette.

Nothing could have delighted a woman who took dollhouses

seriously all her life more than this undertaking. Upstairs in her Oak Spring Garden Library, a Victorian dollhouse—one of several she owned—stands in a window, flanked on one wall by a portrait of the nineteenth-century Kentucky statesman Henry Clay and on the other by a large closed bookcase filled with Paul's gift, the volumes of fairy tales illustrated by Arthur Rackham. Practical as Bunny often was, the boundary between reality and make-believe could still become as joyfully permeable as the looking glass Alice scrambled through—or the glass door Hubert opened leading into the *potager*. In a dollhouse or in the model of the Potager du Roi, Bunny could immerse herself in a tiny world where she was in complete control.

By early July 1991 the model, which included a number of small human figures, was finished. But two weeks later a dissatisfied Bunny asked Lablaude if he "could change the figures?" She and Hubert felt they were "not as exquisite as the Jardin itself." Lablaude wrote back that, as per Bunny's wishes, the figures of "the gardeners and the horse-carriage that add an 'agricole' touch" would remain, but he would remove the figures of "le marquis et la marquise" as Mrs. Mellon had asked.

Bunny remained the rare person who had retained her childhood sense of the importance and possibilities of imaginative play. She did not want company in this imaginary garden. *She* was to be the only visitor who entered through the king's gate. *She*, not some marquise, would walk the rows of the *potager*. The gardeners, however, were to be honored.

In the hours that she spent in the real *potager*, she worked along-side the present-day gardeners. Whatever her hurdles with the French language—and they were considerable—she got to know the skilled, knowledgeable men who worked there. She worked *with* them, almost as an apprentice; they must have taught her some of the finer points of La Quintinie's book, by hand and on the ground. This was exactly what she loved—the biggest of visions and the finest points of craft.

Hubert de Givenchy was crucial to the project. As one of the top couturiers in the world, let alone Paris, he made the Potager du Roi restoration fashionable. His clients in America as well as throughout Europe were happy to contribute. As the owner of a great country house himself, Hubert also had clout as a historical preservationist. In 1993, as his major retirement project, he took on the presidency of the French branch of the World Monuments Fund (WMF).

He had already sent Bunny a twelve-page, single-spaced fax, a history of the *potager* with comparisons to other notable kitchen gardens. When Gregory Usher, president of the École de Gastronomie Française Ritz-Escoffier, asked her to chair one of the galas that fueled the restoration over the years, she accepted, but only "as long as M. de Givenchy is with me." Together the two worked hard, fundraising to "faire revivre Le Potager du Roy," gathering a varied group of supporters that included French aristocrats, American expatriates, grand garden lovers and gardeners, cooking schools like the École de Gastronomie, and the chefs and farmers of the American Institute of Wine and Food (*Le Potager du Roy* was, after all, about food production). The 1993 publication of *Versailles: Le Potager du Roy, ou, manière de montrer le lac des Suisses et le balbi*, by Yves Périllon, with a preface by Babelon and a foreword by Bunny, helped spread the word.

Once, when I arrived for a weekend visit in Virginia, Bunny, who seemed very tired (she was, after all, eighty-four years old at the time), said she'd been "fighting and faxing with Hubert" all day about the smallest details of an upcoming Potager fundraiser.

When in 1972 Bunny had first seen the Grille du Roi, the king's private gate into the *potager*, she described it as surrounded by "carts, hot frames, potting sheds, straw matting, and a small foundry ready to repair broken tools." The gate itself was, as an official report said, "in a very poor state of conservation."

On the first of December 1994, in the freezing gray fog so typical of an Île de France winter, just like the weather on that late afternoon in 1972, Hubert de Givenchy stood in front of the restored gate and was presented with a big gold key about ten inches long. (Another would be given to Bunny, who could not be there that day.) The gate that led to the Pièce d'Eau des Suisses swung open, and the crowd dispersed. As Hubert walked away, he kept opening the presentation box to look at his key, smiling.

In August 1992 the architect Lablaude had sent Givenchy the World Monuments Fund's "Avant-Programme de Restauration de la

Grille du Roy" that included an estimate and timeline for completion. By the end of September, with a note to Bunny that Hubert signed with a heart and "love et du tendresse" (one of their customary valedictions in writing to each other), the relevant pages were in her hands. For the maquette, either out of her own Lambert money or from the allowance that Paul gave her annually, she had paid what seems to me the rather modest sum of $132,304.49 (or about $245,105.62 in 2020 buying power). For the larger sum to restore the gate, she turned to her husband.

As happened with Bunny's Schlumberger jewels or even the biggest blowouts from Givenchy's couture house every spring and fall—expenditures a great deal loftier than the gate restoration—it was apparently Paul Mellon's pleasure to pay the expenses. Even the lawyer Stoddard Stevens could hardly disapprove of such a solid project, amply documented and politely requested, that involved both Versailles and the World Monuments Fund.

In today's world of transitory relationships and easy divorce, Paul's amused, long-standing devotion to his wife—what *would* she think of next?—may seem incomprehensible. Yet Paul seems to have enjoyed being sent on even the most exacting of her errands. When he was dispatched to Asprey, the lofty jeweler on New Bond Street in London, on some unnamed assignment of hers, Paul proudly sent her a postcard that reads, "When I asked for Mr. Harding at Asprey, the man said, 'Well, my name is Harding, sir, what would you wish?' I think if necessary he would go to a leather and glass grinding school to produce your requests."

Besides taking on such small commissions, Paul also obligingly paid for the restoration of the *potager* fountain. Although the gate glittered and gleamed, Givenchy's snapshots of the *bassin* in May 1991 that he sent to Bunny reveal clean water but a dull surface, lifeless without the shine to make it dance. Jackie Kennedy had called Bunny and Paul's gift of the Peale portrait of Jefferson "le comble," the apex of the White House restoration. The Mellons' crowning gesture for the *potager* was to bring the fountain back to life.

In late June 1996, haute American and English gardening society (as well as many who didn't know a snowdrop from a silver dollar), eminent foodies, and a flying wedge of Givenchy's clients and friends headed by Mercedes Bass and Jayne Wrightsman boarded planes to Paris to attend the gala for the opening of the restored Potager du Roi, to make it known, to show it off, and to attract more funding to hire more gardeners.

Bunny recalled her surprise when the gardeners of the *potager*, who had been included along with *le tout Paris*, rose as a body when she entered the tent that had been erected for the gala. They were honoring her for her steadfast work with them and for her considerable horticultural knowledge, more than for her money.

Like Bunny's treasured story of buying her many Rothko paintings off the floor of the dead man's studio, I heard the tale of the gala several times from her, always told with relish and with different details. Once, she said, "The gardeners threw their hats into the air." Hubert, whom I questioned about it, wrote that he didn't remember the presence of the gardeners at the event, but he did recall that Bunny "wore a blue organza cocktail dress of my design." Camilla Chandon, Bunny's goddaughter, confirmed that the mob on that warm evening was dressed to the nines. Bunny didn't need a Givenchy gown to emphasize who she was: the garden with its freshly trained espaliers, the

La Grille du Roi, the solitary remaining original metal gate
at Versailles, shines again.

diamond fountain, the newly gilded gate, and the gardeners' welcome were more than enough.

For her assistance with the Potager du Roi, Bunny received the gilded star of an Officier de l'Ordre des Arts et des Lettres, the sister organization of the French military Legion of Honor. Now France had recognized her, as it had once recognized Stacy Lloyd with the Croix de Guerre.

PART VII

For
Everything
There Is
a Season

22

Osterville and Antigua, Island Havens

A gale force! Bunny in 1960 at the Cape with the journalist Joseph Alsop
and young David S. Bruce, son of Evangeline Bruce and
Ambassador David K. E. Bruce

On a hot summer day in 1995, Eliza and I drove from her house in
Little Compton, Rhode Island, to Osterville, where we found a deeply
shaded courtyard set in the bleached shoreline expanse of sandy land, its
trees and grasses shaped by the constant winds. The smells, the sounds,
and the sights were completely different from those at Oak Spring.

But as Bunny wrote in one of her garden journals, "There is always
a mark or repetition in the work of each gardener," and the same is
true of her architecture. The plan that she and Page Cross worked out
for a summer playground in New England and a winter escape on Antigua was a system marked by beauty, efficiency, privacy, and attention
to detail. Serenity—or at least the appearance of it—was the goal.

The architecture critic Martin Filler, who became friends with Paul Mellon, once asked him how his life had changed over the years. Paul gave a characteristically distant answer, which seems hilarious once you know even a few of the details of Paul's complicated emotional and business life. He pondered a bit, said Filler, and then disarmingly said, "Well, the nineties have been rather like the eighties . . . ," paused and continued, "and the eighties were rather like the seventies . . . ," and so forth.

Bunny was no stranger to New England. Its waterborne landscape had truly come into focus for her when her father chartered a two-masted schooner, the *Sonica*, and organized a family cruise from New York Harbor up the coast to Christmas Cove in Maine. They entered the tiny circular harbor under full sail, and the captain "rounded up into the wind sharply, slowly coming to a stop," wrote Gerard B. "Down went the anchor, and only then did the crew lower the sails." Not long after, in the fall of 1927, he bought the famous three-masted schooner *Atlantic*.

Sailors mostly enter a harbor under engine power and with one sail up, often just a jib. This particular flourish made a huge impression on Gerard B., who later brought a huge J/Boat into crowded Newport Harbor under full sail in a fog in the same way. Though Bunny wasn't one for such showy risk-taking, she did pick up her father's ability to make quick decisions, as well as his delight in presentation and effect.

Her New Hampshire grandparents had summered on the Cape, and Bunny's mother, Ray, after the divorce from Bunny's father and her marriage to her former brother-in-law Mal Clopton, also summered there. Ray continued to spend time there as a widow in the 1950s. Bunny and Paul first rented various "cottages" (what we would consider huge homes) on Cape Cod and then in the early 1950s bought twenty-six acres in Oyster Harbors, as the Osterville Grand Island resort community founded in 1929 was dubbed. A sleepy country club for New England's well-heeled, by 1960 its original membership, mostly Boston Brahmins, had died off. Howard Johnson, the restaurant chain's founder, was ready to swoop in and buy the place for development, but Paul saved the day and bought the entire island.

Paul's ability to control the land wherever he and Bunny lived extended to Dead Neck and Sampson's Island, the sandy sliver that protected their house on the bluff from Nantucket Sound. Evidently—or at least according to an uncredited AP source in Meryl Gordon's book—two thousand tons of Cape Cod sand were brought in to bolster the flattish existing dunes. Paul, an early seashore conservationist, had imported sand and planted dune grasses in a struggle to be near the sea but not in it.

Even before one walked to the windows in the living room to look out at the blue tranquility, ship models and carved wildfowl decoys reminded the visitor that saltwater was near. The Seapuit River ran right below the house, and beyond the barrier islands lay Nantucket Sound and the ocean.

Inside the house, furniture colors and shapes were paler—as if bleached by the sea and salt air—than in Virginia, the furniture lighter in construction, with a lot more wicker and caned pieces, and with weathered blue paint on rustic cupboards and benches. Sister Parish's early decorating touch lingered in the hooked and rag rugs.

Outdoors in the gardens, colors were bright in contrast to the subdued native landscape. A narrow curved bed that ran along the edge of the bluff included orange crocosmia, sunset-colored echinacea, and blue *Salvia farinacea*, along with herbs and tough silvery mulleins. All thrived in the summer sea winds and air.

The main garden was sheltered by a privet hedge, and the soil was prepared by means of the wildly labor-intensive but effective English system of "double digging." The top "spit," or layer of soil, is removed and saved, and what lies beneath is mixed with compost and humus. The mix would be tossed with a garden fork and then the topsoil layer replaced and layered with more sieved compost. This is standard high-class gardening, and it's what Bunny was doing in the White House Rose Garden when she ran into the main "hotline" cable.

The Cape Cod main garden was huge and prideful with its multiple rows and beds of flowers, herbs, and vegetables announcing that it fed many, many people all summer long and produced enough flowers to deck every room. In the garden at Le Jonchet that Bunny designed for Hubert de Givenchy, she would echo the Cape Cod geometry of grass paths and circles that divided the overflowing planted squares, rows, and triangles.

The Cape Cod working garden elements followed Bunny's Oak Spring pattern: a central pavilion flanked by glass houses. This arrangement was augmented on either side by Bunny's nod to George Washington's Mount Vernon—a couple of pepper-pot gazebos like the ones that anchor his flower and vegetable gardens. (Givenchy would also have a pair at Le Jonchet.) One gazebo was used for washing vegetables for the kitchen and the other for herbs that were tied in bunches and hung upside down on pegs on the wall. Different kinds of fences and the wooden wall structure Bunny devised—distressed shingles boxed with a white frame—would also see use at her getaway house on Nantucket.

Complete with brisk sea air and sun, fresh vegetables and fruits, sailboats and sea fogs, Oyster Harbors was a family place, thick with the struggles of young Mellons and Lloyds and Lamberts and their spouses and children comparing themselves to and competing with each other. The summer places of the rich are where such struggles often take place, as the family cast of characters is gathered together without much to occupy themselves. They all loved Cape Cod, however, and Tim Mellon, usually caustic in his childhood recollections, melted enough to say that "everyone got along with everyone; we spent a lot of time shucking corn and shelling peas." Tim recalled how the same people, staff as well as family, came every year to the Cape. Part of that life for all of them was the informality, a contrast to life at Oak Spring.

One similarity, of course, was that the Osterville retreat was also a compound. Putnam House, an eighteenth- or early-nineteenth-century farmhouse on the neighboring cove, had room for fourteen people; the Picnic House, with its winged roof, was where President John Kennedy asked Bunny if she would design a new garden for him outside the Oval Office; and Dune Cottage was a small house with a sheltered pool.

While Dune Cottage was Bunny's retreat, presumably from the hurly-burly of family life, it also contained an adjacent bedroom that, according to Eliza, was intended for Jackie Kennedy. Eliza showed me a secret opening, an almost invisible sliding panel that matched the rest of the handsome, cream-painted wall paneling and was positioned over the bedside table, through which, said Eliza of her mother, "she and Jackie could whisper secrets at night."

Only after Bunny's death and Nancy Collins's discovery in Bunny's Oak Spring bedroom of a similarly hidden recess for the Schlumberger "Breath of Spring" necklace would I really register Bunny's preoccupation with secret hiding places. Even her "cook outs," as she called them, where she could make a cup of tea for herself without summoning any staff, were stationed secretively outside her various bedrooms.

In 1995, a year after Jackie's death, Bunny told me that Dune Cottage was where she and Jackie had talked about Jackie's relationship with Onassis—should she marry him or not? He was pressing her hard, and it was only six months after Robert Kennedy's assassination. The two friends were sitting on the rug in front of the fire on a weekend when most of the other guests were gone. "So I asked her to get out all her jewels, and I brought out mine," Bunny related in her whispering voice. (It's unclear to me why Jackie was carrying so much jewelry on a visit to simple Cape Cod life.) "We tried them all on, bracelets, rings, necklaces, pearls, diamonds, emeralds, rubies, everything, laughing like hyenas till we cried," Bunny said, "and I asked her where hers came from. She said, 'Mostly from Ari.' 'Well, I guess you'd better marry him,' I said." They swept up the jewels, and that was that.

Bunny loved telling this story, I think because she was performing as the wise but mercenary woman of the world, the flippant manager and mistress of men. Only a few people ever glimpsed this Bunny Mellon. One was the late historian William Seale, who over the years from his editorial perch at the White House Historical Association had seen Bunny Mellon come and go as an insider at the White House. (The Historical Association, which has for decades protected, preserved, and provided public access to the rich history of the Executive Mansion, was founded by Jacqueline Kennedy in 1961.) Seale told me, "It is easy to get Mrs. Mellon wrong, to see her as simply a cloistered creature of taste and money . . . but not if one remembers that incredible strain of loyalty and resourcefulness, and her sense of fun and silliness."

Frank Langella later asked Jackie directly why she was marrying Onassis as she boarded the plane for his island of Scorpios with her children. Jackie answered, "I have no choice. They're playing Ten Little Indians. I don't want to be next." Not until 1980 would Jackie find a truly safe harbor with Maurice Tempelsman, an immensely wealthy Belgian-American diamond merchant and financier who eventually moved into her Fifth Avenue apartment, handled her finances, and increased her net worth enormously.

As Bunny described sweeping up the jewels, she also told me that she was the only good woman friend Jackie had. The same was nearly true for Bunny, too, although over the years she had friendships with a few other women: Kitty Wickes, Rosie Fiske, Liza Maugham, Babs Simpson, Evangeline Bruce, Caroline Kennedy—and, above all, her daughter, Eliza.

A photograph of Eliza at the helm of her boat, *Arctic Willow*, sailing from her place in Little Compton to Osterville includes her cat, McIntosh, on deck in a specially tailored blue harness and leash to keep him from falling overboard. The tragedy to be averted was losing McIntosh, the joke was the harness.

When Bunny was in Osterville, every summer morning that she got the chance she sailed her little one-person catboat, designed by Herreshoff, the storied Rhode Island boat builders. Sometimes Bunny would sail her skipjack, the *West Wind*, made locally on Cape Cod in the Crosby Yacht Yard, the oldest existing family-owned wooden-boat builders in America, then in its seventh generation of ownership. A skipjack is a beautiful, shallow-draft oyster dredger that carries a dangerously high amount of sail because it is made to outrun the fast tides that surge in and out of Chesapeake Bay. Sailing a skipjack off Cape Cod, unless you stick to Buzzards Bay or other sheltered waters, may not be the best idea; a skipjack is best handled in those waters by a very experienced sailor. Bunny, who was frightened of flying because of the deaths from airplane crashes in her own family and who worried so much about Eliza in every other regard, was nonetheless comfortable sailing her own boat and letting Eliza sail hers.

Bunny's skipjack sailing to the private Mellon dock on the Cape with
Ned Crosby, grandson of the boatyard's founder, at the helm

Paul sailed his *Cornflower* after lunch, taking with him whatever
friends had come to while away a few summer days by the sea in luxurious comfort. These could include John Baskett, his close friend
and chief art advisor, or Charles Ryskamp, a scholar and collector.
Ryskamp, who knew the Lambert family in Princeton, where he was
a university professor and library curator, then became director first
of the Morgan Library & Museum and, following that, the Frick
Collection (both hold extraordinary stores of beauty and learning
amassed by robber barons like Paul's father). Typically, Ned Crosby,
grandson of the boatyard's founder, brought the Mellons' craft from
their moorings to the private dock for the afternoon sailors and sometimes sailed with them.

Halcyon days. You could call it "legacy sailing." Gerard B. Lambert III, Bunny's nephew, generally known as Jerry but to Eliza as
Barnes, told me his grandfather had left him memorabilia such as the
ship's wheel and the magnificent mahogany-and-brass folding ladder from the *Yankee*, another of Gerard B.'s great racing vessels. For
Bunny, the salty tingle of the sea could be called up by a painting,
such as Eugène Boudin's *Festival in the Harbor of Honfleur*, with its

flag-bedecked ships, bought in 1959 and now in the National Gallery of Art in Washington, D.C.

BUNNY'S OTHER ISLAND was Antigua. In the winter of 1995–96, I spent several days at Oak Spring before going with Eliza and her parents to their retreat there. This trip was an attempt at reunion for the three of them: Eliza's long romantic liaison with Doris Sanders, a divorced woman nineteen years her senior, had done damage to her relationship with her parents.

A freelance journalist who split her time between New York and Paris, Sanders had previously been the partner of the writer Patricia Highsmith. Sometime in the 1980s, Doris and Eliza met, eventually settled into a redbrick house they bought at 97 Barrow Street in Greenwich Village, and spent their summers at Eliza's house in Little Compton. Eliza introduced her stern girlfriend to her family, who accepted her. Eliza's openly acknowledged relationship offered her the freedom to be "out," but it was a governessy freedom. To Eliza's friends, Doris appeared to take every chance to knock Eliza down, to correct her in public, and to isolate her. Paul's goddaughter remembered Bunny telling her, "We felt that Liza had been kidnapped [by Sanders]. We feel like we are the enemy."

Even after Eliza and Doris split in 1992, Eliza remained wary of her mother. So our Antigua weekend began with a needy and nervous Bunny, while Paul was stony. I was there to interview Bunny for the memoir she had agreed to undertake with me, but I was also a buffer.

The three-and-a-half-hour flight landed us at what in the nineties was Antigua's colorful makeshift airport.

"Welcome home, Mr. Mellon," beamed Oscar, the goateed chauffeur.

The desiccated tan countryside we drove through was poor: the island had survived two hundred years of Great Britain's oppression and a slavery economy and was now climbing up to comparative prosperity as a tourist destination. Stretches of the dusty road were lined with mahogany trees, reminders of the original forest, most of which had been timbered off centuries earlier to make the land available for sugarcane.

The Mellons' compound of buildings and gardens at the far eastern tip of the island was officially part of the Mill Reef Club, which the Mellon property adjoined and where they were members. Like the Oyster Harbors Club but with a more exalted international membership, Mill Reef is a gated country club with a high regard for security and amenities. Paul had spent time there since 1947, and in the fifties he bought twenty-six oceanfront acres so Bunny could build a private tropical paradise.

The estate was called King's Leap because, Bunny informed me, the land had been left vacant "in case the king [of England] wanted to land troops there," adding teasingly, "Now it is 'Mr. Mellon's Leap.'" The house sat on a small rise, and, unlike at Apple Hill or Oak Spring or Osterville, it had no entrance courtyard. Instead, a wide path on a shallow incline led up to the heavy front doors of the house. Flat-topped flowering trees that cast waves of high, shifting, lacy shade welcomed us, as did an Antiguan staff. About eight women stood on the steps wearing bright Givenchy uniforms and silky headdresses.

Bunny spent much of each morning planning menus with Cora, the cook, or with other staff members, some of whom came down from Virginia for her stays. Many of the cherished employees at Carter Hall—where Bunny had been queen at nineteen as her mother decamped for Princeton and her beloved and impetuous father left for Boston, where he parlayed the Gillette Blue Blade to fame—had come from local Black families. But behind that scrim of beloved Virginia faces lay the dark vision Bunny had secretly glimpsed in her father's study: photographs of the horrific 1919 Elaine Massacre near his cotton plantation in Arkansas. What Bunny recalled most was the execrable housing provided for cotton workers: one-room tar-paper shacks with newspaper insulation, common throughout the sharecropper South—utterly shocking for a woman who believed that good housing design could actually transform a life. She would forever provide decent housing and health insurance for her employees.

One of her favorites was the eccentric, outspoken, and illiterate

Lena Bradford at Oak Spring. According to Bunny, Lena had never been a house servant; she had worked "in the corn field." Nonetheless, before her interview with Mrs. Mellon for the position of "in-between maid," Mrs. Mellon was told that Lena wanted her to know, "You're not interviewing *her*, she's interviewing *you*."

Lena worked in every capacity for Bunny—including catching her fish for breakfast—for more than forty years. Fascinated by Lena, Bunny described her and her life in a detailed seven-page portrait and attended the woman's crowded funeral. The preacher announced "Sister Lena's" favorite hymn, "Resurrection is free, you better believe it— Resurrection is free," to his congregation, and they sang their hearts out. Lena clearly considered herself to be—and was so considered by Bunny—a free spirit who leapt all obstacles of race, education, and economic status.

For most paying members of the Mill Reef Club, once the red-and-white entrance gate went down behind them, they were enveloped in familiar luxury, and the tiresome outer world was shut out. But Antigua's poverty didn't escape Bunny's notice. On a trip in 1971 she found "unemployment very serious" on the island. Close to Free Town, one of the first freedmen's villages, she started a community garden program, so islanders could grow vegetables for sale to the resort hotels and for themselves. She ordered seed packets for forty different vegetables from Park's Seed Company. Islanders had once grown food on Sundays, their only free day, in a field set aside on each slave plantation, to supplement their scanty imported rations. After emancipation, village markets thrived as a free enterprise system. But Bunny's Freetown garden project needed more attention than she could give it, and a better water supply, so it didn't last. Food supplies on the island are today, as they were then, largely imported, but now the Mill Reef Fund disburses over $9 million annually to help alleviate poverty on Antigua and Barbuda.

A more successful Antiguan enterprise was Bunny's medical laboratory, started in the 1980s for a local hospital and guided by Dr. Bruce Horten, a New York pathologist. It was a medical project for a local hospital, he was told, and they needed a consultant. Only when it appeared that Horten would mix well socially with the Mellons, especially Bunny, was he told who would be doing the hiring. "Oh, Lord, the Mellons . . . difficult and demanding," he protested. "No, no," he was told, "Bunny is a remarkable lady and someone you would like."

Horten took one look at Holberton Hospital and remembers thinking, "What am I doing? Albert Schweitzer would have recognized this old place." But when he saw the new, partially built lab addition, he realized it might work after all.

"Paul [Mellon] was not interested in medical projects," said Horten dryly, though he noted that Paul did in fact contribute funding, "but Bunny was, because of her Lambert pharmaceutical background." Looking back, Horten said, "Bunny was never altogether crisp about things," adding that he worried he might be "a sort of interior decorator for the lab . . . but I also knew that instruments break down, and I had to find a facility somewhere nearby to help out, and so settled on Jamaica as medical partner. I also talked with the Holberton staff to ask them what they wanted; they had already told Bunny that 'the foundation of any hospital is its laboratory.'"

Antigua ended up with a sophisticated lab and a staff pathologist— and a dignified driveway portico designed by Bunny that opened to the new autopsy room, a type of facility before then unknown in Antigua. "Although the hospital has moved to an entirely new site," Horten said, "a plaque exists identifying the lab as a Gerard B. Lambert Foundation project."

But Bunny's time on Antigua was not spent entirely on good works. In March 1981, she invited four friends to King's Leap for a week: Babs Simpson, Billy Baldwin, Walter Lees, and Michael Gardine. Babs and Billy were the stars, Lees and Gardine the satellites. Small, neat, smart, and fearsome, Babs (Beatrice) de Menocal Simpson quietly ruled as the fashion and style editor of the magazine world from 1949 to the end of the twentieth century; by 1981 she had left her twenty-five-year stint at *Vogue* for *House & Garden*, where she spent the rest of her working life. Billy Baldwin had retired in 1973 but continued to be venerated for the clean beauty of his interior design work—and his glittering client list.

Walter Lees, a decorated (as a daring World War II POW escapee)—and decorative—Scot, spent fifty years in Paris as a diplomat and European "extra man." He danced Highland flings with the lonely Duke of Windsor after his abdication and transformed his tiny suite of rooms at the British Embassy into a breathtaking exploration of miniaturized scale. Later, in Hollywood, he met Hubert de Givenchy and, through him, Bunny Mellon.

Michael Gardine, a writer and New York antiques dealer who was the lover of Way Bandy, a famed 1970s New York makeup artist, was embarking on Billy's frothy "autobiography," with Babs as editor. (Billy Baldwin lived out his last years in Gardine's Nantucket house, dying in 1983, two years before Gardine's book was published.) For all three men visiting King's Leap in 1981, this was the tail end of a world as it existed before the AIDS epidemic, so nobody was "out" and certainly nobody wanted to talk about AIDS.

In those days on the island, Bunny, now seventy, had a strong sense of time passing, which she acknowledged when she wrote, "Back again in this house that becomes more and more a part of another century." The orchards she had planted on the nearly waterless island in the sixties were bearing fruit, producing avocados and oranges. Her garden also produced less glamorous vegetables; at one dinner Walter Lees tested, with a bit of trepidation, a "pale beet soup."

"We were all together only a few days" in "a world & time of our own" where "a lovely rhythm exists," wrote Bunny. She demanded that her guests produce daily diary entries for her to compile in a beautifully designed takeaway booklet. That whimsy might have felt pretty overpowering, but Bunny's guests enjoyed the lazy serenity of King's Leap, so different from Cape Cod, where activities seldom ceased. Bunny wrote about "our Antigua family," an echo of Hubert and "the French family"—yet another "family" group bound by interests rather than blood. (When Bunny made her preliminary list for me of those I should interview first about her life, not a single one of her actual relatives was on it.)

Babs Simpson wrote, "For me the house is at its most beautiful in the afternoon from my chair, where one can look across the leafy long shadowed courtyard on one hand, and through the silvery living room out to sea on the other . . . The house is breathing, for everyone is asleep. The light slides into dusk . . . there will soon be music, showers, drinks & activities again . . ."

Gardine rearranged the record collection and put Fred Astaire on the Victrola.

"The room is filled with glorious nostalgia . . . Billy stepped in on his way to the pool—his eyes dancing—we all dance!" wrote Bunny.

The next day she went to St. Croix to "work on Stacy's terrace and courtyard." Bunny's romantic if now platonic relationship with Stacy had never ended, nor did either of them want it to, even though his second wife, Alice Babcock, a good-looking foxhunter from Long Island, had been jealous of Bunny. After Alice's death in 1979, Stacy would marry Virginia "Vidy" Boy-Ed, a carriage-driving enthusiast in Virginia, in 1981; Vidy had no trouble accepting Bunny as her husband's friend.

Everett Hicks popped up from the Mill Reef Club, where he was housed on his visits, and helped Bunny plant six black willows in clay pots at Stacy's St. Croix place. Bunny wrote, "Stacy came back to Antigua with me . . . dinner was especially lovely as Michael told a story of the year before [also on Antigua] touching and full of love about my horse-shoe ring," the one Stacy had given her during their marriage. "Neither Stacy or I will ever forget it . . . It was the night of The Full Moon, the First day of Spring—the Equinox" is how Bunny finished her entry, ending with three little *x*'s.

I believe Bunny was never happier—nor happier with herself—than when she had given pleasure to people she enjoyed and when she knew she had seamlessly pulled off an event, whether it was Eliza's massive debut in 1961 or a short, perfectly orchestrated visit such as this. She was at her best moving in a circle, usually a small one, of those who loved her and were as charmed by her and her productions as her father had been at the sight of Bunny's sister, Lily, who, "from her childhood . . . loved to dress up as a queen" coming "proudly into a room trailing some long fabric she had draped about herself" or when she "put on a beautiful costume to pirouette and dance."

The cheery pathologist Dr. Horten, who moved in Manhattan social circles, also became a frequent guest at the Mellon houses—

acting sometimes as the buffer I sensed myself to be on that January weekend in 1996—and one of Bunny's confidants, someone to whom she could tell the stories of her life. Every year in February and March on the island she imported the kind of companionship she craved— clever, amusing, talented, worshipful, generally male, and apparently unencumbered by a partner of any sexual persuasion. Only occasionally did Bunny relent and ask Hubert's partner, Philippe Venet, or the Dutch antiques dealer Akko van Acker's partner, Ricardo. Throughout the sixties and early seventies, her most romantic tropical getaway remained Schlumberger's rough accommodation on the Îles des Saintes, off Guadeloupe.

With each infatuation, Bunny wanted a partner in some design project that involved his skills and his daily participation *with her*—by letter or, later, fax, and always the phone—about the clinic, or a jewel, or the purchase of a million-dollar book for her library, or the choice of a fabric.

While Bunny was shielding herself with her "families" and platonic but romantic partners, Paul found plenty of room in his life for Dorcas Hardin. The affair that had begun in 1959 or 1960 lasted until his death in 1999. Due to Dorcas's deafness, Paul had to shout on the phone to make himself heard. Like anyone else who knew Bunny, of course I had heard the gossip about those phone calls between the lovers.

I also heard some of those phone calls myself. The airy, open floor plan of the Antigua house meant that even though Paul had a separate bedroom and office suite, hearing his side of some of his conversations with Dorcas was unavoidable. One night, after a particularly fraught dinner, Eliza stormed off, and Paul retired to his own rooms, accompanied by a glass of Ensure carried by Joyce, one of the maids. I sat with Bunny in the pale, high-ceilinged living room as she began to talk against the background of Paul bellowing about his next Tuesday with Dorcas. At one particularly loud burst of laughter, Bunny, who was by this time very practiced in her response to the situation, just paused and said Dorcas's name as if to explain Paul's loudness and to put me at ease.

The next day, as Eliza, Bunny, and I swam in the pool before lunch,

Bunny pointed out the perfect harmony of the shrubs—"cinnamon bushes" she called them (probably some kind of pittosporum)—along the wall that were subtly shaped to echo the humpbacked mountain on the far side of Half Moon Bay. A startlingly white house with a big, sharp-pointed gable stood out in the view, commanding the low neck of the hump—"the only piece of land that Paul didn't buy," said Eliza. "Mummy wanted him to, but a wicked lawyer thwarted her," she added. "This lawyer hated my mother and would have done anything to keep her from having her way."

Stoddard Stevens, the "wicked lawyer," a former Sullivan & Cromwell partner who became Paul's very effective legal bodyguard and sat on the boards of many of Paul's projects, was one of the two people in Paul's longtime employ Bunny could not outwit or overrule. (The other was Beverly Carter, the curator of Paul's art collection at Rokeby and the keeper of his papers, which are now at the Yale Center for British Art.)

To Burton Hersh, the author of *The Mellon Family: A Fortune in History*, Bunny raged, "If I say to Paul, I'd like this and this, Stoddard Stevens will see that it is not done." Paul himself summed up Stevens's protective attitude with an anecdote: "Stoddard regarded anyone connected with me as a potential adversary, and this extended even to the family. As a result, he was not much loved by Bunny, who once asked Jack Barrett whether he thought Stoddard, then in advanced years, would ever die. Jack, who, as Editor of [the] Bollingen Series, had had dealings with Stoddard over a long period, replied 'Bun, I don't think the Lord wants him any more than we do.'"

JOHN VON STADE, an American art dealer who worked with Paul privately on creating the National Museum of American Racing and Hall of Fame in Saratoga Springs, New York, visited Antigua in 1964 and at a glance understood Bunny's determination and ambitions for the place, despite Stevens's efforts to prevent her from "having her way." Von Stade saw the connection between Bunny's extensive produce gardens and the luscious, seven-foot-long still life of tropical fruits by a mid-eighteenth-century French artist, Edmé Jean-Baptiste

A good afternoon at King's Leap: sandy bare feet, a book,
and a luscious tropical fruit painting by the French flower painter
Edmé Jean-Baptiste Douet, one of a pair

Douet, that glowed darkly over the couch in the living room. "She
made up her mind to grow everything that was in the picture," said
von Stade, "and she did it perfectly, on a large plot of about two acres."

What that garden, the leafy orchards, and the profusion of huge
plants in pots signaled was the need for an adequate water supply.
The high, battered stone wall that fell from the swimming pool terrace to the Half Moon Bay beach below is the one reminder of the
old rainwater catchment that once ran under the house. "Mr. Mellon had one of the first private desalinization plants on the island,"
said the Mellons' chief electrician, Skip Glascock, who was flown
down several times from Virginia to sort out problems at King's Leap.
Given that Mellon employees were always expected to find the best,

he added—unsurprisingly, "There were two kinds available, the more expensive one was also more reliable, and so of course Mr. Mellon chose that one."

In the early sixties, Alison Harwood, then a senior editor at *Vogue*, reported that King's Leap was "tropical luxuriance brought to heel." That was what Harwood saw, but Everett Hicks's watering program explains what it took to create that impression. He lists the estate's six gardeners by name, giving very specific orders as to who was to do what, how often—weekends included—and how to water each and every class of plant: trees in ground, weekly and slowly; trees in pots, twice weekly; plants and flowers, daily. (By 2019, according to a regional paper, the island's reservoirs, which usually supplied sixty percent of its water, had run completely dry; the island relied solely on desalinated water.)

Between the two of them, Bunny and Hicks had everything shipped down that was needed that Antigua couldn't supply for her visionary garden, such as osmunda fiber for potting orchids, trays, screens, bamboo stakes, four boxes of "plants from our greenhouse," and even a small watering can. Hicks reached out to the Arnold Arboretum in Boston for a title list of books on the flora of the West Indies to create a library.

It was also imperative, if Bunny was to make the tropical paradise she dreamed of, to provide enough shade for young plants and to train enough labor to care for them. Everett (and Bunny) did find and train enough gardeners to place a straw cover every morning on each herb bed in the trial garden off her bedroom, a cover that was taken off later when the blast of midday sun had passed. Harwood, in the horrible language of the time, cited the "plentiful service from smiling natives" available as one of the draws for Mill Reef residents, along with, she added, Antigua's tranquil history of no "rebellion or uprising."

Besides shade, shelter for living things sometimes also meant getting out of the wind. Coming back one day from lunch at the Mill Reef Club, I realized how relaxing it was to be away from the pressure and whine of the island's incessant gales, because the Mellon house had been placed to block it. Voices and laughter from the far-off kitchen, jasmine in the air, wings rustling as doves landed to bathe in the pool, and below, the soft white beach—all seemed orchestrated to convey a sense of peace. As Bunny went down to the bay to swim before breakfast one morning, she later wrote, she "felt a sense of weightlessness as the water slowly moved, breaking on the sand—the strength of the universe present—a small bird flew by, close to the water—a frail life unafraid."

King's Leap also became a place to recover, to regain strength, and even to absorb tragedy. An overwhelmed Jackie Kennedy came in March 1964, four months after JFK's assassination. Frightened, frozen, and alone, she telegraphed Bunny, "I can't wait." Bunny's efforts to help her friend included producing a parade of Jackie's family—most important, Bobby Kennedy, close as a brother to Jackie—but also Jackie's sister, Lee, and her husband, Prince "Stash" Radziwill. Later, Eliza and her cousin Jerry "Barnes" Lambert came for a few days before leaving for St. Croix to visit Stacy; Caroline Kennedy and little John-John arrived separately the day after the others left. Barnes had noticed how thin Jackie was. In his photographs of a lunch at King's Leap, Bunny sits in her usual totally erect fashion, observing Jackie with concern; Jackie's eyes are clouded and distant above her smile and her cheery, raspberry-colored Lilly Pulitzer shift.

One afternoon not long before Eliza and I were scheduled to head back to New York, she and I walked on the beach and talked over her knotty family situation. She and Doris had split over how Paul's gift of a four-hundred-acre Virginia farm should be treated, and so the deal still hung in the air, unresolved. Paul had also given Eliza a loan to help cover the costs of their separation—a total of half a million dollars, she told me—an amount that included half the estimated value of the Barrow Street house that, apparently, she and Doris had owned in common. (Doris had also negotiated the use for a year of their Paris apartment. It wasn't clear to me that, even with all the legal help available to the Mellon family, Eliza was certain of her facts.) She mentioned the subject before lunch one day, and Paul rather nicely said it was all negotiable.

Then the two of them fought about a poem he had included in his memoir, *Reflections in a Silver Spoon*, published in 1992, that she attributed to someone else. Paul was affronted and managed to make

Eliza look ridiculous. I looked at my plate; Bunny was silent, her brow furrowed.

Paul abruptly disappeared after lunch. Eliza was furious, Bunny alarmed. The afternoon felt paralyzed—immobilized by the fraught land discussion combined with Eliza's feeling that Paul thought she was stupid. Bunny took the two of us on a desultory walk in the garden, where Bunny sliced her leg open when she tripped on a tree's guy-wire. We hurried back to the house silently, Bunny's leg gushing, and Eliza and I watched helplessly while her mother insisted on bandaging her rather awful-looking wound herself.

Much worse for Bunny than any loss of blood was that her husband and her daughter were at odds. Eliza's willingness to come for the weekend had made Bunny feel that she had finally regained Eliza's trust, but now it looked as if she might lose her daughter all over again.

We headed off separately for afternoon naps, and I woke up with a sense of foreboding. Before we gathered for dinner, I was to meet Bunny for another talk about our book. But when we got together, it was clear to me that instead Bunny wanted to process her emotions. She said she was angry that she hadn't heard from Akko van Acker—the Parisian antiques dealer who was her latest obsession—for three days. "He is in Miami!" she exclaimed, meaning, I assumed, that *of course* he should call.

When I tried to change the subject, speculating nervously and foolishly on why Eliza had been with Doris for so long, saying that maybe Eliza had needed a confined relationship and plenty of solitude to realize her potential as an artist, Bunny said crisply, effectively silencing me, "Only the person who goes through things can say why."

At dinner, we three looked at our plates; then Eliza left the table, and Paul summoned me to play Scrabble. Scrabble over at last, I headed for my room in the guesthouse and found Eliza, but I only made things worse when I tried to comfort her. She strode off down the dark driveway in tears as a huge thunderstorm began. I went after her and brought her back, and eventually she calmed down, and the house went quiet.

In the blankly beautiful West Indies sunshine the next morning,

Eliza and I swam in the ocean before breakfast. There was no sign of her mother and no conversation about the previous day's debacle. Improbably, King's Leap, where all the doors were almost always open and the breeze wafted freely through the house, suddenly felt claustrophobic.

By lunchtime, however, Paul and Eliza had worked out a resolution. Or rather Paul, who had spent his business and institutional life cutting through problems like this—often with Stoddard Stevens but never before with his beloved stepdaughter—had solved the problem of the Virginia land deeded to her and Doris Sanders.

Eliza would give back two hundred of the four hundred acres he had given her; land easements and agreements that allowed foot passage and foxhunters without permitting development would cover the entire acreage. I understood nothing about tossing the acres back and forth. It emerged that easements—so dear to Paul's land-conservation instincts—had, according to Eliza, been the real sticking point, because Doris had contested them, wanting to develop the land and build houses to sell—an outrage to Paul. (Much later, I realized that for Bunny, just as for her daughter, finances remained something to be managed by someone else—generally her lawyer, Alex Forger, who was tasked with finding ways for Bunny to do what she wanted to do.)

Paul had then explained to Eliza his reaction to her comments on his poem. And finally all was calm, all was bright, and that evening Paul wore a shirt covered with red hearts (he and Bunny signed their notes to each other with a little red heart), and we drank champagne. The family drama about money and power that we had just been through did not seem to match the happy unrolling of one decade after another, as Paul had described his life to Martin Filler.

23

"A House of My Own": South Pasture on Nantucket

What Bunny created on Nantucket was an exhilarating exercise of every principle of landscape she had discovered for herself. By the time she began building the first structure in 1988, she had repeatedly tested her strengths: her knowledge of siting and scale, abstraction and simplification, and the ability to repeat without being repetitive and to make mistakes boldly and correct them. She certainly also exercised the double-edged sword, money. "That's *perfect*! Let's try this . . ." she once said.

South Pasture was set on a little more than two hundred acres of coastal heathland, pond, bog, old-field terrain, and former sheep pastures. At the crest of the low hill to the north stood what Nantucketers call a "forest," mainly the dark and gnarly scrub oaks that thrive despite fierce and continuous salt-saturated storms and poor soil. Nantucket is a sand bar with a thin covering of earth that erodes quickly, revealing the pale sand almost as soon as a road is cut. This was Bunny's private place, far more private for her than the two houses on Whitehaven Street in D.C. were for Paul. It was the wind-scoured, farthest-point-out-in-the-Atlantic she knew, a reminder of sailing up the New England coast to Christmas Cove in Maine with her family when she was seven years old.

She had purchased the land in 1969 with $200,000 she received in cash from her father's estate (in addition to a tidy trust fund), so her continual insistence that it was the only place that was truly "hers" is no surprise. (Stoddard Stevens disapproved of her spending her in-heritance on the Nantucket property, not that his opinion mattered to her.) It's an exaggeration, however, to say that it was her *only* place—the apartments in Paris were also "hers" in the sense that Paul often stayed in a hotel on his infrequent trips to France.

Until I understood how hard it was for Bunny to continually face down the knowledge of Paul's affair with Dorcas Hardin, I didn't understand how much she needed a place unconnected with him. The residences on—and the differing atmospheres of—the farm, Antigua, Cape Cod, and New York were designed and executed not just for the pleasure of creating them to be just the way she wanted but also with Paul's collaboration to foster the "true, real, and sim-ple happiness" of the life she wanted the two of them to share with guests and family. Bunny, the châtelaine of houses built and per-fectly maintained with Paul's money, was constantly the impresario. Sometimes she wanted to get away from it all. She once said that Nantucket for her was "a vacation from a vacation," meaning a place to escape from Cape Cod.

The adventure started with a picnic rug laid out on the grass above a steep, sandy drop overlooking the South Shore and two of the signa-ture white-cardboard-box lunches that went everywhere with Bunny. She and Jackie would fly over from Osterville, just the two of them, just for lunch. Pure caprice, something Jackie sorely needed and her best friend could provide. Then in 1988 a "picnic house" took the place of the rug—a tiny structure with a roofline just like the archetypal hip roof seen in Stubbs's Newmarket paintings and on many small outbuildings at Oak Spring and throughout Virginia. Other buildings followed, including a main house. I. M. Pei, who was visiting Bunny in her most private retreat, chose the oceanfront site, walking out, the story goes, and saying, "Put it on the bluff!" (Almost all of Bunny's friends were notable, extraordinary, and gifted, which I think was sometimes hard for Eliza, who told me she understood how important these people were so that sometimes she felt quite awed and useless and slow when she was with them.)

The South Pasture complex was nested in mighty clumps of native vegetation—mostly wild bayberry and scrub oak—in a mere lap of lawn with rough-mown fields beyond that. (Those fields and, in fact, the entire property had to be cleared of undetonated ordnance from the U.S. Navy's Tom Nevers Target Area right next door.) A full-scale canvas mock-up of the barn covered with glued plywood was built to move around from location to location on the property. By 1996 the timber frame of the barn was going up, the last of the major structures to be built. Three men were the constants of the construction crew: H. Bancel LaFarge, known as "Bam," Neil Paterson, and Daniel Sutherland.

Chris Westerlund, a longtime member of Bunny's building crew, and H. Bancel "Bam" LaFarge stand in front of a canvas mock-up of the barn in the valley.

The Main House, as it was called, was a 2,500-square-foot cottage with two and a half bedrooms above. The half bedroom had a balcony where Bunny always stepped out to survey "what was going on each morning," said Daniel Sutherland. The birds of the Atlantic Flyway, which runs from the Arctic tundra to South America, stop by Nantucket twice a year, dropping in for food, water, and a brief rest. Sutherland, a landscape photographer, used a few of the shots of birds he'd taken over the years at South Pasture in a book privately printed for Bunny: an improbably blue indigo bunting, a more modest snow bunting, a rufous-sided towhee, and tree swallows by the thousands feasting on bayberries.

Every field had its name, and the native plants were celebrated for their diversity as they flowered in succession. When the front field on the ocean was mowed, the mower carefully cut around the small clumps of wild orange wood lilies (*Lilium philadelphicum*), a prairie native now in decline in New England. In summer, the Forked Pond Valley painted itself with sky-bright patches of blue-eyed grasses, including *Sisyrinchium fuscatum*, one of the three indigenous species of the early-summer flower. *S. fuscatum*, the New England coastal plain species, is now native only to Martha's Vineyard and Nantucket. Two species of everlasting, sweet and pearly, thickened the prairie grasses. Dotted sparsely across the wide land to the north were impenetrable scrub thickets. Bunny, like Christopher Robin, called these clumps by their British name, "spinneys." A narrow sandy path ran to the picnic house and the bluff edge where beach plum and wild rose, *Rosa rugosa*, thrived.

Walls to protect a garden and to mark the house precincts went up. Bunny distressed cedar shingles with paint to look weathered, just as she had once scumbled the stone exterior of Apple Hill with whitewash mixed with clay. In my conversations with her she seldom mentioned the garden itself, focusing rather on the land, the birds, and the freedom she felt. "It's hard to stress how much Mrs. Mellon loved Nantucket," Sutherland told me. "It was such an important chapter in her life and a place where perhaps she was more candid and freer (from her queenly responsibilities) than anywhere else. As it is for so many others, it was her 'soul place.'" To me it seemed that the garden existed to provide vegetables and herbs and some flowers for the house (the idea being that every island farm has a garden patch of necessity), but perhaps it was just as much to show that one *could* garden there, despite the climate and soil drawbacks, like producing the delphiniums she was so proud of on the Cape.

Bunny's sketches of the main house roof profiles and chimney placement were what was built, line for line. A full plywood mock-up was constructed for the kitchen, and the design was altered ten times to get the windows, staircase, fireplace, and walls just right. During the years, the crew working on South Pasture became yet another family for her. "Bunny found her value in the people who were the heart of this place," said Sutherland, who added that they, in turn, he thinks, "dedicated their lives to her, and she knew it."

A farmer to the core, manager Neil Paterson got to know every inch of each field intimately—each patch of little bluestem and goldenrod—as he shaped them. "He became," Bunny wrote, "a great part of creating the world I dreamed of in Nantucket." As an upper-crust Scot from Inverness who was educated at an English public school, he had had the Scottish accent beaten out of him—but not the Scottish temperament. He was blessed with the gentle but sardonic wit that Scots describe as "pawky," and he valued Bunny for one quality above all that not everyone saw in her—her sense of humor—as he wrote in the foreword to Sutherland's book.

His brother, Tim, had emigrated too and took on Bunny's unruly Lloyd grandsons, teaching them manners, helping them have fun outdoors, and keeping them in line. Good-humored Tim Paterson knew discipline from the ground up to the very top: after schooling at Sandhurst, the hallowed British military training school for "Gentlemen Cadets," he then enlisted in the Queen's Highlanders. The Patersons were the kind of well-bred folk Bunny had known from her father's British connections and with whom she felt at home. Both Patersons turned up in kilts at Bunny's funeral.

Bam LaFarge could be called the soul of the South Pasture project. The great-grandson of the painter John La Farge, Bam was educated at Portsmouth Abbey School in Rhode Island and then at Harvard, majoring in anthropology, following up with the Yale School of Architecture. Although he might style himself merely a carpenter, he was, in fact, a master craftsman, as well as Nantucket's eccentric Renaissance man. Large in life and in spirit, as wild as a scrub oak, and with a voice one affectionate local writer described as "gargling," he was a mariner and a self-taught naturalist who spent his entire life on the island, had broad art and intellectual interests, and was consumed by a love for the natural world.

Eleanor Reade, a Nantucket "summer person" from birth, described LaFarge as "a local character, fearsome, kind of a public monument."

He was "a big guy," she went on, "ruddy, good looking in an out-doorsy way, smart, very opinionated, and a perfectionist." She said so because, as a perfectionist and a sailor herself, she had observed Bam take infinite care building a little wooden boathouse, probably only fifteen by fifteen feet, on the LaFarge family's place on Tuckernuck Island as she sailed by.

Bunny loved every aspect of the man, but after years of working together on South Pasture, their friendship broke up over a soffit—the compact wooden overhang that bridges the space between a wall and a roof—on the pool building. For Bunny, it was too wide by an inch or so, not as narrow as those on the other structures. "Everyone, includ-ing me, tried to heal the breach between the two," recalled Daniel Sutherland, "but Bam was done with it." For once it was not Bunny who backed off; it was Bam. He felt he had done his job. After the split Bunny nonetheless saw to it that Bam's work at South Pasture was honored. Set in the pavement outside his workshop adjoining the barn is a beautiful bronze marker: DESIGNED AND WORKED ON BY H. BANCEL LAFARGE.

Sutherland said, "Geometry, that's what she wanted." Because the landscape had so few elements and the structures were so simple, it was easy to figure out how everything lined up with something else, like the top edge of a wall that lined up with the edge of a building many feet away. Even if the lineup went unnoticed, the harmony of parts still existed and could be sensed.

Aesthetically speaking, Nantucket was Bunny's ultimate "Nothing should be noticed" statement. When work on the main house was taking place, the crew put two planks down on the ground as a tem-porary path. At the end of construction, Bunny considered the board path and said, "Just leave it as it is." The planks looked great, and the lawn was laid around them.

"Her first 'insider' connection on Nantucket was with Andy Oates and his partner, Bill Euler," said Sutherland. The two men established Nantucket Looms in 1968, a year before Bunny purchased her land, and when the two gay men had trouble getting a loan for the prop-erty, Paul Mellon stepped in to secure it. At Nantucket Looms, Oates and Euler were on a mission to produce the purity of style in art and daily life that Oates had first seen at Black Mountain College, the experimental school for the arts in North Carolina, where the cream of America's artistic avant-garde of the 1940s and '50s all spent time.

"Andy Oates was one of the few who actually graduated from Black Mountain," said Sam Kasten, who worked at Nantucket Looms and eventually set up shop on his own in 1984. He added, "Bob Rauschenberg was his roommate," and then he tossed out two great Bauhaus names: "Josef Albers was Andy's art teacher, and Anni Albers was his weaving teacher." (The Alberses had left Germany after the Bauhaus was closed down by the Nazis in 1933; the architect Philip Johnson helped them find jobs at Black Mountain.)

When you are very rich and it's widely whispered that you have good ideas as to what to do with all that money, it's easier to get really gifted people interested in your projects. This is what happened to Bunny; geniuses became her employees and often her friends, and at the same time they served as the college and graduate school she never had. Whether or not she knew about the Bauhaus by name before she met Andy Oates, she quickly absorbed the principles, which were already innate within her. The native landscape of Nantucket lends itself to the Bauhaus simplification of design to three elements—line, shape, and color; the designed landscape Bunny created was a translation of the same minimalist ethic. Bunny became one of Andy and Bill's biggest customers. "There was always something on the looms for her," said Kasten, whether it was tablecloths for the opening of the National Gallery's East Building or giant sheer linen curtains woven on ten-foot looms for the Oak Spring Garden Library.

When Kasten visited Oak Spring, he recalled it as "a spiritual and religious experience, and I come from a long line of atheists." About his own work he said, "I'm only interested in timeless design. Just want everything to be made beautifully." I could almost hear Bunny paring things down the same way when she told a reporter in 1969 about her gardens and landscapes: "I don't really like too many flowers about." I can understand her relentless insistence on perfection in even the smallest detail, such as a copper window fitting because it will last forever. When Josef Albers famously said, "Abstraction is real, probably more real than nature," I believe Bunny thought the same, although I doubt anyone but Albers could have articulated it.

Daniel Sutherland, with an art school background and from a New York family that summered on Nantucket, ended up moving to the island full-time to become a professional photographer. His family and the LaFarges were friends, but it was through Neil Paterson that he was invited to Oyster Harbors in the spring of 1991. He was thirty-one years old. Partway through lunch he realized he was being very pleasantly vetted by Paul and Bunny. Danny, as Bunny called him, joined the crew building the main house that year. A photograph of the "topping out party," which takes place when the last bearing roof timber of a new house is in place, shows Sutherland with eleven other tanned and handsome young men in shorts or cutoffs perching on the raw boards, some lifting glasses. Bunny reveled in it all. "Their spouses were not hired," said Sutherland, adding, "Mrs. Mellon loved her men."

The 1991 Nantucket crew raises a glass.

Lunch for Bunny and the crew sometimes took place at a nearby restaurant, the Sea Grille, where camaraderie blossomed at a big round table with a revolving cast of characters. Before the kitchen at the Main House was finished, Bunny sometimes had box lunches flown over from Osterville. Often they would make sandwiches on the kitchen table. In the construction years, said Sutherland, "Bunny always fussed around, wanting to help out." Once, early on, she even brought Rudy Stanish, the omelet king, who persuaded her to sit down and get out of the way by saying, "Madame, let us enjoy you." At Christmastime in the mid-1990s, when construction was going full blast, Bunny would take a room for a party at the historic Jared Coffin House hotel. The entire construction crew was invited, but again, no spouses, even for this festive event. At moments like this I remember a story of a slightly lackluster young Bunny sending bouquets to herself the year she made her debut—just in case her beautiful sister, Lily, received more.

Once the house was habitable, Bunny would come for the night or sometimes a little longer, occasionally staying as long as three days at a time. "After that, everyone got exhausted and crabby," said Sutherland. Bunny continued to add various little houses to the property because, I think, building was like breathing for her—a necessary mental and physical exercise. One little dot of a house became the cook's house for Stanley Champ from Virginia, who flew up with Bunny for eight years running and unobtrusively watched over her when she got very old. Bunny cared for him too, said Stanley, warning him about the possibility of unexploded Navy shells when he walked in her fields. After her dinner she would say, "Go enjoy yourself, Stanley, go out on the town."

By 2001 the bluff was starting to erode, crumbling onto the beach below and out to sea. The next year a very expensive rescue operation ensued to move the house back about four hundred feet from the cliff edge, an intervention that in 2022, in the era of pronounced climate change, is no longer so unusual at upscale beachfront properties. On her birthday in August 2002, Bunny wrote, "Across the Sound my New House on Nantucket has been lifted up on giant steel beams to move it back . . . All the millions of daisies of last year are under the waves."

On October 4, after beating back what she called "various illnesses" (she was ninety-two), she made a trip to the island from Virginia.

"Thank you," she later wrote to Daniel Sutherland, "for twenty-four hours of the happiest day I have [had] in two years. To come back and find such perfection in every corner after the chaos and problems—the house moved—sitting safe and sound with the future joy of design & landscape—the old Cellar a field of green grass . . . Blue sky. Seals in the sea . . . What could have broken my heart, added to all the sadness of Eliza has turned into a future Joy."

Bunny relished being capricious. There was a hiccup in negotiations with the Nantucket Conservation Foundation when, as she wrote to Sutherland, her offer of "100 acres to 'Conservation'" (the Nantucket Conservation Foundation) was queried over her specification that the property be used from time to time for what she called "a Children's [model plane] Airfield." In a huff—and perhaps just as a negotiating ploy—she told Sutherland that instead she had decided to "sell the front land" for development. In the negotiating process Bunny did well, and so did the foundation, which ultimately agreed that the local model airplane club, not coincidentally headed by the man who had moved her house for her, could use her land to fly their aircraft. Nantucketers called it "Lambert Field," a joking reference to the old airfield in St. Louis named after Bunny's birth family.

In April 2007, as Bunny neared her century mark, it was clear that many trees planted at the new house location were losing the struggle for life, so, like the inventive stage designer she was, Bunny sketched a wooden "tree" and its intended setting in a note to Sutherland. Carpenters created an eight-foot-tall version with movable "branches" that was duly "planted" next to a new wall to lend height and form to the garden. In the same note, she wrote that as "the sea throws sand back to the land to build up the banks, we can go on . . . keeping the past and the future living forever."

It is easy to laugh at Bunny and her extravagances or to gape at her amazing jealousies, her possessive desire to be the only woman in the room, or her sudden and sometimes permanent breaks with one friend or another. But what strikes me more is the energy and courage she found in Nantucket in the wake of Eliza's accident. Maybe she believed that if she could beat back the waves, if she could watch the daisies bloom again, her daughter would return to consciousness and to her mother.

By this time Bunny looked for any sign she could call hope. She was a firm believer in auguries, deciding a day was inauspicious for one activity or another depending on her horoscope or what her Virginia psychic, Beverley Newton, told her.

A month after the truck barreled around a corner on Houston Street and struck Eliza in May 2000, a strange thing happened on Nantucket. While Bunny was at Eliza's hospital bedside in New York, Daniel Sutherland, repairing shingles at South Pasture, suddenly found himself more or less "eyeball to eyeball" with a gigantic bird flying in from the ocean. Then it smoothly circled the field and soared back out across the Atlantic. A yellow-nosed albatross, a denizen of the South Atlantic and Indian Oceans, had found its way to New England, and had been sighted repeatedly in the area during the previous month. Grand and strong, with an eight-foot wingspread, and yet somehow comical with a bright yellow stripe running the full length of its nose, this distinctive apparition, Bunny decided, was a "hello" from Eliza on her way back. That didn't seem too unbelievable to Sutherland either.

In 2018, Daniel Sutherland and I stood outside the main house on a new terrace put in by the present owner, Franck Giraud, an art dealer who started working for Bunny after Paul's death. (Giraud was close to Bunny in her last years: he not only bought Eliza's loft on East Tenth Street, but was also extremely helpful to Bunny when she wanted to keep the location of a disputed Degas a secret after Paul's death.) The color of the terrace stone didn't match Bunny's original paving or the house steps, which both matched Nantucket's sand, tone for tone. Almost all building stone is brought in from elsewhere; Bunny brought some of her stone from Virginia and from Jackie Kennedy's house, Red Gate, on nearby Martha's Vineyard, after that place was sold following Jackie's death. At South Pasture, the new garden walls appeared disproportionately heavy—they didn't convey the lightness of Bunny's other projects. Sutherland unwillingly agreed and said, "Some things had become more of a struggle—she didn't have the same energy to push things through."

At ninety-one, Bunny had been forced to decide on a new location for her house when it was moved back from the cliff. "Bunny sat in a chair," Sutherland said. "We laid it out with hammer and stakes." She appeared to be as exacting as ever. "Two degrees this way, two degrees that way," Sutherland said. He noted that on the old site the front elevation of the main house had paralleled the ocean. I asked how Bunny had chosen the new spot, which faces west more directly, and what he thought of that. He said that she had wanted to consider the roll of the land more, and then he reluctantly added, "She did what had to be done." Knowing the place as he did, he went on, he thought the site's geometry regarding the relationship to the other structures . . . suffered because it didn't "feel" right. "Her downward trajectory began with the move."

Rolling along nicely

Moving the house back from the coast and settling it into its new surroundings coincided with the eight years Eliza spent in a persistent vegetative state, and Bunny came less frequently. She didn't want to leave her daughter for more than twenty-four hours at a stretch. Sutherland would tell her about the blue-eyed grass when she asked whether it was in flower or had finished flowering. "What is the land doing, Danny?" she would say on the phone. She wrote ecstatically to him about his book of photographs, which included shots of the original construction process and another sixteen pages about the "house in the air," as Bunny called it, making its way on rollers across the front field, and the final phase of setting it down on its new foundation, safe from the waves.

Bunny was so grateful to Sutherland for becoming her "eyes"—her macular degeneration was beginning—that she gave him a substantial present: Winslow Homer's *Children on the Beach*—little boys perched on an overturned dory, watching the tide and the sails outside the harbor—which she and Paul had bought in 1971. "That painting [had] hung over the fireplace in the kitchen where we ate lunch," said Sutherland. "It was the springboard for all kinds of discussions—about art, history, anything—or sailing—we were all sailors. We were all like-minded spirits, and Bam was our encyclopedia of general knowledge. Just imagine what that was like—picnicking with Mrs. Mellon, with the breeze coming in through the doors, sitting underneath that Winslow Homer." They all hung on Bam's sometimes outrageous proclamations—"Oh Bam, really!" Bunny would say—the crew told their tales of the sea, and Bunny told them about her father's great schooner *Atlantic*.

The Homer had always been protected when Bunny wasn't there. When she was on her way up to the island, a closet where it was kept under lock and key twenty-four hours a day was opened, and security was alerted—"I'm opening the closet now," whoever was in charge of hanging it or taking it down would say. He or she also had to sign in and out.

How was Bunny going to manage the absence of this great work of art in order to give it to Sutherland? Bunny and Paul often moved paintings around their houses, so it wouldn't really have been so unusual for something else to be hung in its place. And the work was one of the twelve Homers Paul had left to Bunny in his 1998 will. So it was, in fact, hers to dispose of, but she still treated her gift as an under-the-table business—a tendency that later came in handy when she characterized her secret contributions to the maintenance of Senator John Edwards's mistress, Rielle Hunter.

Bunny commissioned two landscape paintings of South Pasture from a local artist and replaced the Homer with one of them. *Children on the Beach* was flown in the Mellon plane to Oak Spring, where it was crated up properly and returned to Nantucket. "I never uncrated it," said Sutherland. "I got up my nerve to call Alex Forger [Bunny's personal lawyer] about what I should do, but he was away when I called. When we finally talked, I said I'd called about something else," Sutherland admitted.

In telling me about it, Sutherland sounded shocked, horrified—and, of course, delighted with the gift. Who wouldn't be? But this is where the very rich *are* different from the rest of us. This was far beyond even the casual gift of Jean Schlumberger bracelets to a startled antiques dealer. Sutherland later said that if he had declared the painting on his taxes, the gift tax alone would have wiped him out. "I gave it back to her after mulling it over, moving it around, dealing with the security required," he said. Most of all he worried, despite a signed and dated note from her, that "people would wonder if she really did give it to me. It became a burden." It sold at the auction of her masterworks at Sotheby's in November 2014 for $4.5 million.

Bunny's attempt to give Sutherland the Homer was more evidence that South Pasture was hers, inviolate, in every way. Unlike the houses that were monuments to a shared life, South Pasture offered her the independence she needed.

24

Magnificence in New York, Sorrow in D.C.

The place where Mellon money and power were most unabashedly on display was in New York City. Mary Conover Mellon and Paul Mellon had rented a classic Upper East Side townhouse at 125 East Seventieth Street that they used when they came to New York once or twice a month in the first years of their marriage. According to Paul's memoirs, in 1943 they stayed there while they awaited his wartime assignment overseas and he reported daily to headquarters. They spent many nights roistering with Chauncey Hubbard and other Yale pals, dining at "21," making the rounds of nightclubs, and then falling into bed in the early-morning hours.

After living in that brick house for a few years, Paul and Bunny decided on making some big changes to it. They rented a pair of adjoining apartments in the nearby Carlyle Hotel while the old Seventieth Street brick house and its neighbor in what was arguably Manhattan's most expensive neighborhood were gutted. Bunny made major alterations to their temporary housing, such as changing ceiling heights and having scenic painter Paul Leonard sketch witty silhouettes of furniture on the walls. The renovation process took two years—warp speed by Bunny's standards.

"Page Cross, the architect, is building a house for us on East Seventieth Street," Paul told *The New Yorker*'s "Talk of the Town" in 1963 when he became president of the National Gallery of Art (for the second time, having resigned to go to war). "I used to have a house on the same site, but it got sort of bedraggled."

The new house was anything but bedraggled. Markedly masculine and a bit exotic, the ground-floor decor showcased Paul's interests in England, English country life, and the beauty of animals in movement. Even the small, narrow entry foyer was exciting. George Stubbs's dramatically shadowed *Portrait of a Zebra, standing, turned to the left, in a park* hung over the hall table; the bright spots were her black-and-white-striped belly and gleaming haunch. A polished black limestone blackamoor bust—now at the Yale Center for British Art (as is the *Zebra*)—beautiful, proud, muscled, erect—came next. His pectorals, too, caught the light like a shield. This bust was once supposed to be a portrait from life of "Psyche, an athlete in the employ of the Duke of Northumberland," and he certainly looks the part of any boxer or bodyguard—or an African nobleman or king. In the Mellons' version of the twentieth century, black footmen waited in front halls to open the door.

Next in the architectural lineup came a pale little space cornered with classical pilasters marbleized under the direction of none other than John Fowler, owner with Nancy Lancaster of the London decorator firm of Colefax & Fowler and himself a superb decorative artist. (Leonard and Strom, the scenic painters who got their start with Bunny at Eliza's coming-out party, were flown to England to learn directly from Fowler.) Because of the dark entryway and the intense light farther down the narrow hallway, the alternation of spaces could feel like a run of strobe flashes: dark/light/dark/light. Past Fowler's columns and in the hall proper, straw-colored walls were hung with vivid sketches of animals by Stubbs and Eugène Delacroix.

A few steps farther on and off to the left, light from the outdoors streamed into a jeu d'esprit of wicker, Bunny's city version of her Oak Spring Basket Room. The walls were trellised, as were cornice and ceiling, in narrow strips of honey-colored lath. The floor was almost entirely covered with a tumble of baskets from Bunny's large collection. The room was a trompe l'oeil masterpiece to make you laugh, a garden arcade mimicked indoors. On the walls hung other trompe l'oeil gestures: small panels that were painted as the kind of latticework letter racks found in the halls of well-run Edwardian country houses into which were thrust all the things the house's inhabitants wanted to remember or didn't quite know what do with: envelopes, invitations to the next party, reminder notes, keys, pencils, sketches of flowers, a tiny architectural floor plan, a playing card, a feather.

Bunny's "letter racks," like the objects Fernand Renard painted on the walls of the Oak Spring greenhouse, bore the subliminal message that *you are what you remember and what you hold dear.* The Sotheby's estimate for each panel was $600 to $800; each fetched more than $6,000, for a total of $22,500. They were painted by another English decorative artist, George Oakes, part of the Colefax & Fowler team for special projects, who would also paint the iron chairs at Oak Spring for the Prince and Princess of Wales' 1985 visit.

A narrow central path ran through the heaps of baskets and through a pair of doors into the garden, which was strictly French and urban: an ivy parterre edged with Bunny's standby 'Kingsville Dwarf' box, meaning that the simple-patterned "garden carpet" was composed of just two textures, two slightly varied heights, and two shades of green. Less is more in this case: Bunny knew how to limit herself as well as go the limit. Four stone obelisks held down the "carpet" corners. Fruit trees, along with bulbs and flowering shrubs in narrow borders, served as the garden's seasonal clocks. The white latticed pavilion in a corner with its fleur-de-lis finial acted as an eyecatcher.

Back indoors via the Basket Room garden entry, across the hall was Paul's study and library, a large room densely drag-painted (a process that creates a textured wall pattern) in a watermelon color. In the comfortable dimness, windows framed the brightness of the garden, creating living paintings brought indoors. Paul's desk glistened with every grand desk tool a man could imagine. Over the mantel hung Canaletto's pellucid *Warwick Castle*, now at Yale and evidently one of Paul's favorite works, as he included it in the color pages of his memoir.

Unlike that of most American businessmen, Paul's job was to give away money, and a squadron of able administrators and experts guarded his hoard. Starting in the 1950s, Paul had found a way to organize his life to satisfy himself. "From being a squirrel in a revolving cage, one might say, I became rather a bird dog, a pointer perhaps, guiding others towards various artistic, charitable, and financial efforts that I thought needed undertaking or improvement" was how he described it.

A man born in Pittsburgh with museums in Washington, New Haven, and Richmond that he cherished and to which he gave millions, Paul found New York City convenient but perhaps not lovable, except for the art galleries into which he strolled "to look at pictures" for hours, as he disarmingly wrote. Paul also told a reporter that in reality his office in Washington was where he spent "most of most weeks." His daily urban life, wherever he spent it, was generally separate from Bunny's, as were the lives of most successful men of the period who spent the bulk of their time in the decidedly masculine atmosphere of offices and clubs.

Bunny spent less time in New York than Paul. For both of them Virginia was home and the city a perch, a place in between, somewhere to entertain, to house guests, a place from which to survey the gallery scene and, for Bunny, to do some shopping. Christmas for Bunny involved not only tirelessly visiting antiques shops, often incognito, for just the right thing but also purchasing small Schlumberger items—including the famed enameled bangles—in what amounted to wholesale quantities for many startled and delighted people.

Sam Kasten said, "She was obviously extravagant, frivolous, and more. But she was also brilliant, a world-class designer, and she certainly had her moments of real decency. I think her care of artisans speaks to that. Not typical in that stratosphere. I have been crushed by powerful people in my life as an artisan; never by Bunny."

MUCH OF THE cubic footage of this expensive city real estate was—air. A column of air five stories high ascended over the garden that occupied the heart of the complex; a terrace on the third floor added still more open space. Consequently, the house had three exposures, a great rarity in any city. Inside, ceilings so high had surely not been built in New York since the Gilded Age.

After a short ride up in the small white elevator at the end of the front hall—with a single tiny Ben Nicholson on the wall—the Mellons' private house started on the third floor. (The kitchen and some staff rooms were on the second floor.) I asked Dr. Bruce Horten what his first impression was of the New York house. "The magnificent cut flowers—never too tall—in the vestibule," he said, then stopped and added, "and the security. You couldn't get any farther without somebody checking on you. The elevator was a bit claustrophobic, but afterwards you found yourself upstairs in the light that poured in through French windows with four still lifes by the Italian painter and printmaker Giorgio Morandi on the way to the living room, where Bunny's chair stood next to a wall hung with small Degas sketches."

Over the living room mantel hung a beautiful John Singer Sargent portrait, *Miss Beatrice Townsend*, a twelve-year-old whose little terrier rests on her hip, cuddled against the red satin sash that emphasizes the girl's small waist. Beatrice Townsend's eyes take you in carefully; she is not commanding but curious; she is neither bold nor impudent— instead, she appears to be at ease and assured, her eyebrows slightly raised. Sargent had a way with painting children, especially girls who were leaving childhood to approach adulthood. Any woman looking at that portrait feels a wave of answering curiosity and—later, once she knows the story—sorrow; Beatrice died two years after Sargent painted this portrait.

Andrew Mellon bought the painting in 1936; eventually he gave it to Paul, who bequeathed it to the National Gallery of Art in 1999, leaving it first to Bunny in her life estate. Bunny, writing to the then-director of the NGA, Earl A. Powell III, in 2006, the year the New York house was put on the market and the painting went to the museum, noted that it was "the only picture that father Andrew Mellon gave him."

Much seems wrapped up in this work: Andrew Mellon's bruising treatment of his son over the years, Paul's memory of that treatment, and Bunny's fascination with depictions of solitary women and girls, perhaps a form of self-recognition.

Sargent's painting looked at home against a soft background of peach/orange strié. Bunny had darkened her palette for this city dwelling, choosing stronger colors than any she used at Oak Spring,

Oyster Harbors, or King's Leap. The dining room was treated with a complex layered coating of deep cobalt. Manet's *George Moore in the Artist's Garden*, now also at the NGA, held its own between two windows, and Manet's vine-covered trellis fence brought his garden into the room. A spectacular terrace ran the full width of the living and dining rooms and was reached through French doors.

Outdoors on the terrace Bunny again became a master of make-believe: again she used wooden trellising that ran wild, climbing the wall of the neighbor's house, up, up, up from the terrace floor. That tall expanse was also broken by optical illusions, even a couple of false-perspective oeils-de-beouf, or circular "windows," that echoed the real window and door embrasures they faced on the Mellon house wall. Screening off a neighbor's wall was hardly news in New York City, but this involved true legerdemain.

Bunny and Paul had suites on the fourth floor, while guest rooms were on the fifth, along with additional staff quarters. Bunny's touch hovered over each guest even if she herself was absent: Sam Kasten and his Nantucket Looms colleague and Bunny's close friend Andy Oates were invited to Antigua and spent a night in the New York house before flying to the Caribbean. "Bunny wasn't there, nor was she going to be in Antigua," said Kasten on the phone, "but on the bedside table was a bud vase . . . with a white flower, a sprig of spring flowers, lily of the valley, from Virginia." Kasten choked up as he remembered Bunny's note, written in her hand, and what it meant to him that she had thought to do this. "Dear Sam, I hope you have a wonderful time in Antigua . . ."

At the palace of Versailles, courtiers were honored to be given rooms or even the merest corners of rooms—marks of favor from the king. The Seventieth Street house could not accommodate all the many members of the Mellon retinue who came and went over the years, but the chosen few, such as Hubert de Givenchy, had "their" rooms, though others also sometimes used them. Kenneth Battelle, New York society's hairstylist, and Leonard and Strom, the scenic painters, were stowed in the building across the street, another townhouse that was cut up into apartments. So was interior designer Bruce Budd at the beginning of his thirteen-year career with Bunny, before he was given the carriage house on the next block. Paul also bought a townhouse right around the corner at 713 Park Avenue that he used as an office.

The Mellons were by no means the only storied American family to buy up real estate in the neighborhood. East Sixty-Third Street and surrounding thoroughfares provided spaces for Jock Whitney, Paul's friend at Yale and neighbor in Virginia, who became as notable in American racing and Thoroughbred breeding as Paul. Later he became Paul's ally as trustee at the National Gallery and an art collector himself.

Whitney's first wife was Bunny's Millwood playmate Liz (Mary Elizabeth) Altemus; his second was Babe Paley's sister Betsey, one of the three fabled Cushing sisters of Boston. Bunny told me what she thought about "all the social people in New York," and was determined not to see herself in that category. She saw Babe Paley as a symbol of New York high society in general (a symbol, in fact, she perfectly embodied).

It's no wonder, then, that Bunny had a reputation for being icy and distant in the circles she moved in. She thawed completely only for Jackie Kennedy, who, by the time the Mellon house was finished in 1966, had been living in New York with her children for more than a year after the assassination of the president. She and Bunny were both temporarily living at the Carlyle Hotel while Jackie's apartment at 1040 Fifth Avenue (facing Central Park and the Metropolitan Museum) was being renovated.

Closer to each other than to their own sisters, they now were living only floors apart. Bunny had been emotionally distant from her sister, Lily Lambert Fleming McCarthy, since childhood and would remain so. Lee Radziwill supported Jackie in her trials, but nonetheless strains in their relationship were apparent. In 1962, after a lunch with Radziwill, Truman Capote had said to Cecil Beaton, "My God, how jealous she is of Jackie."

The pleasure of excluding others likely played no small part in Bunny's relationship with Jackie. An Emily Dickinson poem eerily sums up that friendship. It begins: *"The Soul selects her own Society— /*

Then—shuts the Door . . ." It ends: "*I've known her—from an ample nation— / Choose One— / Then—close the Valves of her attention— / Like Stone.*"

I think Bunny considered New York's social turf a challenge that she could meet and beat on her own terms. Some of those terms are laid out visually in a 1977 *W* piece by the late André Leon Talley (then making his ascent in the fashion and style world to become creative director at *Vogue*) about who owned Schlumberger jewels and how many and what they had cost. The article includes pictures of eight of Schlumberger's most prominent and fashionable patrons: Evangeline Bruce (the only non–New Yorker); Françoise de Langlade, a Condé Nast editor and wife of the fashion designer Oscar de la Renta; the art collector and philanthropist Kitty Miller; the fashion editor Diana Vreeland; the fashion icon Lady "Slim" Keith; the socialite Nan Kempner; Bunny; and, of course, Jacqueline Kennedy. All are photographed either in luscious "at home" outfits or at a party, and all are looking prettily at the camera—except for Bunny, who owned the store as regards Schlumberger pieces. Bunny is seen in a very small candid shot and in profile (which she preferred). She appears to be moving fast across what is clearly an Upper East Side street wearing navy blue street clothes (Givenchy and a matching hat) and clutching a sheaf of papers. "Take *that!*" is what the photo says to me.

At 125 East Seventieth Street, Bunny's parties were generally small—Bruce Budd wrote me to say that he "often thought the New York house, with its intimate 'French' rooms, was more about them, really, a house for just Paul and Bunny—for small gatherings— for conversation. The dining table, when not used, had only four chairs around it." The only big celebratory space was the terrace— occasionally used to full advantage, as it was once when the cabaret singer and pianist Bobby Short came to play. Bunny, never at a loss for a way to make a performance perfect, simply had a piano moved out there through the French doors.

Whether the events were small or large, those with knowledgeable eyes knew what they saw. After the eminent art historian Colin Eisler came for lunch with Paul and Bunny, he told a friend, "I recognized their china as Chantilly and was terrified that if I dropped the heavy eighteenth-century pistol-handled knife on the plate, that would have meant about seven hundred dollars' worth of broken china."

Then there were the table linens. "I lived in the Mellons' New York house on Seventieth Street while my mother [Liza Maugham] was fixing up her house there," recalled Bunny's goddaughter Camilla Chandon. She was accompanied by Florrie, her mother's lady's maid, "who was part of our family—oh, that was part of an older time— having a lady's maid," added Chandon hastily. Florrie was most impressed by the amazing Porthault linens.

Later Givenchy and Bunny designed magnificently countryish white or blue table linens, each embroidered at one corner with a little cloud, a cabbage, or a tree motif inspired by an old Rouen plate they both loved. Schlumberger also designed several sets of linens marked with the same entwined initials he had created to conceal inside Bunny's many Givenchy pocketbooks. All these linens were from the French workshop of Nicole de Montesquieu, who also worked for the Duchess of Windsor. Why, you might ask, do I record the social altitude of these minor details? To help you understand to what lengths Bunny was prepared to go for the pleasures of collaboration and perfection. She was spinning a life with her friends, and it didn't matter what it cost.

In New York, Bunny spent a lot of time privately with Jackie, shopping, lunching, talking books and theater and art. She was there for the big events too. When Jackie's sister gave her a "coming-out party," Jackie's first big public outing in 1965, Bunny was there. And she and Jackie together presided over the benefit opening of a private Schlumberger exhibition at the Wildenstein Gallery. "All the social people in New York," whom Bunny didn't want to bother with, were, of course, in attendance.

When Jackie's children were almost grown (Caroline was taking Sotheby's renowned art appreciation course in London, and John Jr. was working his way through the Collegiate School on the Upper West Side), Jackie wanted to find something else to do. In 1975, the journalist Jimmy Breslin, her old friend, said, "You should work as an editor. What do you think you're going to do, attend openings for the rest of your life?"

Jackie started that year as a consulting editor at Viking Press. Barbara Burn, then an editor there, told me that on Jackie's first day she was asked by Tom Guinzburg, her boss, to take the new hire to lunch. Burn blithely named her usual reservation at the Carlyle—"Burn, two"—only to be ignored by the starstruck maître d', who seated them at a table big enough for eight. Later Jackie worked at Doubleday; in total she produced over a hundred books, working into the early 1990s, even as she underwent treatment for her cancer.

During those decades, Bunny made start after start on her memoir, leaving each draft unfinished, although Jackie encouraged her repeatedly. To me it appeared that once Bunny got past describing her childhood, which seemed to have a certain clarity for her, events and emotions would surface that felt too complex for her to explain. Bunny's impulse was never to look back, only forward. When I asked her yet again about her divorce from Stacy, she answered me by saying that even Lily Guest—an old friend, the wife of famed polo player Raymond Guest, and a longtime Washingtonian with a country house not far from Upperville—had pressed her on the subject, saying, "But, Bunny, you must say something so we can take sides." Bunny said she told Lily, "All that 'he is a bad boy, I am a good girl'; I wouldn't have any of it."

NO MATTER HOW old or young, whoever was invited within the nimbus of Bunny Mellon's infinitely detailed world would, at one point or another—and maybe only fleetingly, precariously—be astounded by the pleasure of surprise.

For one Foxcroft classmate the surprise happened the week after Christmas in 1956. I was staying with the Mellons in New York; Eliza and I had both turned fourteen. A revival of one of the last of the great revues, *The Show Is On*, produced by the Shuberts, had opened on Christmas Day. Everyone had written a song, including the Gershwins, Rodgers and Hart, and Harold Arlen. About the original 1936 production, Brooks Atkinson in *The New York Times* said that Vincente Minnelli, who conceived and staged this love letter to Broadway, had pressed all the material into "a luminous work of art." A spotlit Bea Lillie swung out over the orchestra on a wire, sitting in a half-moon above our heads (we were, of course, midorchestra in perfect seats). She kicked off one of her glittery silver slippers, which fell down close by—just not quite near enough to grab. She spoofed Josephine Baker's "A Message from the Man in the Moon," singing a parody of the tune about "our celestial neighbor." Eliza was hooked by the magic of Broadway songs for the rest of her life. Maybe she (and I) didn't have a clue about Josephine Baker, but we could tell Bea Lillie was making a joke.

The next morning the magic continued. In one of the guest rooms in the old house, up at the top, on the fifth floor, looking out over the nearest rooftops along Seventieth Street with a window that faced east to the late-December sunrise, a maid came in with a breakfast tray. I had never had breakfast in bed unless I was sick. I had no idea where Eliza was.

On my tray was a three-inch-high pile of the thinnest crêpes, not that I knew that word at the time. At that moment the sun's rays hit the stack of pancakes, running across the golden top, slanting down the lacy, curled brown edges, highlighting each one. Even syrup, usually my favorite thing about pancakes, was nothing compared to that sight, my most lasting memory of the Mellon house on East Seventieth Street.

MULTIPLE RESIDENCES GAVE Paul and Bunny the privacy and space they needed to carry on their complicated relationship. In D.C., Paul lived a virtually separate life in a stately, seven-bay, neo-Georgian brick house that backed up, appropriately enough for a man who loved England and collected British art, on the garden side of the British ambassador's residence, located on Embassy Row. The 3055 Whitehaven Street home was designed by Nathan C. Wyeth, the Carrère & Hastings architect who also designed the West Wing of the White House and created the Oval Office.

At Whitehaven Street, Paul conducted his business affairs and had his almost-weekly evenings with Dorcas Hardin. In a neighboring, equally grand brick house, also designed by Wyeth, Paul stashed many of his favorite works of art, including Paul Cézanne's *Boy in a Red Waistcoat*, purchased in 1958, when Paul was fifty and his marriage with Bunny was just entering its new "partnership," as he styled it.

Kalorama Circle, farther in toward the center of D.C. than Whitehaven Street, had provided Bunny with her first experience of life in the nation's capital. As Mrs. Stacy Lloyd she had stayed at her father's house awaiting Eliza's birth in November 1942. Both that house and the one on Whitehaven Street are in D.C.'s Northwest district, a major residential hub of the city's power elite. After the Obama and Trump presidencies, both the Obamas and Ivanka Trump and Jared Kushner all lived on Kalorama Circle, which lies just off Embassy Row on Massachusetts Avenue, far from the intimate social cauldron of little brick houses in Georgetown.

Sally Bedell Smith, in *Grace and Power*, perfectly situated Paul and Bunny in the Washington, D.C., of that period, when Bunny, as Jackie's friend and mentor as well as a member of the White House Fine Arts Committee, was quietly designing and planting the Rose Garden in addition to advising Jackie on details such as replacements for the "ghastly brass doorknobs" at the White House. The Mellons, wrote Bedell Smith, were "the twentieth-century equivalent of Edith Wharton's van der Luydens, who 'stood above all of them' and 'faded into a kind of super-terrestrial twilight': shy and gentle, the ultimate in discernment, seldom seen on the party circuit." Bedell Smith goes on to quote Marion "Oatsie" Charles, a powerful D.C. and Newport hostess: "The Mellons didn't have to inhabit anyone else's world. Everyone had to come to them."

Bunny staged an occasional grand dinner at Whitehaven Street, such as that before the opening of the 1985 exhibition *Treasure Houses of Britain*, for which flowers, plants, and even trees were trucked in from the Rokeby greenhouses. D.C., while often enjoyable, also represented work for Bunny, such as designing the White House gardens or teaching the White House staff how to create seventeenth-century still lifes in the flower room she installed at the Executive Mansion. Both were comparatively solitary occupations, and she was the boss,

Dear Bunny—
An evening made nice because you were here—
Fondly- Nancy

First Lady Nancy Reagan; Princess Alexandra, the Honourable
Lady Ogilvy; Bunny; and Gloria Vanderbilt party at the White House
on April 19, 1983. "An evening made nice because you were here,"
wrote the First Lady on the photo sent to Bunny.

as she also was when she designed a layered green garden with eight
kinds of boxwood to front the baldly modernist cinder-block house
that the journalist Joseph Alsop built in Georgetown (perhaps partly
to scandalize his neighbors).

Less pleasurable, perhaps because less solitary or creative, were the
galas and dinners at the National Gallery in which she participated
until 1985, when Paul retired as chairman and he and Bunny ceased
lending works of art from their own houses. At these events Bunny
was always by choice the producer and never the star player, often pre-
ferring to be driven back to Upperville after an event. In an important
sense both the White House and the National Gallery were protection for Bunny in a D.C. where, as one observer said, "Dorcas Hardin
owned Georgetown."

Seven Georgetown ladies ran the capital's cultural institutions and social life—and its powerful gossip mill. What Sally Quinn, the journalist and wife of *The Washington Post*'s Ben Bradlee and later also a member of what Ronald Reagan dubbed "The Georgetown Ladies' Social Club," said on her blog about those old days is now a bromide: "The people who did the entertaining were women who today would have a career, and what they did for a living was to bring people together."

About the Georgetown political scene in the 1950s and '60s, Evan Thomas, author of *The Very Best Men: Four Who Dared: The Early Years of the CIA,* said to an interviewer, "They sort of put down Eisenhower as being dull, Midwestern, wore bad suits, didn't know the right wines." Georgetown, male and female, *did* know: most of them by birth or marriage belonged to what Joseph Alsop once called "the WASP Ascendency," the tight society of families who went to the same New England schools, belonged to the same clubs, and married one another. Thomas also described the players of JFK's Georgetown as "sharper and cooler . . . liberal interventionists . . . who wanted to save the world by conquering the world."

Georgetown's top women were just as sharp and cool as their men. They knew how to conquer D.C. Most had status because of their husbands' positions, but they also had power of their own. Besides Oatsie Charles, the group included "Polly" Wisner, the widow of the early CIA star Frank Wisner (she then married the columnist Clayton Fritchie); Katharine Graham of *The Washington Post*; Lorraine Cooper, the wife of the multi-term Kentucky Republican senator and ambassador John Sherman Cooper; Polly Kraft, the wife of Joseph Kraft, the columnist and speechwriter for John Kennedy in his election year; Susan Mary Alsop, Joseph Alsop's wife; and the political activist and diplomat Pamela Harriman, famed for her multiple dalliances, three marriages, and Democratic political clout in the 1980s. (Bunny once said to me that she hadn't wanted to become close to Harriman, who had a house not far away in Virginia, as she was sure Pamela would try to steal Paul.) Graham had briefly been friends with Bunny in the 1960s, but for never-disclosed reasons their relationship cooled. Only Evangeline Bruce was Bunny's true intimate, the one who was privy to Bunny's heartaches.

Like all of JFK's sexual affairs, Paul Mellon and Dorcas Hardin's arrangement was never covered by the press, although it seems that everyone in D.C. knew about it. "Dorcas was fun! Easy. It was a very open relationship," recalled Janet Bruce, David and Evangeline Bruce's daughter-in-law, who had been one of a party of four women, including Dorcas and Polly Wisner Fritchie, who went on a shopping tour together in New York. Jim, the Mellons' chauffeur, had driven them around.

Katharine Graham reportedly threatened her reporters to ensure a kind of official privacy for Paul's affair, saying, "If a single line appears in [the] paper about this, that reporter will be out of a job before the ink is dry on the page." Graham had publicly acknowledged her friendship with Bunny only by noting its breach, calling her "my then-friend Bunny Mellon" in print without saying what had happened. Graham protected Paul and Dorcas, which thus in a sidelong sense protected Bunny as well.

Little slipped by these Georgetown women. Meryl Gordon quoted Oatsie Charles as telling her that when David Bruce mentioned Paul and Dorcas at a dinner, she "nearly broke [her] neck rushing downstairs to tell Lily Guest and Hallie Covington." Once Janet Bruce wore a cabochon ruby ring to a luncheon. Katharine Graham spied it. "Schlumberger," she said. "Evangeline's?" Janet Bruce told me that Bunny had given Evangeline not only the ruby ring but also two other cocktail rings, a cabochon emerald and a diamond beehive, all Schlumberger.

Who were Bunny's real friends in D.C.? Jackie Kennedy topped the list even before she became First Lady; after she moved to New York in 1964 she remained Bunny's closest confidante until her death thirty years later. Evangeline Bruce was an ally and a closemouthed one. Bunny did talk with her friends and family about Dorcas, but when she did so she cast the affair mostly as a tiresome joke. Bunny and Vangie's close, loving relationship was played out in a different key and, of necessity, carried on in a voluminous correspondence. Vangie was constantly away, a partner in her husband David's extensive diplomatic career. Her maddeningly undated letters to Bunny about friends, children, gardens and plants, servants, travel, and doctors seldom ventured beyond the humdrum, but they had meaning for Bunny simply because they *existed*.

The rope of those letters from Evangeline, so steady, funny, gossipy, comforting, and sometimes worldly, helped carry Bunny across her abysses of pique, rage, sorrow, and loneliness. Vangie counseled Bunny, for instance, that Marie-Hélène Bouilloux-Lafont really *was* her loyal friend and could be trusted. (Bunny had felt that Marie-Hélène got in the way of her relationship with Hubert.) Vangie agreed that, yes, Adele Astaire's grandchild *was* difficult. And every once in a while Vangie wondered discreetly how her friend was doing: "Write and tell me if the three days are happy ones."

Occasionally, in the few letters Bunny wrote back, she opens up, as she did in writing to Vangie's son, her godchild David S. Bruce, about her long relationship with his parents. Bunny said, "Everything connected with your father & mother are wonderful Happy Memories." Again and again, to others and also to her godson, she mentions how lonely she had been, and how David as well as Evangeline had been her support: "Your father often befriended me in Paris when I was alone—we were both at the Crillon & had dinner together at the end of a day." Before Bunny got her own apartment on Avenue Foch she was still finding her way in Paris.

Katharine Graham, born less than a decade after the other Georgetown women's mafia, left that cloistered world behind when she became the publisher of the family newspaper, *The Washington Post*. In her autobiography, *Personal History*, she tackled how she—and Bunny, though not Vangie—had been brought up to think that "women were intellectually inferior to men . . . not capable of managing anything but our homes and our children . . . Pretty soon this kind of thinking—indeed this kind of life—took its toll . . . most of us *became* somehow inferior . . . largely silent, unable to participate in conversations and discussions," producing "in women—as it did in me—a diffuse way of talking." Bunny's scattershot delivery was a version of this "diffuse way of talking."

Vangie, far better educated than Bunny and at ease in the complicated diplomatic universe, wrote to Bunny in witty, indirect language about an opulent daily life that didn't include much more than a whisper of sorrow or irony. Reading these letters today is a translator's work. Vangie and Bunny's mid–twentieth century seems like another country, one that requires a different currency and a passport. But every once in a while both sorrow and irony intruded. In the mid-1950s, just when Bunny and Paul's crisis was coming to a boil and before Paul's affair began, Vangie encouraged Bunny in a letter to find a different and more solitary road without Paul. Vangie wrote, "La faculté de donner à l'existence le sens d'une aventure où la solitude elle-même est une poésie." *The ability to give one's life a sense of adventure when solitude is its only poem.*

Bunny's friend Evangeline Bruce,
who knew the world and its troubles

Perry Wheeler, Bunny's right hand in creating the Rose Garden and many others, was also a comrade and a real confidant. She wrote to him about her heartache and rage over Dorcas, even as the two of them continued steadily to improve the gardens of Paul's house at 3055 Whitehaven Street. Making a garden is such slow work that the intention, whatever it is at the start, is often outrun by the reality of events.

In 1960, Wheeler's memos to her dealt mainly with the essential details of perfecting the garden and grounds—thinning trees, redesigning the top of a brick wall, providing labels for all new trees and shrubs, planting lavender, installing wires to support a clematis. But Bunny's eye could always spot the need for a perfect addition. Black garden furniture was to be painted a beautiful gray-green, the color of the leaves and smooth bark of *Corylopsis sinensis* var. *sinensis*, the fragrant early-spring-flowering Chinese winter hazel, a shrub that Bunny had just seen and bought at her favorite place to shop for plants, Henry Hohman's Kingsville Nursery in Maryland. As Wheeler wrote to Hohman, "Mrs. Mellon would like to reserve more." In fact, she asked for all he had. No half measures for Bunny Mellon.

But by 1966, Bunny was being forced to take in the reality that Paul's affair was no flash-in-the-pan romance—it was still going strong after five years. A flourishing Whitehaven Street, like Oak Spring, would offer Paul "the true, real, and simple happiness of life"—the happiness that Bunny knew how to provide that she felt Dorcas Hardin had taken away.

Paul, however, was the man who reportedly said, "Pleasure is the engine of civilization." He was used to getting what he wanted, and in 1966 Dorcas was the pleasure he wanted most, not beautifully painted gray-green garden furniture or even coziness at the farm—although I believe he didn't see why he couldn't have both. Sometimes his promise to Bunny, "You will be Mrs. Paul Mellon, and you will have all the money you want," must have rung harshly in her ears.

The first years of Paul and Dorcas's affair were also the Kennedy years, years that had brought a new level of moral relativity to Washington, D.C.—not that extramarital affairs were in any way unheard of before that. Cecil Beaton confided to his diary that Jackie had known of her husband's infidelities and had told her sister of them. And if Lee Radziwill knew, then surely Bunny knew.

More than anything else, her February letter to Wheeler had expressed how much she longed for protection and comforting: "Don't you find one has to tighten one's friendships and let very few in?" In her letter, Bunny then moved swiftly onto much safer ground: planning an event. "Do you think that Mr. Young [at the White House] would lend me the vermeil bamboo center dishes for our Party?" she asked Perry.

Perry Wheeler knew about the shame, distress, and heartache Bunny went through, and ultimately maybe he knew too much for her comfort. No clear reason was ever expressed for the break between them, but Perry was eventually asked to give up Spring Hill, the house he had built on land at the farm that he'd been given.

The 1966 National Gallery exhibition, *French Paintings from the Collections of Mr. and Mrs. Paul Mellon and Mrs. Mellon Bruce*, essentially marked the end of the couple's most intensive collecting period together. Both Bunny and Paul told me they continued always to consult each other on most purchases, wandering into the other's bedroom with an auction catalogue to discuss a bid, or mentioning a particularly delectable painting seen in Paris, or revising the changing displays in their houses. The late sixties saw Bunny quite insistently putting a good face on her marriage with the "Nothing should be noticed" article in *The New York Times* in 1969.

The 1970s kept Bunny busy in D.C. with National Gallery galas, including the opening of the East Building, but they also saw a change in the woman Bunny was becoming: someone with an apartment on Avenue Foch in Paris; someone who became a Democrat because she detested Richard Nixon, while her husband remained a Republican; a woman to whom her husband for the first time gave $500,000 annually to be spent on charity without having to ask him for funds; someone who found more time to spend with Jackie Kennedy anywhere but in D.C.; and the woman who hired the young graduate student Dita Amory (later a prominent curator at the Metropolitan Museum of Art) to help organize her book collection at the farm, the first real step forward toward the monumental Oak Spring Garden Library. (Ground was broken in 1976, but Edward Larrabee Barnes was busy with other projects, so the work was completed in 1981.)

The 1980s saw Paul retiring, while Bunny increasingly organized projects and events away from Washington, such as the Oak Spring Dairy, the marriage of Caroline Kennedy to Edwin Schlossberg on Cape Cod (where Bunny first met Robert Isabell), and, in 1989, the publication of her first library catalogue, *An Oak Spring Sylva*, and the first public exhibition, *An Oak Spring Garland*, of a small number of her library holdings, at Princeton University. In her foreword to the small exhibition catalogue Bunny looked back at her childhood in

Princeton, New Jersey, but clearly she was moving forward to a new sense of self-definition.

Bunny, who had been collecting books seriously since the 1950s, had perhaps only now realized her library would be her own lasting monument, not just a handsome botanical collection but a living institution to pair with the living garden below the hill.

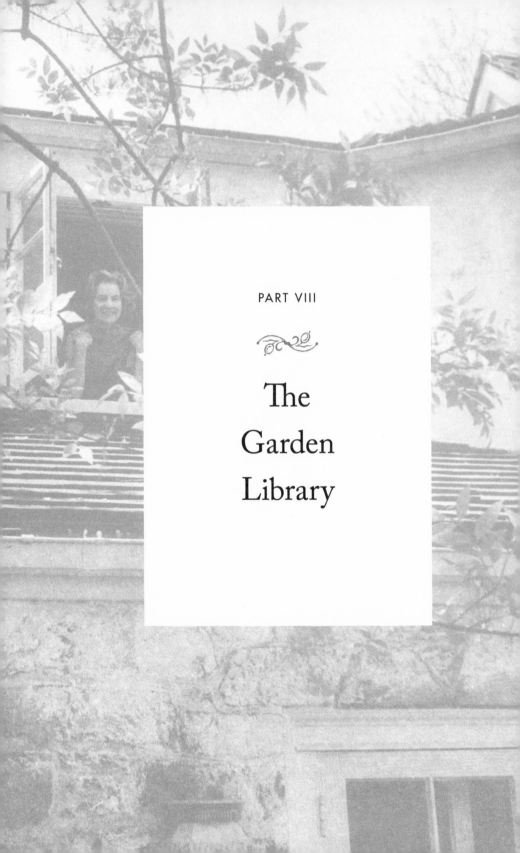

PART VIII

The
Garden
Library

25

A House of Books

Though no one would have called her "literary," Bunny owned thousands of books. The four catalogues that the Oak Spring Garden Library published comprise an enviable record of someone who responded to beauty on the page in interconnected fields: horticulture, botany, design, and global exploration of the plant world (all of which require illustration of some kind). Visual learning was key for her. Could she have had dyslexia? Casual remarks that she was never seen with a book in her hands might support the idea, and many people born a century ago lived out their lives with undiagnosed reading deficits that they triumphantly overcame and turned to their advantage without ever discussing it.

I corresponded with Dita Amory, Bunny's first librarian and now the Curator in Charge of the Robert Lehman Collection at the Met, to ask her about something Bunny had said to me: "Sometimes people don't think I know anyone *or anything*, and then they find out that I do, and that is always interesting." Amory disagreed with my hunch that Bunny may have had some sort of reading disability, writing:

> How could someone who collected extraordinary books, in and out of the library, suffer that impairment? She often quoted literature as well, though I can't think of an example. I never saw her reading, but that is no surprise, as I was her employee, and we had much to discuss. I attribute that self-deprecating quote to a fragile ego, especially in the company

of academics. She always regretted not having a college degree (and her honorary degree from RISD late in life must have meant the world to her).

Did Bunny believe that she had to find a way to define herself separately from Paul? She lived most of the decades of their long marriage designated in their art collections and loans as "and Mrs. Paul Mellon." Although with Paul's willing assent and generous funding, she herself had amassed the holdings of what would become the Oak Spring Garden Library. Finally, after Paul's death and in planning for her own, she arranged to sell at auction most of what art hadn't been previously sold or given away, determined that the proceeds would fund a foundation named after her father and, through it, cement the library's future, her own monument and memorial, and that of her own family, the Lamberts.

The skylit modernist shard of whitewashed local stone standing on the hill above Little Oak Spring holds a collection of more than 19,000 objects, including rare books, manuscripts, and works of art dating back to the fourteenth century. In what Bunny called "the main book room," an airy gallery about one-and-a-half times the length of an Olympic swimming pool, light surges in from all four sides.

On the walls hang still lifes by the seventeenth-century Flemish painter Daniel Seghers, a Pissarro, and a Winslow Homer, some now shown in reproduction because the originals were sold at Sotheby's to fund the library. The major works are interspersed with dozens of lesser, garden-related works—nineteenth-century watercolors and washes, twentieth-century flower paintings, and a primitive of a log cabin, a reminder of rustic Millwood—the Virginia village that little Lord Brooke, Bunny's English "war child" and later the Earl of Warwick, had once described as a "Tobacco Row"—and of Paul and Bunny's first days and nights together in the old Fletcher log cabin.

On the walls also hang photographs of Tuffy and Eliza and some of Eliza's strong and enigmatic paintings and collages. Foxcroft's handsome Miss Charlotte Haxall Noland poses against an oak tree wearing formal hunting gear: beautifully tied stock, and a pair of the big pale wash leather gloves that can stand a lot of soap and water and saddle soap to keep clean and flexible. The skirt of her sidesaddle habit is just visible at the bottom of the shot; her long-lashed hunting crop is in her hands. She looks thoughtful but also ready to school her pupils on how to follow their fox.

A 1930s watercolor by the then–ragingly fashionable artist Rex Whistler of a costume for the Empress Josephine for *The Private Life of Napoleon Buonaparte*, one of a series of sketches for a London theatrical, exhales the giddy air of the international society that Bunny Lloyd had been part of as a teenager. The Whistler also recalls Evangeline Bruce, who, after her long stint as America's perfect Mme Ambassadress, wrote a fine-textured double biography of Napoleon and Josephine—"an improbable marriage," Bruce called it—based on their letters.

Bunny gave Miss Charlotte Noland (1883–1969), founder and headmistress of Foxcroft School, pride of place in the library.

A grand piano is dwarfed by the size of the room, which is shortened by an open mezzanine at one end and divided by groups of furniture—fruitwood, painted or upholstered. Loose linen slipcovers, some in a white-and-red windowpane check woven for Bunny by Nantucket Looms, invite settling into a deep chair to read a good book.

A copy of the magisterial Rothko *Untitled*, 1955 (sold privately before the Sotheby's 2014 auction), brings more sunlight into the space. The upper bookcases are accessed by a spiral stair and catwalk as well as by a rolling ladder, its gleaming brass feet and fittings shined weekly by librarian Tony Willis's brother, Ricky Willis, also a member of the library staff. Several hundred feet of rare books are housed in limed oak cupboards running along the west wall. The oak was cut and aged on the farm.

Elizabeth Banks, a top English landscape architect, came to visit Oak Spring in 2018. A historian and a redoubtable gardener, Banks was also the first woman president of the Royal Horticultural Society in England. I asked her about her impression of the library.

She wrote to me that it was first "an excitement in what's hidden. And then you open another cupboard—still more hidden." (In one staff office Banks was asked to open what looked like a file drawer, only to find a suite of tiny, fully furnished dollhouse rooms inside.) She loved the size of the big room, its "lightness. The lightness of the baluster, of the catwalk shelves. The effort to make a library into a room."

What she appreciated most were the books housed in the closed cabinets, books "that were hidden not because Mrs. Mellon was ashamed of them, or even only because it helped preserve them (which is true). But because she didn't want to make a certain kind of show, the display of learning and knowledge seen in other rich people's libraries." Banks knows what she's talking about, having once worked for a very prestigious private library herself.

How had Bunny gotten started? Two very different books struck her imagination at almost the same time when she was young, pointing her in the two major directions her Garden Library has taken. One led to the world of plants, gardens, and design; the other to nature, science, and exploration.

The first book is the British horticulturist Robert Furber's *The Flower Garden Display'd, in Above Four Hundred Curious Representations of the Most Beautiful Flowers; Regularly Dispos'd in the Respective Months of Their Blossom*, a florilegium, as these gatherings of botanically correct images are called, that was published in London in 1734. Bunny was captivated by Furber's exuberant hand-colored engravings when she was ten years old, as she told Lucia Tongiorgi Tomasi, the eminent art historian who wrote two of Oak Spring's four remarkable descriptive catalogues. Today *The Flower Garden Display'd* retains pride of place as Bunny's first rare-book purchase. Although she bought other editions and went on to buy more and more Furbers in

Robert Furber, *The Flower Garden Display'd* (London, 1734), title page. Bunny's first rare-book purchase not only names the plants but also gives instructions on growing them. Pinks, martagon lilies, and canterbury bells all bloomed in her gardens.

the encyclopedic way of many good collectors, this modest quarto volume is the copy that Tony Willis pulled from the shelf time after time for Bunny to marvel over where it had led her.

Furber's engravings show off the best of what would become the American ideal of the traditional English garden, the flower bed and border. Furber's floral extravaganza presents the garden month by month; he also gives how-to directions on the cultivation of plants in "green-houses, hot beds, glass-cases, open borders or against walls."

The Garden Library holds hundreds of books of this how-to-have-your-own-garden sort, from Furber right on through to the best of the present day. Even those whom landscape gardener Beatrix Farrand dismissively called "the exclusively delphinium-minded," meaning those not interested in garden history or design, can find plenty to read. More than ten thousand "modern books" (printed after 1900) are shelved along the catwalk shelves and elsewhere in the library, including the research and work spaces on the lowest floor and in the study wing.

The second seminal book was yet another precious gift from Grandpa Lowe, probably presented during one of the summers when Bunny visited him in Fitchburg, Massachusetts. The pocket-sized *Flower Guide, Wild Flowers East of the Rockies*, by the New England ornithologist and naturalist Chester Albert Reed, would have been useful to Bunny after a ramble across Lowe's birthplace farm in New Hampshire too. The *Flower Guide* was published in 1907 and again in 1920, when Bunny was ten, and she said she carried it with her everywhere for many years.

Today, instead of Reed a hiker would have Peterson and McKenny's *A Field Guide to Wildflowers of Northeastern and North-central North America* on her cell phone. Both Reed and Peterson offer a beginning naturalist the correct nomenclature and identification drawings she needs in order to be familiar with wild plants and their habitats. In the library, a copy of one of the unassuming *Field Guides*—hardly a rare book—sits handily on a long sideboard with other useful volumes, only feet away from a tiny scrawl of a letter from Thomas Jefferson about pumpkin seeds. Presiding over this display is one of the Rokeby Farm gardener George Shaffer's usual offerings from the big greenhouses—in February, perhaps a pot of forced tulips the color of a flame to let you know spring will eventually come.

The great medieval and Renaissance herbals in the collection as well as the works of exploration, travel, and natural history owe their presence in part to Reed and to Bunny's unfailing curiosity about the natural world beyond the garden gates. The library also holds a manuscript copy of Konrad von Megenberg's *Buch der Natur*, circa 1350, an encyclopedic tour of natural history as it was known at the time, rich with tempera illustrations.

What added another powerful direction to Bunny's collecting was her love for the world of nursery rhymes and stories that she had read first in childhood, when she wasn't outdoors making a garden of her own. In the preface to her first Oak Spring catalogue, *Sylva*, Bunny wrote:

> I will never forget the illustrations and drawings of Beatrix Potter's greenhouses, flower pots, and potting sheds, Kate Greenaway's verses and books, in which fruit trees full of apples and pears hang over pale brick walls, Boutet de Monvel's precise drawings with the music of French nursery rhymes written across pictures of bridges, tall, square, French houses, and trees planted in rows like soldiers. But of all these my favorite illustrator was H. Willebeek Le Mair. Her pictures in *Songs of Childhood*, Robert Louis Stevenson's *A Child's Garden of Verses*, and other books were a young gardener's delight— walls, topiary trees, fruit arbors, sand dunes, and fields of wild flowers.

Bunny's preface opens with the image of Willebeek Le Mair's "Little Jumping Joan," a small barefoot girl leaping into a field of wildflowers. Bunny dedicated *Sylva*, which gathers the descriptions of books about trees, to her grandfather, a man who planted an arboretum of native trees, hoping his grandchildren would see them. Bunny kept his notes on the subject.

The fairy tales to which Bunny was drawn were those illustrated by Arthur Rackham or Edmund Dulac. In her mind she wandered among "Rackham's knarled [*sic*] oaks and apple trees, willows and windswept hills, and Dulac's medieval turrets where ladies embroidered and planted carnations, roses, and herbs as men battled in the distant landscape." Dulac owed some of his inspiration for turrets and ladies, roses and carnations, to fifteenth-century books of hours, devotional volumes such as the ones in the library.

To be whimsical and fey and to hope that she could make her life somehow be a fairy tale was as much a part of Bunny as her stubbornness and her insecurities. After her death, that taste for whimsy lingered in the library as part of its charm for quite a while as the institution began its transformation under the guidance of Sir Peter Crane.

Bunny would have been delighted when a gardener who had been at Oak Spring for decades appeared with a cupful of garden worms for the injured young crow that a library staff member was nursing along until it could fly. (Staff called the bird Russell Crowe.) Arthur Rackham wouldn't have blinked at the sight of that large black bird—which eventually did fly off, healed—as it hopped crookedly along the tiled floor of the library.

By 1975 rare books and fragile ephemera were everywhere at Oak Spring and the Brick House, with no room for more. Where to put the sumptuous 1565 copy, with its gold and silver highlights and more than nine hundred woodcuts, of Pietro Andrea Mattioli's commentaries on Pedanius Dioscorides's *De Materia Medica*? (Mattioli's work includes the first European description of tobacco and the first description of lilacs as they arrived from Persia.) Where to put the fifteen elephant folio volumes, each two feet tall and illustrated with 176 watercolors, part of Johann Simon Kerner's huge *Hortus Sempervirens*? Where to safely house the 1511 compendium *Hortus Sanitatis*, a beautiful herbal with a fore-edge painting (a scene painted on the edges of book pages) by Titian's nephew?

Dita Amory came to Oak Spring when she was twenty-four years old in 1978. She was finishing up her master's degree at the Institute for Fine Arts at New York University. At Oak Spring there were "books under the bed, books in the Brick House basement, books in the cellar—of course too attractive to call it a basement," said Amory.

"I flew down for the day," she recollected. "We both knew by the end of the interview that I was right for the job! I started a month later, in June 1978. I would wait three and a half years to actually work in the library, as construction was slow."

Besides the language of art history, Dita Amory also spoke from birth the language of great American gardens and fortunes. Her great-grandparents, John S. Phipps (of Pittsburgh's U.S. Steel) and Margarita Grace (of the gigantic American firm Grace Shipping Lines), created a 140-acre country estate for themselves on Long Island that still retains a 1906-style aura of roses, lawns, lindens, and handsome luxury. No wonder Dita Amory, who grew up in Old Westbury, felt at home when she arrived at Oak Spring for that interview.

She said the hiring process was quite informal: "I was hired to collect all the books," she told me over lunch, adding, tongue-in-cheek, that she was chosen because "Bunny wanted a housekeeper with a smile!" (She later said that the job was one that any seasoned librarian would have coveted and that she, as an art historian not trained as a librarian or an archivist, felt lucky to get the position.) Serious about making her own way in the world, Amory didn't tell Bunny about her family background, because she wanted to get the job on her own merit—which she did. Bunny loved the story when Amory told her several months after she started work.

Turn over any stone and you'll find that everyone in this privileged world is somehow "known" to one another, whether in sport or high culture. Besides exercising power when they felt like it, this elite also had the time, money, and energy to perfect their talents, whether it was creating a great botanical collection or becoming a ten-goal polo player.

Given the Mellons' relationship with Pittsburgh, which was always a sore subject with Pittsburghers, because Bunny never wanted to spend any time there, an artless story about the impetus for the library building program is worth repeating. (Paul, who didn't like Pittsburgh either, had to spend part of every week there on Mellon business, the original source of his wealth.)

Dita Amory told me that Paul and one of the Hunts, perhaps Roy A. himself or one of his sons, were flying together to or from a business meeting in Pittsburgh, where Paul was on the Alcoa board. On the flight Paul complained that every building in Virginia bulged with garden books. "What, Bunny doesn't have a library?" crowed his companion. "Why, Paul, you must give her one!" (The Hunts had watched Roy A.'s wife, Rachel McMasters Miller Hunt, amass her great botanical library in the 1950s.)

Architect H. Page Cross's long run of hand-in-glove collaborations with Bunny had ended with his death at age eighty-five in 1975. Bunny, moving with the times, looked to modernism for her new design and chose Edward Larrabee Barnes as her architect in 1976. "Ed Barnes was distracted by other clients, like IBM—he designed their building on Madison and Fifty-Seventh Street," said Amory, explaining why the library took so long to be completed. "Mrs. Mellon was integral to the design process and should be credited with much of the library as we know it."

Bunny's first sustained brush with modernism as a movement had come through Andy Oates and Bill Euler. She appreciated the beauty of abstraction perhaps most notably through the Rothko color-field works she bought in 1970, the greatest of which was hung in the library. What else surely contributed to her familiarity with modernism was her friendship with I. M. Pei as it developed during the 1970s, the years that the East Wing of the National Gallery (opened in 1978) was under construction.

Edward Barnes had studied with Walter Gropius and Marcel Breuer at Harvard in the 1930s and credited his decision to become an architect with visits to residences in Massachusetts that both men had designed. While Barnes became most famous for great corporate buildings, such as IBM's, and for his white art palaces, notably the Walker Art Center in Minneapolis, he had also designed what the *New York Times* reporter Douglas Martin called "a village of shingled cottages," the Haystack Mountain School of Arts and Crafts in Deer Isle, Maine. The school was later recognized by the American Institute of Architects as "an early and profound example of the fruitful and liberating fusion of the vernacular building traditions with the rationality and discipline of Modern architecture." The clean, clear congregation of architectural forms that comprises the Oak Spring Garden Library similarly calls on vernacular and modernist traditions. Anything but institutional, it blends in with the other buildings of the "farm" without copying them.

The original building—Bunny's "main book room"—was finished in 1981 and is anchored by the two-story China Tower, which holds Bunny's second-floor office. The building is sunk into the hillside like a traditional banked barn, with a cobbled ramp to the north that leads to a rooftop terrace. Two full stories emerge on the south, where the former main entrance, a pair of sliding doors, is marked by a sundial set high on the wall. Walking through those doors into a low-ceilinged, tile-floored space to face a short flight of steps doesn't prepare you for the big event: the soaring space and cascade of light into the 246-foot-long room at the top of the stairs, perhaps the finest effect that Bunny ever masterminded. Today, visitors enter through what was called the Study Wing, which was designed by a fledgling architect from Upperville, Thomas Beach, and finished in 1997. Together the two sections form an L shape surrounded by orchards. One big old sycamore shades the roofs from the western sun.

Cary Jackson, the library's building contractor, had originally met Paul Mellon in the Virginia hunting field. Jackson's company then built Foxcroft School's large indoor riding ring as well as the school's new library, dedicated in 1969 to the memory of Audrey Bruce Currier, Paul's niece. Construction was slowed not only by Barnes's preoccupation with other projects but also by the Mellons' obsession with perfection. Jackson, wearied by the countless visits to Oak Spring, told his wife, Ann, that the library job was his most drawn-out project *ever.* "Every week he had to go to lunch with the Mellons to discuss 'progress,'" said Ann Jackson after her husband's death. "Sometimes Paul wasn't there," she added, "and "if Mrs. Mellon was displeased with the 'progress,' lunch could be grim."

Ann Jackson also said wryly that the Mellons were "certainly very detail-oriented." Once Paul and Bunny and Cary Jackson flew together in the Mellon plane to visit the manufacturer for an entire day just to check on the custom-made bronze window frames. Finally, and most time-consuming, Ann Jackson said, "the stone walls could not have any glint of mica in them [even though they were to be whitewashed]—one wall was taken down and rebuilt three times."

Ron Evans, the head of the outdoor crews at the farm, had initially worked for Cary Jackson on the library, starting in 1976 with the first excavation. He became a Mellon employee as the library was completed, and he worked for the Mellons until 2004. On the phone with me, he added another detail about those bronze window frames. "After the building was up, and the windows were installed—each cost about five grand—Mrs. Mellon didn't like how the big window on the east wall near the Rothko looked," Evans said. "So we did it again. We closed up that window, and it is buried inside the wall. It's still there. We ordered another one. Mrs. Mellon had a saying: 'The impossible only takes longer and costs more.'"

Bunny was following her father's example: Gerard B. had the front elevation of his Princeton house, Albemarle, mocked up repeatedly, complete with columns, until he was satisfied. Although this same story of repetition until it's right—which is often considered "needless expense"—is told repeatedly about Bunny, I have to ask, why not? Her oft-repeated motto, "It is wasteful to be mediocre," was her justification for the perfect thing she wanted. Bunny and Paul shared this obsession: he is the one who decided to wait two years for the right marble for the East Building of the National Gallery of Art to become available again. Seeking this kind of perfection was both a means of self-definition and a way of life for these people.

Of all the homegrown Virginians Bunny found to work for her, Tony Willis, her librarian, was definitely the star. "My father, Fred Willis, was the foreman for the Oak Spring property painting department for about thirty years," said Tony, "and when I met Dita Amory I was eighteen years old and helping my mother clean the Brick House." Tony, who rarely talks about himself, did manage to add, "I loved books and maps and knowledge." Amory, who noted what a smart young guy he was, said to Bunny, "You should have him here [meaning the library]." Tony's family had moved from a hillside farm to the village of Rectortown, which is not far from Oak Spring, in 1959.

I visited the old Willis family homestead, now a bramble-covered mound of brick, timbers, and tin just off a dirt road, Carr Lane. The six-foot-high clay banks on either side of the land tell you about all the wagons that wore down this deep track over centuries of migration and war. The trajectory from Carr Lane to Tony's library office is almost incalculable, although his manner is still Southern soft, and you can hear rural Virginia in his voice. Today for an important visitor he may wear the black turtleneck, black jacket, and dark-rimmed glasses that could fool you into thinking he is an artist or an architect, but more often he's in a short-sleeved checked cotton shirt. He is a comforting person, always on an even keel and prone to jokes and puns. As the years closed in on Bunny, and other library employees came and went—and especially after Eliza's accident, when Bunny seldom left her daughter for more than twenty-four hours—Tony was more than a comfort; he was (and is) a mainstay. At the rare cocktail hour in the library when he and Bunny and Nancy Collins got together, the daiquiri ritual included her toast, "Here's to little old us"—the heart of Bunny's Oak Spring.

Once it was clear that Tony Willis was a keeper, he was sent to the University of Virginia to the Rare Book School, and in 1999, after Paul's death, Bunny sent Tony to Europe to meet her important book dealers to tell them the library would be moving right along with its acquisitions.

Because Bunny knew everyone wanted to meet her, she devised ways to find out if she wanted to meet *them*. When the local architect Thomas Beach was contacted by Reverend Davenport of Trinity Episcopal Church about an extension to the rectory, Beach said that the reverend told him that "even though [I] had never met Mrs. Mellon that I should get in touch with her first." He tried, got no response, and that was that—until two weeks later, when Bunny called Beach for a smaller project: to renovate a log cabin on the property. "Mrs. Mellon had wanted to find out what kind of guy I was," said Beach, who subsequently worked on other projects with her on Nantucket as well as at Oak Spring, culminating in the library's Study Wing. "My partner, Hardee Johnston, and I made a cardboard model of our first design to show her," said Beach. "She actually tore it apart, used her scissors to cut up the pieces, stacked them, and put them back together. Her way. She said, 'Try this.'"

Beach wrote to Bunny in 2005, laying out his education at her hands by simply stating, "I look back at how naive I was and how little I knew before I knew you." To this day Beach acknowledges that "Mrs. Mellon knew more about architecture than I'll ever know."

Frank Langella, in his electrifying eulogy for Bunny at Trinity Church in 2014, described how she'd adopted a green young man from Bayonne, New Jersey, and taught him about the world. His first lesson came in 1961, he wrote in a memoir, *Dropped Names*, when he and Eliza were both working at the Cape Playhouse in Provincetown. He and Eliza were in a relationship; they both later "moved on to other partners, marriages, and divorces," he wrote, while remaining friends. That June day, Bunny had driven from Oyster Harbors with a picnic basket for herself and Eliza. While Bunny was waiting for Eliza to wash up, she had instantly won Langella over, completely and forever.

That summer, Langella often visited Oyster Harbors. One day, Bunny asked him to read aloud as they sat with Eliza and some Foxcroft friends. Bunny wanted to hear some passages from a book of philosophy (surely an odd choice for a beachside summer day with a bunch of eighteen-year-olds). "When I came to the name of the French philosopher René Descartes . . . I spoke it as I saw it, Dess-Cart-Tees," Langella remembered. Everyone laughed—he didn't know why. Later that day, he recounted, "Bunny said, 'Frank, would you read me that passage again? It was so interesting, particularly the part that refers to Descartes.' And she pronounced it properly as in: Daycart. She had found a way to correct my ignorance and preserve my dignity as casually as if she were opening a packet of sugar."

On a visit to Oak Spring in the 1980s, Bunny took me to the library to show it off. I was on my way to becoming a garden historian and in the middle of the Radcliffe Garden History Seminars, working on a paper about a hidden corner of the Grand Trianon gardens. The library books were pure catnip: pages of books of hours, herbals, hand-colored florilegia on vellum, luscious Redouté roses, and most of all, the giant French garden plans. Looking out a window from the mezzanine level, I rather self-importantly said, "I see a perfect horizontal stripe of wall." Bunny answered, "But if you come down lower, you'll see the tree." She wanted me to understand that our perception of space changes as we move, that it is a progression. We talked about how she had learned that and who had taught her; it was the first time I heard her say, "Johnny [Schlumberger] and I learned without being taught"—something she repeated when we swam in the shady end of the pool in Antigua.

Through some of the 2,500 or so rare books, which are classified as those published between 1501 and 1900, you can track the phenomenon of the seventeenth-century Dutch tulip craze, which expanded exponentially and crashed in less than fifty years. This financial ruin left behind not only the watercolors of Jacob Marrel's *Tulpenboek* of 1642 but also a list of tulip bulbs with their names and prices—

mundane for most people but something that any gardener would love to pore over.

Paintings and prints of specimens created over the centuries when botanical illustration was a primary means of education document the back-and-forth between classification and aesthetics. The great florilegia make you catch your breath not only with the scientific accuracy and limpid transparency of the hand-colored plates but also with their title pages wreathed in flowers. Other images reveal the forthright domination of nature in sixteenth- and seventeenth-century Italian and French garden geometry, while still others unroll the sweep of the eighteenth-century English landscape, a mirror of the growing British imperium.

Not one but four of Humphrey Repton's famed early-nineteenth-century "Red Books" stand boxed on the shelves. Each one contains eerie foldout before-and-after images of Repton's proposals for various country estates, each book a sales prospectus showing the owner or possibly other clients how to eradicate entire ancient villages that spoiled their desired viewsheds in order to remake their demesnes in the new nineteenth-century mode of well-behaved lawn, water, and wood, with a garden peeping out here and there.

What hangs on the library's walls can also spur original research. As the art historian Lucia Tongiorgi Tomasi glanced up from the descriptive entries she was writing for the Oak Spring *Flora* catalogue (published in 1997), her eyes often rested on a pair of unusual oil panels dated 1614, the signed work of a little-known Italian artist, Girolamo Pini. Each is spangled with a riot of flowers, stems, leaves, and bulbs, each plant a newcomer to Europe during the Age of Discovery. The common names are listed on a trompe l'oeil scroll in each painting. The unusual rich brown background, a reminder of the common earth that even such rarities must spring from, highlights the fragility of the blossoms. Bunny bought the works in 1979 when they appeared at auction, disgorged from a Cornish manor.

One of the most revered scholars in her field, Tomasi at the start nonetheless knew little about Girolamo Pini. Over time she discovered that Bunny's two paintings are replicas of a pair of Pinis held by the Musée des Arts Décoratifs, Paris. Then another Pini, also a painter, turned up: Giovanni, a still-life artist of about the same date who was working in Florence, the great center for science and thus for accurate botanical illustration. Were the two men related? Girolamo is generally thought to have come from Pistoia, less than fifty kilometers from Florence.

Color was the clue to another discovery. The use of brown as a background color was as rare as the flowers were in their time. The sight of Bunny's two brown paintings eventually unearthed Tomasi's memory of a large millefleur tapestry with a similar background that has hung in Pistoia since the sixteenth century. Tomasi hypothesized that the brown tapestry ground might have struck Pini as just the right thing for his masterful paintings. And for whom did he paint the replicas? She continues to look for the next clue.

If you want to explore women botanical artists and how they struggled to learn techniques and to make names for themselves, you can begin with the intrepid early naturalist and scientific illustrator Maria Sibylla Merian (1647–1717), Jacob Marrel's German-born stepdaughter, who spent five years in Suriname drawing insects as they metamorphosed—from pupa to wing—and their plant hosts. Another woman artist who found her own path was hardworking Elizabeth Blackwell (1707–1758), a Scot who made money selling watercolors of the medicinal plants she was allowed to see in the Chelsea Physic Garden. Blackwell even bought her husband's release from debtors' prison with her proceeds. Seventy-two Blackwells are now in the Oak Spring Garden Library.

Bunny collected pieces by a few twentieth-century women artists as well, whose work she found in a variety of different ways. Sophie Grandval-Justice (b. 1936) arrived via the broad avenue of textile design and fashion; Hubert de Givenchy introduced Bunny to the French artist's work. Before long, Bunny had commissioned her to create a modern-day watercolor herbal. Forty-eight of her images illustrate a handful of kitchen vegetables and herbs, Bunny's choice of pear varieties, and Bunny's ubiquitous "small herb trees" in clay pots, among other subjects. The library also holds other Grandval compositions. One, a two-foot-tall dandelion head, is depicted against a detail of its khaki-green heavily veined leaf. It is not in any traditional sense a "botanical painting," although it is accurate in every taxonomic detail. Instead, it reminds one of the dream world of Henri Rousseau, whose small *Flowers of Poetry* stops the visitor for a brief reverie along the heavily trafficked passageway to the back kitchen.

When the photographer Fred Conrad of *The New York Times* arrived in 1982 to shoot the library for the paper, Bunny sat for him in a high-backed country chair with one of her large florilegia open on her knees, a severe and diligent reader protected by her absorption in a book, wearing a Givenchy cotton skirt, the light streaming over her shoulder. This particular Bunny Mellon appears as a student, perhaps like her friend Kitty Wickes "of New York, Paris, and Newport," as her engagement announcement read, who attended both Columbia University and Sarah Lawrence College before disappearing into a happy married life with a husband and three children in 1938. Kitty Wickes was Bunny's ideal, a woman who had been allowed to go to college.

Bunny is deep into a rare Dutch florilegium, the *Phytographia curiosa* of Abraham Munting, the seventeenth-century Dutch botanist who commissioned the work and named his botanical garden the "Paradise of Groningen."

Sadly, in Bunny's mind, many considered her not very intelligent and certainly not learned. I think proving herself—to herself as well as to others, but without ever saying so—gave her energy, especially when she focused on the library, the creation that uniquely stands as her life's legacy.

"Life is like a puzzle. It depends on how you look on it," Bunny wrote in one of her journals in 1970. "If you continue with a basic value—one thing makes another work.—without the right piece another would not fit.—The picture or design in the end may be like an abstract painting—but it will tell the story of a life."

Part of the larger puzzle of this life as it is seen in the library, and throughout the house, and in every one of Bunny's houses, are the images of solitary women standing or sitting—and dreaming. (Most were gifts to the National Gallery of Art or sold in the 2014 Sotheby's auction.) Georges Seurat's shadowy conté crayon drawing, *Femme Tenant un Bouquet*, a Christmas gift from Paul in 1956, may be the earliest such acquisition. In the living room at Oak Spring it was hung next to the bar, something seen every day. I see part of Bunny's inner power as coming from the sense that she *was* alone, like Alain-Fournier's traveler stumbling through the foggy woods to find the forever-vanishing château in *Le Grand Meaulnes*. The book's hero never found the party or the partygoers again; Bunny was always hunting for the perfection she could not quite find. (The book was one of Bunny's talismans: she bought twelve copies of a beautiful oversize illustrated edition and gave one to Jackie.)

Augustus John's *Dorelia in the Garden at Alderney Manor*, painted in 1911, was not the last in the long series of portraits of solitary women that Bunny and her husband bought, but it was the one that she was to use directly as a stand-in for herself, as a self-portrait: Bunny had *Dorelia* printed as the frontispiece of her funeral program. Every such portrait, including Henriette Willebeek LeMair's joyful *Little Jumping Joan* from Bunny's childhood, was a way for Bunny to define her inner self. In the case of *Dorelia*—if we except Dorelia McNeill's bowl-cut black hair and bangs—it's very like a portrait of Bunny's physical self as well.

To explain how the Mellons differed in their tastes and their approaches, in their direction and reach, from other major American philanthropists and collectors, the art historian Colin Eisler gave more or less the answer that John Walker at the National Gallery had offered in his memoir, that the Mellons "were buying what pleased them to see in their houses; other collectors were building 'collections.'"

Bunny knew that to have a great botanical library, she needed a backbone of the great, rare, beautiful works on trees, fruit, flowers, and herbs—the basis of her four catalogues. Bunny wanted the other pieces of the puzzle as well: if you have this, then you need that too. It's a scientific requirement to be compendious, to have everything needed to be able to compare and contrast specimens.

In 2002, Bunny took Paul Richard, the art critic at *The Washington Post*, on a tour of the Oak Spring Garden Library in the course of his covering the National Gallery's exhibition *The Flowering of Florence: Botanical Art for the Medici*. (The concept of the show explicitly honored Bunny's career as a landscape architect and gardener and as a connoisseur and collector of botanical art; Lucia Tongiorgi Tomasi was the co-curator.) Richard, who worshipped Paul, found Bunny cold and uncongenial in general, but on that occasion she came alive, he said, as they went through what was on the walls and between the covers of the rare books she showed him.

Richard mentioned how Bunny talked about a painting in the exhibition—not one of hers—of all the varieties of lemons grown in Florence in a certain period. This was an example for Richard of how great collectors want to have "the whole lot." As he told the story, I thought to myself that collecting "the whole lot" is a scientist's habit, a way to survey and understand the world.

Competition and Colleagues

"When the time came to plant my own fruit trees," wrote Bunny,
"I made a search for books of instruction . . . I found my prize . . . the 1821
Jardin Fruitier by Louis Claude Noisette."

Bunny was not the only rich American woman buying botanical books when she began to collect seriously in the 1950s. Therese O'Malley, an eminent garden and landscape historian, singled out two other wealthy American women, both a generation older than Bunny, who amassed similar important libraries in the twentieth century. The garden library of Mildred Barnes Bliss (1879–1969) at Dumbarton Oaks in Washington, D.C., was advancing in the late forties; and already by 1913, Rachel McMasters Miller Hunt (1882–1963) of Pittsburgh had started collecting rare botanical books. Between them, the three "actively scooped up every flower book on the market," said O'Malley.

These three American women—Hunt, Bliss, and Bunny Mellon—were amassing their own intellectual capital, independently making book choices on gardens, gardening, architecture, landscape and landscape design, herbal medicine, botany and botanical art and science, horticulture, agriculture, travel and exploration, apiculture, and whatever else they (and their advisors) felt was relevant to their private assemblages. They shaped their libraries for their own use and pleasure so that each woman's collection and the building that housed it became the equivalent of Virginia Woolf's "room of one's own." But they also had the idea that what they built would eventually serve a wider public and wider research interests.

At Oak Spring, the garden itself was Bunny's most private domain. O'Malley, on her initial visit to the library, said, "I thought she was one of the gardeners," when she met Bunny for the first time—appropriately enough—in the enclosed garden. "She was stooped over in one of her blue smocks and hats. Then she stood up." O'Malley continued, "Bunny told me that she wanted to see 'handicrafts'—she was talking specifically about pruning—raised 'to the status of an art.'"

Bunny manicures the espaliered apple on the south wall of
Paul's study at Oak Spring.

The woman who did so many things wanted others to appreciate fully a skill she had learned on her own and from books.

The three women took their collections and programming in different directions. Hunt's botanical library was the germplasm of the Hunt Institute for Botanical Documentation, which focuses on the history of botany and all aspects of plant science and classification. Long before the Oak Spring Garden Library produced four catalogues highlighting works in the collection, Bunny would have been familiar with Hunt's *Catalogue of Botanical Books in the Collection of Rachel McMasters Miller Hunt*, two volumes of descriptive entries with essays on the materials (published in 1958 and 1961).

Mildred Bliss's garden library began as one part of a three-part complex, what she called "a home for the humanities"—that is, the classical European humanities as we have thought of them for more than a thousand years. The Blisses had lived in France throughout World War I and had seen rampant destruction. Part of the expatriate arts community that included Edith Wharton and Bernard Berenson, they wanted to make Dumbarton Oaks a safe place in America for the humanities and the arts as war loomed again. Dumbarton Oaks became what O'Malley called "the cradle in this country of the field of garden history," which didn't become publicly recognizable as a separate "history" until quite late in the twentieth century, and then mostly because of the garden and landscape studies program at Dumbarton Oaks initiated in 1972.

As early as 1949, a year after Bunny and Paul married, Mildred Bliss and Bunny Mellon were in Paris at the same time, buying books. That was also the same year that Bliss began to assemble her garden library in earnest. Polite letters went back and forth between the two women's secretaries. By the 1960s, the art appraiser Willis Van Devanter, Paul's rare books librarian since 1957, had begun working with Bunny to manage the flow of her correspondence and offerings from dealers. Bliss, born in 1886, was twenty-four years older than Bunny. An institution herself by 1967, Bliss reached out to Bunny to bring the British botanical artist Margaret Mee to Oak Spring.

In the 1950s, Mee, born in 1909, a modern-day Maria Sibylla Merian, had sounded an early alarm about the destruction of Brazilian rain forests that she had witnessed firsthand. Bunny bought four of Mee's watercolors. On the sheet depicting a small wild tree orchid, *Epidendrum vesicatum*, with pendulous foliage and delicate, starlike flowers, Mee penciled in the location, Ubatuba, north of São Paulo in the Mata Atlântica. That long strip of once-lush rain forest running along the mountainous Brazilian coast has now been deeply fragmented by international commercial loggers and soy farmers. Bunny's library holds information on and images of many such endangered plants and regions.

Bliss died in 1969; the following year Dumbarton Oaks invited Bunny to join its garden advisory committee, the first woman (besides Bliss herself) to serve in that capacity. Bunny served for four years, carrying on for two years after the garden and landscape studies program was formed in 1972. The committee members included some faces very familiar to Bunny, such as those of Perry Wheeler, the landscape architect who had assisted her on many projects, and Willis Van Devanter. Charles Ryskamp, Paul's accomplished, amusing, polymath friend whose Princeton garden Bunny designed, joined the Dumbarton Oaks overall board of advisors in 1970, the year after he became director of the Morgan Library and Museum in New York, one of the nation's most prestigious smaller institutions.

The people Hunt, Bliss, and Mellon assembled around them on their boards and committees were chosen primarily for their outstanding professional skills in the arts, humanities, and sciences. However, they also took enjoyment seriously. Nancy Mitford, in her biography of Madame de Pompadour, takes on the subject of pleasure at Versailles, which she describes as an "unedifying but cheerful spectacle of several thousand people living for pleasure and very much enjoying themselves . . . in the great wonderful palace, its windows opening wide on the fountains, the forest and the western sky." In the twentieth century, whether at Dumbarton Oaks or Oak Spring or wherever else this kind of rarefied society gathered, many working parts made the enterprise work.

One "working part" in the early years of Bunny's garden library was twenty-seven-year-old Van Devanter. He worked for the Mellons for seventeen years and later became recognized as one of the world's top manuscript appraisers, evaluating and helping place the papers of many notable Americans, including Reverend Martin Luther King, Jr. (Bunny had only to reach out to Paul to receive the best assistance.)

Almost as soon as Paul hired him, Van Devanter recognized that dealers knew that Bunny was also collecting books—botanical books—and that a feeding frenzy was going on. Van Devanter met regularly with Paul on Saturday mornings at the Brick House, Paul in full hunting kit, ready to chase the fox and to check out Bunny's proposed purchases. One morning, young Van Devanter told Paul, "Mrs. Mellon was chiseled" over the purchase of a certain manuscript, adding that he advised Paul (who was probably already aware of this bit of sage advice before 1957) always to make an offer instead of asking what the price was. "Paul gave me full permission, however, to open up the collecting field to wherever the best was."

Like other collecting cognoscenti, Bunny implicitly trusted any recommendation from Handasyde "Handy" Buchanan at Heywood Hill, the Mayfair bookshop where Nancy Mitford had worked during World War II. Despite the onslaught of war and London's pinched and embattled condition, what Nancy's sister Deborah, the late Duchess of Devonshire, remembered about the atmosphere of the shop was, "It was the best fun in the world." John Saumarez Smith, another passionate bookman who worked at Heywood Hill for thirty years, said, "Handy is the one who knew the bibliographic materials for all botanical publications and wrote reference works on the great flower books."

About Bunny as a collector, Van Devanter said, "I did not have to tell her about the virtues of an item. I would send a little memorandum and leave it for her." In the days of paper catalogues and snail mail, Van Devanter said he "was her eyes and ears at every auction; I sent her every dealer catalogue. Ours was a businesslike arrangement." He recalled also that "very few people were as aggressive as Bunny was in acquiring. She bought everything in sight," although never anything, Van Devanter added, that was second-rate. Van Devanter also remembered, "She often found very small things interesting—something that cost £20." Bunny always wanted to be sure that a new acquisition, large or small, would "fit" with what she already owned. Provenance mattered too, of course. The importance of owning a first edition copy of Jean de La Quintinie's *Instructions pour les jardins fruitiers et potagers* was enhanced by adding a copy of the first English translation by John Evelyn, the great seventeenth-century English writer, memoirist, and gardener.

"She kept her books at Oak Spring, right where she could see them," Van Devanter continued. "She put them where she could find what she wanted." People often asked him why he hadn't done a catalogue (like the four descriptive catalogues that Oak Spring published later). "I told them that the speed at which things were coming in—six to eight items a week—made it impossible." Tony Willis confirmed that at the time Van Devanter left in 1972 and until Dita Amory arrived in 1974, one room at the Brick House, where Van Devanter had been stationed and where Bunny's books were received for shelving, was entirely filled with stacks of books under consideration.

Bunny never talked about money with Van Devanter. "Mrs. Mellon would say—as she also said to dealers and booksellers that I spoke with—'I don't know, you must ask Paul.' Paul would ask, 'Is it reasonable?' and if I said yes, he would buy it." Often, because Bunny was away so much of the time, Van Devanter couldn't reach her when something great came up for auction. When he heard news that an especially important item was to be sold in Czechoslovakia, he said to Paul, "We can't wait on this." Paul's answer: "Well, I'll buy it for her as a present."

As Paul saw his wife's collection expand beyond the botanical, he began to transfer many works of natural history, travel, and exploration from the Yale Center for British Art to Oak Spring. Shortly before his death in 1999, he gave her his prized complete double elephant folio Audubon *Birds of America* for their last wedding anniversary together.

From the 1970s onward, as the Mellons became near-mythic figures, Oak Spring became ever more private. The sprightly Van Devanter often stood in for Bunny when gardeners and bibliophiles came to visit, presiding over the luncheons, teas, book displays, and walks through the garden. Nonetheless, Bunny knew it was important to make her presence and her collection known. In 1967 she had been elected to the board of the New York Botanical Garden (NYBG) and—although she was not by temperament at all a committee woman—she served on the grounds committee between 1968 and 1970. The Garden Library joined the Council on Botanical and Horticultural Libraries in 1978 and lent works to three NYBG shows over the years while contributing to other exhibitions as well.

A small but breathtaking display of Bunny's treasures, *An Oak Spring Garland*, was held in the Princeton University Library in 1989 to celebrate the publication of Oak Spring's first descriptive catalogue, *Sylva*. The modest gray paper cover featured Maria Sibylla Merian's garland of flowers and their supporting cast of insects. In 2016, NYBG's LuEsther T. Mertz Library showed off the breadth of Bunny's collecting with *Redouté to Warhol, Bunny Mellon's Botanical Art*. Sir Peter Crane, president of the newly constituted Oak Spring organization, wrote an introduction, while Tony Willis, Susan M. Fraser, the Mertz librarian, and Lucia Tongiorgi Tomasi contributed essays.

Given the value and importance of the collection, internal organization was remarkably informal at the Oak Spring Garden Library, answering only to Bunny. The officers of the first library board included Kenneth I. Starr, the Mellons' trusted financial advisor before he swindled his many wealthy and celebrity clients in a massive Ponzi scheme in 2010; Bunny's then-secretary, Anita Engel; Bunny's lawyer, Alex Forger; and Tony Willis. Later, in 1993, the Oak Spring Garden Library was incorporated with only Bunny and Forger as directors. In 2016, it was transferred in its entirety to the Oak Spring Garden Foundation when Sir Peter Crane arrived from Yale to become president.

Making an official link with another institution was seriously considered: Dumbarton Oaks itself was one, the Alderman Library at the University of Virginia another, while the National Gallery of Art was the major contender for a number of years. But the Garden Library has stayed put at Oak Spring, anchored in Bunny's gardens and landscape, and is now evolving from a private institution into the Oak Spring Garden Foundation (OSGF), a research organization, with the Garden Library and the property itself together as the driving forces. As a library, Bunny's cherished assemblage displays the interests of a serious gardener that, together with those of a great book and art collector, support one another in a specific regional and rural setting. Susan Fraser, vice president of the New York Botanical Garden and director of the LuEsther T. Mertz Library, said Bunny Mellon's "amazing collection . . . rivals any private library in the world."

In 1956, when Beatrix Farrand shut down her Reef Point gardens and closed the associated library at her summer house in Maine, donating its contents to the University of California, she did so partly because "its use [is] problematical in a place distant from other educational surroundings of like caliber." Now, thanks to the internet and to very substantial funding, the meaning of the word "distant" has changed for the Oak Spring Garden Library. The $215 million proceeds of Bunny's much-ballyhooed Sotheby's sale in November 2014 went to the Gerard B. Lambert Foundation. Now, in 2022, the web of connections with the outside world is thickening with the arrival at Oak Spring of the next generation of artists and scholars on fellowships.

Today Bunny Lambert Lloyd Mellon's Oak Spring Garden Library—her great legacy—is stretching out in many different directions through an array of people, plants, and projects at www.osgf.org. On the foundation's website is news that the Google Institute is partnering with the OSGF to offer images from the library to the public. In her brief history of the Dumbarton Oaks Garden Library, Therese O'Malley quotes the critic Walter Benjamin on the real test of a library. He wrote, "The most distinguished trait of a collection will always be its transmissibility." This will apply equally at Oak Spring as it has at Dumbarton Oaks.

The outer world didn't intrude much on the library in the years following its construction (1976–1981). The White House gardens Bunny had designed and planted were behind her, being maintained by others. The Kennedy and King assassinations, which had affected her so profoundly, were history; the war in Vietnam was over; the nation celebrated its bicentennial; Nixon had been impeached; and Jimmy Carter was the new president when ground for the library was broken. When Reagan arrived in the White House in 1981, Nancy

Reagan asked Bunny for some advice on the Rose Garden, and she and Paul were invited to White House dinners, but as storied public figures, not as intimates.

Women's rights moved forward without much attention from Bunny. While feminists marched, lobbied, and protested for equal rights, Alex Forger asked Bunny about her assets. In 1977, as an answer, Paul sent a long list of her jewels to her lawyer. Eventually and in addition to the many gifts of every kind that Paul gave her, Bunny received half a million dollars annually for charitable spending, but disposition of the rest of the estate—the houses and the money needed for their upkeep, the works of art, and all else—had to wait until after Paul's death.

During those same five years of library construction came the opening of the National Gallery's East Building in 1978, an event brilliantly stage-managed by Bunny wearing her impresario hat. The Yale Center for British Art, Paul's other monument, designed by Louis I. Kahn, opened as well. By 1980, Bunny had conquered a bout of illness—probably cancer—and was seen again at Hubert's Paris openings. Jackie, living mostly in New York, was hired by Tom Guinzburg at Viking Press as an editor; in 1982, with the large settlement Alex Forger had engineered for her from Onassis's estate after his death in 1975, she bought a house on Martha's Vineyard, only a hop from Cape Cod. Bunny helped with both decor and gardens. Eliza, long divorced from Derry Moore, struggled with her mother for her own independence during those years and had her first show of her artwork in New York at the Betty Parsons Gallery in 1976. Meanwhile, public and private book purchases continued, as did the realization of the shape of the Garden Library as a setting for them. The writer Paula Deitz's 1982 front-page *New York Times* interview with Bunny helped the library and Oak Spring itself go public.

The mission statement about interdisciplinarity on the Oak Spring Garden Foundation website, www.osgf.org, reads: "Integrative approaches bring together sciences, humanities, and social sciences for their mutual benefit and to realize the full potential of Bunny Mellon's legacy." The library website introduction describes a collection that "mainly encompasses works relating to horticulture, landscape design, botany, natural history, and voyages of exploration. There are also components relating to architecture, decorative arts, and classical literature." By the time a reader finishes reading those three sentences, she will understand how lucky we are that Bunny recognized many works and objects for the library that in the 1950s, when she began to collect in earnest, seemed to have little to do with "gardens" or "libraries."

Bunny's hunter-gatherer method of buying what pleased her served her well at a time when the history of gardens and gardening as sensitive and accurate barometers of culture seemed tangential to art historians and botanists alike. The library's fantastically broad range of objects and works of art exemplifies not only Bunny's vaunted taste, but also her disregard for material value. Having limitless funds can lead to sloppy choices—solid gold bathroom fixtures, for example—or to strange but discriminating ones, such as Bunny's purchase of eight four-times-life-size painted papier-mâché flowers that were used to illustrate sexual reproduction in plants for Viennese classrooms in the late nineteenth century. These odd, florid shapes are displayed in a bookcase next to a Louis XIV stone fireplace and a restrained nineteenth-century American portrait. It all looks just fine.

One of Bunny's great gestures for the Oak Spring Garden Library was placing a large birdbath at the bottom of a severely vertical stone staircase leading to the flat roof terraces. The birdbath's sculptor, William Edmondson, son of people once enslaved in Tennessee, was the

On a Garden Library terrace, stone doves perch to dip and drink at the rim of a monumental waist-high rough limestone trough.

first Black American artist to receive a solo show at MoMA (1937). Against the weathered, whitewashed stone, Edmondson's masterpiece looks as if it might fit well in the courtyard of some Mediterranean farmstead, but it is not at all out of place on the Virginia flagstones. The peace of Edmondson's eloquent work, set in this quiet corner, is biblical.

Bunny spotted the piece in a Sotheby's catalogue in 2000 and called her decorator, Bruce Budd, who bought it for $236,750. "Probably it should have sold for more," he said, "but I was the only bidder." (Luckily for Bunny, the work was overlooked by most buyers, who were there to bid on lots of American furniture.) Budd also remembered that one of the birds "broke off, post sale, at the auction house, and everyone there was afraid to take responsibility for it. When I finally told Bunny what had happened, she didn't seem at all concerned: 'Oh, let's just send it to the National Gallery. They'll take care of it.' And that was it."

Getting things done anywhere and everywhere, even when she was ninety—because she *could*—is a reminder of the undaunted twenty-one-year-old Bunny described by Stacy Lloyd as a woman who went "flashing across the grey wet hills with the rain beating down . . . the way we did one Friday a long time ago . . . Yet you did not care at all." Stacy was writing about a cold December rainstorm, and he was more concerned about Bunny getting soaked than she was. The same person is visible in what Bruce Budd remembered as her unconcerned acceptance of privilege and power: "They'll take care of it."

PART IX

Meetings
and
Farewells

27

"Le Plus Parisien des Antiquaires Hollandais"

At the Potager du Roi gala in 1996, Bunny had table-hopped, sitting down with the gardeners at one moment and then abandoning her seat of honor next to Hubert de Givenchy to sit with Akko van Acker, the Dutch antiques dealer living in Paris who was her newest obsession and her neighbor on the rue de l'Université. Hubert was not pleased, or that is how Akko remembered it. Bunny had found a new "magic balloon," someone to amuse and entertain her, someone to flirt with and fantasize about, the kind of social creature that Paul had felt so uncomfortable with in Bunny's 1948 London. In this case, Paul quite unexpectedly liked Akko very much, writing to him from Oak Spring in 1996 after his visit that "he would be welcome here any time. You are very invigorating for Bunny and a great pleasure for me. Come back soon."

At first Akko had seemed utterly insignificant to Bunny, merely a means to an end. Hubert had called him "to say a friend of his was coming in—he had seen something in my shop that he knew she would like—a chaise longue—very simple." By the time Bunny got to Akko's shop, it was already sold: "I told him that was all right, probably God didn't want me to have it anyway." They talked for more than two hours. It turned out he spoke "perfect English," she wrote, and she then asked him, "Why did you make me speak shaky bad French?" His only answer was a smile, the first of Akko's teasing and enigmatic responses. She left for Virginia the next day, where she found a fax waiting to tell her that the chaise had reappeared and was for sale. She phoned him and asked him what he looked like—he had just been merely someone in a shop, she wrote, but when "the witching spirits caught me," she became flustered and entranced and literally couldn't remember. All he said was "Five fingers less than Hubert," playfully meaning he was short, and added, "I send you two photos, one at work, one at play."

When I saw at the Oak Spring Garden Library the five fat folders of faxes between them that spanned some twenty years, my heart leaped—then sank as I leafed through them. Where boxes of Hubert's correspondence bulge with hundreds of lovingly chosen cards, notes, and sketches sent back and forth, along with thousands of swatches from the House of Givenchy for her couture, here instead were one-liners on thin fax paper.

Some part of my disappointment came from my own expectations: I thought of Bunny as surrounded by friends from the heights of international society or creative accomplishment, and no wonder. Her friends were titled, rich, and famous, from "Brookie," the Earl of Warwick; or Nancy Lancaster, founder of Colefax & Fowler; or Jackie Kennedy Onassis; to stars and designers like Hubert or Johnny, or, in her old age, Whoopi Goldberg and Donna Karan. She also had real friends on her enormous staff, people she loved for their loyalty, eccentricity, and plainspoken qualities: David Banks and Lena Bradford, the Black Virginians who taught her what they knew about life; her first personal maid when she became Mrs. Paul Mellon, Nelly Jo Thomas; Nancy Collins, the nurse who cared for Bunny to her last hours; and Tony Willis, the librarian who helped her realize her own monument. Often her friends were "country people," Black and white, meaning from a different social universe. I sensed that what Bunny had no time for was the vast middle, the average, what the French call "le moyen," those without spark or accomplishment—which included most of upper-crust American society, who were either bewildered or insulted by her refusal to accept them.

By the time Bunny met Akko, she had outlived two of the Three Musketeers of Style who had introduced her to Paris and to fashion. Akko did not have the lightning-strike Spanish rigor of Balenciaga, who died in 1972, the year she bought her Avenue Foch apartment.

Nor did he have the sexy animal power of Schlumberger, who died in 1987. Or the elegance of Hubert, who retired from the House of Givenchy in 1993. "Maybe you will have more time to garden?" Bunny wrote to him upon his retirement. But Hubert took on the chairmanship of Christie's and dozens of licensing arrangements, and eventually he gave up on the elaborate kitchen and cutting gardens that Bunny had designed for him in the woods at Le Jonchet and replaced them with a plain flat lawn. Bunny would never recapture the fever pitch of emotion and ideas that she had enjoyed over the years with these major creative talents.

By the time she met her Dutch antiques dealer in 1993, Bunny and Hubert had been friends for a quarter of a century, and he had intimately shared his deep love of France with her. On a weekend at Le Jonchet in the seventies they must have talked about the French lyric poet François Villon, because in her journal she jotted *Le Testament*, the title of Villon's collection that includes his "Ballade des dames du temps jadis," that melancholy celebration of vanished queens, saints, heroines, and virgins in history and myth—with its refrain, "Mais òu sont les neiges d'antan?"—"O where have they gone, the snows of long ago?"

Bunny may well have known this poem, but to talk about it with Hubert carried an added charge. She, Bunny, was the lucky one who could picture herself as one of Villon's noble ladies of times gone by. It sounds like she had Hubert all to herself that day they discussed the poet, and he was wearing, she wrote, "bare feet—blue jeans—shirt."

Hubert then took her to the French hideout of his friend David Ogilvy, the British advertising tycoon, where she fell for 'Wedding Bells,' a double-flowered blush rose that climbs to nine feet. She met Ogilvy's houseguest, the flamboyant socialite Countess Afdera Franchetti, onetime wife of Henry Fonda and a friend of Audrey Hepburn, Hubert's muse. (Franchetti allegedly had a short fling with JFK the very week he became president in 1961.) Bunny scribbled in the names of some more gray-leaved plants in Ogilvy's garden and came back to earth at Le Jonchet by concluding her entry with, "Planted hedge at Hubert's." French poetry, racy society, roses and hedges—and a romantic friendship—made for a heady mix.

Was Akko up to this? It would turn out that when Bunny needed comfort, strength, and simple human understanding to deal with her daughter, Eliza, lying unconscious after she was hit by a truck in Manhattan, it would be Akko who remembered "la fête des meres"—Mother's Day—in 2000, right after Eliza was hurt. He hoped that since he couldn't be with her that Robert Isabell (by then Bunny's newest love interest) could cheer her up a little, "as I can't play the fool as well from far away." Akko's primary role would be as the madcap jester and lovable rogue who made Bunny laugh.

I had felt increasing dismay over Bunny's repetitive behavior, with first this infatuation and then that, each one invariably an interesting and talented man in the arts, usually the decorative arts and usually gay, and always supplanted by the next one. I began to see them almost as teenage crushes. I was also unnerved by the startling variations she told of some of the most important events of her life. After her death in February 2014 and under contract to write her biography, I dug into the details and the deeper I got, the harder I found it to believe some of her stories or to blindly keep admiring the woman I had once so respected. Now here was this archly sycophantic antiques dealer; what was I to make of him? But even through his mundane fax exchanges with Bunny, it became clear that Akko helped ground her in her most painful experiences. At Easter, when Paul was recovering from a particularly agonizing struggle with his failing health, Akko simply wrote to her, "I hope you have a lovely day and Paul is well and he has many happy days to come without pain!"

It mattered just as much that he was fun when she needed fun—and was a great gossip. Like her friend and ally on the White House Rose Garden job, the landscape architect Perry Wheeler, Akko had a sharp eye for the absurd. He could be counted on to report that in St. Tropez the philanthropist and socialite Betsy Bloomingdale, wife of Alfred Bloomingdale of the eponymous department store, "is going to the beaches with her gigantic diamond ring," or to make a little joke about the sex-and-shopping novelist Judith Krantz's purchase of a vast Paris apartment in a "*bordel* particulier" instead of "hôtel particulier."

Bunny found a renewed and different energy with Akko. Nonetheless, she did understand that she was getting old, and she dealt with it—as only she could—by building something. "I look forward to mid-July when I can stay in Cape Cod day after day and move mostly in my sailboat," she wrote on a June day in Upperville. "This winter I built a new boat suitable to my age and strength. It is small & pretty about 15 feet long built of wood there is a great sense of freedom like skiing," and she dashed off a quick sketch of a sailboat.

By the next time she came to France, even while she retained her apartment at 84, avenue Foch she had begun to work on her newly

purchased Number 15, rue de l'Université, just a block from Akko's shop. Coming in from the airport in 1993, she asked her chauffeur to slow down in front of the shop, and she wrote in her diary, "And suddenly there he was." Still not sure, she asked, "'Are you Akko?'—he was so attractive I got out and sent the car on." They walked together the rest of the way to her door. An excited eighty-three-year-old Bunny, girlish as ever in romance, had lost her heart *again*.

With ruddy skin, quizzical eyebrows, thick blondish-brown hair, gleaming white teeth, and that enigmatic

Akko and Bunny spent hours on the phone.

smile, Akko seemed younger than his fifty years. Although he was not tall and elegant like "le grand Hubert," Akko van Acker was lively in a way that enlivened Bunny. On the Parisian social ladder, too, he ranked way below Hubert, and even in the roster of antiques dealers Akko wasn't at the top either. Yet, as Bunny told it, he "ran away from Holland and began supporting himself with incredible taste for antiques."

Soon Hubert was asking her, "What are you doing with this antique dealer?" Akko told me, and she answered, "You have six or seven very rich ladies when you come to New York [Hubert naturally kept up with his couture clients everywhere, something Bunny was unwilling to recognize]—Am I not allowed to have one friend on my own?"

I asked Akko, "Did Hubert think you stole Mrs. Mellon?" and he answered benignly, "There was room for me in her life." He relished telling me that when he visited Bunny on Antigua and the phone rang, Bunny, who was in the bathroom, said, "Akko, would you answer it?" It was Hubert. Bunny and Akko were both delighted when he asked, "What are *you* doing there?"

Unlike courtly Hubert, who protected himself with "the French family" against any move on Bunny's part to become physically intimate, Akko was more forthright, letting her know that he wasn't available to do what she wanted him to do because he was gay. I pressed him on Bunny's attitude toward sex, and he answered that indeed "elle etait portée sur la chose"—meaning she was not obsessed, exactly, but was very "carried toward it" and had trouble conceiving of a romance (which is how she thought of her relationship with Akko) that didn't include physical intimacy. Bunny rather dryly also told Akko that for pleasure "she preferred gay men; I never get bored. I prefer them to macho men who jump all over you."

Akko told me that Bunny "liked caresses, wanted physical touch," but he was worried because "how far she would go I didn't know." By the time they met in 1993, Akko had been with Ricardo (who doesn't use a last name) since 1984. "I am a gay man," Akko told her, "our relationship is different."

Still, Akko was an escape for Bunny from the past and her memories; he was a fresh start. On Antigua in 1996 (Bunny was then eighty-six), my conversations, intended to help gather material for her memoir, often ran like this one, intended to be about her relationship with the Kennedy family, with me very respectful and Bunny just being Bunny. Sometimes she was one tough interview . . .

Mac: "Now, you are taking care of Caroline Kennedy Schlossberg's children—"

Bunny: "Yes, just the way I once took care of Caroline and John-John. They keep getting younger; I keep getting older."

Mac: "You'll always do this, won't you?"

Bunny: "No, I want to run away with Akko."

At lunch together the day after a long night of her spilling out stories that maybe she wished she hadn't told me, Bunny was very remote. She was also angry that she hadn't heard from Akko for several days. "I no longer have time for people who don't do what I want," she said. "I could cut him off—no, I couldn't cut *him* off," she corrected herself, "but I could cut anyone off who doesn't fit in." As she had done so many times, I thought, wondering if it was now my turn.

She knew that her powers were diminishing, that she was getting old, and was ready to accept at least some limitations, noting, "My apartment [Avenue Foch] is too large for the life I want to lead in Paris. I look forward to change." But she wanted to use all the powers she retained to indulge her own caprices. "She never asked about or considered the cost of things," said Akko. "In my garden is a seat from one of the rides at a country fair—it's madness, a big painted tôle bird with children climbing on its back. Now it's in my garden in St. Tropez. She flew it down."

Akko often accompanied Bunny to events where she needed a companion, preferably someone young, male, and attractive. She took him to England in 1996 for the funeral of her beloved "Brookie," by then the 8th Earl of Warwick, who thought of Bunny, rather than the giddy Rosie Fiske, as his real mother. When a fire broke out in the Chunnel train and Bunny and Akko were trapped for three hours along with eight hundred–odd fellow passengers, what could have been a claustrophobic nightmare was merely another adventure.

Paul's encouragement of her relationship with Akko meant she happily included news about Paul's health and their life together in her faxes to Akko. Soon after moving into her new apartment she wrote from Upperville, saying, "I'm so happy with Paris. The apartment is wonderful. The river is lovely, the flags and la grande grande Rue [meaning the architectural beauty of the rue de l'Université] . . . I am turning around in the air. Paul was fine. Told me I was great to come back for Sunday (I cook Sundays and he loves it)."

Husband and wife grew closer as Paul became increasingly dependent on her. He moved downstairs to what had been his office, still lively with its chartreuse paint; the two of them made sure that from a window he could see his yearlings grazing in a nearby pasture. She hung just the right favorite paintings on the walls, as she had when he had spent time in the hospital.

Bunny shared her happiness with Akko in 1994 about successfully celebrating Paul's eighty-seventh birthday for two days, for once with "the whole family," who "were so pleased that his health and spirit had improved so much." Later that year, after a day of gardening and going through the mail ("rather have you here than the mail"), Bunny wrote to Akko that "Paul appreciated your fax. It is good for everything that he likes you.—Now you can come back every month."

Six months after Paul's death in February 1999, Akko visited Bunny at Oak Spring, enjoying much about life on the farm—"so good simple and warm!" He had seized the chance to pose in his sweats in front of a van Gogh hanging in a corner of the living room, with a teasing smile about being in the company of his illustrious fellow Dutchman.

Akko also accurately noted—using an American phrase that disregards gender—that Bunny's longtime nurse Nancy Collins "was a real 'nice guy' near you." Nancy and the library staff loved having Akko around for a lift and a joke. He saw how the farm and its life were increasingly Bunny's nest, even as she was planning to buy a new plane, a Falcon; that fall, Bunny and Eliza talked about how much time they were going to spend together in Paris. On his visit to the farm, Akko told Bunny that he loved staying with her and spending time in the "divine library where I feel that I might become an intellectual (What a BORE!)."

He teased her unmercifully about her bad French, then signed himself "le grand vilain Hollandais," or "le grand copain vilain Hollandais," which tickled Bunny. Often, more simply, he was "your Dutchman, your French Dutchman, your Dutchie." Akko encouraged Bunny's ingenue friskiness, what he called her unaffected simplicity, writing absurd things to his friend that he knew would appeal to her, such as "Quel adorable fille simple vous étes. Sans shi-shi," after they had spent a few hours together in Paris. She often reverted to her "American country girl" mode with him, her favorite version of herself, signing off, after a successful Garden Library meeting, to Akko as a "Very Happy Wild Girl," with a quick pen sketch of the Blue Ridge Mountains.

Her Paris life was very far away from the Blue Ridge or from any other place she inhabited on the American side of the Atlantic. Finding an apartment on the rue de l'Universite was not just downsizing: it represented the fulfillment of a girlhood dream. The street runs parallel to the Seine only a block away: from the Quai Voltaire where Bunny loved to stroll, the view is of the Pont Neuf and the spires of the Sainte Chapelle and Notre Dame on the Île Saint-Louis. Here was the mix of French Gothic architecture and the beauty of worship that Bunny had

The facade of Number 15, rue de l'Université

held in her imagination ever since she had seen Chartres Cathedral rise out of the mist so many decades before when she was a schoolgirl.

The three-story, late-seventeenth-century *hôtel particulier* at Number 15 is classed as a national historic treasure; the bold honey-colored stone entrance that opens to a central court has been frequently photographed and can be seen on Instagram as a first-class example of the best aristocratic Parisian architecture. More prosaically, this was indeed what they call a *bonne addresse*, one of the finest in Paris, quieter than Avenue Foch, which by the time Bunny left had become a favorite spot for streetwalkers.

In looking for a smaller Paris life, however, Bunny had also left a garden behind. About thirty by ten meters and visible from the living room windows, it had been filled with her standbys—white roses, lavender, pots of herbs, a bay laurel tree, silvery santolina, and strawberries, perhaps grown from those she had taken from Balenciaga's country house in the fifties. Nonetheless, as she moved on to her new, smaller life, she didn't look back, not even at a lost garden (except, perhaps, Apple Hill).

"Paris garden marvelous!" she had exclaimed in her garden journal about a visit to Avenue Foch in July 1982, while at the same time quickly noting with her practiced eye effects that needed sharpening— "impatiens for shock under trees," she jotted, directing also that the laurel tub be kept painted and that tree branches be kept low to screen the view from the street that was visible through a grille. Nothing stabilized Bunny more than immersion in gardening; her favorite plants were an anchor for her.

Not only the Potager gardeners respected and admired this woman's skills and character. When her gardener at Avenue Foch, René Lauvadet, retired in 1990, he wrote her an old-fashioned letter in French to accompany his final detailed invoice, signing off by saying, "I will guard the finest memories of having worked in your service and beg that Madame will accept my most respectful salutations"—all very stiffly formal so far—and then he burst through at the end with an ebullient "& aimer La Nature. Toujours! Beaucoup!"

In 1992, for her new, smaller French life Bunny bought the second floor at 15, rue de l'Université for herself as well as the dormer

Nicolas de Staël's domestic masterpiece, *Le Saladier*, hangs in the salon
of Bunny's new apartment in Paris.

attic floor above it for her servants, plus a couple of cellars and the
all-important parking space in the central courtyard. The renovation
took more than four years, a typical Bunny pace. The American financier and philanthropist Henry Kravis owned the ground-floor garden
apartment; a two-page typed meeting agenda covered the division of
cellar and attic space (Bunny needed room for air-conditioning). Kravis wanted to clean the garden facade, grimy with centuries of soot,
unlike the street front, which had been cleaned at municipal expense
decades before—and in exchange for her agreement he was not only
willing to foot an extra share of the huge expense (perhaps large even
for Kravis) but also to allow equipment for her renovation to enter
through his recently redecorated apartment.

Along with the almost daily hand-holding that Bunny required of
her romantic Dutch friend came the purchase—either from Akko or
through him, and occasionally through Hubert—of furnishings for
her new apartment, the kind of playing house Bunny liked best. "Your
bed is ready and looks very good at its place," Akko wrote about the

final details. "The two chairs are in . . . the walls, the fireplace, the furniture are asking 'où est notre maîtresse?' I said next week she will come and love you all."

Bunny's affection for Akko produced a separation anxiety similar to what an infant suffers when a parent leaves the room and out of sight means gone forever. Akko's presence every day in a phone call or a fax, at least, told her that he was still there and still loved her. "If you don't hear from me, it doesn't mean I'm not thinking about you," he reassured her. Many notes from him spell out where he will be when, along with phone numbers, or when he will be in the shop and free to talk. He is often traveling, he writes, and explains why he can't talk at a certain moment but outlining when he can. Real life does intrude: at one point he wrote, "Sorry to be so 'short' oven door fell off."

For a while, the transatlantic time change meant the fax machine in his and Ricardo's bedroom ground out her messages by night as well as day, so he moved it. "Yes, dear Bunny, you now can send any hour of the night, as I have put the fax in another room. Love, Akko." He didn't have a staff like Hubert's to maintain any sort of distance between them, and the disparity between his life and Bunny's also meant that sometimes he had to lay things out for her, however hesitantly, in a fax. He had to work hard to find items for his shop, to buy and sell, to pay his bills, and he had other clients. He attended antique fairs and shows. It couldn't be all hearts and flowers.

Bunny's way of retaining a man's interest could be primitive; with Akko she resorted to her adolescent ploy of mentioning—or inventing—rivals. "He's sending me buckets and buckets of flowers" is how van Acker told me she put it. In this case it was a real rival, Robert Isabell, whom she had first met in 1985.

The most ticklish subject for Akko, however, was not satisfying Bunny's constant demands to stay in touch; rather, it was about how to get paid for the work he did for her. Ardent protestations of love and requests for payment inevitably sit oddly together. "I spoke with you a little while ago about two items you asked me to keep for you for your new home." He wanted to send her a bill, saying he hopes "it doesn't annoy you that I have to ask you this," signing off rather soberly as "Yours, Akko." Bunny answered his question months later in a fax mostly about an armoire: she reassured him, writing, "Don't worry about mixing business with pleasure. Love, Bunny."

Eventually, money caused the two friends real trouble. When Bunny was ready to leave her Paris life entirely in 2008, she offered her apartment to him as a gift (or at a very low price; there are various versions of this story), and Akko's colleague, an antiques dealer who had formerly worked for him in his shop, ended up with it instead. Bunny was offended enough to cut off Akko for years. When I spoke with Akko about it in a phone interview, he defended himself, saying that, yes, Bunny had offered it to him, but as he wasn't able to sell his own apartment, so "a dear friend of mine bought it [Bunny's apartment]. Voilà la verité." He also told me that Bunny's lawyer, Alex Forger, had told him, "She would have given you a mortgage." Akko ruefully confessed to me, "I could never talk to Bunny about money. I could never have asked her for a mortgage."

Given the general airiness of their faxed conversations about money and the careless grandeur of her ways with him about spending (who paid what to whom?), Akko told me that the buyer of Bunny's apartment gave him a Dutch genre painting "as his commission." Eventually, after raging about him and cutting off communication, Bunny forgave him, and in 2013 they spoke again. She asked him to visit her in Virginia right after Christmas, a visit that never happened, as she died in early March 2014.

Akko's bulging files also hold a thick folding card with beautiful antique prints of pears, a Bunny favorite tree for espaliering. Postmarked Miami 2000, where Akko often spent time with Ricardo, the date is partially illegible, but the message is clear. Akko understood Bunny very well; he loved her and saw her struggles. In plain, Dutch-accented language, he writes, "I do love you, Bunny, because you are so especial! I love you because your name is Bunny and not Mrs. Paul Mellon. You are still so young and full of life, even if it's not always easy."

28

A Long Goodbye to Paul

The doggies and I miss
You at This hour - 7.30.
Hurry on home.
                        Status Quo

Paul and Bunny grew closer in the nineties—he faxed
this to his wife on May 11, 1995.

During the nineties, even as Bunny worked hard on the Potager du Roi with Hubert and fell heavily and instantly for Akko on the rue de l'Université, she dedicated the second Oak Spring Garden Library catalogue—about fruit trees and appropriately titled *Pomona*, for the goddess of orchards—to her husband, who loved his Virginia farm and life in the orchards his wife had planted all around it.

Paul had been diagnosed with prostate cancer in 1983, and while it was clear that it wouldn't kill him immediately, it would not go away. In his usual orderly manner he had then retired as president of the National Gallery in 1985 and set about distributing his assets and his art collection, selling some forty works in 1989 at Christie's and consulting with Bunny about what paintings should stay in their houses after his death as her life estate. By the 1990s, his cancer was advancing, and trips to the Winchester Medical Center were frequent.

Nonetheless, 1993 was bright: With pleasure and certainty, Paul and Bunny even ordered their tombstones for the informal stone-walled enclosure at Trinity Episcopal Church that Perry Wheeler had helped Bunny lay out. Building programs continued that year: Thomas Beach, the young Virginia architect, designed the Garden Library addition with close direction from Bunny.

The following year, 1994, was bleaker. As if Bunny could stave off the loss of her best friend, Jackie Kennedy, by maintaining her own remarkable resilience and energy in the face of the inevitable, she flew to Nantucket to plant trees during the days in May just before Jackie died. She picnicked with her old building crew, dined with her Cape Cod housekeeper, Susan Cabral, witnessed a solar eclipse over the ocean, and worked on details of the library addition. Then she walked alone in the fields that evening before returning to Oak Spring.

On May 19, Jackie died at home in New York City of complications from non-Hodgkin's lymphoma. Bunny had flown from Virginia to be at her bedside with Caroline and John; she noted in her diary that John had quietly drawn the quilt over his mother's body, a traditional, tender act of closure. The Mellon plane brought Jackie's casket to Washington, D.C., where, in Arlington National Cemetery, she was laid to rest next to her husband in the tomb to which Bunny had helped bring so much grace and meaning. Bunny watched the blanket of earth close over her friend while Robert Isabell sat silently by her side. Bunny thanked him for his calm presence, writing, "I hope we meet again, with flowers or without."

What had begun on Cape Cod in 1985—with a sharp glance from Robert Isabell and a hissed "Who is that woman who is telling Mrs. Kennedy what to do?" to the event planner George Trescher as they worked on Caroline Kennedy's wedding—was becoming an engrossing relationship. Bunny had found someone whose gifts as an impresario easily matched her own. The smart, uneducated boy and the smart, uneducated girl more than forty years his senior had both learned how to use eye, instinct, and taste with expertise, elegance, brio—and vast expense—to turn events into momentous and meaningful occasions. Now she had seen his quiet side.

Eliza had watched over her mother and stayed at her side in this time of her bereavement. She came to tea with Bunny at East Seventieth Street the day before Jackie died and then went with her to Jackie's funeral Mass at Saint Ignatius Loyola in New York. Eliza had seen how much her mother needed her, so she remained in town even though she'd made plans to return to Paris. Bunny took a restorative walk in Central Park that afternoon, but Eliza saw that her mother was exhausted and distraught when she returned, so she took her to the Carlyle for drinks—"lovely time," Bunny wrote—and then back to Seventieth Street for dinner together. "Feeling calm again," Bunny wrote afterward. "Eliza was great help." In July, Bunny made a quick trip to Paris to work on her new apartment and have a fitting with Hubert; her life and schedule were back on an even keel.

Serious Scrabble games continued to take place
in Paul's study at Oak Spring.

In 1994, Paul was still strong enough to enjoy himself on occasion. "Paul met me at the plane," Bunny wrote in her daily journal when she returned to the farm from Nantucket, where she'd spent the week carrying out routines to steady herself against the nearness of Jackie's death. One day the couple entertained some of Paul's oldest friends over lunch, buddies who had foxhunted with him for decades all over England and Ireland.

Bunny's close attention was now on Paul: where once she had focused on providing the grandest creature comforts for him, now she cared watchfully for the man himself. "Paul was wonderful—kept up," Bunny recorded in her diary. Although they were both "v. tired" when the lunch guests left, she and Paul were not too tired to miss Sunday supper together in their little Oak Spring kitchen overlooking the garden.

In their eighties, both Paul and Bunny were reaching the age when their friends were dying off in numbers. Bunny saw beloved figures in her life disappear. In December 1994, Stacy Lloyd died after getting tangled up and dragged in the reins of a young horse he was training to pull a cart. The next December, Bunny lost Evangeline Bruce, another tie to her deep past, a cherished relationship that had lasted from Bunny's first marriage through her divorce, her long and difficult years with Paul, and her longings for Hubert and others.

When Bunny and I lunched alone together just after Vangie's death in 1995, Bunny said sadly, "Mac, now I have lost *all* my old friends." She attended Evangeline's funeral in Washington, D.C., with a bunch of lilies of the valley in her hand, even though, Bunny told me, Evangeline's sister, the art historian and woman of letters Virginia Surtees, had said "'No flowers'—oh, what a surprise, given that Evangeline had publicly said that she wanted a big whoop-de-do Christmas funeral if she died near Christmas. I left the bouquet next to the signing book." Bunny sensed that Dorcas Hardin was somewhere around and saw her leave the flowers. "Paul drives me crazy," she said, imitating how he had craned his head around to look for Dorcas in the church. Bunny and Paul's relationship had lasted long enough to transcend an intimate sexual relationship with another person and become deeper, but the hurt was still there.

Although death was the ever-present shadow of these years, gleams of light kept breaking through. In 1997 and 1998, Christopher Ridgeway wrote not one but two articles for *Country Life* about Bunny's library and its contents, the prestigious British journal's first international recognition. Bunny worked with Lucia Tongiorgi Tomasi on her third garden library catalogue, *Flora*, in memory of Jackie. And the men who surrounded Bunny offered continuing reassurance that she was loved, just as the bouquets she had surrounded herself with as a debutante had done: Frank Langella was attentive; Robert Isabell, now Bunny's clear favorite, sent flowers almost weekly; Akko and Hubert called frequently; and Akko faxed almost every day.

Meanwhile, Bunny continued to create celebrations of her life and times with Paul, working up to what I will always think of as a "yard sale" at the Brick House. In the front hall two long folding tables were covered with lamps, vases, table ornaments, paper cutters, pieces of porcelain—figurines, snuff- and patch boxes, inkstands—and many small items of silver. Paul often sent Eliza to the hallowed silversmith James Robinson in New York at Christmastime to buy antique desktop items that might amuse her mother—think stocking stuffers but at an elevated, Mellon, level. After lunch, each guest (there were about one hundred of us) was supposed to choose one object from the dozens and dozens laid out on the tables, a clear-eyed and practical recognition that this life, the lives of Bunny and Paul Mellon, was coming to an end. I chose a soft-paste snuffbox molded in the shape of a little horse whose shoulder and flank are sprigged with painted flowers— and thus it honors both Paul and Bunny. I did see some guests take away more than one object, tucking them under their arms . . .

"Mr. Mellon loved his birthday," said Nancy Collins. For his ninetieth in 1997, Bunny threw not one but two parties at the Brick House, one big and one small. During the first, a tornado watch was called, and everyone evacuated to the Brick House cellars for shelter. Those cellars, crammed with eye-popping stores of furniture and works of art, also provided entertainment until the tornado watch was over.

The second was a party of ten that consisted mostly of intimate family. We lunched in the small, sunny breakfast room at the Brick House. Paul showed he still had an eye for a woman who interested him: this time it was Rhonda Roland Shearer, a sculptor and journalist who founded a nonprofit organization, Art Science Research Laboratory (ASRL), dedicated to making connections between the arts and sciences. Paul helped fund ASRL, which was founded the next year, 1998. Bunny correctly seated Shearer, who held the place of most important guest, at Paul's right, a small but touching detail. Although many had called Bunny insecure, by this time in her life she was confident in herself and her accomplishments.

Shearer, a sparky conversationalist, kept Paul captivated. It should not have been surprising that prominent figures still sought out the Mellons, if only in search of funding. Also at that small table was Shearer's husband and co-founder of ASRL, Stephen Jay Gould, the world-renowned evolutionary biologist and historian of science. The party favor was a large martini glass, in honor of Paul's invariable evening cocktail, marked NINETIETH YEAR, with the date and his initials.

On their fiftieth anniversary, May Day 1998, Bunny had put up a Maypole to celebrate. That June, Paul's doctor told him that he would make it through Christmas, and, according to the art historian John Baskett, "Just after Christmas you won't feel well, and six weeks later you'll be dead." Paul made his last visit to Cape Cod that summer but was too weak to sail.

Paul continued to spend time with his racehorses, such as Fort Marcy,
1970's *Daily Racing Form*'s Horse of the Year, who had lived
in happy retirement in Rokeby's pastures.

Paul died on February 1, 1999, almost to the day his doctor had reportedly predicted. A week later, his gray and yellow American racing colors draped his coffin at Trinity Episcopal Church in Upperville. John Baskett rose to eulogize Paul and his philanthropy; Paul's son, Tim, spoke about family; and Billy Wilbur, Paul's companion on many Virginia Hundred Mile Rides, remembered Paul's love for horses and hunting. (Wilbur was no longer invited to Mellon lunches once he married—a not altogether remarkable occurrence, given Bunny's dislike of wives in general.) The church was jammed, and the interment was thronged with family, friends from near and far, local farmers, and staff. Dignitaries and colleagues, all old friends from institutions Paul had generously supported, were also there.

Both of Dorcas Hardin's children were there at Bunny's request and were given seats up front. From farther back I could see my schoolmate Diana Hardin's red hair. I did not see Dorcas Hardin in the church, but John Baskett later told me she had been invited and had, correctly, declined.

The reception at Oak Spring afterward might have seemed indecently festive, except that most of those there who lifted a glass to Paul knew that he had at last "laid me down with a will"—a line from Robert Louis Stevenson's poem "Requiem," which is carved in its entirety on the back of Paul's handsome tombstone. The last couplet reads: "Home is the sailor, home from the sea / And the hunter home from the hill."

By the terms of Paul's final testament, signed on November 19, 1998, Bunny received $110 million, the new plane Paul had ordered for her (a Falcon 2000), and a large number of artworks outright along with a life interest in many that would stay with her in various houses until her death. She also received the New York house and the carriage house on the next block. God only knows what Mellon money had been expended over his lifetime to create their life together.

Paul distributed over $160 million to art institutions he had long supported: the National Gallery of Art, the Yale Center for British Art that he had founded, and the Virginia Museum of Fine Arts (VMFA). Other bequests that totaled nearly $25 million went to educational institutions—Choate School and Cambridge and St. John's Universities—that had shaped the man he became.

All these gifts were in addition to the help he'd continuously given over the decades in building programs, special projects, and fellowships. Paul Mellon's gifts, exclusive of what he left to his wife, were estimated at over a billion dollars in 1999. He divided 230 paintings between the National Gallery and Yale and left a van Gogh to the VMFA. He gave Dead Neck Island, the little strip of sand dunes facing the house in Cape Cod, to the Audubon Society, along with half a million dollars. Art critic John Russell aptly commented that Paul Mellon had "turned philanthropy into his own personal art form."

One person curiously absent from Paul's funeral was Gerard Barnes Lambert III, Bunny's only nephew and Eliza's first cousin, her longtime buddy, and a family presence for decades. Eliza called him Barnes; almost everyone else called him Jerry. Bunny loved to call him Gerard, the name of both his father, who was Bunny's brother, and of her father.

In 1964, Bunny had invited Barnes to Antigua to help distract Jackie in the months after JFK's assassination. In 1967, Bunny, Eliza, and Barnes sat together for hours after the death of Bunny's father, their grandfather. Slowly, carefully, Bunny had woven a garland for his grave from stiff branches of glossy-leaved magnolia, intensely blue cornflowers from her Virginia hothouses, and unforgettably fragrant paper-white narcissus. A blizzard was blowing in, dropping a pall of white over Princeton. When the wreath was finished at last, Eliza said, "Come on, Barnes, let's go for a walk." That night, the Lambert home was "so crowded," Barnes recalled, "that I slept on a couch in the room with the casket."

Barnes and his family were fixtures of Osterville summers in the 1980s and early 1990s. But at some point perhaps he had loomed as too constant a presence. Maybe some in the family perceived him as trying to inch into position as Paul's son. On his return to Virginia from a January 1996 Antigua visit, Barnes was called by an Oak Spring staff member, who said, "Mrs. Mellon would like you to leave the property immediately." Barnes quickly packed up and left.

As Bunny had done with Liza Maugham—Lady Glendevon—Syrie Maugham's daughter and Bunny's friend from her early London days, she offered no explanation; it was simply necessary that another person she had once loved should disappear from her life.

When Paul died, an Oak Spring staff member phoned Barnes to tell him about the funeral plans, but he never responded. "I knew I wouldn't be allowed to attend," said Barnes, "so I held my own service. The day after the funeral I came to the grave and put a little boat model I had made on it." It's still there, constantly renewed, a small, personal memorial to Paul Mellon.

A larger memorial lies over the hills and westward into the Blue Ridge foothills: Sky Meadows State Park in the northwest corner of Fauquier County. In 1975, Paul had characteristically stepped in without fanfare to save 1,132 acres from a planned luxury residential development and shopping center, purchasing more land in 1991 for a total of 1,860 acres. The day Barnes put his boat model on Paul's grave, he climbed the mountain; high on the trail he found a tin can of flowers on a bench with a note from another hiker saying, "Thank you, Mr. Mellon."

Within a week of Paul's death, a battle royal began for control of the farm, a battle between Bunny and Beverly Carter, Paul's long-serving art curator at the Brick House, a canny, homegrown Virginian from nearby Frederick County who, like Tony Willis at the library, had trained on the job. Carter was responsible not only for the flow of artworks—mostly but not exclusively British art—once John Baskett had returned to England, but also for their condition and documentation while they remained in Virginia. The British art was eventually sent to Paul's museum in New Haven.

Carter and Bunny had been at odds for years, Carter bridling at Bunny's imperious ways and Bunny resisting anyone's control. Now she and Carter were combatants, and Carter saw her chance. She was the one who paid the farm's employees.

Bunny's first move was to order Carter to leave the Brick House immediately, although she apparently was unable to oust her as a Mellon employee. Carter's resounding return volley was a letter to all 130 farm employees—without notifying Bunny—that terminated their employment at once. Bunny promptly wrote her own letter to every-one, telling all farm employees they were to continue as before, that she would advise on any changes with plenty of advance notice, *and that she was now making the decisions.* She changed the name of the property from Rokeby Farms to Oak Spring Farm and hired Alex Forger to extend his scope to handle all her legal affairs, which now included the farm. In a larger sense Bunny had already won. She was on her own.

Bunny tried for some small economies; she was not operating on a seemingly limitless budget like Paul's. She didn't succeed: almost everything continued unchanged at the farm. Bucky Holsinger and Al Reed still crafted teak buckets for the stables, branding the bottom of each with the words "Oak Spring," the date, and the name of the craftsman, then sending them to the farm's metal shop for handles and other hardware. "Everything here is for pleasure," Holsinger said. "Nothing is commercial."

The dairyman and his wife still made hundreds of pounds of cheese annually and groomed prize cows to send to the cattle shows to bring home ribbons. The greenhouses under Rokeby Farms gardener George Shaffer were still growing thousands of seedlings yearly, de-spite a ten percent cutback.

The new Falcon and its pilots were ready to go, and the proper-ties on Nantucket, Cape Cod, Antigua, Paris, and New York were fully staffed. In New York, Bunny bought top-floor space in the Essex House on Central Park South with a commanding view of the majes-tic park for Forger and his new office staff—the first business head-quarters of her own she had ever had.

Robert Isabell, the quiet but glamorous presence at Jackie's 1994 interment at Arlington National Cemetery, now reappeared. Eliza knew her mother could use a new friend and began scheming to help fill Bunny's lonely hours in the wake of Paul's death. And who bet-ter than a man who spoke the language of flowers almost as well as her mother, someone who clearly already admired Bunny? They also shared the same vocabulary of theatrical presentation, of fantasy, of mind-blowing expense-is-no-object extravagance—and impatience with those who didn't get it right.

Bunny would be spending Christmas at her daughter's place in Rhode Island, Eliza told me—the first time for Bunny to be away from Virginia on the holiday, her first without Paul after fifty-one years. Eliza suggested that Robert have a heaping basket of lily of the valley, Bunny's signature flower, and violets, the blossoms of early spring, delivered to her Little Compton doorstep on Christmas Eve. "Mums, there's a big box out here with your name on it," Eliza then said to her mother. Eliza called to tell me about her mother's raptures, and Bunny wrote a special fourteen-page diary with a drawing of the basket of flowers on the cover.

29

Goodbye, Eliza

In 2000, on May 6, a Saturday morning, as Eliza was walking in lower Manhattan, she stepped off a curb and was struck by a truck barreling around a corner onto Houston Street. Still unconscious more than twenty-four hours later, she was wheeled into an operating room at New York-Presbyterian Hospital on Sunday at 9:30 p.m. Ninety-year-old Bunny had arrived from Virginia not long before. To those of us waiting to hear the results of the surgery, Bunny handed out her signature picnic food, which she had brought with her: crustless sandwiches on homemade bread and a small silver shaker of daiquiris. I wondered if Bunny's lifetime of order, discipline, and control powered by great wealth would help her face whatever the outcome might be of Eliza's surgery.

Bunny had heard about her daughter's injury from Nancy Collins on Saturday afternoon shortly after she had arrived back at Oak Spring from her grandson, Stacy's, graduation in Illinois, but she'd known something was wrong just from the look on Nancy's face. "It's Eliza," said Nancy, and she quickly explained what she knew. They packed bags and headed for Dulles—the Mellon plane was being serviced after the flight from the Midwest. Bunny called Robert Isabell en route to New York to tell him what had happened.

Isabell had already been alerted by Milu Rodriguez, the housekeeper in New York both for the Mellons and for Eliza, who told him that Eliza had been taken to St. Vincent's Hospital in Greenwich Village, the emergency care location nearest the site of the accident. Since she hadn't updated her ID from her old address on Barrow Street, no one knew where she was until Rodriguez picked up a message from St. Vincent's, trying to reach a family member, on Eliza's studio's answering machine and called the Virginia household.

Eliza had been pronounced brain dead after a CT scan, and the St. Vincent's resident on duty deemed any surgical intervention useless, but put her on life support. Meanwhile, her brain continued to swell. Isabell called a friend, Dr. Brian Saltzman, who said there was only one man who could possibly help her, the neurosurgeon Jamshid Ghajar, who had been profiled in 1996 in *The New Yorker* for his revolutionary brain trauma treatment. Eliza was transferred to New York-Presbyterian/Weill Cornell Medical Center, where Ghajar started his exam on Sunday evening.

Rodriguez had called everyone she could, and maybe a dozen of us had been sitting in a row facing the operating theater doors when Bunny and Nancy arrived. At 11:30 that night, an exhausted-looking Ghajar came out, still in his scrubs. By inserting a tube—"as thin as spaghetti," he later said—the first step in preventing further injury, he had relieved the mounting pressure on Eliza's brain caused by a large hematoma. But his face seemed to give us little hope.

Bunny asked to see her daughter, and Nancy Collins went in with her. When the two emerged, Bunny told us firmly, "She looks great." Doubtless Bunny was in shock, but I felt she was also relying on her governing dictum to make the best of things. Nancy, a registered nurse, later told me the edema was so extreme that Eliza's cheeks were swollen enough to conceal most of her nose and that Ghajar said that the internal pressure had almost herniated her brain stem.

In the following days, Bunny's utter determination that Eliza would recover almost seemed like magical thinking. But at that point, who was not going to hope, even in the face of Eliza's near-complete paralysis? Eliza had already been intubated, so she couldn't speak even if she had been able.

When the tube was finally removed, she tried to talk, her eyes moved, opened, and closed, and you could see that she was conscious. She could move her left foot, and when you held her hand, it was warm, and she opened and closed it. She smiled, especially when we played music for her. Her private room was filled with dancing sunlight, and the windows overlooked the sparkling East River many stories below. On the walls, treasured artworks that Bunny had brought in so Eliza could see them hung alongside some of her own work. "She is going to talk to us soon," Bunny said often.

Akko faxed Bunny the Thursday following the accident. "Good morning, dearest Bunny and Eliza, I hope you are both waking up and not too tired after this hard, difficult week. God promised to ring the bells for church so you both can pray and ask him why he does this. Maybe he will tell you . . . I don't see why!"

Ann Hudner, an arts administrator at RISD, had been introduced to Eliza in the fall of 1999 by Virginia Lynch, an art dealer who had shown Eliza's work at her Tiverton, Rhode Island, gallery, and Ann and Eliza were dating. I asked Hudner, who became my friend, if they were in love, and she said simply, "We were excited."

Hudner had an extraordinary ability not to presume beyond what she saw as the limits of her new relationship. In the week after the accident, Hudner hadn't really worried that she hadn't heard from Eliza, since she would often go silent, working for days straight in her studio. She only heard the bad news from Lynch days later and immediately called Diane Brown, an art dealer and one of Eliza's close friends in New York. Although both Hudner and Eliza were very private people, Hudner told Brown they were dating. With a smile, Brown later said to me, "Of course, I saw that."

Hudner wrote to Bunny, whom she had never met, to introduce herself and to ask if she could visit Eliza. Bunny said yes. Hudner told me she had no way to understand the situation she found herself in, as Eliza had been careful not to flaunt who her family was. "Even then," Hudner said, "I didn't take in the extent of the Mellons' wealth until I went to Virginia. I had been exposed to celebrity and fame at RISD, meeting people like Robert Redford, Dale Chihuly, and Jenny Holzer, but I was never starstruck. It's just money." Hudner's no-nonsense New England upbringing had kept her steady.

Hudner and Diane Brown spelled each another and Bunny at the hospital in New York. Bunny soon asked Hudner to stay at Seventieth Street when she came for the weekend from Providence, and Hudner's visits gave Bunny the occasional opportunity to fly to Nantucket or Cape Cod for a brief respite from her nearly round-the-clock vigil at Eliza's bedside.

For Hudner, it was in the Seventieth Street home where different realms of reality collided and the surreal began. The staff "would serve me dinner on a tray in that peach-colored living room, where I sat alone under the large Sargent portrait," said Hudner, who finally asked if she could have dinner in the kitchen, saying, "I spend the whole day with someone who can't talk to me, and I can't come home to silence." Grudgingly the staff agreed, and the next night she came to the kitchen "to find her place at the kitchen table set with a tray, with the same silver flatware, the same silver bud vase, the same silver salt and pepper shakers, with dinner again eaten in silence."

Diane Brown had abruptly left her own dinner party when she got the news of Eliza's accident from Rodriguez. She and Eliza had met when Brown included her in a tour to the Venice Biennale soon after Eliza and Doris Sanders separated. A mutual friend had signed Eliza up for the trip, and "when a power outage in Venice due to a storm meant streets were completely black," Brown recalled, "Eliza began to sing 'Hernando's Hideaway' . . . I knew all the words too!"

They instantly became friends. Eliza's new studio on Tenth Street was around the corner from Diane's apartment. The Thursday before the accident, the two friends had just signed the incorporation paperwork for their new project, RxART, a nonprofit organization that, with seed money from Eliza, would commission and place art for children in hospitals nationwide. After Eliza's death, the Lambert Foundation supported RxART with a million-dollar gift.

While Eliza lay in the hospital, everyone was reaching for something, however small, that might carry her back to us—and carry us back to life before May 6, 2000. We were like the Sarajevo Philharmonic cellist Vedran Smailović, who played day after day in the market square in honor of the dead of his besieged city. We were eternally hopeful and never expressed any doubts to Bunny about Eliza's recovery, except for Ann Hudner, who always answered Bunny's quest for reassurance with, "I just don't know."

After six months in the hospital, Eliza was carefully airlifted to the Inova Rehabilitation Center in Mount Vernon, Virginia, then eventually to a house, Spring Hill, at Oak Spring. As was so often the case, Bunny took action first in the landscape to steady herself. On a memo pad, under the title "Life," Bunny wrote, "You've got to play with the cards you are dealt—just play them like a master." On the next page she added "Clean up Spring Hill," then scribbled "Large Boxwood Bush," boxwood ever a support to her spirit and her landscapes. Spring Hill soon had a fully equipped medical suite for Eliza, with rooms for round-the-clock nurses and for Dr. Ghajar, who was flown down from New York City in the Mellon plane for his periodic weekend visits.

Like a bird smashing itself against a windowpane to get out, Bunny tried every means to get Eliza to communicate with her. "If she could just *speak*," Bunny would often remark, "say just a few words, tell us what she wants." When I visited Spring Hill, Bunny and I would sit on either side of Eliza propped up in her hospital bed and hold her hands and talk to her. "See? She knows we're here!" Bunny would say when Eliza's hands reflexively squeezed ours. Family members came to visit—even those, like her first cousin "Barnes" Lambert, who had been banished—to see if their voices, their presence, would make a difference.

One day Bunny had one of her great Agnes Martin paintings, "a big rosy pink one that was mostly kept in a barn," said Ann Hudner, brought to Spring Hill for Eliza to see, experience, and feel its serene vibration. Musicians, including some of the nurses, played for Eliza in the afternoons. Vigorous massage kept her blood circulation going as much as possible. Bunny set up a Maypole every May Day outside the glass wall of Spring Hill. Bruce Budd, her last decorator and a confidant, said Bunny also asked him to find cheerful old quilts to hang on a clothesline and move in the wind. Gentle Jay Keys, a burly farm employee Eliza had been close to, would drive her around in a specially equipped van so she could enjoy the change of scenery from a wheelchair into which she was snugly strapped to keep her upright. But "these changes in her environment never lasted for long," said Hudner, as Mrs. Mellon would say, "'Eliza doesn't like it anymore,'" when she didn't respond.

Akko, second fiddle to Robert Isabell by 2001, tried his best to put Bunny's desperation into perspective and make her laugh, writing in 2002, "Dearest Bunny, I don't think you need a psychologue. *You* will talk him under the table. It's normal you have depressed moments . . . lots of people couldn't face this dramatic period, so your patience, your friends, and me, of course, are there to help you!"

"Everyone was constantly saying, 'Wake up,'" said Hudner. "One day, when I was alone with Eliza, she just looked so sad, and I said, 'You know, Eliza, everyone keeps telling you to wake up, but, if you're tired and you're ready to go to a new life, if you don't want to wake up, you don't have to—you can go to the next life.'"

As Eliza continued to fail, she was moved into Paul's old study at Oak Spring so that Bunny could be even closer to her. But anyone could see that the end was nearing. Bunny shuffled the staff, but the nurses grew surly and frenetic, as they knew whatever happened would be blamed on them. Besides, some of them wanted higher pay once they saw the many luxuries in the main house at Oak Spring. Also, once they understood that Hudner was Eliza's girlfriend, some were scandalized, and Bunny felt she had to send Ann away to keep the peace. "Mrs. Mellon feels Eliza needs time alone," a nurse said to Hudner, who had just arrived for the weekend. "Am I being asked to leave?" she asked. Yes, was the answer. "I said goodbye to Eliza and left within the hour." She would never see Eliza again.

The following week Bunny sent Hudner an apology via FedEx attempting to explain her reasoning. She said Dr. Ghajar had told her Eliza was entering another stage of healing. "She asked me to call her," said Hudner. "I spoke with my mother—whose words to me are still crystal clear. 'She's a mother, Ann, and desperate to do anything, to try anything, to bring her daughter back. Don't add to her sadness. Forgive her.'"

"I called Mrs. Mellon the next day," said Ann, "and forgave her, and we talked and remained in close touch until her death in 2014 . . . My relationship with her was very special. There were many late-night calls when she was at her most raw and vulnerable and just wanted reassurance from me that she was doing the right things. My respect and admiration for her is deep and unshakable." Hudner saw Bunny in person only once more, at Eliza's funeral. "She hugged me so hard and long, I thought the two of us were going to fall over," said Hudner.

For Dr. Jamshid Ghajar, Bunny felt overwhelming gratitude. She trusted him to eventually "bring Eliza back," even if she would only be able to show a few signs of awareness and recognition. It was a difficult situation for Ghajar, who understood the real impossibility of recovery of any kind as time went on. He made weekend trips to Nantucket at Bunny's invitation while she stayed with Eliza in Virginia, and he briefly developed an understanding with Bunny that she would support the creation of a traumatic brain injury center on the island. But Alex Forger adroitly foiled that plan, and Bunny grew disillusioned when she believed that Ghajar had invited a girlfriend (whom he later married) to Nantucket—the place that Bunny considered her solitary preserve—and asked the staff not to tell Bunny. When she found out, her romantic attachment to him ended, although his care of Eliza continued. Bunny's distress over Eliza, her determination to heal her—and her great wealth—allowed her to imagine the world as she wanted it to be. She overcame any internal governor that might have told her about limits to a relationship. But eventually she would support Ghajar's Brain Trauma Foundation with a $200,000 cash bequest in honor of Eliza. It's estimated that she had spent $1.2 million over the previous eight years on Eliza's care. She would also invite Dr. Ghajar to speak at Eliza's funeral.

For much of her life, Eliza had been forced to be what Bunny wished her to be. From the account of the glamorous Bee Dabney Adams, an artist and one of Eliza's two bridesmaids in 1968, I could see how hard it was to resist the whole program. I phoned Dabney, as I had assumed she had been a close friend of Eliza's, but that wasn't really the case—she was closer to Paul and Bunny. In the early 1960s, she said, Eliza hoped she was "headed for the stage . . . that would have upset Bunny terribly. But when Eliza got more interested in painting, Bunny was so excited, she transformed the barn at once into a studio."

How, exactly, had Eliza become interested in becoming an artist? I asked.

"I taught Eliza how to paint," said Dabney. "We went out on horseback with our art equipment for a plein air session. When we came in, I said, 'Look at that painting, a van Gogh of a field. [She was referring to van Gogh's *Wheat Fields at Auvers*, which hung over the living room fireplace.] How many colors can you see in it?' We went out the next day, and she found colors and shadows she hadn't seen before."

Eliza's early artistic efforts often depended on witty double meanings. She sketched pale flowers in chalk on brown cardboard that was, in fact, a flattened long box like those wholesale florists use to send flowers to retailers. Bunny hung the work proudly over her desk in her tower office at the library. On a board cut from a white oak at the farm, Eliza scratched an oak tree under a full moon, with the grain of the wood standing in for the rays of moonlight.

Eliza later said, "Part of working is throwing things away," as she put together pieces for a 1996 exhibition at the Virginia Lynch Gallery in Tiverton, Rhode Island. Appreciating how her daughter worked, because her own creativity followed the same experimental route, Bunny jotted that comment down in her diary. After months of deliberation, Eliza felt she had thrown away enough.

Eventually, she found the camera and a connection with the natural and spiritual world that fed her inspiration as an artist. She believed that her studio in New York City was guarded by the spirit of Eugène Delacroix, the artist she most admired, and was absorbed in her work for days on end, interrupted only by her daily walks along the Hudson River. A found object was often the start of her best art. A photograph of two clouds could become a large collage called *A Kiss*; a crack in the pavement could spark an angel. The slices of light and dark in photographs and paint that Eliza called the "Walking Angels" were the last projects she worked on in the first months of 2000.

Hudner believed the ad hoc character of Eliza's work pushed back against the meticulous planning of her mother's creations. "Bunny drew the boundaries, then pushed the boundaries," she said. "Eliza was reactive; [she] took pleasure in breaking the rules."

Virginia Lynch mounted another exhibition of Eliza's work in 2002. Diane Brown, who co-curated the exhibition, highlighted in the catalogue something Eliza had written in 1998: "The more I pursue, the more I see or discover. It is more than fascinating, and through these spirits, whether in field or studio, I am always seeing and never alone."

One of Eliza's late works, *Red and Green Tango* (1998)
is only 7.5 by 8 inches, but it packs a punch.

Eliza's wedding on May 14, 1968, had stood out for its fairy-tale beauty and lavishness. The reception was attended by more than three hundred, including the widowed Jackie Kennedy, with her two young children as attendants. Paul rented a bigger plane than his own to bring ninety guests from New York to Upperville. But at the small bridal dinner the night before, only four tables assembled at the Mellons' house in D.C.—Lord Moore, the tenth Earl of Drogheda, father of the groom and managing editor of the *Financial Times* for twenty-five years, and his wife, Joan Carr, a concert pianist and legendary London figure; young Lord Brooke, Bunny's wartime ward; plus Eliza's brother, Tuffy, and her half brother, Robin Lloyd, and, for Paul,

Alfred Vanderbilt, Jr., whose horses regularly competed with Paul's in American stakes races. Stacy Lloyd, who would give his daughter away, sat next to his old friend Evangeline Bruce. Gracie Mull Lambert, Bunny's stepmother, widowed the year before by the death of Gerard B., was Paul's dinner partner. Johnny Schlumberger was seated next to Bunny's longtime friend Liza Maugham, now Lady Glendevon. Only two of Eliza's Foxcroft schoolmates were included. One of them, bridesmaid Cristina de Heeren, was the daughter of a friend of Bunny's, the Brazilian Aimée Soto-Maior de Sá, an international fashion figure married to Rodman de Heeren, the great-grandson of John Wanamaker, who founded the eponymous department store. J. Carter Brown, who would become director of the National Gallery of Art a year later, sat at Stacy's table. The dinner was a picture of money and clout, titles, art, and fashion, some guests from Bunny's first group of friends as Mrs. Lloyd, and not many of Eliza's buddies or those of her groom, Derry Moore.

Derry had started a boutique travel agency in New York—who better to organize your travel than an English earl's very cool son with a budding photographer's eye for locations? He was set up with Eliza by the reigning cosmetics king for the rich, Erno Laszlo, whom Bunny patronized. On their first date (a double date with Cristina de Heeren) they went to Roseland, the old dance hall in Manhattan's Theater District, and danced the night away. "Old-fashioned dancing," said Derry; "Eliza loved it, and so did I." It was straight out of the thirties or the forties or even the fifties, a match between two sheltered young people in 1968, one of the most turbulent years in American history.

When Derry and I met again in London in 2015 for this book, I had just seen a Goya show at London's National Gallery of Art. The grotesqueness of the Spanish royal family as seen in Goya's group portraits was fresh in my mind. As Derry and I talked about the Mellons and Eliza, I said that Bunny was in some ways grotesque, that I had feared her as much as I loved and admired her. Derry, who had loved Eliza and thought it was all going to work out (they divorced in 1972), said, "Eliza was incredibly attractive and had enormous charm. And grace. Bunny had grace too. But in some ways it *is* more interesting that she is partly a monster." The isolation of rich families can lead to a kind of insanity, we agreed.

Barnes Lambert remembered sensing Eliza's desperation the morning of her wedding. "Bunny threw a big brunch, but Eliza said, 'I'm not going,' so she and I hid upstairs and ate on the floor. Bunny was furious," according to Barnes. Finally, Eliza was dressed in her Yves Saint Laurent, striking a tiny blow for freedom from her mother's fealty to Balenciaga. Bunny's personal maid, Nelly Jo Thomas, tied the blue sash. The rest of the wedding party headed for Trinity Episcopal Church, where they awaited the bride's entrance for the four o'clock service. "I was ready with the old station wagon," said Barnes, "but Eliza kept saying she didn't want to go through with it, didn't want to get married. Somehow she got in that car . . ." The bride arrived about half an hour late, according to Barnes, and the brief, picture-perfect ceremony took place. At the reception, everyone watched as Eliza and Derry cut the cake in a specially built white lattice pavilion that still stands at Oak Spring next to Bunny's showplace greenhouse, beyond the crab apple allée.

After flying out to Los Angeles, where Eliza loved driving fast on the freeways, the newlyweds settled in Paris. They bought an apartment at 7 Place Dauphine on the Île de la Cité, twenty yards from the Pont Neuf where it crosses over to the Left Bank. (Bunny was still staying at the Crillon back then.) Eliza continued to paint, while Derry was on his way to becoming one of the world's foremost photographers of interiors. (The flat ultimately went to Robin Lloyd, Eliza's half brother [son of Stacy and Alice], as a bequest from Eliza.)

The marriage soon ran into trouble. In December 1971, Eliza wrote a bitter little note to her mother, saying, "I think I am God's *personal* fool." Eliza and Derry divorced after three years. However, Derry laughed when I asked him if he had received the traditional Mellon golden handshake: a lavish settlement. "My father-in-law was not Paul Mellon," he said, adding that while he admired Paul, it was Stacy he thought of as the perfect American gentleman. (Senator John Warner received $10 million on his divorce from Eliza's half sister, Cathy Mellon, and Tim Mellon's divorced wife, Louise Mellon, always a favorite of Paul's, received a seat on the National Gallery of Art board as well as two paintings as a bequest from Paul in his will.)

The reason Eliza had wanted to leave Derry at the altar seems clear enough to me: she was gay. "I knew she preferred girls," said Derry, "but you know how it is, you think you are the exception." He added with a rueful smile, "In those days you thought you could change a girl's mind." I also asked him if he, like me, had heard that Bunny too "liked girls." He said only that when he was on a photo shoot with Sister Parish in the 1980s, he remembered her saying that at Foxcroft Bunny was "always calling out some girl's name in her sleep." We laughed and dismissed it as a schoolgirl crush. The level of Bunny's often headlong enthusiasm for a new friend or acquaintance had led some to wonder, but there is no evidence that she ever had a physical relationship with another woman.

In retrospect, it seems that Bunny had always known Eliza was gay but wasn't worried about it, although Eliza herself told Ann Hudner that when she was younger, well before her marriage, she was sleeping with a woman curator at the National Gallery of Art. When her mother heard about it, she shipped Eliza off to France at once. Decades later, Akko told me that Bunny showed no such prejudice when he spoke with her about Eliza. "When Eliza was in grade school, the school called her to say that Eliza was very rough with the other children and that they could tell that even at such an early age that she preferred girls. 'So what?' said Bunny. They wanted her to take Eliza out of the school and place her elsewhere. 'She stays where she is,' said her mother."

Still early in Eliza's recovery, when Ann and Bunny were sitting in Bunny's bedroom in New York, "we talked about my relationship with Eliza," said Hudner. "I wanted Mrs. Mellon to know that Eliza and I had only just begun to know each other—it had only been nine months." Bunny drew on her own experience, knowing that love, however one defined it, could strike unexpectedly, saying quietly to Hudner, "A month or a day, it doesn't matter—you loved each other, and that's what matters."

Eliza told me that after she and Doris split, her mother had quickly bought a stuffed guard dog, a German shepherd, to sit in the passenger seat of her daughter's car for protection. The dog was funny and awful; the tragedy was that the daughter Bunny protected would be the person she could not protect from death.

Free at last following her breakup with Doris Sanders, Eliza rocketed around and fell for various pretty gym trainers or women she met in gay nightclubs. She even lunged once for me, her boringly heterosexual old school buddy. Once that idea was banished, we continued to go to her favorite haunt, The Firebird, a darkly atmospheric Russian restaurant in a townhouse on Manhattan's Theater Row, where we drank vodka as Eliza told me about her latest crushes and pursuits.

"Eliza was always teasing me, teasing everybody," said Diane Brown. "Once when Bunny said, 'I love Robert Isabell,' Eliza shot back, 'I love Diane Brown.' 'Oh geez,' said Brown to herself, 'now Bunny will think I'm gay too.' And in fact the next time we met, Bunny said, 'Oh you are the Diane Eliza loves!'"

Not long after Eliza's breakup with Doris, another controlling figure appeared in Eliza's life: Odessa (who used no last name), a psychic. She was a heavyset woman with long, kinky dark gray hair and olive skin. She spoke softly in measured tones. Once, when Ann Hudner told Eliza she loved her, Eliza sent her a note saying, "The spirits believe it, as Odessa has told me." Both Eliza and her mother lived in a world swayed by signs, symbols, emotions, and fears of the unknown: Bunny often consulted her astrological chart to see if a day was auspicious for certain activities and called Beverley Newton, a Virginia psychic, daily.

I believe that the few years in the late nineties following Bunny's reunion with Eliza and before the accident had been among the happiest of Bunny's life. "I know what I want to get done," she said. The stars and the spirits—all spirits—had been in harmony. She and Paul had reconciled, and in his increasing weakness Bunny, late into her eighties, had found her competent and deeply caring, nurturing self.

Bunny was recognized for the Potager du Roi as an Officer of the French Order of Arts and Letters and received an honorary doctorate at RISD with Eliza by her side. She gave a million dollars to RISD to honor Tiverton, Rhode Island, gallery owner Virginia Lynch and then managed to break her wrist when she fell at Eliza's place in Little

Compton. In those years, sorrows and tragedies—both those that could be foreseen, such as Jackie's death—or sudden cataclysms, like the deadly plane crash of John F. Kennedy, Jr., and his wife, Carolyn Bessette, over the ocean near Martha's Vineyard—left mourning and turbulent memories in their wake. But those tragic events were finite in a way completely unlike Eliza's yearslong suffering.

After Eliza's accident, nobody provided Bunny with more distractions and affection than Robert Isabell. He had arrived in New York in the late 1970s, bringing with him a startling aesthetic sense that matched—and partly created—the wild, gilded 1980s of New York partying. His best friend was Ian Schrager, owner of Studio 54 with master promoter Steve Rubell. Isabell was the mastermind behind Gayfryd Steinberg's impossibly opulent and thoroughly outrageous million-dollar 1989 birthday bash for her billionaire corporate-raider and art-collector husband, Saul Steinberg, complete with ten tableaux vivants, including a naked actress portraying Rembrandt's *Danaë* welcoming Zeus into her bed. "Yes, it was gross," said the author and TV journalist Barbara Dearing Howar, who was a stunned yet appreciative guest. "But it was [also] fun and wonderful."

Robert Isabell's perfect four-poster-in-a-meadow fantasy for
Bunny's ninetieth birthday

For Bunny in 2000, Isabell concocted a completely different birthday event—a surprise ninetieth for her on the Cape: in the middle of a flowering meadow sat a four-poster bed curtained in pale blue printed cotton where Bunny could recline and hold court. (Ann Hudner stayed with Eliza in New York "so Bunny wouldn't stress.") "Robert even stood a table next to the bed with a telephone so she could receive calls," said Nancy Collins, "and a piano, and blankets on the grass to lie on, and buckets of sunflowers."

A mixed bag of guests included the loyal bunch from the farm—the Mellon plane had swooped down to gather them up; Caroline Kennedy and her husband, Edwin Schlossberg, and their children; Alex Forger; Bunny's favored grandson, "Little Stacy"; and a few of her new friends in the arts such as Wendy Wasserstein, to whom Isabell had introduced her. Although Diane Brown and Wasserstein got there late due to cascading travel disasters en route from New York, and "the party was long over, [and] everyone [else] had left," Bunny was still lying in her blue-curtained four-poster in the field of wildflowers, flirting happily with Isabell. As Brown recalled, "She was having an awfully good time with Robert."

Given the amount of money and effort expended, just as stunning in its own quiet way as the Steinberg party was the winning entry Bunny and Isabell created for the Chicago Botanical Garden's 2002 annual garden show that replicated the atmosphere of the enclosed garden at Oak Spring. Tractor trailers from Virginia hauled in soil, moss, stones, plants from Rokeby's greenhouses, and, for the finial on the slat house enclosure, a pricy antique American eagle figure that Bunny later gave to the city of Chicago. Liz Garvin, Isabell's longtime lighting designer—not incidentally a Chicago McCormick and the cousin of the New York philanthropist Deeda Blair—said, "The sofa feature was made of boxwood and moss. Bunny was pretty frail by then, but she sat on something that kept her gown from being devastated by the damp and held court."

Isabell's private life in Manhattan, however, was far from picture-perfect garden installations in the Midwest. The most legendary of the leather bar/private clubs catering to gay men was the Mineshaft near his house in the Meatpacking District; another he frequented was the Manhole. "I'm sure he participated," remembered one close friend in the 1980s, "but that was not the main thing. He was watching. That was the way he was in life too. He was watching in order to learn."

Bunny had loved going to the trendy disco Infinity with Givenchy in 1976 for a taste of titillation. She was curious about all things connected with style and scene—so, just as she wanted to go clubbing with Hubert, she wanted to hang out with Robert and at least find out about the Mineshaft scene as part of her friend's life.

For Bunny, Isabell was far more than a "walker" or an imaginary lover or a refreshing entry point into a new life or even more than a comfort in the long years of Eliza's quadriplegia. He was her steady friend, and he gave her good, bold advice. In 2006, he asked her about the New York house: "Why don't you sell it? You don't go there anymore." She sold. He encouraged her to write her memoirs and helped her with projects like planning for a public outlet for her Oak Spring Dairy's cheese and milk, though that project was never executed. His weekly flowers never stopped coming. He was her escort at the opening of the Metropolitan Museum Costume Institute's exhibition *Jacqueline Kennedy: The White House Years* in 2001, essentially reintroducing Bunny to a New York that had mostly forgotten her. From 2000 until his death in 2009, Isabell became "the man in her life."

PAUL'S CHEERFUL OLD STUDY, which had become Eliza's bedroom, was the last place I saw Eliza in the winter of 2008, only months before her death. Close to that end, Ann Hudner told me how Eliza once came into a mooring in staid Westport Harbor in Massachusetts, just across the Rhode Island line, where she kept her boat. She brought her beautiful, thirty-eight-foot *Arctic Willow* in under full sail, the music of the Buena Vista Social Club playing at full volume, scandalizing the onshore kibitzers. Duplicating her grandfather Lambert's star turn with *Sonica* in Christmas Cove, Maine, with young Bunny Lambert aboard, Eliza came about, turning on a dime to scoop up her mooring with the skill, grace, and fearlessness of a woman in her element. Still,

Eliza steers her *Arctic Willow* while McIntosh wears a specially tailored blue harness to keep him from falling overboard.

Eliza was always surprised at herself when she did things well, and that was part of her charm.

Eliza died on the morning of May 7, 2008, of pulmonary complications due to pneumonia, and on May 13 we gathered at Trinity Episcopal Church to celebrate her. Oddly enough, or so it seemed to me, Bunny had chosen her newest male friend, Bryan Huffman, a talkative, apple-cheeked decorator from North Carolina, over Robert Isabell to escort her into the church. The nave was reasonably full, although I felt the gulf of years that yawned between Eliza and those who had last seen her before her accident. One of Bunny's beautiful Winslow Homer watercolors, *Sailing a Dory*, was printed on the front of the funeral program: a lone sailor in his little gaff-rigged boat sailing by himself out into the blue—a journey Eliza had been making alone.

All three of Eliza's brothers spoke, as did I. Bunny had asked me to hark back to my Foxcroft days with Eliza, and although much had gone on between us two since then, I stuck to Bunny's request, talking only about the head of school we all shared, Miss Charlotte, and Eliza's pranks. As I spoke, I looked at Bunny, but because of her macular degeneration, I wasn't sure she saw me. She wore a dark beret, a favorite hat in her old age, pinned with a big diamond star. Caroline Kennedy, another daughter figure, sat close to her. Frank Langella wound up the tributes by remembering Eliza in Provincetown, where they had met in 1961, an Eliza always in motion, singing, dancing, wisecracking.

Because I didn't know how many people in the crowd might know Ann Hudner, before we entered the church I had introduced her to a Foxcroft classmate, Cathy Cochran, who had come with me to visit Eliza in her last years. Cathy sat with Hudner, who silently wept through the service. Hudner recently said to me, "Eliza was a special spirit—innocent and sophisticated, straightforward and complex— who wanted to trust love." She paused and added, "But even in that moment of loss, I was relieved that Eliza, who had so fiercely guarded her privacy and independence, only to be surrounded by people twenty-four/seven for eight years, was now at peace and on to her next journey." We all belted out a sturdy hymn we'd sung many Sundays at Foxcroft, "Go forward Christian soldier, Fear not the secret foe." Eliza had met the secret foe, and now she was gone.

I had stayed in the Oak Spring guesthouse the night before, and while the garden looked a bit shaggy and weedy, why should it not in this time of sorrow? In fact, a sharp-eyed guest at the reception that followed saw something else. In the flagged forecourt, usually an immaculate spot, a Marino Marini equestrian statue worth at the time several hundred thousand dollars, lay on its side, half-hidden in weeds. Bunny and her gardeners always curated whatever plants sprouted in the cracks of terraces—the mulleins, the violets, even the odd dandelion— and let some of them grow tall. Here, though, the fallen figure and its surroundings were emblems of sadness and decay.

At the reception at Oak Spring, for which Robert Isabell did the flowers, we talked about almost everything except Eliza's last years. Foxcroft talked to Foxcroft, family to family, horse people to horse people, who had seen what race where. Bunny recalled yet again to Cathy Cochran that she had once dated Cathy's father. It was as if parallel universes glided past each other that day. Most of the family and friends gathered there were unaware that Bunny's escort, Bryan Huffman, had more things on his mind for her than the interment of her daughter. Ninety-nine-year-old Bunny was already deeply embroiled in her secret scheme to fund Senator John Edwards, a "special project" that Huffman had eagerly facilitated.

"I Want to Make a President"

The telephone rang in my Sag Harbor study in the summer of 2011. A reporter from *Newsweek* wanted to know if I could help her reach Bunny Mellon to talk about her contributions to the disgraced senator and presidential candidate John Edwards. The reporter was not interested in the straightforward large and legal contributions to Edwards's PAC, One America, or to his poverty center, but in the reported $725,000 Bunny had donated for his personal expenses, including his haircuts, which started at a few hundred dollars apiece but ultimately ballooned to over a thousand, since the stylist charged for travel. (*Saturday Night Live* did a skit about that to the tune of "I Feel Pretty.")

I flashed back to a day when our classmate Cathy Cochran and I had visited Eliza in the winter before her death. Bunny had walked into the front hall to greet us. She was followed by the hairstylist Kenneth Battelle, with his little dog on his arm. As was his custom, he had been flown down to Oak Spring in the Mellon plane to cut Bunny's hair—and the barely conscious Eliza's as well. "After that," said Bunny, "I'm going into town [The Plains, a tiny village half an hour from Upperville] to get my hair dyed for *nothing*." Not a word was said about the extravagance of having the plane fly down from New York City with Kenneth and back again. "No wonder Bunny doesn't see John Edwards's four hundred dollar haircuts as extravagant," whispered Cathy. By 2007, Bunny was well embarked on her campaign of support for Edwards's candidacy, and by 2011 the haircuts were a small story compared to the rest of what had gone on.

Bunny told me she was perfectly happy to speak with the reporter. I asked her if there was anything in particular she would like to say to the journalist. True to form, Bunny turned my question around and asked, "Mac, what would *you* tell her?" I stammered, "Well, if you're a hundred years old, you get to like whomever you like." I meant it, well aware that Bunny, even though her macular degeneration had reduced the world to shadows, was otherwise in full command of herself. She even seemed to be enjoying the attention. So I gave Bunny's number to Meryl Gordon, since Bunny had given me the okay.

Paul Mellon once said to Martin Filler, the architectural critic who became his friend, "I've arranged things so that Bun can't get into too much trouble after I'm gone." No one, except perhaps Paul himself, could ever have imagined the John Edwards affair.

Bunny had first noticed John Edwards in 2000, when he had been on Al Gore's short list for vice president. In 2003, in the fight for the Democratic nomination for president, he truly captured Bunny's interest as he rolled out his impressive "Two Americas" speech about the abyss between the nation's rich and poor. Bunny wrote an open letter for the local Middleburg newspaper, calling Edwards a "new south wind, clear and fair . . . blowing from the mountains of the Carolinas" and urging Virginia voters in the February primary to vote for him. He lost and ended up as John Kerry's choice for vice president, but George W. Bush won his second term.

In the winter of 2005, the North Carolina decorator Bryan Huffman visited Middleburg, found his way to Bunny's Trinity Episcopal Church in Upperville, then wrote to tell her what a treasure it was. She delightedly tracked him down and called him. Bunny's friendship with Eliza's doctor, Jamshid Ghajar, had cooled, and even though Hubert and Akko—and even Robert Isabell, her latest "romantic" companion—were there for her, they were old friends, while here was a new one. Bunny and Huffman talked about her lifelong love for Chartres Cathedral and France in general and how simple French country churches had been her inspiration for Trinity. The call apparently lasted for ninety minutes. Huffman had passed the first test: he was engaging to talk to. Bunny asked him to come to Oak Spring for lunch, and when he did, she took him to "meet Eliza." At that point Bunny was still convinced that Eliza would regain some degree of herself. She often projected her hopes for recovery on how her daughter responded to visitors and was pleased when those visitors were able to behave as if they were meeting someone in normal circumstances, which was not easy. According to Huffman, Eliza smiled, and Bunny said, "She likes you." Huffman had passed the second test—interacting well with Eliza—and he was sent home with a package of cheese from the Oak Spring Dairy.

Soon they were constantly on the phone together. Bunny reeled out fascinating stories of her colorful past in a kaleidoscopically wealthy world that Huffman could only have dreamed about. Huffman, an intricate dresser, presented himself in the broadly checked shirts and colorful tweeds of a country gentleman and had the North Carolina drawl to go with it all. Like Akko van Acker, he would tease Bunny and make her laugh. He found perfect presents—something that every friend of Bunny and Paul felt was agonizingly difficult on occasion. (Goddaughter Camilla Chandon de Briailles once desperately appeared with a green velvet mouse for Christmas for Paul: he happily perched it on top of a Cézanne in the Oak Spring living room, with its tail hanging down over the painting.) Imagine Bunny's pleasure at unwrapping Huffman's blue and white gros-point pillow embroidered with tiny carrots and the motto YOU'RE NOBUNNY TILL SOMEBUNNY LOVES YOU. Along with Rothkos and Braques, a blue diamond, and sought-after porcelain cabbages, the pillow received a well-deserved full-page illustration in one of the four volumes of Bunny's 2014 four-day sale at Sotheby's.

Major creative figures like Hubert de Givenchy and Johnny Schlumberger had shared their charged artistic milieus with Bunny. Huffman would offer her something different, something she very much wanted: a political role in a presidential election. When Huffman saw that she was following Edwards's campaign obsessively, through a family connection he reached out to Andrew Young, Edwards's top aide, who didn't know who Bunny Mellon was and thought a visit was absurd. Then he googled her. By December 1, 2005, there was John

Edwards, thanks to Huffman and Young, in Bunny's living room at Oak Spring.

It quickly struck Edwards that Bunny Mellon was a historic American figure and that she might support him in the same lavish way she arranged his departure from that first visit: she flew him back to Raleigh in the Mellon plane. To celebrate the meeting, Huffman sent her a bottle of Veuve Clicquot (this to the woman who had a stash of her preferred Nicolas Feuillatte in the refrigerator of every one of her homes). Bunny eschewed her usual daiquiri in favor of a glass from the celebration bottle as she sat with Eliza to pass New Year's Eve. As the year 2006 dawned, Bunny remained convinced that Eliza was communicating with her. For her ninety-sixth birthday on August 8, 2006, Bunny invited only several family members, librarian Tony Willis, and Huffman, now an intimate, to the Oak Spring house.

Bunny again had begun to enjoy a certainty that she was doing something for her country, just as she had done in the Kennedy years, advising Jackie on the White House restoration, creating the Rose Garden, and contributing mightily to the body and soul of the JFK grave at Arlington National Cemetery. After years of seclusion, Bunny was back in the mix.

At this point in her life what she had said about herself—"I know what I want to get done"—met "I want to make a president." The first was something she had said to me; the second she probably said not only to me but also to many others. At last Bunny had reached the place she unconsciously had always sought: there was no one to stop her, although her legal counselor, Alex Forger, would try his best.

Like JFK, "a man insulated from the normal consequences of behavior long before he entered the White House," as the journalist Seymour Hersh wrote in 1997, Bunny was insulated by wealth, position, and ingrained class entitlement. Hubert, who adored Bunny, seldom spoke as directly about her as he did when he told a journalist after her death, "She was spoilt by a marvelous life, but she was intelligent, and open. The spirit she had was her very own spirit. In my studio she'd see the color and the fabric, and she'd say, 'Oh, I'd love to have a dress in that fabric. Can't you make something special for me?'" Givenchy always could, so why couldn't Bunny herself "make something special" of her chosen candidate?

Tony Willis, by then as much Bunny's dear friend as her librarian, was sympathetic to how badly she needed distraction from Eliza's tragedy. He was also alive to the patriotism instilled in her by her grandfather Lowe. If "doing what she could for the country" could be accomplished with a handsome young Kennedy-esque man, so much the better. Frank Langella said that Bunny was forthright with him about how her new "political interest" began. She ruefully but not at all penitently had said, "He was so attractive: white shirt, white pants, sleeves rolled up." And then she made light of the resulting sordid outcome by admitting, "Well, I suppose it's my own damn fault."

EDWARDS'S PACKAGE OF liberal goals, besides eliminating poverty, included caring for the environment, providing universal health care, and espousing women's and gay rights. Thus, on all counts, Edwards seemed like the right liberal Democrat to put in the White House—Bunny was certain of it. Maybe a few American millionaires had taken steps in water management on their estates by recycling water from their gardens. Bunny, by contrast, had not only put sixty acres of her Nantucket property in conservation but would ultimately donate many more (even though these gifts paled against the mighty dedication to saving entire seashores and mountains that Paul's greater wealth allowed him). As for health care, she and Paul had provided benefits for every one of their employees. Bunny was for women's rights in her own particular and personal way; that is to say, she told Louise Whitney Mellon, the first wife of her stepson, Tim: "You have to make your own life . . . Don't make a man your only focus." Bunny had followed her own advice for decades; as she had long ago said to her personal maid, Nelly Jo Thomas, about her long marriage to Paul, "He goes his way, and I go mine," a productive if troubled arrangement that nonetheless ended with some happy years. Gay rights? Bunny didn't seem to hold any prejudice against gay men or women. In banishing Ann Hudner she had chosen to put what she saw as Eliza's care first, accommodating the feelings of her daughter's nurses.

Senator John Edwards fundraises in December 2006
at Bunny's New York City office.

Edwards faced growing threats in Barack Obama and Hillary Clinton as the campaign season went on. Bunny was ready with her support: the first of her three fundraisers took place in mid-December 2006 at her business headquarters in Manhattan's Essex House, where Alexander Forger dutifully forked over his maximum annual legal contribution of $2,300, as did Bunny—piddling sums compared to the legal $2 million she gave to the UNC anti-poverty center and the One America Committee PAC. Edwards officially announced his candidacy later in December from New Orleans in a neighborhood that had been devastated by Hurricane Katrina.

When Edwards's haircuts received widespread publicity, Bunny was furious. She wrote to Andrew Young on April 21, 2007 (in a letter that would be quoted in Edwards's indictment), that "from now on, all haircuts, etc., that are necessary and important for his campaign" were to be billed to her, because "it is a way to help our friend without government restriction." Forger disagreed, quickly informing Young that Bunny, while she would continue to be one of Edwards's loyal supporters, would take on no further campaign commitments.

Enter the campaign's "special project" in the summer of 2007, a request that Bryan Huffman passed on to Bunny from Andrew Young a few months later. The senator needed a commitment of half a million dollars, according to Huffman, in order to get into the White House. No explanation was given about how the money would be spent.

Bunny knew it was pointless to go back to Forger. She decided to steam ahead on her own. She persuaded Huffman that it would be fun to pretend she was buying antiques from his decorating business but that he would actually be funneling the money she gave him to the Edwards campaign, the "special project." Huffman was unable to re-sist, and it sounds like—according to Bunny's testimony—she didn't ask questions about precisely where the money was going. I should add that when I spoke with her about Edwards and then later with Forger about the case after her death in 2014, I had the feeling one of the two of them at least was winking.

Doing things her way and in secret was something Bunny was good at—as with Degas's *Chez la Modiste*, considered one of the artist's best works, the whereabouts of which were unknown for a dozen years after Paul's death. A woman with auburn hair seated before a mirror is try-ing on hats—it is a work of masterful harmony. Malcolm Cormack, the late Paul Mellon Curator at the Virginia Museum of Fine Arts, quoted Paul as saying, "Every time I look at that painting, I think of Bunny." Evidently, it was highly charged with personal associations; Paul sent the work to her in Paris.

After Paul's death in 1999, a brutal legal battle took place over whether the painting would go to the National Gallery or to the VMFA, which won the suit. The next question was, would it remain with Bunny as part of her life interest? In 2001, the VMFA issued a pro forma accession number and wrote a polite but perfunctory letter to Bunny saying that of course she could retain it until her death. But where was it? Only in 2012 did it arrive at the museum with some of the last of the life interest works, but it didn't come from the rue de l'Université apartment (which by then had been sold) or from Oak Spring or any other Mellon residence. There was no note with the packing materials; the sender's label revealed it came from 132 East Seventieth Street, the New York address of one of Bunny's dealers, Franck Giraud. It had been clear by 2001 that Bunny was entitled to keep the work for her lifetime, but from the way she kept its location secret, it was also clear she didn't want anyone else to see it. As her dealer, Giraud had merely followed her orders.

I asked Tony Willis about the *Chez la Modiste* affair: he told me that "people were pestering her [about Paul's artworks]—where will this one go? Where will that one go? She hadn't made up her mind and didn't want to be pushed. So she became her most secret self." In the late 1990s, in a conversation with her about how she and Paul had made decisions regarding where different paintings would go, Bunny told me—and did not explain what she meant (I was too frightened to ask)—that "the National Gallery made a terrible mistake about a Degas, and I'm going to go after them." Following the correspondence between the National Gallery and the VMFA about *Chez la Modiste* convinced me that this was the painting she had in mind.

Over the months, checks drawn against Bunny's personal bank account regularly arrived in Huffman's mail, while Bunny's notes to Huffman described the "furniture" she was buying. The great impresario was treating each "furniture" check as yet another adventure, describing "dining room chairs" or "an antique table from Charleston" to her new accomplice. No one would question Bunny's spending sprees—after all, this was the woman who had bought multiple Rothkos in one afternoon.

Bunny continued to be loyal to her candidate, but she was also uneasy. Due to her very high living expenses, she felt she might be growing short on funds to send covertly to Edwards's campaign and also to support her life in general. Meanwhile, the frenzied 2007 art market would see an overall rise of eighteen percent over twelve months; a loan issued by Bank of America that used the works of art hanging in Bunny's houses as collateral—an idea proposed by Isabell— would ultimately balloon to $250 million. The loan now came in handy for covering her "furniture" expenses. "Isn't it interesting a modern painting may get a Pres. of the U.S," she wrote to Huffman.

A card with an image of Monet's *Woman with a Parasol*, a work Bunny and Paul had given to the National Gallery in 1983, was what she sent to Huffman regarding her new way to finance her projects, including the "furniture" purchases. On the card, a woman (with her little son well in the background) walks in the wind and sun across a hilltop that could be on Nantucket or Cape Cod. Monet conveys a sense of freedom, a freedom Bunny now had to help buy the president of her choice.

It later became clear that Edwards and self-described filmmaker Rielle Hunter had met in a bar in late February 2006. Like JFK, John Edwards has marvelous teeth, and like JFK he knows how to flash them in a marvelous smile. Edwards and Hunter fell into bed together the first night they met; then he hired Hunter to make short films on the campaign trail in order to continue the affair. He and his wife celebrated their thirty years together in 2007 even as Elizabeth Edwards's cancer recurred, but only months later John's affair went public—and continued, despite his denials. It was the same kind of recklessness that JFK had exhibited with the women he brought in almost daily to his White House swimming pool playground, but times had changed. The mudslinging, hysteria, and titillating reporting that had surrounded the presidential candidate Senator Gary Hart in 1987 had made it clear that politicians were now fair game to journalists in a way that had not existed in Kennedy's era.

The *National Enquirer* dug deep, first publishing a story about Edwards's affair on October 10, 2007. "Presidential Cheating Scandal!" ran the banner. Both Bunny and Huffman, so Huffman said, were reassured by a call from Andrew Young saying that the article was pure trash. Then came the second story, on December 19, about a "love child," with a photo of a pregnant Rielle. Andrew Young then lay down for his boss, claiming the child as his. In the wake of the publicity, the Young family and Hunter fled to California to await the baby's birth. Meanwhile, John Edwards was still protesting that his relationship with his wife, Elizabeth, was strong, but he ended his presidential run in January 2008, and Elizabeth Edwards would die two years later.

Senator Barack Obama won the Democratic nomination. Bunny's last check, made out to Huffman for $200,000 for "furniture" in January 2008, wasn't cashed until March. That, according to Meryl Gordon, is what triggered Alex Forger to do some serious research into Bunny's accounts and to talk with the farm staff about Bunny's furniture-buying spree. At Eliza's funeral reception he actually faced down Bryan Huffman, who confessed everything about the phantom furniture and the pipeline to John Edwards.

Bunny had begged Edwards to sit by her side in Trinity Episcopal Church at Eliza's service in 2008, but he refused, saying that he was still too close to the death of his own sixteen-year-old son in a freak car accident in 1996 to attend. Those of us who had heard Bunny's unending enthusiasm for John Edwards wouldn't have been puzzled at his presence, as the full dimensions of the scandal didn't break wide open until several months later. On ABC, Bob Woodruff interviewed Edwards, who admitted to the affair but denied that Hunter's child was his. That interview aired on August 8, 2008, Bunny's ninety-eighth birthday.

On March 20, 2009, FBI agents arrived at Oak Spring for an interview—and Bunny invited them to lunch. According to Alex Forger, Bunny did a star interrogator's turn: she blinded the visitors by seating them on the side of the table that faced the spring sunshine. Because of her own increasingly cloudy vision, Bunny was all too aware of the uncertainties that could be caused by light and shadow.

She sat across from them, perhaps no longer able to clearly make out what hung over the dining room mantel. At any rate, Edgar Degas's seven jockeys heading for the post at a countryside race meeting seemed far from the political scene that now confronted Bunny directly. Forger, who was there, later told me how well Bunny had handled the intimidating visit. By the end of the lunch the FBI was won over, and the North Carolina agent in charge of the investigation of his senator had been added to Bunny's male telephone chat list, like so many other men Bunny found interesting. More or less hat in hand, the FBI team was pleasantly escorted to the door, having learned next to nothing from Bunny.

The FBI returned in November. This time Forger was not present, at their request. They left with Bunny's assertion that yes, John Edwards had thanked her for the cash—indicating that he certainly knew about the money she'd given him. But Bunny did not admit that the money had been used to support Hunter or her baby, adding that, in her view, powerful men always had mistresses. (In January 2010, Edwards finally confessed that Rielle Hunter's child was his, and at that point Elizabeth Edwards filed for a separation, just months before her death.)

"I think [Bunny's] view is, he's a cute guy, and he's allowed to fool around if he likes. The life she's led was all about that kind of thing," I told *Newsweek*'s Meryl Gordon on the phone in the summer of 2011. Bunny was, of course, drawing on her own experience with Dorcas Hardin, but she was also matter-of-fact with her friend Frank Langella about Jackie Kennedy's problems with her husband's infidelities. "She knew all about the women, of course," Bunny told Langella, "but she stuck, and she decided she was going to do a good job. She was a wonderful First Lady."

Bunny had always been dutifully attentive to the details of family life, although her closest "families" were those she created based on friendship. Blood relatives, even those she felt little affinity for, such as her stepson, Tim Mellon, were nonetheless actors in the slow-moving play that took place over the many decades of her life. Not entirely motionless, as in a tableau vivant, they had roles in seasonal festivities and in life events such as weddings and funerals. It was as if by creating a perfect event, Bunny showed she cared. Some family members, like her sister, Lily—largely a shadow of a past Bunny preferred to ignore—were barely present; Bunny did not attend her sister's funeral in 2006.

But in the wake of the John Edwards scandal, Bunny needed her family, and her son and grandsons were there for their aged matriarch. On December 2, 2011, the Mellon plane brought four Lloyds to the Raleigh-Durham airport. Her son, Stacy Barcroft Lloyd III, "Tuffy," and his wife, Anna Cristina "Rickie" Niceta Lloyd, along with Bunny's favorite grandson, Stacy Barcroft Lloyd IV, and Thomas, his elder brother, whom Bunny had essentially dismissed for years, were all there to testify in federal court on her behalf in the trial of Senator John Edwards.

Bunny had grown closer to Thomas and had attended his wedding, Robert Isabell in tow, and by 2010 she had warmed to his toddler daughter, Fiona. Tuffy, whose vision was also imperiled, was moving to Oak Spring, to the old Hunter Barn farmhouse where Bunny would create a sunny library for his collection of rare books, brought from his former D.C. antiquarian bookshop. Bunny's stepson, Tim Mellon, a stoutly conservative Republican, came separately to the North Carolina courtroom to sardonically observe the goings-on. "I had to step over Edwards's shoes at one point," he said on the phone, clearly feeling this was too close to the man for comfort.

Bunny, known as "Witness C," was never asked to appear in the courtroom. She was excused because of her age and frailty. The trial went on for six weeks, and on May 31, 2012, a jury declared that Bunny's 2008 gift of $200,000 to Edwards—the check that had alerted Alex Forger to the subterfuge—was not illegal on the grounds that the gift was given after Edwards had ended his presidential campaign. (Forger had hastily paid gift taxes on the other amounts, punctiliously including late fees.) The jury deadlocked on the other five charges; the judge declared a mistrial and dropped the case.

Even though Bunny was affronted by Edwards's continuing requests for money to clear his debts, which she politely refused, she still kept advising the disgraced candidate, perhaps trying to keep at least part of her political dream alive. She never expressed real disappointment about Edwards, maybe still imagining herself as a potent advisor who had access to levers of power and even writing to him that she had had "strange thoughts of rearranging new plans." She apparently envisioned Edwards and Caroline Kennedy as a winning political team, writing, "Perhaps if you joined with Caroline Kennedy, you could erase memories of the past?"

Bunny also drew on her own skills, adding in a letter to Edwards, "I see it like remaking a garden. Clean it all up and start with a simple design, using the right plants in the right place."

When Barack Obama chose Hillary Clinton as his secretary of state in 2009, Bunny, who detested the former First Lady, wrote, "My feeling is, Obama made a mistake when he invited Hillary Clinton back—it weakens a new image, although in this case she could help with her experiences in other countries." This ninety-nine-year-old woman sitting in her house in Virginia would be stubbornly loyal to her cherished idea of her candidate's worth—never mind the facts.

Such intense loyalty, one of Bunny's strongest attributes, had already sent her headlong into trouble in another direction at the same time. Kenneth I. Starr had been Paul Mellon's accountant for decades, and Bunny had made him treasurer of her newly formed Garden Library board in the 1990s. Bunny stuck with Starr after Paul's death: he and his third wife, Marisa, were part of the select group who celebrated Bunny's surprise ninetieth birthday party at Oyster Harbors in 2000.

By 2008, Jane Stanton Hitchcock, a novelist and playwright who had once been married to William Mellon Hitchcock, Paul Mellon's cousin, and was a friend of Bunny's, had encouraged her mother, Joan Crowley Stanton, to sue Starr for mismanaging her $70 million estate and pouring it into risky ventures. The suit got public attention, but Starr was able to reassure Forger that there was nothing to it except Jane Hitchcock's desire to get her hands on her inheritance. Even though other Starr clients began to pull their money out, Bunny refused to believe that Starr could have done anything wrong. Hitchcock wanted to get hold of Bunny to warn her, but, according to Meryl Gordon, she was told that Bunny would likely not take her call.

According to Starr, at least, Paul had been unsatisfied with his own accountant and had asked a Manhattan florist he used for a recommendation. "Ken Starr" was the answer, and the door was thus opened to a clientele of *Social Register* figures and then to stars of Hollywood, TV, and theater.

Starr steered dazzled prospective clients to special funds he said were open only to the Mellons. The double-page spread that opened Michael Shnayerson's September 2010 *Vanity Fair* article about Starr's lurid downfall and his hapless pole-dancer fourth wife featured headshots of a dozen other willing victims, celebrities from Liam Neeson to Carly Simon to Mike Nichols to Candice Bergen to Al Pacino. Notably, Bunny is not among them, not only because she wasn't a public figure but also because of Alex Forger's remarkable ability to keep his client out of the spotlight. This, Forger told me, was largely because Bunny's legal name was Rachel, which threw the press off for a time.

When nearly $6 million of Bunny's money was moved to an escrow account, Forger asked Starr about it. When Starr said he was bundling her money with that of other clients to invest in a bond venture, Forger told him, "I would prefer you put it back in Treasuries."

When a week passed without action, Starr said there was trouble with the paperwork. Forger, who had seen in 2008 what could happen with Bunny's money as it was morphed into "furniture," called the Manhattan DA's office. The troubles that phone call ultimately revealed were not Bunny's fault, and the cost to her was many times more than that of her support for John Edwards.

It turned out that Starr was running a $59 million Ponzi scheme, juggling accounts and moving money into high-risk ventures in which he had interests, just as Jane Hitchcock had warned. When Uma Thurman, a longtime investor, found out what was going on, according to Shnayerson, she stormed into Starr's office, armed with lawyers. Starr allegedly paid her off with money stolen from other investors, including Bunny. Starr also handled Tuffy's money and that of his sons: Tuffy lost over $10 million, which included a settlement from a suit against St. Vincent's Hospital for Eliza's care. The total losses for Bunny would ultimately be revealed as over $18 million—although this loss would reputedly still leave her quite comfortable with a fortune of at least half a billion dollars.

On Memorial Day weekend in 2010, as the news about Starr broke on the front page of *The New York Times*, the *Vanity Fair* writer James Reginato arrived at Oak Spring. He was on assignment with the photographer Jonathan Becker, known for his worldly, piercing portraits not just of denizens of Hamptons beaches but also of the Yanomami tribesmen in the Amazon jungle and numberless heads of state.

Reginato had previously met his ninety-nine-year-old hostess in April. Armed with an introduction from just the right person—his close friend Robert Isabell—he had been greeted by Bunny in the Oak Spring forecourt, and they drove up to the library together.

Basking in the sunshine of her most famous Rothko, *Yellow Expanse*, in the Garden Library, Bunny had regaled Reginato with her stories of glorious old times: the purchase of her other Rothkos in one fell swoop in 1970; her friendships with the sculptor Diego Giacometti and the designer Hubert de Givenchy; her husband's Jungian analysis; her Pilates practice with the founder of the studio, and so forth. They had then gone out to tour the garden and Reginato was invited back quickly to photograph for his article, which was going to be rushed into print in the August issue.

Events on Reginato's second visit were different: Bunny was shaken by the revelations about Kenneth Starr, but she still turned up in the old green Volvo wagon at the garden entrance to greet Reginato and to give Becker directions as to how to shoot her garden. She said, "This garden is made of love. And details . . . Look for the details." Mid-shoot, Alex Forger arrived to discuss the bad news about Starr. When I spoke with Reginato in the summer of 2019, he was still impressed with how composed Bunny had been, although he later admitted that she had seemed much older and frailer than she had only two months before.

In Becker's photographs Bunny's garden also seems shadowed and older—anyone who had known it in the eighties would have recognized the differences in 2010. Fuzzy with green blobs that had once been pruned precisely, it had become an old-age vision softened by time and no longer tended by the woman who had made it. "Imperfect perfection"—the phrase that Bunny used to convey the ever-changing processes of nature—had become more imperfect. The single lead flower on the conservatory roof meant to look as if it had just fallen from Schlumberger's sculpted bouquet suddenly seemed to have a deeper meaning.

The stories about Bunny's perfect details, so often repeated, were hardening into legend in Reginato's telling. The conceit of blue scillas outlining the shadow of tree branches on the lawn that I had seen with Eliza on a visit to Oak Spring in the 1990s—hadn't Bunny tried them there, as she told me, *before* she planted them at Le Jonchet? Had Paul Leonard really painted shadows on the floors he created to make it look as if the sun were perpetually shining? I checked with Bruce Budd, Bunny's last decorator, who laughed and said it wasn't true. I didn't remember inhaling the fragrance of "apples boiling constantly in the kitchen to fill the house with the smell of the farm" at Oak Spring, but was that because I hadn't paid attention? It's not an unlikely touch for a consummate stage manager like Bunny. A friend in real estate says that some dealers will heat apple cider on the stove or put cookie dough in the oven of a house for sale to create a homey fragrance. If there were apples perpetually on the boil at Oak Spring, was Bunny ahead of her time in practicing aromatherapy?

When I read Reginato's piece, I understood what the biographer James Atlas had encountered when he was some years into his pursuit of the wily Saul Bellow. "For the first time it occurred to me that Bellow wouldn't just sit there and tell me everything I needed to know . . . All he could do was straighten me out about the facts, quite a few of which I'd got wrong—or, as I would discover, *he* had gotten wrong."

I turned back to Bunny's papers, to a bundle of unidentified, undated pages in her own pale and difficult handwriting that she had written to someone, about someone—about her own feelings—about who she thought she was. That much I could make out. But why had she kept these fragments together? Perhaps she intended to use them in her autobiography? I knew only that, because she put them together in one of her private boxes, they had to be important, but to whom was she writing, and about whom?

31

Robert Isabell

On one of those private pages Bunny had written: *"Like the sea just before dark . . . like the first bird that sings in the morning of a day that you have waited for . . ."*

In this stack of papers was a love story. Yet another of Bunny's arm's-length crushes on a younger, gay-or-nay man, I thought at first. But as I looked though the letters, I saw that this relationship was different. If Bunny was crazy about Robert Isabell, apparently he was equally crazy about her. "Love is easy when it is like air or breathing," she wrote to him as their friendship advanced from a doorstep basket of flowers in 2000. Here, perhaps, was someone who could provide Bunny with the same exacting heights of realized fantasy that she had first achieved with Eliza's debut in 1961.

By 2000, her ninetieth year—almost anyone else's extreme old age—Bunny was beyond mere affinities of taste and style. She was fully immersed in a love unlike any of her other close alliances or preoccupations with handsome, much younger men. (For centuries society has accorded active sexuality to old men, straight or gay—but to old women?)

John Edwards was a user as well as a man deeply mired in troubles with his wife and his mistress; both Hubert and Akko were too well defended by loyalty to their longtime partners. No one ever heard anything about Robert Isabell having a boyfriend. He was a loner and liked it that way. With him, Bunny was struggling for a completion that was hard even for her to comprehend. "I have a shell & must stay in it," she wrote to him one April day from New York, asking him if he would understand if she "said I couldn't see you because I had to stay in my shell?" Without her shell, "it was like running naked in the street."

For two decades, Robert Isabell, as the "pre-eminent ringmaster of startling and fantastical events . . . for some of the wealthiest members of New York society," had near-magical powers, wrote the journalist Christopher Mason. In her own fashion and sphere, so had the old empress of a society that no longer knew who she was. Not that Bunny cared what most of the public thought of her: she lived by Emily Dickinson's "The soul selects its own society, then shuts the door," a dictum that had hurt or enraged those once within the tiny, ferocious microcosm of the rarefied social world who had had that door shut in their faces.

As her fellow impresario, Isabell shared many qualities with Bunny. She had a wit that she largely expressed in form and detail, as well as a capacity for hard work. Then, even leaving aside her remarkable gardens, it's worth studying her command of scale, her will to push for what she saw as beautiful and harmonious, and her ability to transform wild flights of imagination into an evanescent reality—all abilities that Isabell could also claim.

They were well matched. Isabell's longtime lighting designer Liz Garvin said, "Robert lived by his eyes, effects, visions. He was dyslexic." Bunny's lifelong grasp of space had privileged her vision over any of her other senses even as her sight dwindled. It meant she could say, "Try it this way," to Thomas Beach, tearing up and remaking his model of the library addition in a minute. This was entirely different from the slow labor—like that of many writers—that she put into draft after draft of her article on the Potager du Roi; into her attempts to write her autobiography; or even into her private journal entries, which are crisscrossed with scratch-outs and insertions.

James Reginato described Isabell—with whom he'd become friends in the early 1990s—as "unpretentious, dry-humored, and kind of shy." A bit like Bunny, he didn't necessarily enjoy the events he had so carefully orchestrated. Ultimately, they both preferred to be voyeurs. In the early winter of 2000, after Paul Mellon's death, I attended a commemoration of Paul's life in the East Building of the National Gallery and sat with Eliza and Bunny. The simple detail that stood out for me was the ruddy sheaves of living wheat shafts that Isabell had used for decoration in homage to Paul, whose wheat-sheaf ensign was carved everywhere at Oak Spring and engraved on his private writing paper. The other notable sight was the handsome, dark-haired Isabell himself, as square-jawed as Clark Kent, walking down the tall, ramped seating to join us as a witness. Wearing one of his classic white suits, he stood out against the gray and blue banker's stripes of the other mourners.

Cathy Graham, an artist and a New Yorker who moves in the social circles that couldn't have imagined a gala designed by anyone but Isabell in the 1980s and '90s, knew Robert for years and watched his relationship with Bunny grow. There was no doubt he was enthralled with her, Graham said. "He was always going on and on with, 'Bunny this and Bunny that.'" According to Graham, he and Bunny spoke on the phone every afternoon (just the way she had depended on Paul's continuing flood of postcards and then faxes or had needed Akko or Hubert to be in constant touch). What did they discuss? What journalists such as James Reginato and Christopher Mason have written about Robert Isabell's relationship with Bunny Mellon leaves us with scattered, rhapsodic remarks about the perfect details and old-time glamour of how Bunny lived, right down to the composition of her mint daiquiris. For me, though, all the time they spent happily together alone in Virginia, New York, or Antigua speaks of a greater depth and intimacy to their relationship.

Bunny and Robert shared a terrible scorn for anyone who didn't understand what the two of them were up to. "He was a guy who could have a queen fit," Liz Garvin told me. "He was famous for it." Close to nearly invisible as a guest at social events, Isabell was a "Mussolini when at work," said Reginato about his friend's relationships with his help and clientele. In 1996, Isabell told *The New York Times*, "You have to be a dictator when running a party . . . If people ask you to turn down the music, and you know it'll ruin the party, you just smile at them and don't turn it down, because you need a hot, sexy dance floor. I often say yes to people and then go ahead and do what I want."

Robert Isabell at his house at 16 Minetta Lane in Greenwich Village

Bunny's program for doing what she wanted was necessarily different, as she wasn't getting paid to succeed. People who tried too hard or
whose projects didn't suit her soon found themselves bewildered and
left behind, like the unfortunate Jacqueline Duhême, an artist who illustrated the works of any number of French poets. In a flurry of enthusiasm and a back-and-forth of Duhême's charmingly painted letters, she
and Bunny planned a whimsical book, a suite of postcards, an Antigua
map project, a tapestry—but none of them came off. Duhême, who had
counted on a payment for a new car—"je n'ai pas beaucoup de sous"—
was left in the lurch and wondering what could have gone wrong.

For Isabell, not long after they became friends, Bunny set down a
disjointed, unfinished—and unsent—manifesto that laid out her feelings for him. "Darling Robert, You have set a sort of forest fire in
me." Since she was eighteen, she told him, "life, as far as love went,
had been a list of hope & dreams & make-believe that carried me
along." She had depended on her imagination and gardening to fill
a void "with excitement & sometimes success." But always, "at day's
end, where dreams are sorted out," she found herself empty again.
"Books I read & feelings inside wished for another emotion beyond
the awareness of nature that surrounded me."

In her private journal entries and in drafts of similar unsent letters on letterhead from her various houses, Bunny wrote to Isabell or about him just as she had about Hubert. But both her understanding of herself and her understanding of this man who, unlike Hubert, was not deftly defended by his own politesse are different from thirty years earlier. Her bits and pieces chronicle two prima donnas, strangely equal, moving hesitatingly toward one another, often wordlessly, with signs, symbols, and gestures.

Bunny wrote about a short weekend they spent alone together in late spring in Virginia: a walk, a nap, a storm, a visit to Eliza at Spring Hill and to Foxcroft to show him the library courtyard she designed, then a drink on the Oak Spring terrace, where the blackbirds shrieked in the trees. "'If they would only stop,' I thought aloud. Without a word he got up, found a stone, threw it high, high in the tree." The birds flew away. "How beautifully you throw a stone." Isabell smiled and answered, "But I can't whistle." She cooked dinner in the Sunday kitchen while he worked on a faulty tape recorder in the living room. Afterward they went back to sit by the fire; he came over to her on the sofa, put his arms around her and his head on her shoulder. "It was the meeting of a child—the love of a man. So many emotions." (Even in her daze of happiness, of course, she didn't fail to notice his red shoes and his blue sweater, like those of a little boy but "beautifully made.")

He was flippant and funny, sending her what must have been ugly or at least outrageous flowers with a note that read, "Dear Bunny, the first flowers imported from *Mars!*" He knew her competitive spirit and teased her about it: about another fashionable hostess who was featured in the press, he wrote, "Bunny, if you dressed like Linda [?], maybe Hubert would decorate *your* new house."

In New York and on Cape Cod they quarreled and made up. "If I didn't love you so much and put you so high, I would not have been so mad," she wrote. Then she gathered herself together: "To understand the negative and be able with courage to change it into the positive, to have made a mistake—to steadfastly try without the fear that you have destroyed everything by the mistake—one seldom kills the whole with a mistake if in time one starts again to build without fear," she wrote to herself. Then, "Do *not* say, that is what I am, I cannot change. If you cannot change for the better, then your storehouse of possibilities is a cold, empty barn."

The dissatisfied young woman Paul had once described as pecking so ragefully at him and criticizing him into stony immobility had learned in her nineties to be flexible. She understood how much solitude Isabell required (just as Hubert had needed time to create his collections), but with Isabell she was much calmer, less needy: "days will go by, calls forgotten—letters unwritten—and he will mean nothing."

For Isabell, son of a Duluth, Minnesota, power company lineman, "Bunny was the ultimate other world," said Liz Garvin. At Oak Spring, when they were alone, Isabell had said to Bunny in astonishment, "You behave like a Noël Coward play!" But in the hothouse world they made for themselves, they grew to understand each other better. "He has given me the absolute certainty of his affection," she wrote in her journal. He told her, "'I am not leaving—I love you so much.'" She had told her former daughter-in-law not to weigh her own self-worth only as it was measured by a man. Bunny had tried to follow her own dictate, but this was the outright validation she needed from Robert.

Isabell didn't need a "French family," that band of friends Hubert used to shield himself from too much Bunny. But sometimes, when he needed a break, Isabell just stayed at home in Manhattan, fooling with his sound system, said Garvin. Happily for Isabell and Bunny, her understanding of the essentials of a "romance" had changed since the Akko van Acker days a dozen years earlier: "To take care without touching," she could now write, "to speak without speech . . . and to give a dream as a present, to have all this, one must be given a love." In Isabell, she really felt she had been given an enduring love.

Whenever Isabell visited Oak Spring, he was given Givenchy's grand "poppy room" on the guesthouse ground floor that was (and is) hung with a festive, large-scale, orange and blue print very unlike the discreet and peaceful D. D. Tillett small geometrics in other rooms. But Garvin told me that Isabell "dreaded going down to Virginia, always feared there would be other people there . . . He had a stutter and liked spending time with the workers on the place rather than the guests."

By 2004, after working on eight Metropolitan Museum Costume Institute galas with *Vogue*'s Anna Wintour—then the annual high-water mark of New York's social life—Isabell was restless. He talked with Bunny about how to change his life. In December she wrote, "Somehow your decision to change course for another direction has influenced me. I'm less worried and feel free—or at least more free— [drawing of grasses without leaves] all the leaves have gone here.—I love you—Bunny."

Isabell's first effort at changing his life was to enter New York's hot real estate market: in 2006 he successfully flipped two buildings in Manhattan's Meatpacking District, his own neighborhood. He wanted to be a developer like the very successful Ian Schrager, co-founder in the 1970s of Studio 54, where Isabell had created phantasmagoric, one-night-stand "theme parties." Liz Garvin said he and Schrager were "best best best buddies." Schrager considered himself Isabell's closest friend. "We loved each other," he said, adding that "he was very, very private. He had a very compartmentalized life. There were things I didn't know about."

Two years later Isabell couldn't have done worse than to buy another pricey run-down building for $45 million. (The building, 837 Washington Street, was only a door away from Mineshaft, one of the S&M clubs he frequented.) He wanted to develop it into studios and high-end office space and reportedly even approached Bunny to consider an investment. But 2008 was the year the market tanked. Everything went wrong: Isabell's clients entertained less and were suddenly more discreet about it, and when he couldn't get approval from the neighborhood landmarks commission to renovate the space, he didn't have enough money to repay the bank. On August 1, 2009, a huge real estate loan was coming due. "He never let on to anyone that he was even slightly worried," wrote the journalist Arthur Lubow.

After organizing parties in the Hamptons for Lally Weymouth, Katharine Graham's daughter, and for the cosmetics heir Jane Lauder, Isabell headed back home to Manhattan on Saturday night of the

Fourth of July weekend, phoning Bunny on the way. After that, no one heard from him for several days, but since he often dropped out of sight, nobody worried at first. But when Bunny hadn't heard from Isabell for more than two days, she called his friend Norma Kamali, telling the clothing designer that she was starting to worry. On July 8, the police broke down the security gate and front door of his house and found Isabell's body. Brian Saltzman, his friend and personal physician and the doctor who had hurried to Eliza's side at the hospital after her accident, came at once and attested to Isabell's death, which was later confirmed as due to a heart attack. Garvin was part of the grim discovery process; apparently there had been a power outage. "Five days, with no air conditioning in July," she said.

Cathy Graham and Alex Forger, who was Isabell's attorney, thanks to Bunny, were his executors. In a world that presumed everyone, including Isabell, was somehow after Bunny's money, it came as a shock to find that his will directed that some of his possessions go to her. And when his estate was sold at Sotheby's in December 2009, part of the $2.6 million went to the Oak Spring Garden Library Foundation.

A week after his death, *New York Social Diary* reported that "Mr. Isabell, it has been said, will be laid to rest at the Mellon family plot next to a church that Paul Mellon built in Upperville, Virginia." That may have been a rumor; other reports claimed that Bunny and Isabell had already picked out his grave site in the old Fletcher farm cemetery at Oak Spring when he came for Eliza's funeral the year before his own death (which, to me, seems an odd thing for a fifty-seven-year-old man in apparent good health to do).

Whatever the facts, Bunny's nemesis at the farm, Beverly Carter, with power in her official capacity as Paul Mellon's executor, and Frederick A. Terry, Paul's co-executor, sprang into action four days later with a letter to the Trinity Episcopal Church Cemetery Corporation, with a copy to Forger. "Since Mr. Isabell was not related in any way to either Mr. or Mrs. Mellon," it stated, "to bury his remains in a Mellon grave site . . . is not permissible." Mellon relatives such as Tim Mellon breathed a sigh of relief; nothing as undignified as burying Bunny's "boyfriend" in the family section of the Trinity graveyard that Bunny had designed was going to happen on their watch.

Fortuitously, in 1948, Paul had bought the rights to bury his family in a small section of the Oak Spring farm cemetery where he had buried his first wife. Typically, he generously added a clause that rights to burial there could include "such close friends or relations as he [Paul] may designate."

Isabell's grave lies under the trees only feet from the millstone pattern that Bunny had set out as a model for JFK's grave site at Arlington Cemetery. Isabell didn't want to be buried underground, and Bunny respected his wishes. His body rests under what looks a bit like a raised medieval tomb, the kind that is often topped by a stony effigy of a helmeted knight in armor lying on his back, hands crossed on his chest, chain-mail-covered toes pointing upward. No such figure exists here, but given what the stash of Bunny's personal papers revealed about her love for her friend Robert, and his for her, it was typically restrained of her to have carved only three majestic words on the stone that for her encompassed the man: "Magical Noble Elusive."

Bunny sent a printed note in answer to the many, many condolence letters she received. Stubbornly, in the face of her encroaching blindness, she also wrote some individual letters of thanks, especially to Isabell's friends who knew how close the two had been. Bunny, in order to make out what she'd asked Tony Willis to say to Norma Kamali, had him copy it out in blue ink in very large letters so she could see what she'd asked him to send: "You were so understanding in sharing the heartbreak and loss of Robert."

Charlotte Moss, a well-known American interior designer and writer who had admired Bunny's style for years, interviewed her at Oak Spring in 2011, three years before her death. Meeting in the lofty library, they talked about books as well as life—among other things, about how Bunny had read all of Thomas Hardy. Bunny pointedly told Moss that her life "has been one of circumstance, and that is one of the themes of Hardy's work." At first this seems like a fantasy—how could a woman with all the money and power in the world, someone who to the last detail planned her gardens and interiors, her events and processionals, including her own funeral, claim she had led a life "of circumstance," meaning, presumably, a life outside her own control?

Though the remark is Bunny at her most abstract and elliptical, it provides a real insight into how she pictured herself. Granted, she checked her astrological chart regularly, believed what it forecast for her, and spoke daily with Beverley Newton, the psychic in nearby Fredericksburg. But you don't have to delve too deeply into Hardy's work to discover that Bunny had other thoughts about fate that allowed her to think the way she did.

Thomas Hardy calls Tess Durbeyfield, his most lovable and tragic heroine, Demeter—the goddess of summer and harvest whose daughter, Persephone, dies but tantalizingly returns from Hades once a year in spring. Tess is not so lucky: she watches her infant son die and buries him herself in a deserted corner of the graveyard. Bunny, perhaps because of her vast ability to control and change most circumstances, was, at least in relation to her daughter, unable to release herself from hope and so clung to the idea, almost to the very last weeks of Eliza's life, that she would regain at least some meaningful consciousness.

Hardy's Tess is a woman who walks "a long and stony highway"; her life is a string of misfortunes. Fate or unkind "circumstance" within the closed fields of Bunny's life—as she saw it—had begun its stony cruelty when she was nineteen and her cousin, twenty-four-year-old George Lea Lambert, the first of her imagined romances, died in a plane crash in 1929. In 2000, a random vehicle forever damaged her brilliant daughter, who died in 2008. Now, in 2011, her sudden and bruising loss was of Robert Isabell. And all she could do was to memorialize him in stone.

32

"I Am Not Afraid"

Bunny has told me before that now she sees only gray clouds, light gray, dark gray, and movement, except close up. This dinner together in her bedroom at Oak Spring in 2012 just before Christmas will be the last time I see her. Drinks first, of course. I sit in one of her low French armchairs, facing her. She sits in the matching chair, close to the end of her four-poster bed, facing me. It is dark. What great painting hangs over the fireplace in this bedroom? I can't make it out.

Ronnie Caison, the longtime butler of this household, brings us our trays. Bunny's hands move confidently over the blue-and-white linen mat and the silver flatware. She picks up her napkin, the right eating utensil, her glass of wine. She does not disturb the tiny salt and pepper shakers because she knows just where they should be, and they are.

I see her complete assurance that everything will be in the right place. I see a lifetime of order and discipline in the domestic arts. But I also see that she is tired. The same salutation she and Tony Willis always made in the library is the toast she uses now: "Here's to little old us." I find that the thrill of being "little old us" with Bunny Mellon never dims.

I hear from her that she has already planned every moment of her funeral and interment; the future endowment of the Gerard B. Lambert Foundation; and a few of the gifts she would bestow on different institutions. Her gifts are very personal, and each has a private purpose: to display Jean Schlumberger at his best, 140 spectacular pieces have gone to the Virginia Museum of Fine Arts. Another gift is a little wave to a friend: a few of her early Chelsea porcelains—so admired by Queen Elizabeth when she came to tea—will join Forsythe Wickes's Collection at the Museum of Fine Arts in Boston, an homage to him and to his daughter, her friend Kitty, who had introduced her to Paris and French life.

Six months after Bunny's death, the monster Sotheby's auction billed as "Property from the Collections of Mrs. Paul Mellon" would net $218 million, more than twice the estimate. The excess was marvelous to behold, and I thought of a remark the painter Lucian Freud had made about Oscar Wilde, that "he had what is always very attractive in anyone, which is self-indulgence carried to extremes."

Much of what was disgorged from all the houses, barns, and storage bins was tattered and worn but so haloed with provenance that even a pair of dated-looking French armchairs, the upholstery so threadbare that the cotton stuffing was sticking out of the armrests, would sell for $50,000, almost four times the high estimate of $15,000. (Paul sat in one of them every evening at Oak Spring.) Bunny's cookbook collection, with an estimate of $800, would go for $17,500.

The estate auction sales figures of other major society personages, such as Jackie Kennedy Onassis and Brooke Astor, had also been driven up by provenance. In Jackie's case it was a desire to own a piece of Camelot; Brooke Astor's public joie de vivre and generosity had made her a lustrous and beloved New York cultural figure. In a sense both women were known quantities, while in Bunny's case her mystique as a tastemaker and legendary collector added to the allure of her deliberately shadowy public presence.

Bunny's auction lasted for five straight days, morning and afternoon, the items on sale lavishly documented in four handsome volumes. Sotheby's split the loot into three categories: major works of art, jewels, and interiors, the last so large an assemblage that it had to be further divided into two volumes, the second of which would run to over one thousand pages. This tremendous outpouring did not, of course, include the thousands of works of art with which Bunny and Paul had previously endowed many institutions.

The National Gallery arrived with almost unseemly haste following her death to pick up her "life estate"—sixty-two treasured works that had remained at Oak Spring until Bunny's death—to join the nearly nine hundred works already there. Included were masterpieces such as van Gogh's *Still Life with Oranges and Lemons with Blue Gloves*. The gloves look very well used; by 2014 the work was hanging in the dining room on the way in from the garden terrace, surely a passing reference to Bunny's prowess as a gardener.

Bunny's gift to her husband had been the creation of a perfectly curated environment, achieved with the help of many renowned artists and interior designers such as Syrie Maugham, Paul Leonard, Colefax & Fowler, Billy Baldwin, and Bruce Budd. The strength of her domestic assemblages depended on simplicity and rigor as well as Paul's limitless resources. Bunny had once quietly said, "I know what I want to get done." And she generally did know, and she generally did get it done, whatever the project. Only the making of a president eluded her.

During the exhibition days at Sotheby's before the gavel fell, it was clear how the bonds between this thing and that thing, between this space and that, had been burst apart by the atomic force of the auction, and by time itself. Bruce Budd had spent thirteen years with Bunny not just as her last interior designer of record but also as a friend and companion in an intense chase for the perfect object or fabric or color that would complete a magic spell. As he climbed from floor to floor of the lavishly produced display, he said, "I was sad, embarrassed. It didn't represent how she lived or what she liked—her taste changed over time; it evolved."

The Gerard B. Lambert Foundation would receive every penny of the $218 million raised, with most of the money going to support the Oak Spring Garden Library. And the Oak Spring Garden Foundation already has projects in the works with the Lambert Foundation following other Bunny goals: a healing garden for children at a Washington, D.C., hospital, and a public park on a triangle of unused land on Nantucket. ("Folks just didn't realize she was a leader of style [who would] spend her life dedicated to nature," said Alex Forger.)

At dinner, Bunny and I talk about Eliza, about the time they planted Madonna lilies at Eliza's house in Little Compton after her breakup with Doris Sanders. And Bunny harks back to her delight and astonishment when the teenage Eliza and I actually found our way from Foxcroft to Oak Spring on horseback on a May afternoon in 1957. We talk about how sometimes she can still outwit her failing eyes: she had her sketches for Tuffy's library addition to nearby Hunter Barn house blown up to tremendous size and darkened the contrast so she can make them out.

She tells me about Memory House, her storehouse for Eliza's art, whose walls are rising at that moment. As it stands completed between the Garden Library and the Broodmare Barn, I silently judge it as the only unsuccessful structure Bunny ever designed: it squats on the hillside with no feature to lift it toward the sky. Maybe that was the point? It was built with a story underground, windowless, mausoleum-type spaces with racks for Eliza's paintings and an easel and paints set up eerily in one corner as if Eliza were about to walk in and pick up her brush.

We don't talk about her remaining family—even those she at last has allowed to become closer to her: her grandsons, Stacy IV and Thomas Lloyd, and Thomas's then-wife Rickie Niceta, or her great-grandchildren, Fiona and Teddy. We don't talk about her uncompleted memoir—or the pain and rage she so transparently expressed to me about Dorcas Hardin. I don't know if Bunny is still writing down her memories and organizing her papers, and I don't ask.

Sometimes Bunny becomes my Aphra Behn, nicknamed the "female Shakespeare," a woman of many secrets, a flamboyant, gifted seventeenth-century playwright, transatlantic traveler, and early novelist—the first woman in England to make a living as a writer—who became a diplomatic spy (code name Astrea) for Charles II of England. Behn's biographical editors, Derek Hughes and Janet Todd, enthralled with Behn but sometimes, like me with Bunny, irate with their inscrutable subject, wrote that Behn was "a lethal combination of obscurity, secrecy, and staginess that makes her an uneasy fit for any narrative, speculative or factual. She is not so much a woman to be unmasked as an unending combination of masks."

As Bunny and I sit together at dinner at Christmastime in 2012, I am unaware that her 128-carat sapphire and diamond "Breath of

Spring" necklace is already hidden in a secret compartment in the window wall of the bedroom we are in. Nancy Collins will discover it by accident as she and Tony Willis begin to inventory the house contents the day after Bunny dies.

I don't stay long with Bunny, but after dinner and before I go off to the guesthouse, we talk about Trinity Church and a friend of hers who had written to tell her that she had been in the Middleburg Thrift Shop, where someone *had got it all wrong*; had said the church was *English* and that *Paul built it*. Bunny merely smiles. Later, when I'm working in Bunny's archives, I find that friend's note in her papers; she kept it, along with the letter Paul wrote to Bunny saying he would pay for the project but that it would be hers alone.

Bunny tells me about her choices for Scripture readings for her funeral service, ones she has loved all her life. I mention that I just heard a remarkable recording of a magnificently hoarse old church singer, accompanied by an out-of-tune piano, chant the verse from Isaiah about the eagle's wings, and that their power reminded me of her: "*Those that wait upon the Lord shall renew their strength. They shall mount up with wings as eagles, they shall run and not be weary, they shall walk and not be faint*" (Isaiah 40:30–31). I realize this is a bit high-flown and stop, but I am not really embarrassed. We, all her remaining friends, are, in fact, coming to make our goodbyes.

Bunny's two religions ran hand in hand: the Bauhaus—simplicity and purity of line in all things—and her established religion, as reflected in Trinity Episcopal Church in Upperville. The parish was established in 1842, and the Mellons' building, the third on the site, opened for worship in 1960. Here the Episcopalians—white upper-crust establishment Protestants in a largely Baptist part of rural Virginia—listened to the seventeenth-century King James version of the Bible.

Here Foxcroft girls roared out hymns such as "Go Forward, Christian Soldier," Miss Charlotte's favorite, which we had sung at Eliza's funeral and would sing again for Bunny. Miss Charlotte's vibrant faith was meat-and-potatoes, with a special stress on doing good works. A Foxcroft girl was supposed to do something with her faith, for heaven's sake, and Bunny did.

In building the new church in the 1950s, Bunny carried out her own vision of Christian faith. Although she had married Stacy in an Episcopalian church in Princeton, neither her mother nor her father had been particularly religious; it was beloved Grandpa Lowe, a stout New England Congregationalist and nature lover in the Thoreau mold, who influenced her early spiritual life. In plain language he wrote something to his favorite grandchild that could stand as Bunny's creed: "God makes all these lovely, beautiful things and gives us the minds and hearts to know about them and to love them."

When she was eleven, Grandpa Lowe gave her an illustrated copy of the twenty-third Psalm, writing a note to his granddaughter: "'The Lord is my Shepherd' is one of my favorite passages, and I hope you will love it." She did—lines from the Psalm were read at her interment and carved on her gravestone. She kept Grandpa's gift in her library, wrapped in white paper tied with a white ribbon, the color white being the symbol of a precious thing to her.

Faith for Bunny *had* to be wrapped in the power of beauty. But the Holy Spirit could be immanent in what humankind made, just as it was in nature. A person seeking the existence of God could even find it in beautifully produced creations—not in nature alone, but in the way a landscape had been designed, or in a perfectly cut suit jacket, or in the smallest architectural details of a church built to the glory of God.

In her projects, Bunny often went straight for her original impulse. For Trinity Church she had started with the French Gothic architecture she first saw as a girl visiting France when the spires of Chartres Cathedral rose out of the morning fog over "the roofs of the rude French houses," as she wrote in her Foxcroft yearbook.

Bunny and H. Page Cross had turned to a less ornamented version of the style and of course a more modest scale. There were to be no flying buttresses, no filigree spires—this was to be a country church, like "the small French churches in villages surrounded by wheat fields, flax, and forests," as Bunny wrote.

She had worked closely with Perry Wheeler on sculpting the Trinity landscape, speaking with him every night on the phone and worrying about how to present the bills to Paul. ("Dearest Perry—I

The church in the open field, where the Mellon graves lie behind
the low stone wall, center right

just kept the bills for my record. & marked them paid. or is this *un-bussinesslike*? Love, Bunny.") "Sammy" Copenhaver, the man with a sensitive touch on a grader, was part of Everett Hicks's team at the farm: he planted most of the trees, including the inspired choice of a drought-resistant native, *Celtis occidentalis*, the hackberry, as the shade tree for the paved main courtyard. Bunny may have been thinking about her grandfather when she chose it, as he mentions hackberries at his New Hampshire mountain farm in a letter to her when she was nine. So maybe the tree was yet another Bunny talisman: it surely is not by chance that a pair of her library's large glazed doors opens to a view of a tree, now a crab apple but originally another giant hackberry armed with the whiskery branches known as witches' brooms.

No theologian but rather a laywoman who knew her Scripture, Bunny loved the earthly world it described, especially certain details of the Old Testament. In one of her garden notebooks (the first dated entry is 1980), she jotted down a quote from the Book of Kings: "And he spake of trees, from the cedar tree that is in Lebanon even unto the hyssop that springeth out of the wall: he spake also of beasts, and of fowl, and of creeping things, and of fishes" (Kings 1:33). Below the quote Bunny added a reference to an article that mentions hyssop by a Reverend Alfred Traverse (1925–2015), a professor of geology and biology at Penn State and a believer in evolution who nonetheless delivered all his lectures in full clerical garb.

An important aspect of Bunny's character that repeatedly saved her from being a complacent, undereducated, rich society woman with time on her hands was her bottomless curiosity. She wasn't satisfied merely to have reliefs of the plants of Virginia on the pew ends of her rarefied French church, or to have an entire bestiary running around the capitals of its stone columns. So why not turn to an important academic botanical authority who would, no doubt, also be familiar with plants in Scripture? She knew, of course, that because of who she was—Mrs. Paul Mellon—if she wrote to Professor Traverse, likely he would answer her, allowing her to make connections that perhaps no one else could have made. Her wealth helped, but her curiosity was key to the enterprise.

Underfoot in the wide church courtyard, the pavement is laid in a scallop pattern (the scallop recalls the pilgrim's search). Sam Kasten, the weaver, remembered Bunny telling him that cobbles should be "tipped on their sides and sunk in the surface so the paving would last forever." "Forever" had been on Bunny's mind when she and Perry Wheeler designed an area behind the church to be the family burial ground. They surrounded it on three sides with low stone walls and added a bench for contemplation, flanked by magnolias and shaded by a crab apple tree. "A biblical walled garden," she called it. In her correspondence with the senior church warden, she didn't overlook the practical, however, mentioning also the need for a daycare center for the congregation.

My last sight of my biographical subject in 2012 was nowhere near the end for Rachel Lambert Mellon. In the months before Bunny's death in 2014, Nancy Collins was still driving her around the neighborhood to peek and even creep up unfamiliar driveways to see what was going on. High over Carr Lane, the ancient sunken track alongside which Tony Willis's family once farmed, a young couple was renovating an old house and building an addition on the hilltop. Mrs. Charles Carroll IV, Geraldine "Bean" Carroll, was sitting on the new stone retaining wall at the top of the drive, and she hopped down, irritated, to tell the slow-moving old station wagon to buzz off, that she'd had enough of curiosity seekers. But somehow she recognized that her visitor was Bunny Mellon before she warned her off, and she politely asked Bunny's advice about the grounds, aware of her fame as an arbiter of taste. Bunny pointed out that the natural landscape she now could see only in her mind was so beautiful, it could speak for itself. What she said was "Keep it simple," which she knew to be the best possible advice in any design situation.

Spring came, and Bunny asked Marci Nadler, a local artist working on the farm, if she would please paint a life-size buttercup for her that she could hold close and be able to see. To her delight, Bunny could. But some of her daily events were becoming challenges as well: Bunny always wanted to visit the library, but sometimes it was just too much for her to get out of the car. Nadler said, "I do remember her looking into the library from the car—Nancy drove it pretty close to the library, and she peered through the car window with her binoculars." Bunny's range had grown smaller.

The pile of books on her bedside table had also shrunk: the volumes she loved the best were small illustrated children's books bound in plump pink or green embossed leather, all nineteenth- or early-twentieth-century publications, some probably from her childhood, and most featuring flowers and gardens. Their size made them easy to hold, and by making out the pictures Bunny could remember the stories, returning her to memory's blissful world of color and fragrance.

Undine in a thunderstorm, an illustration by Arthur Rackham for *Undine*, a novella by William Leonard Courtney. "The wind bloweth where it listeth."

Among the people who kept track of Bunny during her last

years was John Edwards, who called from time to time as if to remind her he was her friend, not just a political creature looking for money and a way out. Edwards's original contact with Mrs. Paul Mellon, Bryan Huffman, also became a true friend. Bunny and Hubert remained in close touch, now mostly on the phone and in faxes that were taken to her and sent to Hubert by Tony Willis. Hubert made fewer trips to Virginia because of his own increasing frailty. But Bunny hadn't lost her exacting sense of who she was. She asked Hubert to please find her blue T-shirts like the ones from Land's End. This was hardly something Hubert de Givenchy might be expected to provide, but he obligingly did so, even when the first lot didn't pass muster and she asked him for ones with wider necks.

Bunny died on March 17, 2014, at home, at one-thirty in the morning, as snow blanketed the garden. The woman who loved the sight of snow falling and loved being snowbound had one last snow, a spring snow, the kind that sinks softly into the ground and encourages seeds to sprout and plants to grow. The family she had regained had gathered around her in the final days, and she had received last rites.

Nancy Collins had kept watch over her on that last night. She called me early the next morning to give me the news and to tell me that on impulse she had asked Bunny a question: "Mrs., are you afraid?" Bunny had turned toward Nancy and said firmly, "No, I am not afraid." Soon afterward she left us, said Nancy.

"She lay in state in the library, and Thomas Lloyd sat next to her coffin," remembered the chief electrician, Skip Glascock, who told me it took two days for all of Oak Spring's employees to come by and pay their respects. "You had to get an appointment," said Glascock, "and they only allowed in fifteen people at a time. She had asked that we tell her our funny stories about her when we came."

Her coffin was draped magnificently in a length of antique crewelwork: Bunny's obsequies were a grand American country version of those of Deborah Mitford Cavendish, Duchess of Devonshire, whose funeral six months after Bunny's in the parish church nearest Chatsworth was attended by six hundred staff, the Prince of Wales, and the Duchess of Cornwall.

Bunny had left instructions that her body was to be clothed in the plain black graduation gown she had worn when she received an honorary doctorate from RISD, a distinction that meant more to her than any other. She asked Tony Willis and Nancy Collins to place Johnny Schlumberger's letters in her hands and to slip Stacy Lloyd's horseshoe sapphire ring on her little finger, along with her wedding rings from Paul. Such talismans told Bunny that despite the sorrows, dents, and cracks of her life, she had loved and been loved.

On the morning of March 28, the day of her funeral, a steady rain fell. Bunny's casket lay in the church aisle. The altar was decked with only two small bunches of flowers from the Rokeby greenhouses. But even though it was Lent, a time in the church year when the altar is traditionally stripped bare, the pastor was happy to bend the rules a little for Bunny.

One of Augustus John's portraits of his common-law wife, Dore-lia McNeill, is what Bunny chose as the frontispiece for her funeral program. *Dorelia in the Garden at Alderney Manor*, painted in 1911 and purchased by Paul and Bunny in 1982, depicts a tall, thoughtful, rather tough-looking woman standing in her garden wearing a long blue and white wash dress with a torn red apron tucked up into her waist. As she takes a break, leaning on her hoe, Dorelia is silhouetted against a white wall like the one surrounding the Oak Spring garden. It's Bunny at work in the garden, as she saw herself and as she wished to be remembered.

The pews bulged with four generations of her family, members of the community, dozens of her employees, and a scattering of famous folk, the small remainder of all those she had known and outlived. From overseas came longtime friends and colleagues such as John Baskett, Paul's cherished friend and co-author of his autobiography, and Lucia Tongiorgi Tomasi, the art historian who wrote two of Bunny's four Garden Library catalogues, *Flora* and *Herbaria*, the second with Tony Willis.

I was late because I had stopped at a dollar store to buy an umbrella, so I stood in the transept entry, which was packed with many of the Oak Spring staff. They were all wearing black, and most of them were in tears. The organ rolled, and the American Boychoir, which had found a home at Bunny's childhood estate, Albemarle, in Princeton, for a number of years, raised their celestial voices as per Bunny's request.

Her son and grandsons all spoke movingly of the woman who was now gone. Stacy Lloyd IV brought his grandmother closest to us when he talked about the simple things she had loved: the smell of grass, the sound of water lapping against the hull of a wooden boat, the feel of wind on her face. He echoed his great-grandfather Lowe when he said, "She has taught me how to find beauty in everything." Bunny's son, Tuffy, standing and speaking with great difficulty, finished with a flash of wit as well as feeling by saying, "I will miss you truly. Be safe, and take care of God." Her grandson Thomas rejoiced that Bunny's long life had let her meet his children, who were fearless with her in a way that he himself had never been able to be as a little boy.

Frank Langella lifted his great actor's voice, filling the church with his love for Bunny, his friend of fifty-three years. He said Bunny had taught "a rough Jersey kid" how to listen, dress, never be vulgar, respect all people, be humble, avoid hubris, write thank-you notes, never boast, be curious, and "above all, be loyal." Tellingly, he said she taught him to "keep your victories and your grief private"—a reminder of the old, tight-lipped WASP way to behave in which Bunny had been raised. He relished a life that had included a parade of famous people but also asked us to remember the "self-promoting interviews she never gave . . . the galas never attended" and "the red carpets she never stepped on." (One red carpet Bunny did set foot on was at the Metropolitan Museum of Art in 2001, when, at ninety-one, dressed in red satin and black lace, she and a proud Robert Isabell strolled into the opening of the Costume Institute's exhibition honoring her friend Jackie Kennedy.) Startlingly, at the end of the tributes, the organ was still, and a short, rosy-faced, curly-haired woman wearing a black dress and a "Bunny blue" scarf stood and sang "The Rose." It was Bette Midler!

One encomium we did not hear that day was that of Caroline Kennedy, then the American ambassador to Japan, who wrote of a Bunny she'd known first as her mother's greatest friend and later as her own friend. Caroline Kennedy began by looking at her godmother with a child's eye. "She is the last of the great trees that held up the sky of my childhood—tall and strong and graceful—spreading shade and sunlight—and protecting us always with love and strength." She reeled out the glamour of Bunny's life—the Rothkos, the severed hotline in the Rose Garden, the parties, the possessions, and the people—and then described the different Bunny she came to know when she grew up, the one who was interested in politics and history.

She ended with Bunny as a powerful and loving fairy godmother: "When I was packing for Japan, I came across a sixpence, wrapped in West Indian cloth, that was our special symbol. When I was ten, I had asked her if she would be my other godmother, and, as usual, she came up with a better idea. I would be her Sixpence Child. If I ever needed her, I was to send the sixpence, and she would come to help me. Bunny has already helped me more than I can say—but I keep it with me all the time."

John Edwards and his daughter Cate had been barred at the church door, even though Bunny had specified that she wanted him to be there. Family members—Thomas Lloyd and especially Tim Mellon—had had enough of the would-be president. Edwards watched Bunny's service on the big screen in the overflow tent. But after the service ended, he stood near the grave, and then—politician that he is—he glad-handed the crowd.

The sky had cleared by the time the casket made its way from the church to the cemetery. The remains of those who had been buried in the Fletcher family graveyard (including Mary Conover Mellon, to whom Trinity Episcopal Church is dedicated) had long since been transferred to this patch of ground framed by Bunny's low stone walls.

Ronnie Caison was the lead pallbearer; another was Jay Keys, the security guard who had driven the stricken Eliza around the farm in her specially equipped van "for a change of scenery." After the prayers and the blessing, Trinity's choir director, a tall Black man in a long white robe, slowly sang "Oh Shenandoah" in a bass baritone. Not a dry eye after that. Bunny had crossed over the river.

Alex Forger and I stood together near one of the stone walls while the interment took place. Then the huntsman of the local Piedmont Foxhounds—smart chestnut horse, scarlet livery—moved forward.

He had been standing quietly with a few hounds, just over the slope of the hill. He blew "Gone Away" on his short copper hunting horn. The string of high, sharp notes told his hounds their quarry had gone away, gone away, gone away forever. Hounds lifted their voices and mourned. They knew what the call meant, and even though most of those listening had not been taught the meaning or the ritual, they caught the thrill and the sadness of finality. Hounds and huntsman slowly walked offstage.

As the crowd left the church, I ran into Cristina de Heeren, one of Bunny's goddaughters, a Foxcroft schoolmate, one of Eliza's bridesmaids, and her neighbor in Paris. Exhausted, we wondered if we should go have a stiff drink someplace, maybe the Red Fox in Middleburg, and skip the funeral lunch. We were so glad we didn't.

In the softened sunlight of the big white tent, there we were, all together, those of us who remained who might carry on Bunny's legacy. What wonderful things might happen in the Garden Library? How should Bunny's landscape work be highlighted in symposia and programs? Was there really a collection of her recipes? Hubert had already planned a costume exhibition of Bunny's clothes designed by his mentor, Balenciaga, in Balenciaga's hometown of Getaria, Spain. Mostly we just beamed at each other, confident that, as Bunny had shown us, there was a way forward.

We toasted her and one another with champagne or with one of her favorite drinks—Bloody Mary or daiquiri. We nibbled traditional Virginia "ham biscuits" and tiny crab sandwiches. We traded Bunny stories: yet again I trotted out her purchase of the stuffed German shepherd "guard dog" that was to ride in the passenger seat of Eliza's car whenever she drove alone. The Paterson brothers wore their kilts and sporrans—Neil, who kept watch over South Pasture on Nantucket, and Timothy, who had reined in the riotous Lloyd boys. Bunny had left instructions to hire caterers so that her staff, who were her friends, could be guests with all her other friends. Lucia Tongiorgi Tomasi's Pisa accent married with the honk of upper-class English trombone, Long Island lockjaw, elegant French flute, Virginia twang, and lush West Indian hush.

When Bunny and Paul had ordered their tombstones in 1993, Paul chose Robert Louis Stevenson's "Requiem," where the poet welcomes death after a happy, well-ordered life with the line, "Glad did I live and gladly die." Bunny, who spent her life attempting to make the visible world perfect in all its beauty and sensuousness and who had raised a church to the glory of God that was perfect in every detail, did not pick lines about the Garden of Eden or a gorgeous verse from any of the Psalms. She chose the incorporeal, the mysticism and uncertainty that flow through the gospel of John 3:8, where the spirit blows wherever it wants to go.

"The wind bloweth where it listeth, and thou hearest the sound thereof but thou canst not tell whence it cometh, and whither it goeth: so is everyone that is born of the Spirit."

Each performance Bunny staged had to be animated by a spirit of its own—the spirit of experience—Eliza's debut, lifted beyond the ordinary by a cult French novel; or by a relationship—an ineffably romantic moment of friendship with Hubert at Le Jonchet: a poem, some roses, a hedge, and Hubert's blue jeans and bare feet; or by her own understanding, which she at last reached with Robert Isabell, that a love could bind "without touching" and in silence.

The spirit of place connects invisible lines running from the living plants in the walled garden to the coruscating portraits of vegetables on early Chelsea porcelain plates to medieval botanical images in the pages of old books in the Garden Library. Either you realize those connections are there, or you don't—it doesn't matter either way: the spirit remains there and available to "everyone that is born of the Spirit." Ironically, that's what, in the end, Bunny's theatrical mastery and entire life were all about: a search for the invisible, the ineffable, the sublime.

Camille Pissarro, *Le pommier à Eragny*

1910   On August 9, Rachel Lambert (hereafter cited as Bunny or RLM) is born in New York City, to Rachel Parkhill Lowe Lambert (1889–1978) and Gerard Barnes Lambert (1886–1967) (hereafter cited as GBL).

1912   On September 18, RLM's brother, Gerard B. "Sonny" Lambert, Jr. (1912–1947), is born.

1913   Bunny summers on Long Island and visits the family of her godmother, Madeline "Aunt Madie" Huntting Cook Dixon, in North Haven.

1913–17   GBL undertakes the creation of a country place, Albemarle, in Princeton, New Jersey, with architect Harrie T. Lindeberg and Frederick Law Olmsted, Jr. (1870–1957) of Olmsted Brothers, Landscape Architects. In his memoir, GBL wrote, "We argued for weeks over a molding for a doorway . . . We loved the problems and did not rush things. The drawings [alone] took from 1913 [when Bunny was 3] to 1915 to complete, and the building took from 1915 to 1917 to build."

1913   GBL buys 21,000 acres in Elaine, Arkansas, as a timber and cotton plantation.

1914   On September 3, RLM's sister, Lily Lambert, is born in New York City.

1917   On April 6, the United States enters World War I.

1918–20   Bunny attends Miss Fine's college preparatory school in Princeton, NJ.

1919   Hundreds of Black workers are murdered in the race massacres at GBL's Elaine, Arkansas, plantation. GBL sells the plantation.

1918–1920s   Bunny spends six weeks of every summer with her maternal grandparents, Arthur Houghton Lowe (1853–1932) and Anne

Parkhill Lowe (1857–1937), in West Rindge, New Hampshire, and Fitchburg, Massachusetts.

1922–23 In the face of financial overcommitments, GBL takes the family to St. Louis for a year. He works for Lambert Pharmacal, the family company that produced Listerine. Bunny is twelve years old.

1923–29 Calvin Coolidge is president for two terms.

1926 Ailsa Mellon (1901–1969), the daughter of Andrew W. Mellon and sister of Paul Mellon (1907–1999), Bunny's second husband, marries David K. E. Bruce (1898–1977).

1926–29 Bunny attends Foxcroft, a girls' preparatory school in Middleburg, Virginia.

1928 GBL sells all his stock in Lambert Pharmacal.
Bunny meets Stacy Barcroft Lloyd, Jr. (1908–1994), her future husband, at a New York debutante party given for Foxcroft classmate Dorothy "Sister" Kinnicutt.

1929 In June, GBL sells out of all financial markets.
The Foxcroft School yearbook, *Tally-Ho*, prints Bunny's short piece about the beauty of Chartres Cathedral.
On June 3, Foxcroft senior Bunny (class of 1929), receives a certificate.
On July 29, RLM's cousin George Lea Lambert (b. 1905) dies. Bunny will send her debut flowers to be placed on his grave.
On Saturday, October 26, Bunny makes her society debut with a small party at Albemarle.
On October 29 ("Black Tuesday"), the stock market crashes
GBL purchases Carter Hall (built 1792), in Millwood, Virginia; hires architect Harrie T. Lindeberg to modernize the house.
On November 20, Bunny's mother holds a large formal tea at Albemarle.

1930 A chaperoned Bunny tours Egypt and parts of Europe, including Turkey, with Foxcroft classmate Kitty Wickes (Poole).

1931 Bunny begins to correspond with Stacy Lloyd.
At twenty-one, Bunny receives $10,000 from GBL, her first independent money.
Paul's father, Andrew Mellon (1855–1937), buys Rokeby, a four-hundred-acre farm in Upperville, Virginia, half an hour away from Carter Hall in Millwood, for his son.

1932 In summer, Bunny travels abroad with Stacy, chaperoned by his parents and siblings; their engagement is announced on September 3.
On October 27, Arthur H. Lowe dies in Fitchburg. Bunny's brother, Sonny, is a pallbearer.
The November 26 marriage of Bunny and Stacy in Princeton is much smaller than originally planned because of Lowe's death.

1933 Bunny and Stacy occupy a house on Philadelphia's Main Line, a surprise gift from his parents.

GBL honors Bunny and Stacy with a ball at Carter Hall on December 30.

Bunny and Stacy move from Pennsylvania to Carter Hall.

Rachel Lowe Lambert and GBL finalize their divorce after two years of separation.

1934 Rachel Lowe Lambert marries Dr. Malvern Clopton, her widowed brother-in-law.

In June, Stacy purchases *The Clarke Courier*, a local newspaper.

1935 The equestrian artist Franklin Smith paints a portrait of Rachel Lambert Lloyd.

Paul Mellon (hereafter cited as PM) marries Mary Conover Brown (1904–1946) in New York City.

1935–36 Jean Schlumberger (1907–1987) begins his career in Paris as a jewelry designer, producing buttons for the couturiere Elsa Schiaparelli.

1936 Marriage of GBL and second wife, Grace Lansing Mull (1899–1993).

On September 23, son Stacy "Tuffy" Lloyd III (1936–2017) is born to Stacy and Bunny at Carter Hall, Millwood.

Bunny was twenty-six. Stacy was running the rural *Clarke County Courier*. American politicians had their heads in the sand. Ordinary Americans were suffering through the Great Depression. Poverty-stricken Americans went shoeless and ate dirt and weeds. Franklin Roosevelt was inaugurated for his second term. In his inauguration speech he spoke about taking care of the third of the American population who were "ill-housed, ill-clad, and ill-nourished."

1937 Death of PM's father, Andrew Mellon (1855–1937), Secretary of the Treasury and founder of the National Gallery of Art (NGA). PM would later follow his father in his NGA involvement and his collecting life with Bunny.

Bunny and Stacy purchase ten acres that adjoin Carter Hall from Mrs. George Burwell and name the property Apple Hill.

1938 Bunny proposes plantings for designer Hattie Carnegie (1880–1956) at Four Winds Ranch in Middletown, New Jersey, purchased by Carnegie in 1936.

PM and Mary Conover Mellon move permanently from Pittsburgh to Virginia.

Apple Hill under construction. Architect: Charles Read of Paoli, Pennsylvania. The landscape architect Ellen Biddle Shipman (1896–1950) designs a garden fence and gate for it.

1939 Apple Hill completed; the Lloyd family moves in.

GBL designs privately subsidized low-income housing in New Brunswick and Princeton.

1939 Bunny and Stacy go to the White House for New Year's Eve dinner.

1940 Bunny designs a large multipart garden in nearby Paris, Virginia, for Emily Milliken Lambert, the former wife of J. Wooster Lambert, GBL's youngest brother. It is Bunny's first paid job.

Bunny works for the 1940 Wendell Willkie presidential campaign. GBL runs the poll research for Thomas Dewey, who loses the nomination to Willkie.

PM and Mary Mellon begin the construction of the Brick House with architect William Adams Delano (1874–1960). The Mellons found the Bollingen Series.

1939–42 Onset of World War II. Hitler invades Poland on September 1; two days later France and Britain declare war on Germany. On December 7, 1941, the Japanese bomb Pearl Harbor, and the following day the United States declares war on Japan.

PM enlists in the U.S. Army. In 1942, David Robin Francis Guy Greville (1934–1996), 8th Baron Brooke (son of Bunny's friend Rosie Bingham Fiske), the future 8th Earl of Warwick, arrives at Apple Hill at age seven and remains for four years as the Lloyds' British "war child." On September 18, 1942, Stacy enlists, serving in the Morale Operations Branch of the OSS in France (OSS headed by David Bruce, PM's brother-in-law). Bunny remains at Apple Hill.

1942 On October 27, Bunny and Stacy's daughter Eliza is born in Garfield Memorial Hospital, Washington, D.C.

1943 PM sails on May 1 on the *Adair* (the former USS *Exchester*) to England, eventually serving with Stacy Lloyd in the Morale Operations Branch of the OSS office in France.

Bunny and her children summer in Watch Hill, Rhode Island, with two English women friends and their children.

1944 On October 17, Gerard B. Lambert III, son of Bunny's brother, Sonny Lambert, and Elsa Cover, is born.

1945 Stacy is demobilized and returns to Apple Hill.

Ailsa Mellon and David Bruce divorce. Bruce marries Evangeline Wall (1914–1995).

1946 Mary Mellon dies on October 6 in the Brick House in Upperville, Virginia, of a heart attack brought on by asthma.

1946–47 Jean Schlumberger opens a small jewelry salon at 21 East Sixty-Third Street in Manhattan.

1947 On October 3, Sonny Lambert dies in a commercial airliner crash.

1948 GBL sells Carter Hall.

On March 9, Bunny's divorce from Stacy is granted in West

Palm Beach, Florida, her temporary domicile with GBL and wife Grace Mull Lambert.

In late March, Bunny asks PM for a delay of their wedding plans. Accompanied by Sister Parish, the American decorator, she sails for England. PM also travels abroad—separately, at Bunny's request. Bunny meets Colefax & Fowler's partner John Fowler and also renews her acquaintance with Fowler's new partner, Virginian Nancy Lancaster (1897–1994), prime exponent of grand country house "shabby chic."

On May 1, Bunny marries PM in Sister Parish's apartment at 24 East Eighty-Second Street in Manhattan.

In July, Bunny, listed as "Mrs. Stacey Floyd [sic]," purchases an Edgar Degas drawing of a jockey from M. Knoedler & Co. in West Palm Beach.

Bunny and PM and their children, Tuffy and Eliza Lloyd and Tim and Cathy Mellon, live in the Brick House.

1949 Stacy Lloyd weds Alice Woodward Babcock (1927–1980), who is an accomplished horsewoman.

1950 Birth of Robin Lloyd to Stacy and Alice Lloyd.
Schlumberger opens his Paris boutique.

1951 Walter Helmer, a pilot, starts part-time employment with PM.
PM funds the construction of Trinity Episcopal Church in Upperville. H. Page Cross (1910–1975), the architect, and Bunny work as a team on the building.

1952 Bunny begins to shape tabletop topiaries while confined to bed rest after a bout of tuberculosis.
Hubert de Givenchy (1927–2018) founds his couture house.

1952/1953 After five years, first strains appear in the Mellons' marriage.

1953 PM employs pilot Walt Helmer full-time.

1954 Bunny meets Cristóbal Balenciaga (1895–1972) and Givenchy in Paris through Jean Schlumberger.

1953–60 Bunny acquires many of her best-known pieces of Schlumberger jewelry.

1954 The United States takes on the Vietnam military effort after the departure of the French. The war will last until the final evacuation of the American Embassy in 1975.

1955 Additions are completed in Virginia to the old Fletcher farm log house, Little Oak Spring, Bunny and Paul's premarital rendezvous; the couple and their children move from the Brick House.
Tuffy Lloyd graduates from the Middlesex School.
Construction begins on twenty-six waterfront acres at King's Leap, Antigua, next to the Mill Reef Club.

1955–57 PM and RLM's house on twenty-six waterfront acres in Oyster

Harbors, Osterville, Massachusetts, is finished. The architect is H. Page Cross. Bunny buys her first Paris apartment.

1957 Bunny begins her twice-yearly visits to Paris for the spring and fall couture collections.

On August 8, Cathy Mellon and federal prosecutor John Warner (1927–2021) marry on Cape Cod.

On October 20, Queen Elizabeth II (1926–) and Prince Philip (1921–2021) come for tea at Oak Spring.

1958 Bunny travels to England and visits Nancy Lancaster's Haseley Court with Evangeline Bruce.

Bunny's old friend Adele Astaire Douglass (1896–1961), now a Virginia neighbor, brings Jackie Kennedy (1929–1994) to Oak Spring for a visit.

late 1950s Schlumberger buys a winter home on Guadeloupe; Bunny visits him there.

1959 Stacy sells Apple Hill and moves to St. Croix full-time because of his wife's polio.

H. Page Cross designs the formal greenhouse pavilion at Oak Spring.

Fernand Renard (1912–1990), a French trompe l'oeil artist, begins painting the interior of the Oak Spring greenhouse pavilion, finishing the next year.

Harvard-trained landscape architect Perry Wheeler (1913–1989) begins working for Bunny at the Mellons' house on Whitehaven Street in Washington, D.C.

1959–60 Schlumberger produces drawings of a flower-filled urn to serve as a weathervane finial for the Oak Spring formal greenhouse pavilion, a design executed in lead by Robert Bradford.

1960 First service is held in Trinity Episcopal Church, Upperville, in honor of Mary Conover Mellon, on September 28.

Eliza receives a certificate of completion from Foxcroft School.

1961 On January 20, John F. Kennedy (1917–1963) is inaugurated.

In April, the CIA launches the Bay of Pigs invasion, a failed landing operation on the southwestern coast of Cuba by Cuban exiles and American forces.

Eliza's million-dollar June 16 debut at Oak Spring; Paul Leonard (1933–2002), the scenic painter for Franco Zeffirelli and others, creates "sets" with William Strom and the artist Madeleine Hughes for the party and goes on to paint floors at Oak Spring, Oyster Harbors, and King's Leap. Leonard becomes a close friend of RLM.

By midyear much of Washington, D.C., society knows that PM is having an affair with Dorcas Hardin, a well-known clothing boutique owner and socialite.

In July, for JFK's state dinner at Mount Vernon for President

Ayub Khan of Pakistan, Bunny provides flowers and arranges them, lends chairs and linens, and pays for the tent to avoid public comment about Mrs. Kennedy's expenditures.

The Soviets begin preparations for the Berlin Wall.

While visiting the Mellons' Oyster Harbors on Cape Cod, JFK asks Bunny to design the White House Rose Garden.

Bunny meets actor Frank Langella (1938–) in Provincetown, Massachusetts; he becomes a lifelong friend.

Bunny is asked to join the White House Restoration Committee. Lawrence Arata, Bunny's Cape Cod upholsterer, is installed on the Executive Mansion's third floor for a year.

As curator for his collection of British art, Paul hires art expert John Baskett (1931–), who moves to Oak Spring and has offices in the Brick House.

1962　On January 24, Bunny sends her Rose Garden plan to JFK. The president approves it in two days, requesting completion within four months.

On April 24, the Rose Garden opens. Its seasonal plantings of annual and biannual bulbs to freshen the beds will continue as a regular program through the following decades.

For thirteen days, the Unites States and the Soviet Union engage in the tense military and political standoff that becomes known as the Cuban Missile Crisis.

1963　In April, the Virginia Museum of Fine Arts (VMFA) names Paul and Bunny "Collectors of the Year," celebrating with an exhibition of 324 paintings and 127 watercolors from Paul's collection of British art.

1960s　Charles Ryskamp (1928–2010), a scholar, collector, and museum director (Pierpont Morgan Library, Frick Collection) begins to spend the month of August with the Mellons on Cape Cod.

1963　Tuffy works for the U.S. Agency for International Development (USAID) after serving in South Vietnam and Peru with Project Hope, a world health humanitarian NGO founded as a hospital ship, the SS *Hope*.

On June 9, Tim Mellon (1942–) weds Susan Tracy.

Bunny begins plans for the White House East Garden with Jackie Kennedy.

Bunny goes to Paris in July, then visits Balenciaga for a weekend, then heads to Sissinghurst, Vita Sackville-West's estate in England with Evangeline Bruce.

The Kennedys' prematurely born son, Patrick, dies, a reminder for Bunny of her three miscarriages.

On October 1, Jackie goes to Greece with her sister, Lee Radziwill (1933–2019), and Aristotle Onassis (1906–1975).

On November 22, President Kennedy is assassinated in Dallas, Texas. Bunny is responsible for the flowers in the Capitol Rotunda, at the Catholic Cathedral of St. Matthew the Apostle, and at the temporary grave at Arlington National Cemetery. At Jackie Kennedy's request, she gathers a small basket of flowers from the Rose Garden for the president's widow to place on the grave.

1964   In early January, Jackie visits the Mellons on Antigua. She visits again in March.

Bunny begins work on the White House East Garden at the request of Lady Bird Johnson (1912–2007), which the First Lady will dedicate in spring 1965 as the Jacqueline Kennedy Garden.

The architect John Carl Warnecke (1919–2010) presents the official design for JFK's permanent grave site at Arlington National Cemetery. Bunny is asked to make tree selections, but her work expands to other areas and lasts until 1967.

Painting in England 1700–1850, from the Collections of Mr. and Mrs. Paul Mellon opens at London's Royal Academy. Thirteen rare works by George Stubbs hang together in a single room.

1965   Bunny publishes an article in *Vogue* magazine. She writes, "Too much should not be explained about a garden. Its greatest reality is not reality, for a garden, hovering always in a state of becoming, sums [up] its own past and its future."

1966   On March 1, U.S. Interior Secretary Stewart L. Udall presents Bunny Mellon with the Conservation Service Award. Over the next years, her other honors will include the Ordre des Arts et des Lettres as an officer, the Royal Horticultural Society's Veitch Gold Medal, the Henry Shaw Award, and the American Horticultural Society Landscape Design Award. She, with PM, will also be recognized for her assistance in the restoration of the Potager du Roi at Versailles in 1995.

On July 28, the Mellons host a birthday party for Jackie Kennedy at Oyster Harbors, Cape Cod. Dinner is prepared by René Verdon, the White House chef in the Kennedy years, who was flown in secretly to surprise Jackie.

For the twenty-fifth anniversary of the NGA, the exhibition *French Paintings from the Collections of Mr. and Mrs. Paul Mellon and Mrs. Mellon Bruce* includes 248 works.

PM gives his collection of British art, valued at $50 million, to Yale University, with an additional $12 million in funding to build a museum.

PM and Bunny move into the enlarged Manhattan house at 125 East Seventieth Street, executed by H. Page Cross, with additional space provided at 165 East Seventieth Street: a carriage house, plus a twelve-car garage and an apartment for Paul Leonard and his partner William Strom.

Tiffany & Co.'s account book records Paul's December 15 purchase as a Christmas gift of what Bunny called Schlumberger's "Breath of Spring" necklace, set with diamonds and multicolored sapphires.

1967   On January 18, Paul's niece Audrey Bruce Currier (1934–1967) and her husband, Stephen (1930–1967), are lost at sea after their small plane disappears over the Atlantic.

On February 27, GBL dies in Princeton, at age eighty-one. Eliza and her first cousin, Gerard B. Lambert III (1944–), sit with Bunny as she weaves her father's funeral wreath.

On March 14, JFK is permanently interred at the new site in Arlington National Cemetery.

Jackie Kennedy rents a home in Mendham, New Jersey; Bunny visits en route to Princeton to see her widowed stepmother, Gracie Mull Lambert.

On May 1, her nineteenth wedding anniversary, Bunny writes to PM that "this is the happiest anniversary I can remember," mentioning their "shared interests" as well as their various "strengths and weaknesses."

In June, PM and Ailsa's gift of $30 million for a new NGA wing, to be designed by I. M. Pei (1917–2019), is announced.

Bunny enters a purchase agreement for two hundred acres on Nantucket's South Shore with a bequest from her late father of $200,000.

Tiffany & Co.'s account book describes Schlumberger's "Medusa," a jellyfish pin, and records that Bunny asked the staff to tell Mr. Mellon that she would like to have it.

1968   On April 4, Martin Luther King, Jr., is assassinated in Memphis, Tennessee. Bunny flies Jackie Kennedy to the funeral at Ebenezer Baptist Church in Atlanta, Georgia, in the Mellon Gulfstream.

Tuffy Lloyd returns from his job as a junior public affairs officer for USAID, is awarded the first W. Averell Harriman Award for his innovative work in Laos, and is then hired by pollster George Gallup, who was familiar with GBL's work as a political canvasser.

On May 1, PM and Bunny celebrate their twentieth wedding anniversary.

On May 15, Eliza marries Henry "Derry" Dermot Ponsonby, Viscount Moore (later the 12th Earl of Drogheda). First cousin Gerard B. Lambert III drives her unwillingly to the church. The Kennedy children are bridal attendants.

In May, riots bring Paris to a halt, and PM writes a worried letter to Eliza, who is there.

On June 3, the syndicated gossip columnist Walter Winchell writes that the Mellons' marriage is on the rocks. The Mellons deny the rumor.

On June 6, RFK (1925–1968) is assassinated at the Ambassador Hotel in Los Angeles, California.

On June 9, Bunny organizes the flowers for the RFK temporary burial plot, located not far from JFK's grave in Arlington National Cemetery.

In October, Jackie Kennedy marries Aristotle Onassis on Scorpios Island.

Balenciaga retires; Givenchy, who becomes Bunny's designer, says, "When you have so much background, knowledge can be reduced to something very simple—deceptively so, of course. Her taste was a very natural taste, elegant, not complicated."

1969   By now, the Mellon family has already made charitable donations amounting to $700 million.

On June 1, Bunny is interviewed by Sarah Booth Conroy for *The New York Times* article "The House in the Virginia Hunt Country That Is Home to the Paul Mellons."

On August 25, Ailsa Mellon dies.

Richard Nixon enters his first term as president.

1970   In January, the NGA breaks tradition by serving food for the first time for the preview of an exhibition of African sculpture. Bunny arranges for the flowers but can't attend, as she had broken her ankle while watering her plants on Antigua.

In the fall, Bunny visits the studio of Mark Rothko (1903–1970) at 157 East Sixty-Ninth Street with Hubert de Givenchy and buys nine works; she returns to the Marlborough Gallery in spring 1971 to buy more.

1971   Rothko's two children sue the Marlborough Gallery and eventually win control of most of their father's paintings and $9.2 million in damages; Bunny hires top lawyer Alexander Forger (1923–) to successfully defend her against any charges or involvement in the case.

Bunny buys *Les Deux Oiseaux*, the first of her many works by Georges Braque (1882–1963).

On July 26, PM's horse Mill Reef, bred in Virginia, wins the English Grand National, and in September the Prix de l'Arc de Triomphe. The victories are followed by a dinner dance for 120 speedily arranged by Bunny at the nightclub Annabel's in London.

Bunny travels along the Greek and Turkish coasts with Givenchy, Marie-Hélène Bouilloux-Lafont, and Philippe Venet (1929–2021), Givenchy's partner.

1972 Eliza and Derry Moore divorce.
On June 17, there is a break-in at the Democratic National Committee headquarters at the Watergate.
The death of Cristóbal Balenciaga unites Bunny and Givenchy, and she offers to make a garden for him at his Manoir du Jonchet, outside Paris. Bunny writes, "I could help you with this . . . we could do better."
Bunny visits Le Potager du Roi, the King's Kitchen Garden, at Versailles, for the first time with Givenchy.
After meeting Richard Nixon (1913–1994), who was running for his second term as president, Bunny announces she will vote for George McGovern.
Bunny owns an apartment at 84, avenue Foch in Paris.

1973 Nixon wins a second term.
Tuffy writes an article about Laos for *The Washington Post*, then works for the columnist Jack Anderson as a researcher for a year.
Eliza buys land in Little Compton, Rhode Island. The journalist Doris Sanders becomes her partner.
On June 1, Nora Mellon (1879–1973), Paul's mother, dies at the age of ninety-four.
Tuffy marries Anne Emmett (b. 1940), whose powerful D.C. family owns Oatlands, another historic Virginia Carter estate like GBL's Carter Hall. Anne's uncle, who is close to PM, was the longstanding first director of the NGA.
In October, Bunny lends six of her Rothkos to the NGA for the dinner before the opening of *Masterpieces of American Art*, and two more to the show itself.

1974 Jean Schlumberger has a stroke that leaves him unable to draw; he sells his Manhattan house and moves to Paris.
Bunny buys one of the "Ocean Park" series by Richard Diebenkorn (1922–1993), the first of nine.
President Richard Nixon resigns following the Watergate scandal.

1975 Aristotle Onassis dies. Jackie hires Bunny's lawyer, Alexander Forger, to win a $20 million settlement from Onassis's estate.

1976 The architect Edward Larrabee Barnes (1915–2004) breaks ground for the Oak Spring Garden Library (OSGL).
Eliza's work is included in a group show at the Betty Parsons Gallery in New York City.
Jackie becomes an editor at Viking Press in New York City.

1977 Carter Hall becomes the headquarters for Project Hope. In the eighties, Bunny renovates the south landscape; the property would be put on the market in 2018.

Alexander Forger asks about Bunny's assets. PM sends a five-page list of her jewels but agrees to give her an annual allowance of $500,000 for charitable gifts.

PM's Yale Center for British Art, designed by the architect Louis Kahn (1901–1974) to hold PM's collections—then encompassing about 1,800 paintings, 7,000 drawings, 5,000 prints, and 16,000 books—opens with an exhibition titled *The Pursuit of Happiness*.

1978   On June 1, the East Building of the National Gallery of Art, designed by I. M. Pei with an initial budget of $20 million that ballooned to more than $100 million, opens.

Dita Amory (1954–), then finishing up her master's degree in art history from the Institute of Fine Arts in New York City, begins working for Bunny as her librarian.

Bunny is reportedly diagnosed with and treated for cancer; she recovers.

1979–82   Jackie Kennedy builds a house, designed by the architect Hugh Newell Jacobsen (1929–2021), on almost four hundred acres on Martha's Vineyard; Bunny edits and transforms the old farm landscape.

1981   Bunny begins to fill the completed old wing of the OSGL with works of art and rare furniture as well as books.

Bunny places her first fax machine in the schoolroom at the end of the garden, far from the house or the library.

Stacy marries his third wife, Virginia Ida Boy-Ed (1922–2006), known as Vidy.

1982   Dita Amory finishes her work at the OSGL and returns to New York City. The scholar John Dixon Hunt briefly becomes academic advisor, followed by Julia Blakely as librarian and then by Tony Willis (1961–) in 1999. OSGL is organized as a private library open by appointment only.

On June 3, "The Private World of a Great Gardener," by Paula Dietz, appears in *The New York Times*.

1983   Randolph Macon College awards Bunny an honorary doctorate in the humanities.

PM, diagnosed with prostate cancer, gives an additional ninety-three paintings to the NGA.

1984   Bunny assembles a dairy herd, hires the dairyman Allen Bassler, designs a label, and begins producing, selling, and distributing milk and two tons of cheese annually.

1985   Bunny founds Nantucket Lightship Preservation, Inc.

In November, Bunny hosts a dinner at Whitehaven Street to celebrate the opening of *The Treasure Houses of Britain* at the National Gallery.

In November, Prince Charles (1948–) and Princess Diana (1961–1997) come for lunch at Oak Spring.

PM and Bunny fund a wing at the VMFA to house their gifts of French Impressionists and British sporting art.

At the NGA's *Gifts to the Nation—Selected Acquisitions from the Collections of Mr. and Mrs. Paul Mellon*, eighty-five of the Mellons' paintings are brought together in a single exhibition. On May 3, PM retires as chairman of the NGA. President Ronald Reagan presents him with one of the first National Medals of Arts.

1985–90 Bunny funds a medical clinic on Antigua, gives $20,000, enlists the New York pathologist Dr. Bruce Horten for assistance. PM also contributes.

1986 On May 28, Bunny meets Robert Isabell (1952–2009), who is working with New York event planner George Trescher (1926–2003). Isabell asks, "Who is this woman who keeps making suggestions?"

On July 19, Caroline Kennedy (1957–) and Edwin Schlossberg (1945–) wed in Centerville, Massachusetts.

1987 Tuffy and Anne divorce; Tuffy closes Lloyd Books, his travel and antiquarian bookshop, which had first opened in downtown Washington, D.C., and moved to Georgetown in 1983.

On August 29, Jean Schlumberger dies in Paris; Bunny visits him two weeks before his death.

1988 Construction of the Picnic House, the first building on Bunny's Nantucket property, South Pasture, begins, by the team of Neil Paterson (1959–) and Henry Bancel "Bam" LaFarge (1950–2015).

1989 *An Oak Spring Sylva*, a catalogue of fifty OSGL books described by writer and editor Sandra Raphael, is published and dedicated to Bunny's maternal grandfather, Arthur Houghton Lowe.

In October, the Leonard L. Milberg Gallery for the Graphic Arts, Princeton University Library, opens *An Oak Spring Garland*, the first public exhibition of selected OSGL holdings to honor the publication of *An Oak Spring Sylva*.

The Mellons' longtime financial consultant Kenneth I. Starr is appointed an officer of the Oak Spring Garden Library board.

1990 In January, *An Oak Spring Pomona*, a catalogue of one hundred books and manuscripts described by Sandra Raphael and dedicated to Paul Mellon, is published.

1991 Sixty acres of Bunny's two-hundred-acre Nantucket property are given to the Nantucket Conservation Foundation.

1992 Eliza and her longtime partner Doris Sanders break up.

PM closes down his breeding operation in Virginia, keeping only a few horses in the pastures for the pleasure of seeing them.

RLM purchases an apartment at 15, rue de l'Université in Paris.

1993–2001 Bill Clinton (1946–) and Al Gore (1948–) serve as president and vice president for two terms.

1993 Purchase of Spring Hill house and acreage from Wheeler and Dr. James Stengle.

The architect Thomas Beach (1950–) designs an addition to the OSGL that includes carrels for scholars and conference space.

On May 1, PM's Sea Hero wins the Kentucky Derby. PM gives RLM a rose from the Run for the Roses garland to celebrate their forty-fifth wedding anniversary.

RLM and PM order their tombstones for the private plot at Trinity Episcopal Church, Upperville, Virginia.

Bunny and Akko van Acker (1942–) meet at his shop in Paris.

1994 On May 19, Jacqueline Bouvier Kennedy Onassis dies in New York City at age sixty-five. The Mellon plane brings the casket to D.C. for burial next to President Kennedy in Arlington National Cemetery. Robert Isabell sits at the grave with Bunny as Jackie is interred.

On December 6, Stacy Lloyd, Jr., Bunny's first husband, dies in Berryville, Virginia, at age eighty-six.

1995 On December 14, Bunny's close friend Evangeline Bruce dies at age eighty-one. Bunny and PM attend her funeral in Washington, D.C.

On January 26, Bunny receives the award of La Croix d'Officier de l'Ordre des Arts et des Lettres from the French government for her work restoring Le Potager du Roi at Versailles.

1996 Hurricane Edouard lasts for eight days in September. Paul and Bunny stay in Oyster Harbors to watch the storm. Eliza sails her boat to safety before the storm begins.

The Virginia Lynch Gallery in Tiverton, Rhode Island, mounts a show of Eliza's work.

The 84, avenue Foch apartment is sold.

1997 *An Oak Spring Flora*, a catalogue of more than one hundred books, manuscripts, prints, paintings, textiles, and ceramics in the OSGL by the art historian Lucia Tongiorgi Tomasi (1939–), is published. It is dedicated to Bunny's "dear and loyal friend, Jacqueline Bouvier Kennedy Onassis."

On June 11, PM's ninetieth birthday is celebrated at the Brick House.

"A Garden Furnished with Books," by Christopher Ridgway, is published in *Country Life* in December 1997 and January 1998, on OSGL's architecture, holdings, and publishing program.

1998 In June, "Oak Spring Splendors," by Martin Filler, a review of the first three OSGL catalogues, *Sylva*, *Pomona*, and *Flora*, and selected OSGL holdings, is published in *House Beautiful*.

PM's last summer on Cape Cod. John Baskett paints a light-hearted watercolor of Paul's medicine cabinet and administers his pain medication.

PM signs his will, giving Bunny the modern masterpieces she had brought into their collection: Rothkos, Diebenkorns, and Braques, as well as many French Impressionist and Post-impressionist works they had collected together. In addition to all the real estate, she receives a life interest in dozens of works that hang in their houses by Seurat, Cézanne, Bonnard, Degas, John Singer Sargent, Winslow Homer, and other artists.

Eliza sells her 97 Barrow Street house and buys a penthouse apartment and studio at 30 East Tenth Street.

1999 On February 1, PM dies at age ninety-one and is buried in the private Mellon plot at Trinity Episcopal Church, Upperville, Virginia.

Beverly Carter, PM's Virginia curator and general manager, notifies Virginia employees following his death that they are dismissed.

Bunny reassures the staff and changes the name of the Virginia property from Rokeby Farms to Oak Spring LLC, thereby announcing her control.

The Rhode Island School of Design (RISD) awards Bunny an honorary doctorate of fine arts.

In July, the single-engine plane piloted by John F. Kennedy, Jr. (1960–1999), who was accompanied by his wife and sister-in-law, crashes into the Atlantic Ocean near Martha's Vineyard, Massachusetts, killing all aboard.

Bunny and Eliza make plans to go to Paris together.

After PM's death Bunny relies increasingly on financial consultant Kenneth I. Starr for advice; she gives him power of attorney.

Bunny spends the first Christmas after PM's death with Eliza at her house in Little Compton, Rhode Island.

2000 Two twenty-eighth-floor apartments are combined at Essex House, 160 Central Park South, as Bunny's headquarters for lawyers Alex Forger and Jane Maclennan.

Bunny's new plane, a Dassault Falcon 2000, is delivered.

The nonprofit organization RxART is incorporated by art consultant Diane Brown and Eliza to place art in pediatric hospitals.

North Carolina senator John Edwards (1953–) is on presidential candidate Al Gore's short list for VP.

On May 6, Eliza is run down by a truck in Manhattan and suffers a severe brain injury, leaving her with quadriplegia and an inability to speak.

On August 9, Bunny celebrates her ninetieth birthday on Nantucket, her party orchestrated by Robert Isabell. A new intimate friend of Eliza's, Ann Hudner, cares for Eliza in Bunny's absence.

2001   Bunny writes a reminiscence for the Metropolitan Museum catalogue of the exhibition *Jacqueline Kennedy: The White House Years* and attends the opening escorted by Robert Isabell.

Spring Hill, one of the houses on Oak Spring Farm, is renovated to bring Eliza out of the hospital and back home.

2002   The Chicago Flower and Garden Show mounts an installation overseen by Robert Isabell and Bunny that replicates the style of the Oak Spring walled garden.

In June, *Angels of Light, Portraits of Shadows*, an exhibition of Eliza's most recent work, opens at the Virginia Lynch Gallery in Tiverton, Rhode Island.

The oceanfront bluff at South Pasture, Nantucket, erodes and crumbles; the main house is moved four hundred feet back from its original location.

2003   Bunny's previously diagnosed macular degeneration worsens; she stops driving.

Bunny signs a new will, leaving $20 million each to Eliza and Tuffy and a Monet to Tuffy. Starr and Forger are named Eliza's guardians. Robin Lloyd, her half brother, is executor.

In her will, Bunny directs the sale of her assets (worth more than $500 million) at auction after her death to fund the Oak Spring Garden Library as her legacy.

Senator John Edwards of North Carolina announces his run for president.

2004   In the February Virginia presidential primary, Bunny runs an ad in *Middleburg Life* for Edwards, who loses to John Kerry (1943–), who then selects Edwards as his nominee for vice president.

2004   The Bush/Cheney ticket beats Kerry/Edwards.

2004–2005   Through his top aide, Andrew Young, and Bunny's new friend decorator Bryan Huffman, Edwards meets Bunny at the farm. She ultimately gives $3 million to Edwards's 2008 campaign and his causes, such as the UNC Chapel Hill Center on Poverty and his PAC, One America Committee.

2006   Bunny's sister, Lily Lambert McCarthy, dies at age ninety-one.

On March 25, Bunny attends the wedding of grandson Thomas Lloyd (1976–) to Anna Cristina "Rickie" Niceta (1970–) in D.C. RLM makes an additional gift of Nantucket land (comprising 110 acres in all) to the Nantucket Conservation Foundation that "protects sand plain grassland and scrub oak barrens habitat and the uncommon species that depend on them."

The New York house at 125 East Seventieth Street is sold for $22.5 million.

Bunny rents a three-room apartment at the Mark Hotel, says redecorating with her longtime friend and decorator Bruce Budd is "like doing a dollhouse."

Bunny's lawyer Alex Forger holds political fundraisers for Edwards in the Central Park South office. Edwards officially announces his run for president.

2007   In April, Edwards aide Andrew Young phones Bunny. She agrees to fund all Edwards's personal expenses; Forger states that federal campaign limitations prevent it. With Bryan Huffman as the shadow recipient, Bunny disguises additional gifts (a total of $750,000) to Edwards's campaign as purchases of antiques over the next year.

Bunny's eyesight deteriorates further; now she can only make out light and shadow, no color.

2008   On February 7, daughter Fiona is born to RLM's grandson Thomas Lloyd and his wife, Rickie.

On May 7, RLM's daughter, Eliza Lloyd Moore, age sixty-five, dies. She is buried on May 13 in the Mellon plot at Trinity Episcopal Church, Upperville, Virginia. Bryan Huffman reveals the antiques scheme to Alex Forger, and it is ended.

Tuffy moves into the Hunter Barn, a house on Oak Spring Farm. Bunny will design a library for him using oversize prints of her drawings as her guides.

2009   Barack Obama (1961–) is inaugurated as president.

An Oak Spring Herbaria, the fourth volume of the OSGL catalogues, is published by Lucia Tongiorgi Tomasi and Tony Willis and dedicated to "My dearest friend & daughter, Eliza Lloyd Moore."

On July 8, RLM's friend Robert Isabell, fifty-seven years old, dies. He is interred in the old Fletcher farm graveyard at Oak Spring.

The 15, rue de l'Université apartment is sold.

2010   On May 27, Kenneth I. Starr is arrested. Records later reveal Bunny had lost approximately $18 million.

On August 9, as Bunny reaches her centenary, her estate is estimated at half a billion dollars, due to appreciating art and other investments.

Construction of Memory House to hold Eliza's paintings and effects begins at the farm.

2011 On April 1, Thomas and Rickie Lloyd's son Edward is born.

RLM's son, Tuffy, grandsons Thomas and Stacy Lloyd IV, Tony Willis, and Alex Forger testify in the John Edwards trial in Raleigh, North Carolina. Edwards is indicted for violating campaign laws in obtaining funding for his mistress and their baby.

2012 Bunny sells the Oyster Harbors main house for $19.5 million to Bill Koch but gives the associated Dune Cottage to Tuffy. She retains the properties on Nantucket and Antigua, fully staffed, until her death.

2014 On March 17, Bunny dies at age 103 at Oak Spring shortly after one-thirty in the morning as snow blankets the garden. Her will expresses her hope that her extensive botanical library will remain at Oak Spring Farm, and that it will be used for public benefit. Her large collection of Schlumberger jewelry now joins the Schlumberger objects previously given to the Virginia Museum of Fine Arts before her death. Other items that she held in life estate, or that were specified in her will, are also distributed. The contents of her home are sold in a five-day Sotheby's auction in November. After all taxes and other expenses are paid, the proceeds pass to the Gerard B. Lambert Foundation, a philanthropic and grant-making nonprofit organization named for her father. The Lambert Foundation provides the funds that enable the Oak Spring Garden Foundation to operate in perpetuity, including caring for the library and developing other programs focused on plants, gardens, and landscapes.

On March 28, Bunny's funeral service is held in Trinity Episcopal Church, Upperville, Virginia. Her body is interred in the Mellon plot in the graveyard.

NOTES

1. BECOMING BUNNY

13 *"I was born 92 years ago"*: Rachel Lambert Mellon (hereafter cited as RLM), handwritten, August 9, 2002, witnessed by Robert Isabell, Oak Spring Garden Library (hereafter cited as OSGL).

13 *Her birth certificate doesn't give*: State of New York Certificate and Record of Birth No. 45619.

15 *In just seven years annual profits*: "Lambert Pharmaceutical," AdAge, September 15, 2003, http://adage.com/article/adage-encyclopedia/lambert-pharmaceutical/98741/.

15 *had turned the troubled firm*: "Gerard Barnes Lambert," *Encyclopedia Britannica*, www .britannica.com/biography/Gerard-Barnes-Lambert.

15 *Lily "was a very beautiful baby"*: Gerard B. Lambert (hereafter cited as GBL), *All Out of Step: A Personal Chronicle* (New York: Doubleday, 1956), 73.

17 *"fighting with you over anything"*: MacKubin letters to Rachel Lambert, OSGL.

17 *About her father*: RLM, "My Father," extensive notes on their relationship, five typed pages, box 53, OSGL.

17 *"I was surrounded by beautiful things"*: Ibid.

17 *Bunny said that her mother*: I interviewed Bunny Mellon over the course of two years, 1995–96. She would not allow herself to be recorded, and she didn't like having me take notes. After our sessions together I set down her comments in a notebook. All quotes noted as MKG 1995/1996.

17 *"Being a child not much noticed"*: RLM, "My Father."

18 *"We had the top floor"*: MKG 1995/1996, phone interview notes, November 27, 1999, and March 23, 2000.

19 *Bunny's uncle Albert*: GBL, *All Out of Step*, 21.

19 *George Lea Lambert, Albert's son*: For the quote, see Nancy Collins, Bunny's nurse, who became the OSGL archivist when the papers were reorganized after Bunny's death.

19 *The plane dived to the ground*: GBL, *All Out of Step*, 38.

19 *He urged her to stand up*: Arthur H. Lowe (hereafter cited as AHL) to Rachel Lambert, September 9, 1919, OSGL.

19 *One wonders if anyone else*: GBL, *All Out of Step*, 134.

20 *"Don't let either kind"*: AHL to Rachel Lambert, October 9, 1921, OSGL.

20 *"Don't be [completely] unselfish"*: AHL to Rachel Lambert, August 12, 1924, OSGL.

20 *The colored pictures of totem poles*: Rachel Lambert, "A Visit to the Land of Totem Poles," 27, OSGL.

21 *"Dear Bunny, Your grand-pa"*: AHL to Rachel Lambert, September 21, 1918, OSGL.

21 *Bunny missed him*: RLM, reminiscence of a trip to Lowe's New Hampshire cabin, handwritten, one of many versions, n.d., OSGL.

21 *"My dear Bun, I loved your fairy story"*: AHL to Rachel Lambert, n.d., OSGL.

21 *Writing later from her splendid house*: RLM to AHL, n.d., OSGL.

22 *"This was the best part"*: Ibid.

22 *"Space, and how to use it"*: RLM, another reminiscence, n.d., OSGL.

22 *At Albemarle*: John Charles Olmsted to the U.S. Forestry Service, October 1918, Olmsted Archives, Frederick Law Olmsted National Historic Site, Brookline, MA.

22 *Later, when Bunny was designing*: RLM, "My Father."

23 *In Fitchburg alone*: "Parkhill Manufacturing Company Collection," *Women, Enterprise & Society*, Harvard Business School, www.library.hbs.edu/hc/wes/collections/labor/textiles/content/1001955839.html.

23 *As chairman*: *Tariff Information, 1921: Hearings Before the Committee on Ways and Means, House of Representatives, on Schedule I Cotton, and Manufactures Of*, 66th Cong. (1921) (statement of Mr. A. H. Lowe, representing the consolidated tariff committee of cotton manufacturers, Fitchburg, Mass.).

24 *At the same time*: "Mrs. Mellon's Childhood," n.d. and unsigned, typed, OSGL.

24 *And among Bunny's anecdotes*: RLM, undated reminiscence, OSGL.

24 *Although Lambert hoped*: GBL, *All Out of Step*, 239–50.

25 *The three of them*: *Foxcroft Alumnae Bulletin*, June 1941, 35, Foxcroft School Archives, Middleburg, VA.

25 *How Lambert ran his polling*: For RLM's campaign contributions see chapter 30, "I Want to Make a President."

25 *Lambert proudly contends*: GBL, *All Out of Step*, 253.

26 *"Dear Old Bun"*: AHL to Rachel Lambert, February 12, 1921.

26 *Lincoln apparently said this*: Francis B. Carpenter, *The Inner Life of Abraham Lincoln, Six Months at the White House*, facsimile reproduction (New York: Hurd and Houghton, 1867), 258–59.

26 *She needed Grandpa Lowe's*: Mayo Clinic, "Narcissistic Personality Disorder," www.mayoclinic.org/diseases-conditions/narcissistic-personality-disorder/symptoms-causes/syc-20366662.

2. CRAFTING HAPPINESS

29 *hardwood dance floor*: *Carter Hall: A Landscape History*, prepared for the Garden Club of Virginia, 2013, Megan N. Turner, preparator, 54.

30 *Bunny's father had bought*: GBL, *All Out of Step*, 138; Robin Karson, Library of American Landscape History, client list organized geographically, http://lalh.org/wp-content/uploads/2012/05/ContributorGuidelines_ManningClientsList.pdf; Susanne Williams Massie and Francis Archer Christian, *Homes and Gardens in Early Virginia* (Richmond: Garrett and Massie, 1932), 297; Stuart E. Brown, Jr., and Ann Barton Brown, *Carter Hall and Some Genealogical Notes on the Burwell Family* (Berryville: Virginia Book Company, 1978).

30 *"I took this seriously"*: RLM reminiscence, OSGL.

31 *Atlantic was but the first*: GBL, *All Out of Step*, 159–75.

32 *Such visits stoked*: Rachel Lambert, "Chartres," in *Tally-Ho* (Foxcroft yearbook, 1929), 62, Foxcroft School Archives, Middleburg, VA.

32 *The American debutante*: MKG 1995/1996.

33 *They replaced*: Brown and Brown, *Carter Hall and Some Genealogical Notes*.

33 *Relations with the firm*: *Carter Hall: A Landscape History*, 54–62.

34 *Later, at Oak Spring*: Ibid.

34 *And she listened*: MKG 1995/1996; Nancy Collins interviews, 2015 and 2020.

35 *Bunny later wrote*: RLM, "My Father"; Encyclopedia of Arkansas, "Elaine Massacre of 1919," www.encyclopediaofarkansas.net/encyclopedia/entry-detail.aspx?entryID=1102, accessed September 5, 2017; GBL, *All Out of Step*, 73–79; Grif Stockley, *Blood in Their Eyes: The Elaine Race Massacres of 1919* (Fayetteville: University of Arkansas Press, 2001).

36 *"All my love, precious"*: Stacy Barcroft Lloyd, Jr. (hereafter cited as SBL), to Rachel Lambert, postmarked Ardmore, Pennsylvania, January 6, 1932, OSGL.

3. "THE MOST BEAUTIFUL PLAYBOY"

37 *"He was the most beautiful playboy"*: MKG 1995/1996.

38 *Ivy membership*: GBL, *All Out of Step*, 186.

38 *F. Scott Fitzgerald's 1920*: Matthew J. Bruccoli, *Some Sort of Epic Grandeur: The Life of*

F. Scott Fitzgerald, 2nd rev. ed. (Columbia: University of South Carolina Press, 2002), 125; quoted in Wikipedia entry "This Side of Paradise."

38   *"Grace is the greatest artistic effect"*: Nelson W. Aldrich, Jr., *Old Money: The Mythology of America's Upper Class* (New York: Alfred A. Knopf, 1988), 105.

39   *Rapid heartbeat*: "Heart Failure Signs and Symptoms," Heart.org, www.heart.org /HEARTORG/Conditions/HeartFailure/WarningSignsforHeartFailure/Warning -Signs-of-Heart-Failure_UCM_002045_Article.jsp#.WW3kllKZNqw.

39   *"do please be careful"*: SBL to Rachel Lambert, October 8, 1931, OSGL.

40   *"Some day we will go out"*: SBL to Rachel Lambert, December 10, 1931, OSGL.

40   *"So my darling"*: SBL to Rachel Lambert, January 7, 1932, OSGL.

41   *"Must stop"*: SBL to Rachel Lambert, February 19, 1932, OSGL.

41   *The bride wore*: "Lloyd-Lambert," *Philadelphia Inquirer*, November 27, 1932, 7; George Trescher included Bunny's remark about orchids in his notes on Caroline Kennedy's wedding plans, May 28, 1986, OSGL.

42   *He wrote, "I crossed"*: GBL, *All Out of Step*, 186.

42   *On October 30*: "Lloyd-Lambert Wedding Plans Are Announced," *Philadelphia Inquirer*, October 30, 1932, 54.

42   *Among the banks*: Fitchburg Sentinel, October 29, 1932.

43   *"The boulders"*: RLM, a reminiscence of a trip to Lowe's New Hampshire cabin, hand-written, one of many versions, n.d., OSGL.

43   *Hidden "producer"*: RLM, "My Father," includes a section on the Olmsted firm and her design for the White House Rose Garden, OSGL.

43   *"Secretly, we looked"*: MKG 1995/1996.

44   *Maugham's brilliantly lit drawing room*: GBL, *All Out of Step*, 29; Elizabeth Lambert, "Syrie Maugham: Famously White Rooms for an English Innovator," *AD*, posted December 31, 1999, www.architecturaldigest.com/story/maugham-article-012000.

44   *"We have found"*: MKG 1995/1996.

44   *"Mr. Morris"*: Ibid.

45   *Stacy bought*: Rachel Lloyd, "Chewing and Sucking Bugs," *Clarke Courier*, May 6, 1938.

46   *In 2014*: Abram Brown, "175 Years Later, the Mellons Have Never Been Richer. How'd They Do It?," *Forbes*, July 20, 2014, www.forbes.com/sites/abrambrown/2014/07/08/175 -years-later-the-mellons-have-never-been-richer-howd-they-do-it/?sh=1ff165657489. Also see: David Cannadine, *Mellon: An American Life* (New York: Alfred A. Knopf, 2006); Burton Hersh, *The Mellon Family: A Fortune in History* (New York: William Morrow, 1978).

46   *The purchase*: In 1931, Andrew Mellon purchased Rokeby for his wife, Nora, and she subsequently sold it to their son, Paul. In 1936, Paul bought Oak Spring with its log cabin, building "The Brick House" as his residence for his first wife. See Michael Gaige, *An Oak Spring Landscape: History, Ecology, and Management at the Oak Spring Garden Foundation* (Upperville, VA: Oak Spring Garden Foundation, May 2018), 54, https:// issuu.com/osgf/docs/osg_mg_final_220.

47   *"The years of habit"*: Paul Mellon with John Baskett, *Reflections in a Silver Spoon* (New York: William Morrow, 1992), 149.

47   *In one of his kinder descriptions*: Ibid., 65.

47   *Not only would he find*: For the full memorandum, see ibid., 149–51.

49   *The couple married*: William McGuire, *Bollingen: An Adventure in Collecting the Past* (Princeton, NJ: Princeton University Press, 1989), 5, 6–9; Mellon, *Reflections*, 143–47.

49   *Mary said*: McGuire, *Bollingen*, 13.

49   *The Georgian-style mansion*: For architectural drawings of the Brick House and Staunton Hill, see https://findingaids.library.columbia.edu/ead/nnc-a/ldpd_3460565.

4. THE MYTHOLOGY OF CONTENTMENT

51   *"She terrorized"*: Lady Charlotte Fraser to RLM, March 7, 1996, OSGL.

51   *His mother's family*: David Robin Francis Guy Greville (1934–1996), 8th Baron Brooke, 8th Earl of Warwick, memoir (hereafter cited as Brooke memoir) includes seventeen pages on years spent in Virginia as a child, 1999, OSGL.

51   *"The village was Millwood"*: Ibid.

51   *"At a farm party"*: Ibid.

52 *Finally, Liz stuck her head*: MKG 1995/1996.
52 *"When my son, Stacy, was born"*: RLM, five-page memoir fragment, n.d., beginning "It was a summer's day," OSGL.
54 *To this day*: In 1939, the land tax for Apple Hill lists buildings valued at $10,000. The buildings surrounding the stable yard follow the pattern of the outbuildings at Carter Hall behind the main house.
54 *It was her first attempt*: Lucy W. Burwell, widow, and George H. Burwell, Jr., to Stacy B. Lloyd, Jr., and Rachel L. Lloyd, his wife, February 26, 1937, Clarke County Deed Book No. 24.238.
55 *Shipman created several gardens*: Ellen McGowan Biddle Shipman Papers, 1914–1946, Mapcase Folder 81, Collection Number 1259, Mrs. Stacy Lloyd, Millwood, Virginia, Division of Rare and Manuscript Collections, Cornell University Library: Two construction plans: entrance and picket fence.
55 *The concept*: OSGL holds seven works by the English garden historian Eleanour Sinclair Rohde. *My Garden Note Book* (London, 1936) includes invoices from nurseries and landscape services, a photo of SBL notes on plantings at Apple Hill based on Rohde's descriptions, and RLM's inscription on the half title: "Planted at 'Apple Hill,' Millwood in Clarke County, Virginia, by Rachel Lambert Lloyd 1939."
56 *"And we snowballed"*: Brooke memoir, OSGL.

5. LONDON, WAR—AND WOMEN

60 *It is typical*: Sheriff's Sale of Valuable Personal Property, public notice, July 30, 1941.
60 *A couple of steeplechase friends*: Mellon, *Reflections*, 193.
61 *He offered to buy an ambulance*: Meryl Gordon, *Bunny Mellon: The Life of an American Style Legend* (New York: Grand Central Publishing, 2017), 104.
61 *The much-cherished Eliza*: Interview with Nancy Collins, December 2015.
61 *Acting as*: David K. E. Bruce, ed. by Nelson D. Lankford, *OSS Against the Reich* (hereafter cited as *OSS*) (Kent, OH: Kent State University Press, 1991), 8.
62 *Donovan and Bruce*: Nelson D. Lankford, *The Last American Aristocrat: The Biography of Ambassador David K. E. Bruce, 1898–1977* (New York: Little, Brown, 1996), 136.
62 *Bruce's biographer*: Nelson D. Lankford, "Introduction," *OSS*, 11.
62 *Rosie offered*: Rose Bingham Greville Fiske (hereafter cited as RBGF) to Rachel Lloyd, October 10, 1942, OSGL.
62 *Bruce, not given*: *OSS*, 19.
63 *Not that she had*: Brooke memoir, OSGL.
63 *The cable*: RBGF to Rachel Lloyd, cable, November 5, 1942, at GBL house, Kalorama Circle, OSGL.
63 *"Stacy is away"*: RBGF to Rachel Lloyd, January 8, 1943, OSGL.
63 *On March 4*: RBGF to Rachel Lloyd, March 4, 1943, OSGL.
64 *She also asked*: Ibid.
64 *"I believe Rosie"*: SBL to Rachel Lloyd, April 2–5, 1943, OSGL.
64 *By August 1943*: RBGF to Rachel Lloyd, August 14, 1943, OSGL.
64 *In her cable*: RBGF to Rachel Lloyd, August 30, 1943, OSGL.
64 *He and Stacy*: Mellon, *Reflections*, 198, 201–207.
65 *Other London landmarks*: West End at War, www.westendatwar.org.uk/page_id__152_path__0p2p.aspx.
65 *"It seemed very natural"*: *OSS*, 17.
66 *P. G. Wodehouse*: Lunched at Bucks with Stacy Lloyd, July 19, 1944, *OSS*, 112, http://leagueofclubchefs.com/bucks-club.
66 *Rosie herself left around two*: Both quotations in this paragraph are from RBGF to Rachel Lloyd, February 19, 1943, OSGL.
66 *"It overwhelmed everything"*: Kay Summersby Morgan, *Past Forgetting: My Love Affair with Dwight D. Eisenhower* (New York: Simon and Schuster, 1975), 76.
66 *Or, as the American journalist Harrison Salisbury*: Lynne Olson, *Citizens of London: The Americans Who Stood with Britain in Its Darkest, Finest Hour* (New York: Random House, 2011), 388.
67 *Stacy hastened*: SBL to Rachel Lloyd, March 13, 1943, OSGL.
67 *"Valerie came over"*: Georgiana McCabe interview, December 2014.

67   *When Bunny insisted*: SBL to Rachel Lloyd, July 5, 1943, OSGL.
68   *Brookie, who was often*: Camilla Chandon de Briailles, memories of Bunny Mellon at Watch Hill, email, June 27, 2017.
68   *Bunny later recollected*: MKG phone conversations with Bunny Mellon, 1999–2003.
69   *Bunny, who admired*: MKG 1995/1996.
69   *They are those*: Philip Hoare obituary of Lady Glendevon, *Independent*, January 30, 1999; "Liza Glendevon Was a QueerSpawn," Poppycock, May 8, 2012, http://poppycockdc .blogspot.com.
69   *"I long for a letter"*: RBGF to Rachel Lloyd, August 14, 1943, OSGL.
69   *Stacy's reassurances*: SBL to Rachel Lloyd, March 13, 1945, OSGL.
69   *Bunny told me*: MKG 1995/1996.

6. THE FIELD OF WAR

70   *When in September*: Mellon, *Reflections*, 204.
72   *Bruce also visited*: OSS, 173–75.
73   *Bruce's reports*: Janet Bruce, David Bruce's daughter-in-law, personal communication.
73   *London lay*: OSS, 74–77.
73   *He got firsthand*: Ibid., 77, 142.
73   *In nearby Saint-Malo*: Ibid., 137–38.
74   *Bunny had no idea*: "History of WWII Infiltrations into France," www.plan-sussex-1944 .net/anglais/pdf/infiltrations_into_france.pdf.
74   *"Here and there"*: OSS, 150–51.
74   *Stacy and he concocted*: Ibid., 152.
74   *On August 18*: Ibid., 154–55.
74   *At one point*: Ibid., 159.
74   *In Chartres itself*: Ibid., 153.
75   *"C'est la guerre"*: Ibid., 167.
75   *Stacy and his team*: Ibid., 188.
75   *He was thin*: OSS Colonel K. D. Mann to David Bruce, October 24, 1944, OSS declassified files on Stacy B. Lloyd, Jr.
75   *In his letter*: Colonel Mann to David Bruce, November 25, 1944, OSS declassified files on Stacy B. Lloyd, Jr.
75   *Stacy telegrammed*: SBL to Rachel Lloyd, telegram, December 6, 1944, OSGL.
75   *Ten days later*: SBL to Rachel Lloyd, January 16, 1945, OSGL.
76   *Valerie Churchill-Longman*: Mellon, *Reflections*, 210–13.
76   *"Weather was a weapon"*: Evan Andrews, "8 Things You May Not Know About the Battle of the Bulge," History, December 6, 2019, www.history.com/news/8-things-you-may -not-know-about-the-battle-of-the-bulge.
76   *Paul wrote later*: Mellon, *Reflections*, 219.
76   *By now, Paul had been*: Paul Mellon discharge record, OSS declassified files on Paul Mellon.
76   *He sailed on May 22*: Mellon, *Reflections*, 220.
77   *Certainly he felt*: Gordon, *American Style Legend*, 128.
77   *But there in Millwood*: Legion of Merit Recipients. Fred L. Borch III, *Medals for Soldiers and Airmen: Awards and Decorations of the United States Army and Air Force* (Jefferson: McFarland & Company, 2013).

7. THE CHASE AND THE WEDDING

78   *"They kept her body sitting up"*: Nelly Jo Thomas interview, March 10, 2015. All subsequent Thomas quotes in this chapter are from this interview.
79   *Mary, only forty-two*: McGuire, *Bollingen*, 114.
79   *Paul was "restless and irritated"*: Mellon, *Reflections*, 220.
80   *De Rougemont wrote*: McGuire, *Bollingen*, 76–79.
80   *He finishes his description*: Mellon, *Reflections*, 224.
80   *Whatever the nature*: Ibid., 224.
81   *"Bunny answered"*: Martin Filler, personal communication, July 2014.
81   *Mary guided him*: Mellon, *Reflections*, 165.
82   *Edward M. M. Warburg*: Derry Moore, phone conversation, November 25, 2014.
82   *In Virginia the pair*: Twelve letters in the Garden Library written by Paul Mellon (here-

after cited as PM) to Rachel Lambert between March 15 and April 6, 1948, when both were traveling (separately) are not available for quotation, spring 1948.

83   *"The bride will be"*: St. Louis Post-Dispatch, "Mrs. Rachel Lambert Lloyd Granted Divorce in Florida," March 9, 1948: "Mrs. Rachel Lambert Lloyd, daughter of Mr. and Mrs. Gerard B. Lampert [sic] today was granted a divorce from Stacey Barecroft [sic] Lloyd of Millwood, VA. Reports are current in social circles here that Mrs. Lloyd will marry Paul Mellon, Pittsburgh financier and son of the late Andrew W. Mellon. An agreement for property settlement and custody of the two children was not made public. The children are Stacey [sic] Lloyd III, 11, and Eliza. They [Stacy Lloyd Jr. and his wife Bunny Lloyd] were married in 1932 and separated last fall, her attorney said. Since then Mrs. Lloyd has been living with her parents in Palm Beach and Lantana."

83   *Sleepless nighttime hours*: PM to Rachel Lloyd, spring 1948.
84   *Paul felt*: PM to Rachel Lloyd, spring 1948.
84   *Paul cautioned her*: PM to Rachel Lloyd, spring 1948.
85   *Years later*: Marriage Service, stock printed form booklet, 5 by 7.5 inches, Reformed Church in America, standard service, contains church certificate, Paul Mellon, Rachel Lambert Mellon. Witnesses: Richard (?) L. Clopton, Dorothy M. (?) Parish, 24 E. Eighty-Second St., New York, NY, on the first day of May.
85   *In a shipboard letter*: PM to Rachel Lloyd, spring 1948.

8. THE MARRIAGE AND THE TROUBLES

86   *"When I came over the mountains"*: RLM memoir fragment, typed, n.d., OSGL.
87   *Randy wanted to make sure*: MKG 1995/1996.
88   *She had few illusions*: Tim Mellon, phone conversation, notes, January 17, 2019; MKG 1995/1996.
89   *The original plan*: RLM typed history of building the church [Trinity], October 15, 1978, OSGL.
90   *Travelers, he wrote*: NOTE RLM, introduction, printed pamphlet for Trinity Church; Donald D. Hook, "In Upperville, The Upper Crust: Trinity Church in Meade Parish, Upperville, Virginia," *Anglican and Episcopal History* 64, no. 3 (1995): 399–403, www .jstor.org/stable/42611728, accessed October 18, 2020.
90   *He underscored*: PM to RLM, March 17, 1953, OSGL.
90   *Then, as a man*: RLM reminiscence of the building program, manuscript and typed versions, 1948, OSGL.
91   *In 1957*: RLM reminiscence of her first meeting with Cristóbal Balenciaga in 1957 through Jean Schlumberger. "One time when I was in London he [Schlumberger] sent over the head fitter of Balenciaga to take my measurements and make a maquette. Later that fall he sent me two dresses and a ¾ length black coat for autumn in a fascinating black fabric. I have to admit I loved it. It was the beginning of going to Balenciaga." RLM, OSGL.
91   *A chastely beautiful*: Virginia Museum of Fine Arts, Schlumberger Exhibition Checklist 2018, accession number 2015.116, ca. 1952; the Verdura apple tree brooch was sold at the Sotheby's sale of RLM possessions in November 2014.
92   *In the 1990s I had begun:* Mellon, *Reflections*, 225.
92   *They had had*: MKG 1995/1996.
92   *Along with everyone else*: Sarah Booth Conroy, "The House in the Virginia Hunt Country That Is Home to the Paul Mellons," *The New York Times*, June 1, 1969.
92   *That article*: Julie Miller, *"The Crown*: The Scandal That Rocked Queen Elizabeth and Prince Philip's Marriage," *Vanity Fair*, December 9, 2017, www.vanityfair.com/hollywood /2017/12/queen-elizabeth-prince-philip-affair-eileen-parker-the-crown-netflix.
92   *"Our marriage"*: MKG 1995/1996.
92   *"Paul broke with Jung"*: Mellon, *Reflections*, 341–45.
92   *At the same time*: Ibid., 342.
93   *As for therapy*: Jonathan Metzl, "'Mother's Little Helper': The Crisis of Psychoanalysis and the Miltown Resolution," *Gender and History* 15, no. 2 (August 2003): 240–67.
93   *Instead, she continued*: MKG 1995/1996.
93   *The reasons he gave*: MKG 1995/1996.
93   *"Then I asked Paul"*: MKG 1995/1996.
94   *"Standing alone in the hall"*: RLM, memoir fragment beginning with this phrase, OSGL.

95   *Bunny saved*: PM correspondence with RLM 1952–55 is not available for quotation.
95   *What Bunny wanted*: Mellon, *Reflections*, 341–45; PM correspondence with RLM 1952–55, OSGL.
95   *He made at least one more unguarded plea*: Ibid.
96   *In addition to being courageous*: MacKubin letters, OSGL.
96   *In* Reflections: Mellon, *Reflections*, 224–26. Also see Burton Hersh, *The Mellon Family*, 407, quoting RLM: "'Paul and I married because I felt I could help him,' Bunny states now, flatly. 'We became partners to help one another, and we remained that.'"
96   *Bunny told me that after the rift*: MKG 1995/1996.
97   *"Dorcas was fabulous-looking"*: Kathe Gates McCoy, phone call and email notes and follow-ups, February 16, 2018, May 8, 2019.
97   *"When my younger sister"*: Lucie Kinsolving, phone call and email notes and follow-ups, May 2019.
98   *When Paul was eighty-four*: John Russell, "Paul Mellon's Life in Art: Understated, Oversubscribed," *The New York Times*, March 10, 1991; PM to Rachel Lloyd, spring 1948, not available for quotation, OSGL.
99   *For Paul, being "careful"*: Mellon, *Reflections*, 225.
99   *About Hubert she wrote*: RLM, private travel journals, mostly undated and unpaginated, kept by RLM beginning in the 1970s.
100 *Bunny flew off to Tunisia*: RLM travel diary entries, Givenchy notebook number 2, 5½ by 9¾ inches, covered in a blue-and-white flowered fabric, 31–35. One of three similar notebooks.

9. FINDING THE WAY

103 *The intrepid Dorothy McCardle*: Dorothy McCardle, "Mellons Give Million Dollar Party," *Milwaukee Journal*, June 22, 1961, and "A Mere Million for a Deb Party," *The Baltimore Sun*, July 16, 1961.
104 *"Everybody always spoke"*: Billy Baldwin with Michael Gardine, *Billy Baldwin: An Autobiography* (New York: Little Brown, 1985), 317.
104 *Among others at Eliza's ball*: Amy Fine Collins, "A Taste for Living," *Vanity Fair*, August 18, 2014, www.vanityfair.com/style/2014/09/niki-de-gunzburg-profile.
105 *"Son accent est incontestablement"*: Madame Bourdet-Pléville to RLM, March 8, 1961, OSGL.
105 *A French friend of Hubert*: Marie-Hélène Bouilloux-Lafont to RLM, November 11, 1962, OSGL.
105 *In Paris, her mother's friends*: Madame Bourdet-Pléville to RLM, November 10, 1960, OSGL.
106 *Alix Clark, a classmate*: Alix Clark Diana, phone and email, May 7, 2019.
107 *She had "big dark beautiful cow eyes"*: Kathe Gates McCoy, phone and email notes, February 16, 2018, and May 8, 2019.
107 *We had, of course, discovered*: Queen Elizabeth and Prince Philip visited Oak Spring on October 20, 1957; the queen, a noted Thoroughbred breeder and racehorse enthusiast, wanted to see Paul Mellon's stables.
107 *A month or so before*: RLM memoir fragment, n.d., n.p., regarding the queen's planned visit and RLM's worries about her own responses.
108 *But Eliza caught*: Nancy Collins to MKG, April 2019.
108 *Eliza was essentially indifferent*: Derry Moore, phone notes, May 2019.
109 *Her mother had forcibly dragged*: Alain-Fournier (Henri-Alban Fournier), *Le Grand Meaulnes* (first English publication 1928), was reissued in 1972 in an illustrated limited edition (Paris: Paris Editions/Michèle Trinckvel), of which RLM purchased twelve copies.
109 *The day after Eliza's party*: Evangeline Bruce to RLM, June 2, 1961, OSGL.
109 *Bunny and Evangeline*: Conversation with Janet Bruce, February 7, 2019.
109 *Bunny was grateful*: RLM to EB, n.d., OSGL.
110 *Billy Baldwin*: Baldwin with Gardine, *Billy Baldwin*.
110 *He noticed*: Ibid., 318.
111 *When she drove off*: Evangeline Bruce to RLM, June 2, 1961, OSGL.
112 *"D.C. was power"*: Kathe Gates McCoy, phone and email notes, February 16, 2018, and May 8, 2019.

112   *By the time that nineteen-year-old*: The affair began in 1959, according to McCoy, phone conversation, May 8, 2019.

113   *"One day"*: Lucie Kinsolving to MKG, phone and email notes, May 29, 2019.

113   *Bunny told me*: MKG 1995/1996.

114   *"The only person"*: RLM to MKG, early January 1996, less than a month after Evangeline's death on December 14, 1995.

10. LIFE IN PICTURES: DEGAS—AND ROTHKO AND BRAQUE

116   *The description*: M. Knoedler & Co., Painting Sales Book #14, 373, July 1948, 362 Worth Avenue Gallery, West Palm Beach [Florida], CA2928 88. Drawing by Edgar H. G. Degas, 9½-by-12 inches, *Jockey*, 575-, stamped "LL Degas," sold to Mrs. Stacey Floyd [*Floyd* later corrected to *Lloyd* in entry and entered correctly in index]; the entry was changed on January 31, 1949, to include "now Mrs. Paul Mellon."

116   *The inscription on the packaging*: *Seated Jockey*, black chalk drawing, 12⅜ by 9¾ inches unframed, Virginia Museum of Fine Arts #99.104. On the envelope, dated VMFA 6/17/99, the date of accession, the drawing is described as "gift to Mr. Mellon from Mrs. Mellon," n.d.

117   *In 1955*: Mellon, *Reflections*, 274.

117   *In these curiously constructed creatures*: Ibid., 274.

117   *On February 3, 1956*: John Walker, February 3, 1956, "memo for the files," Curatorial Files, National Gallery of Art: "Mr. Mellon telephoned me this morning and we discussed the Degas waxes offered by Knoedler & Company. Mr. Mellon authorized me to make an offer through Mr. Coe Kerr of Knoedler & Company for these waxes."

118   *"At waist height, unframed"*: William Waller to MKG, text message, February 18, 2018.

119   *Bunny's take on a garden*: RLM, "Green Flowers and Herb Trees," *Vogue*, December 1965.

119   *They didn't write letters*: Paul Richard, "Paul Mellon, Reveries & Riches: Stepping Down as Chairman of the National Gallery," *The Washington Post*, May 2, 1985.

119   *Paul told the Mellon family biographer*: Burton Hersh, *Mellon Family*, 428–29.

119   *The art critic Meyer Schapiro*: Meyer Schapiro and Milton S. Fox, consulting ed., *Cézanne* (New York: Harry N. Abrams, 1952), 9–10.

119   *Paul's agent at the Sotheby's auction*: Mellon, *Reflections*, 272.

120   *"I think it is often"*: John Walker, *Self-Portrait with Donors: Confessions of an Art Collector* (Boston: Little, Brown, 1969), 192.

120   *She could always fly out*: Lunch with Bruce Budd, friend and RLM's interior decorator for thirteen years, July 2014.

120   *As a talisman*: See Lucia Tongiorgi Tomasi with Tony Willis, *Paul and Bunny Mellon: Visual Biographies, The Trompe l'Oeil Paintings at Oak Spring, Virginia* (Upperville, VA: OSGF, 2020), 54, which illustrates all Renard's works in the greenhouse vestibule, painted in 1959–60 to represent "the *studiolo* of a Renaissance scholar and student of the science of nature."

120   *The dilemma that Bunny lived out*: John Berger et al., *Ways of Seeing* (New York: Viking, 1973), 46.

121   *"The Mellons"*: Walker, *Self-Portrait with Donors*, 192.

121   *She turned instead*: Gordon, *American Style Legend*, 405.

121   *Over lunch*: Telephone interview and notes, Derry Moore, November 25, 2014.

122   *That year, Paul and Bunny*: *French Painting from the Collections of Mr. and Mrs. Paul Mellon and Mrs. Mellon Bruce, Twenty-Fifth Anniversary Exhibition* (Washington, DC: National Gallery of Art, 1966).

122   *John Walker thanked the three donors*: John Walker, *Self-Portrait with Donors*, "Introduction."

122   *As one reporter wrote*: Ymelda Dixon, "Lord Clark Star of the Triple Header," Washington, D.C., *Evening Star*, November 24, 1969.

122   *"Chaque collection doit avoir"*: Hubert de Givenchy (hereafter cited as Givenchy) to RLM, June 30, 1971, OSGL.

123   *In his first letter*: Givenchy to RLM, October 17, 1969.

124   *Their daughter, Béatrice Badin*: Jean-Noël Liaut, *Hubert de Givenchy: Entre vies et légendes* (B. Grasset, 2000).

124   *By April 20 of that year*: Museum of Modern Art, "Memorial to Mark Rothko," www

.moma.org/momaorg/shared/pdfs/docs/press_archives/4441/releases/MOMA_1970_Jan
-June_0038_39.pdf.

124 *But Bunny, in telling me*: MKG 1995/1996.

124 *Hubert recalled*: "'One day Mrs. Mellon sent me a postcard of a marvelous Rothko painting from the collection of the architect Philip Johnson . . .' Soon after, in February 1970,
Rothko committed suicide. Mrs. Mellon wrote to Givenchy and asked if he would like
to visit Rothko's studio next time he came to New York." Susan Moore, "Hubert de
Givenchy (1927–2018)," *Apollo: The International Art Magazine*, March 13, 2018; www
.apollo-magazine.com/hubert-de-givenchy-1927-2018/.

124 *"Canvases were in a pile"*: MKG 1995/1996.

125 *Givenchy, with a much smaller budget*: Moore, "Hubert de Givenchy (1927–2018)."

125 *The memory stuck*: MKG 1995/1996.

125 *"I kept calling [to give them the numbers]"*: MKG 1995/1996.

125 *"How much I liked"*: Givenchy to RLM, postmarked September 11, 1970, Mac Griswold
translation, OSGL.

126 *These two paintings would eventually be sold*: Marion Maneker, "Private Sale of Two Rothkos and a Diebenkorn from Bunny Mellon Estate Estimated at $300m," *Art Market
Monitor*, September 5, 2014, www.artmarketmonitor.com/2014/09/05/private-sale-of
-two-rothkos-and-a-diebenkorn-from-bunny-mellon-estate-estimated-at-300m/.

126 *"The lawyers came after me"*: MKG 1995/1996.

126 *They also took a commission*: Grace Glueck, "Rothko Art Dispute Ends Quietly After Fifteen Years," *The New York Times*, August 20, 1986, www.nytimes.com/1986/08/20/arts
/rothko-art-dispute-ends-quietly-after-15-years.html.

126 *After yet another visit to Marlborough*: RLM entries, Givenchy notebook, number 2 of 3,
5½ by 9¾ inches, covered in a blue-and-white flowered fabric, 31–35.

127 *She continued*: Ibid.

127 *Eliza told me*: Eliza Lloyd Moore, conversation, 1995.

127 *At once Hubert organized a trip to Provence*: Blue flower-print diary, travel entry from
Beauvais to Maeght, May 30, 1971, RLM (Givenchy) 20–25, OSGL. All subsequent
RLM quotations in this chapter are from this diary entry.

128 *Accompanying the two*: MKG interviews with Barrie McIntyre, archivist of Colefax &
Fowler, September 2015.

128 *But in 2012, Hubert told*: Moore, "Hubert de Givenchy (1927–2018)."

11. BUNNY AND THE MODERN MUSEUM

130 *"Mrs. M. hung it in Eliza's quarters"*: Tony Willis to MKG, spring 2018.

131 *Joseph J. Krakora*: Krakora, phone interview notes (hereafter cited as Krakora), March 5,
2018.

132 *The Sculls were fresh*: Anna Louie Sussman, "How the Scull Sale Changed the Art Market," April 26, 2017, Art Market, www.artsy.net/article/artsy-editorial-three-ways
-single-auction-1973-changed-art-market.

132 *Paul Mellon, president of the gallery*: Paul Richard, "Mid-Century Exhibit: A First for the
National Gallery of Art," *The Washington Post*, August 29, 1973.

132 *The exhibition*: Ibid.

133 *Paul Richard was not an admirer*: Paul Richard, phone interview and emails, March 17,
2018.

133 *Richard notes that the NGA*: Ibid.

133 *After Martin Luther King, Jr., was assassinated*: Denise Kersten Wills, "'People Were out of
Control': Remembering the 1968 Riots," *Washingtonian*, April 1, 2008, www.washingtonian
.com/2008/04/01/people-were-out-of-control-remembering-the-1968-riots/.

133 *"The NGA was saying"*: Paul Richard, phone interview and emails, March 17, 2018.

133 *She had flown Jackie Kennedy*: RLM account, "Martin Luther King's Funeral," 2003,
OSGL.

134 *"No food allowed"*: "The Mellons Give a Dinner at National Gallery," *The New York Times*,
January 27, 1970.

134 *When Russia sent priceless Impressionists*: Dorothy McCardle and Sally Quinn, "The
Marking of a Historic Occasion," *The Washington Post*, March 30, 1973.

135   *Genevra Higginson*: Genevra Higginson, phone interview and notes (hereafter cited as Higginson), April 3, 2018.

135   *Joseph Krakora thought* Treasure Houses: Krakora, March 5, 2018.

135   *"The Gallery had invited"*: Higginson, April 3, 2018.

135   *One Friday night*: Betty Cuniberti, "'Treasure Houses of Britain Exhibit': Royal Fever Has Them Reeling on the Potomac," *Los Angeles Times*, November 4, 1985, www.latimes.com/archives/la-xpm-1985-11-04-vw-211-story.html.

136   *When the prince and princess of Wales*: Krakora, March 5, 2018.

137   *in 1985, Leonard*: MKG 1995/1996.

137   *"He always knows just"*: Ymelda Dixon, "Mellons Hosts at Gallery Lunch," *The Washington Evening Star* and *Washington Daily News*, September 16, 1972.

137   *"Let the painting"*: Jacqueline Trescott, "Art Explained: Mark Leithauser, Chief of Design, National Gallery of Art," *The Washington Post*, February 19, 2011.

138   *He estimated that*: Paul Richard, "Mellon Gives 93 Art Works: Gift to National Gallery Includes 50 Paintings," *The Washington Post*, January 28, 1983.

139   *Mary Morton, described Bruce's attitude*: Mary Morton, "Ailsa Mellon Bruce: Collector and Patron of the National Gallery" (hereafter cited as Morton), a talk given by Mary Morton, curator of French paintings at the National Gallery of Art, at the Legion of Honor, San Francisco, March 29, 2014.

139   *About Ailsa Bruce*: Ibid.

139   *"Mrs. Jack [Gardner]" reveled*: Isabella Stewart Gardner Museum, "Collection," www.gardnermuseum.org/experience/collection.

140   *Louisine took the lead*: Alice Cooney Frelinghuysen, Gary Tinterow, et al., *Splendid Legacy: The Havemeyer Collection* (New York: Metropolitan Museum of Art, 1993).

140   *Jane later recalled*: Carol Vogel, "An Art Collection Grows on a Maryland Farm," *The New York Times*, August 18, 2003, www.nytimes.com/2003/08/18/arts/an-art-collection-grows-on-a-maryland-farm.html.

140   *In talking about the NGA's East Building*: Georgiana McCabe interview, February 2, 2018.

141   *She pointed out*: Higginson, April 3, 2018.

141   *Evangeline Bruce reported*: EB to RLM, May 16, no year, letterhead 1405 34th Street NW, DC (Bruce address), OSGL.

142   *Jackie Kennedy was there*: Barbara Gamarekian, "Capital Gives All for Art," *The New York Times*, May 31, 1978.

143   *Such apparently "flawless performances of effortlessness"*: Robert Motherwell with Robert Bigelow and John E. Scofield, "A Journal of Collaboration Presented by E. A. Carmean, Jr.: Reconciliation Elegy," quoted by Mary Camille Beckman in "Effort and Effortlessness in Motherwell's 'Reconciliation Elegy,'" *Michigan Quarterly Review*, January 15, 2014, *MQR* blog.

143   *Motherwell also explained*: Beckman, "Effort and Effortlessness in Motherwell's 'Reconciliation Elegy.'"

143   *I. M. Pei understood*: I. M. Pei to Bunny Mellon, January 12, 1979, OSGL.

143   *But still earlier*: Carter Wiseman. *I. M. Pei: A Profile in American Architecture* (New York: Harry N. Abrams, 2001).

144   *She had indeed*: RLM to I. M. Pei, February 6, 1997; I. M. Pei to RLM, October 1978 and December 17, 1996, all OSGL.

145   *Sometime in the 1970s*: "Billy Baldwin Remembers Heaven, Hell, and Cole Porter," *Interview*, n.d. The artist Brigid Berlin (1939–2020), who worked the front desk at Andy Warhol's Factory for thirty-five years, was also a staff member of Warhol's *Interview*, transcribing jaunty interviews such as this one between I. M. Pei and Billy Baldwin. Sometimes she took credit herself under the nickname Brigid Polk (because she freely administered sizable "pokes" of amphetamines to all who asked).

12. JOHNNY AND THE JEWELS

146   *Sexy and feline*: MKG 1995/1996.

147   *Once, she told me*: MKG 1995/1996.

147   *Bunny went home*: MKG 1995/1996.

147   *"Darling," said Rosie*: MKG 1995/1996.

147   *"Finally," said Bunny*: MKG 1995/1996.

147 *The Tiffany order book*: Visit with Allen Nissim, The Tiffany Salon, Tiffany & Co., to view the "Tiffany Salon Books," 1996–2002, which record not only the individual orders but also the commentary between Tiffany staff and PM and RLM. The Virginia Museum of Fine Arts includes 361 Schlumberger items (drawings, jewelry, and decorative objects), gifts of RLM evaluated in 2015 at $9.5 million.

148 *"He always wore black"*: MKG 1995/1996.

149 *who measured her*: Bunny memoir fragment, OSGL.

149 *Later that year*: Bunny memoir fragment, OSGL.

149 *"The seamstress fussed"*: Ibid.; all RLM quotes in the next five paragraphs are from the same document.

151 *Another time, Mlle Tamisier*: Bunny's remembrance that begins "Life has been good to me," OSGL; Igor Uria Zubizarreta, collections director, Cristóbal Balenciaga Museum, *Rachel L. Mellon Collection*, exhibition catalogue (Getaria, Spain, 2017), 23–24, for Balenciaga invoices and wardrobe costs, 25 for Tamisier instructions. See also exhibition *Rachel L. Mellon Collection*, May 27, 2017–January 25, 2018, 21–45.

151 *"A solitary rack"*: RLM, "The Brown Linen Dress," in Victor Skrebneski and Laura Jacobs, *The Art of Haute Couture* (New York: Abbeville Press, 1995), 20–21.

153 *Catherine the Great*: Diana Scarisbrick, "Imperial Splendour: Catherine II and Her Jewelry," *All That Glitters* (Sotheby's blog), October 25, 2016, www.sothebys.com/en /news-video/blogs/all-blogs/all-that-glitters/2016/10/imperial-splendour-catherine -the-great-and-her-jewllery.html.

154 *Nancy thought it would be*: Nancy Collins to MKG, conversation, December 2017.

155 *"We would go to a house"*: RLM to Walt Helmer, October 5, 2010.

156 *"Johnny is a realist"*: Vivienne Becker, *The Telegraph*, London, November 21, 2013, www .telegraph.co.uk/luxury/jewellery/16106/jean-schlumberger-the-first-rock-star.html.

157 *"So much love darling"*: Schlumberger to RLM, Bisdary House, Gourbeyre, Guadeloupe, March 10, 1974, OSGL.

157 *"Johnny and I learned"*: MKG 1995/1996.

157 *"I know how much"*: Janette Mahler to RLM, June 25, 1987, OSGL.

158 *"But you know"*: Luc Bouchage to RLM, September 7, 1987, OSGL.

158 *"I am sure you can"*: Luc Bouchage to RLM, March 18, 1989, OSGL.

158 *She had offered*: Landmarks Preservation Commission, June 7, 1988, Designation List 204 LP-1630, http://s-media.nyc.gov/agencies/lpc/lp/1630.pdf; RLM to Luc Bouchage and Bouchage to RLM, n.d., Wednesday night, three pages with her sketch of a proposed addition to Schlumberger's house. Bouchage drove up to Hyde Park with Niki (de Saint Phalle) and is "full of ideas. looked at every stoop from Manhattan to Hyde Park." The house elevation as sketched by RLM has a garden. Mr. Engel is the builder. Sketch shows a Dutch door, a greenhouse attached to the wall, windows, steps, and bush, OSGL.

159 *He should have one counter*: Ibid.

13. CLOTHES AND THE MAN

160 *"Minds that create"*: RLM, memoir fragment that begins "Life has been good to me," OSGL.

161 *"Sometimes they need"*: MKG phone conversation with William Waller, February 18, 2018.

162 *Once, when she knew*: Bouilloux-Lafont correspondence, OSGL.

162 *When I asked Bunny*: MKG 1995/1996.

163 *"There were two little purses"*: Phone notes and emails: MKG, phone, email, and personal interviews, Camilla Chandon de Briailles, 2015–18.

163 *Her relationship*: PM to RLM, April 5, 1952, OSGL.

163 *In my few conversations*: Notes, Tuffy Lloyd, summer 2014; phone conversations, Tim Mellon notes, January 17, 2019.

164 *The pages were*: Givenchy to RLM, October 1970, OSGL.

164 *He fell for the Manoir*: "Château du Jonchet," Wikipedia, https://en.wikipedia.org /wiki/Château_du_Jonchet; Mitchell Owens, "Hubert de Givenchy's Manoir du Jonchet Is as Breathtaking as His Designs," *Architectural Digest*, August 6, 2018, https:// www.architecturaldigest.com/story/hubert-de-givenchys-manoir-du-jonchet-is-as -breathtaking-as-his-designs.

166 *But why did she order*: Invoice, Alice Cadolle, Paris dressmaker, 14 Rue Cambon,

made-to-order girdles, brassieres, all-in-ones, negligees, lingerie, bathing suits, to RLM, April 30, 1980, OSGL.

167 *In 1970*: Janette Mahler to RLM, n.d., 1970, Givenchy papers, OSGL.
167 *Bunny was a hands-on teacher*: Nelly Jo Thomas interview, March 10, 2015.
168 *She knew Bunny's heartaches*: Ibid.
168 *Although Bunny might*: Nancy Collins, conversation with MKG, July 2018.
168 *But most of all*: RLM, personal journal, *"Je suis si heureuse."*
169 *Then he says*: Givenchy to RLM, February 27, 1973; translation by MKG and Lindsay Nolting, OSGL.
169 *In September 1986*: Givenchy to RLM, September 24, 1986, OSGL.
169 *"I am not happy"*: Givenchy to RLM, n.d. but shortly after his mother's death on September 10, 1976, OSGL.
169 *"For hours on end"*: Carol Mongo, "Paris Fashion Homage to Givenchy," *Paris Voice*, June 1995.
170 *"He's my good friend"*: *The Washington Post*, September 16, 1970.
170 *"And that a shock"*: RLM entry, the first entry in a small blue notebook, OSGL.
170 *The first "Actual Black Male Supermodel"*: Bernadine Morris, "A Festive Presentation of Givenchy's Styles," *The New York Times*, April 29, 1976.
171 *"She'd come in"*: https://archive.nytimes.com/www.nytimes.com/books/first/h/haden -party.html.
171 *"His sensitivity"*: RLM journal entry (blue flower-print diary), October 2, 1970, OSGL.
171 *"See you this evening"*: Givenchy to RLM, postcard, n.d., OSGL.
171 *"And as gay men"*: MKG and Derry Moore phone conversation, notes, December 12, 2017.
172 *"You are a marvelous friend"*: RLM to Givenchy, September 23, 2010, OSGL.

14. AN AMERICAN PASTORAL

176 *Then, if she wasn't*: Baldwin with Gardine, *Billy Baldwin*, 320.
176 *While Paul's activities*: Mellon, *Reflections*, 259.
177 *In one of her garden notebooks*: RLM, garden notebook 4, OSGL.
178 *He added that for Bunny Mellon*: John Barnes, phone interview, March 25, 2014.
179 *Tuffy told me*: Interview with Stacy B. "Tuffy" Lloyd III, July 10, 2014.
181 *"After dinner my mother-in-law"*: Eliza Maugham to RLM, from London, n.d. but after 1957, when Queen Elizabeth and Prince Philip visited Oak Spring, OSGL.
182 *rightly described as being about "nothing"*: Nigel Gosling, "English Genius in Flower," *The Observer*, December 20, 1964, 15.
182 *For the English art historian*: Martin Myrone, "George Stubbs—Between Market, Nature and Art," in *George Stubbs 1724–1806: Science into Art*, 2010, ed. Herbert W. Rott (Munich: Bayerische Staatsgemäldesammlungen, Prestel Verlag), 9–15.
182 *"Is it cut up"*: RLM, "Garden Notebook Nine" in the series of photocopies as sent to me by Nancy Collins, OSGL.
182 *"This changes"*: RLM, garden notebook 9, OSGL.
182 *"There seemed to be"*: Paul Mellon, "A Collector Recollects: Remarks by Paul Mellon at the Opening of the Exhibition, *Painting in England, 1700–1850*" (Richmond: Virginia Museum of Fine Arts), 1963, privately printed.
184 *The place still felt*: MKG 1995/1996.
184 *"It included a record"*: Phone interview with Frederick "Skip" Glascock. Jr., September 18, 2018.
184 *"Paul, Paul, come over here!"*: Ibid.
185 *"He would come down"*: Interview with William Keyser, Jr., March 10, 2015.
185 *In Meryl Gordon's biography*: Gordon, *American Style Legend*, 196.

15. SAY IT WITH FLOWERS: THE WALLED GARDEN

189 *They reduced the height*: RLM, "Green Flowers and Herb Trees," *Vogue*, December 1965.
190 *Paul agreed*: PM to RLM, April 3, 1952, OSGL.
191 *"When I was just married"*: MKG 1995/1996.
192 *"Then Babe called me"*: MKG 1995/1996.
192 *By 1948*: Inventory of Residence, "Apple Hill," Millwood, Virginia, February 10, 1948, OSGL.

193   *On seeing*: RLM, garden notes, two pages, n.d. but probably the 1960s, when David Bruce served as ambassador to Great Britain (1961–69). List of twenty-one flowering plants.

193   *Still later*: RLM blue personal diary, July 1963, OSGL.

193   *It was actually the first*: Madeline Huntting Cook Dixon (1890–1976) was Bunny's godmother. Bunny's mother, Rachel Parkhill Lowe Lambert (1889–1978), was godmother to Francis Cook Dixon (1921–1997), Madeline Dixon's third child. Both women had attended the Farmington School in Connecticut. The prominent Huntting and Cook families of Sag Harbor owned several houses in North Haven (then part of Sag Harbor), in one of which lived Madeline Dixon and her husband, Theodore (1883–1959). Bunny's parents rented summer houses in East Hampton and Southampton when she was a child but doubtless also visited the Dixons, since the mothers were close and remained so. Thanks to Christopher P. Dixon. For the mention of Bunny's godmother, see RLM, "Preface," *An Oak Spring Sylva: A Selection of the Rare Books on Trees in the Oak Spring Garden Library* (Upperville, VA: Oak Spring Garden Library, 1989), Sandra Raphael, descriptor, xv–xvii, xv.

193   *She also remembered*: RLM, garden book 2, entry 4, OSGL.

193   *"It was during these hours"*: RLM, typescript reminiscence that begins "It was a summer's day," which covers the Kennedy visit to Osterville and tree planting in New Hampshire with her grandfather Lowe, OSGL.

193   *At his waterfront property*: In 1995–96, Bunny, with the assistance of Perry Wheeler, designed and installed a garden and landscape that included shadblow and bayberry plantings, for a total cost of $9,924.71, OSGL.

195   *The outlines*: *The Brick House, Upperville, Virginia* (privately printed for Oak Spring: Upperville, VA, n.d.), 4–5, OSGL; Rokeby, *Oak Spring Landscape*, 168, OSGL.

195   *Before the taste*: RLM, garden book 6, 11–14, OSGL.

196   *He also always had*: Nancy Collins, personal communication, August 2018.

196   *"What she is really doing"*: RLM to Perry Wheeler, n.d., Perry H. Wheeler Collection, Archive of American Gardens (hereafter cited as AAG), Smithsonian Institution Archives.

196   *She gave*: Conroy, "The House in Virginia Hunt Country."

197   *She offered him*: Sam Kashner, "A Clash of Camelots," *Vanity Fair*, September 2009; Wikipedia, "The Death of a President."

198   *Bunny once told*: Tony Willis, personal communication, July 2014.

199   *And after all those*: RLM, garden notebook 10, "notes for Garden Book," 27, OSGL.

199   *Bunny often mentions*: Ibid.

199   *Self-sown everywhere*: Poppies from Gerald van der Kemp at Giverny, RLM, garden book 10, OSGL; Gerald and Florence van der Kemp correspondence, OSGL; Paul Lewis, "Gerald Van der Kemp, 89, Versailles' Restorer," *New York Times*, January 15, 2002, www.nytimes.com/2002/01/15/arts/gerald-van-der-kemp-89-versailles-restorer.html.

200   *And then there was Everett Hicks*: Everett C. Hicks, *The Washington Post*, September 22, 2011; Emily Langer, "A Local Life: Everett Hicks, 93, Arborist Who Cared for Mellon Family's Trees," *The Washington Post*, October 18, 2011.

200   *Hicks's arbor*: SL to RLL, March 22, 1943, OSGL.

200   *Rokeby's is slightly over*: Greenhouse square footage from gardener Todd Lloyd, August 30, 2018, OSGF.

201   *"I prefer"*: Charlotte Moss, "The Eloquence of Silence," *The New York Times Style Magazine*, June 12, 2014, www.nytimes.com/2014/06/12/t-magazine/rachel-bunny-mellon-final-interview-virginia-estate.html.

201   *Bunny was once again following*: See Judith B. Tankard, *The Gardens of Ellen Biddle Shipman* (New York: Harry N. Abrams, 1997).

203   *In her address to the school*: "The Profile of an Alumna," *Foxcroft* magazine, Summer 1990.

205   *Bunny's niece, Lily Norton*: Phone conversation, summer 2019.

205   *However, Carnegie and her husband*: Notice of purchase by John Zanft, *The New York Times*, February 3, 1937.

205   *"We agreed"*: Paula Dietz, "The Private World of a Great Gardener," *The New York Times*, June 3, 1982; RLM caption draft for a Hattie Carnegie exhibition at the New York Fashion Institute of Technology, January 23, 1996, OSGL.

205   *Bunny Lloyd designed a garden*: Appleton P. Clark, Jr., to Emily J. Lambert, June 12,

1934, 464 acres, Deed Book 140, 46, Warrenton, VA (property is in Fauquier and Loudoun Counties); Lily Norton, phone conversation, summer 2019.

206   *She wrote that every garden*: RLM, garden notebook 10, OSGL.

206   *In his memoir*: Mellon, *Reflections*, 270–71.

206   *Dr. Bruce Horten*: Horten, phone interview, June 2019; MKG 1995/1996; Gordon, *American Style Legend*, 336.

206   *John Baskett*: Baskett email to MKG, July 7, 2014.

207   *Two typed pages*: Typed résumé, two pages, OSGL.

208   *"Finally," she wrote*: RLM, garden book 9, 14, OSGL.

16. WALKING THROUGH THE HOUSE

209   *"I walked into"*: Interview and notes, Georgiana McCabe, December 2014.

209   *"On another visit"*: Ibid.

210   *Georgiana had never forgotten*: Ibid.

210   *"Mrs. hired families"*: Nancy Collins, personal communication, January 2015.

211   *Sam Kasten*: Phone interview, notes, November 1, 2018.

212   *Bunny Williams*: Phone interview, notes, October 6, 2014.

213   *Bill Keyser, the Oak Spring head painter*: Interview, notes, December 28, 2015.

214   *Paul did the washing-up*: John Baskett interview, notes, November 4, 2015.

214   *Bunny was fascinated*: RLM, n.d., two pages: her hand, a Christmas note, recipient unknown (if sent).

214   *"Design is about discipline and reality"*: Christopher Mason, "Master Class: Too Much Beige: Interior Decorator Has Some Strong Words for Young Designers," *New York*, April 12, 2004, http://nymag.com/nymetro/shopping/homedesign/features/n_10144/; Bruce Weber, "Albert Hadley, High Society's Decorator, Dies at 91," *The New York Times*, March 31, 2012, www.nytimes.com/2012/03/31/us/albert-hadley-interior-decorator-to-high-society-dies-at-91.html.s.

215   *Candy Camp, a Foxcroft classmate*: Mac Griswold, "The Art That Paul Mellon Couldn't Part With," *The New Yorker*, February 15, 1999, 29–30; 1997 interview with Paul Mellon.

216   *To the right of the fireplace*: Tim Mellon, Paul's son, remembers the bar door as always open; phone interview and notes, January 12, 2019.

216   *No, said Feuillatte:* Nicolas Feuillatte correspondence, 1977–2004, OSGL.

217   *Babs told me*: Phone interview, notes, July 2014.

218   *"They are some of the finest wares"*: Phone interview, emails, notes, with Errol Manners, E & H Manners, London, December 15, 2015.

17. BUNNY AND JACKIE: A FRIENDSHIP

223   *They met in 1958*: MKG 1995/1996; RLM, "Jacqueline Bouvier Kennedy: A Reminiscence," in *Jacqueline Kennedy: The White House Years, Selections from the John F. Kennedy Library and Museum* (hereafter cited as *White House Years*) (New York: Metropolitan Museum of Art and Bulfinch Press, 2001), 13.

224   *The two women*: Seymour M. Hersh, *The Dark Side of Camelot* (New York: Little, Brown, 1997) 226–46.

224   *Kennedy biographer Sally Bedell Smith*: Sally Bedell Smith, *Grace and Power: The Private World of the Kennedy White House* (New York: Random House, 2004), xxiv.

224   *Bunny said that Jackie*: RLM to George Trescher, October 26, 1995, OSGL.

225   *Bunny answered him*: Ibid.

225   *Bunny contrived not to understand*: Ibid.

225   *The two shared*: Bedell Smith, *Grace and Power*, 117.

225   *J. B. West, chief usher*: J. B. West, *Upstairs at the White House: My Life with the First Ladies* (New York: Coward, McCann & Geoghegan, 1973), 217.

225   *Billy Baldwin, albeit a shameless gusher*: Baldwin with Gardine, *Billy Baldwin*, 322.

226   *Sally Bedell Smith quotes Jackie*: Bedell Smith, *Grace and Power*, 6.

226   *Billy Baldwin, who saw Bunny at work*: Baldwin with Gardine, *Billy Baldwin*, 320.

226   *In 2004 in the opening essay*: Arthur M. Schlesinger, Jr., "Jacqueline Kennedy in the White House," *White House Years*, 3.

226   *One small but bracing example*: MKG 1995/1996.

227   *The historian William Seale*: Phone conversation, notes, December 9, 2014.

229 *Bunny told me*: MKG 1995/1996.

229 *Repeatedly in her letters over the years*: Jacqueline Onassis to RLM, June 21, 1969, OSGL, with permission.

229 *She classed her deception*: Phone conversation, notes, with RLM about Edwards, July 2011.

229 *Joseph Campbell, the twentieth-century writer on myth*: Phone interview with the writer Wendy Gimbel, conversations on Jacqueline Kennedy Onassis, Campbell, and the semiotics of clothes and the nature of fame, during the summer months from 1995 to the present.

229 *The two women often celebrated*: Poems of Emily Dickinson Selected and Annotated with a Commentary by Louis Untermeyer and Illustrated with Drawings by Helen Sewell (New York: Limited Editions Club, 1952), inscribed, OSGL.

230 *"Nobody really notices"*: Phone call, notes, Sam Kasten, November 1, 2018.

231 *Bunny and Jackie often turned*: Jacqueline Kennedy Onassis (hereafter cited as JKO) to RLM, April 10, 1976, OSGL.

231 *Another note from Jackie*: JKO to RLM, n.d. but found in RLM's 1977 daily diary, OSGL.

231 *When in 1989*: JKO to RLM, n.d. but 1989 from internal evidence, OSGL.

231 *In turn, after 1979*: Two-page memorandum, n.d. but after 1981, for Red Gate Farm, with details for the main house and barn surrounds, the hillside by the garage, general pruning and planting, planting, editing, and clearing for views from the patio and behind the main house, OSGL; RLM to JKO, n.d., re: importance of a bed, and JKO to RLM, n.d., both OSGL.

232 *Only Bunny could have thought*: Gordon, *American Style Legend*, 244–45.

232 *One day these gems*: Rachel Garrahan, "Celebrating a Jeweler's Legacy," *The New York Times*, March 24, 2017.

233 *Bunny considered white*: Nancy Collins conversation about the significance for Bunny of white and blue, January 2015; Hamish Bowles, "Defining Style: Jacqueline Kennedy's White House Years," *White House Years*, 59.

233 *Wendy, who knew Jackie well*: Wendy Gimbel, conversations on JKO.

18. A GARDEN FOR THE PRESIDENT

235 *"The President was precise"*: RLM, garden notebook 9, OSGL.

235 *Columnist Joseph Alsop*: Joseph W. Alsop, recorded interview by Elspeth Rostow, June 18, 1964 (25), John F. Kennedy Library Oral History Program.

237 *Bunny's detailed planting plans*: "Planting Plan, West Garden, Executive Mansion, Washington, D.C.," Scale ¼" = 1–0', November 13, 1962 (rev. March 4, 1963), OSGL, reproduced pp. 54–55 in William Seale, "President Kennedy's Garden: Rachel Lambert Mellon's Redesign of the White House Rose Garden," *Journal of the White House Historical Association* (now *White House History Quarterly*), #38 (hereafter cited as Seale, #38), 38–66.

237 *She herself was well aware*: Perry Wheeler to RLM, March 8, 1962, OSGL.

237 *Bunny might have thought back*: RLM, five-page memoir fragment, n.d., beginning "It was a summer's day," OSGL.

238 *As was usual every summer*: RLM, five-page memoir fragment beginning "It was a summer's day," OSGL; Katharine Graham, *Personal History* (New York: Alfred A. Knopf, 1997), 286; garden notebook 1, 1, OSGL.

239 *"How can I cope"*: RLM, "Draft Outline: History of the Rose Garden," Rachel Lambert Mellon Collection, Oak Spring Garden Library," n.d., 3, OSGL.

240 *Wheeler's ability*: "Perry Wheeler," *Shaping the American Landscape*, vol. 2, Pioneers of American Landscape Design Series (Charlottesville: University of Virginia Press, 2009); Cultural Landscape Foundation, "Perry Wheeler," https://tclf.org/pioneer/perry-wheeler; Smithsonian Institution, http://gardens.si.edu/collections-research/aag-wheeler-collection.html; Perry H. Wheeler to Mr. and Mrs. Paul Mellon, December 2, 1959.

240 *It's clear he hadn't received*: RLM to Wheeler, June 27, 1963, OSGL; RLM to Wheeler, n.d, Wheeler addendum: "Dearest Perry—Enclosed is my second little—I think it is alright—. Thank you for delivering it. Please forgive the haste. With much love, Bunny" and "Revised—was returned to Mrs. Mellon," all OSGL.

240 *Bunny described him*: RLM, "Jacqueline Bouvier Kennedy: A Reminiscence," *White House Years*, 14.

240 *West actually became*: J. B. West to RLM, April 5, no year, OSGL.

241 *While the Rose Garden project*: Perry Wheeler to RLM, November 22, 1961, Perry H. Wheeler Collection, AAG, Smithsonian Institution Archives.

242 *In her essay about the Rose Garden*: RLM, "Jacqueline Bouvier Kennedy: A Reminiscence," 15.

242 *In a long letter to Bunny*: Perry Wheeler to RLM, March 8, 1962, OSGL.

242 *According to Linda Jane Holden's book*: Linda Jane Holden and Roger Foley, *The Gardens of Bunny Mellon* (New York: Vendome, 2018), 141.

243 *"We got our way"*: Holden and Foley, *Gardens of Bunny Mellon*, 242, from Holden's interview with RLM, June 14, 2010.

243 *But the Rose Garden*: Perry Wheeler to RLM, November 22, 1961, Perry H. Wheeler Collection, AAG, Smithsonian Archives.

243 *In this case*: RLM, "President Kennedy's Rose Garden," in *Journal of the White House Historical Association* 1, no. 1 (1983); Seale, #38, 36–77.

244 *"The scene was suddenly alive"*: RLM, "President Kennedy's Rose Garden," *Journal of the White House Historical Association* (now *White House History Quarterly*) 1, no. 1 (1983).

244 *For her part*: Seale, #38, 36–77.

244 *Two weeks later*: Seymour Hersh, *Dark Side of Camelot*, 202–221.

244 *Curiously, there was little mention*: *The Washington Post*, May 8, 1962, quoted in Seale, #38, 66.

244 *By early October*: Gordon, *American Style Legend*, 214.

244 *Then, in mid-October*: Seymour Hersh, *Dark Side of Camelot*, 341–71.

245 *The next autumn*: Memorandum from Mrs. Mellon to Mr. Williams of things discussed on Monday, September 9, 1963, Perry H. Wheeler Collection, AAG, Smithsonian Institution Archives.

246 *At Jackie's request*: Bedell Smith, *Grace and Power*, 351; Baldwin with Gardine, *Billy Baldwin*, 356–57; Barbara Leaming, "The Winter of *Her* Despair," *Vanity Fair* online, October 2014, adapted from *Jacqueline Bouvier Kennedy Onassis: The Untold Story* (New York: St. Martin's, 2014).

246 *"It was a hard decision"*: Rachel Lambert Mellon, "The Jacqueline Kennedy Garden: An Oasis for the Side of the White House," *House & Garden*, October 1984, 164–69.

247 *The April 1965 opening*: "The Jacqueline Kennedy Garden," The White House Museum, www.whitehousemuseum.org/grounds/kennedy-garden.htm; Holden and Foley, *Gardens of Bunny Mellon*, 253–59; Winzola McLendon, "Mrs. Kennedy's Garden Will Flower," *The Washington Post*, September 9, 1965.

247 *And then she had acted*: PM to RLM, April 3, 1952, OSGL.

247 *As then-president*: RLM typescript, "My Father."

248 *Leon Zach (1895–1966)*: Charles A. Birnbaum and Stephanie S. Foell, eds., *Shaping the American Landscape: New Profiles from the Pioneers of American Landscape Design Project* (Charlottesville: University of Virginia Press, 2009); RLM, "My Father" includes a description of her meeting with Zach, OSGL.

248 *"I explained that its garden"*: See the Olmsted Research Guide Online (ORGO), Job #7630, Lambert/Albemarle. Jacob Sloet, a principal on the job, was described in a letter of recommendation by John Charles Olmsted, stepson of Frederick Law Olmsted and a partner in the Olmsted landscape architecture firm, as having "a pleasing personality and you or any of your assistants would find him a congenial co-worker."

248 *Zach smiled*: See the Olmsted Research Guide Online (ORGO), Job #7630, for Sloet's involvement in the design and execution of the Lambert job in Princeton.

248 *"I'd think to myself, my goodness"*: MKG 1995/1996.

249 *He must have admired what he saw*: Basil Taylor, *Painting in England 1700–1850* (London: Royal Academy of Arts in London, 1964), catalogue.

249 *Bill Keyser, the longtime head painter at Oak Spring*: Keyser interview, notes, March 10, 2015.

249 *He then "had talked too much"*: RLM to Joan Holt, December 11, 2000, OSGL.

19. "AMERICA'S COUNTRY HOUSE"

251 *When Jackie asked her*: RLM, *White House Years*, 13.

251 *In the essay Bunny wrote*: Ibid., 14.

251 *It seems far more likely*: MKG 1995/1996.

252 *"There is a huge dresser"*: Kay Graham to RLM, n.d., OSGL.

252 *As the restoration began*: RLM, *White House Years*, 13, 14.

253 *Neither "Black Jack" Bouvier, Jackie's father*: Chairs from Ramsey, December 1959, 13,752.45 includes shipping and duty 4,247.71., OSGL.

253 *When* The Washington Post *noted*: Marie Smith, "Christmas Magic Comes to White House," *The Washington Post*, December 13, 1961.

254 *The tree was an irresistible draw*: JKO to RLM, December 13, 1961, OSGL, with permission.

254 *Knowing it was imperative*: James A. Abbott and Elaine M. Rice, *Designing Camelot: The Kennedy White House Restoration* (New York: Van Nostrand Reinhold, 1998), 25. William Seale, *The White House: History of An American Idea* (Washington, DC: White House Historical Association, 1992), is consulted throughout this section.

255 *Jackie understood why*: JKO to RLM, December 9, 1962, OSGL, with permission.

255 *Following the gauzy thread*: Melissa Naulin, "A Suite for the Nation Restored to Its Original Splendor: Regilded and Reupholstered, the Historic White House Bellangé Suite Begins Its Third Century," *White House History Quarterly: The Journal of the White House Historical Association*, no. 56, 6–23.

255 *In a 1997 unpublished reminiscence*: RLM to A. Robert Towbin, n.d., re: winning the Classics Division of the Atlantic Challenge Cup in 1997, OSGL.

256 *The surviving armchairs*: Recent scholarship indicates that the original upholstery may have featured a "design of laurel," as described in the 1817 bill of lading, rather than an eagle; the current upholstery features a laurel wreath and a crown imperial flower (*Fritillaria imperialis*), based on a fabric sample owned at the Musée des Tissus in Lyon, France, and a similarly upholstered suite of furniture marked by Bellangé now at Buscot Park in England. Naulin, "Suite for the Nation," 15–16 and notes 36, 37, 38, 39.

256 *From the first, Jackie wanted Bunny*: Mrs. Francis Henry (Jeannette) Lenygon to RLM, October 8, 1961, with notes appended by RLM, OSGL.

256 *As for the contents of the library*: James T. Babb to Mrs. John F. Kennedy, April 24, 1963, copy, OSGL.

257 *It's not clear that Bunny*: Abbott and Rice, *Designing Camelot*, 24; JKO to RLM, December 9, 1962, OSGL, with permission.

257 *The museum closed in 1829*: "Treasures of the White House: Thomas Jefferson," White House Historical Association, www.whitehousehistory.org/photos/treasures-of-the-white-house-thomas-jefferson; White House Museum, "Jeffersonian Enhancements 1801–1809," www.whitehousemuseum.org/special/renovation-1801.htm; Press release, Jacqueline Bouvier Kennedy Onassis Personal Papers, Textual Materials, Pamela Turnure Files, Subject files: White House: Paintings: Rembrandt Peale, "Thomas Jefferson," JBKOPP-SF035–026, John F. Kennedy Presidential Library and Museum, Boston.

257 *William Voss Elder III*: Jacques Kelly, "William Voss Elder III, White House Curator," *Baltimore Sun*, April 21, 2014, www.baltimoresun.com/obituaries/bs-md-ob-william-elder-20140421-story.html.

258 *Parish, who by 1961 was well established*: Abbott and Rice, *Designing Camelot*, 151.

258 *Jackie was undaunted*: J. B. West, *Upstairs at the White House*, 199–200.

258 *John Sweeney, then Winterthur's senior curator*: "Letters from Jackie: A Personal Piece of Camelot," *Winterthur Museum, Garden & Library* blog, http://museumblog.winterthur.org/2015/01/23/letters-from-jackie-a-personal-piece-of-camelot/.

258 *When he said*: H. F. du Pont, in Abbott and Rice, *Designing Camelot*, 21.

259 *However, although her language was different*: RLM in "The House in Virginia Hunt Country," 196.

259 *The role of the third major figure*: "La Maison Blanche," chap. 3 in Abbott and Rice, *Designing Camelot*.

259 *J. B. West remembered*: Ibid., 117.

260 *But Boudin left his fingerprints*: "The Private Dining Rooms," chap. 11 in ibid., 153–61.

260 *"Well, they are absolutely unbelievable"*: JKO to RLM, December 9 and 12, 1961, OSGL, with permission.

260 *Bunny later wrote*: RLM, *White House Years*, 14.

261 *In July 1962, Tiffany & Co. had written to Bunny*: L. P. Hoagland, vice president of Tiffany & Co., to RLM, July 19, 1962, OSGL; JKO to RLM, December 12, 1962, OSGL, with permission.

261 *"Some people give State Rooms"*: JKO to RLM, December 9, 1962, OSGL, with permission.

262 *Bunny taught the chief floral designer*: White House Historical Association Facebook page, March 11, 2017.

262 *As she left the mansion*: JKO to Lady Bird Johnson, January 3, 1964, quoted in Bedell Smith, *Grace and Power*, 518.

262 *"when Mrs. Kennedy started"*: Lawrence J. Arata recorded interview by Pamela Turnure, 1964, six pages, John Fitzgerald Kennedy Library, www.jfklibrary.org/sites/default/files/archives/JFKOH/Arata%2C%20Lawrence%20 J/JFKOH-LA-01/JFKOH-LA-01-TR.pdf.

263 *He stayed for another two years*: Jean R. Hailey, "Upholsterer for the White House Dies," *The Washington Post*, September 14, 1979.

263 *Most people thought it was silk*: Arata interview with Pamela Turnure.

263 *Quickly she telegraphed Perry Wheeler*: Paul Leonard, "Bunny Dearest," unpublished essay, 2002, quoted by Gordon, *American Style Legend*, 222.

264 *"I arrived at the North Portico"*: RLM, *White House Years*, 15.

264 *She made sure that the overwhelming tide*: RLM interview, William Manchester Papers, Special Collections and Archives, Wesleyan University, Middletown, CT.

264 *Ben Bradlee, JFK's close friend*: Bradlee interview, William Manchester Papers; Bedell Smith, *Grace and Power*, 501.

264 *Jackie then asked Bunny*: RLM interview, William Manchester, William Manchester Papers.

265 *Jackie called the Peale portrait*: JKO to RLM, December 12, 1961, OSGL, with permission.

20. ARLINGTON CEMETERY: PORTRAIT OF A LANDSCAPE GARDENER

267 *Until the 220-year-old Arlington Oak*: J. D. Leipold, "Fallen Centuries-Old 'Mother Oak' Lives on Through Saplings at Arlington," *Army News Service*, April 27, 2012, www.army.mil/article/78839/fallen_centuries_old_mother_oak_lives_on_through_saplings_at_arlington.

268 *Her first active work on the project*: John Carl Warnecke to RLM, March 6, 1964, OSGL.

268 *Isamu Noguchi advised getting rid of the flame*: "Artists at Odds on Kennedy Job," *The New York Times*, October 7, 1964.

269 *When President Kennedy's naval aide*: Jacqueline Kennedy to Tazewell T. Shepard, captain, U.S. Navy, November 29, 1962, White House Rose Garden scrapbook, OSGL, with permission.

269 *So that Bunny could have a secret laugh*: Jacqueline Kennedy to Tazewell T. Shepard, ibid.; Perry Wheeler to RLM, February 8, 1966, Perry H. Wheeler Collection, AAG, Smithsonian Institution Archives.

269 *Such experience in dealing with bureaucratic power*: C. J. Robin, chief, Engineering Division, authorized representative of the contracting officer, Dept. of the Army, Norfolk District Corps of Engineers, to Alan H. Rider, John Carl Warnecke and Associates, re: night lighting, December 14, 1966, copy, JFK 7, OSGL; Lieut. Col. Carlyle H. Charles, Corps of Engineers, authorized representative of the contracting officer, Dept. of the Army, Norfolk District Corps of Engineers, OSGL.

270 *"Since we are anxious"*: RLM to Michael Painter, September 29, 1966, OSGL.

270 *After a look at an unsuccessful marble sample*: Perry Wheeler to RLM, n.d., OSGL.

270 *It wasn't until five years after the assassination*: Carl O. Romberg, president, McLeod & Romberg Stone Co., Inc., to Laurence C. Barber, Chief of Engineers, U.S. Army, Washington 25, D.C., September 30, 1968, Perry H. Wheeler Collection, AAG, Smithsonian Institution Archives.

270 *In the scrapbook*: Jacqueline Kennedy, gift to RLM, April 19, 1963, White House Rose Garden scrapbook, OSGL, with permission.

270   *As was often the case*: O. D. Garland to Perry H. Wheeler, October 17 and November 7, 1966, Perry H, Wheeler Collection, AAG, Smithsonian Institution Archives.

270   *A memo from Bunny*: RLM to Michael Painter, September 29, 1966, Perry H. Wheeler Collection, AAG, Smithsonian Institution Archives.

271   *Bunny and Jackie together*: O. D. Garland (The Antiquarium Antiques) to RLM, December 28, 1966, re: the old millstone, OSGL.

271   *In 1967, John Warnecke*: J. C. Warnecke to RLM and RLM to J. C. Warnecke, March 18, 1967, Perry H. Wheeler Collection, AAG, Smithsonian Institution Archives.

271   *When I saw the photograph*: Holden and Foley, *Gardens of Bunny Mellon*, 269.

271   *At last various jerry-built solutions*: "Man Found at Grave Died of Heart Attack," *The Washington Post*, December 7, 1982.

272   *In the Garden Library*: Carlyle H. Charles, LTC, Corps of Engineers, authorized representative of the contracting officer, etc., re: Eternal Flame visibility studies, to JCW, January 10, 1967, OSGL; Alan A. Rider to RLM, re: visibility studies, January 17, 1967, OSGL; Perry Wheeler to RLM, July 11, 1967, re: a trial of the flame to take place "in the evening around 9:00 o'clock," OSGL, copy sent to Mellon residence, Osterville, Perry H. Wheeler Collection, AAG, Smithsonian Institution Archives.

272   *For Jackie, who in 1961*: Beatrice Gormley and Meryl Henderson, *Jacqueline Kennedy Onassis: Friend of the Arts* (New York: Simon and Schuster, paperback ed., 2002), 142–43.

272   *"I tried your suggestion"*: RLM to J. C. Warnecke, March 18, 1967, Perry H. Wheeler Collection, AAG, Smithsonian Institution Archives.

272   *Wheeler asked someone*: Note from Wheeler, addressee not noted, but probably J. C. Warnecke, n.d., Perry H. Wheeler Collection, AAG, Smithsonian Institution Archives.

272   *"The men working on this project"*: RLM to J. C. Warnecke, March 18, 1967, Perry H. Wheeler Collection, AAG, Smithsonian Institution Archives.

273   *Irvin Williams found some specimens*: John Carl Warnecke & Associates—Landscape Section, "The Approved List of Plant Materials for John F. Kennedy Grave (Now in Contract)," October 26, 1966, OSGL; A. E. Gude, A. E. Gude Sons Co., to Everett Hicks, list of forty-seven trees and shrubs, total cost $9,945, n.d. but year is clearly 1966, Perry H. Wheeler Collection, AAG, Smithsonian Institution Archives.

273   *Hicks, an arboriculturist*: Everett C. Hicks to RLM re: maintenance, March 10, 1967, OSGL.

273   *Everett Hicks, recognizable*: Everett C. Hicks, *The Washington Post*, September 22, 2011; Langer, "A Local Life: Everett Hicks, 93, Arborist Who Cared for Mellon Family's Trees."

273   *"I think the grading"*: Michael Painter, Warnecke firm, to RLM, November 30, 1966, Perry H. Wheeler Collection, AAG, Smithsonian Institution Archives.

274   *He wrote to Bunny*: J. C. Warnecke to RLM, March 14, 1967, Perry H. Wheeler Collection, AAG, Smithsonian Institution Archives.

274   *Bunny answered Warnecke's letter promptly*: RLM to J. C. Warnecke, March 16, 1967, Perry H. Wheeler Collection, AAG, Smithsonian Institution Archives.

275   *Jackie wrote to Bunny*: JKO to RLM, March 17, 1967, OSGL, with permission.

275   *Robert Kennedy, in a letter written shortly after his brother's death*: Robert Kennedy to RLM, from Jacqueline Kennedy, White House Rose Garden scrapbook, OSGL, with permission.

275   *In a long letter she wrote to Bunny*: JKO to RLM, June 21, 1968, OSGL, with permission.

276   *She wrote to Jean Schlumberger*: Jacqueline Kennedy to Jean Schlumberger, August 1968, by permission, OSGL. The design for a plaque was never realized.

21. LE POTAGER DU ROI

279   *Until she bought*: Marie-Hélène Bouilloux-Lafont to RLM, March 28, 1962, OSGL.

280   *The stands at Longchamps*: James Brown, "U.S.-Bred Mill Reef Choice in French Arc de Triomphe Today," *The New York Times*, October 3, 1971.

280   *"It was late autumn"*: RLM, "Mrs. Mellon's Secret Garden," *House & Garden*, June 1988.

280   *down "a pebbled ramp"*: Ibid.

281   *Standing in the centuries-old royal kitchen garden*: Ibid.

281   *"Woven into its painted blue ironwork"*: Ibid.

281 *And here Bunny had also unmistakably found*: RLM, "a gardener's conception of *Le Grand Meaulnes*," draft of a foreword, April 1993, to Jacques de Givry and Yves Perillon; introduction, Jean-Pierre Babelon, *Le Potager du Roi, ou, Montrer le lac des Suisses, le potager et le balbi (l'esprit des lieux)* (Paris: JDG Publications, 1993), OSGL.

282 *In the Oak Spring Garden Library is an undated guidebook: Monsieur de la Quintinie a la Grille du Roy*, n.d., École Nationale Supérieure d'Horticulture, inscribed "Bunny Mellon Paris 1972," enclosure: a pass for Hubert de Givenchy and a guest to visit the *potager*, September 29, 1973, OSGL.

284 *The entire operation is overseen*: Catharine Reynolds, "Where Versailles Grew Its Veggies," *The New York Times*, September 11, 1994.

285 *His fame as a master gardener grew*: Wikipedia, "Jean-Baptiste de La Quintinie," https://fr .wikipedia.org/wiki/Jean-Baptiste_de_La_Quintinie.

286 *"Jean de La Quintinie became"*: RLM to Bertrand de Vignaud de Villefort, n.d., OSGL.

286 *In her* House & Garden *article*: RLM, "Mrs. Mellon's Secret Garden."

287 *De Margerie, who had been head of the museums*: Nina Hyde, "To Be Perfectly French," *The Washington Post*, February 23, 1985.

287 *Bunny proposed*: RLM to Jean-Pierre Babelon, June 2, 1990, OSGL.

287 *By September of that year*: RLM to Pierre-André Lablaude, September 28, 1990, OSGL.

288 *Lablaude wrote back*: RLM to Pierre-André Lablaude, July 15, 1991; Lablaude to RLM, August 1, 1991, OSGL.

288 *As one of the top couturiers in the world*: See Françoise Mohrt, *The Givenchy Style* (New York: Vendome Press, 1998).

289 *When Gregory Usher, president of the École de Gastronomie Française Ritz-Escoffier*: Gregory Usher to RLM, May 22, June 5, 1991, OSGL; RLM to Usher, OSGL; David Sassoon and Bonnie Burnham, *World Monuments Fund: The First Thirty Years* (New York: Christie's, 1996), 78–79.

289 *The gate itself was*: World Monuments Fund, "The First Thirty Years," www.wmf.org /sites/default/files/article/pdfs/World%20Monuments%20Fund_The%20First%20Thirty %20Years.pdf.

289 *As Hubert walked away*: Photo prints of the opening of the Grille du Roi at the Potager du Roi, December 1, 1994, OSGL.

290 *For the larger sum*: Estimate maquette: $38,250, Jean-Pierre Babelon to RLM, July 3, 1990, OSGL; final payment, July 15, 1991, RLM to Pierre-André Lablaude, OSGL; Pierre-André Lablaude, chief architect of Historic Monuments, Château of Versailles, "Avant-Programme de Restauration de la Grille du Roy" (Paris: World Monuments Fund France and the National Museum and Domaine of Versailles and the Trianon, 1992), "Estimation Sommaire des Travaux," OSGL; Givenchy to RLM, September 28, 1992, OSGL.

290 *When he was dispatched to Asprey*: PM to RLM, n.d., OSGL.

290 *In late June 1996*: Suzy Menkes, "Givenchy, Vegetable Gardener," *International Herald Tribune*, June 25, 1996, www.nytimes.com/1996/06/25/style/IHT-givenchy-vegetable -gardener.html.

291 *They were honoring her*: MKG 1995/1996.

291 *Hubert, whom I questioned about it*: Phone message relayed to MKG by Veronique Benitah, Givenchy's secretary, and James Taffin, Givenchy's nephew, Givenchy to MKG, July 2015.

291 *Camilla Chandon, Bunny's goddaughter*: Emails, summer 2018.

291 *Bunny didn't need a Givenchy gown*: See six photos of the Grille du Roi and the Bassin at the Potager du Roi taken by Givenchy, OSGL.

22. OSTERVILLE AND ANTIGUA, ISLAND HAVENS

296 *The architecture critic Martin Filler*: Phone and in-person conversations with Filler, summer 2014.

296 *They entered the tiny circular harbor*: GBL, *All Out of Step*, 155.

297 *Evidently—or at least according to an uncredited AP source*: Gordon, *American Style Legend*, 168.

298 *Tim Mellon, usually caustic*: Tim Mellon, January 17, 2019.

298 *Part of that life*: In January 2019, Tim Mellon read sections of my manuscript about Oak Spring and its stages of construction as he remembered them as a child and made comments on Cape Cod as well.

299 *Even her "cook outs"*: Visit to Carter Hall with Nancy Collins, September 2014.

299 *They swept up the jewels*: MKG 1995/1996.

299 *Seale told me*: MKG notes 1995/1996; interview with William Seale, summer 2014.

300 *Jackie answered*: Frank Langella, *Dropped Names: Famous Men and Women as I Knew Them, A Memoir* (New York: Harper Perennial, 2013), 122.

300 *The same was nearly true for Bunny*: MKG 1995/1996.

300 *A skipjack*: Information from Gerard B. "Barnes" Lambert III, summer 2016.

302 *"We felt that Liza had been kidnapped"*: Phone calls and notes, summer 2017.

303 *But behind that scrim of beloved Virginia faces*: Stockley, *Blood in Their Eyes: The Elaine Race Massacres of 1919*.

303 *What Bunny recalled most*: MKG 1995/1996.

304 *Nonetheless, before her interview with Mrs. Mellon*: Related by Nancy Collins, summer 2018.

304 *Lena clearly considered herself*: RLM, "If you get me started talking about Lena," seven-page typed transcription, n.d., but internal evidence points to before 1994, OSGL.

304 *On a trip in 1971*: RLM, blue and green Antigua journal entry, June 24–28, 1971, OSGL; RLM to Geo W. Park Seed Co., Inc., February 28, 1972, OSGL; Desmond Brown, "Hoping to Save Millions, Antigua Turns to Backyard Gardening," Inter Press Service, June 18, 2012, www.ipsnews.net/2012/06/hoping-to-save-millions-antigua-turns-to-backyard-gardening/.

305 *"No, no," he was told*: Dr. Bruce Horten, phone interviews, January 4 and 14, 2019.

305 *"Although the hospital has moved"*: Dr. Bruce Horten, phone interview, January 5, 2019.

305 *In March 1981*: Matthew Schneier, "Babs Simpson, Taste-Making Fashion Editor at Vogue, Is Dead at 105," *New York Times*, January 7, 2019, www.nytimes.com/2019/01/07/obituaries/babs-simpson-dead.html; Walter Lees Foundation, "Walter Charles Lees," www.walterleesfoundation.org.uk/about-walter.html; Baldwin with Gardine, *Billy Baldwin*, xi–xvi.

306 *"We were all together"*: RLM, Simpson, and Baldwin quotations in paragraphs below from "Notes of Five Friends on the Island of Antigua," 1981, OSGL.

307 *She was at her best*: GBL, *All Out of Step*, 131.

308 *At one particularly loud burst*: MKG 1995/1996.

309 *A startlingly white house*: MKG 1995/1996.

309 *To Burton Hersh*: Burton Hersh, *Mellon Family*, 519.

309 *Paul himself summed up*: Mellon, *Reflections*, 348.

310 *"She made up her mind"*: John von Stade phone conversation with Eleanor Weller Reade, May 14, 2016, notes to MKG; MKG phone conversation with von Stade, May 31, 2016.

310 *"Mr. Mellon had one of the first private desalinization plants"*: Skip Glascock, phone interview and notes, January 7, 2019.

311 *In the early sixties*: Alison Harwood to Mrs. Vreeland, Condé Nast Publications, Inc., Paul Mellon House . . . Mill Reef Club, Antigua, n.d., "NO ONE supposed to see this" in red, OSGL.

311 *That was what Harwood saw*: Glascock, phone interview, January 7, 2019.

311 *He lists the estate's six gardeners by name*: Everett Hicks, memorandum to grounds maintenance men at Mellon Property General Grounds Program, February 1964; noted: the document was checked by RLM, OSGL.

311 *Hicks reached out*: Book list of what is in library, February 18, 1964, and in care of Everett C. Hicks, OSGL.

311 *Harwood, in the horrible language of the time*: Harwood to Vreeland, 3, 6, OSGL.

312 *As Bunny went down to the bay*: RLM, diary entry, n.d., OSGL.

312 *Frightened, frozen, and alone*: JKO to RLM, OSGL, by permission.

312 *Bunny's efforts to help her friend*: Gordon, *American Style Legend*, 229–31.

312 *In his photographs*: MKG interviews, phone conversations with Gerard B. Lambert III, notes, emails, November 14, 2017, through 2020.

314 *By lunchtime*: From unknown, recap of a note, July 18, 1993, to Mr. Tyson Van Aiken,

221 Governor St., Richmond, regarding Eliza's four-hundred-acre farm in Virginia, Paul asked for easement, she said no, as she "is not too much on legal views . . . a charming person but frightened and naive, can you help explain how it would benefit her," OSGL.

23. "A HOUSE OF MY OWN": SOUTH PASTURE ON NANTUCKET

315 *"That's perfect!"*: Daniel Sutherland to MKG, Nantucket interview, November 20, 2018.

316 *She once said*: A remark she often repeated, said Nancy Collins, personal communication.

316 *I. M. Pei, who was visiting*: Sutherland interview, November 20–25, 2018.

317 *The half bedroom*: Ibid.

318 *In summer, the Forked Pond Valley*: RLM to Neil Paterson, March 24, 1996, courtesy of Daniel Sutherland.

318 *"It's hard to stress"*: Sutherland email, February 12, 2019.

319 *He was blessed*: Neil Paterson, foreword, *South Pasture Memories: Reminiscences in Pictures, Photography by Daniel Sutherland*, privately printed, 2007.

319 *Bam LaFarge could be called*: "Remembering Bam," *Nantucket Chronicle*, March 10, 2015, www.nantucketchronicle.com/forums/nantucket-insiders/remembering-bam.

319 *Eleanor Reade, a Nantucket "summer person"*: Phone interviews and texts, ECWR to MKG, January and February 2019.

320 *"Everyone, including me"*: Interviews and correspondence with Daniel Sutherland, 2016–19.

320 *The two men established*: Gordon, *American Style Legend*, 279.

321 *"Andy Oates was one of the few"*: Sam Kasten, phone interview, November 1, 2018; Wikipedia, "Black Mountain College."

321 *"There was always something"*: Kasten, phone interview, November 1, 2018; follow-up emails, December 2018–February 2019.

321 *When Kasten visited Oak Spring*: Kasten interview, November 1, 2018.

321 *I could almost hear Bunny*: Conroy, "The House in Virginia Hunt Country."

322 *When Josef Albers famously said*: *Arts/Canada* 23 (1966): 46.

323 *At moments like this*: Nancy Collins, personal communication, summer 2018.

323 *One little dot of a house*: Stanley Champ, phone interview, February 2019.

323 *On her birthday in August 2002*: RLM, August 9, 2002, birthday letter, copy, recipient unknown, OSGL.

324 *"Thank you," she later wrote*: RLM to Daniel Sutherland, October 4, 2002, courtesy of Daniel Sutherland.

324 *There was a hiccup in negotiations*: RLM to Daniel Sutherland, July 14, 2004, courtesy of Daniel Sutherland; additional information from Nantucket conservation lawyer Arthur Reade.

324 *In the same note*: RLM to Daniel Sutherland, April 6 and May 9, 2007, courtesy of Daniel Sutherland.

325 *A yellow-nosed albatross*: E. Vernon Laux, "A Wayward Albatross Soars On," *The New York Times*, June 12, 2000.

326 *"Her downward trajectory"*: Sutherland emails, February 2019.

327 *So it was, in fact, hers*: RLM to Daniel Sutherland, gift letter, August 22, 2007, courtesy of Daniel Sutherland; Gordon, *American Style Legend*, 369.

328 *Most of all he worried*: RLM to Daniel Sutherland, August 22, 2007, gift of Winslow Homer's *Boys on the Beach*, as she called it, courtesy of Daniel Sutherland.

24. MAGNIFICENCE IN NEW YORK, SORROW IN D.C.

329 *They spent many nights roistering*: Mellon, *Reflections*, 194–95.

329 *"I used to have a house"*: Geoffrey T. Hellman, "Paul Mellon," *The New Yorker*, October 5, 1963, 41.

331 *The Sotheby's estimate*: *Interiors*, vol. 3 of *Property from the Collection of Mrs. Paul Mellon*, 4 volumes (New York: Sotheby's, 2014), November 22 and 23, 2014, lots #1376, 77, 78.

331 *Back indoors via the Basket Room garden entry*: The New York section owes much to a conversation with Bruce Budd, August 11, 2018.

331 *"From being a squirrel"*: Mellon, *Reflections*, 346–47.

332 *A man born in Pittsburgh*: Hellman, "Paul Mellon," 41.

332   *Sam Kasten said, "She was obviously extravagant"*: Sam Kasten to MKG, November 13, 2018.

333   *I asked Dr. Bruce Horten*: Phone interview, January 4, 2019; follow-up and notes, January 14, 2019.

333   *Bunny, writing to the then-director of the NGA*: Rachel Lambert Mellon to Earl A. Powell III, June 20, 2006, copy of the letter in NGA curatorial files, and note 4; National Gallery of Art, "John Singer Sargent, *Miss Beatrice Townsend*," www.nga.gov/collection/art-object-page.96999.html#provenance; NGA Accession #2006.128.31.

334   *"Dear Sam, I hope you have"*: Kasten interview, November 1, 2018.

335   *She saw Babe Paley as a symbol*: MKG 1995/1996.

335   *In 1962, after a lunch*: Quoted in Bedell Smith, *Grace and Power*, 284.

335   *It begins*: Emily Dickinson, "The Soul Selects Her Own Society," Poets.org, www.poets.org/poetsorg/poem/soul-selects-her-own-society-303.

336   *"Take that!" is what the photo says*: André Leon Talley, "Today's Treasures," *W*, November 11–18, 1977.

336   *At 125 East Seventieth Street*: Bruce Budd emails, January 2019.

336   *Whether the events were small or large*: Colin Eisler to Susana Torruella Leval, email, November 22, 2015.

337   *She was accompanied*: Camilla Chandon interviews, phone calls, and emails, 2015–16.

337   *All these linens were from the French workshop*: Interiors, vol. 3 of *Property from the Collection of Mrs. Paul Mellon*.

337   *In 1975, the journalist Jimmy Breslin, her old friend*: Nancy Bilyeau, "Jackie Kennedy's Third Act," *Town & Country*, August 18, 2017.

338   *Burn blithely named*: Barbara Burn, phone interview, January 29, 2019; Burn, personal reminiscence, email, January 29, 2019.

338   *Bunny said she told Lily*: MKG 1995/1996.

338   *About the original 1936*: William A. Everett and Paul R. Laird, *The A to Z of the Broadway Musical* (Lanham, MD: Scarecrow Press, 2009), 314.

339   *The 3055 Whitehaven Street home was designed*: Julia Blakely, "The Myths of the British Embassy II: The Location with Lutyens," Landscape of a Washington Place, November 19, 2014, https://washingtonembassygardens.wordpress.com/2014/11/19/the-myths-of-the-british-embassy-ii-the-location-with-lutyens/.

340   *Sally Bedell Smith, in* Grace and Power: Bedell Smith, *Grace and Power*, 108.

340   *The Mellons, wrote Bedell Smith*: Ibid., 105.

340   *Bedell Smith goes on*: Ibid., 105.

340   *Both were comparatively*: Kathy Orton, "The Modern Home That Scandalized Georgetown," *Washington Post*, February 23, 2018, www.washingtonpost.com/news/where-we-live/wp/2018/02/23/the-modern-home-that-scandalized-georgetown/.

341   *In an important sense*: Janet Bruce, phone conversation, February 5, 2019.

342   *What Sally Quinn*: Maureen Orth, "When Washington Was Fun," *Vanity Fair*, November 5, 2007, www.vanityfair.com/news/2007/12/socialDC200712.

342   *About the Georgetown political scene*: Booknotes, *C-SPAN Booknotes*, interview with Evan Thomas, author of *The Very Best Men: The Daring Early Years of the CIA*, program air date December 17, 1995, www.booknotes.org/FullPage.aspx?SID=68051-1.

342   *Georgetown's top women*: Mitchell Owens, "A Personal Appreciation of Marion 'Oatsie' Charles," *New York Social Diary*, December 26, 2018; Claudia Levy, "Polly Fritchey Dies," *The Washington Post*, July 11, 2002, www.washingtonpost.com/archive/local/2002/07/11/polly-fritchey-dies/828ee107-5c37-4f78-a19f-f2c1ea76dad8/?utm_term=.2abd3b06b213; MKG 1995/1996.

343   *"Dorcas was fun!"*: Janet Bruce, phone conversation, February 5, 2019.

343   *Katharine Graham reportedly threatened*: Graham, *Personal History*, 286.

343   *Meryl Gordon quoted Oatsie Charles*: Gordon, *American Style Legend*, 268.

343   *Janet Bruce told me*: Janet Bruce interview, August 30, 2015.

344   *Occasionally, in the few letters Bunny wrote*: RLM to David S. Bruce, December 26, 1995, Janet Bruce Collection.

344   *Again and again, to others*: Ibid.

344   *In her autobiography,* Personal History: Graham, *Personal History*, 416–17.

345   *Vangie wrote*: Evangeline Bruce to RLM, n.d. but written on 67 Rolandstrasse Bad

Godesberg [Berlin] letterhead, which Bruce heads with "American Embassy." They had arrived for his German posting in 1957. Janet Bruce translation.

346   *A flourishing Whitehaven Street*: RLM to Perry Wheeler, February 15, 1966, n.d.; only a single page exists of this letter, numbered as "6." Perry H. Wheeler Collection, AAG, Smithsonian Institution Archives.

346   *Sometimes his promise to Bunny*: MKG 1995/1996.

346   *Cecil Beaton confided to his diary*: Cecil Beaton, unpublished diary, June 1968, Beaton Collection, St. John's College, Cambridge, copyright the Literary Executors of the late Sir Cecil Beaton, quoted by Bedell Smith, *Grace and Power*, xxiii.

346   *"Do you think that Mr. Young"*: RLM to Perry Wheeler, February 15, 1966.

25. A HOUSE OF BOOKS

351   *Amory disagreed*: Dita Amory email to MKG, March 10, 2019.

353   *The Whistler also recalls*: Evangeline Bruce, *Napoleon and Josephine: An Improbable Marriage* (New York: Scribner, 1995).

354   *She wrote to me*: Elizabeth Banks email to MKG, January 26, 2018.

354   *The first book*: Oak Spring Garden Library database/ID RB0532, Robert Furbur (ca. 1674–1756), *The Flower Garden Display'd*, etc., printed 1734.

354   *Bunny was captivated*: Lucia Tongiorgi Tomasi, "Bunny Mellon: Collector and Gardener," in *Redouté to Warhol: Bunny Mellon's Botanical Art* (Upperville, VA: Oak Spring Garden Foundation, and New York: New York Botanical Garden, 2016), exhibition catalogue.

355   *Even those whom landscape gardener Beatrix Farrand*: Beatrix Farrand to Mildred Bliss, May 26, 1947, Beatrix Farrand File, Rare Book Collection, Dumbarton Oaks; see Therese O'Malley, "Mildred Barnes Bliss's Garden Library at Dumbarton Oaks," in James Nelson Carder, *A Home of the Humanities: The Collecting and Patronage of Mildred and Robert Woods Bliss* (Washington, DC: Dumbarton Oaks Research Library & Collection, 2011), 143.

357   *In the preface to her first Oak Spring catalogue*: RLM, "Preface," *Sylva*, xv.

357   *Bunny dedicated Sylva*: RLM, "It was a summer's day," typescript, mention of Lowe, tree planting, and his grandchildren, 3, OSGL.

358   *By 1975 rare books*: Bunny bought the Mattioli in 1962 and the Kerner in 1963; the Rackham collection was a gift from Paul in 1971.

358   *At Oak Spring there were*: Dita Amory interview, May 8, 2015.

358   *"I flew down for the day"*: Email correspondence, Dita Amory, March 3, 2019.

359   *She said the hiring process*: Amory interview, May 8, 2015; emails, March 3, 2019.

359   *Serious about making her own way*: Wikipedia, "John Shaffer Phipps," https://en.wikipedia .org/wiki/John_Shaffer_Phipps.

359   *Paul, who didn't like Pittsburgh either*: Mellon, *Reflections*, 349, 353.

359   *Dita Amory told me*: Amory emails, March 3, 2019.

359   *The Hunts had watched*: Roy A. Hunt Foundation, "Our Story," http://rahuntfdn.org /about-us/our-foundations-history.

360   *"Mrs. Mellon was integral"*: Amory interview, May 8, 2015.

360   *While Barnes became most famous*: Douglas Martin, "Edward Larrabee Barnes, Modern Architect, Dies at 89," *The New York Times*, September 23, 2004.

361   *"Every week he had to go to lunch"*: Ann Jackson, phone interview, April 13, 2017.

361   *Finally, and most time-consuming*: Jackson, phone interview, April 13, 2017.

361   *"After the building was up"*: Ron Evans, phone interviews, summer 2019.

362   *"My father, Fred Willis"*: Tony Willis, interview and notes, March 4, 2019; Amory interview, March 4, 2019.

363   *When the local architect Thomas Beach*: Beach, phone interview, March 8, 2019.

363   *Beach wrote to Bunny in 2005*: Beach to RLM, August 16, 2005, OSGL.

363   *His first lesson came in 1961*: Langella, *Dropped Names*, 344.

364   *"When I came to the name"*: Langella, *Dropped Names*, 344.

365   *One of the most revered scholars in her field*: Interview, email, copy of notes corrected by Tongiorgi Tomasi, March 14, 2019.

366   *Tomasi hypothesized*: Tongiorgi Tomasi, phone interview, March 14, 2019.

366   *If you want to explore*: Oak Spring Garden Foundation, "Women Botanical Artists," www.osgf.org/women-botanical-artists.

367   *This particular Bunny Mellon appears as a student*: "Forsyth Wickes, Art Collector, 88," *New York Times*, December 21, 1964, www.nytimes.com/1964/12/21/archives/forsyth -wickes-art-collector-88-lawyer-had-been-lecturer-at.html.

367   *a rare Dutch florilegium*: Vellum binding; 245 engraved and etched plates, all colored by hand (Amsterdam, 1713).

367   *"Life is like a puzzle"*: RLM, linen-bound journal entry, 3, November 25, 1970, OSGL.

368   *Augustus John's* Dorelia: *Dorelia in the Garden at Alderney Manor*, Augustus John, Yale Center for British Art, Paul Mellon Collection, Accession number 54271-B2014.5.85.

368   *To explain how the Mellons differed*: Colin Eisler to Susana Torruella Leval, email, November 22, 2015.

26. COMPETITION AND COLLEAGUES

370   *"When the time came to plant"*: Rachel Lambert Mellon, preface, xxiii, *An Oak Spring Pomona, a Selection of the Rare Books on Garden Fruit in the Oak Spring Garden Library Described by Sandra Raphael* (Oak Spring Garden Library, Upperville, VA, 1990).

370   *The garden library of Mildred Barnes Bliss*: O'Malley, "Mildred Barnes Bliss's Garden Library at Dumbarton Oaks," in Carder, 145, 151.

371   *O'Malley, on her initial visit to the library*: Therese O'Malley, phone and email interview, February 15, 2016.

372   *An institution herself*: O'Malley, "Mildred Barnes Bliss's Garden Library at Dumbarton Oaks," 146.

373   *Bunny's library holds*: Ibid.; Katherine Tyrrell, "Botanical Artists: Margaret Mee," *Making a Mark* (blog), April 9, 2009, https://makingamark.blogspot.com/2009/04/botanical-artists -margaret-mee.html.

373   *Charles Ryskamp*: Dumbarton Oaks, "Who Was Who at Dumbarton Oaks, 1940–2015," www.doaks.org/research/library-archives/dumbarton-oaks-archives/historical-records /who-was-who-at-dumbarton-oaks-194020132015; Charles Ryskamp correspondence, OSGL.

373   *Nancy Mitford, in her biography*: Nancy Mitford, *Madame de Pompadour* (New York: Random House, 1953), 104.

373   *One "working part"*: Phone interviews and emails with Willis Van Devanter, March 26, 27 and April 3, 2019.

374   *John Saumarez Smith*: Interviews, phone calls, and email correspondence, November 2015, February and June 2016.

376   *A small but breathtaking display*: Sandra Raphael, *An Oak Spring Garland, Illustrated Books, Prints, and Drawings from the Oak Spring Garden Library* (Upperville, VA: Oak Spring Garden Library, 1989).

376   *In 2016, NYBG's LuEsther T. Mertz Library*: *Redouté to Warhol*, exhibition catalogue.

376   *The officers of the first library board*: Michael Shnayerson, "All the Best Victims," *Vanity Fair*, August 3, 2010.

376   *In 2016, it was transferred*: Communication with Sir Peter Crane, OSGF director, April 15, 2019.

377   *Susan Fraser, vice president*: On the opening of *Redouté to Warhol*, exhibition catalogue, October 8, 2016.

377   *In 1956, when Beatrix Farrand*: O'Malley, "Mildred Barnes Bliss's Garden Library at Dumbarton Oaks," 143, note 20; www.osgf.org/blog/2019/3/6/beatrix-farrand-an -ecological-designer.

377   *In her brief history*: Walter Benjamin, "Unpacking My Library," in *Illuminations* (New York: Schocken Books,1969), 66.

377   *When Reagan arrived*: Gordon, *American Style Legend*, 322–23.

378   *In 1977, as an answer*: Ibid., 301.

380   *Bunny spotted the piece*: William Edmondson, *Birdbath*, Sotheby's, October 13, 2000, invoice #0055; Bruce Budd email, December 15, 2016.

380   *Getting things done anywhere*: SBL to Rachel Lambert, postmarked Ardmore, December 10, 1931, OSGL.

27. "LE PLUS PARISIEN DES ANTIQUAIRES HOLLANDAIS"

383 *"Le Plus Parisien"*: *Vogue Décoration Edition Internationale #39* gushed over Akko, calling him *"le plus parisien des antiquaires hollandais"* and *"le plus fantasque des magiciens."*

383 *In this case*: PM to Akko van Acker, fax, December 8, 1996, courtesy of Akko van Acker.

383 *Hubert had called him:* Phone interview, notes, Akko van Acker, May 16, 2017.

383 *It turned out*: RLM memoir fragment, n.d., OSGL.

384 *All he said*: RLM, ibid.

385 *"Maybe you will have"*: RLM to Givenchy, n.d., OSGL.

385 *On a weekend at Le Jonchet*: RLM, garden notebook 8, 1, *"Faire le mainage [menage] et le Testament,"* OSGL.

385 *It sounds like*: RLM, garden notebook 8, 1, OSGL.

385 *Hubert then took her*: Garden notebook 12, 15; Michele Masneri, "Interview with Afdera Franchetti," *Vogue Italia*, December 2017, 220, OSGL.

386 *He could be counted on*: Van Acker to RLM, birthday card, 2006, and van Acker to RLM, July 13, 1994, OSGL; Veronica Horwell, Judith Krantz obituary, *Guardian*, June 27, 2019, www.theguardian.com/books/2019/jun/27/judith-krantz-obituary.

387 *"This winter I built a new boat"*: RLM to van Acker, fax, May 1, 1994, OSGL, and fax, June 30, no year visible, OSGL.

387 *Coming in from the airport*: 15, rue de l'Université, was purchased in 1993, alterations completed by 1994, OSGL.

388 *Yet, as Bunny told it*: RLM memoir fragment, n.d., OSGL.

388 *I asked Akko*: Van Acker, phone interview, June 8, 2017.

388 *I pressed him*: Ibid.

388 *Akko told me*: Ibid.

388 *On Antigua in 1996*: MKG 1995/1996.

389 *At lunch together the day after*: MKG 1995/1996.

389 *"My apartment [Avenue Foch] is too large"*: RLM memoir fragment, n.d., re: leaving Avenue Foch apartment, OSGL.

389 *"She never asked"*: Akko van Acker, phone interview, June 8, 2017.

389 *When a fire broke out*: Keith Dovkants, "800 Trapped in Chunnel for Three Hours," *London Evening Standard*, February 20, 1996, with RLM note "On this train returning from David [*illeg: Brooke?*] service with Akko," OSGL.

389 *Soon after moving*: RLM to van Acker, n.d., OSGL.

390 *Bunny shared her happiness*: RLM fax, van Acker, n.d. but probably 1996, OSGL.

390 *Later that year*: RLM to van Acker, June 13, 1994, OSGL; RLM to van Acker, October 20, 1994, OSGL.

390 *Six months after Paul's death*: Van Acker fax to RLM, November. 23, 1999, OSGL; phone interview with MKG, June 8, 2017.

390 *Akko also accurately noted*: Van Acker fax to RLM, November 23, 1999, OSGL.

390 *He teased her unmercifully*: Van Acker fax to RLM, February 24, 1997, OSGL.

391 *Akko encouraged Bunny's ingenue friskiness*: Van Acker fax to RLM, n.d., OSGL.

391 *She often reverted*: RLM to van Acker, October 29, n.d., OSGL.

392 *More prosaically*: Jean Pierre Babey, "Expert's Valuation Report Concerning Two Apartments and Their Annexes," for 15, rue de l'Université, December 2008, OSGL; Akko van Acker, phone interview, September 19, 2019.

392 *About thirty by ten meters*: RLM memoir fragment, n.d., re leaving Avenue Foch apartment, OSGL; Akko van Acker, phone call description of Avenue Foch garden; Prévosteau et Fils, plant lists to RLM, OSGL.

392 *"Paris garden marvelous!"*: Garden book 10, July 1, 1982, 13, OSGL.

392 *When her gardener at Avenue Foch*: René Lavaudet to RLM, May 30, 1990, OSGL.

392 *In 1992, for her new, smaller French life*: RLM, unsent draft letter to an owner of another apartment at 15, rue de l'Université, August 11, 1992, OSGL.

393 *"Your bed is ready"*: Van Acker to RLM, fax, April 5, OSGL. The year date is wrong on many of the messages sent or received on the Oak Spring fax machine: this one is dated 2012, after she had sold the apartment, so the correct year date is not known, only that she was still setting up house in 1994–95, as per information from OSGL.

394 *Many notes from him*: Van Acker to RLM, "Hope you don't find me too much talking about business," May 17, 1994, OSGL.

394   *Real life does intrude*: Van Acker to RLM, faxes, June 16, 1994, and May 1997, OSGL.
394   *"Yes, dear Bunny, you now can send"*: Van Acker to RLM, June 13, 1994, OSGL.
394   *"He's sending me buckets"*: Van Acker phone call, September 15, 2019.
394   *"I spoke with you"*: Van Acker fax to RLM, February 7, 1993, OSGL.
394   *Bunny answered his question*: RLM to van Acker, Upperville garden fax, May 17, 1993, OSGL.
395   *When I spoke with Akko*: Acker, phone interview, June 8, 2017; the apartment was sold in 2009, as per OSGL.
395   *Eventually, after raging about him*: Acker, phone interviews, May 16, 2017, and August 17, 2018; MKG conversation with Tony Willis, OSGL.
395   *Akko's bulging files*: Van Acker to RLM, folding postcard, n.d., but after May 2000 (Eliza's accident), OSGL.

28. A LONG GOODBYE TO PAUL

397   *As if Bunny could stave off*: RLM, blue daily diary, May 7–15, 1994, OSGL.
397   *"I hope we meet again"*: RLM to Robert Isabell, May 29, 1994, OSGL.
397   *What had begun on Cape Cod*: George Trescher, notes, May 28, 1986, OSGL.
398   *"Feeling calm again"*: RLM, blue daily diary, May 16–22, 1994, OSGL.
398   *In July, Bunny made a quick trip*: RLM, blue daily diary, July 5–9, 1994, OSGL.
399   *"Paul was wonderful"*: RLM, blue daily diary, May 7–15, 1994, OSGL.
399   *"Mac, now I have lost"*: MKG 1995/1996.
400   *I did see some guests*: MKG 1995/1996.
400   *For his ninetieth in 1997*: Nancy Collins, interview, notes.
400   *The second was a party of ten*: MKG 1995/1996.
401   *That June, Paul's doctor*: London interview with John Baskett, November 2015; Bruce Budd phone call, summer 2015.
402   *Wilbur was no longer invited*: Personal communication.
402   *I did not see Dorcas Hardin*: John Baskett interview, November 2015.
402   *Paul distributed over $160 million*: Eric Gibson, "A Patron Who Gave as Good as He Got," *The Wall Street Journal*, February 3, 1999.
403   *He divided 230 paintings*: Paul Richard, "Paul Mellon's Final Gifts," *The Washington Post*, February 11, 1999.
403   *Art critic John Russell*: John Russell, "Paul Mellon, Patrician Champion of Art and National Gallery," *The New York Times*, February 3, 1999.
403   *When the wreath was finished at last*: Gerard B. Lambert III, phone interview, November 14–15, 2017.
403   *On his return to Virginia*: Gerard B. Lambert III, phone interview, November 14–15, 2017.
404   *When Paul died*: Gerard B. Lambert III, phone interview, November 14–15, 2017.
404   *The day Barnes put his boat model*: Gerard B. Lambert III, continued email and phone correspondence to 2019.
405   *Bunny promptly wrote her own letter*: RLM, letter to staff, February 26, 1999, OSGL; MKG, conversation with Eliza Lloyd, February 2000.
405   *"Everything here is for pleasure"*: Vicky Moon, "Polished to a Shine and Ready for Visitors: Mellon's Rokeby Farm a Highlight of Annual Tour at Elite Stables," *The Washington Post*, May 23, 2002.
405   *The dairyman and his wife*: Allen Bassler, dairyman and cheese maker, to RLM, May 28, August 5, and August 16, 2002, OSGL.
405   *The new Falcon and its pilots*: Gordon, *American Style Legend*, 372.
406   *Eliza called to tell me*: RLM to Robert Isabell, *A Journal for Robert While He Was Away for New Year's*, a fourteen-page small diary, dated New Year's 2000–2001, with the 2000 basket of flowers sketched on the cover, OSGL; Bunny Mellon, "How Bunny Mellon Met Robert Isabell," *W* magazine, September 2009.

29. GOODBYE, ELIZA

407   *In 2000, on May 6, a Saturday morning*: Milu Rodriguez, phone calls, Sunday, May 7, 2000.
407   *"It's Eliza"*: Nancy Collins, notes, June 2017.

408   *Isabell called a friend, Dr. Brian Saltzman*: Malcolm Gladwell, "Conquering the Coma," *The New Yorker*, June 30, 1996.

408   *By inserting a tube*: PBS, *Nova Online*, "Coma," www.pbs.org/wgbh/nova/coma/ghajar.html.

408   *Nancy, a registered nurse*: MKG interview with Nancy Collins, spring 2017.

409   *Akko faxed Bunny*: Van Acker to RLM, May 13, 2000, OSGL.

409   *I asked Hudner*: Assembled Ann Hudner phone and email notes, June 5, 2016, through December 7, 2020.

409   *With a smile*: Diane Brown, phone notes, April 13 and 24, 2017.

409   *"Even then," Hudner said*: Hudner notes.

410   *The staff "would serve me dinner"*: Hudner notes.

410   *"A mutual friend"*: Diane Brown notes.

410   *After Eliza's death, the Lambert Foundation*: Diane Brown notes; Robin Scher, "RxArt Receives $1 M. Gift, Largest in History," *ARTnews*, February 2, 2016, www.artnews.com/art-news/news/rxart-receives-1-m-gift-largest-in-history-5764/.

410   *We were like*: John F. Burns, "The Death of a City: Elegy for Sarajevo—A Special Report; A People Under Artillery Fire Manage to Retain Humanity," *The New York Times*, June 8, 1992.

411   *On a memo pad, under the title "Life"*: Original cataloguing order, box #53, item 18, reviewed by MKG December 10, 2014, small lined pad, blue paper, 8 by 5 inches, top sheet reads "life." "You've got to play with the cards you are dealt—just play them like a master."—evidently written after Eliza's accident, as the next page says, "Clean up Spring Hill Large Boxwood Bush," with lists of phone numbers. Also instructions on how to play a tape recorder.

411   *Bruce Budd, her last decorator*: Bruce Budd email, October 3, 2019.

412   *Akko, second fiddle*: Van Acker fax to RLM, January 27, 2002, OSGL.

412   *"Everyone was constantly saying"*: Hudner notes.

412   *She would never*: Hudner notes.

412   *"I spoke with my mother"*: Hudner notes.

412   *"I called Mrs. Mellon the next day"*: Hudner notes.

413   *Bunny grew disillusioned*: RLM to Alexander Forger, draft of a letter, August 29, 2005, OSGL.

413   *But eventually she would support*: Maria di Mento, "No. 8, Rachel Lambert (Bunny) Mellon," *The Chronicle of Philanthropy*, February 8, 2015.

413   *In the early 1960s, she said*: MKG phone interview with Bee Dabney Penati Adams, September 29, 2016.

413   *"I taught Eliza how to paint"*: Dabney interview, September 29, 2016.

414   *Eliza later said*: RLM, blue personal diary, OSGL.

414   *"Bunny drew the boundaries"*: Hudner notes.

414   *"The more I pursue"*: "Eliza Moore: Photographs/Paintings," Virginia Lynch Gallery, Tiverton, Rhode Island, June 23–July 21, 2002.

415   *But at the small bridal dinner*: Seating plans for the bridal dinner on May 13, 1968, OSGL.

416   *"Old-fashioned dancing," said Derry*: Derry Moore, phone conversation, November 25, 2015.

416   *"But in some ways it is more interesting"*: MKG interview with Derry Moore, November 15, 2015, and later phone conversations and emails through 2019.

417   *"Bunny threw a big brunch"*: Phone conversations and emails with Gerard B. Lambert III, November 14 and 15, 2017, and February 22, March 4, March 6, and March 16, 2018.

417   *After flying out to Los Angeles*: Cristina de Heeren interviews, emails, calls, 2015–2017.

417   *In December 1971*: Eliza to RLM, December 6, 1971, OSGL.

417   *"My father-in-law was not Paul Mellon"*: Derry Moore, phone conversation, November 25, 2015.

417   *Senator John Warner received*: "Navy Head and Wife Divorce," *Chicago Tribune*, August 23, 1973; Paul Richard, "Paul Mellon's Final Gifts," *The Washington Post*, February 11, 1999.

418   *"I knew she preferred girls"*: Derry Moore, November 15, 2015; phone conversations and emails through 2019.

418   *In retrospect, it seems*: Phone calls with Ann Hudner, June 6, 2016, and October 18, 2018.
418   *Decades later, Akko told me*: Van Acker, phone call, June 8, 2017; email, June 15, 2017.
418   *Still early in Eliza's recovery*: Hudner notes.
418   *Eliza told me that after*: A story Eliza told me in the mid-1990s, although I never saw the dog!
419   *"Eliza was always teasing me"*: Diane Brown notes.
419   *Once, when Ann Hudner told Eliza*: Hudner notes.
419   *"I know what I want"*: MKG 1995/1996.
420   *"Yes, it was gross"*: Martha Sherrill, "Billionaire's Birthday Party the Talk of the Town," *South Florida Sun Sentinel*, August 23, 1989.
421   *"Robert even stood a table"*: Nancy Collins emails, October 2019.
421   *"the party was long over"*: Diane Brown notes.
421   *"The sofa feature"*: Phone interview with Liz Garvin, December 15, 2016.
422   *"I'm sure he participated"*: Arthur Lubow, "All Yesterday's Parties," *New York*, October 11, 2009.
422   *In 2006, he asked her*: RLM to MKG re: Isabell's advice on the New York house, 2006.
423   *Eliza was always surprised*: Hudner notes.
424   *Hudner recently said to me*: Hudner notes.

30. "I WANT TO MAKE A PRESIDENT"
427   *True to form, Bunny*: Phone conversation with RLM, July 2011.
427   *Paul Mellon once said*: Martin Filler email to MKG, April 12, 2014.
428   *According to Huffman*: Gordon, *American Style Legend*, 396.
428   *By December 1, 2005*: Ibid., 399.
429   *Bunny eschewed her usual daiquiri*: Ibid., 400.
429   *At this point in her life*: MKG 1995/1996.
429   *Like JFK, "a man insulated"*: Seymour Hersh, *Dark Side of Camelot*, flap copy.
429   *Hubert, who adored Bunny*: Jo Ellison, "A Cultivated Taste: The Bunny Mellon Auction," *Financial Times*, November 14, 2014.
430   *Tony Willis, by then as much Bunny's dear friend*: Tony Willis conversation, notes, spring 2019.
430   *Frank Langella said that Bunny was forthright*: Langella, *Dropped Names*, 341.
430   *Bunny was for women's rights*: Gordon, *American Style Legend*, 326.
430   *Bunny had followed her own advice for decades*: Nelly Jo Thomas interview.
431   *She wrote to Andrew Young*: RLM to Andrew Young, April 21, 2007, OSGL.
431   *Enter the campaign's "special project"*: Gordon, *American Style Legend*, 409.
432   *I should add that*: RLM phone call, Christmastime 2010, and Alexander Forger, phone call, September 2014.
432   *Paul sent the work*: As of May 17, 2001, the work was inventoried in Bunny's Paris apartment.
432   *In 2001, the VMFA issued*: Malcolm Cormack, Paul Mellon Curator, Virginia Museum of Fine Arts, to Frederick A. Terry, Esq., Sullivan & Cromwell (representing Rachel Lambert Mellon), regarding the Degas painting *At the Milliner's*, June 6, 2000: "The Museum does not really want to seize this lovely painting from Mrs. Mellon . . . the Museum is willing to allow Mrs. Mellon to enjoy the painting during her life if a document, sufficient under the laws of France and the United States, affirming the Museum's title . . . were suitably signed and filed"; Malcolm Cormack, "Gift Consideration," May 2001; VMFA accession date May 17, 2001.
433   *I asked Tony Willis*: Conversation and notes, Tony Willis, 2017; MKG notes 1995/1996.
433   *Meanwhile, the frenzied 2007 art market*: "The Speculative Bubble in the Art Market Reaches Its Peak in November 2007," Artprice.com, January 21, 2008, www.artprice.com/artmarketinsight/the-speculative-bubble-in-the-art-market-reaches-its-peak-in-november-2007.
433   *The loan now came in handy*: RLM to Bryan Huffman, July 2007, quoted in Meryl Gordon, courtesy of Huffman, *American Style Legend*, 411.
433   *A card with an image of Monet's* Woman with a Parasol: National Gallery of Art, "Claude Monet, *Woman with a Parasol—Madame Monet and Her Son*, 1875," www.nga.gov/collection/art-object-.

434 *It was the same kind*: Seymour Hersh, *Dark Side of Camelot*, 226–46.

434 *The* National Enquirer *dug deep*: Rick Egusquiza, "Presidential Cheating Scandal!" *National Enquirer*, October 10, 2007; Alan Butterfield et al., "John Edwards Love Child Scandal," *National Enquirer*, December 19, 2007; Gordon, *American Style Legend*, 402, 412, 413.

434 *At Eliza's funeral reception*: Gordon, *American Style Legend*, 417, 419.

435 *On ABC, Bob Woodruff interviewed Edwards*: Bob Woodruff, "John Edwards Interview," ABC News.com, August 8, 2008.

435 *Bunny did a star interrogator's turn*: Alexander Forger, conversation, notes, September 2014.

435 *They left with Bunny's assertion*: Gordon, *American Style Legend*, 429.

436 *"She knew all about the women"*: Meryl Gordon, "Bunny Mellon the Secret-Keeper," *Newsweek*, July 25, 2011; Langella, *Dropped Names*, 351.

437 *"I had to step over Edwards's shoes"*: Tim Mellon, January 17, 2019.

437 *She apparently envisioned Edwards and Caroline Kennedy*: RLM, draft of a letter to Edwards, n.d. but after 2008, and notes also n.d. but after 2009, OSGL.

438 *Bunny stuck with Starr*: Diane Brown notes.

438 *Hitchcock wanted to get hold of Bunny*: Gordon, *American Style Legend*, 417.

438 *According to Starr, at least*: Shnayerson, "All the Best Victims."

438 *Notably, Bunny is not among them*: Forger, phone conversation, August 2014.

438 *When nearly $6 million of Bunny's money*: Shnayerson, "All the Best Victims"; Gordon, *American Style Legend*, 434.

439 *It turned out*: Shnayerson, "All the Best Victims"; Gordon, *American Style Legend*, 434.

439 *On Memorial Day weekend in 2010*: James Reginato, "Bunny Mellon's Secret Garden," *Vanity Fair*, August 2010.

439 *Basking in the sunshine*: Ibid.

440 *She said, "This garden is made of love"*: Ibid.; MKG phone interview with James Reginato, summer 2010.

441 *"For the first time"*: James Atlas, *The Shadow in the Garden, A Biographer's Tale* (New York: Parthenon Books, 2017), 241.

31. ROBERT ISABELL

442 "Like the sea just before dark": A half page, dated November 12, no year, on 125 East Seventieth Street letterhead. One of eight letters or diary entries, none dated, some as long as three pages, that Bunny kept together, are all to or about Robert Isabell or about her own emotions. They are identified in these notes as RLM, Isabell papers, OSGL, and postdate *A Journal for Robert While He Was Away for New Year's, 2000–2001*, which she illustrated with drawings in pencil. The letters probably continue until his death, in 2009. Bunny and Isabell had met on May 28, 1986, when he attended a meeting in New York with Jackie Kennedy Onassis and George Trescher, the New York event planner, to work out the decorative scheme for Caroline Kennedy's wedding on July 19.

442 *"Love is easy"*: RLM, Isabell papers, OSGL.

442 *No one ever heard anything*: Liz Garvin, phone interview, 2016.

442 *"I have a shell & must stay in it"*: RLM, Isabell papers, OSGL.

443 *For two decades, Robert Isabell*: Christopher Mason, "He Said It with Flowers," *The New York Times*, July 17, 2009.

443 *Isabell's longtime lighting designer*: Garvin interview, 2016.

443 *James Reginato described Isabell*: James Reginato, "Flower King," *W*, September 1, 2009.

444 *What did they discuss?*: Ibid.; Cathy Graham and Anne Bass interview, December 2016; Mason, "He said It with flowers."

444 *"He was a guy"*: Garvin interview, 2016.

444 *"You have to be a dictator"*: Reginato, "Flower King," quoting Isabell from an earlier article in *The New York Times*, 1996.

445 *In a flurry of enthusiasm*: Jacqueline Duhème correspondence 1988–2008, OSGL.

445 *For Isabell, not long after they became friends*: RLM, Isabell papers, OSGL.

446 *Bunny wrote about a short weekend*: RLM, Isabell papers, OSGL.

446 *He was flippant and funny*: January 6, 2003, a note to accompany flowers, OSGL.

446 *He knew her competitive spirit*: Isabell to RLM, n.d., OSGL.

446 *In New York and on Cape Cod*: RLM, Isabell papers, OSGL, including all quotations in this paragraph.

447 *She understood how much solitude*: RLM, Isabell papers, OSGL.

447 *For Isabell, son of a Duluth, Minnesota*: Liz Garvin interview, 2016.

447 *"He has given me"*: RLM, Isabell papers, OSGL.

447 *But sometimes, when he needed a break*: Garvin interview, 2016.

447 *Happily for Isabell and Bunny*: RLM, Isabell papers, OSGL.

447 *But Garvin told me*: Garvin interview, 2016.

448 *In December she wrote*: RLM to Isabell, postmarked Cape Cod, sent to him at 410 West Thirteenth Street, December 9, 2004, OSGL.

448 *Liz Garvin said*: Garvin interview, 2016.

448 *Schrager considered himself*: Lubow, "All Yesterday's Parties."

448 *"He never let on"*: Ibid.

449 *On July 8, the police broke down*: Reginato, "Flower King."

449 *Garvin was part*: Garvin interview, 2016.

449 *A week after his death*: "Robert Isabell, the Highly Successful Floral Designer," *New York Social Diary*, July 13, 2009.

449 *Whatever the facts*: Beverly Carter and Frederic A. Terry, Jr., Executors of the Estate of Paul Mellon, to Officers and Directors Trinity Church Cemetery Corporation, July 16, 2009, copy of letter courtesy of Tim Mellon.

450 *Fortuitously, in 1948, Paul had bought*: Deed of Release, T.G.F. Slater et al. to Paul Mellon, January 30, 1948, with a plat of the half-acre Fletcher family burying ground appended, with the Mellon area set-aside in question, citing the Fauquier County deed for "Oak Spring Farm" to Paul Mellon, dated November 17, 1936, Deed Book 143, 364, in which the family burying ground is exempted as per the original will of Robert Fletcher, July 4, 1845, Will Book No.19, 298. Copy Deed of Release, Fletcher plot plan, courtesy of Tim Mellon; George Nicholas Slater to RLM, affidavit granting permission to bury Robert Isabell in the Robert Fletcher Cemetery located at "Little Oak Spring," August 9, 2009, State of Virginia, Fauquier County, Registration No. 136896, copy of affidavit courtesy of Tim Mellon.

450 *Charlotte Moss*: Moss, "The Eloquence of Silence," *The New York Times Style Magazine*, June 2014.

451 *But you don't have to delve*: Ellen O'Connell Whittet, "Thomas Hardy's Rule-Breaking Heroines," *Ploughshares*, October 17, 2017.

32. "I AM NOT AFRAID"

453 *Bunny's auction*: "Masterpieces from Mr. and Mrs. Paul Mellon Bring Depth to National Gallery of Art's French and American Collections," *The New York Times*, May 23, 2014.

454 *The gloves look very well used*: Bruce Budd, personal communication, May 2020.

454 *Bruce Budd had spent thirteen years*: Bruce Budd, phone conversation, 2019.

454 *"Folks just didn't realize"*: Ellison, "A Cultivated Taste: The Bunny Mellon Auction."

455 *Behn's biographical editors*: Derek Hughes and Janet Todd, *The Cambridge Companion to Aphra Behn* (Cambridge: Cambridge University Press, 2004), 1–10.

456 *Later, when I'm working*: RLM reminiscence of the building program, manuscript and typed versions, 1948, OSGL.

457 *When she was eleven*: Arthur Lowe to Rachel Lambert, 1921, OSGL.

457 *For Trinity Church she had started*: *Tally-Ho!* (Foxcroft yearbook, 1929), 62.

457 *"Dearest Perry—I just kept the bills"*: RLM to Perry Wheeler, n.d., Perry H. Wheeler Collection, AAG, Smithsonian Institution Archives.

458 *"Sammy" Copenhaver, the man with a sensitive touch*: RLM to Clive Copenhaver, February 13, 1963, cc Perry Wheeler, Charles Pecora, OSGL.

458 *Bunny may have been thinking*: Arthur Lowe to Rachel Lambert, September 9, 1919, OSGL.

458 *Below the quote*: James B. Riding, William G. Chaloner FRS, Martin B. Farley, Fredrick J. Rich, and Paul K. Strother, "A Biography and Obituary of Alfred Traverse (1925–2015)," *Palynology* 40, no. 2 (2016): iii–xi, doi: 10.1080/01916122.2016.1164980.

459 *Sam Kasten, the weaver*: Sam Kasten, phone interview, November 1, 2018.

459   *In her correspondence*: Duffy Rathbun, senior warden of Trinity Episcopal Church, to RLM: "The vestry is pleased with the site for the "biblical walled garden'" (in his note Rathbun alludes to her plans for the cemetery and daycare center), handwritten note, Trinity Church letterhead: n.d., OSGL.

459   *Mrs. Charles Carroll IV, Geraldine "Bean" Carroll*: "Bean" Carroll to MKG, September 2015.

460   *Nadler said, "I do remember her"*: Marci Nadler, February 4, 2015.

460   *The pile of books on her bedside table*: List of bedside books from Tony Willis, December 8, 2014.

461   *She asked Hubert to please find*: RLM to Givenchy, n.d., OSGL; Guy Trebay, "Inside Bunny Mellon's World," *The New York Times*, November 19, 2014.

461   *She called me early the next morning*: Nancy Collins, phone call to MKG, March 17, 2014.

461   *"She lay in state in the library"*: Skip Glascock, phone interview, September 18, 2018.

463   *Her son and grandsons all spoke movingly*: MKG recollection of the service, March 28, 2014.

463   *One encomium we did not hear*: Caroline Kennedy Schlossberg, "Eulogy for Bunny Mellon," with permission, OSGL.

INDEX

ILLUSTRATION CREDITS

2   Toni Frissell, photographer. Library of Congress, Prints and Photographs Division, Courtesy of Oak Spring Garden Foundation, Upperville, VA (*hereafter OSGF*)

16   OSGF

18   Gottscho-Schleisner Collection, Library of Congress, Prints and Photographs Division

27   Boots OSGF. Photo courtesy Mac Griswold

28   *All Out of Step, A Personal Chronicle*, by Gerard B. Lambert, page 138. Doubleday & Company, Inc., Garden City, New York, 1956

29   Gottscho-Schleisner Collection, Library of Congress, Prints and Photographs Division

31   Permission of the Gerard B. Lambert Foundation

34   OSGF

36   "Mrs. Stacy B. Lloyd on Buberry," Francis L. Smith, OSGF

37   Permission of the Gerard B. Lambert Foundation

41   Ira L Hill Collection, Archives Center, National Museum of American History, Smithsonian Institution/Permission of the Gerard B. Lambert Foundation

48   Chatham University Chronological Photograph Files

50   Mac Griswold, photographer

53   "Tuffy Lloyd's Christening 1937," book of photographs. Permission of the Gerard B. Lambert Foundation

54   "Tuffy Lloyd's Christening 1937," book of photographs. Permission of the Gerard B. Lambert Foundation

60   Bettmann / Getty Images

66   Stacy Lloyd to Rachel Lloyd, March 13, 1943, permission of the Gerard B. Lambert Foundation. Photograph Mary Evans Picture Library

68   Lotte Jacobi, photographer, courtesy of Camilla Chandon de Briailles

70   Permission of the Gerard B. Lambert Foundation

72   John F. Kennedy Presidential Library and Museum

85   Photographer unknown

87   Gottscho-Schleisner Collection, Library of Congress, Prints and Photographs Division

88   Thomas Neil Darling photograph, courtesy of the Fun Shop, Middleburg, VA

97   Gerald Martineau / *The Washington Post* / Getty Images

100   OSGF

106   OSGF

108   Alain-Fournier, *Le Grand Meaulnes* (1913), lithograph Braziller, Editions Michèle Trinckvel, limited edition of 350 copies, Paris, 1989

110	OSGF
115	Virginia Museum of Fine Arts, Richmond, VA
123	OSGF
138	Courtesy of National Gallery of Art, Washington, D.C., Gallery Archives
142	Courtesy of National Gallery of Art, Washington, D.C., Gallery Archives
148	Bruce Davidson / Magnum Photos
152	OSGF
156	Photographer unknown
161	OSGF
165	OSGF
166	OSGF
175	Jon Lam for Sotheby's
179	Jon Lam for Sotheby's
181	Fred Conrad / *The New York Times* / Redux
186	Jon Lam for Sotheby's
187	Jon Lam for Sotheby's
194	Max Smith, courtesy of Oak Spring Garden Foundation
204	OSGF
208	OSGF
211	Michael Dunne, OSGF
215	Michael Dunne, OSGF
216	Jim Morris, OSGF
219	Michael Dunne, OSGF
223	Michael Dunne, OSGF
227	Courtesy of Gerard B. Lambert III
230	Photograph by Randall Hagadorn / Courtesy of Gerard B. Lambert III
234	Bettmann / Getty Images
236	OSGF
238	John F. Kennedy Presidential Library and Museum
241	John F. Kennedy Presidential Library and Museum
253	John F. Kennedy Presidential Library and Museum
255	Bruce White for the White House Historical Association
260	Bruce White for the White House Historical Association
267	Guillermo Olaizola / Shutterstock.com
284	Photograph by Jacques de Givry
291	Photograph sent to Bunny Mellon by Hubert de Givenchy / OSGF
295	OSGF
301	OSGF
310	Joshua Greene © 2021 / www.archiveimages.com
317	daniel-sutherland.com
322	daniel-sutherland.com
326	daniel-sutherland.com
341	Ronald Reagan Presidential Library and Museum
345	Photographer unknown / Courtesy of Janet P. Bruce
353	Louise Dahl-Wolfe Archive / Gift of the Louise Dahl-Wolfe Trust. © 1989 Center for Creative Photography, Arizona Board of Regents (93.72.90).
355	OSGF
367	Photograph by Fred Conrad / *The New York Times* / Redux